Growing Together
Personal Relationships across the Life Span

Understanding personal relationships throughout the life course is one of the most crucial issues in the behavioral and social sciences. This book brings together perspectives from different disciplines on individual development and personal relationships across the life span. The book addresses two pertinent dimensions of personal relationships: 1) structures of relationship networks (e.g., kin vs. non-kin, peripheral vs. intimate, short-term vs. long-term) and 2) processes (i.e., change or stability) and outcomes of personal relationships across the life span. The book stimulates discussion of personal relationships as resources for and outcomes of individual development throughout the life course. Different qualities of personal relationships serve as catalysts for individual development. At the same time, relationship qualities reflect changes of developing individuals. The book does not give exclusive priority to one phase of the human life span. Rather, each chapter addresses social development across the entire life span from childhood to later adulthood.

Frieder R. Lang is Professor of Developmental Psychology at the Martin-Luther-Universität Halle-Wittenberg. His research is on self-regulatory and control processes in social relationships across the life span. He has published numerous journal articles and book chapters. He was a Fellow at the Max-Planck Institute for Human Development and has worked as a member of the Berlin Aging Study since 1994. The German Research Foundation (DFG) has funded his research project on successful aging and life experience (1996–1999, together with Margret M. Baltes). He has received several awards for his work. Among these is the Margret Baltes Award for Early Career Achievement in Behavioral and Social Gerontology from the Gerontological Society of America in 2000.

Karen L. Fingerman is Associate Professor of Child and Family Studies and Berner Hanley University Scholar at Purdue University. She has conducted research and published numerous scholarly articles on positive and negative emotions in social relationships. The National Institute on Aging as well as the Brookdale Foundation has funded her work. She received the Springer Award for Early Career Achievement in Research on Adult Development and Aging from Division 20 of the American Psychological Association and the Margret Baltes Award for Early Career Achievement in Behavioral and Social Gerontology from the Gerontological Society of America in 1999.

ADVANCES IN PERSONAL RELATIONSHIPS

HARRY T. REIS
University of Rochester

MARY ANNE FITZPATRICK
University of Wisconsin-Madison

ANITA L. VANGELISTI
University of Texas, Austin

Although scholars from a variety of disciplines have written and conversed about the importance of personal relationships for decades, the emergence of personal relationships as a field of study is relatively recent. *Advances in Personal Relationships* represents the culmination of years of multidisciplinary and interdisciplinary work on personal relationships. Sponsored by the International Association for Relationship Research, the series offers readers cutting-edge research and theory in the field. Contributing authors are internationally known scholars from a variety of disciplines, including social psychology, clinical psychology, communication, history, sociology, gerontology, and family studies. Volumes include integrative reviews, conceptual pieces, summaries of research programs, and major theoretical works. *Advances in Personal Relationships* presents first-rate scholarship that is both provocative and theoretically grounded. The theoretical and empirical work described by authors will stimulate readers and advance the field by offering up new ideas and retooling old ones. The series will be of interest to upper division undergraduate students, graduate students, researchers, and practitioners.

OTHER BOOKS IN THE SERIES
Attribution, Communication Behavior, and Close Relationships
Valerie Manusov and John H. Harvey
Stability and Change in Relationships
Anita L. Vangelisti, Harry T. Reis, and Mary Anne Fitzpatrick
Understanding Marriage: Developments in the Study of Couple Interaction
Patricia Noller and Judith A. Feeney

Growing Together

Personal Relationships across the Life Span

Edited by

FRIEDER R. LANG

*Martin-Luther-Universität
Halle-Wittenberg*

KAREN L. FINGERMAN

Purdue University

CAMBRIDGE
UNIVERSITY PRESS

MT

PUBLISHED BY THE PRESS SYNDICATE OF THE UNIVERSITY OF CAMBRIDGE
The Pitt Building, Trumpington Street, Cambridge, United Kingdom

CAMBRIDGE UNIVERSITY PRESS
The Edinburgh Building, Cambridge CB2 2RU, UK
40 West 20th Street, New York, NY 10011-4211, USA
477 Williamstown Road, Port Melbourne, VIC 3207, Australia
Ruiz de Alarcón 13, 28014 Madrid, Spain
Dock House, The Waterfront, Cape Town 8001, South Africa

http://www.cambridge.org

First published 2004

Printed in the United States of America

Typeface Palatino 10/12 pt.   *System* LATEX 2$_\varepsilon$ [TB]

A catalog record for this book is available from the British Library.

Library of Congress Cataloging in Publication Data

Growing together : personal relationships across the lifespan / edited by Frieder R. Lang,
Karen L. Fingerman.
    p.   cm. – (Advances in personal relationships)
Includes bibliographical references and index.
ISBN 0-521-81310-7
1. Interpersonal relations.   2. Developmental psychology.   I. Lang, Frieder R., 1962–
II. Fingerman, Karen L.   III. Advances in personal relationships (Cambridge, England)
HM1106.G76   2003
158.2 – dc21   2002041683

ISBN 0 521 81310 7 hardback

11/23/05

To Margret M. Baltes with gratitude

Contents

List of Contributors

Rebecca G. Adams
Department of Sociology, The University of North Carolina at Greensboro, P. O. Box 26170, Greensboro, NC 27402-6170

Hiroko Akiyama
Institute for Social Research, 426 Thompson St., Ann Arbor, MI 48109-1109

Toni C. Antonucci
Department of Psychology, University of Michigan, 525 East University, East Hall, Ann Arbor, MI 48109-1109

Victoria Hilkevitch Bedford
Department of Psychology, Indiana University, 1701 Circle Drive, Rawles Hall, Bloomington, IN 47401

Hans-Werner Bierhoff
Department of Psychology, Ruhr-Universität Bochum, D-44780 Bochum, Germany

Fredda Blanchard-Fields
School of Psychology, Georgia Institute of Technology, 274 5th Street, Atlanta, GA 30332-0170

Rosemary Blieszner
Department of Human Development, Virginia Polytechnic Institute & State University, 313 Wallace Hall, Blacksburg, VA 24061

Heike M. Buhl
Department of Psychology, University of Jena, Am Steiger 3/Haus 1, 07743 Jena, Germany

Susan Turk Charles
Department of Psychology and Social Behavior, University of California, Irvine, 3340 Social Ecology II, Irvine, CA 92697-7085

Carolyn Cooper
School of Psychology, Georgia Institute of Technology, 274 5th Street, Atlanta, GA 30332-0170

Eric L. Daleiden
Child and Adolescent Mental Health Div., Hawaii Department of Health, 3627 Kilauea Ave., Honolulu, HI 96816

Karen L. Fingerman
Child Development and Family Studies, Purdue University, 1269 Fowler House, West Lafayette, IN 47907-1269

Robert O. Hansson
Department of Psychology, University of Tulsa, 600 South College, Lorton Hall 307, Tulsa, OK 74104

Bert Hayslip, Jr.
Department of Psychology, University of North Texas, P.O. Box 311280, Denton, TX 76203-1280

Frieder R. Lang
Institute of Psychology, Martin-Luther-Universität Halle-Wittenberg, Brandbergweg 23A, D-06099 Halle a. d. Saale, Germany

Elizabeth S. Langfahl
Department of Psychology, University of Michigan, 525 East University, East Hall, Ann Arbor, MI 48109-1109

Shahrzad Mavandadi
Department of Psychology and Social Behavior, University of California, Irvine, 3340 Social Ecology II, Irvine, CA 92697-7085

Franz J. Neyer
Department of Psychology, Humboldt-Universität zu Berlin, Oranienburger Str. 18, D-10178 Berlin, Germany

Peter Noack
Department of Psychology, University of Jena, Am Steiger 3/Haus 1, 07743 Jena, Germany

Karen A. Roberto
Center for Gerontology, Virginia Polytechnic Institute & State University, Blacksburg, VA 24061

Karen Rook
Department of Psychology and Social Behavior, University of California, Irvine, 3340 Social Ecology II, Irvine, CA 92697-7085

Martina Schmohr
Department of Psychology, Ruhr-Universität Bochum, D-44780 Bochum, Germany

Dara Sorkin
Department of Psychology and Social Behavior, University of California, Irvine, 3340 Social Ecology II, Irvine, CA 92697-7085

Michelle L. Stevenson
Center for Gerontology (0426), 237 Wallace Hall, Virginia Polytechnic Institute & State University, Blacksburg, VA 24061-0426

Keiko Takahashi
Department of Psychology, University of the Sacred Heart, 4-3-1 Hiroo Shibuya-ku, Tokyo 150-8938, Japan

Brenda L. Volling
Department of Psychology, University of Michigan, 525 East University, East Hall, Ann Arbor, MI 48109-1109

Laura Zettel
Department of Psychology and Social Behavior, University of California, Irvine, 3340 Social Ecology II, Irvine, CA 92697-7085

Acknowledgments

We are grateful to Donna Ballock, Shelley Hosterman, Sara Moorman, Anne Schmidt, and Franziska Reschke for assistance with manuscript preparation. We thank Phil Laughlin at Cambridge University Press for his encouragement as we put together this volume and his kind responses to our many queries. We thank John Yeazell for assistance in coming up with a title for the book.

Editorial work on this book took place while Frieder R. Lang was supported by the Alice Aeppli Stiftung, Zürich, Switzerland, and Karen L. Fingerman was supported by funds from the Brookdale Foundation and by grant AG17916-01A, "Problems between Parents and Offspring in Adulthood," from the National Institutes on Aging.

Clearly, no book addressing personal relationships throughout the life span would be possible without a rich array of supportive ties. We are grateful to our friends, family, and colleagues for their support and encouragement. And we reserve special thanks to Bryce and Lillian Yeazell and to Clarissa and Gesine Lang who took us to the park and inspired this book.

1

Coming Together: A Perspective on Relationships across the Life Span

Karen L. Fingerman and Frieder R. Lang

This chapter introduces a life-span perspective on personal relationships by emphasizing how the structure, processes, and outcomes of relationships are interwoven with human development. The social arena serves as a metaphor for changes and continuities individuals experience in their social partners, activities, and goals over the life span. We consider mutual influences between individual development and relationship partners, including 1) individual changes, 2) the development of relationships themselves, and 3) the context of the larger social network. A life-span understanding of personal relationships considers the structure of relationships (e.g., the types of social partners individuals of different ages interact with), the processes underlying personal relationships (e.g., personality, motivation for social contact, cognition), and the outcomes or precursors of relationship change across the life span.

We, the editors of this book, are parents of young children. As a result, when the weather allows it, we spend considerable time at our local parks and frequently have the opportunity to observe a microcosm of life-span relationships. People of all ages engage in activities, from sitting under a tree watching the clouds, to playing softball in mixed groups of adults and children. Our little ones vie for attention among the other children who run around the slide or swings. Older children throw balls or participate in organized activities. A group of teenagers sit apart and listen to music on a portable compact disc player. Multiple generations come together for a family picnic. Young couples hold hands as they stroll. A community league plays weekly soccer games. A middle-aged couple expresses fatigue as they chase a grandchild. And one particular older gentleman reminisces alone as he feeds the birds. These patterns can be found in the city and the countryside all over Europe, Australia, Asia, Africa, and the Americas. The pervasiveness of social ties from birth to old age is evident to us on such gentle summer evenings. Of course, not all people spend their weekends at the park; the neighborhood park may be dangerous in some communities or nonexistent in some cultures. Yet the type of park we describe illustrates the complex nature of relationships across the life span.

Our personal relationships span decades, generations, cultures, and even continents. Each liaison is embedded within larger familial, institutional, societal, and cultural contexts. Personal relationships accompany us at each phase of life, yet the overall social network changes over time. We retain ties to our parents and siblings as we move through infancy, childhood, adolescence, and adulthood. A few of our childhood pals become lifelong friends, some live in the vicinity (and we run into them at the market from time to time), but others move on and remain distant memories from class photographs. After high school, we make new friends, some of whom remain close for life, some of whom we lose again, some of whom we fall in love with, and others with whom we lose contact. Sometimes we meet someone who has been the friend of a very good friend; and we are surprised how small the world is. (And this may remind us that we even belong to "networks" of personal relationships without our overt knowledge.) Over time, we establish ties to coworkers or colleagues. Later in life, we may experience the loss of an "old friend," for deliberate, or for not so controllable, reasons. At the same time, in-laws and grandchildren may become new members of our families. These ties serve certain functions in the social world we inhabit: they provide entertainment, they inspire or encourage us, they help us with daily tasks, they make demands, and they influence our evaluations of other people and of ourselves. This volume addresses such changes and continuities in personal relationships across the life span.

At all stages of the life course, personal relationships accompany, set forth, or hold back developmental progress. At the same time, social relationships arise from and are important outcomes of individual growth. Whether due to maturation, life experience, or social context, individuals of different ages bring different capacities to their relationships. A two-year-old child cannot aspire to be the type of friend a seven-year-old child can easily be. In young adulthood, romantic partners engage in sexual behaviors beyond the physical maturation of pre-adolescent children. Likewise, middle-aged adults provide mentorship to youth reflecting their accumulated knowledge. In sum, social ties shape and emerge from human development. In this manner, individuals and their social worlds are woven together throughout life.

This chapter introduces our central purposes for editing this volume on personal relationships across the life span. We submit the notion that a life-span conceptualization of personal relationships must be grounded in understanding relational structures, processes, and outcomes. First, we discuss the meaning of personal relationships and how such ties are defined. Next, we outline the challenges scholars confront in taking a life-span developmental approach to understanding social ties. Then, we provide a rubric for this volume and explain how the structure of the social world, the processes involved in maintaining social ties, the precursors of these ties, and the outcomes of social ties vary across the life span. Family and friendships, peripheral and intimate ties, short-term and long-term relationships, threaded together in different configurations at different points in life, constitute the "structure" of individuals' social worlds. The term "process" refers to processes underlying and arising from relationships, including individuals' emotional and cognitive capacities, their personalities and predispositions, and their motivation to engage in relationships with other people. Finally, "outcomes" include the benefits and costs of an individual's social ties (e.g., satisfaction or anger, instruction or obstruction, support or demands, well-being, and health). We recognize that individuals' capacities and characteristics also serve as precursors to relationship formation and maintenance, but for the sake of simplicity we refer to these matters as "outcomes" here. We consider how these three aspects of relationships fit together across the life span.

THE MEANING OF PERSONAL RELATIONSHIPS

Human beings are inherently social creatures. Indeed, the capacity and need for affiliation may be an evolved psychological mechanism that contributes to better reproductive fitness of the human species (e.g., Axelrod, 1985; Baumeister & Leary, 1995; Buss, 1999, Neyer & Lang, 2003). At the most basic level, social ties are necessary for humans to have children and raise those children. Yet, individuals' social ties persist beyond these basic functions to include a wide array of partners. As adults, we may serve multiple roles in multiple relationships. We are simultaneously romantic partners, parents of growing children, children of older parents, relatives of in-laws and siblings, neighbors, and co-workers. A myriad of relationships persists at stages of development where autonomous functioning is possible and sometimes even at high cost to the individuals involved. Consideration of how and why individuals maintain such ties throughout life warrants consideration.

The social world includes many levels of social interaction. Intimate dyads, family units, workplace organizations, larger ethnic groups, social institutions, and the cultural milieu may have an impact on individual development. This volume focuses more specifically on personal relationships and their role in human development. The term "personal relationships" implies that individuals have social connections to specific people who affect their lives. Such a focus pursues the meaning of social ties at an individual rather than a societal level. Elsewhere, scholars have argued that relationships involve repeated interactions or interdependencies between social partners (e.g., Bronfenbrenner & Morris, 1997; Kelley et al., 1983). We do not constrain "relationships" under such a premise of active engagement. Rather, certain social ties may involve few exchanges, and may be based primarily on individuals' cognitive representations (e.g., Fingerman, Chap. 8, this volume). This approach considers a fetus in the womb, a child's tie to a stuffed elephant, an older adult's ties to a friend from college whom he has not seen in decades, and even ties to friends and relatives who have passed away. Indeed, the chapters in this volume consider personal relationships in the broadest sense, from individuals' representations of their closest, most intimate social partners to the array of social partners who constitute the background of everyday life. We use the terms "social relationships" and "social ties" interchangeably with the term "personal relationships," in keeping with an interdisciplinary and inclusive approach to the topic.

A "social arena" serves as a metaphor for the interweaving of social ties as they come and go throughout an individual's life. An arena character- izes a large area for social contact. If we think of a traditional Roman arena, activities may vary from highly structured games to interactions surround- ing market days to loose conversation arising from a spontaneous meeting of two partners. Even the same game may look different if the players in- volved are young children versus older adults. In this manner, we attempt to disentangle the structure of the social network (the people who are in the arena) from the activities involved, and from the larger cultural and social structures that support or inhibit these ties. We consider the social arena as a metaphor for the many configurations, the dynamics and the activities associated with social ties across the life course. The social arena is potentially available to all individuals, while at the same time it is used in particular and individualized ways. From a life-span perspective, the so- cial partners present in the arena at any given time may vary – some of the people may remain the same, but others come and go. We can observe the interplay between the structure (partners in the social arena), the processes (interactions that take place in the arena), and the outcomes (of being in the arena). Individuals alter the nature of the arena while the arena, in turn, changes the individuals. It is this image of a social arena that guided us throughout the course of editing this book, from the initial brainstorming of ideas to the final proofreading.

The literature regarding personal relationships typically addresses such topics as commitment, communication patterns, relationship maintenance, exchanges of social support, intimacy, emotional qualities, and cognitive representations of relationships (e.g., Auhagen & Von Salisch, 1996; Duck, 1998). Current conceptions of the social arena do not fully encompass a sense of human development underlying this flow of social ties, however. Volumes that have linked the topics of social ties and development have broadened our understanding of these topics (e.g., Hartup & Rubin, 1986; Turner, 1996), but additional work remains to pull together scholarship addressing human development and personal relationships. Elsewhere, scholars have linked historical and social events to individual development through the life-course perspective (e.g., Caspi, Elder, & Bem, 1987; Elder, 1998a, 1998b). Chapters in this volume touch on these issues but look more specifically at individuals in transactions with their social partners. We consider such questions as how the infant's singular fascination with the mother in the first year of life relates to the widow's needs for assistance with transportation and emotional support at the end of life, and how the small child's refusal to come to dinner when called by his father differs from the feelings of efficacy that adults derive from a loving romantic partner.

ASPECTS OF THE SOCIAL ARENA

A life-span perspective on relationships requires us to consider the larger social arena. All people tied to a specific target individual are located somewhere in that arena. Take, for example, a graduate student working on an advanced degree. To understand her relationships, we consider her romantic partner, her father and her mother with their respective families of origin, her stepparents or in-laws, her brother and his best friends, her past and her current friends, her current classmates and teachers, her former schoolmates, her past and her current neighbors, and the lady who sells a newspaper to her at the train station each morning. Anyone who is or has been related to this student is a member of this social progression. We are interested in the people in the arena, how these people are positioned relative to the student, and how they are positioned relative to each other. From a life-span perspective, we are also interested in how this structure varies from infancy to later life, and even before birth and after death. We consider the precursors and implications of such age differences and how social ties arise from and influence life goals and tasks. We ask why some persons are in the social arena whereas others are not.

Different people in the social arena appear to be associated with different developmental processes and outcomes in the individual's life course. As such, we may ask when and why individuals of different ages choose to interact with different types of social partners and how they interpret their social partners' behaviors. Using our student as an example, to whom does she turn when she is upset about a personal problem? How do other students enhance her feelings about her academic abilities? The student may expect her romantic partner to support her when she is upset about a family member's problems, and she may turn to her advisor to open professional doors for her. The things the student seeks from her social partners are different at this stage of her life than when she was in elementary school and will change again when she has completed her degree and has students and a family of her own.

Indeed, the social arena may be marked by change and variability throughout life. The scientific endeavor asks what happens when an individual behaves in certain ways, and what happens when people who are located in the individual's social arena behave in certain ways. We may wonder how the student's behaviors affect other people and vice versa. In this realm, we might be interested in microgenetic, interpersonal transactional, ontogenetic, or even phylogenetic processes as they occur within the individual's social arena. In sum, the social arena might be illustrated using a three-dimensional cube encompassing the array of relationships, the psychological processes, precursors, and outcomes underlying these changes in relationships. Mechanisms of change over time might be illustrated on a continuum from micro to macro-level influences.

Figure 1.1 illustrates the interweaving of structure, processes, and outcomes in a life-span perspective on personal relationships. We also include mechanisms of change that might instigate associations between

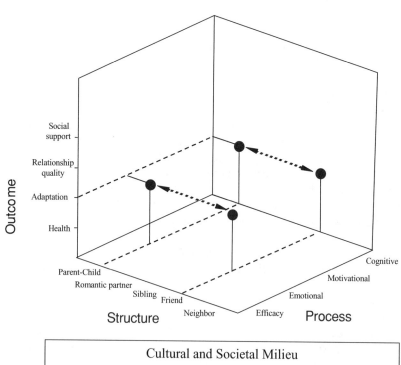

FIGURE 1.1. Personal Relationships across the Life Span: A Cube Model of Classifying Perspectives.

these features of relationships from the microgenetic to evolutionary level influences. These terms (e.g., structure, process, outcomes) and categories are presented to provide an organizing framework for this volume. Research on personal relationships typically focuses on specific pieces of this cube. For example, as can be seen in Figure 1.1, researchers may be interested in the ontogenetic development of emotional aspects in the mother-child tie in adolescence or in middle adulthood or across the life span. Alternately, the health benefits of ties to family may be compared to the health benefits of friendships in late life. One may ask whether cognitions play a different role in transactions between romantic partners than between friends over time. Furthermore, we refer to health, adaptation, and relationship quality loosely as "outcomes" of relationships, cognizant of the fact that these variables are also precursors to different types of relationships.

The mechanisms of change involve a variety of theoretical explanations for mutual influences between individuals and their social partners over time. Microgenetic influences are described in an understanding of behavioral genetic influences on relationships (Bierhoff & Schmohr, Chap. 5, this volume), social structures and technologies clearly shape different relationships and the effects of those relationships on individual development (see, in this volume: Adams & Stevenson, Chap. 15; Antonucci, Langfahl, & Akiyama, Chap. 2; Blieszner & Roberto, Chap. 7), and evolutionary pressures may influence the types of romantic partners individuals seek or the attachment that parents form with young children (Bierhoff & Schmohr, Chap. 5, this volume; Takahashi, Chap. 6, this volume). Each chapter describes multiple mechanisms that may contribute to interactions between individuals and their social partners. These and other chapters also consider the benefits or harms individuals derive from those ties.

Of course, the cube offers only a rough, analytic distinction between the structure, processes, precursors, and outcomes of relationships for a purely illustrative purpose. Cultural and socioeconomic contexts clearly influence these dimensions of the social arena. Culture shapes individuals' opportunities for different types of relationships, the salience and importance of those ties, as well as the micro and macro processes that guide those relationships over time. For example, in parts of China, an older woman's tie to a daughter-in-law may provide more support than her relationship to a grown daughter, whereas in the United States, the opposite is usually the case (Fingerman, 2002; Fischer, 1983). In addition, the emotional meanings and motivations underlying these ties vary across cultures; young women in the United States and China experience differing degrees of obligation toward their mothers and mothers-in-law. Finally, precursors of relationships and outcomes that arise from relationships, such as health and well-being, exist in cultural settings as well. We conceptualize the social arena as lying within larger social and cultural structures. Indeed, one aim of this volume was to present a cross-cultural collection on personal relationships. We brought together scholars from North America, Europe, and Asia. Some chapters touch on personal relationships in Germany, China, Japan, Korea, France, the United States, and Kenya. Others focus predominantly on culture (e.g., Antonucci, Langfahl, & Akiyama, Chap. 2; Takahashi, Chap. 6), or discuss cultural perspectives with regard to a specific topic in the personal relationships literature.

In sum, the triarchy idea of structure, process, and outcome provides a heuristic for discussing personal relationships across the life span. The "cube" model of personal relationships offers a useful tool for uncovering constraints and limitations in existing knowledge about personal relationships. Authors consider changes and continuity in relationship structures, processes, and outcomes that bring the social world to the fore of human existence throughout life.

THE SOCIAL ARENA IN A LIFE-SPAN CONTEXT

Of central interest in this volume is how and why relationships change or remain the same across the life span. On the surface, the infant's playful engagement with his parents seems starkly different from the matriarch's family gathering with her children, children-in-law, grandchildren, and great-grandchildren. A life-span perspective on personal relationships articulates how and why these relationships change over time and also considers continuities in individuals' lives. Individuals may maintain ties to a family friend from childhood into adulthood. For example, a young child who attends dinner at this friend's house may refuse an hors d'oeuvre that is offered. Yet, as the individual enters college and visits the family friend, the nature of their interactions may be transformed – this young adult brings a new perspective on politeness that necessitates eating smoked fish or other proffered delicacies. A life-span perspective in the social domain also reaches beyond the view that life stretches from birth to death. For example, certain relationships (such as ties between parents) exist prior to an individual's birth, and many relationships transcend death (such as a widow's tie to a deceased spouse). In this volume, we consider three levels of change and continuity in personal relationships, involving 1) the individual, 2) the relationship, and 3) the larger social network.

First, at the individual level, we might consider the person as a developing entity who possesses relationships. This approach takes a psychological bent and the individual is the unit of investigation. Individual development is addressed with regard to such issues as personality development (Neyer, Chap. 12), competence (Hansson, Daleiden, & Hayslip, Chap. 13), motivation for social ties (Lang, Chap. 14), cognitive representation of relationships (Blanchard-Fields & Cooper, Chap. 11), and emotional processes (Charles & Mavandadi, Chap. 10; Takahashi, Chap. 6).

In considering individuals from a life-span perspective, it is important to think about how we measure change and continuity. Nearly three decades ago, theorists noted that investigations of individual change across the life span must reflect complexities inherent to the meaning of chronological age (Wohlwill, 1973). Indeed, age (e.g., position in the life span) serves as a marker of: 1) changes within the individual; 2) differences associated with birth in a specific historical cohort; and 3) individuals' positions within the social structure. Some scholars have taken a psychological approach by emphasizing differences in the capacities individuals of different ages bring to their relationships (Lang, 2001; Marsiske, Lang, Baltes, & Baltes, 1995). For example, researchers have examined how individuals' needs and goals at specific stages of life are associated with their desire for social contact (e.g., Lang, 2001; Lang & Carstensen, 1994, 2002). Alternately, sociologists have taken a life-course perspective, considering an individual's age as an indicator of cohort and role position within society. For example, interest in the baby boomer cohort's relationships with their parents may focus on how middle-aged adults with many siblings handle their parents' aging. Likewise, in age-graded societies, age serves as a marker of the types of roles and daily environment individuals are likely to occupy. In industrialized societies, children attend schools, middle-aged adults go to work, and older adults may be retired. As such, individuals of different ages possess different abilities, experiences, and goals and bring those capacities and experiences to their social ties.

Second, relationships might be considered as developing units in their own right, with a mutual influence between partners and the relationship. The dyadic relationship includes areas of continuity and change over time. For example, friends who have known each other for years can ask for favors, read one another's mood, and go without contact for prolonged periods of time without damage to the relationship, whereas a budding friendship requires greater investment of time and politeness (Blieszner & Roberto, Chap. 7, this volume). Of course, individuals' ages and relationship duration are associated; relationship partners are often of like age – adolescent youth with adolescent friends, older parents with older children, older wives with older husbands, and so forth. As a result, it is difficult to disentangle individual age and relationship duration. Therefore, we must consider how partners' developmental tasks interface with different phases of relationship development.

Finally, as a larger unit of analysis, the social network itself changes over time. Families expand or contract as members marry, divorce, have children, have grandchildren, or pass away. Social networks reflect the changing life circumstances of the individual; children's horizons expand when they enter school settings outside the family, widows confront new challenges as they renegotiate ties to existing friends and family members as single adults (Morgan, Neal, & Carder, 1997). Moreover, personal ties are set in different constellations of social partners. The adolescent's budding romance takes place within the larger peer network, whereas the widow's new romance may be centered in a family constellation involving grown children and grandchildren.

This volume examines multiple aspects of relationships in a life-span framework. Chapters consider changes at the individual, relationship, and social network levels. Further, reciprocal influences on change are described – how social partners influence one another over time, how the relationship influences individual development, and vice versa. In sum, this volume considers the importance of development in understanding personal relationships. In many cases, we use age as a correlate of skills, position in society, or relationship status. Focusing on age alone, however, is not sufficient for understanding personal relationships, their continuities, and changes in a life-span context. We address time more generally in this volume as a variable in the social domain.

EXISTING KNOWLEDGE ABOUT PERSONAL RELATIONSHIPS ACROSS THE LIFE SPAN: CONSTRAINTS AND LIMITATIONS

The authors who contributed to this volume present unique integrations of specific topics pertaining to personal relationships. Comprehensive studies of the social domain from birth to death are not evident in extant literature. These authors confronted several challenges in pulling this literature together. Two principal challenges are described here, 1) divisions within the disciplines that study human development, and 2) difficulties in assessing noncomparable phenomena.

With regard to disciplinary challenges, a life-span understanding of personal relationships must pull together the fields of child development, adult development, gerontology, family science, and personal relationships, to name a few. These fields are themselves multidisciplinary, and include psychologists, sociologists, demographers, anthropologists, geneticists, biologists, physiologists, policy analysts, and other scientists. Scholarship addressing relationships has become increasingly fragmented and segregated by topic over the past fifty years (Fingerman & Bermann, 2000). Yet each field has acquired knowledge about particular aspects of relationships. Integration of scholarship sheds light on the meaning of the social arena throughout life.

With regard to phenomenological issues, people of different ages possess different capacities and goals. Differences between infants, children, adolescents, and adults of different ages challenge researchers who wish to study relationships across this broad age span; for example, researchers have to use different methodologies for children and for older adults. Difficulties of designing studies that could encompass such a wide range of individuals hamper studies of relationships from birth to death. In the next section, we describe historical and disciplinary distinctions that present challenges to integrating the literature examining personal relationships across the life span.

DIFFERENT HISTORIES OF THE STUDY OF CHILD AND ADULT DEVELOPMENT

There is a long history of interest in life-span development. In Germany, life-span perspectives on human development date back to the eighteenth century. Johan Nikolaus Tetens (1777) is considered one of the founders of the field of developmental psychology (P. Baltes, Staudinger, & Lindenberger, 1999). Throughout the twentieth century, developmental psychologists in Germany and the United States elaborated the perspective of lifelong ontogeny (e.g., Bühler, 1933/1935; Erikson, 1950; Hall, 1922; Thomae, 1959). Yet empirical research addressing relationships over the life span has not yielded a comprehensive understanding of how social partners affect individuals of different ages and vice versa.

Empirical studies on age differences in personal relationships are embedded in the distinct fields of child development and adult development. These two fields differ with regard to their degree of understanding of phenomena of interest. The field of child development has a longer history than the field of adult development. Scholars such as Jean Jacques Rousseau expounded theories about how and why children develop as early as the 1700s (Ariès, 1962; Hilgard, 1987). The modern study of child development began in the late nineteenth century, however, catalyzed by the rising interest in evolutionary theory as well as by societal concerns for the welfare of children. The early years of the study of children involved observational and experimental methods for assessing children and the instigation of longitudinal studies that continue to have an impact on the field of human development today (Hilgard, 1987). Furthermore, from the start, scholars who studied child development were interested in relationships between parents and children, instigating a relationship perspective in the field.

By contrast, the study of adult development and aging began more recently; the Gerontological Society of America was founded in 1945 and involved only a small cadre of interested scholars at that time. Although many well-known longitudinal studies on development that were started in the twenties, thirties, and forties of the twentieth century have become studies on aging as the participants grew old over the decades, only a few scholars have attempted to examine relationship processes in these studies (e.g., Carstensen, 1992; Field, 1981).

Although both fields of human development are relatively young in comparison to more established fields of study (e.g., mathematics), differences in their etiologies have had an impact on the way in which scholars conceptualize topics of interest. We know more about children's social worlds than we do about adults' social worlds. Attempts to extend theories that address children to understand adults have been hampered by complexities in conceptualization and measurement. For example, scholars in the 1980s and 1990s attempted to understand how early internalized working models of the social world derived from infant attachment relationships might extend into adults' romantic ties (Hazan & Shaver, 1987, 1994; Main, Kaplan, & Cassidy, 1985). Yet, despite abundant empirical studies, it has been difficult to establish continuities in attachment patterns throughout life (Levitt, 2000). A challenge of this volume was to disentangle discontinuities as well as describing continuities in social ties, based on a disparate literature.

DISPARATE FIELDS OF STUDY

Adding to these early historical differences in the fields of child and adult development, the past fifty years have seen both increasing dissection of scholarly topics across and within the behavioral and social sciences (Fingerman & Bermann, 2000; Hinde 1997) as well as increasing efforts to integrate the entire life span in the developmental sciences (e.g., Carstensen, Graff, & Lang, 2000). For example, certain professional societies (i.e., International Society for the Study of Behavioral Development, Society for the Study of Human Development) attempt to bring together scholars from across fields of human development. However, in many academic settings, a fragmented approach to the life span remains dominant. A cursory examination of job advertisements reflects the dissection of the life span; in the United States it is still rare to find a university advertising to hire a scholar who studies the "life span."

Furthermore, research interests on social relationships vary considerably depending on life phases. Research on social relationships in childhood often addresses different issues than research on social relationships in late adulthood or in adolescence. For example, we know a great deal about parents and children in early life and at the end of life, but we know relatively little about this tie when offspring are young adults. We know a great deal about friendships in childhood and old age, but gaps in knowledge about friendships in middle adulthood persist (e.g., Blieszner & Roberto, Chap. 7, this volume). With regard to young adults, romantic ties and marriage receive greatest attention. Scholars interested in late life have tended to consider intergenerational relationships or the larger social network and support functions social partners may provide. Clearly, relationships are not as discontinuous as the extant literature on these topics; individuals have ties to their parents well into adulthood and children value their friends beginning in early childhood, but the literature remains uneven. A life-span perspective on personal relationships must pull together disparate information about the processes underlying social ties.

Of course, these biases are not arbitrary. It is not simply that researchers who study infants drew the relationship "mother" in a lottery, and researchers who study teenagers drew "peer group." Rather, the salience of different relationships varies at different points in the life span; more salient relationships receive more research attention. Children are embedded in families with parents and siblings. Young adults may live alone or with a romantic partner. Middle-aged adults may confront a myriad of ties to generations above and below them as well as to coworkers, neighbors, and siblings. As such, a life-span understanding of the social arena seeks to understand how and why the salience of social ties varies over time.

Given the state of empirical inquiry concerning human development, the authors who contributed to this volume provide integration across noncomparable literatures. As such, this volume ties up the continuities in a discontinuous literature and a discontinuous social world.

METHODOLOGICAL AND PHENOMENOLOGICAL CHALLENGES

The complexities involved in putting together a life-span portrait of the social domain go beyond bringing together scholars from different areas of study. People of different ages have different skills, capacities, goals, and needs. These skills, capacities, and goals shape their social behaviors, their perceptions of their relationships, and their responses to researchers' queries. As such, a life-span understanding of the social domain is hampered by inherent conceptual challenges. In this section, we describe difficulties in finding comparable ways to measure children's and adults' relationships and difficulties in recruiting people of different ages to participate in research.

Social processes that are highly salient in the social world at one point in time may be dormant or disappear altogether at another point in time. Sibling rivalries provide an example. In early childhood, many siblings are keenly aware of disparities in their treatment across a variety of domains, such as privileges, discipline, and companionship (Dunn & Plomin, 1990). By middle adulthood, such issues may be less important or more global; siblings may be aware of which party the parent favors but less concerned with the meaning of that favoritism or the domain in which it takes place (Bedford, 1992; Bedford & Volling, Chap. 4, this volume; Davey, Fingerman, & Jenkins-Tucker, 2002; Suitor & Pillemer, 1997). In late life, as parents require care, earlier patterns within the family may resurface (Connidis, Rosenthal, & McMullin, 1996; Fingerman & Bermann, 2000). Such complexities are inherent to the social domain and cannot be treated simply as confounds. Methodological and sampling challenges further cloud these matters.

Social scientists have approached an understanding of personal relationships using a variety of methodologies such as self-report, clinical, observational, experimental, and indirect or projective measures. Each of these methodologies provides information about personal relationships and their functions, but a full integration of methodological approaches across the life span does not exist in current literature. The difficulties involved in conducting research on personal ties have been enumerated elsewhere (Duck, 1996; Mangen & Bengtson, 1988). Relationships involve dynamics between multiple partners in multiple settings; efforts to disentangle the individual, the relationship, and the context of the relationship have presented insurmountable methodological challenges (Mangen, 1995). To add to these complexities, a life-span perspective on personal relationships must consider continuities and discontinuities in these phenomena.

Again, the fields of child development and adult development are separated by a gulf with regard to methodologies. Researchers in the field of child development have tended to rely on observational, experimental, and other-party reports of social behaviors. With the exception of marital research (where observational methodologies are commonly used), researchers interested in adults' personal relationships have relied primarily on self-report instruments. Again, a number of factors prevent researchers from using the same methodologies to study different periods of the life span. For example, a scholar might be interested in how self-understanding contributes to individuals' behaviors in relationships. Yet individuals of different ages engage in different types of social behaviors, possess varying degrees of self-understanding, and respond in different ways to questions. Children may play with their friends in front of a video camera without thinking about the fact that they are being observed, whereas adults might feel self-conscious in such a context. By contrast, adults can respond thoughtfully to questions that involve decisions using seven-point scales, whereas a child might rapidly tire of such questions. The issues of response pattern and age cannot be disentangled.

To illustrate these points, consider the different meanings of behaviors when manifested by individuals of different ages. A five-week-old baby who cries may be hungry, whereas a seventy-year-old woman who cries may be grieving. Personal relationships complicate matters further. Behaviors that occur in normal transactions between partners in one context and at one age may have a dramatically different meaning between partners of another age. For example, in the first months of life, a parent feeds the child at the breast or by holding a bottle, cuddling the child close. By middle childhood, a parent who fed a child in such a manner would be highly abnormal. Such clear instances of variability in behavioral meaning are obvious to researchers. Yet more subtle variations exist. A young adult daughter greatly values her mother's advice and input, whereas a middle-aged daughter or older mother might find such input intrusive

(Fingerman, 2000, 2001; Lang & Schütze, 2002). Researchers must identify behaviors that serve as indicators of similar phenomena at different points in the life span.

Of course, the best approach to study changes in personal relationships across the life span would involve examination of the same subjects or the same relationships over time. Unfortunately, extant longitudinal studies tend to have less information about personal relationships than about cognition, achievement, and socioeconomic factors (e.g., Baltes & Mayer, 1999; Schaie, 1996). Therefore, researchers interested in personal relationships across the life span are often forced to rely on cross-sectional studies. Even then, few studies encompass the entire life span. In addition, difficulties in sampling may deter even the most determined life-span researchers.

Children and adolescents may be easier to identify and sample than infants and adults. The neighborhood school provides a basis for socioeconomic background and other characteristics of school-age samples. College students are also readily available and are probably the most researched subgroup in the population. A content analysis of recent articles published in major journals examining person relationships revealed age biases, with 24% of studies relying solely on college student samples. These biases appear to reflect pragmatic issues in sampling, rather than researchers' deeply held preferences about the importance of young adulthood in the study of relationships (Fingerman & Hay, in press). Researchers must take greater pains to obtain samples of adults outside the college milieu. Middle-aged adults have many demands on their time and may be reticent to participate in in-depth studies that could provide important information about personal relationships.

Finally, personal relationships vary dramatically from one birth cohort to the next. Historical events, technologies, size of birth cohort, and beliefs about relationships influence the nature of personal ties. As an example, in the early twentieth century parenting manuals advised mothers not to play with their infants or toddlers for fear of overstimulating them (Hilgard, 1987). Parenting guides in the early twenty-first century provide recommendations for the best toys for parents and children to play with starting at birth (e.g., Leach, 1997). Differences in parents' ties to their children may stem from such changing societal values. Yet studies of age differences in parent-child ties are rarely able to measure such cohort-based differences.

Given the difficulties of conducting research from a life-span perspective and the challenges of investigating personal relationships, it is not surprising that researchers and theorists have shied away from integrating research across the life span. A central goal of this volume is to provide a foundation for theory building and future research. This goal also involves efforts to differentiate and integrate disparate fields of study, varying foci in research, and disparate methodologies.

STRUCTURE, PROCESSES, AND OUTCOMES OF PERSONAL
RELATIONSHIPS ACROSS THE LIFE SPAN: AN INTEGRATION
OF RESEARCH ON PERSONAL RELATIONSHIPS

Despite the challenges scholars confront in pulling together research on relationships across the life span, each chapter in this book deals with the structure of relationships, the processes that occur within those relationships, and the individual precursors and outcomes of those ties for individual development. All chapters in this volume address precursors and outcomes of personal relationships across the life span. However, some of the chapters focus on specific structures of social ties (e.g., the parent-child dyad, sibling relationships, the social convoy), while others emphasize specific processes that occur in personal relationships (e.g., social cognition, motivation, emotion regulation). Consequently, we organized this volume in two large sections: The first section contains chapters that focus on the structures of personal relationships. The second section includes chapters that explore and discuss specific processes in personal relationships.

We recognize that our conceptualization imposes false distinctions on relationship phenomena; obviously these issues are intertwined – structure, processes, and outcomes cannot be separated empirically. In this volume, we organized chapters under these two overarching themes, but the authors treated all three dimensions of the cube presented in Figure 1.1. For example, we placed the chapter examining coping and adaptation as a process within relationships (Rook, Sorkin, & Zirkel, this volume, Chap. 9), yet widowhood provides a relationship structure. Likewise, we treat relationships between parents and children as a structural element of the social arena (Noack & Buhl, Chap. 3), but we are aware of processes underlying this tie and its impact on individual well-being.

STRUCTURES AND OUTCOMES OF PERSONAL RELATIONSHIPS

The structure of the social arena involves individuals, personal relationships, and the aggregate of those relationships (family, social network, social institutions, community). Few personal relationships begin at birth; the structure of the social world gradually shifts from infancy through childhood, adolescence, and early and later adulthood. Some types of relationships (e.g., intimate romantic partnerships, professional colleagues) only emerge after childhood. Even when individuals engage with the same social partner throughout life (a sibling, a parent) interaction patterns with that social partner may vary dramatically. In this volume, we consider two features of the structure of relationships, 1) the types of social partners individuals of different ages encounter, and 2) the nature of the specific relationship (parent, sibling, friend) over time.

Biological, psychological, and social structural factors generate age differences in the structure of the social arena across the life span. In this regard, we might consider: 1) fertility/fecundity and mortality patterns; 2) individuals' choices or selection of partners; and 3) social roles or social norms for relationships. Biological constraints (e.g., fertility and mortality) set parameters on the structure of the social network, particularly with regard to family ties. Family ties reflect the facts that humans have biological children only after puberty, that fertility decreases dramatically in the second half of life, and that most people die before the age of one hundred. As a result, the majority of individuals under the age of fifteen in the United States and Europe have a living grandparent, whereas almost no individuals over the age of sixty do. Individuals under the age of ten are not raising their biological children, nor are most women over the age of sixty (for statistics on intergenerational patterns in the United States, see Fingerman, Nussbaum, & Birditt, in press). Societies also set parameters on the relationships individuals maintain. For example, in age-graded societies, individuals of similar age experience the transition to marriage or leadership roles in society simultaneously (e.g., Kenyatta, 1962; Shostak, 1981). In industrialized societies, public education may place children in school settings and adults in the workforce. As a result, individuals of different ages have the opportunity to interact daily with different social partners.

Variability in social partners is not simply a matter of availability, however. Individuals of different ages also choose to interact with different types of social partners (Fingerman & Birditt, in press; Lang, 2001). In young adulthood, romantic partners and friends may take precedence, whereas in midlife and late life, ties to family may be important. In this volume, we consider how and why individuals choose to interact with different social partners at different ages.

In addition to the types of relationships individuals of different ages encounter, we consider how the structure of a particular relationship changes over time. This perspective on the lifelong development of social relationships is most prominently identified in the now-classic social convoy model of social relationships. In Chapter 2 of this volume, Antonucci, Langfahl, and Akiyama provide an overview of the dynamics between relationships and individual development. They point out that traditional views of social relations as predictors of well-being and other outcome variables must be complemented by recognition that in many cases social relations are in themselves an outcome. This approach also points to the specific processes that determine the course and quality of social relationships across the life span. Certain relationships exist from the start of life and persist into adulthood. (Ties to parents, siblings, cousins, and other family members fit this category.) Other types of relationships may begin in childhood or adulthood (friendships and romantic partnerships serve as an example of these types of ties). As such, chapters in this volume consider variability across the life span with regard to the parent-child tie (Noack & Buhl, 2003, Chap. 3), sibling ties (Bedford & Volling, Chap. 4), affective family ties (Takahashi, Chap. 6), romantic ties (Bierhoff & Schmorr, Chap. 5), friendships (Blieszner & Roberto, Chap. 7), and a variety of social partners to whom individuals feel little bond or affiliation (Fingerman, Chap. 8).

PROCESSES AND OUTCOMES IN PERSONAL RELATIONSHIPS

The processes underlying personal relationships influence why, how, and under what conditions individuals benefit from relationships with others. Examination of such processes includes the important insight that social relationships may entail both risks and chances for individuals, particularly in situations where they confront stress (Rook, Sorkin, & Zirkel, Chap. 9). From a life-span perspective, this issue also entails the question how and why the processes underlying relationships change or remain stable as individuals develop from birth to late life. Individuals' physical, cognitive, and emotional capacities vary at different ages, and these differences contribute to differences in their relationships. Several chapters in this volume pull together research on personal relationships with other phenomena in the social and behavioral sciences such as emotions and health (Charles & Mavandadi, Chap. 10), social cognition and attributions (Blanchard-Fields & Cooper, Chap. 11), personality development (Neyer, Chap. 12), and motivation (Lang, Chap. 14). Hansson, Daleiden, and Hayslip (Chap. 13) suggest that individuals' ability to access, initiate, and maintain appropriate relationships reflects their relational competence. These chapters indicate that processes and dynamics of relationships arise from features of the individuals involved and from the relationship itself.

Over the past two decades, theorists have also devoted particular attention to personality processes and individual differences that contribute to changes in relationships and in the general configuration of the social network (Hansson, Daleiden, & Hayslip, Chap. 13; Lang, Chap. 14; Neyer, Chap. 12). Such a focus usually involves personality or motivational processes and also points to the specific outcomes of personal relationships. In other words, age and life experiences set parameters on individuals' capacities, social roles, and relationship styles, but individual temperament and personality contribute to the relationships as well. Individuals of different ages vary in their approaches to relationships and the relationships themselves vary as a function of the individuals.

Processes also refer to transactions that occur within relationships over time. We might ask, how do individuals respond to what others do or say to them? Recent historical developments introduce technological processes that may affect the nature of personal relationships. Adams and

Stevenson (Chap. 15) describe the ways in which transportation, computers, telephone, and other technologies contribute to the maintenance and dissolution of relationships throughout the life span. The premise that relationship processes involve technologies beyond the individuals is not new; as Adams and Stevenson point out, the Pony Express allowed for transmission of information across vast distances over two hundred years ago. Yet the pervasiveness of technological communication has increased dramatically in recent years, and has become a process of communication within many relationships as a result.

PERSONAL RELATIONSHIPS, THE SOCIAL ARENA, AND HUMAN DEVELOPMENT

This volume focuses on the reciprocal interface between individual development and personal relationships. We consider the ways in which personal relationships arise from and have an impact on individual development. Relationships and development are intricately woven together in a dance of influence. Over fifty years ago, Erikson noted that individual development arises from and affects subsequent individual development (Erikson, 1950). Early relationships set a foundation for trust and exploration, which in turn may shape subsequent relationships (Ainsworth, 1979; Bowlby, 1969). On a more complex level, we explore how personal relationships may improve or hinder an individual's development across domains. A purpose of this volume is to stimulate discussion of social relationships as resources for, and outcomes of, human development.

In sum, throughout life, individuals have different social ties, they bring different capacities to those social ties, and they take away different things from those social ties. Personal relationships themselves arise from transactions between social partners over time and develop in their own right. The interplay between development and the social arena warrants increased attention. This book brings attention to these matters from a life-span developmental perspective.

References

Adams, R., & Stevenson, M. (2003). A lifetime of relationships mediated by technology. In F. R. Lang & K. L. Fingerman (Eds.), *Growing together: Personal relationships across the life span* (Chap. 15). New York: Cambridge University Press.

Ainsworth, M. D. S. (1979). Infant-mother attatchment. *American Psychologist, 34,* 932–937.

Antonucci, T. C., Langfahl, E. S., & Akiyama, H. (2003). Relationships as outcomes and contexts. In F. R. Lang & K. L. Fingerman (Eds.), *Growing together: Personal relationships across the life span* (Chap. 2). New York: Cambridge University Press.

Ariès, P. (1962). *Centuries of childhood.* New York: Vintage Press.

Auhagen, A. E., & Von Salisch, M. (1996). *The diversity of human relationships* (Translation of German volume published in 1991). Cambridge: Cambridge University Press.

Axelrod, R. M. (1985). *The evolution of cooperation.* New York: Basic Books.

Baltes, P. B., & Mayer, K. U. (Eds.) (1999). *The Berlin aging study: Aging from 70 to 100.* New York: Cambridge University Press.

Baltes, P. B., Staudinger, U. M., & Lindenberger, U. (1999). Lifespan psychology: Theory and application to intellectual functioning. *Annual Review of Psychology, 50,* 417–507.

Baumeister, R. F., & Leary, M. R. (1995). The need to belong: Desire for interpersonal attachments as a fundamental human motivation. *Psychological Bulletin, 117,* 497–529.

Bedford, V. H. (1992). Memories of parental favoritism and the quality of parent-child ties in adulthood. *Journal of Gerontology, 47,* S149–S155.

Bedford, V. H., & Volling, B. L. (2003). A dynamic ecological systems perspective on emotion regulation development within the sibling relationship context. In F. R. Lang & K. L. Fingerman (Eds.), *Growing together: Personal relationships across the life span* (Chap. 4). New York: Cambridge University Press.

Berkman, L. F., Glass, T., Brissette, I., & Seeman, T. E. (2000). From social integration to health: Durkheim in the new millennium. *Social Science and Medicine, 51*(6), 843–857.

Bierhoff, H.-W., & Schmohr, M. (2003). Romantic and marital relationships. In F. R. Lang & K. L. Fingerman (Eds.), *Growing together: Personal relationships across the life span* (Chap. 5). New York: Cambridge University Press.

Blanchard-Fields, F., & Cooper, C. (2003). Social cognition and social relationships. In F. R. Lang & K. L. Fingerman (Eds.), *Growing together: Personal relationships across the life span* (Chap. 11). New York: Cambridge University Press.

Blieszner, R., & Roberto, K. A. (2003). Friendship across the life span: Reciprocity in individual and relationship development. In F. R. Lang & K. L. Fingerman (Eds.), *Growing together: Personal relationships across the life span* (Chap. 7). New York: Cambridge University Press.

Booth, A., & Johnson, D. R. (1994). Declining health and marital quality. *Journal of Marriage and the Family, 56*(1), 218–223.

Bowlby, J. (1969). *Attachment and loss: Vol. 1. Attachment.* New York: Basic Books.

Bronfenbrenner, U., & Morris, P. A. (1997). The ecology of developmental processes. In W. Damon (Ed.), *Handbook of child psychology* (5th ed.) (pp. 993–1028). New York: Wiley.

Bühler, C. (1935). *From birth to maturity.* London: Kegan Paul. (German original published in 1933: *Der menschliche Lebenslauf als psychologisches Problem*).

Buss, D. M. (1999). *Evolutionary psychology: The new science of mind.* Needham Heights, MA: Allyn & Bacon.

Carstensen, L. L. (1992). Social and emotional patterns in adulthood: Support for socioemotional selectivity theory. *Psychology and Aging, 7,* 331–338.

Carstensen, L. L., Graff, J., & Lang, F. R. (2000). Psychology's contributions to gerontology. In J. M. Clair (Ed.), *Multidisciplinary perspectives on aging: Progress and priorities* (pp. 29–48). Amityville, NY: Baywood Publishing Company.

Caspi, A., Elder, G. H., & Bem, D. J. (1987). Moving against the world: Life-course patterns of explosive children. *Developmental Psychology, 23,* 308–313.

Caspi, A., & Silva, P. (1995). Temperamental qualities at age three predict personality traits in young adulthood: Longitudinal evidence from a birth cohort. *Child Development, 66,* 486–498.

Charles, S. T., & Mavandadi, S. (2003). Social support and physical health across the life span: Socioemotional influences. In F. R. Lang & K. L. Fingerman (Eds.), *Growing together: Personal relationships across the life span* (Chap. 10). New York: Cambridge University Press.

Chatters, L. M., & Taylor, R. J. (1993). Intergenerational support: The provision of assistance to parents by adult children. In J. S. Jackson & L. M. Chatters (Eds.), *Aging in Black America* (pp. 69–83). Thousand Oaks, CA: Sage.

Connidis, I. A., Rosenthal, C. J., & McMullin, J. A. (1996). The impact of family composition on providing help to older parents: A study of employed adults. *Research on Aging, 18,* 402–429.

Davey, A., Fingerman, K. L., & Jenkins-Tucker, C. (2002). Within-family variability in representations of past relationships with parents. Manuscript under review.

Duck, S. W. (Ed.) (1996). *Handbook of personal relationships* (2nd ed.). New York: Wiley.

Duck, S. W. (1998). *Human relationships* (3rd ed.). London: Sage Publications.

Dunn, J., & Plomin, R. (1990). *Separate lives: Why siblings are so different.* New York: Basic Books.

Elder, G. H. (1998a). The life course as developmental theory. *Child Development, 69,* 1–12.

Elder, G. H. (1998b). The life course and human development. In R. M. Lerner (Ed.), *Handbook of child psychology, Volume 1: Theoretical models of human development,* pp. 939–991. New York: Wiley, Inc.

Erikson, E. K. (1950). *Childhood and society.* New York: W.W. Norton.

Field, D. (1981). Retrospective reports by healthy, intelligent elderly people of personal events of their adult lives. *International Journal of Behavioral Development, 4,* 77–97.

Fingerman, K. L. (2000). "We had a nice little chat": Age and generational differences in mothers' and daughters' descriptions of enjoyable visits. *Journal of Gerontology: Psychological Sciences, 55,* P95–P106.

Fingerman, K. L. (2001). *Aging mothers and their adult daughters: A study in mixed emotions.* New York: Springer Publishers.

Fingerman, K. L. (2003). The consequential stranger: Peripheral social ties across the life span. In F. R. Lang & K. L. Fingerman (Eds.), *Growing together: Personal relationships across the life span* (Chap. 8). New York: Cambridge University Press.

Fingerman, K. L. (in press). The role of offspring and in-laws in grandparents' relationships with their grandchildren. *Journal of Family Issues.*

Fingerman, K. L., & Bermann, E. (2000). Applications of family systems theory to the study of adulthood. *International Journal of Aging and Human Development, 51,* 5–29.

Fingerman, K. L., & Birditt, K. S. (in press). Do age differences in close and problematic family networks reflect the pool of available relatives? *Journal of Gerontology: Psychological Sciences.*

Fingerman, K. L., & Hay, E. L. (2002). Searching under the streetlight: Age biases in the personal and family relationships literature. *Personal Relationships, 9,* 415–433.

Fingerman, K. L., Nussbaum, J., & Birditt, K. S. (in press). Keeping all five balls in the air: Juggling family communication at midlife. In A. L. Vangelisti (Ed.),

Handbook of family communication. Hillsdale, N.J.: Lawrence Erlbaum Associates.

Fischer, L. R. (1983). Mothers and mothers-in-law. *Journal of Marriage and the Family, 45,* 187–192.

Hall, G. S. (1922). *Senescence: The last half of life.* New York: Appleton.

Hansson, R. O., Daleiden, E. L., & Hayslip, B. Jr. (2003). Relational competence across the life span. In F. R. Lang & K. L. Fingerman (Eds.), *Growing together: Personal relationships across the life span* (Chap. 13). New York: Cambridge University Press.

Hartup. W., & Rubin, Z. (Eds.) (1986). *Relationships and development.* Hillsdale, NJ: Lawrence Erlbaum.

Hazan, C., & Shaver, P. R. (1987). Romantic love conceptualized as an attachment process. *Journal of Personality and Social Psychology, 52,* 511–524.

Hazan, C., & Shaver, P. R. (1994). Attachment as an organizational framework for research on close relationships. *Psychological Inquiry, 5,* 1–22.

Hilgard, E. R. (1987). *Psychology in America: A historical survey.* Orlando, FL: Harcourt Brace Jovanovich.

Hinde, R. A. (1997). *Relationships. A dialectical perspective.* Hove, East Sussex, UK: Psychology Press Publishers.

Kelley, H. H., Berscheid, E., Christensen, A., Harvey, J. H., Huston, T. L., Levinger, G., McClintock, E., Peplau, L. A., & Peterson, D. R. (1983). *Close relationships.* New York: W. H. Freeman.

Kenyatta, J. (1962). *Facing Mount Kenya: The tribal life of the Gikuyu.* New York: Vintage Books.

Lang, F. R. (2001). Regulation of social relationships in later adulthood. *Journal of Gerontology: Psychological Sciences, 6,* P321–P326.

Lang, F. R. (2002). The filial task in midlife: Ambivalence and the quality of relationships with old-aged parents. In K. Pillemer & K. Luescher (Eds.), *Intergenerational ambivalences: A new perspective on parent-child relations in later life.* Elsevier/JAI press.

Lang, F. R. (2003). Social motivation across the life span. In F. R. Lang & K. L. Fingerman (Eds.), *Growing together: Personal relationships across the life span* (Chap. 14). New York: Cambridge University Press.

Lang, F. R., & Carstensen, L. L. (1994). Close emotional relationships in late life: Further support for proactive aging in the social domain. *Psychology and Aging, 9,* 315–324.

Lang, F. R., & Carstensen, L. L. (2002). Time counts: Future time perspective, goals, and social relationships. *Psychology and Aging, 17,* 125–139.

Lang, F. R., & Schuetze, Y. (2002). Adult children's supportive behaviors and older parents' subjective well-being – A developmental perspective on inter-generational relationships. *Journal of Social Issues, 58,* 661–680.

Leach, P. (1997). *Your baby & child: From birth to age five.* New York: Alfred A. Knopf.

Levitt, M. J. (2000). Social relations across the life span: In search of unified models. *International Journal of Aging and Human Development, 51,* 71–84.

Main, M., Kaplan, N., & Cassidy, J. (1985). Security in infancy, childhood, and adulthood: A move to the level of representation. *Monographs of the Society for Research in Child Development 50, Serial 209.*

Mangen, D. J. (1995). Methods and analysis of family data. In R. Blieszner & V. H. Bedford (Eds.), *Aging and the family: Theory and research* (pp. 148–177). Westport, CT: Praeger Publishers.

Mangen, D. J., & Bengtson, V. L. (Eds.), (1988). *Measurement of intergenerational relations*. Newbury Park, CA: Sage Publications.

Marsiske, M., Lang, F. R., Baltes, P. B., & Baltes, M. M. (1995). Selective optimization with compensation: Life-span perspectives on successful human development. In R. Dixon & L. Bäckman (Eds.), *Psychological compensation: Managing losses and promoting gains* (pp. 35–79). Hillsdale, NJ: Erlbaum.

Morgan, D. L., Neal, M. B., & Carder, P. C. (1997). Both what and when: The effects of positive and negative aspects of relationships on depression during the first 3 years of widowhood. *Journal of Clinical Geropsychology, 3,* 73–91.

Neyer, F. J. (2003). Dyadic fits and transactions in personality and relationships. In F. R. Lang & K. L. Fingerman (Eds.), *Growing together: Personal relationships across the life span* (Chap. 12). New York: Cambridge University Press.

Neyer, F. J., & Lang, F. R. (2003). Blood is thicker than water: Kinship orientation across adulthood. *Journal of Personality and Social Psychology, 84,* 310–321.

Noack, P., & Buhl, H. M. (2003). Child-parent relationships. In F. R. Lang & K. L. Fingerman (Eds.), *Growing together: Personal relationships across the life span* (Chap. 3). New York: Cambridge University Press.

Rook, K. S., Sorkin, D., & Zirkel, L. (2003). Stress in social relationships: Coping and adaptation across the life span. In F. R. Lang & K. L. Fingerman (Eds.), *Growing together: Personal relationships across the life span* (Chap. 9). New York: Cambridge University Press.

Schaie, K. W. (1996). *Intellectual development in adulthood: The Seattle longitudinal study*. New York: Cambridge University Press.

Shostak, M. (1981). *Nisa: The life and words of a !Kung woman*. Cambridge, MA: Harvard University Press.

Suitor, J. J., & Pillemer, K. (1997, November). "Mom always loved you best": Preliminary findings from a pilot study of within-family differences in parent-adult child relations. Paper presented at the Gerontological Society of America annual meeting, Cincinnati, OH.

Takahashi, K. (2003). Close relationships across the life span: Toward a theory of relationship types. In F. R. Lang & K. L. Fingerman (Eds.), *Growing together: Personal relationships across the life span* (Chap. 6). New York: Cambridge University Press.

Tetens, J. N. (1777). *Philosophische Versuche über die menschliche Natur und ihre Entwicklung*. Leipzig: Weidmanns Erben & Reich.

Thomae, H. (1959). Entwicklungsbegriff und Entwicklungstheorie [Definition of development and developmental theory]. In H. Thomae (Ed.), *Entwicklungspsychologie*. Göttingen: Hogrefe.

Turner, J. (Ed.) (1996). *The encyclopedia of relationships across the life span*. Westport, CT: Greenwood Publishing.

Wohlwill, J. F. (1973). *The study of behavioral development*. New York: Academic Press.

2

Relationships as Outcomes and Contexts

Toni C. Antonucci, Elizabeth S. Langfahl,
and Hiroko Akiyama

In this chapter we provide a broad overview of how culture influences all aspects of social relations. We consider the interpretation of social relations as both outcomes of individual and situational experiences as well as contexts within which a broad range of development occurs. We suggest that the traditional view of social relations as predictors of well-being and other outcome variables needs to be complemented by the recognition that in some cases social relations are in themselves an outcome. And finally, as life-span developmental psychologists we emphasize the importance of recognizing the continuing influence of development and the dynamic nature of social relations both as outcomes and predictors.

In this chapter we explore how relationships can be outcomes of individual and life experiences as well as contexts within which a broad range of development occurs. At the same time social relations also influence important mental and physical outcomes over the life course. We propose that the conceptualization of relationships as both outcomes and contexts of development provides a unique insight into the complex and multidimensional potential of relationships. Relationships are outcomes, in the sense that personal and situational characteristics of the individual shape the type of relationships an individual needs or seeks, the kinds of support exchanged, and the ways in which those relationships are evaluated. Characteristics of the individual and the situation affect the way individuals initiate, develop, maintain, and sometimes end relationships across their life span. But relationships also serve as a context of individual development. They shape consequent physical and mental health from infancy through adulthood. The convoy model of social relations over the life course usefully illustrates those characteristics that shape relationships as outcomes as well as how social relations provide a context that fundamentally influences well-being. We begin first with a brief overview of the convoy model.

THE CONVOY MODEL OF SOCIAL RELATIONS

The convoy model of social relations is offered as a useful heuristic for conceptualizing the multifaceted and long-term nature of individuals' close relationships (Kahn & Antonucci, 1980). Individuals are thought to move through life with a "convoy" of relationships, which may exhibit both stability and discontinuity, and which also influences their socialization and development (Antonucci & Akiyama, 1987). The convoy model integrates the concepts of social network structure, social support and support satisfaction, as well as characteristics of the person and the situation, to facilitate the examination of social relations from a life-span perspective. The relationships that compose an individual's convoy can be conceptualized as "outcomes" of development, although continuously subject to change associated with both individual development and relationship development. Both the existence of a relationship and relationship quality can be viewed as outcomes. Relationships are also contexts, as individuals' convoys provide support for challenges and demands throughout the life span, thus facilitating individual well-being and development. However, convoy members themselves may also be the source of challenges and demands.

An individual's social convoy is usually composed of a variety of relationships across the life span. Individuals often organize their relationships hierarchically. Thus, the convoy model distinguishes relationships that are very close, somewhat close, and less close. Under optimal conditions, the convoy can be conceptualized as a protective layer of social relationships that works to guide, socialize, and encourage individuals throughout their lifetime. Different relationships in an individual's convoy may serve different functions, including the exchange of aid, affective support and affirmation, or encouragement (Kahn & Antonucci, 1980). However, it is important to acknowledge that support from individuals and the social convoy as a whole is not always associated with positive outcomes. Relationships can serve as contexts for exchanges that foster maladaptive behaviors (e.g., drinking or drug buddies) or simply do not provide enough support to foster adaptive or positive outcomes (e.g., for health behaviors such as exercise or a healthy diet) (Kahn & Antonucci, 1980).

The convoy model recognizes that personal and situational characteristics shape the individual and affect their social relations. In this sense relationships are outcomes in that they are influenced by properties of the person, such as age, gender, race, education, and personality, and by properties of the situation, such as role expectations, demands, daily hassles, and resources. Individuals with certain specific personal characteristics (e.g., older, less educated, female, minority group member) will likely have social networks, exchange social support, and be satisfied with support relations in ways that are distinctly different from individuals with different personal characteristics (e.g., younger, more educated, male, majority group member). Similarly, people who occupy extremely demanding roles or are confronted with numerous daily hassles will develop social networks, support exchanges, and be satisfied with support that is distinctly different from people who live in non-stressful, non-demanding circumstances. Thus, social relations are the outcomes of specific personal and situational characteristics. But there is a continuation in the chain of events and an individual's social network; social support and support satisfaction are, in turn, hypothesized to provide the context which additively and multiplicatively influences and contributes to an individual's health and well-being (Antonucci, Akiyama, & Merline, 2001).

Although the fact that social relations vary over time has been recognized for some time, much less recognized is how culture provides a context for this influence. The influence of personal characteristics such as age, gender, and SES on social relations differs across cultures. Support needs and opportunities for individuals also vary across time and place. It is clear that social convoys, including all aspects of convoys – personal and situational characteristics, support relations, and well-being – are culturally situated. We illustrate this perspective in Figure 2.1. As can be seen, culture provides the overarching framework within which the social convoy

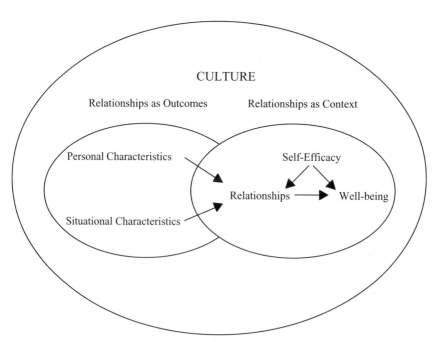

FIGURE 2.1. Relationships as Outcomes and Contexts of Development.

operates. In the following section we provide illustrative examples to demonstrate how culture shapes both the development and interpretation of social relations.

CULTURAL INFLUENCES ON SOCIAL RELATIONS

Often social behaviors and social relations are studied as though they were the same in all cultures and contexts. This is clearly not true. There are circumstances where the same social network composition or behavior could be interpreted quite differently. Consider the following examples of identical network size, composition, and behavior interpreted quite differently depending on the cultural perspective or the eye of the beholder.

While the actual size of social networks appears to be relatively stable across the life span, social network size has been documented to vary by culture. The majority of cross-sectional and longitudinal survey research on social networks across the life span has been conducted in North America, Europe, Japan, and to a limited degree, China (e.g., Antonucci, Lansford et al., 2001; Ruan, Freeman, Dai, Pan, & Zhang, 1997; Wellman & Wortley, 1989). There seem to be cultural differences in the size of social networks. Some cultures or religions encourage large families, and because of the predominance of kin in individuals' social networks, this may be associated with mean differences in size. For example, both Mexican Americans and Mormons have a tendency to have large families; both will likely have larger social networks across the life span than someone from a British or Chinese background where families tend to be smaller and social networks might also be smaller. In all these examples, while certain characteristics are the same (i.e., large or small families), other characteristics represent very different cultures (e.g., Mexican-Americans vs. Mormons, British vs. Chinese). Hence, it is clear that culture provides a context within which to interpret characteristics and circumstances.

Alternatively, it may not be cultural preferences but cultural experiences that shape network size. As a result of World Wars I and II both Germany and Japan have much smaller numbers of men in certain birth cohorts and many more who never married as well as widowed women in these same cohorts. More recently in some African nations, AIDS has ravaged the eighteen-to-forty-year-old population, reducing social network size by leaving elders childless and younger children orphaned (Roughton, 2000). These network size changes in the different cultures have direct and devastating effects on the availability of support providers at critical junctions across the life span.

Other cultural influences relate to the interpretation of behavior. Consider the following example. An American mother of Lebanese descent who describes her ten-year-old son as shy notes different reactions to her son's shy behavior at the mall. She encounters an American acquaintance and while they chat the acquaintance tries to begin a conversation with the preteen. However, he does not respond and seems uncomfortable, and the acquaintance tries to make him feel more comfortable by telling his mother, "Don't worry about it – he's just shy." However, when the Lebanese American mother and her son later encounter an acquaintance from the local Lebanese American community, the son's behavior is interpreted differently. When the ten-year-old behaves in exactly the same manner, the acquaintance is offended. The same behavior is now interpreted negatively, since it is customary for younger people in the Lebanese American community to greet and respond to adults. This is considered appropriate, respectful behavior. Later, when she thinks about the incident, the mother realizes that she and her husband, who themselves daily move between the American and the Lebanese American communities, have allowed their son to exhibit this unresponsive behavior. The behavior is labeled "shyness" in the broader American culture, but is perceived as disrespectful by the Lebanese community. She now sees that they need to encourage him to exhibit friendly, respectful behavior even though he feels shy, so that his behavior is appropriate in both cultural contexts. An alternative, of course, would have been to exhibit the appropriate behavior for each context.

The senior author spent a sabbatical year in France where her children went to French schools and learned both the French language and various French expressions. By the end of the year, they were quite proficient in the French language and with that well-known double-shouldered, utterly uncaring French shrug, which although non-verbal, is clearly accompanied by the thought, "I don't know, I don't care, it's not my business, and I can't be bothered." This may be common behavior in France, but it was not very well received when these same children came back to the United States and to an American elementary school that considered this French national shrug both rude and defiant. The senior author had to sit her children down and explain how they needed to modify their behavior for their American teachers.

As these examples illustrate, social behaviors may be consistent across contexts, but there may be important differences in how these behaviors are perceived and interpreted. Socially adept individuals recognize these contextual differences and adjust their behavior accordingly. The degree to which individuals are able to make these adjustments, and feel satisfied with their supportive relationships and with their general social acceptance, is likely to vary and to be an important factor in mental and physical health outcomes. Many individuals may find themselves negotiating multiple social contexts. It is these people especially who need to recognize the influence of culture.

RELATIONSHIPS AS OUTCOMES ACROSS THE LIFE SPAN

Personal Characteristics

As the convoy model suggests, personal characteristics of individuals such as gender, race/ethnicity, and socioeconomic status are associated with different relationship outcomes, specifically differences in social network structure, such as size and composition, across the life span (Antonucci, 2001; Kahn & Antonucci, 1980). Additionally, personal characteristics can both directly and indirectly influence the exchange of support within the context of individual relationships and across social networks. As the individual develops over time there are associated changes in his or her social relationships. This life-span individual development, in turn, is associated with changes in social networks, such as network size and composition as well as changes in the exchange of support. The parent-child relationship is different when the child is an infant and the parent a young adult as compared to when the child is a middle-aged adult and the parent a member of the oldest old (see Fingerman, 2001).

Gender and Social Relations across the Life Span. Gender differences in social relations across the life span also represent an example of how personal characteristics influence the outcome of social relations. The association of gender and social relations is quite complex and is also influenced by culture (see Best & Williams, 2001). The social networks of both men and women are usually composed of the same relationships, for example, parents, spouse, child, and friends (Antonucci, 1994, 2001). However, evidence suggests that the quality, nature, and function of women's and men's social relationships may differ. Data from an extensive study of German elders is illustrative. While Smith and Baltes (1998) did not find gender differences in network size among older Germans, they found gender differences in the types of support that individuals felt they provided to others. Even in old age, women considered themselves primarily to be providers of emotional support, while men reported providing more instrumental support. These gender differences, no doubt, transcend many cultures.

Gender differences influence relationships throughout the life span, and earlier life decisions, in conjunction with gendered patterns of social relations, can have very negative effects later in life. Barker, Morrow, and Mitteness (1998) considered gender differences in the informal social networks of older urban African Americans. Their findings indicated that men who were no longer married to the mother of their children were especially disadvantaged in the size and composition of their social network. The children of the estranged father were more likely to maintain ties with their mother than with their father, perhaps reflecting the stronger emotional ties that children were able to maintain with their mothers. The pattern of Barker et al.'s (1998) finding is not unexpected, and would likely be replicated in other populations. The caregiving role of women in many contexts may serve to maintain and strengthen social ties across the life span.

Race/Ethnicity and Social Relations across the Life Span. Racial, ethnic, and cultural factors can influence social relations across the life span. There is increasing interest in examining the social relations of different racial and ethnic groups, as such groups have historical and contemporary life experiences that may differentially shape their social relations (Harevan, 1994). This is especially evident in the United States, which is characterized by much cultural variability, making it possible to examine how racial, ethnic, and cultural membership affects individuals' social relations within a diverse society. In the convoy model, racial or ethnic identity is considered to be a property of the person, but also indicates membership in a larger group, making it both a personal characteristic and a cultural/structural context. The ways in which racial and ethnic differences are associated with changes in social relations across the life span create an added layer of complexity. We now explicitly address these associations.

There is evidence that there are racial and cultural differences in social networks across the life span, although these differences may be moderated by personal and relationship characteristics, such as age and closeness of relationships. For example, U.S. findings suggest that Blacks have smaller social networks than their White counterparts, perhaps due to the greater likelihood of Whites being married and to the shorter life expectancy of Blacks (Ajrouch, Antonucci, & Janevic, 2001; Pugliesi & Shook, 1998). Ajrouch, Langfahl, and Antonucci (2001) examined racial differences in social networks and found that although Black respondents had smaller social networks overall than Whites, Blacks and Whites reported approximately the same number of close relationships. Blacks and Whites did differ in the number of somewhat close relationships. Whites reported more somewhat close relationships, although these relationships were less geographically proximal and characterized by less frequent contact than Black respondents' relationships were (Ajrouch, Langfahl, & Antonucci, 2001). There is less support for racial differences among older adults, however. Ajrouch, Langfahl, and Antonucci (2001) and Peek and O'Neill (2001) found no significant race differences in total network size among older adults. Differences in network characteristics early in life may disappear when life circumstances, such as marital status, converge. These findings point to the complexity of race differences and highlight the importance of considering personal characteristics across the life span.

While there are differences in social relations associated with race, ethnicity, and culture, there are also a number of similarities in social relations across cultural and racial/ethnic groups. One obvious commonality is the type of relationships typically identified as close. Across groups, people most often report being close to their parents, spouse, and children (Antonucci, Lansford et al., 2001; Wenger, 1997). However, in the United States, certain groups are perceived to differentially rely on support from close family, extended family, friends, and religious and organizational groups. Among African Americans, family, extended family, and the church have been documented as important sources of support (Krause & Van Tran, 1989; Taylor & Chatters, 1986; Taylor, Chatters, & Jackson, 1997). It can be argued that strong family ties are important sources of support among all racial and ethnic groups. However, a strong identification with family members and a desire to exchange support with family members (i.e., "familism") is an important cultural value for many ethnic groups in the U.S., including African Americans, Hispanics, and Asian Americans (Chen & Lan, 1998; Freeberg & Stein, 1996).

The cultural value of familism may be related to structural and functional characteristics of support networks. Individuals who value familism and feel that their families are an important source of support turn to nuclear and extended family members for support, and feel obligated to provide support to their family. However, the degree of support exchanged by family members may vary by acculturation (Rodriguez & Kosloski, 1998; Sabogal, Marin, Otero-Sabogal, & Marin, 1987). For some cultural groups, the family context is the most valued and interactions within this context make important contributions to individual well-being (La Roche, 1997). This reliance upon family for support is also associated with costs. For example, caregivers may experience emotional, physical, and financial burdens when caring for family members, especially if they underutilize outside support resources (John, Resendiz, & De Vargas, 1997; Purdy & Arguello, 1992; Youn, Knight, Jeong, & Benton, 1999). However, as individuals and their families become more acculturated or upwardly mobile, they may become more likely to seek formal instrumental support, although they may still highly value family relationships.

Socioeconomic Status and Social Relations across the Life Span. A final group of individual characteristics that have been increasingly recognized include indicators of SES such as education, work status, and income, which are known to be differentially associated with social relations across the life span (Antonucci, 2001; Antonucci, Ajrouch, & Janevic, in press; Mirowsky & Ross, 1999). Education, income, and other SES indicators are directly associated with a variety of individual outcomes across the life span, such as health, cognitive functioning, and physical and emotional well-being (Adler, Boyce, Chesney, Cohen, Folkman, Kahn, & Syme, 1994; Rautio, Heikkinen, & Heikkinen, 2001; Seifer, 2001). Socioeconomic status can influence social relations and health both directly and indirectly, through the neighborhoods individuals live in, schools children attend, work experiences, the resources of social network members, etc. (Leventhal & Brooks-Gunn, 2000). Social relationships are important contexts for the exchange of support that facilitates well-being regardless of SES; however, lower SES is associated with smaller, more strained social networks, and with network members who themselves require more support (Antonucci, 2001; Krause & Borawski-Clark, 1995). The experience of economic hardship itself can negatively affect family relationships, as fostering relationship quality may become less important than succeeding in the day-to-day tasks of making ends meet (Gomel, Tinsley, Parke, & Clark, 1998).

Situational Characteristics

Although implied thus far and implicitly addressed, we turn now to the explicit consideration of properties of the situation. Roles, expectations, and environmental characteristics also affect social relations in conjunction with personal characteristics and the broader cultural context. For example, a Chinese study illustrates how cultural context and the primacy of certain roles affect individuals' social relations. This study provides evidence that macrolevel (governmental) changes are linked to microlevel changes in individuals' social networks. Specifically, Ruan et al. (1997) examined changes in the structure of social networks in the third largest city in China, Tianjin, based on a 1993 replication of a survey conducted in 1986. Over the seven-year period, there was a significant decrease in the average number of relationships identified as "discussion partners," (i.e., strong relationships). Specifically, they found a decrease in the average number of kin and coworkers identified as strong relationships while there was a significant increase in the average number of friends and "others" identified as strong. The authors suggested that prior to the emergence of the new market economy in China, workplace ties were extremely important, since individuals generally had lifelong employment and the workplace provided benefits and resources that kin were unable to provide. Increased economic stability and decreased job stability both eroded the importance of the workplace as a long-term primary context for the development of strong supportive relationships and expanded opportunities in the private sector and for socialization outside of the workplace (Ruan et al., 1997).

Contrast this with Lai's (2001) examination of social networks in Shanghai, China. Lai suggested that state controls were weaker in Shanghai, leading to less reliance on the workplace and, therefore, less dependence on coworkers for support. It was found that spouse and parents/parents-in-law were an important source of support, while support from coworkers was less important. Although both Ruan et al. (1997) and Lai (2001) caution that the links between social relations and macrolevel forces like state control and increases in the market economy are only hypothesized, their findings do highlight the ways in which economic and cultural forces have the potential to shape individuals' social relations, in terms of the ties individuals develop and maintain, and the function and importance of those ties.

On a less macro level, we know that people whose work or personal lives are particularly stressful or demanding are likely to seek social relations that will help them alleviate the demands they are experiencing. There is now an accumulating literature on the social relations of caregivers indicating that high-quality supportive relationships can significantly offset the stress burden of long-term caregivers (Aneshensel, Pearlin, Mullan, Zarit, & Whitlatch, 1995). Similarly, a recent study of older people in four nations, France, Germany, Japan, and the United States, indicates that people who are coping with the resource deficits of widowhood, financial strain, or health problems are likely to have social relations with different characteristics than those who are not experiencing these same deficits (Antonucci, Lansford et al., 2001).

Social relationships, defined by Reis, Collins, and Berscheid (2000), represent a context of mutual influence in which relationship partners engage in a series of social interactions over time. Social relations are both the outcome of individuals' situational and personal characteristics as well as the predictors of mental and physical health outcomes. Much of the literature has examined how both quantitative and qualitative aspects of social relations affect various outcomes. This literature has accumulated over the years and is both persuasive and compelling. We briefly turn to that literature next.

RELATIONSHIPS AS CONTEXT AND PREDICTORS OF OUTCOMES

Documentation of the significant predictive relationship between social relations and mortality by Berkman and Syme (1979) is often considered a turning point in the field. While researchers suggested this association for decades, documentation of it using longitudinal data and controlling for a number of known sociodemographic covariates finally convinced a large number of researchers that this was an important association. Additional research quickly followed replicating the mortality finding and adding morbidity (including both physical and mental health). Several extensive reviews are available (Antonucci, 2001; Bowling & Grundy, 1998; Seeman, 2000); therefore we will not review this literature in any detail but rather turn to a few specific examples that particularly demonstrate social relations as context and predictors.

George, Blazer, Hughes, and Fowler (1989) and Oxman, Berkman, Kasl, Freeman, and Barrett (1992), using American samples, examined different aspects of social relations and their effect on morbidity, specifically depression. Both of these studies, one in North Carolina and one in Connecticut, demonstrated that qualitative indicators of social relations were better able to predict depressive symptomatology than quantitative aspects of social relations. Antonucci, Fuhrer, and Dartigues (1997) replicated this finding with a representative sample of older people in southwestern France. These data suggest a pattern indicating that while different aspects of social relations (e.g., size and quality) are related to outcomes, some clearly account for a higher proportion of variance in the outcome of interest than others. Interestingly, whereas culture often shapes social relations, this finding seems to be robust across different cultures. Of course, while quality is a generic term, it may very well be that the assessment of quality is directly influenced by the context within which it is being assessed. For example, in environments where intergenerational coresidency is expected, high-quality intergenerational relationships may not be achievable if the coresidency expectation is not met. On the other hand, evidence does exist that coresidency itself is likely to have a negative effect on some supportive relationships (van Tilburg, Gierveld, Lecchini, & Marsiglia, 1998). Other negative effects of social relations have been documented. Women appear to not always benefit from more numerous and involved social relationships. For example, at midlife when many women have multiple ties and multiple roles, these relationships can be associated with increased demands, which can negatively affect well-being, although these same relationships can also be the source of support (Antonucci, 1994; Antonucci, Akiyama, & Lansford, 1998; Lynch, 1998; Turner & Turner, 1999).

Vaillant, Meyer, Mukamal, and Soldz (1998) raised the question, "Are social supports in late midlife a cause or result of successful physical aging?" It seems very likely that the answer to this question is both. People who reach midlife with positive support relationships are much more likely to be in good health. At the same time, being in good health increases the likelihood that an individual will remain connected, engage in adaptive health behaviors, and will consequently maintain a successful aging trajectory.

Accumulated evidence points to the importance of having supportive relationships, and the consequences of not having a social network, though this is likely a rare phenomenon. For example, in a sample of older Japanese, Takahashi, Tamura, and Makiko (1997) identified "lone wolves," individuals who lacked affective ties, and found that lone wolves had lower levels of well-being than individuals with affective ties. A reasonable hypothesis is that having a support network across the life span is important for health and well-being across cultures. Thus, it may be important to determine if the relative stability of social networks across the life span is evident in a variety of cultures and, if not, to determine what the individual and societal consequences are.

While much research has documented how different characteristics of the social network, the support exchanged, and support quality affect outcomes, the field has offered much less by way of explanatory mechanisms. In the following section we offer the support/efficacy model, which provides one explanatory mechanism for how different aspects of support relations influence mental and physical health. This is a life span cumulative model that suggests that it is the occasion of positive, satisfactory exchanges with significant others over time that conveys to the individual that they are persons of ability and worth who are capable of achieving both proximate and distal life goals.

SUPPORT/EFFICACY MODEL

The convoy model outlines what influences the development of social relations and how social relations might be associated with an individual's health and well-being. However, this model does not address the possible mechanisms that account for this association. Antonucci and Jackson (1987) proposed that self-efficacy might be one of the mechanisms through which social support affects an individual's health and well-being. According to this hypothesized model, individuals, under optimal conditions, receive support from their relationship partner. The relationship partner holds positive beliefs about the support recipient's ability, worth, and capability, and is motivated (by norms, prior help given, ability, opportunity, etc.) to communicate those beliefs to the support recipient. The support provider's beliefs and motivations influence his or her supportive behavior, that is, the provision of instrumental and emotional support and affirmation. It also influences the support provider's communication and beliefs about the support recipient *to* the support recipient. The support received and the perception of that support by the support recipient then develops in the support recipient a positive sense of self, ability, and self-worth that accumulates and translates into feelings of self-efficacy, which then positively affects health and well-being.

This complex hypothesized model of support and efficacy within a relationship context highlights the ways in which past relationship history and individual motivations, i.e. context, influence exchanges of support and in turn, self-efficacy, health, and well-being. However, self-efficacy is influenced not only by interactions with one relationship partner, but also by the multiple relationships that compose an individual's social network. It may be that there is consistency across relationships. Individuals could receive and perceive similar support that fosters their sense of self-efficacy, or they may, in a sense, receive contradictory messages from different relationships. For example, adolescents may receive contradictory messages about their ability to be successful in school. Parents may communicate to their children throughout their lifetime that they are capable and intelligent, a good student. When confronted by a single bad grade or teacher who feels no confidence in an adolescent with this prior experience, the adolescent, based on a lifetime of encouragement and efficacy, will be much better able to overcome the particular negative circumstance and rely on his or her own sense of ability and self-worth. Another adolescent whose parents have never been confident in their child's intellectual ability and who have communicated those feelings to their child is much more likely when confronted by a bad grade or failing class to assume that the child does not have the ability to succeed and that previous parental messages or predictions are now being fulfilled (Christenson, Rounds, & Gorney, 1992; Eccles & Harold, 1996).

While this is only one example, it is clear that it can easily be generalized. People occupy a variety of roles, such as child, spouse, parent, employee, and volunteer. They may receive adequate support for some roles but not for others. Women with traditional sex role socialization experiences report feeling more efficacious in traditionally female roles such as mother or nurse but much less efficacious in the roles of CEO or doctor. Because of the specific and developmental nature of the support/efficacy model, people can clearly be made to feel efficacious in certain domains, such as work, but less efficacious in other domains, such as parenting.

Linking the Support/Efficacy and Convoy Models

The support/efficacy model and the convoy model are essentially over-lapping models, as it is hypothesized that self-efficacy is one mechanism through which social support affects health and well-being. An intrigu-ing extension of these models, however, is to consider the ways in which an individual's self-efficacy may then directly and indirectly affect factors such as properties of the situation, social network, and social support, thus influencing later support satisfaction, self-efficacy, health, and well-being.

Integrating the convoy and support/efficacy models makes explicit the notion that context matters in relation to the types of activities and en-deavors for which and from whom individuals are likely to receive sup-port. On most college campuses today, both female and male premedical college students are likely to receive encouragement to become doctors, but today, even as thirty years ago, there are some communities in which females would be encouraged to become nurses and males to become doc-tors. Consider two teenage boys who are both fascinated by planes. One boy's father is a car mechanic and he encourages his son to become an airplane mechanic. The other boy's family has a history of serving in the armed forces, so they encourage him to apply to the Air Force Academy in order to become a pilot. Both boys are being supported in their love of planes but the context of their families directs them in their respective career paths. Gender, historical time, family history, and other factors all serve as contexts that shape the expectations and support exchanges with others in fundamental ways. Larger societal contexts as well as relationship contexts, cultural norms and expectations, community characteristics, and relationship quality are all likely to impact the expectations and motivations of support providers, satisfaction of the support recipient, and their sense of efficacy and well-being.

Evidence has been accumulating in support of the efficacy model. In a longitudinal study of low-income single mothers, Green and Rodgers (2001) found support for a reciprocal relationship between self-efficacy and social support. Specifically, they found that a sense of efficacy was associated with the feeling that there was someone to turn to for instrumental support and advice, and being able to obtain instrumental support and advice was associated with increased self-efficacy. In addition, while emotional support was not associated with changes in self-efficacy, it was related to a decrease in the mother's stress level (Green & Rodgers, 2001). Lang, Featherman, and Nesselroade (1997) found that people who felt supported, as measured by perceived support availability, had higher levels of self-efficacy than those who did not. These findings are consistent with the convoy and support/efficacy models. Different types of social support may facilitate a sense of efficacy, increasing individuals' ability to obtain the support they need, and directly influence stress levels and well-being.

It is also useful to recognize that the kind of exchanges that are described in the support/efficacy model often occur within the family context. Families often provide the context within which individuals experience their earliest social relations and from which they develop a sense of efficacy about themselves. The link between family support and the individual's self-efficacy is demonstrated by the types and quality of relationships that the individual creates as they move from the exclusive world of the family to the broader world of family, community, and society. Just as Bronfenbrenner (1986) places the developing individual in context, the intersection of individual and family development occurs in a larger context. The timing and nature of both the developmental tasks individuals are expected to master and how they will develop and enter into family relationships, from family of origin to current family, are all culturally situated. However, in different countries around the world and in a nation as culturally diverse as the United States it is important to recognize that there is much variation in what is perceived as normative by developing individuals and their families.

A life-span developmental perspective particularly informs this view. We have noted earlier in this chapter that social relations change as the individual develops. Relationships (e.g., mother-child and husband-wife) certainly change as people age. We have also noted that relationships affect well-being, that people with better social relations tend to benefit from these relationships as demonstrated by better physical and mental health. While these associations are perhaps more widely recognized and accepted, we wish to make one final point. This point, too, emerges from our life-span perspective but also recognizes the dynamic nature of human relationships.

We have noted that individuals develop and change over time and that this affects their social relations, which, in turn, affects their well-being. However, this suggests a simple unidirectional framework that we do not think is accurate. The directional change referred to above (personal/situational characteristics $\rightarrow$ social relations $\rightarrow$ well-being) is simply part of an ongoing chain of events. Thus, well-being (physical and mental health) affects individual and situational characteristics, which affect social relations and well-being. An example may be helpful.

Consider a healthy middle-class, middle-aged woman (personal characteristics), employed at a local company in a demanding but satisfying job (situational characteristic), who is relatively well integrated into a social world of family, friends, and coworkers (social relations), and who is in good health (well-being). Suddenly, she becomes the caregiver (i.e., change in situational characteristics) for an aging parent recently diagnosed with advanced Alzheimer's disease. The literature on caregiving is informative (Aneshensel et al., 1995). The demands on her time become overwhelming. Although there are other children, she becomes the family-designated caregiver and gets little help from others. Her cultural background mandates provision of care by family members despite the possibility of formal paid services. Consequently, there are changes in her social relations. Relations with her siblings become strained, and her relationship with her mother is forever changed. She has little time for her spouse and children. She loses her job. She is tired all the time, is not eating well, and feels very stressed. Her mental and physical health deteriorates. She becomes very depressed; her mental health is changed. This depression leaves her unable to engage in enjoyable social interactions with family and friends and she begins to withdraw from others. Her circle of social relations becomes smaller, there are fewer people with whom she exchanges supportive interactions and she is significantly less satisfied with her life. The cycle of influence repeats itself but now the results are quite different. Because she is caregiving and is ill, she now has no time for all her other social relations, which eventually dissipate, leaving her even less well physically or emotionally. Needless to say, this once efficacious individual becomes increasingly less so. The point to be made here is that personal/situational characteristics, social relations, and well-being are in a continuing interactive sequence of associations that are fundamentally dynamic in nature.

FUTURE RESEARCH

A great deal is known about the importance of social relationships, both as outcomes and as contexts for individual development and well-being.

However, more research is needed to examine how larger contextual factors, such as culture, shape social relations. As we noted in our discussion of the social convoy model, the relationships that make up individuals' social convoys provide support as individuals negotiate life's challenges and demands. However, it is clear that in addition to personal and situational characteristics, the larger cultural context influences the challenges individuals face, the kind of support they need, seek, and provide, as well as who provides the support given to them. Thus, more research is needed to fully understand the ways in which culture both directly and indirectly influences social relations, in conjunction with other personal and situational characteristics.

Though we focus on the need for further examination of the influence of contextual factors and social relations, we also suggest that it may be possible to identify processes that operate similarly across persons. For example, the support/efficacy model suggests that social relations can foster a sense of self-efficacy and in turn, well-being. Future research should explore the ways in which processes may operate similarly across persons, while the specifics of social relations, such as the size of the social network, support expectations within certain relationships, and relationship quality, may vary. By simultaneously considering variations in social relations across contexts and similarities in processes, we may reach a deeper understanding of how optimal outcomes can be reached by multiple pathways, bounded by cultural, personal, and situational factors.

In addition to the need to explore the role of context, it is also important to continue to recognize and further explore social relationships from a life-span perspective. In order to understand how social relations are both outcomes and contexts it would be useful to explore the association between context, social relations, and well-being longitudinally. We suggest that these associations are not unidirectional, but instead are dynamic and bidirectional. A variety of methodological approaches may offer insights into these dynamics. Longitudinal survey research with representative populations has documented important linkages between social relations and well-being, as well as insights into how social relations are influenced by personal and situational characteristics. In addition to continued research utilizing representative samples, our understanding of how cultural factors interact with personal and situational factors could be increased by a focus on specific racial and ethnic groups. We note that others have also recognized the need for the study of the many racial and ethnic groups represented in the U.S. population, and as a result there appear to be increased funding and research opportunities to explore social relations and health in different populations. We reiterate that what we learn by exploring different populations also teaches us much about our own.

The study of social relations would also benefit other methodological approaches, such as daily experience methods, in-depth interviews, and qualitative approaches (Gable & Reis, 1999; Reis et al., 2000). We believe that the study of social relations is less meaningful when considered out of context, and that a variety of ecologically valid approaches can increase our understanding of variations, processes, and outcomes of social relationships.

CONCLUSION

In this chapter we have made a simple but, we believe, critically important point: social relations are both affected by the personal and situational characteristics of the individual and provide a context that influences physical and mental health outcomes. Related to this point is our view that in order to understand social relationships the culture and context within which they occur must be considered. Similarly, it is also important to recognize that social relations, at any one point in an individual's or family's history, must be considered within a life-span multigenerational perspective. We offer the support/efficacy model as one illustrative model of the mechanism through which support has the pervasive effects that have been documented across time, relationship, and outcome. With the importance of social relationships now so well documented, we must move forward to better understand how these relationships are effective. We believe that this goal cannot be reached without the fundamental understanding of context and the dynamic nature of these associations across the life span.

Acknowledgments

We gratefully acknowledge the following source of support: SES, Social Support and Health, NIH Grant R01-AG17520-02.

References

Adler, N. E., Boyce, T., Chesney, M. A., Cohen, S., Folkman, S., Kahn, R. L., & Syme, S. L. (1994). Socioeconomic status and health. *American Psychologist, 49,* 15–24.

Ajrouch, K. J., Antonucci, T. C., & Janevic, M. R. (2001). Social networks among Blacks and Whites: The interaction between race and age. *Journal of Gerontology: Social Sciences, 56B,* S112–S118.

Ajrouch, K. J., Langfahl, E. S., & Antonucci, T. C. (2001). Close relationships and social networks: A Black-White comparison. Presented at the Annual Meeting of the Gerontological Society of America, Chicago, IL.

Aneshensel, C. S., Pearlin, L. I., Mullan, J. T., Zarit, S. H., & Whitlatch, C. J. (1995). *Profiles in caregiving: The unexpected career.* San Diego, CA: Academic Press, Inc.

Antonucci, T. C. (1994). A life-span view of women's social relations. In B. F. Turner & L. E. Troll (Eds.), *Women growing older* (pp. 239–269). Thousand Oaks, CA: Sage Publications, Inc.

Antonucci, T. C. (2001). Social relations: An examination of social networks, social support, and sense of control. In J. E. Birren (Ed.)., *Handbook of the psychology of aging* (5th ed., pp. 427–453). San Diego, CA: Academic Press.

Antonucci, T. C., Ajrouch, K. J., & Janevic, M. R. (in press). The effect of social relations on the SES-health link in men and women aged 40 and over. *Social Science and Medicine.*

Antonucci, T. C., & Akiyama, H. (1987). Social networks in adult life and a preliminary examination of the convoy model. *Journal of Gerontology, 42,* 519–527.

Antonucci, T. C., Akiyama, H., & Lansford, J. E. (1998). The negative effects of close social relations among older adults. *Family Relations, 47,* 379–384.

Antonucci, T. C., Akiyama, H., & Merline, A. C. (2001). Social relations at midlife. In M. Lachman (Ed.), *Handbook of midlife development* (pp. 571–598). New York: John Wiley & Sons.

Antonucci, T. C., Fuhrer, R., & Dartigues, J. (1997). Social relations and depressive symptomatology in a sample of community-dwelling French older adults. *Psychology and Aging, 12,* 189–195.

Antonucci, T. C., & Jackson, J. S. (1987). Social support, interpersonal efficacy, and health: A life course perspective. In L. L. Carstensen & B. A. Edelstein (Eds.), *Handbook of clinical gerontology* (pp. 291–311). New York: Pergamon Press.

Antonucci, T. C., Lansford, J. E., Schaberg, L., Smith, J., Baltes, M., Akiyama, H., Takahashi, K., Fuhrer, R., & Dartigues, J. (2001). Widowhood and illness: A comparison of social network characteristics in France, Germany, Japan, and the United States. *Psychology and Aging, 16,* 655–665.

Barker, J. C., Morrow, J., & Mitteness, L. S. (1998). Gender, informal social support networks, and elderly urban African Americans. *Journal of Aging Studies, 12,* 199–222.

Berkman, L. F., & Syme, S. L. (1979). Social networks, host resistance, and mortality: A nine-year follow-up study of Alameda County residents. *American Journal of Epidemiology, 109,* 186–204.

Best, D. L., & Williams, J. E. (2001). Gender and culture. In D. Matsumoto (Ed.), *The handbook of culture and psychology* (pp. 195–222). New York: Oxford University Press, Inc.

Bowling, A., & Grundy, E. (1998). The association between social networks and mortality in later life. *Reviews in Clinical Gerontology, 8,* 353–361.

Bronfenbrenner, U. (1986). Ecology of the family as a context for human development: Research perspectives. *Developmental Psychology, 22,* 723–742.

Chen, H., & Lan, W. (1998). Adolescents' perceptions of their parents' academic expectations: Comparisons of American, Chinese-American, and Chinese high school students. *Adolescence, 33,* 385–390.

Christenson, S. L., Rounds, T., & Gorney, D. (1992). Family factors and student achievement: An avenue to increase students' success. *School Psychology Quarterly, 7,* 178–206.

Eccles, J. S., & Harold, R. D. (1996). Family involvement in children's and adolescents' schooling. In A. Booth (Ed.), *Family-school links: How do they affect educational outcomes?* (pp. 3–34). Hillsdale, NJ: Lawrence Erlbaum Associates, Inc.

Fingerman, K. L. (2001). *Aging mothers and their adult daughters: A study in mixed emotions.* New York: Springer Publishers.

Freeberg, A. L., & Stein, C. H. (1996). Felt obligations towards parents in Mexican-American and Anglo-American young adults. *Journal of Social and Personal Relationships, 13,* 457–471.

Gable, S. L., & Reis, H. T. (1999). Now and then, them and us, this and that: Studying relationships across time, partner, context, and person. *Personal Relationships, 6,* 415–432.

George, L. K., Blazer, D. G., Hughes, D. C., & Fowler, N. (1989). Social support and the outcome of major depression. *British Journal of Psychiatry, 154,* 478–485.

Gomel, J. N., Tinsley, B. J., Parke, R. D., & Clark, K. M. (1998). The effects of economic hardship on family relationships among African American, Latino, and Euro-American families. *Journal of Family Issues, 19,* 436–467.

Green, B. L., & Rodgers, A. (2001). Determinants of social support among low-income mothers: A longitudinal analysis. *American Journal of Community Psychology, 29,* 419–441.

Harevan, T. K. (1994). Aging and generational relations: A historical and life course perspective. *Annual Review of Sociology, 20,* 437–461.

John, R., Resendiz, R., & De Vargas, L. W. (1997). Familism as explicit motive for eldercare among Mexican American caregivers. *Journal of Cross-Cultural Gerontology, 12,* 145–162.

Kahn, R., & Antonucci, T. C. (1980). Convoys over the life course: Attachment, roles, and social support. In P. B. Baltes & O. J. Brim (Eds.), *Life-span development and behavior* (Vol. 3, pp. 253–286). New York: Academic Press.

Krause, N., & Borawski-Clark, E. (1995). Social class differences in social support among older adults. *The Gerontologist, 35,* 498–508.

Krause, N., & Van Tran, T. (1989). Stress and religious involvement among older blacks. *Journal of Gerontology: Social Sciences, 44,* S4–S13.

Lai, G. (2001). Social support networks in urban Shanghai. *Social Networks, 23,* 73–85.

Lang, F. R., Featherman, D. L., & Nesselroade, J. R. (1997). Social self-efficacy and short-term variability in social relationships: The MacArthur successful aging studies. *Psychology and Aging, 12,* 657–666.

La Roche, M. (1997). The association of social relations and depression levels among Dominicans in the United States. *Hispanic Journal of Behavioral Sciences, 21,* 420–430.

Leventhal, T., & Brooks-Gunn, J. (2000). The neighborhoods they live in: The effects of neighborhood residence on child and adolescent outcomes. *Psychological Bulletin, 126,* 309–337.

Lynch, S. A. (1998). Who supports whom? How age and gender affect the perceived quality of support from family and friends. *The Gerontologist, 38,* 231–238.

Mirowsky, J., & Ross, C. E. (1999). Well-being across the life course. In A. Horwitz (Ed.), *A handbook for the study of mental health: Social contexts, theories and systems* (pp. 328–347). NY: Cambridge University Press.

Oxman, T. C., Berkman, L. F., Kasl, S., Freeman, D. H., & Barrett, J. (1992). Social support and depressive symptoms in the elderly. *American Journal of Epidemiology, 135,* 356–368.

Peek, K. M., & O'Neill, G. S. (2001). Networks in later life: An examination of race differences in social support networks. *International Journal of Aging and Human Development, 52,* 207–229.

Pugliesi, K., & Shook, S. L. (1998). Gender, ethnicity, and network characteristics: Variation in social support resources. *Sex Roles, 38,* 215–238.

Purdy, J. K., & Arguello, D. (1992). Hispanic familism in caretaking of older adults: Is it functional? *Journal of Gerontological Social Work, 19,* 29–43.

Rautio, N., Heikkinen, E., & Heikkinen, R. (2001). The association of socio-economic factors with physical and mental capacity in elderly men and women. *Archives of Gerontology and Geriatrics, 33,* 163–178.

Reis, H. T., Collins, W. A., & Berscheid, E. (2000). The relationship context of human behavior and development. *Psychological Bulletin, 126,* 844–872.

Rodriguez, J. M., & Kosloski, K. (1998). The impact of acculturation on attitudinal familism in a community of Puerto Rican Americans. *Hispanic Journal of Behavioral Sciences, 20,* 375–390.

Roughton, B. (2000, March 26). The orphans of AIDS: More than 9 million children in Africa have lost their parents to AIDS, and with 23.3 million Africans now infected with HIV, that number is expected to triple over the next decade. *The Montreal Gazette,* p. C4.

Ruan, D., Freeman, L. C., Dai, X., Pan, Y., & Zhang, W. (1997). On the changing structure of social networks in urban China. *Social Networks, 19,* 75–89.

Sabogal, S., Marin, F., Otero-Sabogal, R., & Marin, B. V. (1987). Hispanic familism and acculturation: What changes and what doesn't? *Hispanic Journal of Behavioral Sciences, 9,* 397–412.

Seeman, T. E. (2000). Health promoting effects of friends and family on health outcomes in older adults. *American Journal of Health Promotion, 14,* 362–370.

Seifer, R. (2001). Socioeconomic status, multiple risks, and development of intelligence. In J. Sternberg (Ed.), *Environmental effects on cognitive abilities* (pp. 59–81). Mahwah, NJ: Lawrence Erlbaum Associates, Inc.

Smith, J., & Baltes, M. M. (1998). The role of gender in very old age: Profiles of functioning and everyday life patterns. *Psychology and Aging, 13,* 676–695.

Takahashi, K., Tamura, J., & Makiko, T. (1997). Patterns of social relationships and psychological well-being among the elderly. *International Journal of Behavioral Development, 21,* 417–430.

Taylor, R. J., & Chatters, L. M. (1986). Patterns of informal support to elderly Black adults: Family, friends, and church members. *Social Work, 31,* 432–438.

Taylor, R. J., Chatters, L. M., & Jackson, J. S. (1997). Changes over time in support network involvement among Black Americans. In R. J. Taylor (Ed.), *Family life in Black America* (pp. 293–316). Thousand Oaks, CA: Sage Publications, Inc.

Turner, H. A., & Turner, R. J. (1999). Gender, social status and emotional reliance. *Journal of Health and Social Behavior, 40,* 360–373.

Vaillant, G. E., Meyer, S. E., Mukamal, K., & Soldz, S. (1998). Are social supports in late midlife a cause or a result of successful physical ageing? *Psychological Medicine, 28,* 1159–1168.

van Tilburg, T., Gierveld, J., Lecchini, L., & Marsiglia, D. (1998). Social integration and loneliness: A comparative study among older adults in the Netherlands and Tuscany, Italy. *Journal of Social and Personal Relationships, 15,* 740–754.

Wellman, H., & Wortley, S. (1989). Brothers' keepers: Situating kinship relations in broader networks of social support. *Sociological Perspectives, 32,* 273–306.

Wenger, C. (1997). Review of findings on support networks of older Europeans. *Journal of Cross-Cultural Gerontology, 12,* 1–21.

Youn, G., Knight, B. G., Jeong, H., & Benton, D. (1999). Differences in familism values and caregiving outcomes among Korean, Korean American, and White American dementia caregivers. *Psychology and Aging, 14,* 355–364.

3

Child-Parent Relationships

Peter Noack and Heike M. Buhl

The chapter gives an overview on the development of the relationships of parents and their offspring. While the selection of issues addressed is not meant to be comprehensive, the chapter focuses on conceptualizations and findings of particular relevance: Individuality and relatedness, the active role that parents and their offspring play in shaping their relationship, the importance of a biographical perspective on relationship development, and contextual influences on child-parent relationships. The chapter concludes with consideration of directions for future research.

Child-parent relationships are special. This is obviously true on an individual level. For example, children see their parents as outstanding people – at least up until the transition to adolescence. Likewise, some parents are infatuated with their children and expect much of their sons and daughters, sometimes to the point of overtaxing their abilities and patience. At the same time, child-parent relationships, in general, have features that give them a particular significance. As compared to other types of relationships, bonds between parents and their offspring are of an extremely long-standing nature. Moreover, when parents and children interact, aspects of socialization and education tend to play a more important role than is the case among siblings, friends, or romantic partners. Finally, it has to be recognized that child-parent relationships represent an intergenerational constellation.

Relationships between children and parents surpass most other relationships in *duration*. We take Germany as a case in point. With an average age at first childbearing of close to twenty-eight years (Engstler, 1998) and a life expectancy of over eighty years (Statistisches Bundesamt, 2001), German mothers and their children share more than half a decade of their lifetime. The modal father faces about six years less shared time when his first child is born. Of course, there is considerable variation within Germany, and the figures are somewhat different for second or later born children. We are also aware of the fact that ages at the birth of the first child as well as life expectancies are comparably high in Germany. Still, most parents and children spend several decades together or apart in their relationship. We explicitly refer to years spent apart in recognition of the fact that relationships between parents and children continue to exist even in the absence of contact.

Following the same line of thought, we want to question the seemingly obvious definition of the birth of a child as the starting point of a child-parent relationship as well as of the death of a parent (or a child) as its end. There are indications that a relationship begins to develop as early as during the months of pregnancy. Findings of a longitudinal study that accompanied young couples starting soon after conception through the time after birth (Gloger-Tippelt, 1991) are a case in point. The way in which the pregnant women could relate to the prenatal child and the extent to which they were able to have a vivid mental representation of it were predictive of aspects of the later relationship with the newborn baby. Likewise, parental influence does not stop when parents die (Klass, Silverman, & Nickman, 1996). Considerations such as "I cannot do this. My parents would not have approved of it" are but an example of how the relationship may survive at least on a representational level. A similar point could be made with regard to the death of children (e.g., Wheeler, 2001). Clearly, we proceed on the assumption that subjective representations are a constitutive aspect of close relationships. Taking this perspective, child-parent relationships truly enjoy an outstanding longevity only paralleled by sibling relationships.

Among parental tasks, the *socialization* of their children figures prominently besides the provision of physical and emotional security. It does not challenge the widely accepted understanding of socialization as a bidirectional process (Maccoby, 1992; Schaffer, 1999) to suggest that socialization in the family involves a constellation of roles characterized by an uneven distribution of power. The quality of socialization varies with the child's age. We want to claim, however, that the socialization of children remains an issue far beyond the first two decades of life. This includes children's wishes to influence their parents' lives and development as well as actual child effects on parents.

Although not feasible to the parent-child tie, many processes of selection and de-selection that occur in other types of relationships (e.g., Kandel, 1978; Yamaguchi & Kandel, 1997) may contribute to increased similarity between relationship partners. The socialization process may also result in shared similarity. Furthermore, even though the fact that family members share genes is well known, findings of behavioral genetic research (e.g., Plomin, 1994; Rowe, 1994) have only slowly drawn attention to the importance of the genetic linkage between parents and children. In her provocative critique of methodological shortcomings of studies on parenting, Harris (1998) recently pointed to the possibility that many findings interpreted in terms of parental influence on children could result from genetic similarity. It is not necessary to agree with Harris's fundamental doubts concerning effects of parental child rearing to acknowledge the peculiarity of the genetic linkage in the family. Besides, for instance, temperamental and intellectual similarities, this linkage seems to also affect the perception of child-parent relationships for which a substantial amount of heritability was identified (e.g., Plomin et al., 1989).

Parents and children not only have different roles in the process of socialization but also represent *two generations*. This is true in the sense that the relationship partners belong to different cohorts and thus differ in the conditions of their upbringing and experiences. Given the considerable variation in cohort background depending on parents' age at childbirth, the intergenerational constellation could be more important on the level of partners' perceptions distinguishing parent and child generations than on the level of chronological age differences. In the majority of families with children, this constellation is accentuated by the presence of one or more siblings and, as a consequence, of evolving generational subsystems (Kreppner, Paulsen, & Schuetze, 1982) that cut across and interact with the child-parent subsystem.

Longevity, socialization and genetic similarity, and the intergenerational character of the relationship are not the only important features of the bonds between children and their parents, and they are typical of child-parent relationships but not specific for them. Still, we believe that the constellation of these features sets the stage for child-parent interactions across the life span. We will come back to this when trying to delineate aspects of an integrative model of child-parent relationships under a life-span perspective. We will shortly review research on different periods of child-parent relationships organized according to the life-span development of children. The juxtaposition of previous research and our conceptual ideas will result in suggestions for future research presented in the final portion of this chapter. Given the spatial restrictions of the chapter, we will mostly confine ourselves to a discussion of parents and their biological children who do not face nonnormative challenges such as chronic illness or physical handicaps. Moreover, we acknowledge that we will not consistently consider a cross-cultural perspective as much of the research we will report originates from North America and Western Europe. We believe that the diversity of child-parent relationships beyond what we will be able to report deserves a discussion in its own right.

CHILD-PARENT RELATIONSHIPS ACROSS THE LIFE SPAN

Despite the limited scope of our review, there is no way to arrive at a comprehensive account of research on child-parent relationships across the life span. Reading the body of literature accumulated during decades would be far more than a life-span endeavor. This is true even though scholarly efforts have greatly varied depending on the (children's) age groups of concern. For instance, developmental psychology began as the psychology of child development, expanding its interest to the second decade of life and more recently to also address late adulthood. Accordingly, there is a wealth of studies on individual development in childhood and adolescence and also on the quality and changes of close relationships during these periods of the life span. Clearly less is known concerning child-parent relationships later in life.

As we lack long-term longitudinal studies on child-parent relationships, we report on research concentrating on the different periods of the life span. The respective selection is not meant to be representative but aims at highlighting issues and lines of research that we consider particularly important concerning a given phase of the family biography.

Birth and Infancy

The extension of the family due to the birth of a first child can be considered a normative transition. In Germany (Engstler, 1998), for instance, more than half of the households are comprised of one or more children below the age of majority (18). Up to now, however, the number of women not becoming mothers has been about a quarter of the adult female population, and the figures are rising. It should be noted that the percentages of households experiencing this transition to parenthood is higher in most other European countries and in the United States.

The birth of the first child places strong *adaptation demands* on a couple, which challenge partners' coping abilities. For example, the marital subsystem has to adjust to provide space for the child, child rearing and household tasks have to be coordinated, and relationships with other family members have to be reorganized. This includes relationships with the partners' parents who, then, also assume the role of grandparents (McGoldrick & Carter, 1982). At first glance, many young parents seem to be overwhelmed by the transition, as suggested by significant declines in marital satisfaction (e.g., Cowan, Cowan, Herring, & Miller, 1991; Jurgan, Gloger-Tippelt, & Ruge, 1999; Wallace & Gotlib, 1990; cf. Glenn, 1990). However, research employing more elaborated designs (Schneewind, 1995) point to the importance of adopting a differential perspective. It seems to be those couples, in particular, who had comparably low levels of satisfaction prior to the birth of their first child who experience a severe deterioration of their relationship after becoming parents, whereas a slight effect of the opposite direction can be observed among those who were happy before the transition. The same research also underscores the importance of considering comparison groups. Young parents who gave mixed reports on their marital satisfaction, for instance, show the same trajectory of their relationship quality as a parallel group married for the same duration but without children (cf. McHale & Huston, 1985).

Cognitive processes seem to play an important role in the adaptation to parenthood. Young fathers and mothers both report more problems if they arrive at a negative balance of gains and losses due to the birth of the child and tend to see their partner as responsible for resulting restrictions (Reichle & Montada, 1999). More factors, however, influence the satisfaction of the young women. Those who had anticipated the restrictions due to parenthood were less affected. The latter finding adds to the observation that cognitions prior to the birth of the child have effects on the adaptation to the new situation as mentioned earlier in this chapter (Gloger-Tippelt, 1991). Summarizing, concurrent and anticipatory cognitions during pregnancy seem to play an important role concerning the subsequent satisfaction in the marital partnership and in the child-parent relationship that, in turn, show a close association (Kalicki, Peitz, Fthenakis, & Engfer, 1999).

Although the number of studies focusing on the transition to parenthood is limited, there is a plethora of research addressing the child-parent relationship during its early phase. Theorizing on the *attachment* between children and parents (Ainsworth, 1979; Bowlby, 1969) has been particularly influential in shaping our views on this period of the family biography. The basic tenet is that affectionate ties develop in the course of caregiver-child interactions that provide an important basis for the exploration of the world and the future social and emotional development of the child. Part of the reason why attachment has attracted so much scholarly attention is its long-term stability (Waters, Weinfield, & Hamilton, 2000) and the variety of domains affected, as well as the practical implications as evidenced in the vivid debate as to whether early institutional childcare severely undermines child-parent relationships and the further individual development of children (e.g., Belsky, 1986; Phillips, McCartney, Scarr, & Howes, 1987).

The theory posits that a key element in the interaction of children and their mothers (or other caregivers) for secure attachment to develop is maternal sensitivity, that is, prompt and adequate maternal responses to children's signals and communications. In a meta-analytic study, De Wolff and van Ijzendoorn (1997) could, indeed, show a substantial, albeit moderate, association between maternal sensitivity and mother-child attachment paralleled by a similar association in the father-child dyad, which was, however, less pronounced (Van Ijzendoorn & De Wolff, 1997). Additional evidence is provided by an experimental intervention (van den Boom, 1994) (with positive consequences on attachment relationships) in which mothers with irritable infants were successfully trained to sensitively attend to their children's behaviors. Still, these robust findings could easily obstruct the view on the infants' contributions to the development of attachment (van den Boom, 1997). Likewise, further conditions influencing the development of this central aspect of child-parent relationships as well as contextual moderators affecting this process need to be considered (e.g., Thompson, 1997).

Preschool and Elementary School Age

In research on the socialization of children, *parenting styles* play a particularly prominent role. While studies on parenting effects on adolescents are as numerous as research focusing on children before the pubertal transition, systematic inquiry into the workings of parenting typically starts during the preschool and elementary school years. Drawing on Baumrind's (e.g., Baumrind & Black, 1967) seminal work, developmentalists often describe parenting in terms of warmth and engagement as well as of demandingness and control. In more recent approaches (cf. Steinberg, 1990), the control dimension is conceptualized in a more differentiated way, distinguishing behavioral control in a narrow sense and psychological control (as opposed to autonomy granting). Often, these two or three dimensions are combined to represent different styles of parenting, such as authoritative parenting, characterized by high levels of warmth, behavioral control, and little psychological control, and authoritarian parenting, characterized by little (or medium) warmth, and both behavioral as well as psychological control.

Most empirical findings converge in pointing to the beneficial effects of authoritative parenting. In child-parent relationships where this general pattern of socialization prevails, children tend to have a more positive self-concept, they are more successful in meeting academic demands, and they are less likely to indulge in problem behaviors (Lamborn, Mounts, Steinberg, & Dornbush, 1991). Despite some variations depending on the larger context, this pattern holds across various ecological niches as defined by family structure, socioeconomic status, and cultural background (Steinberg, Mounts, Lamborn, & Dornbush, 1991). Recently, however, some doubts have been voiced addressing two issues in particular. First, little attention has been paid to influences that children might exert on their parents' behavior. If directions of effects are tested on the basis of longitudinal data, there is evidence that parents respond to children's behavior (e.g., Noack & Kracke, 2002). Second, it has been pointed out that the conceptualization of behavioral control in terms of parental monitoring as operationalized by parents' knowledge about their children's activities, friends, and leisure places could have resulted in a misinterpretation of findings. Findings of more differentiated analyses suggest that trust and open communication in the family, on the one hand, are reflected by parental knowledge about their children and, on the other hand, account for a good deal of the positive effects of authoritative parenting (Stattin & Kerr, 2000; Kerr & Stattin, 2000). Thus, parenting research seems to be on the way toward a more comprehensive understanding of child-parent relationships.

For many children, starting daycare, preschool, or elementary school means entering a context beyond the family, without parental guidance, for the first time. This is not only a challenge for the children. The family as a whole has to master the more complex constellation of relationships. Taking a Bronfenbrennerian perspective (e.g., Bronfenbrenner, 1979), parents have to deal with influences of exosystems when their children interact with teachers and classmates and are affected by experiences in the classroom. More important, parents are called upon to contribute to the formation of a new mesosystem, that is, links between the family and the educational institution and its representatives. Participation in school activities, attending parents' meetings, and establishing contacts with teachers are some examples of relevant activities. Lively bonds between families and the institution figure prominently among the features of "good schools" (Fend, 1998) and, at the same time, seem to strongly facilitate children's academic success (Griffith, 1996; Grolnick & Slowiaczek, 1994).

It should be noted that preschools and schools differ markedly from the family and several other informal social contexts. What these institutional contexts typically have in common is sometimes referred to as "universalism" (vs. "particularism"), that is, schools have explicit rules and regulations as the basis of interaction, focus on the student role rather than on the individual in a holistic sense, and enact consequences of children's behavior that are more closely linked to outcomes than to intentions (Hofer, 1992). Of course, schools vary a good deal as to the extent to which they are governed by universalistic principles, as do child-parent relationships in the extent to which they operate in a particularistic way. It can be assumed that the children's ecological transition will be particularly difficult if the situation they encounter in the classroom is quite different from the children's experiences with parents (Hansen, 1986).

Adolescence

A major theme of the adolescent years is *autonomy*. The notion of autonomy includes individual competencies such as self-determination and self-regulation as well as relational aspects (Steinberg, 2001). Thus, child-parent relationships are a major arena where autonomy development takes place. They provide opportunities to, for example, acquire and try out competencies and, at the same time, these relationships change themselves as part of the development of autonomy. In earlier theorizing, detachment from parents was seen as the prime goal of adolescent autonomy development (Blos, 1979). Some authors postulated conflict between adolescents and their parents as a necessary means to this end. However, empirical findings have seriously questioned these ideas (Laursen, Coy, & Collins, 1998). Socioemotional bonds linking children and their parents seem to remain basically intact during the second decade of life despite heightened levels of conflict. Rather, conflicts center on mundane issues and are mostly not severe. The number of families continuously experiencing strong tension is low and only rarely do these problems between parents and children start all of a sudden at the onset of adolescence without any childhood precursors (Stattin & Klackenberg, 1992).

Still, adolescence is a challenge for child-parent relationships. As posited by Youniss and other advocates of *individuation* theory (Grotevant & Cooper, 1985; Youniss & Smollar, 1985), parents and children have to master a transformation of their relationship leading from the unilateral patterns of childhood to a reciprocal, more egalitarian structure at the transition to adulthood. According to Youniss, sound socioemotional bonds are not only possible during this time but are an important condition facilitating the transformation. Empirical findings show that in the majority of families, parents and adolescents are successful in keeping their connectedness (socioemotional aspect) on a high level, while individuality in the family (structural aspect) increases across the years (Noack, Oepke, & Sassenberg, 1998; Noack & Puschner, 1999).

It would, however, contradict popular wisdom to expect the transformation of parent-child relationships to be completed by the age of majority (18). Although data on the distribution of power in child-parent relationships document considerable relative gains on the part of sons and daughters during adolescence, a balance of power is not reached until some time during the third decade of life (Buhl, 2000; Noack & Buhl, 1999).

Early Adulthood

Studies on *social support* that document the asymmetry of give and take between young adults and their parents add to the assumption that the individuation of child-parent relationships continues well into early adulthood: Young people aged twenty-five to twenty-nine receive particularly high levels of support in terms of advice, services, and gifts followed by a steady decline across subsequent periods of the life span. However, the decrease of receiving gifts and money and, to some extent, parental advice is less steep than the decline of other types of support such as services provided by parents (Cooney & Uhlenberg, 1992). This state of affairs is reflected in family members' perceptions. Fathers, for example, continue to see themselves as an authority, provider, protector, and teacher of their children during the third decade of life. Nevertheless, the processes are not fully unidirectional but characterized by some interdependence (Lewis, 1990). Emotional support on the part of young adults seems to become increasingly salient for parents during the adulthood years (Bertram, 1995). Parents' perceptions of received emotional support even go beyond what their children acknowledge giving (Veevers & Mitchell, 1998). So there is a continuous exchange of support with variations depending on type of support as well as on children's and parents' age.

Thus, both partners, children and parents, continue to deal with the task of changing their relationship into one between autonomous adults. *Biographical transitions* to be negotiated by sons and daughters in their twenties (Marini, 1984) set the pace for transformations in the relationship. Most research has focused on the move out of the parental home that is uniformly observed to result in a decline of conflict as well as in increases of attachment and intimacy (e.g., Berman & Sperling, 1991; Dubas & Petersen, 1996; Flanagan, Schulenberg, & Fuligni, 1993; Papastefanou, 2002). By the same token, a growing number of ILYA ("incompletely launched young adults"; Goldscheider & Goldscheider, 1999; Singh, Williams, & Singh, 1998) share living arrangements with their parents that seem to be unsatisfactory for both parties involved and to include conflicts (Schnaiberg & Goldenberg, 1989) partly because of asymmetrical patterns of support (Spitze & Ward, 1995).

Even though there is some indication that the transition to work life is the most consequential one concerning the child-parent relationship (Roberts & Bengtson, 1993), only a few investigators have addressed this issue. Existing findings suggest a growing distance between parents and their adult children once the latter have entered the workforce (Buhl, Wittmann, & Noack, under review; Scabini & Galimberti, 1995). However, the effects of the child's employment status seem to vary depending on gender. Kaufmann and Uhlenberg (1998), for example, report on a negative effect of daughters' work hours on the relationship with fathers whereas the opposite was observed concerning young males at work. Finally, examinations of the effects of children's marriages point to an increase of connectedness and mutuality in the child-parent relationship (Frank, Avery, & Laman, 1988; White, Speisman, & Costos, 1983). With the birth of the sons' or daughters' first child, observations are consistent concerning an increase of social support given by the (grand)parents (Cooney & Uhlenberg, 1992; Rossi & Rossi, 1990). Inconsistent findings with regard to other aspects of the relationship (Buhl, 2000; Fischer, 1981; Graebe & Luescher, 1984; Neyer, 1999) could result from cohort differences in the interpretation of the role of young mothers and fathers.

Middle Adulthood

Because of increased life expectancies, the time between sons' and daughters' entry into middle adulthood and the death of their parents has extended considerably. Thus, many middle-aged children have very old parents and feel obligated to take on caregiving responsibilities. While the last section focused especially on changes in the children's lives connected with biographical transitions, families with middle-aged children face changes related to the biography of the older generation: leaving the labor force, declining health, losing friends or the partner to death.

There is a lot of contact between middle-aged children and their parents with an impressive proportion of 40% of the elderly having frequent face-to-face contact with an adult child (Lye, 1996). In a recent German survey, 75% of the participating elderly parents reported one or more contacts per week with offspring (Kohli & Kuehnemund, 2000). Regarding relationship quality, there seems to be a high level of regard (e.g., Fingerman, 2000).

Research interests related to this period of the family life cycle primarily concentrate on *social support* and *caregiving* (Alan, Blieszner, & Roberto, 2000). Many middle-aged children, especially women, give physical assistance to their elderly parents (e.g., Lye, 1996; Rossi & Rossi, 1990). About 44% of those beyond eighty years of age experience care from their daughters. By the same token, one of the most important predictors of institutionalization is childlessness (Zank, 2002). This new dependency goes along with changing roles (Dobson & Dobson, 1991) and can cause a loss of parents' psychological well-being and self-esteem (Marks, 1995). Moreover, many middle-aged adults are in a sandwich situation if they are caring for elderly parents and children simultaneously (e.g., Raphael & Schlesinger, 1993).

As a theoretical framework, Bengtson and colleagues (e.g., Bengtson, 2000; Bengtson & Roberts, 1991; Parrott & Bengtson, 1999) formulated and elaborated empirically a theory of intergenerational solidarity with strong interrelations among normative integration (family roles and familial obligations), frequency and patterns of interaction, and affection. Luescher and Pillemer (1998) additionally underline that intimate relationships, in particular, can be conflictual at the same time and formulated the concept of "intergenerational ambivalence."

Looking for sources of tension, Fingerman (1996) differentiated between developmental differences such as different perceptions of the primacy of the relationship, and other contents (Clarke, Preston, Raksin, & Bengtson, 1999). In fact, developmental differences go along with negative views of the relationship.

A last important role change is related to *parental death*. Although the death of a parent is very likely when children are middle-aged, little research has addressed effects on adult children, especially in comparison with effects on minor children. Umberson and Chen (1994) compared bereaved adult children (death of a parent within the last three years) and minor children who had not experienced the death of a parent. They showed that the death of a parent appears to be a very stressful life event. However, some groups of children were more affected than others. For example, divorced children or children with an emotionally supportive father were more adversely affected by death. In some cases there even was a reduced level of distress as observed with daughters whose deceased fathers had mental health problems. Regarding mothers' functional status, Umberson and Chen reported an interaction with the child's gender: Death of unimpaired mothers did not affect sons' levels of distress, but did affect daughters' levels of distress. Death of impaired mothers did not affect daughters, but it did affect sons. To sum up, the effect of parental death depends on the parent-child relationship and the child's living situation. In comparison with living parents, deceased parents are evaluated more positively after parental death and there even may be more perceived closeness and influence. The time since death does not affect the child's reported attachment (Shmotkin, 1999). Thus, some findings suggest that child-parent relationships survive parental death (Bedford & Blieszner, 1997).

ASPECTS OF AN INTEGRATIVE MODEL

As the previous pages have shown, various approaches have been employed to capture child-parent relationships. Conceptual frameworks as well as relationship aspects addressed in empirical studies vary in part depending on the period of the life span of concern. Consequently, existing models with a more comprehensive scope typically refer to the family as a whole and remain quite abstract. This is true of three theoretical frameworks that are often drawn upon to conceptualize structural and dynamic features of the family across the life span, namely family systems theory (Minuchin, 1985), family biography theory (McGoldrick & Carter, 1982), and family stress theory (McCubbin & Patterson, 1983). Obviously, an attempt on our part to fill this gap would be bound to fail. Instead, we will try to delineate a set of aspects that from our point of view are of critical importance for research that will contribute to an adequate understanding of child-parent relationships across the life span.

Individuality and Relatedness

The tension between balancing relatedness, on the one hand, and the nature of relationship partners as individuals with goals, experiences, and images of themselves pointing beyond roles in a given dyad (or triad), on the other hand, is a basic characteristic of any close relationship. As outlined by Benjamin (1974), who refers to affiliation and interdependence, both aspects are orthogonal dimensions. So a friendship or child-parent relationship may be characterized by a high degree of relatedness *and* individuality.

Because of differential use of both of these concepts, it seems useful to clarify our understanding of them (Grotevant & Cooper, 1985; Honess & Robinson, 1993; Lewis, 1990; Nydegger, 1991; Ryan & Lynch, 1989; Steinberg, 2001; Steinberg & Silverberg, 1986; Sternberg, 1986; Wintre, Yaffe, & Crowley, 1995; Youniss & Smollar, 1985). Relatedness of two persons can

be found in different areas. First, a socioemotional aspect, sometimes referred to in terms of affection or attachment, can be distinguished. This is
often reflected in interrelated behavior such as shared activities and verbal
intimacy. Second, a cognitive part of relatedness exists, such as commitment and obligation, e.g., for instrumental support.

Individuality as a second pivotal dimension of close relationships
should be distinguished from autonomy as a construct on the individual level. On the one hand, the balance of power between children and
parents and the interdependency of support can be considered structural
aspects of individuality. On the other hand, there is a sociocognitive aspect
including perceptions of the partners as equals, the valuing of autonomy,
reciprocity, and perspective-taking ability.

Taking the two-dimensional conceptualization as the point of departure, we argue that important features of human relationships (e.g., Hinde,
1993) such as power, intimacy, commitment, and satisfaction can be seen
as subordinated aspects of individuality and relatedness. It has to be acknowledged, however, that conflict, which seems to be closely associated
with relatedness, could be of a somewhat different nature. Personal relationships that are particularly close, such as child-mother relationships
(vs. child-father relations) or spousal relationships (vs. relations of cross-
gender friendship dyads), may show considerable levels of conflict. Constellations of closeness and conflict could result from the fact that conflict
seems to operate sometimes as a mechanism fostering relationship development toward a desired state. The case of the child-parent relationship
during adolescence stands as an example (Laursen, 1995; Tesson & Youniss,
1995).

Looking at parents and their children in terms of individuality and relatedness shows that their relationships are quite special. They start out with
a heavy emphasis on the relatedness dimension, and then show substantial
change during the further course of the family biography as a consequence
of the individual development of parents and children. Psychoanalytic theorizing posits, first, a process of individuation in early childhood (Mahler,
Pine, & Bergman, 1975) that is attributed to the child's recognition of self
and mother as separate individuals. It should be noted, however, that this
concept has not remained undisputed (e.g., Dornes, 1993). Erikson (1959)
postulated autonomy to be the central issue of the subsequent years of
childhood. Erikson's view corresponds to everyday observations of, for
instance, practical aspects of individuality, such as parents having the goal
of children learning to eat independently. Still, timetables of independence
differ interculturally (Hess, 1980). Despite considerable intercultural as
well as interindividual variation, in general, levels of individuality in the
child-parent relationship reached during the first decade of children's lives
remain limited. Suffice it to say that children in this age bracket lack the

cognitive prerequisites to distinguish their father or mother as a person from the parental roles they play in the family.

Research points to adolescence as the period in the life course when the balance between relatedness and individuality is at stake (e.g., Steinberg, 2001). Most theoretical views agree about an increase of individuality during adolescence. With relatedness, however, conceptualizations vary, claiming either the start of the breakup of bonds linking parents and children or a transformation of their relationship. Neo-analytic scholars, for instance, suggest a "second process of individuation" (Blos, 1979) that does not necessarily imply dramatic relationship conflicts but will lead to detachment as its result. More recent interpretations of individuation (Youniss & Smollar, 1985) assume that a constellation of stable connectedness and an increase of individuality characterize relationship development. From this point of view, the socio-emotional quality of the child-parent relationship is considered to be the basis for negotiating changes in individuality. Empirical studies favor this position, yielding evidence for healthy families and fewer problems in the course of adolescent identity development as a consequence (e.g., Alan, Hauser, & Bell, 1994; Grotevant & Cooper, 1985).

Theorists suggest that relationship transformation moves toward a constellation of high levels of connectedness *and* individuality as the final state of individuation is reached in adulthood, resulting in a "peer-like" relationship of adult children and their parents (Smollar & Youniss, 1989). Empirical findings mostly corroborate these assumptions. The relationship is perceived as a close one showing considerable continuity from adolescence to early adulthood (e.g., Lye, 1996; Schneewind, Ruppert, & Harrow, 1998; Tubman & Lerner, 1994) while aspects of individuality increase (e.g., Hoffman, 1984; Noack & Buhl, 1999; Wintre, Yaffe, & Crowley, 1995). It should be noted, however, that even 26-year-old young adults seem not to have truly peer-like relationships with their parents (White, Speisman, & Costos, 1983). Likewise, sons and daughters in their thirties see their relative power to be smaller than their fathers' (Buhl, 2000). As regards relatedness, several studies point to a modest age-graded decrease that is associated with young adults' biographical transitions such as first parenthood (Buhl, Wittmann, & Noack, under review; Kaufman & Uhlenberg, 1998; Neyer, 1999; Scabini & Galimberti, 1995).

When parents reach old age, increases in parental dependency have an impact on relatedness and individuality in the family. As is the case during adolescence, elevated levels of conflict do not necessarily go along with reduced relatedness in this period of the family life cycle (Luescher & Pillemer, 1998). As mentioned earlier, relatedness seems to remain a relevant dimension for understanding child-parent relations even beyond parental death (Shmotkin, 1999).

Relationships between Active Individuals

Even though our focus is on the dyad, an adequate understanding of child-parent relationships has to account for the fact that they are made up of two people with individual perceptions and individual goals that they each actively pursue. Children's as well as parental goals could address their relationship or the partner in the relationship, but also point beyond the dyad. Obviously, the extent to which the other's goals are realized or even interpreted correctly and whether goals and perceptions of parents and children converge varies between relationships and across time. As pointed out earlier, a change of mutual perceptions from seeing the other mainly in terms of her or his role in the relationship, that is, child or parent, toward a more individualized perspective is a crucial aspect of increasing individuality in the course of relationship individuation during adolescence (Youniss & Smollar, 1985). More generally, the child-parent relationship at each given point in time represents a unique constellation of individual characteristics.

Taking a life-span perspective, developmental features deserve particular attention. Again, sons' and daughters' adolescent years are an illustrative case in point. A good deal of negotiations in the child-parent dyads address the developmental agenda of the adolescent offspring. Mostly, disagreements arise not over developmental goals per se, but rather regarding the question of the appropriate timing of developmental milestones. Research on developmental timetables (Feldman & Quatman, 1988; Noack & Kracke, 1992) directly focusing on this issue shows that paternal timetables typically define later ages for the majority of transitions than do adolescents' agendas. Mothers partly side with fathers in this respect, and partly take an in-between position. To a certain extent, timetables specifying developmental issues reflect expectations shared in a society or culture. At the same time, they are affected by individual development such as children's physical maturation or changes in cognitive abilities (Havighurst, 1972). Likewise, more general orientations, depending on personality characteristics such as temperamental factors, can be assumed to be of influence. Underscoring the role of active individuals in child-parent relationships, we thus do not suggest considering only individual goals or even only those goals parents and children consciously pursue. We rather want to point out that any child-parent relationship represents a constellation of a variety of individual characteristics of which developmental ones could be of special interest. Of course, different patterns of constellation vary in their likelihood. For instance, genetic similarity between parents and their children as well as previous interactions, namely socialization, can be assumed to result in a certain correspondence between relationship partners.

Still, there are systematic deviations from this general tendency. A prominent example is addressed by the developmental stake hypothesis

(Bengtson & Kuypers, 1971; cf. Giarusso, Stallings, & Bengtson, 1995). In fact, there is ample evidence that perceived relationship quality varies between children and parents. Fathers and, to a greater degree, mothers, typically see child-parent relationships in more favorable terms than do their sons and daughters (e.g., Fingerman, 1995; Schneewind, Ruppert, & Harrow, 1998). This particular discrepancy does not seem to put their relationships at risk. In general, however, empirical evidence suggests viewing the extent of divergence between parents' and children's perceptions and expectations as an indicator of the socioemotional quality of their relationships. High levels of disagreement often predict individual problems and conflict in the relationship (e.g., Ohanessian, Lerner, Lerner, & von Eye, 1995).

Observing a linkage between children's and parents' discrepant perceptions and expectations, on the one hand, and individual and relationship problems, on the other hand, does not necessarily imply linear associations. Although it seems plausible to assume a direct correspondence between agreement and harmony or conflict in the child-parent relationship, the issue could be more complex when it comes to individual development. For example, there are indications that a certain divergence of perspectives fosters children's development, whereas full agreement does not. In a longitudinal study of adolescent self-esteem, Fingerle (2000) provided evidence showing that neither low nor high disagreement of perspectives affected sons' and daughters' self-esteem. Rather, medium-level divergence predicted subsequent changes.

So far, we have focused on perspectives on the child-parent relationship or the individual from the viewpoint of the children. We will now turn to the developmental constellation in the family. Parents and their children necessarily go through different periods of the life span that can be a source of tension, as Fingerman (1996) pointed out when introducing the term 'developmental schism.' Taking Erikson's (1959) theoretical framework of psychosocial development as an example, parents with children up until early adulthood would typically have to address the issues of having reached a certain balance or plateau. For many a parent this means coping with indications of one's own limitations and stagnation. Older parents have to struggle with the finiteness of life and the evaluation of their own biography, which can be rejected but not changed. Their children pass through several phases of development that cannot be explicated in detail here. However, in each instance, the pivotal issues to be dealt with, such as the question of identity and one's place in society or intimacy and isolation, are quite different from those critical for their parents. As Erikson's comprehensive perspective on life may appear to be quite metaphorical to some, it could be instructive to make the issues more concrete. For instance, sons and daughters experience pubertal maturation when, at least in most Western countries, their parents have typically passed their peak of reproductive capability. Obviously, there are different ways to respond to this developmental constellation. While some parents might take pride in the youthful power of their children, the contrast could accentuate feelings of loss among others and even cause envy. A psychological crisis on the parental end of the relationship seems not to be an atypical result (Steinberg & Steinberg, 1994). In fact, there is some indication that the coincidence of pubertal maturation in daughters and menopause in their mothers, in particular, can be threatening and problematic for the latter (Graber & Brooks-Gunn, 1996). Given the scarcity of relevant research, this finding should be interpreted with caution. From our point of view, however, it is quite illustrative for our idea about developmental constellations in child-parent relationships and their possible consequences. By the same token, the feebleness of aging parents might be a burden for middle-aged children in more than a practical sense. At the same time, it might foster sons' and daughters' anxious attempts to overcome possible stagnation in the middle of their lives.

Divergences in goals, perceptions, or developmental phases do not typically drive children and parents apart. Processes of explicit or implicit negotiation are the more likely consequence. It is also in this sense that we refer to active individuals in the child-parent relationship, that is, individuals who try to influence each other in their interactions.

Relationship Biography

Looking at child-parent relationships under the perspective of relationship biography, we do not introduce completely new ideas. Various transitions in the biography of a child-parent relationship are closely linked to individual development, namely of the child, which has already been referred to in the previous section. Children's physical and cognitive development in the wake of puberty and the resulting challenges for the relationships with mothers and fathers are a case in point. From our point of view, however, adopting a biographical perspective as suggested by family life-cycle models (McGoldrick & Carter, 1982) offers additional insights.

Conceptualizing relationship development in biographical terms points to a typical sequence of challenges that have to be jointly negotiated and mastered. Theoretical approaches to appropriately capture the dyadic nature of attempts to deal with these challenges are rare. Bodenmann (e.g., 1997) introduced the concept of dyadic coping going beyond individual-level conceptualizations. The concept has been successfully applied to interactions in marital relationships and their consequences for relationship development (Bodenmann, Charvoz, Cina, & Widmer, 2001; Gottman & Levenson, 2000). An adaptation to the peculiarities of child-parent dyads could offer a promising avenue to a better understanding of the development of child-parent relationships.

Norms applying to particular periods of the development of child-parent relationships underscore the relevance of a biographical perspective. For example, parents of preschool or elementary schoolchildren are expected to accept challenges and to respond flexibly to attempts of their sons and daughters to influence the mother or father. However, a situation where children try to educate or explicitly guide their parents would raise serious concern. By the same token, parents with teenage children are expected to keep up intergenerational boundaries. An abdication of the parental role has been repeatedly pointed out as a problem of, for example, those divorced mothers who treat their sons or daughters like a peer or partner (Glenwick & Mowrey, 1986; Minuchin, 1985; Vines, 1998). At the same time, a continuation of earlier dependencies on parents into the adulthood years of the children is widely seen as an off-time state of the child-parent relationship. Regardless of considerable variations, ideas concerning an adequate timing of a launching phase are shared in many societies and are reflected in the concept of "incompletely launched young adults" or ILYA (Schnaiberg & Goldenberg, 1989).

Finally, we want to point out an additional correspondence of a biographical perspective on the individual and the child-parent relationship. With regard to the individual, the failure to master challenges that are typical of a given period of the life span seems to decrease the likelihood of successfully negotiating future biographical transitions. This notion of sequential dependencies in the course of individual development is a central claim of, for instance, Havighurst's (1972) concept of developmental tasks as well as of Erikson's (1959) theory of psychosocial development. We want to suggest that similar sequential dependencies characterize the development of child-parent relationships. Again, the individuation of child-parent relationships during adolescence (Youniss & Smollar, 1985) may serve as an example. An individuated relationship would combine relatedness and individuality. While it can be disputed whether individuation is mostly complete by early adulthood, a balance of both relationship aspects is eventually reached in many families. It can be assumed that, for instance, an imbalance due to a lack of individuality has consequences in the future. Such a constellation should be predictive of later problems when a growing neediness of parents due to feebleness or disease results in reversed dependencies (Lewis, 1990). Adult children may then not be able to assume and master their new responsibilities or to enjoy their gain of power at the expense of their mothers and fathers (Blenkner, 1965).

We acknowledge that a biographical perspective on child-parent relationships borrows heavily from conceptualizations of individual and family biographies. Does it make sense to apply these ideas to the dyadic level? From our point of view, the differential pace of development of child-mother and child-father relationships in the modal family suggests the usefulness of such a conceptualization. Again, the transformation of child-parent relationships during adolescence provides a good example. Typically, the state of individuation of the child-mother relationship surpasses the state of transformation of the child-father relationship (e.g., Noack & Buhl, 1999; Youniss & Smollar, 1985). Likewise, dyadic development differs depending on children's gender when elderly parents need assistance. In this situation, daughters show stronger feelings of responsibility and higher levels of involvement than sons (Lye, 1996; Rossi & Rossi, 1990). At this point, we can only speculate about the usefulness of elaborating the biographic notion to accommodate variations as a function of child and parental gender.

Child-Parent Relationships in Context

Taking a systems view on child-parent relationships, a first type of context to be considered is located *within the family*. Even within a small nuclear family comprised of one child, a mother, and a father, three dyads can be distinguished. In this case, for example, the parental dyad and the father-child dyad provide contexts for the child-mother relationship. Moreover, it seems to make sense to look at the family triad including the child-mother dyad as a further context. At first glance, it may not be obvious whether this apparently analytic decomposition of the family offers any insights. However, there is ample evidence reported in the parental separation literature suggesting detrimental effects of marital conflict and hostility on child-parent relationships (Schwarz & Noack, 2002). Likewise, studies on effects of financial deprivation on child development point to the mediating role of impaired spousal relationships and resulting problems in child-parent interactions (e.g., Conger & Elder, 1994). Further evidence is provided by research into child-parent interactions in the dyadic situation as compared to behavior shown when the other parent is present (Deal, Hagan, Bass, Hetherington, & Clingempeel, 1999; Gjerde, 1986). Typically, fathers and mothers seem to behave differently depending on whether the situation is dyadic or triadic. Thus, within-family contexts of parent-child relationships seem to make a difference.

It should be noted that the character of intrafamily dyadic relationships, namely their salience and boundaries, are subject to change in the course of family development. Such changes become particularly obvious when a new member enters the family system. For example, Kreppner and colleagues (Kreppner, Paulsen, & Schuetze, 1982; Papastefanou, 2002) postulate a three-step process of family adaptation during the first two years after the birth of a second child. While the first step serves to integrate the new family member into the family including, for instance, an intensification of the relationship between the father and the older child, the search for a new balance in the extended family is the major challenge during the second phase. The process typically results in the formation of salient parental and sibling subsystems that can be assumed to affect mutual perceptions of family members as well as interactions in all six dyads.

Besides work based on family systems theory, behavior-genetic research has drawn attention to influences of siblings on child-parent relationships. While the concept of nonshared environment as introduced by behavior geneticists (e.g., Dunn & Plomin, 1991; Reiss, Hetherington, Plomin, Howe, et al., 1995) includes contexts beyond the family, it has certainly underscored the importance of considering differential aspects of socialization as experienced by siblings within families. The presence of a sibling may alter behavior within a given child-parent dyad. It definitely provides a frame of reference for the perception of child-parent relationships. Broadening the perspective on child-parent relationships only a bit by incorporating siblings or even further kin such as the grandparents thus results in a considerable increase of complexity that is only rarely addressed by empirical research.

Comparably more attention has been paid the workings of *meso-system* and *exo-system* effects (Bronfenbrenner, 1979, 1989) linking the child-parent relationship with contexts beyond the family. Starting with Melvin Kohn's (1963; Kohn, Naoi, & Schoenbach, 1990) seminal work, evidence has been accumulated for effects of conditions at the parental workplace on processes of child rearing in the family (Crouter & McHale, 1993). It has been suggested that cognitive challenges and opportunities for self-direction at work, in particular, affect parental values that, in turn, are assumed to influence parents' goals for socialization. Similarly, children's experiences in school seem to indirectly impact on child-parent relationships. Students' problems in mastering academic demands figure prominently among the reasons for child-parent conflict (Wild & Hofer, 2002). Even when students are more successful, school leaves its imprints on child-parent relationships. For example, in school systems where homework is a regular part of the workday, parents can hardly avoid getting involved. At least in Germany, the average parent, mostly the mother, is engaged in some homework surveillance on a regular basis which, however, varies depending on the social status of the family, child age, and subject area (Oswald, Baker, & Stevenson, 1988). Giving efficient support is difficult, as the quantity and quality of parent-teacher cooperation is often low (Krumm, 1998). Anglo-American examples show that improvement is feasible and yields positive effects in terms of academic outcomes (cf. Griffith, 1996). The concept of school-based home instruction exemplifies effects of the school context on child development mediated by child-parent interactions.

Despite the considerable body of literature on family-peer linkages, most empirical research has addressed effects on friendship and peer group relationships (Noack, 2002). Clearly less is known concerning influences of the reverse direction affecting child-parent relationships. This state of research may come as a surprise given widely recognized theoretical assumptions that suggest an important role played by peers. For example, taking peculiarities of the peer context such as similarity and equality as the point of departure, individuation theory (Youniss & Smollar, 1985) sees sons' and daughters' experiences among peers as one of the triggers of the transformation of the child-parent relationship during adolescence. The dearth of studies addressing this idea clearly calls for future research.

Finally, child-parent relationships are embedded in *macro-systems*, that is, societal and cultural conditions that are assumed to affect parents and their children mostly by way of influences on more proximal contexts. While only rarely doubts are voiced concerning the pervasive effects of macro-contextual conditions, research setting out to elucidate the concrete workings of societal influences faces serious methodological challenges. Studies following the typical empirical approaches of comparisons across societies or of comparisons across time within a given society often fall short of disentangling the plethora of potentially relevant characteristics on the macro level (Silbereisen, Robins, & Rutter, 1995). Institutions and laws could be expected to impinge on child-parent relationships as could informal norms, belief systems, and value orientations shared in a country or culture. Obviously, conclusive research requires differentiated conceptualizations that spell out the relevant processes mediating societal effects. Research drawing on the values-of-children framework (Hoffman, 1987; Nauck, 2001) may serve as an example. It is guided by the assumption that cultures vary as to the kind of value typically attached to children, such as instrumental values or expectations of love and companionship. As a consequence, reproductive behaviors as well as goals for child socialization and parenting strategies are expected to vary. The hypothesis can be tested on a population level as well as by following individual-level approaches as was the case in a cross-cultural research project. A continuation of this work that includes new data assessments has just been started (Nauck, 2002) and promises not only to replicate the earlier findings but also to test the central hypotheses by way of historical comparison based on social change in the focused societies during the last twenty-five years.

FUTURE DIRECTIONS

In our overview of child-parent relationships across the life span as well as in the discussion of focal aspects to be considered in models of relationship development, we have already identified various challenges for future research. Some periods of relationship development have attracted considerable scholarly attention while others deserve more extensive empirical examination. In particular, our knowledge is quite limited concerning the phase after children have entered early adulthood and before elderly parents become more needy. At the same time, we have pointed out that more research on child-parent relationships is necessary that takes into account the complexity of the dynamics of interacting family subsystems in context. Instead of further elaborating on these shortcomings, we want to draw attention to two other issues, namely the scarcity of longer-term longitudinal studies and the failure to elucidate the origin and consequences of multiple perspectives on child-parent relationships.

Much of what we presently know about child-parent relationships is based on cross-sectional data or information yielded by short-term longitudinal studies. A life-span perspective on relationship development calls for more research capturing extended phases in the course of child-parent relationships. In particular, studies that focus on transitional periods and shed light on their early precursors as well as on their late consequences promise to considerably broaden our understanding. Research reported by Stattin and Klackenberg (1992) is illustrative in this respect. Based on data on the emotional quality of relationships in Swedish families taken from a prospective, longitudinal study of children from birth to maturity, the authors cast doubt on the popular assumption that child-parent relationships swiftly deteriorate when children reach puberty. Continuity of the emotional quality from childhood to adolescence seems to be the typical developmental pattern in child-mother relationships as well as in child-father relationships. Addressing a different period of relationship development, Schneewind, Ruppert, and Harrow (1998) analyzed an unusual data set. Following up a sample first contacted sixteen years earlier, when the children were in mid-adolescence (Schneewind, Beckmann, & Engfer, 1983), they were able to analyze stability and change of various aspects of child-parent relationships. As many of the children had in the meantime become parents themselves, the intergenerational transmission of, for instance, parenting could also be examined. These studies as well as further examples of long-term longitudinal research (e.g., Belsky, Jaffee, Hsieh, & Silva, 2001; Silverstein et al., 2002) convincingly demonstrate the payoff of this demanding and laborious avenue to a more adequate understanding of child-parent relationships.

Divergent perceptions of child-parent relationships are not only a methodological issue. Certainly, it can be grossly misleading to rely only on self-reports of a child or a parent when trying to capture aspects of their relationship. However, we want to suggest that even findings based on more elaborate operationalizations such as treating multiple perspectives as indicators of a relationship construct may only tell half the story. All these approaches proceed on the (implicit) assumption that there is one relationship reality. From our point of view, it might be promising to look at converging and diverging perspectives not only in terms of a methodological challenge but also as a substantive issue. It seems plausible to assume that the extent to which parents and children agree in the perceptions of their relationship is not randomly distributed among child-parent dyads.

Some findings addressing adolescent-parent relationships suggest, for example, variations depending on sons' or daughters' age (Lanz, Scabini, Vermulst, & Gerris, 2001), and on the state of relationship transformation during adolescence (Collins, 1991). Likewise, we would expect that the extent of child-parent agreement has consequences on the individual as well as on the dyadic level. Even though findings from several studies are concordant with this hypothesis, they rely on cross-sectional (Carlson, Cooper, & Spradling, 1991; East, 1991) or longitudinal correlations (Ohannessian et al., 1995) that do not address directed effect. Further work is clearly needed to elucidate the role played by the subjective realities of child-parent relationships.

References

Ainsworth, M. S. (1979). Infant-mother attachment. *American Psychologist, 34,* 932–937.

Alan, J. P., Hauser, S. T., & Bell, K. L. (1994). Longitudinal assessment of autonomy and relatedness in adolescent-family interactions as predictors of adolescent ego development and self-esteem. *Child Development, 65,* 179–194.

Alan, K. R., Blieszner, R., & Roberto, K. A. (2000). Families in the middle and later years: A review and critique of research in the 1990s. *Journal of Marriage and the Family, 62,* 911–926.

Baumrind, D., & Black, A. E. (1967). Socialization practices associated with dimensions of competence in preschool boys and girls. *Child Development, 38,* 291–327.

Bedford, V. H., & Blieszner, R. (1997). Personal relationship in later life families. In S. Duck (Ed.), *Handbook of personal relationships* (pp. 523–539). New York: Wiley.

Belsky, J. (1986). Infant day care: A cause of concern. *Zero to Three, 6,* 1–9.

Belsky, J., Jaffee, S., Hsieh, K.-H., & Silva, P. A. (2001). Child-rearing antecedents of intergenerational relations in young adulthood: A prospective study. *Developmental Psychology, 37,* 801–813.

Bengtson, V. L. (2000). Beyond the nuclear family: The increasing importance of multigenerational bonds. *Journal of Marriage and the Family, 63,* 1–16.

Bengtson, V. L., & Kuypers, J. A. (1971). Generational difference and the developmental stake. *Aging and Human Development, 2,* 249–260.

Bengtson, V. L., & Roberts, R. E. L. (1991). Intergenerational solidarity in aging families: An example of formal theory construction. *Journal of Marriage and the Family, 53,* 856–870.

Benjamin, L. S. (1974). Structural analysis of social behavior. *Psychological Review, 81,* 392–425.

Berman, W. H., & Sperling, M. B. (1991). Parental attachment and emotional distress in the transition to college. *Journal of Youth and Adolescence, 20,* 427–440.

Bertram, H. (1995). Die Sicherheit privater Beziehungen [Security in close relations]. In H. Bertram (Ed.), *Das Individuum und seine Familie. Lebensformen, Familienbeziehungen und Lebensereignisse im Erwachsenenalter* [The individual in the family] (pp. 91–156) (DJI: Familien-Survey 4). Opladen: Leske + Budrich.

Blenkner, M. (1965). Social work and family relationships in later life with some thoughts on filial maturity. In E. Shanas & G. F. Streib (Eds.), *Social structure and the family* (pp. 46–59). Englewood Cliffs, NJ: Prentice Hall.

Blos, P. (1979). *The adolescent passage*. New York: International Universities Press.

Bodenmann, G. (1997). Dyadic coping: A systemic-transactional view of stress and coping among couples: Theory and empirical findings. *European Review of Applied Psychology/Revue Européenne de Psychologie Appliquée, 4*, 137–141.

Bodenmann, G., Charvoz, L., Cina, A., & Widmer, K. (2001). Prevention of marital distress by enhancing the coping skills of couples: 1-year follow up study. *Swiss Journal of Psychology, 60*, 3–10.

Bowlby, J. (1969). *Attachment and loss: Vol. 1. Attachment* (rev. ed.). Harmondsworth: Penguin.

Bronfenbrenner, U. (1979). *The ecology of human development*. Cambridge: Harvard University Press.

Bronfenbrenner, U. (1989). Ecological systems theory. In R. Vasta (Ed.), *Six theories of child development* (pp. 185–246). Greenwich, CT: JAI.

Buhl, H. M. (2000). Biographische Übergaenge und Alter als Determinanten der Eltern-Kind-Beziehung im Erwachsenenalter [Biographical transitions and age as determinants of parent-child relationships in adulthood]. *Zeitschrift fuer Soziologie der Erziehung und Sozialisation, 20*(4), 391–409.

Buhl, H. M., Wittmann, S., & Noack, P. (under review). *Eltern-Kind-Beziehungen studierender und berufstaetiger junger Erwachsener.* [Parent-child relationships of university students and working young adults].

Carlson, C. I., Cooper, C. R., & Spradling, V. Y. (1991). Developmental implications of shared versus distinct perceptions of the family in early adolescence. *New Directions for Child Development, 51*, 13–31.

Clarke, E. J., Preston, M., Raksin, J., & Bengtson, V. L. (1999). Types of conflicts and tensions between older parents and adult children. *The Gerontologist, 39*(3), 261–270.

Collins, W. A. (1991). Shared views and parent-adolescent relationships. *New Directions for Child Development, 51*, 103–110.

Conger, R. D., & Elder, G. H., Jr. (1994). *Families in troubled times. Adapting to change in rural America.* New York: Walter de Gruyter.

Cooney, T. M., & Uhlenberg, P. (1992). Support from parents over life course: The adult child's perspective. *Social Forces, 71*(1), 63–84.

Cowan, C. P., Cowan, P. A., Herring, G., & Miller, N. B. (1991). Becoming a family: Marriage, parenting, and child development. In P. A. Cowan & E. M. Hetherington (Eds.), *Family transitions* (pp. 79–109). Hillsdale, NJ: Erlbaum.

Crouter, A. C., & McHale, S. M. (1993). The long arm of the job: Influences of parental work on childrearing. In T. Luster & L. Okagaki (Eds.), *Parenting: An ecological perspective* (pp. 179–202). Hillsdale, NJ: Erlbaum.

Deal, J. E., Hagan, M. S., Bass, B., Hetherington, E. M., & Clingempeel, G. (1999). Marital interaction in dyadic and triadic contexts: Continuities and discontinuities. *Family Process, 38*, 105–115.

De Wolff, M. S., & van Ijzendoorn, M. H. (1997). Sensitivity and attachment: A meta-analysis on parental antecedents of infant attachment. *Child Development, 68*, 571–591.

Dobson, J. E., & Dobson, R. L. (1991). Groups for caretakers of older adults. Changing roles: An aging parents support group. *Journal for Specialists in Group Work, 16*(3), 178–184.

Dornes, M. (1993). *Der kompetente Saeugling. Die praeverbale Entwicklung des Menschen* [The competent infant. Preverbal development of human beings]. Frankfurt/M.: Fischer.

Dubas, J. S., & Petersen, A. C. (1996). Geographical distance from parents and adjustment during adolescence and young adulthood. In J. A. Graber & J. S. Dubas (Eds.), *Leaving home: Understanding the transition to adulthood* (pp. 3–19). San Francisco, CA: Jossey-Bass.

Dunn, J., & Plomin, R. (1991). Why are siblings so different? The significance of differences in sibling experiences within the family. *Family Process, 30*, 271–283.

East, P. L. (1991). The parent-child relationships of withdrawn, aggressive, and sociable children: Child and parent perspectives. *Merrill-Palmer Quarterly, 37*, 425–443.

Engstler, H. (1998). *Die Familie im Spiegel der amtlichen Statistik* [The family as reflected by public statistics]. Bonn: Bundesministerium für Familie, Senioren, Frauen und Jugend.

Erikson, E. H. (1959). *Identity and the life cycle*. New York: International Universities Press [German ed.: 1973].

Feldman, S. S., & Quatman, T. (1988). Factors influencing age expectations for adolescent autonomy: A study of early adolescents and parents. *Journal of Early Adolescence, 8*, 325–343.

Fend, H. (1998). *Qualitaet im Bildungswesen. Schulforschungen zu Systembedingungen, Schulprofilen und Lehrerleistungen* [Quality in school education]. Weinheim: Juventa.

Fingerle, M. (2000). Übereinstimmung globaler Selbsteinschaetzung von Jugendlichen und ihrer Einschaetzung durch die Eltern. Konsequenzen für die Selbstkonzeptentwicklung [Agreement of adolescents' self-concept and parental perceptions]. Unpublished Ph.D. thesis, University of Jena.

Fingerman, K. L. (1995). Aging mothers' and their adult daughters' perceptions of conflict behaviors. *Psychology and Aging, 10*, 639–649.

Fingerman, K. L. (1996). Sources of tension in the aging mother and adult daughter relationship. *Psychology and Aging, 11*(4), 591–606.

Fingerman, K. L. (2000). "We had a nice little chat": Age and generational differences in mothers' and daughters' descriptions of enjoyable visits. *Journal of Gerontology, 55B* (2), P95–P106.

Fischer, L. R. (1981). Transitions in the mother-daughter relationship. *Journal of Marriage and the Family, 43*(3), 613–622.

Flanagan, C., Schulenberg, J., & Fuligni, A. (1993). Residential setting and parent-adolescent relationships during the college years. *Journal of Youth and Adolescence, 22*(2), 171–189.

Frank, S., Avery, C. B., & Laman, M. S. (1988). Young adults' perceptions of their relationship with their parents: Individual differences in connectedness, competence, and emotional autonomy. *Developmental Psychology, 24*(5), 729–737.

Giarusso, R., Stallings, M., & Bengtson, V. L. (1995). The intergenerational stake hypothesis revisited: Parent-child differences in perceptions of relationships

20 years later. In V. L. Bengtson et al. (eds.), *Adult intergenerational relations: Effects of societal change* (pp. 227–296). New York: Springer.

Gjerde, P. F. (1986). The interpersonal structure of family interaction settings: Parent-adolescent relations in dyads and triads. *Developmental Psychology, 22*, 297–304.

Glenn, N. D. (1990). Quantitative research on marital quality in the 1980s: A critical review. *Journal of Marriage and the Family, 52*, 818–831.

Glenwick, D. S., & Mowrey, J. D. (1986). When parent becomes peer: Loss of intergenerational boundaries in single parent families. *Family Relations, 35*, 5–62.

Gloger-Tippelt, G. (1991). Zusammenhaenge zwischen dem Schema vom eigenen Kind vor der Geburt und dem Bindungsverhalten nach der Geburt bei erstmaligen Muettern [Associations between the schema of the firstborn child prior to birth and attachment behavior after birth]. *Zeitschrift für Entwicklungspsychologie und Pädagogische Psychologie, 23*, 93–114.

Goldscheider, F., & Goldscheider, C. (1999). *The changing transition to adulthood. Leaving and returning home.* Thousand Oaks, CA: Sage.

Gottman, J. M., & Levenson, R. W. (2000). The timing of divorce: Predicting when a couple will divorce over a 14-year period. *Journal of Marriage and the Family, 62*, 737–745.

Graber, J. A., & Brooks-Gunn, J. (1996). Reproductive transitions: The experience of mothers and daughters. In C. D. Ryff & M. M. Seltzer (Eds.), *The parental experience in midlife* (pp. 255–299). Chicago: University of Chicago Press.

Graebe, S., & Luescher, K. (1984). Soziale Beziehungen junger Eltern [Social relationships of young parents]. *Zeitschrift für Sozialisationsforschung und Erziehungssoziologie, 4*(1), 99–121.

Griffith, J. (1996). Relation of parental involvement, empowerment, and school traits to student academic performance. *Journal of Educational Research, 90*, 33–41.

Grolnick, W. S., & Slowiaczek, M. L. (1994). Parents' involvement in children's schooling: A multidimensional conceptualization and motivational model. *Child Development, 65*, 237–252.

Grotevant, H. D., & Cooper, C. R. (1985). Patterns of interaction in family relationships and the development of identity exploration in adolescence. *Child Development, 56*, 415–428.

Hansen, D. A. (1986). Family-school articulations: The effects of interaction rule mismatch. *Educational Research Journal, 23*, 643–659.

Harris, J. R. (1998). *The nurture assumption.* New York: Free Press.

Havighurst, R. J. (1972). *Developmental task and education* (3rd ed.). New York: McKay.

Hess, R. D. (1980). Maternal expectations for mastery of developmental tasks in Japan and the United States. *International Journal of Psychology, 15*, 259–271.

Hinde, R. (1993). Auf dem Wege zu einer Wissenschaft zwischenmenschlicher Beziehungen [Toward a science of interpersonal relationships]. In A. E. Auhagen & M. Salisch (Eds.), *Zwischenmenschliche Beziehungen* (pp. 11–36). Göttingen: Hogrefe.

Hofer, M. (1992). Die Familie mit Schulkindern [Families with school kids]. In M. Hofer, E. Klein-Allermann, & P. Noack (Eds.), Familienbeziehungen [Family relationships] (pp. 171–193). Göttingen: Hogrefe.

Hoffman, J. A. (1984). Psychological separation of late adolescents from their parents. *Journal of Counseling Psychology, 31*, 170–178.

Hoffman, L. W. (1987). The value of children and childrearing patterns. *Social Behaviour, 2*, 123–141.

Honess, T., & Robinson, M. (1993). Assessing parent-adolescent relationships: A review of current research issues and methods. In A. E. Jackson & H. Rodriguez-Tome (Eds.), *Adolescence and its social worlds* (pp. 47–66). Hillsdale, NJ: Erlbaum.

Jurgan, S., Gloger-Tippelt, G., & Ruge, K. (1999). Veraenderungen der elterlichen Partnerschaft in den ersten 5 Jahren nach der Elternschaft [Changes in marital relations during the first 5 years after parenthood]. In B. Reichle & H. Werneck (Eds.), *Übergang zur Elternschaft* [Transition to parenthood] (pp. 37–51). Stuttgart: Enke.

Kalicki, B., Peitz, G., Fthenakis, W. E., & Engfer, A. (1999). Passungskonstellation und Anpassungsprozesse beim Übergang zur Elternschaft [Processes of fit and adaptation during the transition to parenthood]. In B. Reichle & H. Werneck (Eds.), *Übergang zur Elternschaft* (pp. 129–146). Stuttgart: Enke.

Kandel, D. B. (1978). Homophily, selection, and socialization in adolescent friendships. *American Journal of Sociology, 84*, 427–436.

Kaufman, G., & Uhlenberg, P. (1998). Effects of life course transitions on the quality of relationships between adult children and their parents. *Journal of Marriage and the Family, 60*, 924–938.

Kerr, M., & Stattin, H. (2000). What parents know, how they know it, and several forms of adolescent adjustment: Further support for a reinterpretation of monitoring. *Developmental Psychology, 36*, 366–380.

Klass, D., Silverman, P. R., & Nickman, S. L. (Eds.) (1996). *Continuing bonds: New understandings of grief*. Philadelphia: Taylor & Francis.

Kohli, M., & Kuehnemund, H. (Eds.). (2000). *Die zweite Lebenshaelfte. Gesellschaftliche Lage und Partizipation im Spiegel des Alten-Survey* [The second half of life]. Opladen: Leske + Budrich.

Kohn, M. L. (1963). Social class and parent-child relationships: An interpretation. *American Journal of Sociology, 68*, 471–480.

Kohn, M. L., Naoi, A., & Schoenbach, C. (1990). Position in the class structure and psychological functioning in the United States, Japan, and Poland. *American Journal of Sociology, 95*, 964–1008.

Kreppner, K., Paulsen, S., & Schuetze, Y. (1982). Infant and family development: From triads to tetrads. *Human Development, 25*, 373–391.

Krumm, V. (1998). Elternhaus und Schule [Parental home and school]. In D. H. Rost (Hrsg.), *Handwoerterbuch Paedagogische Psychologie* (pp. 81–85). Weinheim: Beltz.

Lamborn, S., Mounts, N., Steinberg, L., & Dornbush, S. M. (1991). Patterns of competence and adjustment among adolescents from authoritative, authoritarian, indulgent, and neglectful families. *Child Development, 62*, 1049–1065.

Lanz, M., Scabini, E., Vermulst, A. A., & Gerris, J. R. M. (2001). Congruence on child rearing in families with early adolescent and middle adolescent children. *International Journal of Behavioral Development, 25*, 133–139.

Laursen, B. (1995). Conflict and social interaction in adolescent relationships. *Journal of Research on Adolescence, 5*, 55–70.

Laursen, B., Coy, K. C., & Collins, W. A. (1998). Reconsidering changes in parent-child conflict across adolescence: A meta-analysis. *Child Development*, 69, 817–832.

Lewis, R. A. (1990). The adult child and older parents. In T. H. Brubaker (Ed.), *Family Relationships in later life* (pp. 68–85). Newbury Park, NJ: Sage.

Luescher, K., & Pillemer, K. (1998). Intergenerational ambivalence: A new approach to the study of parent-child relations in later life. *Journal of Marriage and the Family*, 60, 413–425.

Lye, D. N. (1996). Adult child-parent relationships. *Annual Review of Sociology*, 22, 79–102.

Maccoby, E. E. (1992). The role of parents in the socialization of children: An historical overview. *Developmental Psychology*, 28, 1006–1017.

Mahler, M., Pine, F., & Bergman, A. (1975). *The psychoanalytical birth of the human infant*. New York: Basic Books.

Marini, M. M. (1984). The order of events in the transition to adulthood. *Sociology of Education*, 57, 63–84.

Marks, N. F. (1995). Midlife marital status differences in social support relationships with adult children and psychological well-being. *Journal of Family Issues*, 16(1), 5–28.

McCubbin, H. J., & Patterson, J. M. (1983). The family stress process: The double ABCX model of adjustment and adaptation. *Marriage and Family Review*, 6, 7–37.

McGoldrick, M. S. W., & Carter, E. A. (1982). The family life cycle. In F. Walsh (Ed.), *Normal family processes* (pp. 167–195). New York: Guilford.

McHale, S. M., & Huston, T. L. (1985). The effects of the transition to parenthood on the marriage relationship: A longitudinal study. *Journal of Family Issues*, 6, 409–434.

Minuchin, P. (1985). Families and individual development: Provocations from the field of family therapy. *Child Development*, 56, 289–302.

Nauck, B. (2001). Der Wert von Kindern fuer ihre Eltern. "Value of Children" als spezielle Handlungstheorie des generativen Verhaltens und von Generationen-beziehungen im interkulturellen Vergleich [The value of children. "Value of Children" as a specific theory of goal-directed action of reproductive behavior and of intergenerational relationships in cross-cultural comparison]. *Koelner Zeitschrift für Soziologie und Sozialpsychologie*, LIII, 407–435.

Nauck, B. (2002). http://www.tu-chemnitz.de/phil/soziologie/nauck/index.htm.

Neyer, F.-J. (1999). Die Persoenlichkeit junger Erwachsener in verschiedenen Lebensformen [The personality of young adults in different living arrangements]. *Koelner Zeitschrift für Soziologie und Sozialpsychologie*, 51(3), 491–508.

Noack, P. (2002). Familie und Peers [Family and peers]. In M. Hofer, E. Wild, & P. Noack (Eds.), *Lehrbuch Familienbeziehungen* (pp. 143–167). Göttingen: Hogrefe.

Noack, P., & Buhl, H. M. (1999). Relations with parents and friends during adolescence and early adulthood. Unpublished manuscript, University of Jena.

Noack, P., & Kracke, B. (1992). Developmental timetables for adolescence. Similarities and differences between adolescents, their mothers, fathers, and friends. Poster presented at the Sixth European Conference on Developmental Psychology, Seville, Spain, September.

Noack, P., & Kracke, B. (2002). Problem behavior and parenting: Child rearing behavior as a dependent variable? Paper presented at the 4th Conference of the International Academy of Family Psychology, Heidelberg, Germany, April.

Noack, P., Oepke, M., & Sassenberg, K. (1998). Individuation in Familien mit Jugendlichen nach der deutschen Vereinigung [Individuation in families with adolescents after German unification]. *Zeitschrift für Sozialisationsforschung und Erziehungssoziologie, 2*, 199–214.

Noack, P., & Puschner, B. (1999). Differential trajectories of parent-child relationships and psychosocial adjustment in adolescents. *Journal of Adolescence, 22*, 795–804.

Nydegger, C. N. (1991). The development of paternal and filial maturity. In K. A. Pillmer (Ed.), *Parent-child relations throughout life* (pp. 93–112). Hillsdale, NJ: Erlbaum.

Ohanessian, C. M., Lerner, R. M., Lerner, J. V., & von Eye, A. (1995). Discrepancies in adolescents' and parents' perceptions of family functioning and adolescent emotional adjustment. *Journal of Early Adolescence, 15*, 490–516.

Oswald, H., Baker, D. P., & Stevenson, D. L. (1988) School charter and parental management in West Germany. *Sociology of Education, 61*, 255–265.

Papastefanou, C. (2002). Die Erweiterung der Familienbeziehung und die Geschwisterbeziehung [The extension of the family relationship and the sibling relationship]. In M. Hofer, E. Wild, & P. Noack (Eds.), *Lehrbuch Familienbeziehungen* [Family relationships] (pp. 192–215). Göttingen: Hogrefe.

Parrott, T. M., & Bengtson, V. L. (1999). The effects of earlier intergenerational affection, normative expectations, and family conflict on contemporary exchanges of help and support. *Research on Aging, 21*(1), 73–105.

Phillips, D., McCartney, K., Scarr, S., & Howes, C. (1987). Selective review of infant day care research: A cause for concern. *Zero to Three, 1*, 18–21.

Plomin, R. (1994). *Genetics and experience: The interplay between nature and nurture.* Thousand Oaks: Sage.

Plomin, R., McClearn, C. E., Pedersen, N. L., Nesselroade, J. R., & Bergeman, C. S. (1989). Genetic influence on adults' ratings of their current family environment. *Journal of Marriage and the Family, 51*, 791–803.

Raphael, D., & Schlesinger, B. (1993). Caring for elderly parents and adult children living at home: Interactions of the sandwich generation family. *Social Work Research and Abstracts, 29*(1), 3–8.

Reichle, B., & Montada, L. (1999). Übergang zur Elternschaft und Folgen: Der Umgang mit Veraenderungen macht Unterschiede [Transition to parenthood and its consequences: The way of dealing with changes makes a difference]. In B. Reichle & H. Werneck (Eds.), *Übergang zur Elternschaft* (pp. 205–224). Stuttgart: Enke.

Reiss, D., Hetherington, E. M., Plomin, R., Howe, G. W. et al. (1995). Genetic questions for environmental studies: Differential parenting and psychopathology in adolescence. *Archives of General Psychiatry, 52.*

Roberts, R. E. L., & Bengtson, V. L. (1993). Relationships with parents, self-esteem, and psychological well-being in young adulthood. *Social Psychology Quarterly, 56*(4), 263–277.

Rossi, A. S., & Rossi, P. H. (1990). *Of human bonding. Parent-child relations across the life course.* New York: De Gruyter.

Rowe, D. C. (1994). *The limits of family influence.* New York: Guilford.

Ryan, R. M., & Lynch, J. H. (1989). Emotional autonomy versus detachment: Revisiting the vicissitudes of adolescence and young adulthood. *Child Development, 60*, 593–606.

Scabini, E., & Galimberti, C. (1995). Adolescents and young adults: A transition in the family. *Journal of Adolescence, 18,* 593–606.

Schaffer, H. R. (1999). Understanding socialization: From unidirectional to bidirectional conceptions. In M. Bennett (Ed.), *Developmental psychology* (pp. 272–288). Philadelphia: Psychology Press.

Schnaiberg, A., & Goldenberg, S. (1989). From empty nest to crowded nest: The dynamics of incompletely launched young adults. *Social Problems, 36*(3), 251–269.

Schneewind, K. A. (1995). Familienentwicklung [Family development]. In R. Oerter & L. Montada (Eds.), *Entwicklungspsychologie* (pp. 128–166). Weinheim: Beltz.

Schneewind, K. A., Beckmann, M., & Engfer, A. (1983). *Eltern und Kinder* [Parents and children]. Stuttgart: Kohlhammer.

Schneewind, K. A., Ruppert, S., & Harrow, J. (1998). Personality and family development: An intergenerational longitudinal comparison. Mahwah, NJ: Erlbaum.

Schwarz, B., & Noack, P. (2002). Scheidung und Ein-Elternteilfamilien [Divorce and single-parent families]. In M. Hofer, E. Wild, & P. Noack (Eds.), *Lehrbuch Familienbeziehungen* (pp. 312–335). Göttingen: Hogrefe.

Shmotkin, D. (1999). Affective bonds of adult children with living versus deceased parents. *Psychology and Aging, 14*(3), 473–482.

Silbereisen, R. K., Robins, L., & Rutter, M. (1995). Secular trends in substance use: Concepts and data on the impact of social change on alcohol and drug use. In M. Rutter & D. J. Smith (Eds.), *Psychosocial disorders in young people* (pp. 490–543). Chichester: Wiley.

Silverstein, M. C., Wang, H., Giarusso, R., & Bengtson, V. L. (2002). Reciprocity in parent-child relations over the adult life course. *Journal of Gerontology, 57B,* 3–13.

Singh, B. K., Williams, J. S., & Singh, B. B. (1998). An examination of extended family residence sharing predispositions in the United States: 1973–1989. *Marriage and Family Review, 27*(1/2), 131–143.

Smollar, J., & Youniss, J. (1989). Transformations of adolescents' perceptions of parents. *International Journal of Behavioral Development, 12,* 71–84.

Spitze, G., & Ward, R. (1995). Household labor in intergenerational households. *Journal of Marriage and the Family, 57,* 355–361.

Statistisches Bundesamt (2001). *Weitere Zunahme der Lebenserwartung* [Further increase of life expectancy]. http://www.statistik-bund.de/presse/deutsch/pm2000/p4470022.htm

Stattin, H., & Kerr, M. (2000). Parental monitoring: A reinterpretation. *Child Development, 71,* 1072–1095.

Stattin, H., & Klackenberg, G. (1992). Family discord in adolescence in the light of family discord in childhood: The maternal perspective. In W. Meeus, M. de Goede, W. Kox, & K. Hurrelmann (Eds.), *Adolescence, careers, and cultures* (pp. 143–161). Berlin: De Gruyter.

Steinberg, L. (1990). Autonomy, conflict, and harmony in the family relationship. In S. S. Feldman & G. R. Elliott (Eds.), *At the threshold* (pp. 255–276). Cambridge: Harvard University Press.

Steinberg, L. (2001). *Adolescence* (6th ed.). New York: McGraw Hill.

Steinberg, L., Mounts, N., Lamborn, S., & Dornbush, S. M. (1991). Authoritative parenting and adolescent adjustment across various ecological niches. *Journal of Research on Adolescence, 1,* 19–36.

Steinberg, L., & Silverberg, S. B. (1986). The vicissitudes of autonomy in early adolescence. *Child Development, 57*, 841–851.

Steinberg, L., & Steinberg, W. (1994). *Crossing paths: How your child's adolescence triggers your own crisis.* New York: Simon & Schuster.

Sternberg, R. J. (1986). A triangular theory of love. *Psychological Review, 93*, 119–135.

Tesson, G., & Youniss, J. (1995). Micro-sociology and psychological development. *Sociological Studies of Children, 7*, 101–126.

Thompson, R. A. (1997). Sensitivity and security: New questions to ponder. *Child Development, 68*, 595–597.

Tubman, J. G., & Lerner, R. M. (1994). Continuity and discontinuity in the affective experiences of parents and children: Evidence from the New York longitudinal study. *American Journal of Orthopsychiatry, 64*, 112–125.

Umberson, D., & Chen, M. D. (1994). Effects of a parent's death on adult children: Relationship salience and reaction to loss. *American Sociological Review, 59*, 152–168.

van den Boom, D. C. (1994). The influence of temperament and mothering on attachment and exploration: An experimental manipulation of sensitive responsiveness among lower-class mothers and irritable infants. *Child Development, 65*, 1457–1477.

van den Boom, D. C. (1997). Sensitivity and attachment: Next steps for developmentalists. *Child Development, 68*, 592–594.

van Ijzendoorn, M. H., & de Wolff, M. S. (1997). In search of the absent father–meta-analyses of infant-father attachment: A rejoinder to our discussants. *Child Development, 68*, 604–609.

Veevers, J. E., & Mitchell, B. A. (1998). Intergenerational exchanges and perceptions of support within "boomerang kid" family environments. *International Journal of Aging and Human Development, 46*(2), 91–108.

Vines, D. S. (1998). A conceptualization of divorced single-mother families from a structural perspective. *Dissertation Abstracts International: Section B, 59*, 0462.

Wallace, P. M., & Gotlib, I. H. (1990). Marital adjustment during the transition to parenthood: Stability and predictors of change. *Journal of Marriage and the Family, 52*, 21–29.

Waters, E., Weinfield, N. S., & Hamilton, C. E. (2000). The stability of attachment security from infancy to adolescence and early adulthood: General discussion. *Child Development, 71*, 703–706.

Wheeler, I. (2001). Parental bereavement: The crisis of meaning. *Death Studies, 25*, 51–66.

White, K. M., Speisman, J. C., & Costos, D. (1983). Young adults and their parents: Individuation to mutuality. In H. D. Grotevant & C. R. Cooper (Eds.), *Adolescent development in the family* (pp. 61–76). San Francisco: Jossey-Bass.

Wild, E., & Hofer, M. (2002). Familien mit Schulkindern [Families with children in school]. In M. Hofer, E. Wild, & P. Noack (Eds.), *Familienbeziehungen* [Family relationships] (pp. 216–240). Göttingen: Hogrefe.

Wintre, M. G., Yaffe, M., & Crowley, J. (1995). Perception of Parental Reciprocity Scale (POPRS): Development and validation with adolescents and young adults. *Social Development, 4*, 129–148.

Yamaguchi, K., & Kandel, D. B. (1997). The influence of spouses' behavior and marital dissolution on marijuana use: Causation or selection. *Journal of Marriage and the Family, 59*, 22–36.

Youniss, J., & Smollar, J. (1985) *Adolescent relations with mothers, fathers, and friends.* Chicago: The University of Chicago Press.

Zank, S. (2002). Familien mit Kindern im mittleren Erwachsenenalter [Families with children in middle adulthood]. In M. Hofer, E. Wild, & P. Noack (Eds.), *Familienbeziehungen* [Family relationships] (2nd ed.) (pp. 290–311). Göttingen: Hogrefe.

4

A Dynamic Ecological Systems Perspective on Emotion Regulation Development within the Sibling Relationship Context

Victoria Hilkevitch Bedford and Brenda L. Volling

This chapter presents a dynamic ecological systems model of emotion regulation. We focus on the course of the sibling relationship across the life span, making note of the connections between individuals' developing capacity to regulate their own emotions and the interpersonal nature of the sibling relationship. We introduce the concept of emotion other-regulation and note how siblings attempt to regulate their own emotions through attempts to influence others. We lay out a developmental timeline showing how parents regulate the relationship between their children during early childhood and how this parental control is slowly relinquished over time such that older children, adolescents, and adults become more responsible for the interpersonal regulation in their sibling relationship and, in turn, their own emotion self-regulation.

An ecological perspective on human development underscores the importance of examining child and adult development within multiple contexts and the necessity of examining intraindividual change along with change in the family, community, and cultural contexts in which individuals live. This volume is devoted to understanding change in personal relationships over time from the early years of childhood through the later years of adulthood. In the current chapter, we use a dynamic ecological systems perspective to examine the sibling relationship as a context for the development of emotion regulation in both childhood and adulthood. Development is defined according to the principles of the life-span perspective. Thus, development is lifelong, multidimensional, multidirectional, and contextual (Baltes, 1987).

We begin this endeavor by reviewing current theoretical perspectives that emphasize relationships as developmental contexts in the infancy and child literature. The specific focus, consequently, is on attachment theory, parent-infant interaction, and the early development of emotion regulation. We then argue that other family relationships are important developmental contexts and that the sibling relationship may be an especially relevant family relationship context in which not only children, but adults as well, experience intense emotions. This experience has consequences for individual development. We then present a dynamic ecological systems model that outlines our position on the interdependence between emotion self-regulation, emotion other-regulation, and interpersonal regulation by acknowledging that siblings, through their interactions with one another, can create very different relationship contexts that can either promote or undermine the individual's development of self-regulation strategies. Next we provide a review of some of the literature in both childhood and adulthood supporting our contention that human development involves a dynamic, transactional process between individuals and the social environment and that sibling relationships are an important part of that process. Finally some case studies of sibling relationships are given to illustrate the model of development presented.

RELATIONSHIPS AS DEVELOPMENTAL CONTEXTS FOR EMOTION REGULATION IN INFANCY

Several current developmental perspectives underscore social relationships as developmental contexts (Berscheid, 1999; Collins & Laursen, 1999; Dunn, 1993; Hartup & Laursen, 1999). Individual development is seen as interdependent with the social transactions taking place in one's closest and significant relationships. Much of the work in this area has focused on early mother-infant interactions (Sroufe, 1996) and the fact that although young infants have rudimentary strategies available to regulate physiological arousal, it is the support and responsivity of the mother in her interactions with her young infant that helps the child regulate emotional arousal (Sameroff & Emde, 1989). In essence, the parent-infant relationship is seen as a coregulatory system. Cassidy (1994) has proposed that the coregulation observed in early parent-infant attachment relationships serves as the basis of subsequent self-regulation strategies. Specifically, infants learn different emotion self-regulation strategies based on their early experiences interacting with a parent who is sensitive, inconsistently available, or rejecting. Cassidy (1994) proposes that when caregivers are emotionally available and respond sensitively to the infant's signals, the infant not only develops a secure infant-parent attachment, but the child also develops the capacity for an open and flexible expression of emotions. This means that the child is able to express the full range of emotions and none of the emotional expressions are grossly exaggerated or inhibited. Moreover, infants can use the parent as a secure base and feel free to explore their environment. Similarly, parental responsiveness, mutually shared positive affect, and sensitivity to the infant's cues not only leads to a secure attachment relationship between the mother and infant, but also to the eventual development of self-regulation, inhibitory control, and conscience (Kochanska &

Askan, 1995). Insecurely attached infants, however, develop different patterns of emotion regulation based on their affective experiences during parent-infant interaction. Infants whose emotional needs have been rejected by the caregiver are more likely to develop an insecure-avoidant attachment and develop a regulatory strategy whereby they minimize their emotional expression so as not to risk further rejection and anger from the parent. Infants whose mothers are inconsistently available to meet the infant's needs are more likely to develop an insecure-resistant attachment and develop a regulatory strategy in which negative affect is heightened in an effort to gain the attention of an unavailable caregiver. In brief, the quality of early coregulation as reflected in parent-infant interaction determines the child's internalization of either competent or dysfunctional emotion regulation strategies in subsequent relationships in later years.

Beyond the Parent-Infant Dyad

To the extent that early coregulation in parent-infant interaction is underscored as the social origins of the young child's emotion regulation strategies, it is notable that so little research considers other possible relationship contexts as contributing to the child's emotion regulation. Children, as well as adults, spend a considerable part of their life interacting with a myriad of social partners both within (e.g., fathers, grandparents, siblings) and outside the family of origin (e.g., peers, teachers). Unfortunately, very little work on children's emotion regulation has focused on other relationship contexts beyond the mother-infant dyad. In the current paper, we focus on the sibling relationship as an influential context for the development of emotion self-regulation. Sibling relationships in childhood and adulthood represent a wide range of emotional experiences. Rivalry, conflict, and aggression are commonplace between siblings in both childhood and adulthood, but so are laughter, cooperative play, humor, and kindness (Dunn, 1988; Shortt & Gottman, 1997). Sibling exchanges can be highly charged angry confrontations one minute and involve teaching, concern, and helpfulness a short time later. Who cannot recall children tormenting and teasing a younger sibling and then find them a few minutes later protecting this same sibling from the neighborhood bully? Adults can take emotional risks in their sibling relationships that they would not attempt in voluntary friendship relationships for fear that the latter would dissolve (Bedford & Avioli, 2001). We will argue that the sibling relationship is a developmental context in which children and adults alike learn to regulate emotion. Further, we will focus on the interdependency between the development of self-regulation and interpersonal regulation, defined as the ability to regulate one's social relationships. We will also introduce the concept of emotion other-regulation, a component of interpersonal regulation.

A Model of Interpersonal Regulation and Self-Regulation of Emotions

Tomkins (1962, 1963) claims there are four goals for emotion regulation: (1) to minimize negative affect; (2) to maximize positive affect; (3) to decrease affect inhibition; and (4) to feel competent in one's ability to achieve these goals. Magai and Passman (1997) point out that relationships with other people are the primary source of "feeling good" and "feeling bad," suggesting that the close relationships that individuals have with others is a significant context in which these goals for emotion regulation are achieved.

Those researchers who study children's emotional development emphasize that the eventual goal of socialization is for the child to internalize a set of parental standards so that parental control lessens over time as the child's self-control increases over time (Kochanska, 1991; Kopp, 1989; Sroufe, 1996). It is around the preschool years that one starts to see children using self-regulation strategies in their attempts to inhibit behavior and comply with parental requests (Kochanska, Tbjekes, & Forman, 1998). However, even with the advent of more mature forms of self-regulation in preschool, social relationships and the interpersonal context continue to exert significant influence on an individual's ability to regulate emotional arousal across the life span. Unfortunately, the interpersonal contributions to the development of emotion regulation seem to have been overlooked at the expense of the search for children's self-regulatory abilities. Emotion regulation, according to Thompson (1994), refers to "the extrinsic and intrinsic processes responsible for monitoring, evaluating, and modifying emotional reactions, especially their intensive and temporal features, to accomplish one's goals" (p. 28). Emotion regulation, therefore, includes internal and external processes, yet much of current research in this area has emphasized internal regulatory processes such as the focused attention, attentional shifting, or effortful control the individual uses to regulate emotional arousal. What is missing from more contemporary perspectives of emotion regulation is the appreciation of the external processes or interpersonal context in which the individual functions and which more than likely gives rise to the emotional experience in the first place (Campos, Campos, & Barrett, 1989).

In the present paper, we propose a model of emotion regulation that situates the individual within social relationships, in this case, the sibling relationship. Our model underscores the interdependence between interpersonal regulation and intrapersonal regulation. In Figure 4.1, we present a dynamic ecological systems model of emotion regulation as applied to the sibling relationship. In this model, both siblings interact over time to mutually influence one another's social and emotional competence, which, in turn, creates a relationship context that either maintains or undermines

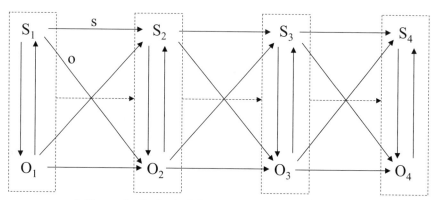

FIGURE 4.1. A Dynamic Ecological Systems Model of Interpersonal, Self-, and Other-Regulation in Sibling Relationships. *Note*: S = sibling 1 (self) ; O = sibling 2 (other).

these competencies over time. Bidirectional arrows indicate that through their interactions with one another, one sibling (S) and the other sibling (O) not only influence each other as individuals, but, also, their interaction creates a relationship dynamic that now provides a context for future interactions. This process is denoted in the figure by the hash-marked box encompassing both the older and younger siblings. Through their interactions with one another, siblings establish a relationship that can become a supportive context for the development of competent emotional functioning or can contribute to the individual's inability to regulate emotions in a socially acceptable and openly flexible manner. Furthermore, the behavior of one sibling (S) affects that sibling's behavior at subsequent points in time, as seen in path *s*. This sibling also affects the behavior (and emotions) of the other sibling (O) over time, as seen in path *o*, which we refer to as emotion other-regulation. Moreover, the hash-marked arrows running through the middle of the figure linking the boxes indicate that the processes not only involve individuals influencing each other within and across time, but that there is also a relationship dynamic based on past interactions (i.e., relationship history) that travels over time with the individual siblings and provides an interpersonal context for the development of self-regulation.

Sibling Relationships in Childhood and Processes of Interpersonal Regulation

Several areas of research can be summoned to support this model and our contention that emotion self-regulation, no matter how old the individual, is affected by and affects interpersonal regulation, which in turn continues to affect individual development. We will provide examples of current research that show how the interpersonal relationship between siblings can influence the development of emotion self-regulation on the part of both siblings. Further, we will present research documenting the important role of other social partners in regulating the sibling relationship in the early years of childhood until children have the ability to maintain the affective nature of their own relationships with one another. In other words, we move beyond the dyadic relationship context to incorporate a more complex network of interpersonal regulation that involves multiple social partners.

Anger, Conflict, and Aggression. Research on both preschool and adolescent siblings has documented the toll of aggressive sibling interaction on children's social and emotional competence (Garcia, Shaw, Winslow, & Yaggi, 2000; MacKinnon-Lewis, Starnes, Volling, & Johnson, 1997; Patterson, 1986). Patterson (1986) has proposed a sibling-trainer hypothesis in which he claims that fighting between siblings provides the opportunities for children to acquire and practice social aggression and coercion. Children learn and practice aggression within their sibling relationship and the continuing exchange of aggressive behavior between siblings ensures that coercion, anger, and contempt continue to characterize the sibling relationship. Patterson speculates that during an extended interchange of negative behaviors, either of the siblings can increase the intensity of their coercive and hostile behavior. Should one of the siblings then back off, this increases the likelihood (through negative reinforcement) that the other sibling will continue to employ a strategy in which he or she increases the intensity of coercive behavior in future interactions. It can soon become a vicious cycle between individuals and the relationship context in which they live. Patterson also notes that the development of aggression in this type of social interchange is a gradual process that takes some time, underscoring how the employment of self-regulation strategies can change over time in an effort to adapt to the interpersonal demands of the situation. Initially, the negative interchanges between siblings may include high rates of noncompliant behaviors, then nonphysical aggressive behaviors such as yelling and teasing will begin to emerge as one or both siblings begins to increase the intensity of negative behaviors. Finally, physical aggression including pushing, shoving, hitting, and attacking with objects will surface as each of the siblings increases their coercive behaviors. What is important to emphasize here is that no matter who "started it," both siblings, by their participation in this hostile and coercive social exchange, become increasingly aggressive.

Patterson's work on the sibling-trainer hypothesis is relevant for our argument of the interpersonal and intrapersonal dynamics of emotion regulation in several other ways as well. First, Patterson points out that it is through disruptions in parental discipline that these sibling-child exchanges begin. Parents may ignore the situation hoping the children will work it out themselves, fail to punish aggressive behavior when it starts or punish misbehavior inconsistently, and reinforce the behavior by responding with a neutral or positive behavior (e.g., talking or not responding). In each case, the coercive exchanges between siblings can increase in magnitude and frequency and these hostile interchanges become more difficult for parents to manage over time. Not only is the sibling relationship context, then, particularly influential in determining the individual's self-regulation and vice versa, but third-party intervention can further alter the social dynamics between the children, a topic we pick up later in this chapter. Once again, we see how individuals can influence and be influenced by the interpersonal contexts in which they live.

Patterson's work on sibling aggression also underscores how important the interpersonal context is for interpreting emotional expression. In uncovering the sequence of behaviors that transpired between siblings to predict aggressive outbursts, Patterson noted that whereas sibling teasing may have initiated a negative interchange, one of the sibling behaviors that served to escalate the aggressive interaction was the sibling's *laughter* in response to the child's teasing or negative physical behavior. Why is this important? We often assume that laughter is an expression of positive affect, happiness, or joy. Patterson's work clearly demonstrates how important it is to consider the interpersonal context in which an emotional display is observed. Laughter is not always part of a positive emotional experience and in this case can actually serve to escalate negative affect between two individuals.

Further, several sibling researchers have also noted that whereas girls, in general, are much less aggressive than boys, within the context of the sibling relationship girls may be just as likely to participate in verbal and physical aggression as boys. Patterson (1977) noted that even though over 50% of the hitting that was given or received during coercive interaction was between male siblings, younger siblings, particularly younger sisters, were the primary instigators for the initiation and maintenance of a coercive interchange with their older brothers. The point to be underscored here is that there appear to be certain situations, in this case the instigation of sibling conflict, where girls are just as involved in coercive behaviors as boys, and as a result, are just as much in need of learning how to regulate extreme negative affect as are boys.

The Role of Individual Characteristics and the Sibling Relationship Context

Research on sibling temperament has also documented the significant role of individual characteristics in determining the quality of one's social relationships and the consequences of these social experiences in determining individual development. Stoneman and Brody (1993), for instance, studied children's temperament and sibling conflict. They were particularly interested in whether children with difficult temperaments (e.g., higher activity level, higher negative reactivity) would have more sibling conflict. Similar to the work of Munn and Dunn (1986) with preschool siblings, when both siblings had difficult temperaments, there was more conflict than if neither child had a difficult temperament. Thus, children with difficult temperaments will be exposed to more sibling conflict than those without difficult temperaments and this will undoubtedly affect the individual children's developmental outcomes. What is interesting about the work of Stoneman and Brody (1993) is the demonstration that similar child characteristics can create very different interpersonal contexts depending on which sibling has the difficult temperament. Stoneman and Brody created four sibling groups based on the temperament of the older and younger sibling. These groups included dyads in which the older sibling had a difficult temperament and the younger did not, as well as dyads in which the younger sibling had a difficult temperament and the older did not. They were interested in learning whether the presence of a sibling with a calm and easy disposition would be a protective factor and decrease the likelihood of sibling conflict even though the other sibling had a difficult temperament. The answer was both yes and no. When younger children had difficult temperaments and the older did not, there was less conflict between siblings. However, when the older sibling had a difficult temperament and the younger did not, sibling conflict was as high as that found in the dyads in which both siblings had difficult temperaments. The conclusion drawn was that, because older siblings tend to be leaders and younger siblings followers, the older sibling had more influence in determining the quality of the relationship that developed. Thus, depending on the child's age and birth order, different children will be influenced differently by the relationship context in which they interact with their sibling; siblings do not share the exact same experiences within this relationship environment (Dunn & Plomin, 1991).

Support, Cooperation, and Prosocial Behaviors. In addition to the evidence suggesting that aggressive and coercive interaction between siblings can lead to difficulties with emotion regulation for the two individuals involved, there is also evidence to suggest that supportive, mutually positive exchanges between siblings have positive benefits for the individual children. For example, Munn and Dunn (1986) observed preschool children interacting with their toddler siblings when the younger was 18 months old and again when they were 24 months old. When older siblings were more giving and cooperative at 18 months, the younger siblings showed more cooperative behavior at 24 months. Similarly, when 18-month-old younger siblings showed more friendly behavior toward their older siblings, the older siblings were more giving and cooperative toward the younger sibling six months later, and were more likely to use distraction and conciliating behaviors during sibling conflicts rather than more extreme forms of conflict behaviors such as physically prohibiting the younger sibling and using physical aggression. Not only did the sibling relationship provide the social context in which the younger child may have acquired cooperative and prosocial behavior, but these cooperative behaviors when expressed months later in interaction with the older sibling also maintained the positive and supportive context that would continue to facilitate the younger child's prosocial development. When sibling conflict did erupt between these children, older siblings were more caring and sensitive in how they handled conflict than were children in less cooperative and friendly sibling relationships.

The quality of the sibling relationship also plays a role in the frequency of cooperative and pretend play between siblings. Some scholars have argued that cooperative and pretend play may facilitate a child's understanding of others' beliefs and feelings (e.g., Harris & Cavanaugh, 1993; Taylor, Cartwright, & Carlson, 1993) and several investigations have found that children with siblings, particularly older siblings, appear to be better at mastering "theory of mind" tasks than those without siblings (Jenkins & Astington, 1996; Perner, Ruffman, & Leekam, 1994; Ruffman, Perner, Naito, Parker, & Clements, 1998). Youngblade and Dunn (1995) have demonstrated that preschool siblings are more likely to engage in cooperative pretend play when mothers describe the relationship as friendly. Children were also involved in more social pretense and expressed a greater diversity of pretend themes during play when more positive affect was exchanged between siblings. Further, participation in pretense with one's sibling was correlated with the younger 33-month-old sibling's emotional understanding; that is, their ability to understand the affective perspective of another person. As Youngblade and Dunn (1995) note, "the findings argue against interpreting development solely in terms of continuity in *individual child* characteristics and suggest, rather, that we should consider seriously the developmental importance of the child's social experiences" (p. 1486). Of course, the direction of effects in this study is difficult to discern because it may be that social pretense facilitates children's social cognition or that children with a greater understanding of others' emotions are better able to engage in joint pretense with a social partner. In any case, children's understanding of others' emotions is one component of a child's developing emotional competence and undoubtedly plays some part in children's ability to regulate emotional expressions in line with cultural display rules (Saarni, 1997). In this regard, Volling, McElwain, and Miller (2002) recently found that children's emotional understanding predicted the older sibling's ability to regulate jealousy responses when interacting with their mothers and younger siblings. Collectively, these findings underscore once again the interdependent nature of self-regulation and interpersonal regulation in sibling relationships.

Although the previous examples focused on young children, there is also evidence suggesting that there are positive consequences for younger siblings in the early adolescent years as well when their relationship with an older brother or sister is described as close and warm. Tucker, Updegraff, McHale, and Crouter (1999) were interested in whether the older sibling's personal characteristics and the quality of the sibling relationships were related to the younger sibling's empathy. Given the asymmetry between siblings with respect to power and influence, Tucker and her colleagues hypothesized that older siblings would have more influence on their younger siblings' development than vice versa. This seemed to be the case because younger brothers were more empathic when their older brothers were also more empathic and their relationship was described as warm and positive. Younger sisters were more empathic when they had empathic older sisters, but also when their older sisters directed more anger at and had more fights with their younger sisters. The reason for this relation was not clear, but as Tucker et al. (1999) explain, it may be adaptive for younger sisters to be aware of the older sister's angry emotional state in order to protect or defend themselves. It's also possible that being the recipient of another's angry emotions and verbal attacks can be hurtful and elicit painful feelings that promote an awareness of one's own as well as others' feeling states. Again, what is important to note here is that the relationship context helps give meaning to the emotions and behaviors expressed, and these findings clearly demonstrate that anger or interpersonal conflict between siblings does not automatically translate into angry and aggressive outcomes for the individuals involved.

Sibling Relationships in Adulthood and Processes of Interpersonal Regulation

Next we extend the previous discussion to adulthood. Before we begin, however, we digress to provide background information on the development of emotion regulation in adulthood.

Emotion Regulation Development in Adulthood. As in the child literature, emotion regulation development in adulthood emphasizes the individual processes involved despite the fact that emotions are experienced in social contexts (Carstensen, Gross, & Fung, 1997). We review a recent conceptualization of adult development of emotion self-regulation, and we also introduce the concept of emotion *other*-regulation.

Emotion self-regulation appears to follow a developmental trend in adulthood. Labouvie-Vief and Medler (2002) proposed a two-process model. One process involves affect dampening for the purpose of optimizing positive affect and minimizing negative affect. Maximal positive affect is not always the aim, it should be noted, because high levels can be maladaptive for some individuals (see Labouvie-Vief & Medler, 2002). The dampening process occurs when the system receives a signal that there is deviation from equilibrium. The system takes palliative action to restore the original state. In this process, therefore, high levels of arousal are not especially desirable whether positive or negative. There is considerable empirical evidence that adults indeed become increasingly effective at emotion dampening as they grow older. Some affect-regulating processes are defined as "response focused" (Carstensen et al., 1997, p. 339; Gross, 1998). These are the management strategies used once emotions have been aroused. The more adaptive strategies, such as those described by Labouvie-Vief and Medler, are "antecedent focused." One kind of antecedent focused strategy, which adults become increasingly competent at employing, is to alter the thought process about the potentially disturbing situation. Coping and defense mechanisms are used that allow individuals both to reinterpret and to positively appraise conflict situations (Diehl, Coyle, & Labouvie-Vief, 1996). Another kind of antecedent focused strategy is to modify the environment. Adults also become increasingly adept at this strategy of creating environments that aid in affect optimization (Lawton, 1989). They may limit their exposure to environments that are potentially provocative of undesirable emotion. Or they may increase their exposure to environments that elicit positive emotions. The second process described by Labouvie-Vief and Medler involves affect amplification. In the face of negative affect, instead of dampening it, the system opens itself to experiencing it. The aim of this process is not to maintain equilibrium, but to magnify the affective experience. The purpose of this magnification is to move the affect system toward "innovation and change." This process requires a deliberate effort, and results, ultimately, in the development of new capabilities, namely, to integrate positive and negative emotions. For instance, a person may feel justifiably angry toward a person whose actions are provocative yet feel compassion as well. Recent studies suggest that the development of this emotion regulation ability to process complex emotions follows an inverted U curve. It increases during adulthood, peaks during midlife, and then declines (Labouvie-Vief & Medler, 2002)

Whereas most of the emotion control literature focuses on the individual's self-regulation, even in social situations, another aspect of emotion regulation within a social dyad is the emotion regulation of the partner. Emotion regulation of others can take many forms. Some forms may be deliberate or intentional, as in the case of "social control" when friends deter one's risky behavior (Rook & Ituarte, 1999), or social support, when friends cheer each other up. Other forms of emotion other-regulation may be unintentional. Some ways in which people regulate the emotions of others are by means of social activities that initiate, magnify, or dampen emotional arousal in their social partners, whether positive or negative (e.g., telling jokes, picking a fight, giving succor). Another source of regulating the emotions of the social partner is through one's emotional expression, such as affect displays. Such expressive displays may elicit similar feelings in others through contagion (Keltner, 1996). Thus, the sadness of one partner may elicit sympathetic tears in the other partner ; laughing may initiate laughter. Emotion displays also convey messages that regulate the social partner's emotion (e.g., Magai & Passman, 1997). For instance, a display of anger may elicit fear in the partner. Emotions are also expressed verbally, a tendency that appears to vary systematically by age (e.g., Labouvie-Vief, Devoe, & Bulka, 1989 ; Lawton & Albert, 1990, cited in Magai & Passman, 1997). Emotion regulation of partners through verbal emotion expressions is amply illustrated in the marriage literature, as when one partner's intense emotional expression elicits emotional withdrawal from the other (Levenson, Carstensen, & Gottman, 1994).

It would seem that adults increase their use of emotion other-regulation in later years because they grow in their ability to disinhibit emotional expression. Unlike adults of other ages, older adults demonstrate little correspondence between their knowledge of cultural rules for emotion display and applying those rules to their own emotion expression (Malatesta & Kalnok, 1984). In fact, older adults appear to be more emotionally expressive when aroused than younger adults (Malatesta-Magai, Jonas, Shepard, & Culvert, 1992). As for verbal expression of emotions, middle-aged adults are more likely to acknowledge their inner emotional experiences and describe their emotions more vividly than younger adults (Labouvie-Vief et al., 1989). Older adults show a similar trend (Lawton & Albert, 1990, cited in Magai & Passman, 1997). At the same time that adults are becoming more emotionally expressive, however, their emotion self-regulation processes are showing increased competence. Add to the mix a rise of emotion complexity experience, particularly through midlife. The result would appear to be the potential for the judicious exercise of emotion regulation of others and through a variety of channels (verbal and nonverbal), and elevated salience of emotion regulation processes in close relationships. We now turn to the interpersonal context in the model.

Disinhibition and Dampening of Emotion. We illustrate the dynamic ecological systems model in adulthood in the areas of emotion disinhibition and emotion dampening. We know that emotions become more salient as adults grow older, as they express emotions more openly, and both processes are adaptive (Carstensen et al., 1997). The sibling relationship, given its ascribed status, is likely to be an important social context in which to learn these behaviors. At the same time, affect dampening competencies improve with age, and the negative consequences of disinhibition experiences in the sibling relationship may contribute to the development of this dimension of emotion regulation.

Adult sibling relationships may function as a training ground in emotion cognition, if the relationship is a secure one. Alternatively, the adult sibling relationship may foster emotion dampening, when to disinhibit emotions may trigger negative experiences. Shortt and Gottman (1997) compared facial and physiological affect during sibling interactions between sibling pairs who differed in degree of relationship closeness (close, distant, and mixed). Close siblings, when talking about positive topics, showed not only more positive affect, but more negative affect as well, than did distant siblings. Apparently close relationships offer the security that allows for the disinhibition of negative affect during such discussions. Distant siblings, on the other hand, cannot take this risk, no doubt due to the fragility of the relationship. To maintain these relationships, affect dampening is more advantageous. On the other hand, when sibling partners talked about topics of disagreement, close siblings displayed more positive affect, specifically more affection and more validation than did distant pairs. No doubt these close siblings have a particularly strong investment in preserving this valued relationship. They will not allow a disagreement to compromise it. Distant siblings appear to lack this motivation when disagreeing.

These examples illustrate the importance of context (degree of closeness) in these adult relationships for disinhibiting and for dampening emotional expression. The consequences of these experiences may influence the sibling partners' personal development in terms of their flexibility of emotion expression, and their sibling's development in understanding and responding to these emotions, and these experiences add to the history of the relationship in shaping its qualities.

Regulation of the Sibling Social Environment and Its Influence on Development

The sibling relationship, like all relationships, consists of two individuals whose characteristics, behaviors, and emotions converge to determine the nature of the sibling relationship. In this section, we consider how interpersonal regulation (regulation of the quality of the sibling relationship) influences the development of emotion self-regulation. We will begin with the parents' role in this process when their children are young. We will follow the relinquishing of that role when adolescent offspring have the cognitive capabilities to develop coping skills that allow them to strive toward achieving the quality of the relationship with their siblings that they desire or to reject the relationship. In adulthood other motives may supplant personal preferences in response to life events and norms governing expectations from siblings.

Infancy and Childhood. Not all interpersonal regulation is contained within the confines of a dyadic relationship. Indeed, a developmental systems model of emotion regulation underscores the complexity of interpersonal relationships and the ways in which individuals manage their relationships and the relationships of others in an effort to manage affect. This is particularly the case when we think of the development of sibling relationships from early childhood throughout adolescence and into adulthood. Toddler and preschool-aged siblings are still too young to independently manage their own affect as well as the affect in their relationship. They must rely on parents to manage sibling conflict and hence, their relationship. Parents attempt to manage their children's relationships with one another until children are eventually mature enough to manage the affect in their own relationships. The goal for most parents with respect to sibling interaction is to reduce levels of negative affect, conflict, and aggression and to increase levels of sharing, cooperation, and positive affect. This goal of decreasing negative affect and increasing mutually shared positive affect seems to be a cornerstone of emotion regulation (Tomkins, 1962) and relationship management (Sroufe, 1996; Tronick, 1989). The developmental systems model acknowledges that children form relationships with other family members, namely their siblings, and parents are responsible initially and throughout much of childhood for managing the affect in those relationships.

As noted, parents socialize their young children in the family to get along with one another, to share with one another, and to develop close relationships with one another. However, young children are not adept at managing their early relationships, so parents must do this for them. Parenting that is warm, affectionate, emotionally focused, and sensitive to the individual needs of both children is associated with cooperative and caring sibling relationships (Brody, Stoneman, & McCoy, 1992; Dunn & Kendrick, 1982). Parenting that is harsh, rejecting, coercive, and favors one child over another is related to sibling conflict and aggression (Brody et al., 1992; Dunn & Kendrick, 1982; Volling & Belsky, 1992). The parents' management of sibling interaction (i.e., interpersonal regulation) is crucial in determining the interpersonal context in which the two young children interact and, eventually, the development of the children's emotion self-regulation. Sibling relationships also contribute to the emergence of emotion self-regulation and may actually be the interpersonal context in which young children first learn to regulate powerful emotions such as jealousy and anger (Volling, McElwain, & Miller, 2002).

Adolescence. As children approach adolescence, they now have the cognitive maturation necessary to use more sophisticated cognitive coping strategies and to employ these in the service of their interpersonal goals. The growth of emotion regulation in adolescence is not only a function of the child's increasing ability to shift attention away from disturbing thoughts, or to contemplate more pleasurable moments, or to distract oneself by engaging in an energizing activity. It also involves the sophistication and social manipulation of relationship environments. Adolescents, through means of their own positive affect and supportive behavior, can now create and maintain a warm and friendly sibling relationship that encourages the growth of interpersonal understanding and a desire to continue one's relationship with the sibling. Whereas early sibling relationships may have been maintained primarily through family ties and parental encouragement, the possibility of the self voluntarily forming a supportive friendship with one's sibling becomes possible with the advent of adolescence. Alternatively, aggressive or abusive behavior that fuels sibling conflict creates an angry and aversive interpersonal context that the adolescent may soon actively choose to avoid. It should not be surprising then to observe adolescents with a childhood history of stormy sibling relationships spending far fewer hours in the company of their sibling and far more hours in the company of friends. The adolescent, unlike the young child, can now make decisions and choices about their own behavior that have significant developmental consequences for them, their relationships, and the partners in these relationships. Parents must increasingly turn more control of the sibling relationship over to their children as they get older, with the hope that as young adulthood approaches, their children will acquire the necessary self-regulation skills to monitor and control the emotion in their own interpersonal relationships with one another. This balance between self and interpersonal regulation will continue to have prominence in adulthood when parental management of the relationship is no longer sought or encouraged.

Adulthood. Adult siblings may have the final say in whether they maintain friendly and supportive contact with one another, keep a cool distance, or continue a raging battle. In general, however, it appears that siblings become increasingly salient in the course of adulthood (e.g., Gold, 1989), and that siblings seem to be adept at reframing negative experiences in the relationship as ultimately benefitting them (Bedford, Volling, & Avioli, 2000 ; Bedford, 1998). However, social norms suggest that there exist a set of implicit sibling roles, "tasks of siblingship" (Goetting, 1986, p. 703), the fulfillment of which may require the sibling partners to stretch outside of their comfort zone in relation to one another. Goetting defines these tasks of adulthood as (a) to support each other's adult role choices and enactment (young adulthood), (b) to cooperate in decision making and caring for older parents in declining health (middle adulthood), and (c) to engage in coreminiscence (late adulthood). The formation of these tasks and their potential role in the development of emotion regulation in adulthood follow.

Goetting posits that during the life course siblings are confronted with a series of tasks related to normative role sequences in adulthood. These tasks require the partners to engage in "specific prosocial observed and expected behaviors" relevant to specific life course periods (p. 704). As life progresses, these tasks of siblingship change in response to the role transitions and life events typically encountered. Adult siblings' development may be enhanced by the interpersonal regulation challenge of fulfilling these tasks of siblingship. Particularly when the sibling relationship is distant or conflictual, but the partners are motivated to meet the tasks of siblingship, they may find that their usual emotion regulation strategies are not adequate. Under such circumstances, the tasks may provide the impetus for development of new emotion regulation strategies within the sibling system.

In young and middle adulthood, when siblings no longer coreside, their contacts become more voluntary. When they establish families of procreation and/or careers the sibling tie is often mediated by the needs of these activities and relationships. The siblingship task is "to transform the childhood tasks of nurturance, caretaking, and teaching" of the sibling (Goetting, 1986, p. 707) to the task of providing the sibling with the socio-emotional support needed to enact adult roles, such as parent, worker, and child of aging parents. The early adulthood expression of this task is highly variable due to its voluntary nature. Thus, its expression may vary from one extreme of merely keeping informed about one another, often through the parent (kin-keeper), to the opposite extreme of daily contact (Goetting, 1986).

The empirical literature on young adult siblings indicates that they tend to maintain interest in each other, but that the relationship is relatively dormant during this period in which many new roles are initiated. When no direct contact occurs, parents mediate, as in childhood, by keeping each sibling informed about the other (Bedford, 1995). This lull in contact may be an effective emotion dampening strategy for siblings who are particularly conflictual or distant. The strategies of affect dampening and complexity have only begun to increase in competence, and may not be up to the task of maintaining a desirable emotional tone at this period of the life for such cases. The potential for sibling strife is high in societies with nuclear family structures and individualistic values. The competitive atmosphere fostered under these conditions may render the partners' spouses, children, and career status as fodder for reactivating early rivalries, as well as memories of resentments over parental unfairness, whether real or imagined (Bedford, 1989). Thus, reduced contact may be an effective strategy for dampening the expression of negative emotions (Bedford, 1995).

An example comes from a longitudinal study of adult sibling relationships (Bedford, Rains, & Guseilla, 2000). One woman's behavior toward her sister illustrates this dynamic. Early in the study, at age thirty, Margaret was trying to provide emotional support to her sister who was divorced, had dropped out of college, and was caring for young children. The sister was unreceptive and the relationship was strained. Margaret was, in fact, busy with her own agenda, and no doubt her affect communicated it. Margaret was successful in all the areas in which her sister was not, and from this "superior" position was doling out advice. Meanwhile, Margaret was angry at the favoritism her mother was showing by planning, in her will, to leave more money to the needy sister, rather than to her, the "good" sister. We see in the interactions between the sisters that Margaret lacked the emotion regulation capabilities to complete the siblingship task of young adulthood, namely, to give her sister the socio-emotional support that would empower her to make good decisions. Instead of saying "you should do (or feel) thus and so" she might try listening and observing her sister kindly and with an open mind, take notice and acknowledge her sister's potential strengths.

In middle adulthood, the siblingship task of supporting one another is more demanding than the young adult task, because the role is a shared one, parent care. Thus, "siblings must turn to one another in a spirit of unity in order to adequately carry out critical responsibilities to their parents" (Goetting, 1986, p. 709). Such responsibilities may include monitoring and caring for frail parents, making arrangements for their burial and its sequalae, including settling the parental estate. In middle age, then, contact is essential. Emotion regulation strategies cannot rely on geographic or temporal separation. Thus, siblings are challenged to develop emotion regulation strategies that permit sufficient congeniality to make and carry out joint decisions. Consequently, this task may provide the impetus for important maturation of emotion regulation. It is well known that proximity reactivates sibling rivalry (e.g., Laverty, 1962) and proximity cannot be avoided during this phase of development when parent care is of central importance to the family. Even congenial sibling relationships offer unique emotion regulation challenges. As peers, siblings expect equality in what each contributes to the relationship (Hochschild, 1973 ; Bedford & Avioli, 2001). Thus, there is frequently strife over who is doing more, over one sibling excluding others, etc. Despite the potential for or expression of negative emotions the siblingship task requires that the relationship remain highly functional. Having to sustain a successful working relationship under these conditions requires exercising complex emotional processes.

Emma and her sister exemplify this situation. Emma always worshipped her older sister. It was also agreed that Emma's sister would take care of their mother, who lived near her, when the occasion arose. When this happened Emma was horrified with the way her sister handled their mother. This was a blow to Emma, because she did not remember ever feeling critical of her admired older sister. Nonetheless, eventually Emma managed to broker a better living arrangement for her mother (and without alienating her sister), despite her anger and disappointment toward her.

Goetting identified one task of siblingship in old age, coreminiscing (Ross & Milgram, 1982). Sharing childhood memories together contributes to a sense of integrity (Erikson, 1963). The process involved in coconstructing their shared past is often described as a highly satisfying experience (e.g., Gold, 1989; Ross & Milgram, 1982). Emotion regulation competencies at this age are related to affect dampening, primarily through antecedent-focused means, whether using cognitive coping strategies or environmental manipulations. Reminiscing may be one example of cognitive coping, in that in the coconstruction of the past, negative experiences are transformed into positive ones (Goetting, 1986).

Socioemotional selectivity theory reinforces this developmental pattern (Carstensen, 1992). Accordingly, as adults near the end of life, they exercise emotion regulation strategies that assure satisfying emotional experiences. They use the anticipatory strategies of selecting fewer social partners by maintaining contact with those to whom they are particularly close. Family members, such as siblings, and old friends are typical choices. The complex nature of many of these relationships in late life, such as those described here in the case of siblings, is not addressed directly by the theory. It is possible, however, to extrapolate from the principles of the theory to understand why relationships like siblings become those of choice in later life. As mentioned earlier, highly familiar relationships are easier to regulate than more novel ones because the partners know what may initiate negative as well as positive exchanges. Thus, it is relatively easy to create satisfying intimate interactions.

THE DYNAMICS OF CHANGE

In the final section of this chapter, we consider how change in the dynamic ecological system of emotion regulation occurs. Specifically, we offer a heuristic for understanding the mechanism by which a pair of siblings and their relationship may contribute to developmental change in one another's emotion regulation system and to change in their relationship. We then use three cases from a longitudinal study of brothers to illustrate variations on change and stability in the system.

So far, we have described how siblings may contribute to the development of emotion regulation strategies of one another. Earlier in the chapter, we presented a model of emotion regulation development within the sibling relationship that acknowledges the interrelationships among the sibling partners, their relationship and its history (Fig. 4.1). Accordingly, the emotion regulatory behaviors of the sibling partners and their relationship function as one system. No one component or subsystem is inherently dominant over the others. Now we make an addition to the model that provides a heuristic for understanding the mechanism of development. Synergetics, the physics of complex systems, offers such a heuristic (Thelan, 1989). We will borrow three constructs from synergetics that provide tools to elucidate the intersystemic processes that account for developmental change that are implied, but not explained, by the dynamical ecological systems model. These constructs are attractor, phase shift, and control parameter.

When we represent the emotion regulation process as stable, stability is relative. In the synergetic metaphor, all systems are in a state of flux. The attractor symbolizes this concept of stability. The "attractor" is a kind of homeostasis or "constrained region" of behavior. Rather than constant, an attractor has a limited range of variability. The attractor is "flexibly assembled within certain organismic constraints and the demands of the context or task" (Thelan, 1989, p. 85). Thus, in its attractor state, the sibling partners' emotion regulation strategies and the relationship qualities are in flux as they interact with one another, responding and influencing one another within a pattern that does not vary greatly.

Change can be explained with respect to the attractor state. Change occurs when an attractor is destabilized or an attractor is rendered more stable. When this occurs, a "phase shift" takes place. Thus, the metaphor allows us to differentiate between change that is a patterned fluctuation and a genuine alteration of the pattern. Siblings may have an elaborate pattern of emotional interaction but because the pattern does not deviate, it is stable, in an attractor state. We give a hypothetical example to illustrate these terms. Cindy and her sister follow an elaborate emotion regulation pattern whenever they meet, usually at a family function. First, they excitedly catch up on one another's lives, spilling out information in a burst of excitement. But inevitably the mood changes, as a competitive spirit arises and old resentments spill out. Soon, tempers flare and they part in anger, only to start over again at the next family function. This repetitive pattern illustrates an attractor state, despite its variability of emotion regulation patterns. A phase shift occurs when this pattern is broken. For instance, the sisters' mother becomes disabled and Cindy takes the initiative to approach her sister about eliminating the negative phase of their interaction pattern. Her sister is willing to give it a try. They talk over their grievances; when Cindy's sister begins the provocative phase, Cindy points this out to her. Her sister accepts the feedback, and they manage to maintain good feelings throughout their visit. It appears they have broken out of the previous pattern. If they sustain this change, a phase shift in their emotion regulation process has occurred.

The synergetic heuristic also underscores the *cause* of change, the "control parameter." The control parameter is an element that is introduced to the system that is responsible for the phase shift. The phase shift can take place gradually (linearly) or suddenly (discontinuously) (Thelan, 1989).

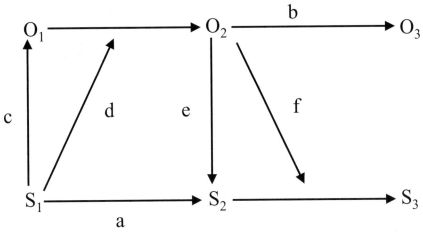

FIGURE 4.2. A Deconstruction of the Intersection between Inter- and Intraindividual Processes of Emotion Regulation. *Note* : S = sibling 1 (self) ; O = sibling 2 (other).

In this case a parent's decline appeared to be the ingredient that initiated the phase shift, followed by Cindy's initiative within the sibling interaction. Thus, the mother's physical decline and frailness represents a control parameter that brought about change in system.

In Figure 4.2, we present a deconstruction of the interface between intra- and interindividual processes within adult sibling relationships. S (self) and O (other) represent each sibling's state and the demands of the other sibling. Thus, the sibling's input is a potential control parameter to the partner's emotion regulation development. Other elements related to the sibling relationship may also function as control parameters, which are represented by the box enveloping the sibling pair and arrows connecting them in Figure 4.1. These include the relationship history (e.g., close or distant relationship), tasks of siblingships, and parental interference. We are not reproducing them in Figure 4.2 for the sake of simplicity. Instead, we take this opportunity to examine the interface between the sibling partners and the emotion regulation process used. We artificially deconstruct the parallel processes of the interlocking systems of the sibling partners so that we can analyze the components. Thus, parallel processes appear as a linear sequence of interactions.

Emotion self-regulation processes of S and O are seen in paths a and b, respectively. From S's perspective, emotion other-regulation is seen in path c, where S influences O's emotions directly, and in path d, where S influences O by altering O's self-regulation process (indirectly). Paths e and f show O's direct and indirect influence of S's emotions. It is possible that these paths of emotion regulation are deliberate actions or outside of the awareness of one or both of the partners.

The subscripts in Figure 4.2 represent the time dimension. After the first phase of the interaction, S and O's states may have altered. Consequently, their regulation of self and other may have changed. The partners' regulation processes reflect the accumulation of modifications that have been taking place since the beginning of their interaction. As this process continues through time it describes a trajectory of continuities, permutations, and, perhaps, phase shifts. Thus, the model can account for change in the relationship and for change in emotion regulation strategies within the sibling relationship. As long as variations in the trajectory of emotion regulation behaviors remain within an established pattern, they are attractors, representing continuity. When a phase shift occurs, these behaviors deviate from this pattern. For instance, a likely control parameter in the child literature that transforms teasing into aggressive outbursts is laughter (Patterson, 1986). In the adult literature, normative life events that affect siblings may function as control parameters, such as the death or disability of a parent.

Examples of Emotion Regulation in Midlife Brothers. To illustrate the dynamics of change requires analyses of single cases for which there are longitudinal data with multiple data points. We draw upon a rough approximation of such data from a sixteen-year longitudinal study of the quality of adult sibling relationships, specifically, several cases of middle-aged brothers (Bedford, Rains, Ramogatsis, & Smith, 2001). Five waves of data were collected at four-year intervals. Data consisted of narratives about siblings in response to TAT-like stimuli, the Sibling Thematic Apperception Test (Bedford, 1989). Each of six stimulus cards consisted of a pair of brothers in an ambiguous situation. The men were requested to tell a story about what was happening. The sixteen-year span began in early middle age and ended in late middle age (approximately the early forties to late fifties). Using a grounded-theory method of analysis, themes were identified for each brother relationship and their trajectories were tracked over the sixteen-year period. Thus, perturbations within themes could be followed including linear changes, continuities, and discontinuities, such as the emergence of new themes, disappearance of old themes, and transformations of themes. We will give two extreme examples of the dynamic over time. The first example demonstrates a pattern of failed attempts at self and other emotion regulation and no phase shift. The second example demonstrates a flexible pattern of emotion regulation that eventuates in a phase shift toward emotion regulation strategies that sustain a recognizably more positive and less negative relationship.

The regulation of emotions in Joe's relationship with his brother illustrates the repetition of a failed strategy over the course of sixteen years. Joe's brother had problems with alcoholism, which elicited distress in Joe. Joe felt responsible for his brother and tried to regulate his behaviors through social control, namely, trying to talk him out of his addictive behavior. Not surprisingly, Joe's brother was unresponsive to his efforts. This pattern represents an attractor state. Despite attempted interventions on the part of Joe to change this pattern, the pattern persisted. For instance, Joe longed for the brother of his childhood, which motivated him to either "cure" his brother or to contort his own thinking to believe that his brother was the good one and he himself was the bad one. In fact, Joe was highly successful in his career, whereas his brother had failed to finish high school. Joe's brother ignored Joe's effort to help, and Joe's cognitive reversal strategy only reinforced his own depression, rendering him less effective in dealing with his brother. Joe's emotion self-regulation strategies were self-destructive (fostering depression) and his other-regulation strategies were ineffective. Nor was he able to regulate the effect his brother had on his own emotions. Although Joe admitted that he could not help his brother, he would not stop trying. No doubt a central problem for Joe was his emotional goal for the relationship – to return to the longed-for sibling relationship of his childhood. As long as he pursued this goal, he would not have to mourn the loss of such a relationship. Thus, he had a stake in the status quo despite his professed desire to help his brother.

At the other extreme is Bud. During the course of the study, his relationship with his brother shifted from one pattern to a decidedly different one. Initially, Bud's descriptions of the relationship centered on creating distance between them, individuating, and making comparisons (in education, jobs, finances, wives). Bud expressed negative feelings, such as hostility and distrust, but also feelings of affiliation and emotional closeness. By Wave 4, however, the relationship weighed significantly on the side of positive emotions, and by Wave 5, negative aspects of the relationship had essentially disappeared. Thus, the course of Bud's relationship represents a phase shift. The control parameter that accounted for the phase shift appears to be Bud's flexibility and openness to change at crucial times. This ability did not make a sudden qualitative change in the relationship; the change was gradual. In addition to the increase of positive affect and decrease of negative affect over the sixteen years, the brothers accumulated a history of shared experiences that seemed to cement the relationship, creating a shared legacy. Initially, sharing was barely noticeable, but it accelerated throughout the sixteen years. Thus, a gradual accumulation of shared experiences enriched the relationship over time, both in reminiscences and in contemporary experiences. Some of the reminiscing was about their family experiences in childhood, as when they had to visit a dreaded aunt but behaved themselves for their mother's sake. A contemporary experience was sharing a period of anxiety while waiting together as a parent was undergoing surgery.

As for the control parameter, Bud exhibited this ability for flexible, open acceptance early on. For instance, when the relationship was highly negative, Bud tended to expect negative behaviors from his brother. But when Bud saw his brother display good qualities, he was not too proud to admit that he had misjudged him. Later, Bud was able to forgive his brother for an indiscretion. Another example of flexibility occurred after a prolonged disagreement. Suddenly Bud realized that his brother was right and admitted it openly. These reversals are reminiscent of the young adult siblings described earlier, who, when close, expressed positive emotions when they talked about problematic topics (Shortt & Gottman, 1997). It was not clear in Bud's case, however, if the relationship would become more negative, remain ambivalent, or move toward a more positive direction. It is clear, however, that Bud developed emotion regulation processes that could sustain emotion complexity and use emotion dampening to achieve an optimal relationship with his brother. It is plausible that Bud's desire for a highly positive and supportive relationship helped him to develop the emotion regulation strategies needed to achieve it. We can assume that the relationship history and his brother's emotion regulation strategies played a role in this development. We can be sure that Bud's maturing emotion self-regulation contributed importantly to shaping the quality of this very satisfying sibling relationship.

CONCLUSION

We have shown how emotion regulation development, launched within the infant–primary caregiver context, is not simply internalized in early childhood but continues to develop within relationship contexts. We have chosen to target the sibling relationship, one that is often neglected in family and social psychology literatures despite its being a primary relationship throughout life. We have shown how siblings, first with the help of parents and then on their own, create a social context that can undermine or promote individual self-regulation strategies. We demonstrated how siblings, as cognitive abilities mature, make use of them to modify their interactions and to accomplish normative tasks of siblingship throughout adulthood, such as caring for aging parents. We have offered a dynamic ecological systems perspective that provides a model for understanding how change in emotion regulation processes could occur. To test the model and advance our understanding of the developmental process of emotion regulation within the social context of siblings, empirical studies are needed. These studies of adult sibling relationships will need to make use of direct observation techniques in order to observe whether the kinds of processes described here that were derived from sibling story narratives are accurate. The larger, ecological context of the sibling relationship should also be included in the design of such sibling studies. Another direction of future study is to explore the feasibility of applying the Dynamic Ecological Systems perspective to other social relationships. This endeavor will help to establish whether it is a general model with applications for other long-term relationships.

References

Baltes, P. B. (1987). Theoretical propositions of life-span developmental psychology: On the dynamics between growth and decline. *Developmental Psychology, 23,* 611–626.

Bedford, V. H. (1989). A comparison of thematic apperceptions of sibling affiliation, conflict, and separation at two periods of adulthood. *International Journal of Aging and Human Development, 28,* 53–65.

Bedford, V. H. (1995). Sibling relationships in middle adulthood and old age. In R. Blieszner & V. H. Bedford (Eds.), *Handbook on aging and the family* (pp. 201–222). Westport, CT: Greenwood.

Bedford, V. H. (1998). Sibling relationship troubles and well-being in middle and old age. *Family Relations, 47,* 369–376.

Bedford, V. H., & Avioli, P. S. (2001). Variations on sibling intimacy in old age. *Generations, 25,* 34–40.

Bedford, V. H., Rains, S. E., & Guseilla, K. J. (2000, August). Midlife changes in TAT stories about siblings: A prospective study. Paper presented at the 108th annual meeting of the American Psychological Association, Washington, DC.

Bedford, V. H., Rains, S. E., Ramagotsis, S., & Smith, C. (2001, November). Simultaneous trajectories of continuity and change in relationships between middle-aged brothers. Paper presented at the meeting of the Gerontological Society of America, Chicago.

Bedford, V. H., Volling, B. L., & Avioli, P. S. (2000). Positive consequences of sibling conflict in childhood and adulthood. *International Journal of Aging and Human Development, 51,* 53–67.

Berscheid, E. (1999). The greening of relationship science. *American Psychologist, 54,* 260–266.

Brody, G. H., Stoneman, Z., & McCoy, J. K. (1992). Associations of maternal and paternal direct and differential behavior with sibling relationships: Contemporaneous and longitudinal analyses. *Child Development, 63,* 82–92.

Campos, J., Campos, R., & Barrett, K. (1989). Emergent themes in the study of emotional development and emotion regulation. *Developmental Psychology, 25,* 394–402.

Carstensen, L. L. (1992). Social and emotional patterns in adulthood: Support for socioemotional selectivity theory. *Psychology and Aging, 7,* 331–338.

Carstensen, L. L., Gross, J. J., & Fung, H. H. (1997). The social context of emotional experience. In K. W. Schaie & M. P. Lawton (Eds.), *Annual review of gerontology and geriatrics,* Vol. 17 (pp. 325–352). New York: Springer.

Cassidy, J. (1994). Emotion regulation: Influences of attachment relationships. *Monographs of the Society for Research on Child Development, 59*(2–3), 228–249.

Collins, W. A., & Laursen, B. (Eds.) (1999). *Relationships as developmental contexts. The Minnesota symposia on child psychology,* Vol. 30. Mahwah, NJ: Erlbaum.

Diehl, M., Coyle, N., & Labouvie-Vief, G. (1996). Age and sex differences in strategies of coping and defense across the life span. *Psychology and Aging, 11,* 127–139.

Dunn, J. (1988). *The beginnings of social understanding.* Cambridge, MA: Harvard University Press.

Dunn, J. F. (1993). *Young children's close relationships: Beyond attachment.* Newberry Park, CA: Sage Publications.

Dunn, J., & Kendrick, C. (1982). *Siblings: Love, envy, and understanding.* Cambridge, MA: Harvard University Press.

Dunn, J., & Plomin, R. (1991). Why are siblings so different? The significance of differences in sibling experiences within the family. *Family Process, 30,* 271–283.

Erikson, E. H. (1963). *Childhood and society.* New York: Norton.

Garcia, M. M., Shaw, D. S., Winslow, E. B., & Yaggi, K. E. (2000). Destructive sibling conflict and the development of conduct problems in young boys. *Developmental Psychology, 36,* 44–53.

Goetting, A. (1986). The developmental tasks of siblingship over the life cycle. *Journal of Marriage and the Family, 48,* 703–714.

Gold, D. T. (1989). Sibling relationships in old age: A typology. *International Journal of Aging and Human Development, 28,* 37–51.

Gross, J. J. (1998). Antecedent and response-focused emotion regulation: Divergent consequences for experience, expression and physiology. *Journal of Personality and Social Psychology. 74,* 224–237.

Harris, P. L., & Cavanaugh, R. D. (1993). Young children's understanding of pretense. *Monographs of the Society for Research on Child Development, 58* (1, Serial No. 231), v–92.

Hartup, W. W., & Laursen, B. (1999). Relationships as developmental contexts: Retrospective themes and contemporary issues. In W. A. Collins & B. Laursen (Eds.), *Relationships as developmental contexts. The Minnesota symposia on child psychology* (Vol. 30, pp. 13–35). Mahwah, NJ: Lawrence Erlbaum.

Hochschild, A. R. (1973). *The unexpected community.* Berkeley: University of California.

Jenkins, J. M., & Astington, J. W. (1996). Cognitive factors and family structure associated with theory of mind development in young children. *Developmental Psychology, 32,* 70–78.

Keltner, D. (1996). Facial expressions of emotion and personality. In C. Magai & S. McFadden (Eds.), *Handbook of emotion, adulthood, and aging* (pp. 385–401). San Diego: Academic.

Kochanska, G. (1991). Socialization and temperament in the development of conscience. *Child Development, 62,* 1379–1392.

Kochanska, G., & Askan, N. (1995). Mother-child mutually positive affect, the quality of child compliance to requests and prohibitions, and maternal control as correlates of early internalization. *Child Development, 68,* 94–112.

Kochanska, G., Tbjekes, T. L., & Forman, D. R. (1998). Children's emerging regulation of conduct: Restraint, compliance, and internalization from infancy to the second year. *Child Development, 69,* 1378–1389.

Kopp, C. (1989). Regulation of distress and negative emotions: A developmental view. *Developmental Psychology, 25,* 343–354.

Labouvie-Vief, G., Devoe, M., & Bulka, D. (1989). Speaking about feelings: Conceptions of emotions across the life span. *Psychology and Aging, 4,* 425–437.

Labouvie-Vief, G., & Medler, M. (2002). Affect optimization and affect complexity: Modes and styles of regulation in adulthood. *Psychology and Aging, 17,* 571–587.

Laverty, R. (1962). Reactivation of sibling rivalry in older people. *Social Work, 7*, 23–30.

Lawton, M. P. (1989). Environmental proactivity and affect in older people. In S. Spacapan & S. Oshamp (Eds.), *The social psychology of aging* (pp. 135–163). Newbury Park: Sage.

Lawton, M. P., & Albert, S. M. (1990, August). Affective self-management across the life span. In A. J. Zautra (Chair), "The longitudinal study of elder health and well-being," symposium conducted at the meeting of the American Psychological Association, Boston.

Levenson, R. W., Carstensen, L. L., & Gottman, J. M. (1994). The influence of age and gender on affect, physiology, and their interrelations: A study of long-term marriages. *Journal of Personality and Social Psychology, 67*, 56–68.

MacKinnon-Lewis, C. E., Starnes, R., Volling, B. L., & Johnson, S. (1997). Perceptions of parenting as predictors of boys' sibling and peer relations. *Developmental Psychology, 33*, 1024–1031.

Magai, C., & Passman, V. (1997). The interpersonal basis of emotional behavior and emotion regulation in adulthood. In K. Warner Schaie & M. P. Lawton (Eds.), *Annual review of gerontology and geriatrics* (pp. 104–137), Vol. 17. New York: Springer.

Malatesta, C., & Kalnok, M. (1984). Emotional experience in younger and older adults. *Journal of Gerontology, 39*, 301–308.

Malatesta-Magai, C. Z., Jonas, R., Shepard, B., & Culvert, C. (1992). Type A personality and emotional expressivity in younger and older adults. *Psychology and Aging, 7*, 551–561.

Munn, P., & Dunn, J. (1986). Siblings and the development of prosocial behavior. *International Journal of Behavioral Development, 9*, 265–284.

Patterson, G. R. (1977). Accelerating stimuli for two classes of coercive behaviors. *Journal of Abnormal Child Psychology, 5*, 334–350.

Patterson, G. R. (1986). The contribution of siblings to training for fighting: A microsocial analysis. In D. Olweus, J. Block, & M. Radke-Yarrow (Eds.), *Development of antisocial and prosocial behavior* (pp. 235–261). New York: Academic Press.

Perner, J., Ruffman, T., & Leekam, S. R. (1994). Theory of mind is contagious: You catch it from your sibs. *Child Development, 65*, 1228–1238.

Rook, K. S., & Ituarte, P. H. G. (1999). Social control, social support, and companionship in older adults' family relationships and friendships. *Personal Relationships, 6*, 199–211.

Ross, H. G., & Milgram, J. I. (1982). Important variables in adult sibling relationships: A qualitative study. In M. E. Lamb & B. Sutton-Smith (Eds.), *Sibling relationships: Their nature and significance across the life span* (pp. 225–249). Hillsdale, NJ: Erlbaum.

Ruffman, T., Perner, J., Naito, M., Parkin, L., & Clements, W. A. (1998). Older (but not younger) siblings facilitate false belief understanding. *Developmental Psychology, 34*, 161–174.

Saarni, C. (1997). Emotional competence and self-regulation in childhood. In P. Salovey & D. J. Sluyter (Eds.), *Emotional development and emotional intelligence* (pp. 35–66). New York: Basic Books.

Sameroff, A. J., & Emde, R. N. (Eds.) (1989). *Relationship disturbances in early childhood: A developmental approach.* New York: Basic Books.

Shortt, J. W., & Gottman, J. M. (1997). Closeness in young adult sibling relationships: Affective and physiological processes. *Social Development, 6,* 142–164.

Sroufe, L. A. (1996). *Emotional development: The organization of emotional life in the early years.* New York: Cambridge University Press.

Stoneman, Z., & Brody, G. H. (1993). Sibling temperaments, conflict, warmth, and role asymmetry. *Child Development, 64,* 1786–1800.

Taylor, M., Cartwright, L. E., & Carlson, S. M. (1993). A developmental investigation of children's imaginary companions. *Developmental Psychology, 29,* 276–285.

Thelen, E. (1989). Self-organization in developmental processes: Can systems approaches work? In M. R. Gunnar and E. Thelen (Eds.), *Systems and development. The Minnesota symposia on child psychology* (Vol. 22, pp. 77–117). Hillsdale, NJ: Erlbaum.

Thompson, R. A. (1994). Emotion regulation: A theme in search of definition. *Monographs of the Society for Research in Child Development, 59* (2–3, Serial No. 240), 25–52.

Tomkins, S. S. (1962). *Affect, imagery, consciousness, Vol. 1: The positive affects.* New York: Springer.

Tomkins, S. S. (1963). *Affect, imagery, and consciousness, Vol. 2: The negative affects.* New York: Springer.

Tronick, E. Z. (1989). Emotions and emotional communication in infants. *American Psychologist, 44,* 112–119.

Tucker, C. J., Updegraff, K. A., McHale, S. M., & Crouter, A. C. (1999). Older siblings as socializers of younger siblings' empathy. *Journal of Early Adolescence, 19,* 176–198.

Volling, B. L., & Belsky, J. (1992). The contribution of mother-child and father-child relationships to the quality of sibling interaction: A longitudinal study. *Child Development, 63,* 1209–1222.

Volling, B. L., McElwain, N. L., & Miller, A. L. (2002). Emotion regulation in context: The jealousy complex between young siblings and its relations with child and family characteristics. *Child Development, 73,* 581–600.

Youngblade, L. M., & Dunn, J. (1995). Individual differences in young children's pretend play with mother and sibling: Links to relationships and understanding of other people's feelings and beliefs. *Child Development, 66,* 1472–1492.

5

Romantic and Marital Relationships

Hans-Werner Bierhoff and Martina Schmohr

According to the hierarchical model of love, Lee's (1973) love styles may be subdivided into passionate and companionate love. From the perspective of life-span theory of control that differentiates selective and compensatory control, new insights on the development of love styles are derived. The goal of partnership formation depends on age-graded opportunity structures. Age-normative factors influence the chances to fulfill tasks with respect to the initiation and maintenance of a partnership. Passionate love is more easily realized in early than in late adulthood. In later adulthood, disengagement from goals related to passionate love and increased emphasis on companionate love are expected. A review of empirical findings tends to support these assumptions.

Hardly anywhere is the rivalry between lay insights and scientific knowledge as strong as in the area of romantic and marital relationships. We all know or expect to know from our everyday experience what this kind of relationship means. We have our personal insights and implicit theories about what characterizes a successful marital relationship and about the conditions under which a romantic relationship is formed. For example, people tend to equate marital relationship with romantic love. In addition, they assume that romantic love emerges immediately after the first contact has been established (love at first sight; Averill, 1985).

Other implicit assumptions refer to the development of romantic and marital relationships across time. From self-observation we are convinced that love changes over time. We feel that a personal relationship has developed somewhat across, say, five or ten years. Some say that the relationship becomes more mature, while others say it grows empty over time. Some say the relationship offers them support, referring to their marital relationship as the most important element in their social support system. Others say the relationship limits their autonomy and restricts their social activities, reducing the number of new social contacts.

In the following we will discuss issues related to these implicit theories from a scientific point of view, which have emerged in the relatively new research tradition of empirical investigations of close relationships. We start with a definition of romantic relationships, present a hierarchical model of love, and follow the development of love from childhood to late midlife. The structure of this discussion is derived from the life-span theory of control by Heckhausen and Schulz (1995) that emphasizes the influence of opportunity structures. Opportunity structures are characterized by cultural, social, or biological conditions that determine the probability for realizing a specific goal or developmental task. Whereas this discussion focuses on age-graded processes, which are essentially assumed to be representative for people in general, we also take an individual-difference perspective and examine differences in the development of love depending on gender and sexual orientation. To amplify what has been stated about age-graded love styles in general, we describe results of cross-sectional and longitudinal studies presenting some data on the stability and change of love styles that have not yet been published. In the concluding discussion we come back to the implicit theories of laypeople outlined in the introduction.

The present overview focuses almost exclusively on love attitudes and their development across the life span. Although we are aware of other important characteristics and processes of romantic and marital relationships (e.g., marital quality, relationship behavior, emotion regulation), we concentrate on love for two reasons: First, it would go beyond the scope of this chapter to treat these myriad aspects and, second, scientific theories as well as personal experience consider love a central characteristic of romantic and marital relationships. The attention that is paid to this aspect of romantic relationships is high, at least in Western culture. As Hatfield and Rapson (1993) noted in their preface to *Love, Sex and Intimacy*, "love" is as magical a word in American culture as "money." Under the precondition that the assessments refer to the same relationship partner, love attitudes show a remarkable stability and are unaffected by present mood. Love attitudes – as a system of traits based on the interaction with a particular relationship partner – are connected with different features of romantic relationships, for example, sexual attitudes, relationship satisfaction, and duration of partnership (cf. Bierhoff & Klein, 1991).

A personal relationship can be described as a social interdependence between two persons (P and O) that is characterized by going beyond social role prescriptions and becoming more personal. A romantic relationship fulfills the following criteria (cf. Levinger, 1980, 1994): P and O like each other, engage in mutual self-disclosure, have insight into each other's personal feelings, emphasize the uniqueness of the relationship in terms of specific norms and symbols that are something special, and adopt an altruistic orientation toward each other. Depending on how far these tendencies go, the overlap between the interests, activities, preferences, and habits of the persons involved increases from minor intersection to major intersection.

Whereas this definition refers to personal relationships in general, romantic relationships are defined more narrowly in that the attraction between the two persons has something to do with love. As we will argue below, love is a multidimensional concept encompassing several quite independent orientations toward the loved person. Suffice it to say that one facet of love or another (e.g., romantic love, best-friends love) must be involved in a romantic or marital relationship. Therefore, the term *romantic relationship* is not restricted to relationships based on romantic love. It is equally possible that other forms of love are the basis of the relationship.

Romantic and marital relationships are complex phenomena. Partners perceive the combination of feelings, thoughts, and behavioral tendencies occurring in close relationships as unique and personal. Therefore, research in the field of intimate relationships is often confronted with the opinion that such an idiosyncratic experience is difficult to measure. Nevertheless, the study of love has flourished during the last twenty-five years, as documented by hundreds of published articles on the topic. Using the database of PsychINFO from January 1999 to January 2002, we found over two thousand references published using the keyword "marriage" and over a thousand publications connected to the keyword "love." The positive development of this scientific area is based on great interest and the consideration given to critical questions concerning the issue of internal and external validity of the measurement of love by questionnaire (Amelang, 1991; Hendrick & Hendrick, 1997; Bierhoff & Grau, 1999).

These scientific activities have resulted in an increasing body of knowledge about romantic and marital relationships, their determinants and consequences. Because researchers have focused on the couple in their search for factors contributing to relationship beginning, relationship satisfaction, and stability (cf. Berscheid & Reis, 1998), they have often overlooked the possibility that close relationships are resources for and outcomes of individual development. Does the conception of love change within individual development across the life span? We already know that individual development depends on opportunities offered by the social world and that romantic relationships are one important part of this social world. Are different dimensions of love connected with changing opportunity structures throughout the life course?

Since most of the studies in the field of romantic and marital relationships are carried out with students, this research does not contribute much to knowledge about stability and change of love across the life span. In this chapter we offer a theoretical overview of existing literature and data that may help to bridge this gap. In the first step we will discuss the meaning of love on the basis of the hierarchical model of love by

Barnes and Sternberg (1997). In addition, we turn to the measurement of love emphasizing the approach by Lee (1973) and Hendrick and Hendrick (1986; Hendrick, Hendrick, & Dicke, 1998). In the second step we will delineate a hypothesis on the link between age and love using the approach of age-adjusted control processes (Heckhausen & Schulz, 1995; Wrosch & Heckhausen, 1999). Finally, we will describe the results of studies addressing our hypothesis of age-graded love styles. We will consider most of the life span including adolescents, young adults, middle-aged adults, and late adults.

HOW DO VARIOUS ASPECTS OF LOVE RELATE TO EACH OTHER? AN INTEGRATIVE HIERARCHICAL MODEL

As already mentioned above, empirical studies and theories on romantic and marital relationships have become so great in number that the need for a theoretical structure arises. In response to this need, Barnes and Sternberg (1997) have developed a hierarchical model of love that takes into account the level of generality of the different theories.

On the basis of this model it becomes possible to integrate numerous constructions of love that have emerged in the field of interpersonal attraction. As a consequence, the theories are no longer seen as different conceptions standing unconnected next to each other, but as associated vertical levels of differentiation.

Barnes and Sternberg's new integrative model distinguishes between three main kinds of theories that represent the different levels of the hierarchy: unifactorial (love as a single dimension), multifactorial (love consists of a few primary and equally important factors), and multiple cluster (love as a set of characteristic features). In more detail, the first level represents love as an undifferentiated whole. This conceptualization of love is favored by theorists like Rubin (1970). On the next level of love, two facets are considered: passionate love and companionate love. Berscheid and Walster (1974) originally described this contrast by comparing a more irrational type of loving with a more rational type of loving. Hatfield and Rapson (1993) define passionate love as a state of intense longing for union with another including appraisals, subjective feelings, expressions, physiological processes, action tendencies, and instrumental behaviors. While reciprocated passionate feelings are associated with fulfillment and ecstasy, unrequited love goes hand in hand with emptiness, anxiety, or despair, meaning that passionate love can be either pleasurable or painful. Unlike this "hot" emotion, which is characterized by high arousal, companionate love is associated with a warm-hearted relationship, emphasizing intimacy and commitment in which passion plays only a minor role. Apart from these differences, companionate love is a complex functional whole like passionate love and includes all the components (appraisals, feelings, etc.)

mentioned above. Hatfield and Rapson define companionate love as the affection and tenderness we feel for those with whom our lives are deeply entwined.

The love styles described by Lee (1973) are located on the next lower level of the hierarchical model. In the following, they will be considered in more detail. In his multidimensional approach Lee (1973) goes beyond Berscheid and Walster's (1974) two love forms in that he differentiates between six love styles. It is assumed that love styles are changeable, although there is a tendency to keep a particular style over a longer period of time.

Lee distinguishes between the following love styles.

- *Romantic love (Eros)* refers to immediate attraction to the loved person as expressed in the ideal type of love at first sight. Physical beauty, handsomeness, and sexual passion play an important role in the development of this love style.
- *Game-playing love (Ludus)* represents a variation of passionate affection where seduction, sexual freedom, and sexual adventure stand in the foreground. The attitude toward longer-term relationships tends to be avoidant and hesitant.
- *Best-friends love (Storge)* develops from a previous friendship. Mutual interests, mutual trust, and tolerance characterize the interpersonal orientation.
- *Possessive love (Mania)* is an extreme version of romantic love as it accentuates passionate and seemingly irrational relationship behavior. Idealization and possessiveness are connected to strong feelings that can be positive (achieving fusion with the partner) as well as negative (as in jealousy).
- *Pragmatic love (Pragma)* represents a certain contrast to the emotional ebullience of possessive love because rational considerations help determine the choice of partner. The relationship is intended to create desirable living conditions or serve particular ends (e.g., end loneliness, have children).
- *Altruistic love (Agape)* exists where partners are prepared to make sacrifices for each other. Lovers who ascribe to this style of love are prepared to put their own aims and desires last if this contributes to the well-being of their partner.

Romantic and possessive love resemble passionate love, whereas pragmatic and best-friends love are similar to companionate love (Hatfield, 1988). Corresponding to these assumptions, the hierarchical model of love assumes that love may be subdivided into passionate and companionate love. Eros, Ludus, and Mania can be summarized under passionate love, whereas Pragma, Storge, and Agape are examples of companionate love. Eros, Ludus, and Mania all refer to emotional experiences that focus on passionate love. In contrast, Pragma, Storge, and Agape focus on practical goals related to the partnership. Therefore, they are best summarized under the heading of companionate love.

In the following we delineate the basic proposition on the level of passionate love and companionate love across the life span. By implication this assumption applies to Eros, Ludus, and Mania (examples of passionate love) and to Pragma, Storge, and Agape (examples of companionate love). This means that our hypothesis is expressed on a higher level of abstraction (passionate and companionate love), whereas the data we present refer to love styles and are therefore on a more concrete level.

Continuities and Discontinuities in Attachment

Another important area of theory and research, which is related to love research but has taken its own direction, is the study of attachment processes (cf. Shaver & Clark, 1996). Love and attachment share conceptual commonalities, but they also have some differences. For example, possessive love and the anxious-ambivalent attachment style, which was described by Ainsworth, Blehar, Waters, and Wall (1978), are conceptually overlapping (Bierhoff & Grau, 1999). In contrast, other love styles (e.g., best-friends love, pragmatic love) have no counterpart in attachment theory (Levy & Davis, 1988); furthermore, the emphasis on the distinction between secure and insecure attachment is also not found in the theory of love styles. It is likely that security of attachment is very much associated with personality dynamics (cf. Shaver & Brennan, 1992).[1]

Although we do not go into attachment theory in any detail, it is useful to summarize what attachment research has found with respect to age-graded development (Koski & Shaver, 1997). Attachment researchers emphasize the continuities in the development of attachment, but they also acknowledge certain differences comparing different phases over the life span. The assumption of continuity results from the fact that attachment styles are seen as a function of the behavior of primary caregivers. If circumstances stay more or less the same and the attachment experiences are of the same quality for a substantial time period, a child develops internal working models of self and relationship partners. These working models are cognitive representations that guide future behavior and relationships, and in this manner may establish a certain continuity (Bretherton & Munholland, 1999). From this point of view, relationships with parents may foster or inhibit experiences in adolescence and early adulthood that are important for the formation of individual identity and romantic relationships.

---

[1] In this chapter we focus instead on relationship *attitudes*. We do not go into the question of personality ramifications of relationship experiences, which is an issue of its own (see Neyer, Chapter 12 in this volume).

In the following life phases, differences based on developmental changes emerge. For example, cognitive abilities contribute to the improvement of the communication pattern. Whereas infants display certain patterns of distress (anxiety, anger, withdrawal from others) in response to separation, older children acquire skills that allow them to adopt the perspective of others and express themselves verbally. The early behavioral indicators are transformed into more complex patterns of cognitive, linguistic, and empathic skills. As a consequence, the intensity of attachment behavior decreases, and the behavior becomes more flexible (Koski & Shaver, 1997). Whereas infants require continuing support, a secure older child, adolescent, or adult is usually able to cope with negative events even when the attachment figure is temporarily not available.

Another reason for discontinuity of attachment style is that attachment experiences toward different attachment figures may be discordant. Empirical studies with infants show divergent attachment styles in reference to fathers and mothers (Bowlby, 1995). Collins and Read (1994) argue that individuals develop a hierarchy of working models. A set of generalized models for particular classes of relationships (e.g., family members, peers) are at the top of the hierarchy and models for individual relationships at the lowest level (e.g., father, romantic partner). In addition, the roles that an individual assumes change over the life span (e.g., dependent child, autonomous adult, caring parents), and in most cases parents are replaced by intimate partners as principal attachment figures in adulthood (Bretherton & Munholland, 1999).

Development of Relationship Experiences across the Life Span

People are confronted with life tasks associated with certain phases of their biography. Such developmental tasks are derived from biological and cultural factors that influence individual expectations and aspirations. An example of such a developmental task that is limited with respect to a certain time frame is childbearing. In this chapter we suggest that to initiate and maintain a romantic or marital relationship may also be considered a developmental task that is related to a certain phase in the biography of the individual. The experience of romantic relationships at different ages might be affected by the presence or absence of this developmental task.

This idea has been developed further by Wrosch and Heckhausen (1999) who argue that the realization of life goals depends on opportunity structures that increase or decline depending on age. They propose that a developmental task refers to a normative age range implying more or less rigid age boundaries. These developmental deadlines identify the moment from which the chance for goal attainment deteriorates. A combination of biological, sociostructural, and age-normative factors determines age-graded constraints in opportunity structures. An example is females' limited age range for childbearing. Biological factors determine age-graded constraints on women's fertility. Other examples for changing opportunity structures include the sociostructural factors determining the chance for starting a successful career because many companies offer jobs only to people under a certain age. The goal of partnership formation is characterized by age-graded opportunity structures too, because the chances of finding an appropriate partner are higher in early adulthood than in late midlife. Studies support the assumption of reduced opportunities for partnership formation in late midlife (e.g., Braun & Proebsting, 1986; Teachman & Heckert, 1985) because by this time most people are involved in long-term relationships and therefore are not available for those who want to start a new intimate relationship. Age-normative conceptions about the timing of marriage and procreative intentions result in a smaller chance to find a new partner in late midlife. A lower societal acceptance of a new partnership in later life resulting from negative age stereotypes may also reduce the probability to form a new relationship. This might be particularly true for passionate relationships.

As a consequence, age-normative factors exert an influence on the chances to fulfill certain expectations with respect to the initiation and maintenance of partnerships. Partners may adapt to this opportunity structure and adopt the strategy to set age-related goals in their partnership. Thus, an opportunity-structures theoretical paradigm and control theory are used for explaining changes in attitudes and behavior. Similar concepts have been discussed in reference to children. For example, Case (1987) describes children's control structures through four stages in the course of their development. Heckhausen and Schulz (1995) have distinguished between selective control strategies, which serve the realization of goal attainment, and compensatory control strategies, which are used as a technique of goal disengagement. Additionally, their life-span theory of control proposes two basic processes: primary and secondary control. Striving for primary control involves attempting to change the external world so that individual needs and desires can be fulfilled. In contrast, secondary control is characterized by the attempt to change personal motivation, emotion, and cognitive representations so that these psychological states, which can be summarized with the term "inner world," fit the opportunities offered by the external world. Both of these control processes are selective, directed to goal attainment, and are functional at a stage in the life course when individuals have enough time as well as favorable opportunities to attain the aspired goal (Wrosch & Heckhausen, 1999). If the circumstances are advantageous but internal resources prove to be insufficient to reach the goal, compensatory primary control processes, which are characterized by seeking social support or external assistance, may be required.

But these preconditions will not remain as favorable throughout the whole life course. If in the course of time the more or less strict normative age range for the realization of a developmental task is passed without having attained a specific goal, the opportunities become fewer and the constraints greater. Therefore, it seems adaptive for the individual to activate compensatory secondary control strategies characterized by protecting motivational and emotional resources through the use of self-enhancing strategies or goal disengagement. Goal deactivation – as one kind of compensatory secondary control strategy – may help the person to find other life domains with more favorable opportunity structures. Substituting goals may be a successful way of avoiding negative consequences resulting from the low probability of attaining the original goal. Empirical evidence for opportunity-related shifts in individuals' control processes has been found to be related to health (Wrosch, Heckhausen, & Lachman, 2000) and childbearing (Heckhausen, Wrosch, & Fleeson, 2001). Recently, studies have shown that particular components of perceived control are differently associated with subjective well-being across the adult life span (Lang & Heckhausen, 2001). This stresses the point that developmental changes over the life course are related to different processes and strategies, especially if we assume that life satisfaction or enhancement of positive affect are goals, which are more or less consciously striven for. If these changes adjust an individual to the situation and its particular conditions, one question remains that is the focus of this chapter: Is this adaptive regulation with respect to age applicable to the task of forming and maintaining a romantic/marital relationship? Passionate love probably is the developmental goal that people generally try to realize because it is expected to lead to sexual union, perhaps even to marriage and family (Hatfield & Rapson, 1993). As stated above, it seems plausible that the opportunities for forming a passionate relationship deteriorate in later adulthood. In order to protect motivational and emotional resources it might be adaptive to shift from goal engagement to goal disengagement in reference to passionate love and instead intensify the engagement with a kind of love that offers a more favorable opportunity structure. Companionate love includes little passion but a great deal of commitment and intimacy. There is no reason to assume that the chances to realize commitment and intimacy become worse in later adulthood. Common sense implies that commitment and intimacy might increase with relationship duration. The next section presents a review of studies that follow the idea of a changing emphasis of love styles throughout the life course.

Age-Graded Love Styles

In the beginning of this section we focused on some results on the relation between age and love. If there is an age timing of opportunity structures, it is likely that partners' love orientation changes over their life span. For example, younger partners are likely to be involved in highly romantic relationships, whereas older partners may emphasize friendship and solidarity. Therefore, a possible age-related sequence is that the emphasis on passionate love in early adulthood is replaced by an emphasis on friendship and cooperation in late midlife. This contention is in agreement with sociobiological theory (cf. Shackelford & Buss, 1997), which argues that younger partners, especially younger women, are orientated toward passionate feelings more strongly than older partners.

Butler, Walker, Skowronski, and Shannon (1995) compared college-aged and middle-aged participants using an age of 25 as a cutoff value for group assignment. Their data indicated that older respondents report less endorsement of possessive and altruistic love than younger respondents. A limitation of the results was that age-related decrease in altruistic love was more pronounced in females than in males. For the other four love scales no main effect or interaction effect involving the age variable was found. Montgomery and Sorell (1997), who gave the Love Attitudes Scale to 250 adults in four different family life stages, found differences in the endorsement of the six love styles among the four groups depending on life stage. These results are of interest to our question because the authors report that age and life stage were strongly correlated and revealed nearly identical patterns of associations for love attitudes. Specifically, differences in love attitudes between college-age single youth and the older married groups occurred. The younger group consisted of non-married, childless, young adults, ranging in age from seventeen to twenty-four, who reported being presently in love. They showed higher scores in game playing and possessive love than married, childless people under the age of thirty, married people, ranging in age from twenty-four to fifty, with school-age children, and married people ranging in age from fifty to seventy.

Yancey and Eastman (1995) report on a study comparing undergraduates and older adults (over the age of twenty-nine) on love styles and life satisfaction. Assessments of the older sample were similar to those of the undergraduate women but not to the undergraduate men. The young men responded in a somewhat distinctive fashion because game-playing love was correlated positively with life satisfaction for them, whereas it was correlated negatively for the other groups.

The results mentioned above indicate that love styles change over time but do not demonstrate a common pattern. Although this conclusion is partly due to the fact that the studies refer to different aspects (love styles, connection between love styles and satisfaction), there is another problem that makes it difficult to interpret the results of these studies. All studies described above are cross-sectional, thereby confounding effects of age and cohort. In one of the few longitudinal studies, Sprecher and Metts (1999) demonstrated that romantic beliefs were positively associated with love and that participants' scores indicated a slight decline in romanticism over time. However, romanticism did not predict changes in love, commitment, or satisfaction.

However, it is possible that people in late midlife turn to goals like the fulfillment of common interests as a compensatory secondary control strategy when the availability of romantic experiences diminishes. Consequently, love styles may presumably be related to age. Whereas it is assumed that passionate love is highest in early adulthood and decreases afterwards, the importance of companionate love is assumed to increase in a compensatory way. This might be considered as an example of a compensatory secondary control strategy. Referring to opportunity structures and compensatory secondary control strategy, our hypothesis implies that we consider different developmental mechanisms in the ontogenesis of love. Age is a proxy variable for these developmental mechanisms. From a theoretical point of view, we cannot predict which love styles from the passionate cluster will decrease in importance over the life span and which love styles from the companionate cluster will increase. For example, it might turn out that one passionate love style (e.g., Eros) decreases, whereas one companionate love style (e.g., Pragma) increases. We consider such evidence as empirical support for the assumed compensation of passionate love by companionate love. It is unlikely that all passionate love styles lose importance during midlife while all companionate love styles gain importance. Instead, it is likely that the expected compensation is manifested on the basis of specific love styles. For example, the possibility exists that specific companionate love styles are more easily employed as compensatory devices than others.

Wrosch and Heckhausen (1999) note that some opportunity structures change quite rapidly (e.g., childbearing), whereas others change more slowly (e.g., mate selection). We assume that opportunity structures important for love orientations change only gradually. Although we must admit that opportunity structures with respect to mate selection and starting a romantic affair change very slowly, we hardly doubt that such a deterioration of chances takes place over the life span.

Love styles related to passionate love are assumed to decrease in importance during middle age. This change involves romantic and game-playing love, which are highly passion driven, and possessive love, which is dominated by affection and anxieties about the potential loss of the loved partner. Furthermore, love styles related to companionate love are assumed to become more prominent in later adulthood than in early adulthood. This change involves best-friends love, altruistic love, and pragmatic love. Whereas selfless love is an example of denial of personal needs and urges, pragmatic love is characterized by avoidance of romantic feelings and emphasis on practical considerations.

There are at least two other questions that must be addressed: Are the assumed developmental processes the same in heterosexual relationships and same-sex couples? Or do specific processes take place in gay and lesbian relationships indicating that there are distinguishing developmental features depending on sexual orientation? In addition, another individual difference variable seems to be relevant: gender. Do men and women differ with respect to their experience of love and intimacy? Whereas the discussion up to this point has focused on general developmental processes, we now turn to individual differences connected with sexual orientation and gender.

Differences in the Development of Love Depending on Gender

Are there differences in the experience of love styles between men and women? Much theorizing and public discussion focuses on this issue. Whereas many authors have emphasized gender differences in love from a theoretical perspective, the empirical basis for such statements is rather weak. For example, with respect to love styles only small gender differences are reported (Bierhoff & Klein, 1991; Butler et al., 1995). Hendrick and Hendrick (1995), who found some gender differences (women more oriented to friendship-based love, and men to game-playing love), stressed the need to consider both gender differences and similarities in love within intimate relationships. Stronger gender differences emerge on measures of sexual permissiveness. Although both sexes endorsed some aspects of sexuality to a similar extent, including sex as an emotional experience, men were more sexually permissive than women (Hendrick & Hendrick, 1995). In addition, there are some gender differences in the motivation for sex (Murstein & Tuerkheimer, 1998). Young men's motivation for sex (affection-closeness vs. physical release) was characterized more by physical release than women's motivation for sex, but at a later age women obtained higher scores than men in this choice. Despite this difference, the authors found no significant differences in the scores of men and women on Rubin's Love Scale.

Differences in the Development of Love Depending on Sexual Orientation

Although the processes of control and compensation underlying the development of love and intimacy across the life span are thought to characterize a broad range of close relationships, this is only applicable to gay and lesbian couples if the opportunity structure is more or less the same for them. As Rutter and Schwarz (1996) emphasize, before sexual orientation develops, sexual identity and behavior is socially and biologically constructed. Both sexes are socialized into relationship roles and sexual roles. As a consequence, these gender norms tend to create similarity between homosexuals and heterosexuals of the same sex. Thus, the authors expect more similarities between lesbian and heterosexual women and between gay and heterosexual men than between gay men and lesbians. For this reason, and if we suppose an opportunity structure for homosexuals that resembles that of heterosexuals, it would not be necessary to treat same-sex couples as a specific group from a theoretical point of view.

Rutter and Schwarz described that gays and lesbians engage in finding a partner and forming a committed relationship and that their activities correspond with gender norms. As the authors pointed out, women seek high emotional intensity while men seek low conflict – independent of sexual orientation. While heterosexual couples have to balance the differences between male and female styles, same-sex couples have to deal with the similarities in styles.

Longitudinal data from heterosexual, gay, and lesbian couples show that levels of global commitment to the relationship can be explained in terms of attraction forces and constraint forces (Kurdek, 2000). For all three groups commitment was linked to change in attraction as well as to change in constraint.

After identifying all these similarities, one aspect demonstrates the influence of changing opportunities on the development of relationship attitudes. During the AIDS era attitudes toward nonmonogamy for gay men changed. Rutter and Schwarz (1996) report a reversal in attitudes toward monogamy from the 1970s, when the majority endorsed nonmonogamy, to the 1990s, when the majority considered monogamy as a relationship ideal. Perhaps this change in attitudes toward monogamy is accompanied by a change in game-playing love. But apart from that, monogamous behavior is influenced by age and context. The authors reported that younger men are less likely to be monogamous than older men. Becoming integrated in a gay community, where a greater number of alternative partners are available, reduces the likelihood of monogamous living and loving.

In summary, the hypothesis that the realization of life goals depends on opportunity structures that increase or decline depending on age and therefore that different strategies (selective control vs. compensatory control) are activated over the life span seems to apply to heterosexual as well as to same-sex couples.

Love Styles at Young Adulthood and Midlife – Cross-sectional Data

The central thesis that passionate love styles decrease across adulthood while companionate love styles increase was supported by a study of Bierhoff and Rohmann (2000), who analyzed cross-sectional data. The results were based on a sample of 1,308 respondents who ranged in age from nineteen to fifty-four years, with a mean age of twenty-nine years. Their love styles were measured by the MEIL (Marburg Inventory of Love Styles; Bierhoff, Grau, & Ludwig, 1993), which is a German questionnaire for the assessment of the love styles as described by Lee.[2] On the general response level the mean assessment of love styles indicated that romantic love was preferred most, followed by best-friends love and altruistic love, while the mean scores were lower for pragmatic and game-playing love. In spite of the fact that the correlations among the six scales were quite low, two associations are worth mentioning: Possessive love was positively correlated with altruistic love and willingness to sacrifice was positively associated with romantic love. The correlations among the six love scales were nearly the same for males and females, but the authors also reported that two associations between gender and love styles emerged: Women expressed more possessive love and less altruistic love than men.

With respect to the question of age-related love styles, three significant associations were reported. While pragmatic and altruistic love increased with age, romantic love decreased. These associations fit our assumptions derived from the hierarchical model of love and the idea of opportunity structures, which increase or decline depending on age. Companionate love (represented here by pragmatic and altruistic love style) increased, whereas passionate love (represented here by romantic love style) decreased. Because of the fact that the correlations only reflect the strength of linear relationships, Bierhoff and Rohmann coded age into fourteen levels and entered this recoded age variable as an independent variable in a *MANOVA* with the six love styles as dependent variables.

Their analyses showed a significant age effect, even when the influence of relationship duration was controlled for. In order to interpret these results in reference to our hypotheses, we took a closer look at each single love style. Beginning with the three styles representing passionate love, linear age effects were observed only for romantic love (Eros), which decreased with age (see Fig. 5.1, right panel). The relationship between age and game-playing love (Ludus) was inverted U-shaped. In the middle age range, game-playing love was more important than in younger and older persons. In contrast, the course of possessive love (Mania) did not seem to be influenced by age. So these findings support the assumed development of passionate love only in part. While the decrease in romantic love confirms the assumption quite strongly, the inverted U-shaped course of game-playing love indicates that the suggested decrease started only in

[2] The German Marburg Inventory of Love Styles (MEIL; Bierhoff, Grau, & Ludwig, 1993) consists of six scales relating to the six facets of love described by Lee (romantic love, best-friends love, pragmatic love, passionate love, game-playing love, and altruistic love). Each subscale consists of ten items. The items are rated on nine-point scales anchored by "strongly disagree" and "strongly agree". Results indicate that responses are only minimally influenced by social desirability and participants' moods. The assumed six-factor structure was replicated in several independent studies. Internal consistencies are good or satisfactory.

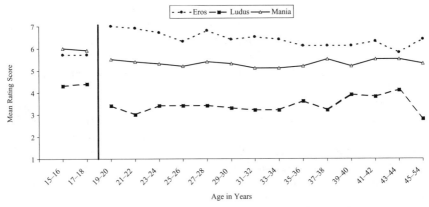

FIGURE 5.1. Mean Assessments of Passionate Love Depending on Age.

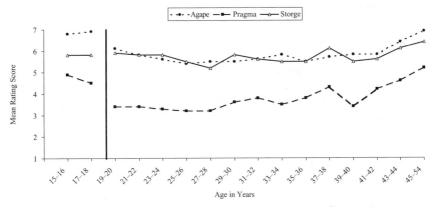

FIGURE 5.2. Mean Assessments of Companionate Love Depending on Age.

late midlife. Contrary to the assumption, no age-graded development was seen for possessive love.

What about the suggested increase of the mean assessments of companionate love depending on age? Results are summarized in Figure 5.2 (right panel). Linear age effects were detected for pragmatic love (Pragma), which increased with age. Altruistic love (Agape) was highest in the older age group, it being lowest in the middle age range and moderately high in the younger age groups. Only minimal age effects were ascertainable for best-friends love (Storge). Similar to the results of passionate love, the empirical data support the assumption only partly. While the linear increase of pragmatic love strongly confirms the hypothesis, the U-shaped course of altruistic love agrees with the hypotheses only for the older age groups. In the case of possessive love, no influence of age was detected.

One shortcoming of this survey is that data from young adolescents are missing. Therefore, to fill this gap we present additional data of 109 German high school students (58 male, 60 female, 1 missing data) ranging in age from 15 to 18 years who were all currently involved in a dating relationship. Duration of relationship varied between one month and five years, mean duration was ten months and duration of one month was the value observed most frequently. These respondents participated in a study at different schools in the area of Düsseldorf, and their love styles were measured with the MEIL. The results are illustrated in Figures 5.1 and 5.2 (left panels). A comparison of the adolescents' responses on the six love scales to the responses of the nineteen-year-olds shows that both change and stability of love styles occur during this early age period. The results indicate that the younger group scored lower on romantic love (Eros). Whereas they only reached a score of 5.7 on a scale that ranged from 1 to 9, the young adults showed a mean assessment of 7. Compared with the older respondents, the pupils showed higher scores on game-playing love (Ludus), possessive love (Mania), altruistic love (Agape), and pragmatic love (Pragma). The mean assessments of best-friends love (Storge) were nearly the same for both groups.

How can these differences and similarities be interpreted? One important conclusion from these results is that, in some aspects, love during puberty seems to be different from the attitudes toward love and intimate relationships during early adulthood. As mentioned above, age-graded opportunity structures may be the reason for decreasing passionate love and increasing companionate love in late midlife, but the reason for changes in love styles in youth is not yet clear. Presumably, the developmental task between fifteen and eighteen years is not the same as in the following years. While in adulthood high romantic love, low game-playing love, and low possessive love make it easier to initiate and maintain a serious partnership and avoid destructive conflicts, puberty does not offer the same opportunity structure. Neither social institutions, normative conceptions, nor biological constraints identify this age category (from fifteen to eighteen years) as a life stage appropriate for intimate relationships and marriage. This phase offers the opportunity to try out different kinds of relationships or partners and to learn through such experience. In particular, high scores of game-playing love and possessive love in combination with low romantic love indicate that individuals between the ages of fifteen to eighteen are somehow keen to experiment. Without broad experiences with romantic relationships, individual preferences dominate the understanding and social construction of love. It seems that such attitudes and behavior should be favorable for gaining experience. This interpretation fits in nicely with the fact that the length of dating relationship reported by fifteen-to-eighteen-year-olds most frequently was one month. So, this early phase is characterized by somewhat different love attitudes. The differences in love styles seem to be age-specific and perhaps best reflect the type of behaviors in adolescence. The love styles at fifteen to eighteen years motivate behavior that seems to be useful as a preparation for later developmental tasks, such as relationship formation, marriage, or childbearing.

Starting Line and Final Stage of Love across the Life Span

So far we have referred to the development of love only during young adulthood and midlife. Are there precursors of love styles in childhood? Is it possible to say something about love styles in relationships in later life? To answer these questions, we examine a broader age range and attempt to give a more comprehensive perspective on the change of romantic relationships and the experience of love.

As we mentioned above, the switch from passionate love to companionate love as a consequence of the change from selective control strategy to compensatory control strategy is assumed to take place gradually. Although there is no specific age when opportunities suddenly become scarce, we expect this process to be more or less irreversible once this process has started. There are no indications for greater opportunities and fewer constraints for starting and maintaining a romantic relationship in later life. So we assume that, once started, the use of compensatory control strategies will remain more or less on the same level or will even get stronger during the following years. Montgomery and Sorell (1997), who investigated changes in the experience of love associated with life-course changes, distinguished four different life stages: college-age single youth, young childless married adults, married adults with children living at home, and married adults with launched children. The last group consisted of persons ranging in age from 50 to 70. This group is expected to score lower on romantic love and higher on best-friends love, pragmatic love, and altruistic love than the younger groups. The results offer some confirmation. Compared to a group of married people ranging in age from twenty-four to fifty, pragmatic and altruistic love were endorsed to a significantly greater extent in the older group. Older people, whose children were launched, experienced less possessive love than college-age young adults. In spite of the fact that predictions for romantic and best-friends love were not confirmed, the results show that persons in the age group from fifty to seventy seem to experience love in a more companionate way than younger people do.

What about the beginning of romantic feelings and conceptions of love? Unlike attachment theory, which claims its influence on specific types of relationships emerging during individual development across the life span (infant-parent relationship, friendships, love affairs), the conception of love seems to focus much more on late adolescence and adulthood. To our knowledge, only the psychoanalytic developmental viewpoint considers intimate loving and sexual feelings as aspects of love experienced by young children (Kaplan, 1991). But there are some indications that children have romantic feelings and acquire some knowledge about romantic love (Simon, Eder, & Evans, 1992).

Connolly, Craig, Goldberg, and Pepler (1999) explored conceptions of cross-sex friendships and romantic relationships in boys and girls ranging in age from nine to fourteen years. Although age and experience were associated with differences in descriptions, the results indicated that even young adolescents who were lacking extensive experiences expressed conceptions that were consistent with adults' views of love and friendship. Therefore, the development from childhood to early adulthood is not necessarily characterized by a radical change in interpersonal conceptions, although biological and cultural factors that influence the age-graded opportunity structures for forming a romantic relationship change enormously at puberty.

On the other hand, the indication of continuity does not mean that the conception of love formed in childhood is permanently fixed for life. Sprecher, Cate, and Levin (1998) compared college students from intact versus divorced families in reference to beliefs and attitudes about love and romantic relationships. Female students with divorced parents were less pragmatic, manic, and altruistic. In reference to males, only one significant difference was found between intact and divorced group. Males from divorced families scored higher on the erotic love style. There were hardly any differences concerning romantic beliefs. For males, there was no difference between intact and divorced group and for females the divorced group scored lower on idealization.

So the findings show some associations between parental marital status and love attitudes, although these associations differ for males and females. But the results do not suggest that the experiences of parental divorce at an early age place children at a disadvantage in connection with the development of love.

All in all these findings give an ambiguous picture. There are some hints for continuity, but it is not clear whether the developmental tasks of childhood are directly linked to the task of forming a romantic relationship. Therefore, in the following we limit our considerations to the experience in intimate relationships beginning in adolescence and later.

A Longitudinal Study on Love Styles over Four Years

Next we consider results from a longitudinal study (unpublished data), which focuses on the hypotheses on age-graded expression of love styles. In this section we will present data on the link between relationship duration, age, and love styles. A sample of 193 respondents (101 women, 92 men) described their attitude toward love in their stable relationship

TABLE 5.1. *Statistics on Love Styles*

	1st Measurement		2nd Measurement			
	M	*SD*	*M*	*SD*	r_{tt}	*N*
Passionate Love						
Eros	6.47	1.79	5.90	1.87	.60***	193
Ludus	2.64	1.43	2.23	1.37	.58***	193
Mania	6.18	1.52	5.88	1.74	.58***	193
Companionate Love						
Agape	5.72	1.73	5.54	1.86	.70***	193
Pragma	4.18	1.56	4.10	1.90	.57***	193
Storge	5.88	1.60	6.39	1.80	.58***	193

Note. $^*p < .05.$ $^{**}p < .01.$ $^{***}p < .001.$

at two measurement points: The first session took place in January 1996, the second one in June 2001. At the first measurement point, respondents ranged in age from nineteen to sixty-five years, with a mean age of thirty-three years. Because respondents with a high educational level are over-represented, the sample is not representative of the general population. Nevertheless, the sample is quite heterogeneous with respect to demographic variables. Respondents were recruited through newspaper articles that included a telephone number to call if the reader was interested in participating in the study; 81% of the respondents had an occupation, whereas 13% were students. In general, the duration of the partnership was quite long. The mean relationship length was almost eight and a half years, ranging from two months to forty-four years; 85% of the respondents lived together and 60% were married. Finally, 35% of the respondents had at least one child.

In Table 5.1 the mean assessments of love styles, the standard deviations of ratings, and the test-retest reliabilities of the love styles over a period of four and a half years are summarized. The reliabilities show that there is substantial stability in individual scores across time. In addition, the reliability coefficients indicate that there is enough latitude for the occurrence of change over time.

As mentioned in the section on the integrative hierarchical model of love, the love styles are organized into two clusters, described as passionate love and companionate love. The hypotheses imply that the passionate-love cluster (including Eros, Ludus, and Mania) decreases over time, whereas the companionate-love cluster (including Agape, Pragma, and Storge) increases. As a consequence, in our sample we expected a decrease of love styles belonging to passionate love and an increase of love styles belonging to companionate love over time. This pattern, which is derived from the idea of compensatory strategies, is expected because in the age range of our sample a shift is predicted from an emphasis on passionate love to an emphasis on companionate love – at least in enduring relationships. "Enduring relationships" refers to whether a relationship remains intact. This meaning of enduring relationships differs from the colloquial meaning, which is that in the course of the relationship over time, nothing changes (cf. Karney, Bradbury, & Johnson, 1999). We assume that stability of relationship is associated with change in relationship-specific attitudes.

Results of a *MANOVA* show that all three passionate love styles decrease over time.[3] The profile is steepest for romantic love (Eros: t $(1,192) =$ 4.78, $p < .001$) and somewhat flatter for game playing (Ludus: t $(1,189) =$ 4.451, $p < .001$) and possessive love (Mania: t $(1,192) = 2,72$, $p = .007$). The statistical analysis reveals that only the main effect of measurement point is significant (F $(1,189) = 50.92$, $p < .001$). In contrast, the statistical interaction between measurement point and love style is not significant, indicating that the general trend of the profile is similar for all three passionate love styles.

An inspection of the companionate love styles indicated that across the $4\frac{1}{2}$-year interval the level of pragmatic love essentially did not change (Pragma: t $(1,191) = 0.64$, $p = .522$), whereas the level of altruistic love slightly decreased (Agape: t $(1,192) = 1.75$, $p = .081$). In contrast, in correspondence with our hypotheses the level of best-friends love increases over time (Storge: t $(1,191) = -4.42$, $p < .001$). This divergent pattern of results is reflected in a significant interaction between measurement point and love style (F $(2,380) = 11.30$, $p < .001$). The interaction concentrated in the linear component was highly significant (F $(1,190) = 19.58$; $p < .001$).

It is evident that the mean level of endorsement of the love style scales is quite different. Whereas romantic love, possessive love, best-friends love, and altruistic love are strongly endorsed, pragmatic and especially game-playing love are endorsed to a much lesser extent. This pattern of results corresponds with other studies (see above). It is reflected in a highly significant effect of love styles, which is equally pronounced in the analysis of the passionate love style cluster, F $(2,378) = 361.37$, $p < .001$ and in the analysis of the companionate love style cluster, F $(2,380) = 98.05$, $p < .001$.

A supplementary analysis was undertaken with respect to age effects. The assumption was that the same pattern of results that was obtained in the longitudinal data would be replicated in regression analysis, in which the love styles are regressed on age of respondents. This is illustrated by the regression analysis on the basis of the first measurement point. As for the longitudinal results, the analysis reveals that age is a significant predictor

---

[3] Love styles were measured by a short version of the MEIL that includes only five items in each subscale. Internal consistencies of the six scales varied from alpha .69 to .89 and are satisfactory.

of pragmatic and possessive love. Whereas the association is positive in the first case, it is negative in the second case. These results partially corroborate the longitudinal results.

CONCLUDING COMMENTS

How do our results contribute to a life-span psychology of social relationships? We have focused on romantic and marital relationships. A first lesson is that love and intimacy are likely to change across the life span. This does not mean that love diminishes over the life span (cf. Hendrick & Hendrick, 2000). Rather, the change in love is based on the fact that love consists of a set of characteristic features that are of varying relevance in different life stages and are therefore adaptive.

On a general level two aspects of love can be identified: passionate love and companionate love (Barnes & Sternberg, 1997). Taking the love styles (Lee, 1973) into account, on a more detailed level the characteristics of each facet can be described by three different love styles. Passionate love includes the love styles romantic love, game-playing love, and possessive love, whereas the companionate-love cluster consists of bestfriends love, pragmatic love, and altruistic love. The identification of these two clusters is of theoretical interest because it shows that different social constructions of love can be integrated into a hierarchical model.

Are there any behavioral patterns in marital relationships that are related to the six love attitudes? Bierhoff (2000) discussed the connection between social circumstances/structural conditions of the relationship and love attitudes. Living together in one apartment, getting married, and having children is connected with a higher level of altruistic and pragmatic love. Therefore, companionate love attitudes and structural conditions seem to be related. Helms and Bierhoff (2001) found that passionate love is related to marital infidelity: While romantic love is negatively related, game-playing love shows a positive correlation with infidelity.

Since developmental tasks and life goals change over the life span, the different aspects of love are functional to realize these goals or – when opportunities become scarce – to buffer the negative effects of missing a life goal (Heckhausen & Schulz, 1995).

We assumed that passionate love would be highest in early adulthood because this cluster of love seems to be functional to initiate and intensify a partnership. Afterwards it will decrease and because of the fewer opportunities to realize a passionate relationship we suppose that the importance of companionate love will increase in a compensatory way. On the basis of these hypotheses, we asked if the different qualities of love present in romantic and marital relationships reflect the changes in individual development.

In an attempt to answer this question, we have considered both cross-sectional and longitudinal data, taking into account the connection between age and love and the change of love across time within a constant relationship.

What do the cross-sectional data indicate? First, it is worth mentioning that some general support of our hypotheses is found in the results. Note that each of the love clusters is represented by three love styles. Because the expected changes are not found for all subdimensions, the data support the assumptions only in part. Although most of the studies presented here measured the complete range of love styles corresponding to those described by Lee (1973), none of the studies found linear age effects for all six of the love styles in one sample.

The hypothesis of decreasing passionate love received support for romantic love (Bierhoff & Rohmann, 2000), possessive love (Butler et al., 1995; Montgomery & Sorell, 1997), and game-playing love (Mongomery & Sorell, 1997). In sum, this seems to be a quite strong confirmation of the assumption that passionate love decreased over time.

The evidence for the hypothesized increase in companionate love is much weaker. On this cluster of love styles Bierhoff and Rohmann (2000) found only an increase of pragmatic love. In addition, they found a U-shaped relationship between altruistic love and age. This additional result stresses the point that if one searches for linear relationships only, relevant aspects of developmental changes may be easily overlooked.

With respect to the analysis of age effects in romantic relationships an important methodological issue is that age and relationship duration are correlated empirically. By computing partial correlations Bierhoff and Rohmann showed that the effects of age on love styles were attenuated but still significant, which indicates that age and relationship duration exert independent influences on love styles. In this chapter we focused on general age-graded processes in romantic and marital relationships, which are mainly based on individual development across the life span.

In addition to this approach on intimate relationships, which stresses resources for and outcomes of individual development, future studies might concentrate on factors more closely linked to relationship development (e.g., relationship duration). If the unit of analysis is the individual, an approach focusing on age of respondents suggests itself. In contrast, if the unit of analysis is the pair, relationship duration is a more suitable criterion of the state of the relationship.

Of course it must be recognized that these cross-sectional data have methodological limitations because age effects are confounded with cohort effects. To compensate this shortcoming, we have also considered longitudinal data. What do these data indicate?

The results of the repeated measurement of love styles over a period of four and a half years showed a stronger confirmation for the hypothesized effect on passionate love than for the hypothesized effect on companionate love. Therefore, the results point in the same direction as in the cross-sectional approach. Scores in all three love scales belonging to the passionate love cluster decreased over time. This trend strongly supported the assumed developmental sequence. Since these data are based on stable relationships, it seems that even individuals in romantic relationships that are not expected to break up in the near future report that their passionate attitude is becoming weaker as they grow older.

In contrast to these results, which were in agreement with our hypotheses on passionate love, the assumed increase of the companionate aspects of love did not appear that clearly in the longitudinal perspective. Pragmatic love and altruistic love did not change to a significant extent; only best-friends love increased within the time frame of four and a half years. The hypothesis that companionate love grows across the life span received support only for best-friends love.

Although the longitudinal approach eliminates the objection that the indicated developmental sequence in relationship-specific attitudes is due to cohort effects, one other methodological effect has to be considered. Repeated measures threaten the internal validity of the analysis because test effects might emerge. Although there was a period of four and a half years between the measurement points, the possibility of test effects cannot be ruled out. The combination of cross-sectional and longitudinal research methods promises to overcome the limitations inherent in each approach.

Our goal has been to integrate individual development throughout the life course with the hierarchical model of love. We assumed that the change in love attitudes across the life span is a consequence of opportunity structures that increase or decline depending on age. The chance of getting involved in highly passionate relationships is greater in early adulthood than in late midlife. Therefore, the growing importance of companionate love in the later life stages might be an expression of compensatory strategies. Best-friends love, pragmatic, and altruistic love might compensate for the somewhat limited occasions to fall in love with intense feelings of passion. The shift in love styles shows that attitude changes may also be important for understanding personal relationships across the life span.

Where do we go from here? An important area for future scientific research might center on the association between the configuration of age-graded love styles and life and partnership satisfaction. If there is a compensatory function in the shift from passion to companionate love, this shift should be associated with positive effects on life and relationship satisfaction. As Wrosch and Heckhausen (1999) report, compensatory strategies do not improve well-being in younger separated adults, but do have a positive effect on older separated individuals. This pattern of results indicates that the fit of strategy and developmental task is important for affective outcomes.

In the introduction we mentioned different implicit assumptions of laypeople about love and the development of love. One insight was that love changes over the course of a relationship. In retrospect we add that there seems to be some truth in this implicit theory. However, our scientific analysis goes further because we can add that the change is focused especially on the passionate love cluster, where a general diminishment of the level of love occurs over time. Whether this change means that marital relationships become more mature or grow empty is a matter of perspective. One could argue that relationships are more mature if age-graded compensatory developments take place, for which we have found only scarce evidence. In contrast, one could argue that relationships are less mature if the decrease in the passionate love cluster is not compensated by other changes in relationship experiences. More research is needed on this question (e.g., whether new goals are pursued in late midlife).

References

Ainsworth, M. D. S., Blehar, M. C., Waters, S., & Wall, S. (1978). *Patterns of attachment: A psychological study of the strange situation.* Hillsdale, NJ: Erlbaum.

Amelang, M. (1991). Einstellungen zu Liebe und Partnerschaft: Konzepte, Skalen und Korrelate. In M. Amelang, H. J. Ahrens, & H. W. Bierhoff (Eds.), *Attraktion und Liebe* (pp. 153–196). Göttingen: Hogrefe.

Averill, J. R. (1985). The social construction of emotions. With special reference to love. In K. J. Gergen & K. E. Davis (Eds.), *The social construction of the person* (pp. 89–109). New York: Springer.

Barnes, M. L., & Sternberg, R. J. (1997). A hierarchical model of love and its prediction of satisfaction in close relationships. In R. J. Sternberg & M. Hojjat (Eds.), *Satisfaction in close relationships* (pp. 79–101). New York: Guilford Press.

Berscheid, E., & Reis, H. T. (1998). Attraction and close relationships. In D. T. Gilbert, S. T. Fiske, & G. Lindzey (Eds.), *The handbook of social psychology* (4th ed., Vol. II, pp. 193–281). New York: Oxford University Press.

Berscheid, E., & Walster, E. (1974). A little bit about love. In T. L. Huston (Ed.), *Foundations of interpersonal attraction* (pp. 355–381). New York: Academic Press.

Bierhoff, H. W. (2000). Partnerschaft im Kontext von Familienkonstellation und Wohnsituation [Partnership in the context of family and living arrangements]. In P. Kaiser (Ed.), *Partnerschaft und Paartherapie* [Partnership and Couple therapy] (pp. 147–156). Göttingen: Hogrefe.

Bierhoff, H. W., & Grau, I. (1999). *Romantische Beziehungen* [Romantic relationships]. Göttingen: Huber.

Bierhoff, H. W., Grau, I., & Ludwig, A. (1993). *Marburger Einstellungsinventar für Liebesstile* [Marburg Inventory of Love Attitudes]. Göttingen: Hogrefe.

Bierhoff, H. W., & Klein, R. (1991). Dimensionen der Liebe: Entwicklung einer deutschsprachigen Skala zur Erfassung von Liebesstilen [Dimensions of love]. *Zeitschrift für Differentielle und Diagnostische Psychologie, 12,* 53–71.

Bierhoff, H. W., & Rohmann, E. (2000). Stability and change in romantic relationships. In J. Heckhausen (Ed.), *Motivational psychology of human development* (pp. 325–337). Amsterdam: Elsevier.

Bowlby, J. (1995). Bindung: Historische Wurzeln, theoretische Konzepte und klinische Relevanz [Attachment: Historical roots, theory and clinical relevance]. In G. Spangler & P. Zimmermann (Eds.), *Die Bindungstheorie. Grundlagen, Forschung und Anwendung* [Attachment theory] (pp. 17–26). Stuttgart: Klett-Cotta.

Braun, W., & Proebsting H. (1986). Heiratstafeln verwitweter Deutscher 1979/82 und geschiedener Deutscher 1980/83 [Widowed and divorced Germans in 1979/82 and 1980/83]. *Wirtschaft und Statistik*, 107–112.

Bretherton, I., & Munholland, K. A. (1999). Internal working models in attachment relationships. In J. Cassidy & P. R. Shaver (Eds.), *Handbook of attachment: Theory, research, and clinical application* (pp. 89–111). New York: Guilford Press.

Butler, R., Walker, W. R., Skowronski, J. J., & Shannon, L. (1995). Age and responses to the love attitudes scale: Consistency in structure, differences in scores. *International Journal of Aging and Human Development, 40*, 281–296.

Case, R. (1987). The structure and process of intellectual development. *International Journal of Psychology, 22*, 571–607.

Collins, N. L., & Read, S. J. (1994). Cognitive representations of adult attachment: The structure and function of working models. In K. Bartholomew & D. Perlman (Eds.), *Advances in personal relationships* (Vol. 5, pp. 53–90). London: Jessica Kingsley.

Connolly, J., Craig, W., Goldberg, A., & Pepler, D. (1999). Conceptions of cross-sex friendships and romantic relationships in early adolescence. *Journal of Youth and Adolescence, 28*, 481–494.

Hatfield, E. (1988). Passionate and companionate love. In R. J. Sternberg & M. L. Barnes (Eds.), *The psychology of love* (pp. 191–217). New Haven, CT: Yale University Press.

Hatfield, E., & Rapson, R. L. (1993). *Love, sex and intimacy: Their psychology, biology, and history.* New York: HarperCollins College Publishers.

Heckhausen J., & Schulz, R. (1995). A life span theory of control. *Psychological Review, 102*, 284–304.

Heckhausen, J., Wrosch, C., & Fleeson, W. (2001). Developmental regulation before and after a developmental deadline: The sample case of "biological clock" for childbearing. *Psychology and Aging, 16*, 400–413.

Helms, L., & Bierhoff H. W. (2001). Laesst sich Untreue durch Geschlecht, Einstellung oder Persönlichkeit vorhersagen? *Zeitschrift für Familienforschung, 13*, 5–25.

Hendrick, C., & Hendrick, S. S. (1986). A theory and method of love. *Journal of Personality and Social Psychology, 50*, 392–402.

Hendrick, S. S., & Hendrick, C. (1995). Gender differences and similarities in sex and love. *Personal Relationships, 2*, 55–65.

Hendrick, S. S., & Hendrick, C. (1997). Love and satisfaction. In R. J. Sternberg & M. Hojjat (Eds.), *Satisfaction in close relationships* (pp. 56–78). New York: Guilford Press.

Hendrick, S. S., & Hendrick, C. (2000). Romantic love. In C. Hendrick & S. S. Hendrick (Eds.), *Close relationships. A sourcebook* (pp. 203–215). Thousand Oaks, CA: Sage.

Hendrick, C., Hendrick, S. S., & Dicke, A. (1998). The love attitudes scale: Short form. *Journal of Social and Personal Relationships, 15*, 147–159.

Kaplan, E. H. (1991). Adolescents, age fifteen to eighteen: A psychoanalytic developmental view. In S. I. Greenspan & G. H. Pollock, *The course of life, Vol. 4: Adolescence* (pp. 201–233). Madison, WI: International Universities Press.

Karney, B. R., Bradbury, T. N., & Johnson, M. D. (1999). Deconstructing stability: The distinction between the course of a close relationship and its endpoint. In J. M. Adams & W. H. Jones (Eds.), *Handbook of interpersonal commitment and relationship stability* (pp. 481–499). New York: Kluwer Academic/Plenum Publishers.

Koski, L. R., & Shaver, B. R. (1997). Attachment and relationship satisfaction across the life span. In H. J. Sternberg & M. Hojjat (Eds.), *Satisfaction in close relationships* (pp. 26–55). New York: Guilford Press.

Kurdek, L. A. (2000). Attractions and constraints as determinants of relationship commitment: Longitudinal evidence from gay, lesbian, and heterosexual couples. *Personal Relationships, 7*, 245–262.

Lang, F. R., & Heckhausen, J. (2001). Perceived control over development and subjective well-being: Differential benefits across adulthood. *Journal of Personality and Social Psychology, 81*, 509–523.

Lee, J. H. (1973). *The colours of love.* Englewood Cliffs, NJ: Prentice Hall.

Levinger, G. (1980). Toward the analysis of close relationships. *Journal of Experimental Social Psychology, 16*, 510–544.

Levinger, G. (1994). Figure versus ground. Micro- and macroperspectives on the social psychology of personal relationships. In R. Erber & R. Gilmour (Eds.), *Theoretical frameworks for personal relationships* (pp. 1–28). Hillsdale, NJ: Erlbaum.

Levy, M. B., & Davis, K. E. (1988). Love styles and attachment styles compared: Their relations to each other and to various relationship characteristics. *Journal of Social and Personal Relationships, 5*, 439–471.

Montgomery, M. J., & Sorell, G. T. (1997). Differences in love attitudes across family life stages. *Family Relations: Interdisciplinary Journal of Applied Family Studies, 46*, 55–61.

Murstein, B. I., & Tuerkheimer, A. (1998). Gender differences in love, sex, and motivation for sex. *Psychological Reports, 82*, 435–450.

Rubin, Z. (1970). Measurement of romantic love. *Journal of Personality and Social Psychology, 16*, 265–273.

Rutter, V., & Schwarz, P. (1996). Same-sex couples: Courtship, commitment, context. In A. E. Auhagen & M. v. Salisch (Eds.), *The diversity of human relationships* (pp. 197–226). New York: Cambridge University Press.

Shackelford, T. K., & Buss, D. M. (1997). Marital satisfaction in evolutionary psychological perspective. In H. J. Sternberg, & M. Hojjat (Eds.), *Satisfaction in close relationships* (pp. 7–25). New York: Guilford Press.

Shaver, P. R., & Brennan, K. A. (1992). Attachment styles and the "Big Five" personality traits: Their connection with each other and with romantic relationship outcomes. *Personality and Social Psychology Bulletin, 18*, 536–545.

Shaver, P. R., & Clark, C.L. (1996). Forms of adult romantic attachment and their cognitive and emotional underpinnings. In G. G. Noam & K. W. Fischer (Eds.), *Development and vulnerability in close relationships* (pp. 29–58). New York: Lawrence Erlbaum.

Simon, R. W., Eder, D., & Evans, C. (1992).The development of feeling norms underlying romantic love among adolescent females. *Social Psychology Quarterly*, *55*, 29–46.

Sprecher, S., Cate, R., & Levin, L. (1998). Parental divorce and young adults' beliefs about love. *Journal of Divorce and Remarriage*, *28*, 107–120.

Sprecher, S., & Metts, S. (1999). Romantic beliefs: Their influence on relationships and patterns of change over time. *Journal of Social and Personal Relationships*, *16*, 834–851.

Teachman, J. D., & Heckert, A. (1985).The impact of age and children on remarriage. *Journal of Family Issues*, *6*, 185–203.

Wrosch, C., & Heckhausen, J. (1999). Control processes before and after passing a developmental deadline: Activation and deactivation of intimate relationship goals. *Journal of Personality and Social Psychology*, *77*, 415–427.

Wrosch, C., Heckhausen, J., & Lachman, M. E. (2000). Primary and secondary control strategies for managing health and financial stress across adulthood. *Psychology and Aging*, *15*, 387–399.

Yancey, G. B., & Eastman, R. L. (1995). Comparison of undergraduates with older adults on love styles and life satisfaction. *Psychological Reports*, *76*, 1211–1218.

6

Close Relationships across the Life Span: Toward a Theory of Relationship Types

Keiko Takahashi

In this chapter I discuss how to conceptualize and study individual patterns of close relationships consisting of multiple significant others. The discussion consists of three parts. First, I review previous research on close relationships to clarify which aspects of social relationships have already been studied and which have not been fully understood. Then I use the affective relationships model to examine how the important, but not sufficiently studied, aspects of social relationships from young childhood to old age can be conceptualized. Finally, I discuss the effectiveness of the typological analysis of this model and future directions of this research.

THE NATURE OF CLOSE RELATIONSHIPS

From the time they are born into society, humans are exposed to a variety of social relationships, and are naturally directed toward having interactions with multiple significant others for their survival, safety, and well-being. However, most researchers have focused on dyadic relationships, such as with the mother in infancy (Ainsworth, Blehar, Waters, & Wall, 1978; Bretherton & Waters, 1985; Cassidy & Shaver, 1999; Kobak & Hazan, 1991), with a friend in childhood (Dodge, Pettit, McClasky, & Brown, 1986; Jones & Vaughan, 1990; Parker & Gottman, 1989; Urberg, Degirmencioglu, Tolson, & Halliday-Scher, 1995), and with a romantic partner in adolescence and adulthood (Hazen & Shaver, 1987, 1990; Shaver, Hazen, & Bradshaw, 1988).

In the last few decades, some researchers have moved beyond this traditional dyadic paradigm and asserted that each individual, from infancy to old age, of both genders, and in every culture, has social relationships consisting of multiple significant others, including their parents, siblings, spouse, children, relatives, peers, friends and others who are close to them (Belle, 1989; Hinde, 1981; Kahn & Antonucci, 1980; Lang & Carstensen, 1994; Lewis, 1982, 1984; Pierce, Sarason, & Sarason, 1996; Takahashi, 1974,

1990a). If we accept the fact that each person has multiple significant others concurrently, we can reasonably extract at least the following three assumptions regarding social relationships: (1) individuals assign different social roles to each of the multiple figures; (2) individuals have their own representation of the framework of social relationships consisting of the multiple social figures; and (3) because individuals select appropriate figures for themselves, there must be individual patterns of the internal framework of social relationships. In the section that follows, we will briefly review to what extent these three assumptions of social relationships have been examined by theories and the empirical evidence.

Articulations of Psychological Functions among Multiple Significant Others

The main goals of having close relationships are to maintain one's survival and feeling of safety, and to enhance one's well-being. In conceptualizing close relationships, researchers have differentiated several sub-goals in terms of functions following Murray's need functions (Lewis, 1982), the key elements of interpersonal transactions (Kahn & Antonucci, 1980), or the categories of relational provisions (Weiss, 1974) through which people achieve their main goals. In addition, researchers have assumed that the psychological functions are assigned to multiple significant figures differently.

If we look at the matter from a different angle, it is assumed that, because of these functional differentiations among figures, a person is able to possess multiple relationships simultaneously. When we consider the mental cost, the distribution of psychological functions among limited numbers of significant others is essential to insure that there will be appropriate and available figures for every expected situation. When a person attaches to only one figure or attaches to everybody, he or she may be overly dependent on or easily influenced by the others accordingly, and this will impair his or her ability to live as an autonomous adult. Thus, it is necessary to describe the whole relationship profile for an individual, in which the psychological functions of each figure must be related to or vary with the assignments of functions of other figures. We should treat all the figures as a related whole in each individual's set of social relationships. In other words, we should conceptualize social relationships by considering both psychological functions and social figures.

There have been the following innovations that promote the conceptualization of multiple social relationships. In studies using a rubric of social support networks, researchers have delineated various categories of social support, such as emotional, informational, and instrumental, and found that many different people supply social support to the recipient in a manner that is cooperative and in which the supporters compensate for each other (Barrera, 1986; Barrera & Ainslay, 1983; Hinde, 1981; Rook, 1987; Weiss, 1974).

Lewis and his colleagues (Feiring & Lewis, 1989, 1991; Lewis, 1982; Lewis & Feiring, 1979) viewed a social space as consisting of many people who fulfill many kinds of social functions. They defined various functions as important; for example, for infants, protection, caregiving, feeding, play, exploration/learning, and social control are considered important. Given these categories, they proposed to describe the entire social map of a child in terms of a matrix of figure by function: a large lattice on which the Y axis represents an array of figures and the X axis represents a variety of psychological functions. Studies applying this device successfully indicated that each child has a variety of social figures that fulfill different psychological functions.

Antonucci and her colleagues conceptualized social relationships as individuals' hierarchical social support networks, using the image of a convoy that surrounds a person over time, in which supporters are distinguished by the degree of importance they have to the individual (Antonucci, 1985; Kahn & Antonucci, 1980). Specifically, these investigators first asked their subjects to map important persons in their lives and to classify them into three concentric circles. Each of the circles was considered to represent a different level of importance to the target person. They then interviewed the subjects as to the functions provided by the designated figures. Their (Antonucci & Akiyama, 1987; Antonucci, Fuhrer, & Dartigues, 1997; Antonucci & Jackson, 1987) and others' studies (Lang & Carstensen, 1994; Lang, Staudinger, & Carstensen, 1998; Levitt, Guacci-Franco, & Levitt, 1993; Levitt, Weber, & Guacci, 1993) revealed features of social relationships more clearly than had previous conventional research. They found that adults nominated eight or nine figures on average and, of these, three or four were placed into the inner circle of people who provided higher proportions of all kinds of support, such as confiding, reassurance, respect, care when sick, and talk when upset, whereas the middle-circle figures provided respect and care when sick, and outer-circle members only provided respect (Antonucci & Akiyama, 1987). This sophisticated research has clearly indicated the existence of the articulations of psychological functions among significant others.

Internal Framework of Close Relationships

It is well documented that humans as young as toddlers have the ability to construct and use mental models that serve to interpret immediate situations, and to select or plan actual and appropriate behaviors in a given context (Bowlby, 1969/1982, 1973, 1980; Bretherton, 1993; Nelson, 1986; Piaget, 1954; Schank & Abelson, 1977). Because of this ability, it is reasonably assumed that social interactions and relationships are *not* synonymous

(Lewis, 1982). We can observe social interactions, but such observation does not necessarily lead to the understanding of close relationships as an integrated system. For this we must somehow access the mental models of social relationships.

Some researchers have posited such mental models of social relationships as relational schema (Baldwin, 1992; Yee, Santoro, Paul, & Rosenbaum, 1996), attachment style (Davila, Burge, & Hammen, 1997; Hazan & Shaver, 1987, 1990; Scharfe & Bartholomew, 1994), or trust (Rempel, Holmes, & Zanna, 1985). Most typical theoretical innovations in the mental models of social relationships may be identified in the attachment theory, although this theory primarily concerns the mother-child, dyadic relationship. These researchers have extended the attachment theory beyond toddlerhood by "a move to the level of representation" (Bretherton, 1985; Main, 1994; Main, Kaplan, & Cassidy, 1985), based on the internal working model proposed by Bowlby (1969/1982, 1973, 1980). They extend the theory by focusing on mental representations of the "current state of mind with respect to attachment experiences," mainly with the mother in childhood (e.g., George, Kaplan, & Main, 1996; Hesse, 1999; Main & Goldwyn, 1998). These devices suggest that we can conceptualize social relationships as representations of actual interactive relationships.

The internal framework provides us not only with the experiences of social figures but also with beliefs about how each figure fulfills each function, by considering what the figure thinks of us and how the figure will respond, in other words, beliefs that come from inferring the figure's mind. Thus, we can hypothesize that the representational framework of close relationships controls the everyday social interactions of each person, although the representations are influenced and changed by the actual interactions.

Individual Patterns of Close Relationships

As individuals select appropriate figures for themselves and assign one or more psychological functions to each of them, it is assumed that there are individual differences in the configurations of a person's framework of close relationships. Some innovative researchers have proposed ways to summarize the detailed information gained from their interviewees about their relationships, beyond the conventional descriptions of normative tendencies.

For example, Antonucci and her colleagues have proposed the total network size or the composition of a network (family vs. friends ratio) as indicators of individual differences in social relationships (Antonucci, Fuhrer, & Dartigues, 1997). Wenger (1991, 1996) and Litwin (2000, 2001) have identified individual network types among elderly citizens based on the frequency of contact with children, friends, or neighbors and their attendance of social activities. Although a quantitative summary of social frameworks is convenient, its use might result in the loss of the essential nature of social relationships represented by the relationship between figures and functions. I believe that indicators based on the quantitative aspects of social relationships are too general and abstract to depict the complexly organized representational framework. Rather, the unique nature of the social relationships of each individual needs to be condensed.

CONCEPTUALIZATION OF CLOSE RELATIONSHIPS

As thus far reviewed, the three assumptions about close relationships have been partly examined and embodied in the recent innovative research described above. The most critical problem that now confronts us is how densely to describe how figures and functions are related to each other in each individual's personal network. In other words, we must take into account the outstanding qualitative characteristics of the individual framework, which consists of multiple figures among which psychological functions are shared, articulated, and divided. At the same time, the detailed, qualitative descriptions of individuals should be categorizable into groups or types for the purpose of understanding general rules in social relationships.

Next, I will discuss the affective relationships model (Takahashi, 1973, 1986, 1990a; Takahashi & Sakamoto, 2000) as an example of an attempt to integrate all three of the assumptions together into one model. This model was constructed in Japan and has been applied not only among the Japanese but also among other Eastern and Western participants (Heo, 2000; Levitt, 2001; Shulman & Scharf, 2000; Takahashi, Ohara, Antonucci, & Akiyama, in press).

Affective Relationships Model

The notion of affective relationships focuses on the core and relatively stable close relationships that are assumed to be important for the survival and well-being of human beings. The affective relationships are defined as those interpersonal relationships that satisfy our needs for emotional interactions with significant others; they include the need for emotional support, exchanging warm attention, and giving nurture. Thus, the affective relationships include a variety of intimate relationships that have been studied under such rubrics as attachment, trust, love, close relationships, and romantic relationships. Because previous research has indicated that purely instrumental supports, such as financial supports and those that provide help in urgent situations, are sometimes unaccompanied by any positive affection (e.g., Iida, 2000; Takahashi & Ohara, 1997), these kinds of support are excluded.

The affective relationships model allows us to conceptualize the important features of close relationships that have been identified only partially by previous research as stated above. More specifically, the following three features characterize the framework of affective relationships in this model.

1. The framework consists of multiple figures that have been chosen by each individual, who assigns to them each of the psychological functions. We can distinguish a variety of psychological functions, from the critical (e.g., asking for emotional support) to the peripheral (e.g., sharing emotional experiences and information) that provide support for an individual's survival and well-being; these figures and functions have been identified in previous studies (Furman & Buhrmester, 1985; Furman, Simon, Shaffer, & Bouchey, 2002; Kahn & Antonucci, 1980; Weiss, 1974).

2. The framework has a clear hierarchical structure, as in the convoy model (Kahn & Antonucci, 1980). That is, there are focal figures that satisfy almost all of the psychological functions, and provide the scaffolding of being for each person by fulfilling the most critical functions. In addition to the focal figures, there is a limited but sufficient number of significant others to satisfy a variety of psychological functions for a stable and autonomous life, so that the focal figures' influence could be reduced by the influence of the others. This structured framework serves to construe the core and relatively stable social relationships. However, it is also assumed that the framework will be transformed through encounters with new and appropriate figures, the loss of figures by separation or death, aging, or development. Thus, it is reasonably hypothesized that each person continuously constructs and reconstructs her or his own framework of affective relationships throughout life.

3. There are individual differences in frameworks, because each person chooses the figures that are most appropriate and available to them to fulfill each of the functions. To highlight these individualities, it is useful to evaluate the importance of a limited number of significant others, in light of their roles in providing a few generally important psychological functions. To summarize the individual nature of social relationships that is captured by these figure-function pairs, we adopt typological classifications. The typological analysis falls midway between case descriptions of individuals and normative descriptions of groups. Such conventional analyses of social relationships are not always appropriate: the former is too concrete and the latter lures us into missing individualities. In the affective relationships model, we use typology and tentatively discern types of frameworks.

Measuring Affective Relationships

The Affective Relationships Scale (ARS). To better define the affective relationships model, a new self-report type of assessment instrument, the Affective Relationships Scale (ARS), was proposed (Takahashi, 1974, 1990a;

Takahashi & Sakamoto, 2000). The ARS is constructed to assess subjective representations of close relationships as a complex set of figure-function pairs, using the same set of questions to ask about supposedly major social figures.

More concretely, the ARS describes multiple close relationships in terms of representations of multiple interpersonal relationships. The ARS requires a subject to give separate ratings on the same set of items, which describes each of six psychological functions. That is, the ARS consists of statements describing concrete affective behaviors that are grouped according to the following six functions: (1) seeking proximity; (2) receiving emotional support; (3) receiving reassurance for behavior and/or being; (4) receiving encouragement and help; (5) sharing information and experience; and (6) giving nurture. Participants are asked to give separate ratings of the 12 items (i.e., 6 functions × 2 items), as shown in Table 6.1, for each of their five to eight figures using a five-point scale from 5 (I agree) to 1 (I disagree). The figures are selected from several social categories based on preliminary studies identifying the most important persons for adults. In most cases, participants are asked to rate the mother, the father, the closest sibling, the closest same-gender friend, the most favored opposite-gender friend or romantic partner, and a respected person, in that order. For married people, the spouse (instead of a romantic partner) and the closest child are included. Thus, the ARS can be flexibly adjusted to different populations by including or excluding figures, depending on the respondents' social and societal conditions and the aims of the research. The ARS is designed to yield two kinds of score: the total score for all twelve items

TABLE 6.1. *Items of the Affective Relationships Scale*

The first series of statements are about your relationship with your mother. For each of the statements, please choose one of the alternatives that best describes how much you agree. (Alternatives and score: 5, Agree; 4, Agree somewhat; 3, Neither agree nor disagree; 2, Disagree somewhat; or 1, Disagree.)

1. I would like to be emotionally supported by my mother.
2. I would miss my mother if she were away.
3. I would like to be with my mother when I feel sad.
4. I would like to be understood by my mother when I have a hard time.
5. I would like my mother and me to share our difficulties.
6. I would like to encourage my mother when she has difficulties.
7. I would like to be with my mother when I need a boost in my self-confidence.
8. I would like my mother and me to share each other's happiness.
9. I would like to be encouraged by my mother when I do something.
10. I would like to be with my mother if possible.
11. I would like my mother to agree with me if I am doing the right thing.
12. I would like my mother to ask me to help when she has difficulties.

for each major figure, and a set of subscores for each of the six functions for each figure. The former reflects the strength of the subject's need for affective behaviors from each figure, and the latter the major functions of that figure.

The Picture Affective Relationships Test (PART). For subjects who have difficulty responding to the ARS, that is, young children, elementary schoolchildren, and very elderly people, a series of picture-type instruments (the Picture Affective Relationships Test, PART) was constructed based on the affective relationships model. The PART consists of two sets of eighteen cards, one for females and one for males. Each card illustrates a daily life situation in which affective behaviors toward another person may be induced. As shown in Figure 6.1, each pair of cards depicts imaginary situations representing each of the same six functions that are in the ARS. During the test session, a subject is instructed to suppose the major figure in the picture was her or himself, then is shown each card and asked to answer the question pertaining to each picture with the name of a person and that person's relationship to the subject (Takahashi, 1978/2000; Takahashi, 2002). Thus, using both the ARS and the PART, we can assess affective relationships over the course of life, from young children to elderly people, based on the same theory.

Affective Relationships Types: Condensing the Individual Patterns of Relationships Described by the ARS and the PART. To condense the rich information obtained for each individual by the ARS or the PART, we have proposed typological classifications as intermediate descriptions of the data between live case depictions and normative summaries of the whole data, because previous findings suggest that there are three groups of people. First, previous studies indicate that one group of individuals includes people who are dominantly concerned with family members and another group includes people who are more concerned with nonfamily members (Antonucci, Fuhrer, & Dartigues, 1997; Litwin, 2000, 2001; Wenger, 1991, 1996). The former conventionally includes the natural family members, i.e., parents, siblings, and children, and the latter typically includes friends of both genders. In fact, correlations of the ARS scores for the various figures indicated that the *r*s among either family or nonfamily members were significantly greater than those between family and nonfamily members (Takahashi & Sakamoto, 2000; Takahashi et al., in press). Moreover, for instance, college students who gave the highest ARS scores for the mother reported that they had no friends of the opposite gender, in contrast to their friend-dominant type counterparts who reported having active interactions with friends including romantic partners (Takahashi, 1974, 1986). However, the differentiation of family members from outsiders will depend on one's subjective definitions of "family." In particular,

"If you got hurt, who would you want to be with?"

(A card for girls)

"If something pleasant happened to you, who would you
like to share it with?" (A card for boys)

FIGURE 6.1. Sample Cards of the PART for Young Children.

the classification of romantic partners or the spouse into the family or
nonfamily cluster will be arbitrary. A romantic partner is initially considered a nonfamily member, but will often, but not always, be considered a
family member after marriage. For the sake of convenience, we will classify the romantic partner as a family member among married participants
hereafter.

In addition to the above-mentioned people who are interested in others,
a third group is made up of persons who are not very interested in other
human beings. Members of this group have been identified in the previous

literature under rubrics such as isolation, withdrawal, loneliness, and attachment disorganization (Main & Solomon, 1990; Rotenberg & Hymel, 1999; Solomon & George, 1999). Respondents to the ARS or the PART can easily be classified into one of these three groups (Family, Nonfamily, and "Lone Wolf") of social relationships.

Moreover, if we look at each detailed description of individuals' close relationships, we find that people have preferences among the most important social figures. For instance, some Family group students express a preference for the mother over other family members. Among Nonfamily group adolescents, we could discriminate two types: same-gender friend dominant and opposite-gender friend dominant students. Thus, we can identify specific types in terms of a dominant, focal figure in both the Family and Nonfamily groups.

After various statistical trials aimed at defining the focal figure, we have tentatively concluded that the most highly scored figure by the ARS or the PART can be regarded as a useful, though simple, indicator of each personal framework. We have described the analytical process in detail elsewhere (Takahashi & Sakamoto, 2000). By identifying the top figure, we can classify respondents into several types, such as Mother type, Child type, Spouse type, and Friend type. These types are also classified into the two major groups, i.e., the Family or Nonfamily group.

Thus, similar to other elaborate measurements such as Antonucci's and Lewis's, the ARS and the PART describe close relationships throughout the life course in considering which figure fulfills which functions, but differ from them in the following respects: (1) the ARS and the PART focus on close relationships with a limited number of significant others, whereas the others ask subjects to nominate all significant figures; (2) they assess mentally represented relationships and not actual interactions, whereas the others do not clearly discriminate the needs of a close relationship from the behaviors associated with it; and (3) they summarize an individual's configuration of personal relationships in terms of a focal figure who fills most of the psychological functions and inevitably provides the most critical function for survival or well-being (Takahashi, 1974). Antonucci has only proposed quantitative norms of individualities, and Lewis has not yet proposed any indices of the patterns of close relationships.

TYPOLOGY OF CLOSE RELATIONSHIPS

In this section, I will examine the empirical evidence for our ability to differentiate individualities by typological classifications. First, by this typology, we found normative distributions of types according to ages and genders that were consistent with previous findings. At the same time, under the normative trends, that is, the changes and expansions of close relationships from the family to nonfamily members, we found all kinds of types throughout the life course. As expected, every significant figure had the potential to be chosen as the focal figure according to individuals' preferences. Second, each group showed different social interactions and narratives that could be theoretically explained based on the results of the test. That is, Family group participants more easily and comfortably interacted with family members and voiced life stories and future plans that mostly focused on family members. In contrast, Nonfamily group individuals showed more ease in interacting with friends of both genders and narrated nonfamily-centered life stories. However, there were no qualitative differences in social adjustment between the two groups of social relationships, probably because each individual possessed a type of psychological scaffolding. In addition to these groups, Lone Wolf type participants were identified across the life span. Operationally, these are people who report a very low affective need for all figures in the ARS, or who don't report a sufficient number of social figures in the PART, saying, "I don't need others because I can do anything by myself," "I am an independent person," or "I have no particular persons." These Lone Wolf types were suffering from loneliness, depression, or low life satisfaction. In the following sections, we examine all these findings in more detail.

Frequencies of Affective Relationships Types across the Life Span

Figure 6.2 shows the proportion of affective relationships types from 3.6-year-old children to elderly people in Japan (Inoue & Takahashi, 2000, 2001; Nagata & Suzuki, 1983; Takahashi & Majima, 1994; Takahashi & Sakamoto, 2000; Takahashi, Tamura, & Tokoro, 1997; Takahashi & Yokosuka, 1997). The types were identified by the ARS for adolescents (junior high school students) to elderly citizens, and by the PART for children, based on the same principle. As the figure indicates, we can discern different types even among three-year-old children.

As Figure 6.2 shows, we found a prominent type for each age group: among very young children, such as three-year-olds, the mother is the dominant figure; as children grow, especially at the elementary school ages, friends of the same gender are very important for many of them; among adolescents, a romantic partner occupies the most significant status; and after marriage, the spouse is reported as an important figure. In addition, we found gender differences in the frequencies of types: among females, there are more Mother types across all ages; among males after high school age, a larger number of Romantic partner or Spouse types were found.

On the other hand, it is worth noting that under these normative developmental trends, that is, the changes of focal figures from family to nonfamily members, each individual constructed her or his own subjective representation of affective relationships. These data suggest that through negotiating with the cultural expectations according to age and/or gender,

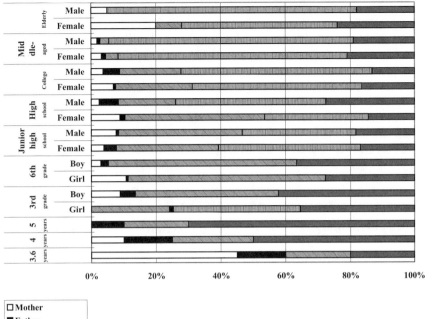

FIGURE 6.2. Distributions of Affective Relationship Types across the Life Span.

individuals voluntarily select suitable social figures for themselves and as-sign appropriate psychological functions to each of them.

It is also assumed that the framework will change as a result of an indi-vidual's encounters with various social experiences, development, and/or aging. The stability of and changes in framework types will be best ob-served in longitudinal studies.

A total of 66 female sophomores (19–21 years old) were assessed for their affective relationships types twice with an interval of seven months. Almost 80% of them were coherently classified into the same group at both assessments. Of the rest, all but 5% reported what they believed to be the causes of the score change for each of the figures. That is, they reported that the occurrence of ordinary contacts (via dating, calling, and writing to) and quarrelling with the figure tended to reduce the score of the target figure; on the other hand, deprivation of contact with the figure, and also special events such as being cared for when sick or having a lengthy conversation leading to deepened understanding or renewed feelings of love, were identified as the reason for increasing the ARS score and changes in the focal figure (Takahashi, 1990b).

Moreover, among 38 middle-aged adults (aged 34–54 years) who were investigated with respect to their social relationships for two years, 7% changed from being in the Family group to the Nonfamily group; these individuals reported a variety of reasons for changing the need strength of affective relationships toward each figure, such as bereavement, the independence of a child, participation in social activities, and aging (Hamanoue, 1999). Twenty-three cancer patients (aged 36–65 years) reported that after an operation, they had a different view of their social networks (Fukui, 1999). Most of these patients said that they were acutely aware of the importance of a focal figure, and changed (either included or excluded) some other figures.

Differences in Behaviors among Affective Relationships Types

Differences among the Types in Social Activities. First, we examined whether the two major groups among kindergarten children, the Family group (i.e., Mother type) and Nonfamily group (i.e., Friend type) children, would interact differently with two different kinds of partners, an age-mate and a female adult (Takahashi, 1997). It was hypothesized that children would more actively and effectively collaborate with the kind of partner who belonged to the same social category as the focal figure in her or his own framework of relationships. That is, we examined whether a Friend type child would show an advantage in interactions with an age-mate stranger, because the friend-dominant framework would help the child anticipate various activities of age-mates and would motivate the child to cooperate with them, and in contrast, whether a Mother type child would show an advantage in interactions with a mother-like adult stranger, because the framework would help the child interact with a female adult. We expected to see a significant interaction effect between the types of affective relationships a child possessed and the kind of partner the child was paired with for a task.

Using the PART for kindergarten children, 20 Friend type, 23 Mother type children, and 43 children who had named both an age-mate and the mother a few times each and served as controls or "neutral" partners to the two identified types of children, were selected from 210 kindergarten children (5–6 years old). The target (Friend type and Mother type) children were asked to participate in two joint problem-solving sessions: one "with-child" and one "with-adult" session. In the with-child session, each same-sex pair of children, one "neutral" partner and the other of either the Friend or Mother type, was asked to build a house together using a 40-piece set of colored blocks. In the with-adult session, the children were asked to accomplish a 42-piece jigsaw puzzle task, and they were told that the puzzle was for elementary schoolchildren and might be a little bit difficult for them, so they were encouraged to ask for help from their adult, female partner. The transcripts of the video recordings were coded with respect to nine indexical behaviors of the target child in interactions with her or his partner. The analysis revealed that four out of the nine Type × Session interaction effects were significant: the Friend type children exhibited more frequent collaborative talk, complimentary behavior, and social referencing, and less frequent noninteractive behavior in the with-child session than in the with-adult session. In contrast, the Mother type children more frequently showed collaborative talk, complimentary behavior, and social referencing, as well as less frequent noninteractive behavior, in the with-adult session than in the with-child session.

Thus, the Friend type children more actively and skillfully interacted with a child stranger than did the Mother type children, but this was not true with the adult partner. These children were more competent in collaborations with child partners than their Mother type counterparts. However, those children who actively interacted with their child partner did not necessarily actively interact with their adult partner, and they were quiet or shy in the with-adult situation. They did not speak to the adult and often ignored her suggestions; all they did was give her a slight nod. In contrast, the Mother type children showed that they were at an advantage in the with-adult session but not in the with-child session. They actively responded to the adult partner's proposals and effectively used her suggestions, to which they did not always respond verbally.

As expected, this study indicates that the preestablished personal framework mediates and affects ongoing social interactions. A study among college students replicates the results. Using 26-week longitudinal data from female first-year college students, we examined how the preestablished framework of affective relationships of an individual student would affect her adjustment to the transition from home to college dormitory and campus life (Takahashi & Majima, 1994). By the ARS we identified 23 Nonfamily group (i.e., Friend type) and 14 Family group students at the time of entrance to college. These two groups were compared with respect to how well they established new social relationships and resolved social conflicts in dormitory and college life during the following 26 weeks. They were asked to report psychological and physical difficulties in adjusting, both in questionnaires and interviews at the 10th and the 27th weeks. The results indicate that Friend type students developed relationships with new fellow students more easily and reported fewer difficulties in making the transition than their Family group counterparts. It is assumed that the Friend types possessed rich representations of relationships with age-mates, and thus had an advantage in adjusting to such age-mate dominant situations as attending a college and living in a dormitory. That is, a Friend type framework fits the transitional circumstance of going to college, whereas the Family group student will show superiority over the Friend type in situations where social interactions are characterized as family-like or intergenerational transactions.

Differences in Social Adjustment. Another line of research has focused on the relationships between the affective relationships types and psychological adjustment and general well-being. In this conceptualization of close relationships, it is hypothesized that humans voluntarily select suitable figures for themselves and assign appropriate psychological functions to each of them. This implies that there should be no differences in the quality of psychological adjustment among individuals displaying different patterns of affective relationships, irrespective of who the focal figure is. It is plausible that each person has a personal framework that will support her or his well-being. However, it is assumed that the Lone Wolf types, who do not have sufficient social resources, would suffer from difficulties in psychological adjustment, as suggested by previous research (Antonucci & Jackson, 1987; Krause, 1987; Lang & Carstensen, 1994; Main & Solomon, 1990; Solomon & George, 1999).

Elementary schoolchildren were investigated to test our hypotheses that there would be no differences in psychological adjustment between children who had the Mother type and Friend type of affective relationships, because in either case their framework would support their well-being, but that Lone Wolf type children would have difficulties in attaining and maintaining such adjustment (Inoue & Takahashi, 2000). A total of 689 elementary schoolchildren of both genders participated in this study: 358 third-graders and 331 sixth-graders. The children were given the PART for elementary schoolchildren and then, based on the results, classified into affective types in terms of the dominant figure. Operationally, a child who answered "self," "anybody," or "nobody" for more than half the cards was designated as a Lone Wolf-type. Among the remaining subjects, the figure who was nominated most frequently was designated as the dominant figure, and the children were classified into types in terms of the dominant figure. If a child did not name any particular figure for as many as three cards, or nominated two or more figures in the same number of cards, she or he was identified as unclassifiable, because it was difficult to identify the primary figure in such cases. For 75% of the participants, one of the figures was identified as being dominant. Among all the children, 11% and 50% were identified as Mother and Friend types, respectively. Consistent with our previous findings among older generations, the dominant figure was assigned most of the psychological functions, especially the functions of emotional support, receiving reassurance for behavior and/or being, and seeking proximity. Twelve percent of the total participants fell into the Lone Wolf type category (17% of the boys and 6% of the girls). The percentage of appearance of Lone Wolves was similar to our samples of college students

(Takahashi & Majima, 1994) and elderly people (Takahashi & Yokosuka, 1997).

After responding to the PART, children were analyzed with respect to three psychological adjustment scales: The loneliness scale for children (Asher, Hymel, & Renshaw, 1984), the self-esteem scale (Rosenberg, 1965), and the self-efficacy scale for children (Sherer et al., 1982). As expected, Lone Wolf type children felt significantly stronger loneliness, were lower in their self-esteem score, and were less confident in their self-efficacy than their Mother type and Friend type counterparts. However, there were no clear differences between Mother type and Friend type children in adjustment scores. This tendency for the Lone Wolf type children to show a higher loneliness score was found for children of both grades and of both genders. The tendency toward lower self-esteem was unquestionable among the third-grade boys and sixth-grade girls. The tendency toward a lower self-efficacy scale was obvious among all the third-graders and the sixth-grade girls.

Consistent with previous research (e.g., Antonucci & Jackson, 1987; Krause, 1987; Lang & Carstensen, 1994), Lone Wolf types in every age group consistently expressed difficulties in social adjustment (Inoue & Takahashi, 1999; Takahashi & Inoue, 2001; Takahashi, Tamura, & Tokoro, 1997; Takahashi, & Yokosuka, 1997). However, we found some but often not statistically significant differences between Family group and Nonfamily group participants in each age group. For example, among college students, Nonfamily group students reported higher psychological adjustment scores and satisfaction in college life than their Family group counterparts (Inoue & Takahashi, 1999). In contrast, among elderly people, Family group people, especially Spouse types, were more highly satisfied with their life than people of the Nonfamily group (Takahashi, Tamura, & Tokoro, 1997). These differences can be attributed to people's social representations within each generation (Moscovici, 1983, 2001). For example, if elderly people tend to have a social representation that ordinary citizens of her or his generation must have a family, then Nonfamily group people would underestimate their own life satisfaction as they lack close relationships with family members. In contrast, if college students have the cultural representation that many of their age-mates have a friend of the opposite gender, Family group youngsters would report lower life satisfaction if they have no such age-mate.

Differences in Life Stories. Another set of studies suggests that the framework of affective relationships functions as a filter both when people retrieve past experiences and when they anticipate their future life. In some of these studies among college students and elderly persons, we aimed to examine how the present framework served to encode and retrieve past experiences of social relationships when the participants narrated their life stories. It is hypothesized that an individual's framework serves to interpret her or his experiences of social interactions and induces the person to reconstruct and make sense of her or his life stories in ways that are consonant with the contents of the present representation of relationships. In short, we sought to test whether happy people would narrate happy life histories whereas unhappy persons would construct sad stories (Ochs & Capps, 1996, 2001; Ross & Buehler, 1994).

Specifically, we tested the following three hypotheses among elderly participants: a total of 134 (79 females and 55 males) over the age of 65. No one had any severe mental or physical disorders and all subjects were literate. The hypotheses were: (1) Lone Wolf type people who were living isolated from other people would focus less frequently on the positive and pleasant and more frequently on conflicts or difficulties in social interactions in their narratives than people who had a sufficient number of social relationships with family members and friends. This was because a Lone Wolf type framework would mostly highlight the negative side of one's life history; (2) in recounting their lives, elderly adults would mostly highlight their relationships with the focal figure at each stage from young childhood to the present; and (3) people would seldom refer to landmark events or turning points that had pushed them onto their pathways of life, because people would tend to construct their life stories in light of, and coherent with, their present framework.

The participants were individually assessed for their affective relationships types by the PART for elderly people, using the same procedure we had used with children. The participants were encouraged to tell their life stories with a focus on their social interactions from young childhood to the present. The narratives of the three types of elderly people, in this case 46 Spouse, 27 Friend, and 17 Lone Wolf types, were analyzed to determine whether each of 14 elements, such as the relationships with each of the family and nonfamily members, the life satisfaction, and the everyday feelings, were touched upon at least once in each life story.

We tested whether the Lone Wolf type participants narrated stories less frequently that concerned the positive and pleasant, and more frequently concerned conflicts or difficulties in social interactions with others, than their Spouse type and Friend type counterparts. The analyses indicate clear differences in the descriptions of the life stories between the Lone Wolf type and other types of participants. That is, Lone Wolf type people described social interactions, with every person both in the present and the past, more negatively and less positively than their Spouse type or Friend type counterparts. In addition, Lone Wolf type individuals often reported that they were not satisfied with their life, not self-confident, and not happy. In fact, 82% of the Lone Wolf types stated that they were not satisfied with their present lives. Most of them said that they felt sad and lonely every day. Moreover, 65% of them were identified as lacking trust in people.

They said that they could not believe other people and they were afraid of being cheated by them, and thus they did not try to develop close relationships with others. In contrast, 56–78% of the Spouse type and Friend type participants reported self-confidence, life-satisfaction, a happy everyday mood, or trust in human beings. In addition, as expected, the Spouse type and Friend type people more often reported pleasant interactions with others and especially with their focal figure. That is, 82–91% voiced positive current feelings and 82–83% did so in relating past experiences toward the focal figure. When we looked at negative descriptions of social interactions, a majority of the Lone Wolf types brought up conflicts, difficulties, or detachment in their present and past interactions with children, friends, and/or others. In contrast, the Spouse type participants did not often cite negative interactions with others, especially with family members, but Friend type people complained of problematic experiences with their children and spouse.

Finally, only 29–41% of the participants referred to landmark events or turning points that might be assumed to have constrained their developmental pathways to the way they experience present social relationships. Rather, the data suggested that each person coped with each life event in a way that reflected her or his individual framework. For example, regarding the same traumatic event, the loss of a child, a Lone Wolf type person said that he was too sad to recover from the separation even today, insisting that nobody could understand how bitter the experience had been. However, a Spouse type participant similarly expressed his sadness over his daughter's death, but at the same time referred to his wife's mental situation: "to the mother as she was, it must be even more heartaching than to me." He reported that after the death of their daughter, he and his wife regularly visited many temples together for a memorial service. He also added, "We appreciate and feel that our daughter is still with us."

In sum, the Lone Wolf type elderly people reported difficulties in maintaining well-being in their life stories. From young childhood to the present, their life stories highlighted mostly negative aspects of social relationships or human nature in the past, the present, and even the future. In contrast, Spouse type and Friend type participants highlighted their stories, both past and present, with pleasant, peaceful, and happy events, especially those involving the focal figure. Thus, the results suggest clear differences in narrations about their life among the types, although we have no evidence whether each type of the narrators interacted differently with those figures in the past and the present.

Similarly, Family group college students included in their life stories interactions with family members, whereas Nonfamily group (i.e., Friend type students) highlighted theirs with interactions with age-mates from young childhood to the present (Takahashi, 1989). Moreover, students of the two groups, especially male students, reported different strategies for coping with hypothetical future life events such as promotions, unemployment, marriage, childbirth, and illness. A greater proportion of Family group students anticipated that their parents would share life events with them; in contrast, Nonfamily group students preferred age-mates as supporters in their future life rather than family members (Kobayashi, 1993).

Thus, each affective relationships type can summarize and anticipate behaviors in a given social context. So far, our studies indicate that individuals' frameworks of affective relationships take very important roles in their interactions with new figures, adjustment to new environments, and narrations of their life stories.

Culture and Close Relationships

A popular conceptual framework, individualism versus collectivism, has often highlighted differences in human relationships between cultures. The individualism versus collectivism concept proposes to plot the various nations on a single continuum, with the two extremes, individualistic and collectivistic, at each end (Markus & Kitayama, 1991; Rothbaum, Pott, Azuma, Miyake, & Weisz, 2000; Triandis, 1995). In this framework, most Western nations are placed close to the individualistic end and Eastern nations near the collectivistic end. Many researchers are accustomed to this global framework of cross-cultural comparisons, although empirical studies and discussions have emerged that challenge this conceptualization of cultures (e.g., Befu, 1980; Gjerde & Onishi, 2000; Hirai, 1999; Hirai & Takahashi, 2000; Matsumoto, 1999; Takano & Osaka, 1999).

Our comparative study of close relationships between Americans and the Japanese, people who have often been considered as representative of individualistic and collectivistic nations, respectively, indicate that this popular framework may offer a heuristic comparative framework but doesn't do any more than that. In particular, when we performed a detailed comparison of the two cultural groups by the ARS, both commonalities and differences in close relationships across the cultures were found. Our findings indicated that nearly half of hypotheses that had been extracted from the individualism versus collectivism concept were true and the others were not only not true, but the people from the two countries were significantly different in the opposite direction (Takahashi et al., in press). These findings suggest that real characteristics of the cultural elements of close relationships are too complicated to describe or explain by the global dichotomous view of cultures.

Furthermore, there is disagreement among researchers about how to compare cultures. Cultural psychologists who are unsatisfied with the traditional cross-cultural comparisons accuse the conventional, direct comparisons of mean scores between cultures of being "methodological behaviorism" (e.g., Greenfield, 1997). In fact, it is from the direct comparisons of scores or frequencies that researchers have established the popular premise, "The Americans are more independent than their Japanese counterparts" (Cousins, 1989; Kashima, Yamaguchi, Kim, Choi, Gelfand, & Yuki, 1995; Triandis, 1989). However, this premise has not always been supported by other studies based on the same or similar questionnaires (Takano & Osaka, 1999). In fact, against the popular expectation, Americans expressed affective need more strongly toward all of the significant others than their Japanese counterparts in our study (Takahashi et al., in press).

Affective Relationships Types in Various Cultural Contexts

Cross-cultural comparisons by the affective relationships types, that is, comparisons of the relative status of each social figure in a personal framework, not the direct comparisons of means, have highlighted differences between the Japanese and American cultures. In this study, American ($N = 547$) and Japanese ($N = 808$) people 20 to 64 years of age were compared. Because the Americans rated significantly and highly as to most of significant others than their Japanese counterparts, we compared the combinations of the first two or three figures, instead of the distributions of the top figure, between the cultures. We found that the combinations of the top figures were very different between the two cultures. That is, among the Americans, the top two figures tended to be nonfamily members: 68% of females and 31% of males include a closest same-gender friend. Among the top three figures, 82% of females and 76% of males included a same-gender friend. In contrast, among the Japanese, a majority of the top two figures were composed of the spouse and a child (46% for females and 51% for males). Eighty-two percent of the top two figures and 60% of the top three figures consisted of only family members, including natural parents and children, and the spouse (Takahashi et al., in press).

These results suggest that the Japanese share a custom of being more concerned with biological, ascribed relationships than their American counterparts. Among the Japanese, the spouse, while not biologically related and initially an outsider, essentially becomes an organic part of the biological family. In contrast, the preference of same-gender friends among the Americans, especially among females, suggests that they are more free from the conventional family concept and more flexible in their selections of social figures than the Japanese, because it is assumed that friends are the most changeable social figures in that they can be added and subtracted at will. We can reasonably assume that sociocultural changes in the United States, urged by women's economic autonomy, the women's movement, and feminist theories, must have an effect on people's definition of family and on their selections of social figures.

Another cross-cultural comparison, between Korean and Japanese college students, indicates differences in the proportion of the appearances of types. That is, a larger number of the Korean students agreed with a traditional patriarchy than their Japanese counterparts. Consistent with their family-oriented beliefs, there was a larger number of Family group and a smaller number of Nonfamily group students (Friend types and Romantic partner types) in Korea than in Japan (Heo, 2000).

TOWARD A THEORY OF CLOSE RELATIONSHIPS

Recent research in close relationships is making advances toward a theory that describes three aspects of the essential nature of human relationships across the life span: (1) humans have multiple significant others to whom they assign different psychological roles; (2) individuals have their own representation of a framework of close relationships consisting of multiple social figures; and (3) there are individual patterns of the internal framework. However, to date, researchers have focused on one or two aspects of the nature of human relationships and have been limited to theorizing about how they are manifested in reality. We propose that social relationships should be conceptualized by integrating all three of the characteristics together. We have examined the ability of the affective relationships model to achieve this goal.

Typology of Close Relationships

To conceptualize an individual's close relationships, a typological analysis was performed. It may be controversial whether we can always identify the individuality of a person's relationships by their focal figures. However, to date, empirical research supports the idea that a typological analysis of affective relationships in terms of the focal figures is effective for understanding the following three groups of people possessing individual differences in social interactions throughout the life span.

First, we can differentiate the subjective representations of the social world held by Family group versus Nonfamily group people. In a given social context that requires certain kinds of social interactions, participants whose focal figures fit the appropriate context show advantages. For example, Nonfamily group (i.e., Friend type) students adjusted to college dormitory life where everyday interactions with age-mates are dominant more easily than their Family group counterparts, because their age-mate dominant framework helped them adjust to the context. Moreover, Friend type children skillfully interacted with an age-mate stranger, whereas Family group (i.e., Mother type) children did well with an adult stranger. Similarly, Family group and Nonfamily group participants retrieved their life experiences differently in centering on their focal figures, and anticipated their future life discriminately, based on their present frameworks. This view shares much in common with the goodness-of-fit model elaborated by Lerner, Baker, and Lerner (1985). Considering the observed match between a given social context and an individual's framework, typological analysis of the affective relationships model seems to be effective in helping us understand the superiority of different types in different situations.

Moreover, we can identify Lone Wolf type individuals using this analysis. The Lone Wolves, who lack sufficient social resources, from childhood to old age more often report maladjustment and dissatisfaction in their life than their Family group and Nonfamily group counterparts.

Universality and Cultural Specificity of the Theory and Assessment Instruments

Is the affective relationships model applicable to cultures other than the Japanese? Are the assessment instruments, the ARS and series of PARTs, useful for subjects in other cultures?

I definitely agree with others that theories and measurements are culture-bound to a large extent. In this vein, we believe that the theory and measurements developed by a Japanese female researcher will highlight different aspects of social relationships than those that have been emphasized using conventional male-dominant and Western-dominant devices. So far, based on the variety of the above-mentioned studies, I can claim that the theory and the assessment instruments of the affective relationships model clearly shed light upon both universal and specific aspects of close relationships across ages, genders, and nations.

It is universal that (1) humans have affective needs for others; (2) there are three major groups of affective relationship frameworks consisting of multiple significant others across cultures, that is, Family, Nonfamily, and Lone Wolf; and (3) the typological analyses can be used to differentiate the social interactions and representations of close relationships. The ARS and PARTs used in different cultures and subcultures will show that the frequencies of certain groups and also specific types vary with cultural conditions. Furthermore, if researchers consider broadening the ARS and the PARTs to include other potentially important social figures and functions for their own subjects who live in different social environments than Japan, they can find facts that are specific to their own culture.

FUTURE DIRECTIONS

The typological analyses shed new light on social relationships but also suggest important tasks for the future. First, we need to look deeper into the methodology for typological analyses; in particular, we need to understand how to identify types both qualitatively and statistically. I agree with others that the focal figures do not always necessarily represent the nature of an individual's framework. At present, we propose the top figure to be useful as a simple and heuristic indicator. Second, we need sufficient data of the ARS and the PARTs from various cultures and subcultures. These data must be indispensable for validating the theory and assessment instruments.

For this purpose, I will draw researchers' attention to the fact that they can flexibly apply the assessment instruments to their cultures by including important figures and functions for their own subjects. Such modifications of both figures and functions will widen the cultural applicability of these measurements to other cultures, and show how close relationships are constrained by sociocultural factors. Third, we cannot yet fully explain why each person constructs one type of affective relationships framework but not another. In particular, we are not sure why nearly 10% of persons across all ages are not very interested in humans, identified here as the Lone Wolf type, against the basic assumption that humans are social. We hope that our ongoing longitudinal research focusing on development of affective relationships and various kinds of developmental niches finds some answers to the questions. Endeavors in these tasks will advance our understanding of the nature of social relationships.

Author's Note

The author is deeply indebted to Giyoo Hatano for his providing constructive and wide-ranging comments on the research and earlier drafts of this manuscript.

References

Ainsworth, M. D. S., Blehar, M. C., Waters, E., & Wall, S. (1978). *Patterns of attachment: A psychological study of the strange situation.* Hillsdale, NJ: Erlbaum.

Antonucci, T. C. (1985). Personal characteristics, social support, and social behavior. In R. H. Binstock & E. Shanas (Eds.), *Handbook of aging and the social sciences* (2nd ed., pp. 94–128). New York: von Nostrand Reinhold.

Antonucci, T. C., & Akiyama, H. (1987). An examination of sex differences in social support among older men and women. *Sex Roles, 17,* 737–749.

Antonucci, T. C., Fuhrer, R., & Dartigues, J. F. (1997). Social relations and depressive symptomatology in a sample of community-dwelling French older adults. *Psychology and Aging, 12,* 189–195.

Antonucci, T. C., & Jackson, J. (1987). Social support, interpersonal efficacy, and health: A life course perspective. In L. L. Carstensen & B. A. Edelstein (Eds.), *Handbook of clinical gerontology* (pp. 291–311). Elmsford, NY: Pergamon Press.

Asher, S. R., Hymel, S., & Renshaw, P. D. (1984). Loneliness in children. *Child Development, 55,* 1456–1464.

Baldwin, M. W. (1992). Relational schemas and the processing of social information. *Psychological Bulletin, 112,* 461–484.

Barrera, M., Jr. (1986). Distinctions between social support concepts, measures and models. *American Journal of Community Psychology, 14,* 413–441.

Barrera, M., Jr., & Ainslay, S. L. (1983). The structure of social support: A conceptual and empirical analysis. *Journal of Community Psychology, 11*, 133–143.

Befu, H. (1980). A critique of the group model of Japanese society. *Social Analysis, 5/6*, 29–43.

Belle, D. (Ed.) (1989). *Children's social network and social support*. New York: Wiley.

Berman, W. H. (1988). The role of attachment in the post-divorce experience. *Journal of Personality and Social Psychology, 54*, 496–503.

Bowlby, J. (1969/1982). *Attachment and loss: Vol. 1. Attachment*. New York: Basic Books.

Bowlby, J. (1973). *Attachment and loss: Vol. 2. Separation*. New York: Basic Books.

Bowlby, J. (1980). *Attachment and loss: Vol. 3. Loss*. New York: Basic Books.

Bretherton, I. (1985). Attachment theory: Retrospect and prospect. *Monographs of the Society for Research in Child Development, 50* (1–2), 3–35.

Bretherton, I. (1993). From dialogue to internal working models: The co-construction of self in relationships. In C. A. Nelson (Ed.), *Memory and affect in development: The Minnesota symposia on child development, Vol. 26* (pp. 237–263). Hillsdale, NJ: Erlbaum.

Bretherton, I., & Waters, E. (Eds.) (1985). Growing points of attachment theory and research. *Monographs of the Society and Research in Child Development, 50* (1–2), Serial No. 209.

Cassidy, J., & Shaver, P. R. (Eds.) (1999). *Handbook of attachment: Theory, research, and clinical applications*. New York: Guilford.

Cousins, S. D. (1989). Cuture and self-perception in Japan and the United States. *Journal of Personality and Social Psychology, 56*, 124–131.

Davila, J., Burge, D., & Hammen, C. (1997). Why does attachment style change? *Journal of Personality and Social Psychology, 73*, 826–838.

Dodge, K. A., Pettit, G. S., McClasky, C. L., & Brown, M. M. (1986). Social competence in children. *Monographs of the Society and Research in Child Development, 51* (1).

Feiring, C., & Lewis, M. (1989). The social networks of girls from early through middle childhood. In Belle, D. (Ed.), *Children's social networks and social supports* (pp. 119–150). New York: Wiley.

Feiring, C., & Lewis, M. (1991). The transition from middle childhood to early adolescence: Gender differences in the social network and perceived self-competence. *Sex Roles, 24*, 489–509.

Fukui, S. (1999). Stability and change of social relationships among cancer patients. Unpublished manuscript.

Furman, W., & Buhrmester, D. (1985). Children's perceptions of the personal relationships in their social networks. *Developmental Psychology, 21*, 1016–1024.

Furman, W., Simon, V. A., Shaffer, L., & Bouchey, H. A. (2002). Adolescents' working models and styles for relationships with parents, friends, and romantic partners. *Child Development, 73*, 241–255.

George, C., Kaplan, N., & Main, M. (1996). Adult attachment interview protocol. Unpublished manuscript, University of California, Berkeley.

Gjerde, P. F., & Onishi, M. (2000). Selves, culture, and nations: The psychological imagination of "the Japanese" in the era of globalization. *Human Development, 43*, 216–226.

Greenfield, P. M. (1997). Culture as process: Empirical methods for cultural psychology. In J. W. Berry, Y. H. Poortinga, & J. Pandy (Eds.), *Handbook of cross-cultural psychology, Vol. 1 Theory and method*, 2nd ed. (pp. 301–346). Boston: Allyn and Bacon.

Hamanoue, K. (1999). Changes and stability of social relationships among middle-aged persons: A two-year longitudinal study in an island. Unpublished manuscript.

Hazan, C., & Shaver, P. (1987). Romantic love conceptualized as an attachment process. *Journal of Personality and Social Psychology, 52*, 511–524.

Hazan, C., & Shaver, P. (1990). Love and work: An attachment-theoretical perspective. *Journal of Personality and Social Psychology, 59*, 270–280.

Heo, K.-O. (2000). Cross-cultural comparisons of social relationships between Korean and Japanese college students. Unpublished manuscript.

Hesse, E. (1999). The adult attachment interview: Historical and current perspectives. In J. Cassidy & P. R. Shaver (Eds.), *Handbook of attachment: Theory, research, and clinical applications* (pp. 395–433). New York: Guilford.

Hinde, R. A. (1981). The base of a science of interpersonal relationships. In S. Duck & R. Gilmour (Eds.), *Personal relationships I: Studying personal relationships* (pp. 1–22). London: Academic Press.

Hirai, M. (1999). Stereotypical views of the Japanese: Differences between myself and others. *Japanese Journal of Experimental Social Psychology, 39*, 103–113 (in Japanese).

Hirai, M., & Takahashi, K. (2000). When your benefit and mine clash: Mental negotiations between selves and others. In G. Hatano, N. Okada, & H. Tanabe (Eds.), *Affective minds: The 13th Toyota conference* (pp. 153–156). Amsterdam: Elsevier.

Iida, A. (2000). Reciprocal social relationships as buffers of life stress among elderly people. *Journal of Health Psychology, 13*, 29–40 [in Japanese].

Inoue, M., & Takahashi, K. (1999, September). Affective relationships types and adjustment to college life. Paper presented at the Meeting of Japanese Psychological Association.

Inoue, M., & Takahashi, K. (2000). Assessing types of social relationships among elementary schoolchildren. *Journal of Japanese Educational Psychology, 48*, 75–84 (in Japanese).

Inoue, M., & Takahashi, K. (2001, November). Developmental transformation of affective types among young children. Paper presented at the Japanese Psychological Meeting.

Jones, D. C., & Vaughan, K. (1990). Close friendships among senior adults. *Psychology and Aging, 5*, 451–457.

Kahn, R. L., & Antonucci, T. C. (1980). Convoys over the life course: Attachment, roles, and social support. In P. B. Baltes & O. B. Brim (Eds.), *Life-span development and behavior*, Vol. 3 (pp. 253–268). New York: Academic Press.

Kashima, Y., Yamaguchi, S., Kim, U., Choi, S.-C., Gelfand, M. J., & Yuki, M. (1995). Culture, gender, and self: A perspective from individualism-collectivism research. *Journal of Personality and Social Psychology, 72*, 1245–1267.

Kobak, R. R., & Hazan, C. (1991). Attachment in marriage: Effects of security and accuracy of working models. *Journal of Personality and Social Psychology, 60*, 861–869.

Kobayashi, K. (1993). Coping with future life events among college students: The role of a preestablished personal framework in the planning future. Unpublished manuscript.

Krause, N. (1987). Life stress, social support, and self-esteem in an elderly population. *Psychology and Aging, 2,* 349–356.

Lang, F. R., & Carstensen, L. L. (1994). Close emotional relationships in later life: Further support for proactive aging in the social domain. *Psychology and Aging, 9,* 315–324.

Lang, F. R., Staudinger, U. M., & Carstensen, L. L. (1998). Perspectives on socioemotional selectivity in late life: How personality and social context do (and do not) make a difference. *Journal of Gerontology: Psychological Science, 53B,* 21–30.

Lerner, J. V., Baker, N., & Lerner, R. M. (1985). A person-context goodness of fit model of adjustment. In P. C. Kendall (Ed.), *Advances in cognitive-behavioral research and therapy,* Vol. 4 (pp. 111–136). New York: Academic Press.

Levitt, M. J. (2001, April). Patterns of social support in middle childhood and early adolescence: Implications for adjustment. Paper presented at the meeting of the Society for Research in Child Development, Minneapolis, MN.

Levitt, M. J., Guacci-Franco, N., & Levitt, J. L. (1993). Convoys of social support in childhood and early adolescence: Structure and function. *Developmental Psychology, 29,* 811–818.

Levitt, M. J., Weber, R. A., & Guacci, N. (1993). Convoys of social support: An intergenerational analysis. *Psychology and Aging, 8,* 323–326.

Lewis, M. (1982). The social network model. In T. M. Field, A. Huston, H. C. Quary, L. Troll, & G. E. Finley (Eds.), *Review of human development* (pp. 180–214). New York: Wiley.

Lewis, M. (Ed.). (1984). *Beyond the dyad.* New York: Plenum.

Lewis, M., & Feiring, C. (1979). The child's social network: Social objects, social functions, and their relationship. In M. Lewis & L. Rosenblum (Eds.), *The child and its family: The genesis of behavior,* Vol. 2 (pp. 9–27). New York: Plenum.

Litwin, H. (2000). Social network type and social support among the old-old. *Journal of Aging Studies, 14,* 213–228.

Litwin, H. (2001). Social network type and morale in old age. *The Gerontologist, 41,* 516–524.

Main, M. (1994, July). A move to the level of representation in the study of attachment organization: Implication for psychoanalysis. Annual lecture to the British Psycho-Analytical Society, London.

Main, M., & Goldwyn, R. (1998). Adult attachment scoring and classification systems. Unpublished scoring manual. University of California, Berkeley.

Main, M., & Kaplan, N., & Cassidy, J. (1985). Security in infancy, childhood, and adulthood: A move to the level of representation. *Monographs of the Society for Research in Child Development, 50* (1–2), 66–104.

Main, M. & Solomon, J. (1990). Procedures for identifying infants as disorganized/disoriented during the Ainsworth strange situation. In M. T. Greenberg, D. Cicchetti, & E. M. Cummings (Eds.), *Attachment in the preschool years: Theory, research, and intervention* (pp. 121–160). Chicago: University of Chicago Press.

Markus, H. R., & Kitayama, S. (1991). Culture and self: Implications for cognition, emotion, and motivation. *Psychological Review, 98,* 224–253.

Matsumoto, D. (1999). Culture and self: An empirical assessment of Markus and Kitayama's theory of independence and interdependence self-construals. *Asian Journal of Social Psychology, 2,* 289–310.

Moscovici, S. (1983). The phenomenon of social representations. In R. M. Farr & S. Moscovici (Eds.), *Social representations* (pp. 3–69). Cambridge: Cambridge University Press.

Moscovici, S. (2001). *Social representations.* New York: New York University Press.

Nagata, C., & Suzuki, M. (1983). Development of interpersonal relationships among kindergarten children. Unpublished manuscript.

Nelson, K. (1986). *Event knowledge: Structure and function in development.* Hillsdale, NJ: Erlbaum.

Ochs, E., & Capps, L. (1996). Narrating the self. *Annual Review of Anthropology, 25,* 19–43.

Ochs, E., & Capps, L. (2001). *Living narratives: Creating lives in everyday storytelling.* Cambridge: Harvard University Press.

Parker, J. G., & Gottman, J. M. (1989). Social and emotional development in relational context: Friendship interaction from early childhood to adolescence. In T. J. Berndt & G. W. Ladd (Eds.), *Peer relationships in child development* (pp. 95–131). New York: Wiley.

Piaget, J. (1954). *The construction of reality in the child.* New York: Academic Press.

Pierce, G. R., Sarason, R., & Sarason, I. G. (Eds.). (1996). *Handbook of social support and the family.* New York: Plenum.

Rempel, J. K., Holmes, J. G., & Zanna, M. P. (1985). Trust in close relationships. *Journal of Personality and Social Psychology, 49,* 95–112.

Rook, K. S. (1987). Reciprocity of social exchange and social satisfaction among older women. *Journal of Personality and Social Psychology, 52,* 145–154.

Rosenberg, M. (1965). *Society and the adolescent self-image.* Princeton: Princeton University Press.

Ross, M., & Buehler, R. (1994). Creative remembering. In U. Neisser & R. Fivush (Eds.), *The remembering self* (pp. 205–235). New York: Cambridge University Press.

Rotenberg, K. J., & Hymel, S. (1999). *Loneliness in childhood and adolescence.* New York: Cambridge University Press.

Rothbaum, F., Pott, M., Azuma, H., Miyake, K., & Weisz, J. (2000). The development of close relationships in Japan and the United States: Paths of symbiotic harmony and generative tension. *Child Development, 71,* 1121–1142.

Schank, R. C., & Abelson, R. P. (1977). *Scripts, plans, goals and understanding.* Hillsdale, NJ: Erlbaum.

Scharfe, E., & Bartholomew, K. (1994). Reliability and stability of adult attachment patterns. *Personal Relationships, 1,* 23–43.

Shaver, P. R., Hazen, C., & Bradshaw, D. (1988). Love as attachment: The integration of three behavioral systems. In R. J. Sternberg & M. L. Barnes (Eds.), *The psychology of love* (pp. 29–70). New Haven, CT: Yale University Press.

Sherer, M., Maddox, J. E., Mercandante, B., Printice-Dunn, S., Jacobs, B., & Rogers, R. W. (1982). The self-efficacy scale: Construction and validation. *Psychological Reports, 51,* 663–671.

Shulman, S., & Scharf, M. (2000). Adolescent romantic behaviors and perceptions: Age- and gender-related differences, and links with family and peer relationships. *Journal of Research on Adolescence, 10,* 99–118.

Solomon, J., & George, C. (1999). *Attachment disorganization*. New York: Guilford.

Takahashi, K. (1973). Development of attachment relationships among female young adults. *Annual review of Japanese developmental psychology*, Vol. 12 (pp. 255–275). Tokyo: Kaneko-Shobo [in Japanese].

Takahashi, K. (1974). Development of dependency among female adolescents and young adults. *Japanese Psychological Research*, *16*, 179–185.

Takahashi, K. (1978/2000). The measurement of affective relationships among young children. Unpublished manuscript. University of the Sacred Heart.

Takahashi, K. (1986). The role of personal framework of social relationships in socialization studies. In H. Azuma, H. Stevenson, & K. Hakuta (Eds.), *Child development and education in Japan* (pp. 123–134). New York: Freeman.

Takahashi, K. (1989, April). Personal history differences between family pattern and age-mate pattern affective relationships among female college students. Paper presented at the meeting of the Society for Research in Child Development, Kansas City, MO.

Takahashi, K. (1990a). Affective relationships and their lifelong development. In P. B. Baltes, D. L. Featherman, & R. M. Lerner (Eds.), *Life-span development and behavior* Vol. 10 (pp. 1–27). Hillsdale, NJ: Erlbaum.

Takahashi, K. (1990b, July). Changes and stability in affective relationships of late adolescence: A short-term longitudinal study. Paper presented at International Conference on Personal Relationships, Oxford.

Takahashi, K. (1997, April). Friends versus Mothers: The role of preestablished relationships in children's joint problem solving. Paper presented at the meeting of the Society for Research in Child Development, Washington, DC.

Takahashi, K. (2002). Assessing close relationships across the life span: Constructing and validating the Affective Relationships Scale and the Picture Affective Relationships Test. *Monographs of University of the Sacred Heart*, *98*, 101–131 [in Japanese].

Takahashi, K., & Inoue, M. (2001, April). Types of social relationships and psychological adjustment in middle childhood: Mother type versus Friend type versus Lone Wolf type. Paper presented at the meeting of the Society for Research in Child Development, Minneapolis.

Takahashi, K., & Majima, N. (1994). Transition from home to college dormitory: The role of preestablished affective relationships in adjustment to a new life. *Journal of Research on Adolescence*, *4*, 367–384.

Takahashi, K., & Ohara, N. (1997, April). Are the Japanese more interdependent?: A cross-cultural perspective on social relationships. Paper presented at the meeting of the Society for Research in Child Development, Washington, DC.

Takahashi, K., Ohara, N., Antonucci, T., & Akiyama, H. (in press). Commonalities and differences in close relationships among the Americans and the Japanese: A comparison by the individualism/Collectivism concept. *International Journal of Behavioral Development*.

Takahashi, K., & Sakamoto, K. (2000). Assessing social relationships in adolescents and adults: Constructing and validating the Affective Relationships Scale. *International Journal of Behavioral Development*, *24*, 451–463.

Takahashi, K., Tamura, J., & Tokoro, M. (1997). Patterns of social relationships and psychological well-being among the elderly. *International Journal of Behavioral Development*, *21*, 417–430.

Takahashi, K., & Yokosuka, A. (1997, November). Types of affective relationships and psychological well-being among Japanese elderly adults. Paper presented at the 50th Annual Scientific Meetings of the Gerontological Society of America, Cincinnati.

Takano, Y., & Osaka, E. (1999). An unsupported common view: Comparing Japan and the U.S. on individualism/collectivism. *Asian Journal of Social Psychology, 2*, 311–341.

Triandis, H. C. (1989). The self and social behavior in differing cultural contexts. *Psychological Review, 96*, 506–520.

Triandis, H. C. (1995). *Individualism and collectivism*. Boulder: Westview Press.

Urberg, K. A., Degirmencioglu, S. M., Tolson, J. M., & Halliday-Scher, K. (1995). The structure of adolescent peer networks. *Developmental Psychology, 31*, 540–547.

Weiss, R. (1974). The provisions of social relationships. In Z. Rubin (Ed.), *Doing unto others* (pp. 17–26). Englewood Cliffs, NJ: Prentice-Hall.

Wenger, G. C. (1991). A network typology: From theory to practice. *Journal of Aging Studies, 5*, 147–162.

Wenger, G. C. (1996). Social networks and gerontology. *Reviews in Clinical Gerontology, 6*, 285–293.

Yee, P. L., Santoro, K. E., Paul, J. S., & Rosenbaum, L. B. (1996). Information processing approaches to the study of relationship and social support schemata. In G. R. Pierce, B. R. Sarason, & I. G. Sarason (Eds.), *Handbook of social support and the family* (pp. 25–42). New York: Plenum.

7

Friendship across the Life Span: Reciprocity in Individual and Relationship Development

Rosemary Blieszner and Karen A. Roberto

The chapter addresses the intersection of individual development and relationship development within the context of friendship. Friendship structures, functions, interactional processes, and outcomes change from infancy to old age according to developmental progression in physical, social, and psychological aspects of being and in conjunction with situational contexts of life. Friend relationships proceed along a continuum of intimacy from acquaintanceship or friendly relations, to casual friendship, to close friendship and reflect phases of existence from initiation to maintenance to dissolution. Based on a developmental theory, we compare friendship processes and outcomes at multiple stages of the life span. The chapter concludes with recommendations for future research on friendship from a life-span perspective.

In Western cultures, friendship is usually defined as a voluntary relationship that encompasses intimacy, equality, shared interests, and pleasurable or need-satisfying interactions. In contrast to family or even neighbor relationships, scholars view friendship as a noninstitutionalized relationship for which the norms are self-defined and fairly loose. Ordinarily, friendship is neither ritualized nor celebrated in the ways that kin ties are formalized. Although it is important to note that in other cultures friendship is more formally defined and institutionalized than in the West, and that friendships in the West actually *are* constrained by social structure and norms, we will not discuss friendship from that perspective here (see Blieszner & Adams, 1992, for that analysis). Rather, we will adopt the typical Western definition of friendship as an informal voluntary relationship, and focus attention on the meanings and functions of friendship across the life span.

Individual Development and the Influence of Relationships

Although seminal discussions of a life-span perspective on human development can actually be traced back to the late 1700s and early 1800s, empirical assessment of developmental processes has a more recent history. Investigations conducted in the late nineteenth century and first half of the twentieth century focused on distinct stages of life, usually childhood and less frequently old age, before the modern conception of life-span developmental frameworks emerged in the 1970s (Baltes & Goulet, 1970; Munnichs & Olbrich, 1985). Life-span developmental theory embraces principles addressing the potential for change throughout life, the multidirectionality of developmental change, the joint occurrence of both developmental gains and developmental losses throughout life, the diversity and modifiability of developmental processes, the influence of sociohistorical and cultural contexts on development, and the multidimensionality of influences on development (Baltes, 1987; Hoyer & Rybash, 1996). Most of the early studies of development examined attributes at the individual level of analysis.

Extending these notions to the connection between individual development and close relationships requires turning to social psychology for historical antecedents of contemporary research approaches. Assessment of the influence of social relationships on personal development has theoretical roots in the work of George Herbert Mead, who elaborated ideas about the self proposed by William James and Charles Horton Cooley in the 1890s and early 1900s. According to Mead (1934), the self develops through language, play, and organized social activities. By participating in social processes, trying on various roles, and recognizing the attitudes and responses of others, individuality emerges (Deutsch & Krauss, 1965). Relationships provide contexts in which many personal skills and competencies are developed (Collins, 1997; Collins & Laursen, 2000). Significant others serve as cognitive, social, and affective resources that promote and challenge development throughout life (Lang, 2001). Both individuals and relationships evolve within cultural contexts that differentially shape personal attributes and emergent interactional dynamics (Lewin, 1948). A person's expressions of acquaintanceship and friendship thus do not occur randomly, but rather are influenced by internalized cultural norms and expectations.

Relationship Development and the Influence of Partners

Views of relationships as developing entities and examination of the influence of individuals on relationship characteristics and processes have a more recent theoretical and empirical basis, stemming from the emergence of the multidisciplinary field of personal relationships studies in the 1980s (Duck & Gilmour, 1981; Hinde, 1979; Kelley et al., 1983a). Personal dispositions, along with relational dynamics and situational contexts, became recognized as important causal conditions that affect interactions and relationships (Berscheid & Peplau, 1983), including such important phase-related processes as initial attraction, interpersonal perceptions and attributions, displays of emotion, methods of handling conflict, self-disclosure, exchanges, and feelings of satisfaction (Auhagen & Hinde, 1997). As individuals develop and refine their physical, cognitive, social, and emotional skills and abilities, their changing capacities as relationship partners affect the properties of their close relationships (Hartup & Laursen, 1993; Kelley et al., 1983b).

Personal relationships themselves became recognized as developing, not static, entities (Adams & Blieszner, 1994; Fehr, 1996). They evolve along a continuum of intimacy from mere acquaintanceship to very close friendship and deeply loving family relationships. Contemporary research on relationship development processes and the impact of individuals on relationships includes, for example, inquiry into the effects of self-disclosure on relationship formation (Dindia, 1997) and study of how each partner's friends affect the marital relationship (Milardo & Helms-Erikson, 2000).

Friendship as the Ideal Relationship for Studying Reciprocal Developmental Influences

As researchers turned from laboratory experiments on isolated attitudes to more ecologically valid investigations of actual relationships, they tended to focus on heterosexual dating and marital relationships. This body of research, though well developed and providing useful insights, represents an incomplete picture of the reciprocal influences of individuals and relationships on one another. Not everyone dates or gets married. Moreover, family relationships, whether constituted by blood or legal ties, entail particular norms and obligations that influence their structure, dynamics, and longevity. Friendship, as a voluntary tie in which people can participate with multiple others simultaneously, and as a relationship that can be present throughout life, provides a unique context for studying reciprocal individual and relationship influences. It provides a pervasive enduring relational milieu in which to examine the intersections of multiple aspects of personal development (physical, cognitive, emotional, social, personality), life stage experiences (during infancy, childhood, adolescence, early adulthood, middle adulthood, and late adulthood), and relationship phases (initiation, maintenance, and dissolution). Indeed, Brown (1991) called it an "ageless relationship" and Matthews (1986) demonstrated the utility of linking analysis of friendship over the life course with analysis of personal developmental transitions.

We note a caveat, however. Many models of individual development and of friendship have limited external validity from a life-span perspective because they are age-restricted. Researchers have seldom examined questions relating to development or friendship through the use of either age comparisons or longitudinal designs; instead they have tended to focus on cross-sectional studies of friendships at a specific life stage. Moreover, perhaps because developmental changes occur most rapidly and are most visible during childhood and adolescence, theorists and researchers have given greater attention to the details of development in the early stages of life. Just as gerontologists drove the formulation of life-span models of development with their questions about antecedents of the behaviors they observed in adulthood and old age (Munnichs & Olbrich, 1985), gerontologists seem to be the intellectual leaders of the movement to examine close relationships from a life-span point of view (e.g., Adams & Blieszner, 1994; Carstensen, Isaacowitz, & Charles, 1999; Lang, 2001; Sherman, de Vries, & Lansford, 2000). The existing conceptual and empirical limitations restrict the research examples that we can present in this analysis. Nevertheless, we believe that useful advances in understanding both personal development and relationship development can be gained from an integrated life-span focus on friendship as opposed to studying relationships only at discrete stages of life.

A LIFE-SPAN DEVELOPMENTAL PERSPECTIVE ON FRIENDSHIP

Taking a life-span perspective on friendship requires theoretical models of individual development and of relationship development. Because study of individual development has a long-standing history, it is easy to find theory relevant to consideration of the connection between personal changes and relationships such as friendship. Erikson's (1950) model of psychosocial development is particularly useful because it provides a theoretical framework for examining individual stability and change in all stages of life. In contrast, theorizing about relationship development is a much newer endeavor, and fewer theoretical guides exist. We offer the Adams and Blieszner (1994; Blieszner & Adams, 1992) conceptualization of relationship structures, processes, and phases as a potential framework for analyzing friendship development across all levels of closeness. We provide an overview of these complementary organizing schemes, and then demonstrate their intersection with research examples. Because readers are more likely to be familiar with Erikson's theory of psychosocial development than with relationship development concepts, we spend relatively more time explaining the latter than the former.

Psychosocial Development

Erikson's (1950) theory of psychosocial development highlights the challenges individuals face as they proceed through the life cycle. In each stage of development, people strive to achieve a creative balance between opposing tensions, using their own instinctive energies and a widening radius of interpersonal relations (Erikson, Erikson, & Kivnick, 1989/1994). As individuals face the focal challenge of each life stage, they also engage in the anticipation of future challenges, reexperience tensions that were inadequately integrated at an earlier stage of life, and reexamine events that were appropriately integrated in the past but are no longer adequate explanations or solutions in their current stage of life. When presenting this framework, Erikson (1982) noted that individual development could not be adequately understood apart from the personal and social contexts in which it comes to fruition. Thus, how individuals respond to these challenges and develop a sense of well-being is strongly influenced by their physical and cognitive abilities, societal norms, and interactions with others.

During the first stage of life, infants learn to depend on their own senses and the trustworthiness of their parents or primary caretakers. Although relationships with others outside of immediate caretakers are at best tangential, the development of trust in self and others during infancy is essential for the development of future relationships, including those with friends. Through simple give-and-take interactions with others, including their peers, toddlers begin to develop a sense of will as they balance the need for autonomy with feelings of shame and doubt.

The third stage of psychosocial development, frequently referred to as the "play age," emerges from more complex and reciprocal interactions with family members and friends. During this stage, preschoolers learn to pursue personal initiative while at the same time balancing the needs and wants of others in their social network. Next, school-age children confront the developmental tension of industry and inferiority. Friends supply emotional support and interpersonal validation that may facilitate children's abilities to adjust and adapt to the challenging demands of school. The sixth stage of development emerges in adolescence, with its basic tension between development of a sense of psychosocial identity and its interplay with role confusion. As individuals proceed through the various stages of adolescence, their friend networks expand and they become more autonomous and independent of their parents.

From the ideological commitments of adolescence emerge intimate connections in adulthood. Young adults strive to balance the need for and risks associated with intimacy as they develop the capacity for commitment to lasting friendships and romantic relationships. In middle adulthood, individuals face the challenges of generativity, or the need to take care of what is being procreated, produced, and created. Friendships provide numerous opportunities for persons to engage in generative activities. During the final stage of development, elders strive for integrity in the face of declining personal resources. Older adults often rely on their friends to serve as guides and companions as they proceed through life's concluding journey (Erikson et al., 1989/1994).

Increases in life expectancy have brought to the forefront additional psychosocial issues not addressed in the original model. Joan Erikson suggested a ninth stage of development (Erikson & Erikson, 1997) in which individuals in advanced old age face new demands, reevaluations, and daily difficulties. As specific life challenges and pleasures are reframed by the inevitabilities of time, interactions between friends may diminish or change, but the emotional closeness developed over time sustains these supportive relationships into very old age (Johnson & Troll, 1994).

Friendship Phases

Just as human development begins with conception, transpires through a variety of experiences and life stages over time, and ends with death, so does development of a relationship have a beginning, a middle, and an ending. Close relationships such as friendship proceed along a continuum of phases, starting with initiation (from acquaintance to casual friend), enduring throughout the maintenance phase (wherein occurs stability, increase or decrease in closeness, and other attributes), and ending with dissolution (termination of the relationship by choice or happenstance). Just as personal developmental trajectories are highly differential and influenced by multiple causal conditions as expressed by life-span developmental theories (Baltes, 1987; Erikson, 1950, 1982), so are relationship trajectories unique across people and relationships. Some friendships grow to deep closeness and persist for decades, others remain casual or are short-lived. Some friendships follow a smooth and gradually increasing pathway of self-disclosure and expressions of trust, others sustain peaks of conflict and discord that restrict closeness and render them vulnerable to suspension. As these examples illustrate, phases of friendship take place over time and encompass a range of structural and interactional outcomes (Adams & Blieszner, 1994; Blieszner & Adams, 1992).

Levinger (1983) conceptualized a five-step developmental sequence for close relationships that can be applied to the phases of friendship. The sequence begins with awareness of or acquaintance with another person, and then continues in what Levinger called the "buildup" of the relationship. Next is continuation or consolidation of the relationship in a relatively durable state. At some point, deterioration or decline in closeness might occur. Ultimately, relationships end through some form of separation or dissolution, or because of the death of one or both partners. In friendship, transitions from one step in the sequence to another are fostered by differential communication strategies (Sias & Cahill, 1998), changes in the amount and breadth of interactions (Hays, 1985), deepening attraction and trust (VanLear & Trujillo, 1986), and, in the case of deterioration, diverging interests and lifestyles or major breaches of friendship norms (Blieszner & Adams, 1998; Wiseman, 1986).

Initiation. According to Foa and Foa's theory of resource exchange (1974), not only must potential friends be aware of one another and motivated to become involved in a relationship, but also certain conditions are required for close relationships to evolve from acquaintanceships. Therefore, in order for potential friends to discover whether they like each other and share valued attributes and interests, it is necessary for them to have repeated interactions, meet in dyads or very small groups, have an appropriate degree of privacy, and interact frequently enough and for a long enough duration to enable them to become comfortable with one another. In the presence of these conditions, the interaction processes that contribute to friendship initiation – such as perceptual judgments of attractiveness and likeability, communication of personal information, and expressions of compatibility – can emerge (Blieszner & Adams, 1992).

Maintenance. Relationship maintenance entails continuing the relationship at a fairly stable level of intimacy, in good relational repair, and in a condition that is satisfactory to the partners (Dindia, 2000). A wide variety of interactional processes and situational conditions build up and consolidate relationships in the maintenance phase. Chief among these are perceptions of similarity on key attributes, discovery of mutually shared interests, forms of self-disclosure deemed appropriate for the type of friendship, intentional efforts to sustain the relationship, emergent feelings of trust and affection, expressions of social and emotional support, and effective strategies for resolving any disagreements (Blieszner, 1995; Blieszner & Adams, 1992; Fehr, 1996; Rawlins, 1994).

As would be expected from the definition of friendship as a voluntary tie, most continuing friendships encompass positive interactions and relationship satisfaction. Even so, discovery of undesirable characteristics of the friend or features of the friendship does not necessarily lead to dissolution of the relationship, although it might diminish feelings of closeness or trust, or frequency of contact. Within the maintenance phase, friendships can be sustained at a range of emotional closeness, from very casual to closest or best friend. Events and situations, as well as developmental changes in the partners, can lead to increases or decreases of affection, confiding, or other attributes of friendship over time. In other words, continuation of a friendship does not necessarily mean that all of its features are stable (Adams & Blieszner, 1998; Blieszner & Adams, 1998).

Dissolution. Friendships end for a variety of reasons, besides incapacitation or death of partners. These include benign neglect, changes in preferences and interests, situational constraints, unresolved conflicts, overt actions such as betrayal, and conservation of emotional energy in the face of physical decline. The strategies used to end relationships purposefully seem to vary by age group (presumably reflecting relational experience), although few studies of friendship endings have been conducted (Blieszner & Adams, 1992, 1998; Carstensen et al., 1999; Fehr, 1996; Rose, 1984).

Influences on Relationship Development. Aside from the interaction processes and environmental and situational conditions that promote or impede movement from one friendship phase to another, key influences on friendship phases are the developmental maturity and social skills possessed by the friend partners. Hallmarks of successful progress in both arenas would be positive resolution of the developmental challenges posed by Erikson – progression through the stages of life with physical and psychological resilience, gains in characteristics and capabilities that foster successful resolution of relational challenges involved in creating and sustaining friendship networks, and loss of characteristics and behaviors that interfere with relational goals.

FRIENDSHIP ACROSS THE LIFE SPAN

In the following section, we review key findings related to the intersections of personal and relationship development within friendship at each stage of life. Note that most of the studies focus on ongoing friendships, which we locate in the maintenance phase. Relatively few scholars have addressed friendship formation and dissolution or transitions from one phase of friendship to another. Moreover, most research on young adulthood stems from samples of college students, such that little is known about friendships of other young adults. Likewise, few studies focus specifically on the middle years of adulthood, particularly compared to the extent of research on friendship in the later years. Despite these uneven features of the friendship literature, we still have a wealth of resources upon which to draw for illustrating reciprocal developmental influences between individuals and their friend relationships.

Friendship before Adulthood

Investigators of friendship in infancy, childhood, and adolescence have concerned themselves with assessing the effects of physical, cognitive, social, and emotional dimensions of development on friend relationships. They have also examined the ways that social institutions such as families and schools affect friend interactions (Minuchin & Shapiro, 1983).

The literature contains analyses of the benefits of friendship for enhancing development and the problems associated with personal and situational characteristics that interfere with having positive friendships (Crosnoe, 2000). Compared to these foci, relatively few studies yield information on specific strategies that children and youth use to establish, maintain, and end friendships.

Infancy and Childhood. By definition, friendship is a voluntary relationship that, we argue, contributes to and supports individual development. As such, interactions among peers in infancy and very early childhood do not completely meet this definition. The potential for relationships in young childhood is embedded in a nexus of other relationships that influence their course (Hinde & Stevenson-Hinde, 1986). Adults regulate social opportunities, select the contexts, and orchestrate subsequent interactions because infants and toddlers do not possess the physical or cognitive capabilities needed to initiate and maintain voluntary relationships. However, the benefits of these friend-like relationships on psychosocial development can be identified through behavioral observations of infants and toddlers interacting with their peers. For example, familiarity with peers reduces inhibition and promotes interpersonal and social responsiveness among infants (Lewis, Young, Brooks, & Michaelson, 1975). Peer familiarity also enhances infants' social development (Becker, 1977) and the play skills of toddlers (Howes, 1988; Mueller & Brenner, 1977). Evolving emotional expressions that result from peer interactions contribute additional evidence for the importance of early friend relationships. Exchanges of smiles and laughter can be observed among young toddlers, suggesting enjoyment and a growing intimacy in their relationships with one another (Ross & Lollis, 1989). Older toddlers often form preferences for affiliating with certain of their peers, implying that they develop specific relationships with some of their companions but not with others (Howes, 1996).

The acquisition of new skills and abilities is reflected in the emergent structure of preschool and school-age children's friendships. Friendship networks are smaller among preschool children and the time they spend with friends is more limited than at later stages of life. Young preschoolers most often select friends with overt characteristics similar to themselves – same age, sex, and racial ethnic group (Aboud & Mendelson, 1996; Schneider, Smith, Poisson, & Kwan, 1997). The environmental context strongly influences the development of friendships at this stage in life. Unless children are involved in the same activities or programs, their friendships are unlikely to persist.

As children develop more sophisticated cognitive and social skills, the nature of their friendships changes to accommodate new personal and interpersonal needs (Brownell, 1986; Buhrmester, 1996; Parker & Gottman, 1989). For example, with the development of language skills, shared

humor and "silliness" contribute to the establishment of positive reciprocal friendships (Howes, 1996). Among older preschool and school-age
children, reciprocities between friends support the attainment of new social skills such as cooperation and conflict resolution. They also begin to
employ finer-grained selection criteria and expand their friend network to
include persons with similar as well as diverse demographic and intrinsic
characteristics.

Cognitive and emotional development in middle childhood changes
children's conception of friendship. Concrete reciprocities lose their centrality as intimacy issues become more important (Youniss, 1980). Although
children of all ages look for companionship from friends, older children
begin to expect intimacy, loyalty, and emotional support from their friendships as well (Newcomb & Bagwell, 1995; Parkhurst & Hopemeyer, 1999).
With the development of these skills and expectations, children's friendships become more durable than they were earlier.

The benefits of actively engaging in friend relationships during childhood are numerous and often long-lasting, reflecting positive resolution
of psychosocial challenges in Erikson's schema. Friends provide children
with self-validation and ego support, emotional security, the opportunity
for self-disclosure, help and guidance, reliable allies, companionship, and
stimulation (Rose & Asher, 2000). Children who have friends are more
socially competent than those who do not; they are more sociable, cooperative, altruistic, and self-confident, and they are less lonely (Newcomb &
Bagwell, 1995).

The magnitude and prominence of friendship benefits are associated
with life stage. For example, friendships of young children focus primarily
on companionship (Parker & Gottman, 1989). Engaging in play activities
is an overarching goal of these friendships. By middle childhood, the role
of friendship expands to include elements of loyalty and assistance. Thus,
it is in middle childhood where self-disclosure begins to emerge as an
important element of friendships (Buhrmester, 1996; Gottman & Mettetal,
1986; Parker & Gottman, 1989). In fact, the most salient social process in
middle childhood is gossiping. For school-age children, gossiping about
peers' unwarranted behavior builds solidarity among both female and
male friends and provides them a venue for acknowledging and managing
their own feelings of inferiority (von Salisch, 1997).

Comparisons of males and females of various ages indicate that friendless children report greater levels of loneliness than children with at least
one close friend (Parker, Saxon, Asher, & Kovacs, 1999; Parker & Seal,
1996). Children seeking professional help for psychosocial problems are
more likely to be friendless when compared to children not seeking help
(Rutter & Garmezy, 1983). However, not all friendships are equal; the quality of the friendship influences its benefits. Children with more supportive
friendships are better accepted in the peer group, more socially competent,

more motivated and involved in school, and exhibit fewer behavioral problems than those with less supportive relationships. Less friendship support or more unresolved conflict in friendships is associated with lower self-esteem, more negative self-perceptions, and greater school difficulties (Parker et al., 1999). Poor peer relationships in childhood are also characteristic of some children who become at risk for emotional and behavioral disturbances in adolescence and adulthood (Hartup, 1992; Rubin, Bukowski, & Parker, 1998).

Adolescence. Friendships become less prescribed and more diverse as individuals achieve greater autonomy, mobility, and independence during adolescence. Advances in cognitive and social development provide adolescents with skills needed to recognize and manage the complexities of friendships. Although relationships in adolescence often appear to be in a constant state of flux, success in forming and maintaining the fairly global and undifferentiated friend groups of childhood begets close friendships in adolescence (Collins & Laursen, 2000).

Collins (1997) described relationships in adolescence as "a microcosm of the impact of individual development on dyadic functioning" (p. 2). As adolescents experience biological, psychological, and social changes, significant qualitative changes occur in the amount, content, and perceived meaning of their interactions and in their expression of positive and negative affect (Collins & Repinski, 1994; Collins & Russell, 1991; Hartup & Stevens, 1997). The emphasis of these friendships shifts toward intimacy and other exchanges that support a sense of self-identity, sensitivity with respect to the needs of others, and maintenance of mutually oriented relationships (Hartup & Stevens, 1997). The expectation for more intimate relationships between friends during adolescence also opens these relationships to greater conflict, and possible dissolution, as a result of accusations of untrustworthy and disrespectful acts, lack of sufficient attention, and inadequate communication. Such conflicts, however, tend to be less disruptive to adolescent friendships than to friendships in earlier stages of life. Conflicts can foster the development of interpersonal adaptation strategies that aid in dealing with the changing capabilities and needs of adolescents (Collins & Repinski, 1994; Hartup, 1995).

Friends in adolescence provide significant support to one another as they cope with the developmental challenges confronting them. The importance of friends as confidants increases substantially during early and middle adolescence, particularly as dependence on parents declines (Buhrmester, 1996). The experiences shared with friends shape and moderate social adaptation, enhance personal competence, and promote the development of identity (Berndt, 1996; Cairns & Cairns, 1994) as well as strengthen and solidify the friendships. Romantic relationships often emerge from the interpersonal network created by friends as cross-sex friendships become more common during mid and late adolescence (Feiring, 1999; Kuttler, La Greca, & Prinstein, 1999).

Some empirical evidence suggests that involvement with friends during adolescence is associated with positive mental health outcomes. Such outcomes are most likely to occur when adolescents have close friends, when their friends follow social norms, and when friendships are supportive and intimate (Hartup & Stevens, 1997). At the same time, adolescent friendships can also promote negative behaviors. For example, among adolescent boys experiencing high stress, friend support encourages both alcohol use and depression; for boys reporting low to moderate stress, only relationships with nonsupportive friends predicted both alcohol use and depression (Windle, 1992). Among girls, friend supportiveness was positively correlated with alcohol use but negatively correlated with depression.

Adult Friendship

In contrast to the focus of the friendship literature related to infancy, childhood, and adolescence, investigators of friendship in adulthood have largely ignored the possible effects of cognitive and physical development and have given restricted attention to the impact of social and emotional development on friend interactions. Rather, the focus has been on conceptions of friendship, structural features of dyadic and network relationships such as number and demographic homogeneity of friends, friends as sources of social support, and various interaction processes that take place between and among friends. Relatively few researchers have examined friendship phases; among those who have, most have concentrated on initiation strategies of college students (Blieszner & Adams, 1992).

Definitions of *friend* and valued characteristics of friends are similar across the adult years. Most people view friendship as an emotionally close relationship that entails affection, shared values and interests, companionship, respect and trust, reciprocity, and support (Adams, Blieszner, & de Vries, 2000; Becker, 1987; Swain, 1989). In general, adults expect their friends to "be there" for them in times of joy and sorrow, to be loyal and committed to the relationship, to honor confidences, and to put their fair share of effort into the relationship (Isaacs, 1999; Rawlins, 1994).

Early Adulthood. The years of early adulthood typically herald significant changes in family and friend ties and personal responsibilities, as compared to those in the adolescence stage of life. Rawlins (1992) pointed out that these changes, as well as an expansion of the social world, yield both exciting opportunities for creating a new personal identity while establishing new friendships and the possibility of experiencing social distress and loneliness. Facing developmental challenges associated with completing formal education, finding a location in which to settle, starting a career, and identifying a primary romantic partner, most persons in their twenties and early thirties turn to friends for role socialization as well as leisure pursuits. Young adults seek companionship, advice, and support from their friends. They find friends at work, in the neighborhood, and within all sorts of community groups where mutual interests can be pursued. It is during this stage of life that individuals discover the importance of qualities such as mutual understanding and support, fondness, affection, and loving intimacy necessary for maintaining and advancing lifelong personal relationships (Matthews, 1986; Roberto & Kimboko, 1989).

Scholars interested in young adult friendship have given attention to the similarities and differences in women's and men's same- and cross-sex friendships. Although members of both genders value similar characteristics in their friends, aspects of friendship are expressed in different ways by women and by men. Women tend to put greater emphasis on self-disclosure and verbal forms of interaction, whereas men usually adopt a more instrumental approach involving shared interests and activities. These preferences led Wright (1982) to characterize women's friendships as "face-to-face" and men's as "side-by-side." The central question related to cross-sex friendships has been whether they inevitably lead to romantic liaisons. Werking (1997), who has conducted the most detailed analysis of cross-sex friendships to date, found that women and men both value such partnerships highly. Thus, in order to preserve them, the friends find ways to negotiate issues of romance and sexuality so they do not interfere with the friendship. They also assign different meanings to their interactions with cross-sex friends as compared to romantic partners; the same words and actions that might express deeper intimacy in a romantic relationship are viewed as expressions of affection and caring in these friendships.

Research by Carbery and Buhrmester (1998) examined the intersection of friendship and developmental stage of early adulthood as indicated by marital and parental status (not married, married without children, married with children). They found a trend indicating that young adults in each successive family role stage relied less on friends and more on spouses for companionship, intimacy, support, and guidance. Those who were parents also secured companionship from their children, further displacing the salience of friendships in satisfying that need. The authors concluded that the functional significance of friends peaks in the singlehood stage of young adulthood.

Although research on adjustment within the early adulthood period supports the contention that friendships are important contributors to well-being (Richardson, 1984; Winefield, Winefield, & Tiggemann, 1992), cross-sectional studies cannot disentangle the effects of relationship experiences per se from other experiences and maturational processes. In an attempt to ascertain long-term effects of friendships, Giordano, Cernkovich,

Groat, Pugh, and Swinford (1998) examined longitudinal data on friend interactions in adolescence and personal outcomes as reported ten years later. They actually found little relationship between amount of intimacy with friends in adolescence and adult characteristics such as higher self-esteem, lower psychological distress, or greater marital satisfaction. Rather, adolescent sociodemographic characteristics and attachment to parents were more strongly related to such outcomes in early adulthood. In a longer longitudinal study with a similar purpose, Bagwell, Schmidt, Newcomb, and Bukowski (2001) reported on thirteen- and eighteen-year follow-ups of fifth-grade children. Young adults who had more adjustment difficulties and higher psychopathological symptoms were also those who were most likely to have been without a reciprocal friendship at preadolescence and most likely to have been named as an undesirable playmate. This more detailed examination of links between early friendship experiences and later well-being, as compared to the study by Giordano and associates (1998), confirmed the expectation that friendship success in childhood fosters adaptation later on in life.

Middle Adulthood. For those leading normative patterns of work and family life, the middle years of adulthood are busy and complicated by multiple and often conflicting role demands. Work and civic responsibilities peak at midlife, while attention or even intensive assistance may be needed by one's parents and other elderly relatives as well as by one's offspring. Hence, middle-aged adults report having fewer friends and spending less time with friends than younger adults do (Adams & Blieszner, 1996). But situational constraints do not typically reduce the importance or closeness of friendship in the middle years (Fiebert & Wright, 1989; Rawlins, 1992) and most middle-aged adults sustain at least some friendships. As in earlier stages, friends of midlife persons provide social and emotional support, serve as models for adapting to developmental transitions, and supply affection and companionship. Friends may be directly involved in expressions of generativity (Antonucci & Akiyama, 1997), either insofar as they require mentoring, or to the extent that they share in efforts to accomplish generative goals such as volunteering to help develop and manage community programs.

Franz, McClelland, and Weinberger (1991) reported a direct study of developmental effects on middle adulthood friendship. Data from a thirty-six-year follow-up of children first assessed at five years of age showed that warm and affectionate relationships with parents predicted positive social accomplishment in midlife. In turn, the more socially adept adults were likely to engage in affiliative behaviors and enjoy good relationships with close friends as well as with family members. They also exhibited higher levels of generativity. Similarly, a thirty-seven-year follow-up study (comparing persons at ages thirteen and fifty) showed that having harmonious peer relations in early adolescence was associated with psychological health in midlife (Hightower, 1990).

Studies of the strategies middle-aged adults use to establish and maintain friendships have not been published, nor are there reports on causes or processes of transition from one phase of friendship to another. Although this lack of attention to friendship phases in middle age is consonant with the general deficit of midlife friendship research, the deficit is curious in that adults have many occasions to make and require new friends. For example, they join community organizations, relocate because of employment opportunities, upgrade homes by moving to new neighborhoods, pursue different hobbies and interests, join support groups, and engage in other activities that afford chances to make friends. They also encounter new situations that could challenge existing friendships, as indicated earlier, yet their means of coping with such challenges has not been investigated.

Late Adulthood. In contrast to the paucity of research on friendship in middle adulthood, many studies of friendship in the final stage of life have appeared. The preponderance of these investigations addresses the effects of friendships on psychological well-being (Gupta & Korte, 1994; Takahashi, Tamura, & Tokoro, 1997; Wenger, 1990), particularly in relation to provision of some form of social support (Matt & Dean, 1993; Rook, 1987).

Whereas some of the role conflicts that might have constrained friendship in the middle years are likely to be reduced in late adulthood, new age-related changes bring other relational challenges. For example, a retired elderly person with no primary child-rearing responsibilities might have more discretionary time to spend with friends, yet might not have the physical health or monetary resources needed to pursue preferred friendship activities. Carstensen's program of research on socioemotional selectivity theory (see Carstensen et al., 1999) addresses the connection between personal development and relationships at the individual level of analysis. Hypotheses that older adults conserve emotional and physical energy by concentrating attention on a reduced number of close relationships, as compared to their past network configuration and interactions, have been confirmed in diverse samples for multiple relationships. Rather than attempting to sustain or re-create a large friendship network, older adults are more likely to retain a few very close friends in their relational sphere, along with key family members. Thus, their social needs are still met, despite reduced resources for accomplishing social goals.

Few studies of late-life friendship have been conducted at the relationship level of analysis; the Adams and Blieszner (1994, 1998; Blieszner, 1995; Blieszner & Adams, 1992, 1998) program of research on friendship structure, processes, and phases and Roberto's studies of exchange and equity in older women's friendships (see Roberto, 1996) illustrate approaches to relational analytic schemes.

Some (but not all) of the older adults in Matthews's (1986) study continued to establish new friends in the later years of life. Jerrome (1981) observed how older women in England went about making new friends. She pointed out that living in age-segregated housing and long-term residence in a neighborhood were conducive to establishing new friendships among women who had lost close ties due to retirement or widowhood. Some of them reactivated lapsed friendships or elevated acquaintances to friend status. Others joined church groups, adult education classes, or special interest groups with the intention of finding friends.

A comparison of long-term and more recent friendships by Shea, Thompson, and Blieszner (1988) revealed differential maintenance strategies for each type of friendship. The elders in this study took expressions of affection as givens in old friendships, whereas new ones required displays of affection to aid their growth and maintenance. The elders valued receiving advice from their old friends and engaged in reminiscing and self-disclosure with them, but they tended to discuss current events and other less personal topics with their new friends. Old friends helped each other as needed, and the elders appreciated the support their long-term friends had provided over the years. Exchanges of help were not a significant part of keeping new friends, however, and the elders who exchanged favors with newer friends expressed a concern about reciprocity that was not evident in their discussions of long-standing friendships.

RECOMMENDATIONS FOR FUTURE RESEARCH

This review of friendship patterns, processes, and outcomes illustrates a strong degree of interdependence between individual development and relationship development. As individuals move through the life span, they reframe or reoperationalize the meanings of psychosocial challenges – such as those related to trust, identity, and intimacy – within the context of expanding and contracting social environments. The pursuit and transformation of friendships is central, not peripheral, to this developmental process. We believe that deeper understanding of development could be realized if researchers were to consider individual development and relationship development not as two separate phenomena, but as mutual, reciprocal forces of maturation.

Expanded Approaches to the Study of Reciprocal Individual and Relationship Development

Most of the studies mentioned in this chapter focus on individuals as friend partners and the impact of having and interacting with friends on those individuals at one point in the life span. Moving from the individual to the relationship level of analysis requires studying both partners within a dyad or multiple members of friend networks and examining cognitive, affective, and behavioral processes that result from their interaction (Blieszner & Adams, 1992). Moving from a static to a developmental perspective requires longitudinal designs involving study of stability and change in personal attributes of friend partners, and of their transitions from one maturity level to another. In complementary fashion, a developmental perspective also entails study of stability and change of relationship attributes within friendship phases, and of transitions from one friendship phase to another.

Another layer of complexity is added when the focus moves beyond a particular friend dyad, and beyond study of the impact of the partners' developmental and interactional processes on their own relationship, to recognition of the broader relationship context within which partners and their friendship exist. Specifically, it is important to consider how persons and relationships outside a particular dyad affect the partners and their friendship. These kinds of effects, too, could be stable or changing over time. Potential influences extend to a broad range of experiential impacts on friends and their friendship.

The following scheme illustrates this sequence of foci and effects and suggests possibilities for new kinds of studies of reciprocal personal and relationship development across the life span.

1. *Effects of earlier personal development on later personal outcomes.* This type of investigation takes place at the individual level of analysis, emphasizing intraindividual development over multiple stages of the life span. The cross-sectional studies cited in the discussion of friendship during infancy and childhood approximate this approach insofar as the results suggest that smiling and playing together teaches infants about the pleasure of reciprocity and practice in cooperating with friends provides a useful social skill. The assumption, grounded in Eriksonian theory, is that early acquisition of social concepts and skills prepares individuals for negotiating relationships successfully later on.

2. *Effects of earlier relationship experiences on later personal outcomes.* These studies also occur at the individual level of analysis, but use relationship-level predictors. It is difficult to find existing research conducted from this perspective, particularly in studies of friendship occurring before adulthood, which tend to focus on individual outcomes. Cross-sectional studies of the contributions of social support obtained from friendships to physical and psychological well-being in adulthood might serve as proxies for this type of research. An explicitly developmental example is the investigation by Hightower (1990) of the impact of early adolescent friendships on midlife mental health.

3. *Effects of earlier personal development on later relationship outcomes.* Studies within this genre occur at the relationship level of analysis, looking at both the individual's relationship experiences and the partner's

relationship experiences. We found no reports of true dyadic friendship analyses, however. A suggestive empirical example, presented earlier, is the research showing that by adolescence, cognitive, social, and emotional development have advanced sufficiently to enable friends to be aware of their own impact on their relationships and of their partners' responses to them personally and to their relationship. A developmental illustration can be found in Adams's (1987) three-year longitudinal study of adaptations elderly women made in their friend networks. Prompted largely by changes in their other social roles, these women adjusted their friend networks and the amount of emotional energy they invested in them in order to pursue new social opportunities and personal goals.

4. Effects of earlier relationship experiences on later relationship outcomes. This type of investigation takes place at the relationship level of analysis, emphasizing intrarelationship development over multiple phases of interaction. Studies of changes and stabilities within particular friendships across the years would reflect this approach. For example, in Roberto's (1997) fourteen-year longitudinal follow-up study, older women reported that changes had occurred in seven of the eleven close friendship characteristics under investigation.

5. Effects of other persons and relationships on a focal relationship. This category of investigation speaks to the relationship level of analysis and highlights extra-dyadic and extra-relationship influences. Examples of studies in this group would be analysis of the effects of the larger friend network on a particular friendship within it, effects of a spouse's characteristics and preferences on a person's interactions with friends, effects of caring for parents on time available for friend interactions, and effects of interactions with work-related friends on the evolution of one's romantic relationship. In this case, ties between extra-dyadic individuals and other relationships would be investigated over time within the context of the personal developmental changes of the partners and of changes within the focal relationship itself. For example, the elderly women in Roberto's fourteen-year longitudinal follow-up study responded to death of beloved friends and loss of such significant relationships by deepening their remaining close friendships, establishing new close friendships, relying on family members for friendship, or distancing themselves from remaining friendships (Roberto & Stanis, 1994).

It is important to point out that simple correlational studies of fairly superficial relationship indicators such as frequency of contact and types of shared activities, even if conducted longitudinally, will not advance understanding of personal and relational development at the level we are advocating. Rather, it will be essential to probe deeply, within the context of life span and relationship theory, into the causal mechanisms that link individual development to relationship outcomes and vice versa. As Crosnoe (2000) observed, finding associations between childhood friendship experiences and adult social success or psychological well-being does not reveal how and why these outcomes occurred. Given the existence of many suggestive studies of friendship throughout the life span that could be used as springboards, the time seems right to begin pursuing multi-method designs, conducted with persons representing various age groups. These programs of research should include multiple members of friend networks, in an effort to capture relationship experiences more fully. Finally, they should persist over short- and long-term assessment periods relevant to developmental and relationship transitions and trajectories in order to examine development directly.

References

Aboud, F., & Mendelson, M. (1996). Determinants of friendship selection and quality: Developmental perspectives. In W. Bukowski, A. F. Newcomb, & W. W. Hartup (Eds.), *The company they keep: Friendship in childhood and adolescence* (pp. 87–114). New York: Cambridge University Press.

Adams, R. G. (1987). Patterns of network change: A longitudinal study of friendships of elderly women. *The Gerontologist, 27,* 222–227.

Adams, R. G., & Blieszner, R. (1994). An integrative conceptual framework for friendship research. *Journal of Social and Personal Relationships, 11,* 163–184.

Adams, R. G., & Blieszner, R. (1996). Midlife friendship patterns. In N. Vanzetti & S. Duck (Eds.), *A lifetime of relationships* (pp. 336–363). Pacific Grove, CA: Brooks/Cole.

Adams, R. G., & Blieszner, R. (1998). Structural predictors of problematic friendships in later life. *Personal Relationships, 5,* 439–447.

Adams, R. G., Blieszner, R., & de Vries, B. (2000). Definitions of friendship in the third age: Age, gender, and study location effects. *Journal of Aging Studies, 14,* 117–133.

Antonucci, T., & Akiyama, H. (1997). Concern with others at midlife: Care, comfort, or compromise? In M. E. Lachman & J. B. James (Eds.), *Multiple paths of midlife development* (pp. 147–169). Chicago: University of Chicago Press.

Auhagen, A. E., & Hinde, R. A. (1997). Individual characteristics and personal relationships. *Personal Relationships, 4,* 63–84.

Bagwell, C. L., Schmidt, M. E., Newcomb, A. F., & Bukowski, W. M. (2001). Friendship and peer rejection as predictors of adult adjustment. In D. W. Nangle & C. A. Erdley (Eds.), *The role of friendship in psychological adjustment: New directions for child and adolescent development* (No. 91, pp. 25–49). San Francisco: Jossey-Bass.

Baltes, P. B. (1987). Theoretical propositions of life-span developmental psychology: On the dynamics between growth and decline. *Developmental Psychology, 23,* 611–626.

Baltes, P. B., & Goulet, L. R. (1970). Status and issues of a lifespan developmental psychology. In L. R. Goulet & P. B. Baltes (Eds.), *Lifespan developmental psychology: Research and theory* (pp. 3–21). New York: Academic Press.

Becker, C. S. (1987). Friendship between women. *Journal of Phenomenological Psychology, 18,* 59–72.

Becker, J. (1977). A learning analysis of the development of peer-oriented behavior in nine-month-old infants. *Developmental Psychology, 13,* 481–491.

Berndt, T. J. (1996). Exploring the effects of friendship quality on social development. In W. Bukowski, A. F. Newcomb, & W. W. Hartup (Eds.), *The company they keep: Friendship in childhood and adolescence* (pp. 346–365). New York: Cambridge University Press.

Berscheid, E., & Peplau, L. A. (1983). The emerging science of relationships. In H. H. Kelley et al., *Close relationships* (pp. 1–19). New York: W. H. Freeman.

Blieszner, R. (1995). Friendship processes and well-being in the later years of life: Implications for interventions. *Journal of Geriatric Psychiatry, 28,* 165–183.

Blieszner, R., & Adams, R. G. (1992). *Adult friendship.* Newbury Park: CA: Sage.

Blieszner, R., & Adams, R. G. (1998). Problems with friends in old age. *Journal of Aging Studies, 12,* 223–238.

Brown, B. B. (1991). A lifespan approach to friendship: Age-related dimensions of an ageless relationship. In H. Z. Lopata & D. R. Maines (Eds.), *Friendship in context* (pp. 23–50). Greenwich, CT: JAI Press.

Brownell, C. A. (1986). Convergent developments: Cognitive-developmental correlates of growth in infant/toddler peer skills. *Child Development, 57,* 275–286.

Buhrmester, D. (1996). Need fulfillment, interpersonal competence, and the developmental contexts of early adolescent friendship. In W. Bukowski, A. F. Newcomb, & W. W. Hartup (Eds.), *The company they keep: Friendship in childhood and adolescence* (pp. 158–185). New York: Cambridge University Press.

Cairns, R. B., & Cairns, B. D. (1994). *Lifelines and risks.* New York: Cambridge University Press.

Carbery, J., & Buhrmester, D. (1998). Friendship and need fulfillment during three phases of young adulthood. *Journal of Social and Personal Relationships, 15,* 393–409.

Carstensen, L. L., Isaacowitz, D. M., & Charles, S. T. (1999). Taking time seriously: A theory of socioemotional selectivity. *American Psychologist, 54,* 165–181.

Collins, W. A. (1997). Relationships and development during adolescence: Interpersonal adaptation to individual change. *Personal Relationships, 4,* 1–14.

Collins, W. A., & Laursen, B. (2000). Adolescent relationships: The art of fugue. In C. Hendrick & S. S. Hendrick (Eds.), *Close relationships: A sourcebook* (pp. 58–69). Thousand Oaks, CA: Sage.

Collins, W. A., & Repinski, D. J. (1994). Relationships during adolescence: Continuity and change in interpersonal perspective. In R. Montemayor, G. Adams, & T. Gullotta (Eds.), *Personal relationships during adolescence* (pp. 7–36). Thousand Oaks, CA: Sage.

Collins, W. A., & Russell, G. (1991). Mother-child and father-child relationships in middle childhood and adolescence: A developmental analysis. *Developmental Review, 11,* 99–136.

Crosnoe, R. (2000). Friendships in childhood and adolescence: The life course and new directions. *Social Psychology Quarterly, 63,* 377–391.

Deutsch, M., & Krauss, R. M. (1965). *Theories in social psychology.* New York: Basic Books.

Dindia, K. (1997). Self-disclosure, self-identity, and relationship development: A transactional/dialectical perspective. In S. Duck (Ed.), *Handbook of personal relationships* (2nd ed., pp. 411–426). Chichester, UK: John Wiley & Sons.

Dindia, K. (2000). Relational maintenance. In C. Hendrick & S. S. Hendrick (Eds.), *Close relationships: A sourcebook* (pp. 286–299). Thousand Oaks, CA: Sage.

Duck, S. W., & Gilmour, R. (Eds.). (1981). *Personal relationships: Studying personal relationships*. London: Academic.

Erikson, E. H. (1950). *Childhood and society* (2nd ed.). New York: W. W. Norton & Company.

Erikson, E. H. (1982). *The life cycle completed*. New York: W. W. Norton & Company.

Erikson, E. H., & Erikson, J. M. (1997). *The life cycle completed* (extended version). New York: W. W. Norton & Company.

Erikson, E. H., Erikson, J. M., & Kivnick, H. Q. (1994). *Vital involvement in old age: The experience of old age in our time*. New York: W. W. Norton & Company. [Original work published 1989.]

Fehr, B. (1996). *Friendship processes*. Thousand Oaks, CA: Sage.

Feiring, C. (1999). Other-sex friendship networks and the development of romantic relationships in adolescence. *Journal of Youth and Adolescence, 28*, 495–512.

Fiebert, M. S., & Wright, K. S. (1989). Midlife friendships in an American faculty sample. *Psychological Reports, 64*, 1127–1130.

Foa, U. G., & Foa, E. B. (1974). *Societal structures of the mind*. Springfield, IL: Charles C. Thomas.

Franz, C. E., McClelland, D. C., & Weinberger, J. (1991). Childhood antecedents of conventional social accomplishment in midlife adults: A 36-year prospective study. *Journal of Personality and Social Psychology, 60*, 586–595.

Giordano, P. C., Cernkovich, S. A., Groat, H. T., Pugh, M. D., & Swinford, S. P. (1998). The quality of adolescent friendships: Long-term effects? *Journal of Health and Social Behavior, 39*, 55–71.

Gottman, J. M., & Mettetal, G. (1986). Speculations about social and affective development: Friendships and acquaintanceship through adolescence. In J. M. Gottman & J. G. Parker (Eds.), *Conversations of friends* (pp. 192–237). Cambridge, UK: Cambridge University Press.

Gupta, V., & Korte, C. (1994). The effects of a confidant and a peer group on the well-being of single elders. *International Journal of Aging and Human Development, 39*, 293–302.

Hartup, W. W. (1992). Conflict and friendship relations. In C. U. Shantz & W. W. Hartup (Eds.), *Conflict in child and adolescent development* (pp. 186–215). New York: Cambridge University Press.

Hartup, W. W. (1995). The three faces of friendship. *Journal of Social and Personal Relationships, 12*, 569–574.

Hartup, W. W., & Laursen, B. (1993). Conflict and context in peer relations. In C. H. Hart (Ed.), *Children on playgrounds: Research perspectives and applications* (pp. 44–84). Albany: State University of New York Press.

Hartup, W. W., & Stevens, N. (1997). Friendships and adaptation in the life course. *Psychological Bulletin, 121*, 355–370.

Hays, R. B. (1985). A longitudinal study of friendship development. *Journal of Personality and Social Psychology, 48*, 909–924.

Hightower, E. (1990). Adolescent interpersonal and familiar precursors of positive mental health at midlife. *Journal of Youth and Adolescence, 19,* 257–275.

Hinde, R. A. (1979). *Towards understanding relationships.* London: Academic.

Hinde, R. A., & Stevenson-Hinde, J. (1986). Relating childhood relationships to individual characteristics. In W. W. Hartup & Z. Rubin (Eds.), *Relationships and development* (pp. 27–50). London: Lawrence Erlbaum Associates.

Howes, C. (1988). Peer interaction of young children. *Monographs of the Society for Research in Young Children, 53* (Serial 217).

Howes, C. (1996). The earliest friendships. In W. Bukowski, A. F. Newcomb, & W. W. Hartup (Eds.), *The company they keep: Friendship in childhood and adolescence* (pp. 66–86). New York: Cambridge University Press.

Hoyer, W., & Rybash, J. (1996). Lifespan theory. In J. E. Birren (Ed.), *Encyclopedia of gerontology* (Vol. 2, pp. 65–71). New York: Academic Press.

Isaacs, F. (1999). *Toxic friends, true friends.* New York: William Morrow and Company.

Jerrome, D. (1981). The significance of friendship for women in later life. *Ageing and Society, 1,* 175–197.

Johnson, C., & Troll, L. (1994). Constraints and facilitators to friendship in late late life. *The Gerontologist, 34,* 79–87.

Kelley, H. H., Berscheid, E., Christensen, A., Harvey, J. H., Hustson, T. L., Levinger, G., et al. (1983a). *Close relationships.* New York: W. H. Freeman.

Kelley, H. H., Berscheid, E., Christensen, A., Harvey, J. H., Hustson, T. L., Levinger, G., et al. (1983b). Analyzing close relationships. In H. H. Kelley et al., *Close relationships* (pp. 20–67). New York: W. H. Freeman.

Kuttler, A. F., La Greca, A. M., & Prinstein, M. J. (1999). Friendship qualities and social-emotional functioning of adolescents with close, cross-sex friendships. *Journal of Research on Adolescence, 9,* 339–366.

Lang, F. R. (2001). Regulation of social relationships in later adulthood. *Journal of Gerontology: Psychological Sciences, 56B,* P321–P326.

Levinger, G. (1983). Development and change. In H. H. Kelley et al., *Close relationships* (pp. 315–359). New York: W. H. Freeman.

Lewin, K. (1948). *Resolving social conflicts.* New York: Harper & Row.

Lewis, M., Young, G., Brooks, J., & Michaelson, L. (1975). The beginning of friendship. In M. Lewis & L. A. Rosenblum (Eds.), *Friendship and peer relations* (pp. 246–273). New York: John Wiley & Sons.

Matt, G. E., & Dean, A. (1993). Social support from friends and psychological distress among elderly persons: Moderator effects of age. *Journal of Health and Social Behavior, 34,* 187–200.

Matthews, S. H. (1986). *Friendships through the life course.* Beverly Hills: Sage.

Mead, G. H. (1934). *Mind, self, and society.* Chicago: University of Chicago Press.

Milardo, R. M., & Helms-Erikson, H. (2000). Network overlap and third-party influence on close relationships. In C. Hendrick & S. S. Hendrick (Eds.), *Close relationships: A sourcebook* (pp. 33–45). Thousand Oaks, CA: Sage.

Minuchin, P. P., & Shapiro, E. K. (1983). The school as a context for social development. In P. H. Mussen (Series Ed.) & E. M. Hetherington (Vol. Ed.), *Handbook of child psychology: Vol. 4. Socialization, personality and social development* (pp. 197–274). New York: John Wiley & Sons.

Mueller, E., & Brenner, J. (1977). The origins of social skills and interaction among playground toddlers. *Child Development, 48,* 854–861.

Munnichs, J. M. A., & Olbrich, E. (1985). Lifespan change in a gerontological perspective. In J. M. A. Munnichs, P. Mussen, E. Olbrich, & P. G. Coleman (Eds.), *Life-span and change in a gerontological perspective* (pp. 3–11). Orlando: Academic Press.

Newcomb, A. F., & Bagwell, C. L. (1995). Children's friendship relations: A meta-analytic review. *Psychological Bulletin, 117,* 306–347.

Parker, J. G., & Gottman, J. M. (1989). Social and emotional development in a relational context: Friendship interaction from early childhood to adolescence. In T. J. Berndt & G. W. Ladd (Eds.), *Peer relationships in child development* (pp. 95–132). New York: John Wiley & Sons.

Parker, J. G., Saxon, J. L., Asher, S. R., & Kovacs, D. M. (1999). The friendship experience in middle childhood and adolescence: Implications for understanding loneliness. In K. J. Rotenberg & S. Hymel (Eds.), *Loneliness in childhood and adolescence* (pp. 201–224). New York: Cambridge University Press.

Parker, J. G., & Seal, J. (1996). Forming, losing, renewing, and replacing friendships: Applying temporal parameters to the assessment of children's friendship experiences. *Child Development, 67,* 2248–2268.

Parkhurst, J., & Hopemeyer, A. (1999). Development change in the source of loneliness in childhood and adolescence: Constructing a theoretical model. In K. J. Rotenberg & S. Hymel (Eds.), *Loneliness in childhood and adolescence* (pp. 56–79). New York: Cambridge University Press.

Rawlins, W. K. (1992). *Friendship matters: Communication, dialectics, and the life course.* New York: Aldine de Gruyter.

Rawlins, W. K. (1994). Being there and growing apart: Sustaining friendships during adulthood. In D. J. Canary & L. Stafford (Eds.), *Communication and relational maintenance* (pp. 275–294). San Diego: Academic Press.

Richardson, V. (1984). Clinical-historical aspects of friendship deprivation among women. *Social Work Research and Abstracts, 20,* 19–24.

Roberto, K. A. (1996). Friendships between older women: Interactions and reactions. *Journal of Women and Aging, 8,* 55–73.

Roberto, K. A. (1997). Qualities of older women's friendships: Stable or volatile? *International Journal of Aging and Human Development, 44,* 1–14.

Roberto, K. A., & Kimboko, P. (1989). Friendships in later life: Definitions and maintenance patterns. *International Journal of Aging and Human Development, 28,* 9–19.

Roberto, K. A., & Stanis, P. I. (1994). Reactions of older women to the death of their close friends. *Omega, 29,* 17–27.

Rook, K. S. (1987). Reciprocity of social exchange and social satisfaction among older women. *Journal of Personality and Social Psychology, 52,* 145–154.

Rose, A., & Asher, S. (2000). Children's friendships. In C. Hendrick & S. S. Hendrick (Eds.), *Close relationships: A sourcebook* (pp. 47–57). Thousand Oaks, CA: Sage.

Rose, S. M. (1984). How friendships end: Patterns among young adults. *Journal of Social and Personal Relationships, 1,* 267–277.

Ross, M., & Lollis, S. (1989). A social analysis of toddler peer relations. *Child Development, 60,* 1082–1091.

Rubin, K. H., Bukowski, W. K., & Parker, J. G. (1998). Peer interactions, relationships, and groups. In W. Damon (Series Ed.) & N. Eisenberg (Vol. Ed.), *Handbook of child psychology. Vol. 3, Social, emotional, and personality development* (pp. 619–700). New York: John Wiley & Sons.

Rutter, M., & Garmezy, N. (1983). Developmental psychopathology. In P. H. Mussen (Series Ed.) & E. M. Hetherington (Vol. Ed.), *Handbook of child psychology. Vol. 4, Socialization, personality, and social development* (pp. 775–911). New York: John Wiley & Sons.

Schneider, B. H., Smith, A., Poisson, S. E., & Kwan, A. B. (1997). Cultural dimensions of children's peer relations. In S. Duck (Ed.), *Handbook of personal relationships* (2nd ed., pp. 121–146). Chichester, UK: John Wiley & Sons.

Shea, L., Thompson, L., & Blieszner, R. (1988). Resources in older adults' old and new friendships. *Journal of Social and Personal Relationships, 5,* 83–96.

Sherman, A. M., de Vries, B., & Lansford, J. E. (2000). Friendship in childhood and adulthood: Lessons across the life span. *International Journal of Aging and Human Development, 51,* 31–51.

Sias, P. M., & Cahill, D. J. (1998). From coworkers to friends: The development of peer friendships in the workplace. *Western Journal of Communication, 62,* 273–299.

Swain, S. (1989). Covert intimacy: Closeness in men's friendships. In B. J. Risman & P. Schwartz (Eds.), *Gender in intimate relationships* (pp. 71–86). Belmont, CA: Wadsworth.

Takahashi, K., Tamura, J., & Tokoro, M. (1997). Patterns of social relationships and psychological well-being among the elderly. *International Journal of Behavioral Development, 21,* 417–430.

VanLear, C. A., & Trujillo, N. (1986). On becoming acquainted: A longitudinal study of social judgement processes. *Journal of Social and Personal Relationships, 3,* 375–392.

von Salisch, M. (1997). Emotional processes in children's relationships with siblings and friends. In S. Duck (Ed.), *Handbook of personal relationships* (2nd ed., pp. 61–80). Chichester, England: John Wiley & Sons.

Wenger, G. C. (1990). The special role of friends and neighbors. *Journal of Aging Studies, 4,* 149–169.

Werking, K. (1997). *We're just good friends: Women and men in nonromantic relationships.* New York: Guilford.

Windle, M. (1992). A longitudinal study of stress buffering for adolescent problem behaviors. *Developmental Psychology, 28,* 522–530.

Winefield, H. R., Winefield, A. H., & Tiggemann, M. (1992). Social support and psychological well-being in young adults: The multidimensional support scale. *Journal of Personality Assessment, 58,* 198–210.

Wiseman, J. P. (1986). Friendship: Bonds and binds in a voluntary relationship. *Journal of Social and Personal Relationships, 3,* 191–211.

Wright, P. H. (1982). Men's friendships, women's friendships and the alleged inferiority of the latter. *Sex Roles, 8,* 1–20.

Youniss, J. (1980). *Parents and peers in social development: A Piaget-Sullivan perspective.* Chicago: University of Chicago Press.

8

The Consequential Stranger: Peripheral Relationships across the Life Span

Karen L. Fingerman

Individuals of all ages encounter social partners with whom they are not intimate (e.g., cousins, classmates, neighbors, church members). Peripheral ties arise in daily life. These relationships link individuals to larger social structures and provide opportunities for cultural models, novel stimulation, identity exploration, and social support. In childhood, peripheral partners provide opportunities to acquire skills not available through familiar social contacts. In adolescence and young adulthood, they help individuals define themselves and provide information about the culture. In midlife, a proliferation of close ties provides a larger number of peripheral ties. In late life, peripheral ties may offer support or provide for "social reminiscence." Discussion addresses the function and meaning of peripheral relationships in comparison to close social ties.

The traffic outside the Henderson Childcare Center at the end of the day is a sight to behold. The lot typically contains only fifteen cars during the day. At 5:00 P.M., a horde of fifty vehicles containing parents descends upon the building. To add to the chaos, there is only one driveway through which cars must both enter and exit. Toyotas park on the sidewalk, Volvo station wagons weave in and out, and inevitably, several Pontiac Grand Ams are locked in their spaces while toddlers find their way from care providers to parents. Yet no one honks. No one shouts. Tempers do not flare. Drivers wait patiently as each vehicle maneuvers back onto the street. These parents are not exceptionally virtuous people. Nor are their children endowed with particular serenity (in fact, tired and hungry children scream vociferously). Rather, the atmosphere in the parking lot arises from the fact that the people in these fifty vehicles are linked to one another; the driver in any given vehicle knows the driver in another vehicle in some manner. Colleagues, friends of friends, neighbors, and care providers are thrown together as they navigate a gauntlet.

These social partners are not intimate. They do not provide social support. In some ways, they are simply strangers who have connections. We might question whether such ties do, in fact, constitute relationships. Scholarly definitions of relationships include ideas of interdependence, interactions between two individuals known to one another, continuity in contact patterns, or people who have an impact on one another (Hinde, 1979, 1995; Kelley, 1983; Noller, Feeney, & Peterson, 2001). Using such definitions, it is possible to configure the ties outside the Henderson building as "relationships." These social partners have an impact on daily mood and well-being, instigate developmental changes, and support stability. Indeed, it is surprising that researchers have focused so little attention on such social contacts who narrowly avoid collision in the parking lot each evening. I use the terms "peripheral ties" in reference to such social partners.

This chapter provides an overview of peripheral social ties. Many chapters in this volume describe the ways in which intimate and close social partners influence individual development. Empirical studies show that parents, children, romantic partners or spouses, siblings, and friends play important roles at different points in individuals' lives (e.g., Antonucci, 2001; Antonucci & Akiyama, 1987; Carstensen, Isaacowitz, & Charles, 1999). Yet, a variety of social contacts exist outside the domain of intimacy. People send cards to their cousins at the holidays, they interact with classmates or coworkers on weekdays, run into friends-of-friends at barbecues in the summer, engage in conversations with the person who cuts their hair, and they grow irritated with a neighbor who throws loud parties. These social partners warrant consideration in a life-span framework.

Specifically, this chapter addresses three questions: 1) Who are members of the peripheral social network and how is this network defined?, 2) How do peripheral ties function across the life span, and are these functions specific to peripheral ties?, and 3) What are the implications of peripheral ties across the life span? There is little research specifically addressing these questions. This chapter draws on literature examining "weak" ties (e.g., Granovetter, 1973), ecological theories of development (e.g., Bronfenbrenner & Morris, 1997), group socialization theories (e.g., Harris, 1995, 2000; Maccoby, 2002), and the scant empirical literature examining neighbors, relationships with coworkers, mentors, and the like. The next section explains how we would define peripheral ties in the social arena.

DEFINING THE PERIPHERAL SOCIAL NETWORK

Individuals have a sense of a hierarchy within close ties (e.g., Kahn & Antonucci, 1980), and this sense of decreasing intimacy extends to provide a continuum from the most intimate relationships to peripheral ties to relative strangers. Obviously, the intimate and peripheral social networks overlap. Social partners move in and out of the two networks (Morgan, Neal, & Carder, 1996). A neighbor who is merely an acquaintance may become a good friend if she has a child at the same time that you do. A coworker who has been a friend may drift away after you are promoted. Furthermore, peripheral partners affect interactions with intimate partners and vice versa. A woman who is respected in the workplace returns home at the end of the day in a pleasant mood to interact with her family. A man with a circle of close friends has the psychological resources to remain calm when dealing with a difficult neighbor. Here I treat peripheral ties as a discrete set of relationships for the sake of discussion. Metaphorically, close relationships are at the center of vision, and peripheral relationships lie in the blurred edges.

Parameters of the Peripheral Network

Although scholars have not considered peripheral ties in a life-span framework, sociologists have examined what they call "weak ties." In so doing, they recognize the difficulties of delineating these ties. Granovetter (1973) dealt with this issue by stating, "It is sufficient for the present purpose if most of us can agree, on a rough intuitive basis, whether a given tie is strong, weak, or absent" (p. 1361). Scholars interested in "weak ties" further specified that these relationships are characterized by infrequent contact, low emotional intensity, and little intimacy (Granovetter, 1973; Marsden & Campbell, 1984). Furthermore, weak ties involve fewer interpersonal similarities than close ties; weak ties involve people who are different from one another (Heider, 1958; Wegener, 1991).

Although definitions of "weak" ties are useful, these parameters do not encompass the array of peripheral partners individuals encounter throughout life. Scholars interested in "weak ties" were specifically interested in the valence of the tie – namely its "weakness." Peripheral ties include a broader array of social partners not limited to individuals who have infrequent contact or little emotional intensity. People encounter classmates, neighbors, and coworkers on a daily basis. Such partners may evoke strong feelings of annoyance or may be pleasant and enjoyable. Further, peripheral partners in school settings, neighborhoods, churches, and workplaces are likely to share high degrees of interpersonal similarities such as social class and shared values. In other words, weak ties fall under the purview of peripheral ties, but the peripheral network encompasses a broader array of social partners who may affect individual well-being and development.

Of interest is also the delineation between close ties and peripheral partners. Objectively, a given individual could be a close tie or a peripheral tie. As an illustration, in many work settings, individuals have a number of friends, but also spend much of the day with individuals whom they view merely as coworkers (Blieszner & Roberto, 2003). A given individual is labeled a "friend" or a "coworker," depending on degree of intimacy and mutual feelings for one another. The "close" nature of a relationship is subjectively defined. For example, Antonucci and Akiyama (1987) assessed close social ties by asking individuals to list "people who are important in your life, not just people you happen to know or be related to." Most people listed romantic partners or spouses, parents, children, close friends, and siblings in response to this query (see Antonucci, 2001), supporting the notion that these relationships are "close" ties; yet, the definition is subjective. In a parallel manner, peripheral ties are social partners to whom individuals do not feel close. On the flipside of Antonucci and Akiyama's (1987) approach, the peripheral network includes social contacts who are not important in the individual's life but who just happen to be related or known to them.

The peripheral network is also distinct in terms of individuals' investment in these ties. Other chapters in this volume suggest selection processes and social skills are inherent to the organization and maintenance of close relationships (Hansson, Daleiden, & Hayslip, 2003; Lang, 2003). Close relationships reflect the partners' personalities, attributes, and emotional affection. Friends are selected based on shared interests and personal attributes; someone cannot arbitrarily stand in as "friend" on a given day. Similarly, even in situations where individuals do not choose a close social partner, such as a parent or sibling, they invest in that specific individual as a close relationship. Although individual behaviors contribute to the nature of the peripheral network, peripheral partners arise in the course of daily life through connections with other people and entry into work or other activities. Of course, some energy is required to leave the house, work, or to be active, but an individual who has few social skills and who is not extraverted may encounter dozens of peripheral partners in the course of daily tasks such as work, child care, a local meeting, and the neighborhood.

A further distinction of peripheral and close relationships involves the degree of formality involved in exchanges. As mentioned previously, many Western languages demarcate the boundaries of close and peripheral social partners through the use of a formal "you" term.[1] Certain peripheral partners entail a degree of formality, such as ties between a health practitioner and patient, a lawyer and a client, a child's tie to a teacher, a worker's tie to a boss, or a church congregant's tie to the pastor. These social contacts are usually defined around specific functions. Some individuals find formality reassuring, and prefer to retain a degree of formality with everyone but their closest friends and family. Of course, not all peripheral ties are formal, but when individuals do retain formality in a relationship in the modern world, the tie is not likely to be close and intimate.

---

[1] Historically, individuals used the formal "you" term with adults of varying degrees of intimacy, including their spouse, whereas the informal "you" was reserved for children and individuals deemed socially inferior. Modern languages have evolved to provide a distinction more clearly demarcating degrees of intimacy rather than social structural hierarchies, although the formal "you" still conveys politeness.

Finally, a parameter must be drawn between peripheral ties and complete strangers. For purposes of understanding these ties as "relationships," peripheral ties must also involve some degree of mutual recognition. It is this recognition that serves as a demarcation between peripheral partners and true strangers. In sum, peripheral partners include the array of social partners with whom individuals interact with mutual recognition, whom they do not consider to be close or intimate, and in whom they invest little of their emotional energy.

Members of the Peripheral Network

Given these parameters for peripheral partners, I next turn to understanding who peripheral partners are and how they fit into individuals' social arenas. Figure 8.1 presents a pyramid of daily social partners based on degree of intimacy. These pyramids are not intended to accurately represent patterns for close relationships – small children may be highly attached to siblings, older adults may have a spouse, and so forth. Rather, these pyramids serve as a heuristic illustrating that social partners who are neither close and intimate nor complete strangers are pervasive in the social arena.

Peripheral partners include people seen on a daily basis and people seen infrequently, people who are annoying and people who are pleasing, people who know other social partners we know and people who do not. We encounter some peripheral partners on a daily basis in work or school settings where we interact around specific tasks, schedules, and routines. Other peripheral partners provide services in formal settings, such as the woman who sells us a newspaper each morning. Still other peripheral partners are friends of friends whom we encounter at large, informal social gatherings at sporadic intervals. We enjoy hearing about their recent travels or their children's exploits, we call them when we search for a job, or we hear about their recent illness from a friend. We might classify peripheral partners along three dimensions: 1) kinship, 2) frequency of contact, and 3) degree of social connection.

There are kin and non-kin peripheral ties. Distant relatives may lie in the peripheral network. Cousins, sons-in-law, grandchildren residing across the country, aunts, uncles, a stepparent acquired in adulthood, and consensual relatives may all be peripheral ties. Consensual relatives are individuals who have agreed to treat one another as family members. For example, some older African American adults treat nieces, nephews, or unrelated adults in the role of a grown child, or as fictive kin (Burton, 1995; Johnson, 1995). Such fictive kin may be close and intimate, or they may be peripheral, depending on circumstances. Indeed, distant kin on the whole are difficult to relegate to either the close or peripheral network without additional information. In a study of nearly two hundred individuals aged 13 to 99, we found that all but two participants listed at least one distant

1. Preschool child's social encounters

2. Young adult's social encounters

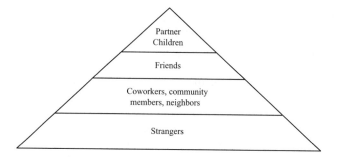

3. Older adult's social encounters

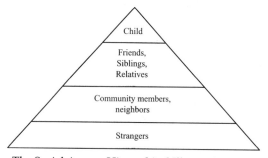

FIGURE 8.1. The Social Arena : Hierarchical Illustrations.

relative as a "close" social partner (Fingerman, Hay, Porfeli, Mayger, & Birditt, 1999). Furthermore, the degree of intimacy between kin may vary across the life span. For example, cousins may play like siblings in childhood but lose touch after they have grown and live farther apart. Finally, as will be discussed, non-kin peripheral partners may seem interchangeable across the life span; the relationship may be based more on roles and functions than on the specific person. Distant kin remain distant kin throughout life, whether they move, see each other solely at big family events, or lose track of one another altogether. Throughout life, cousins retain their relationship as cousins. Coworkers do not. Given the complexities of considering distant kin as peripheral ties, this chapter focuses primarily on non-kin peripheral ties.

With regard to frequency of contact, individuals encounter some peripheral partners on a daily basis and other peripheral partners once a year or even less often. Peripheral partners people encounter frequently may influence their daily mood and distinct aspects of their development. There are three principal contexts for daily encounters with peripheral partners: 1) work or school, 2) shared space or geographic proximity, and 3) organizations and clubs. Peripheral ties arise in structured areas of the social world and include classmates, coworkers, bosses, or clients. It is not that school and work inevitably contain peripheral ties: A small business might involve three workers who share intimate secrets like friends. Rather, peripheral ties are *likely* to arise in these contexts. Geographic proximity is also a driving force behind peripheral ties. College students residing in the same dormitory, neighbors in an apartment building, and nursing home residents come to recognize one another and to enjoy the small talk that accompanies such recognition. Likewise, membership in community organizations, churches or synagogues, and social clubs may provide such daily contacts.

This is not to say that peripheral ties are constrained to daily contacts; individuals also retain peripheral ties with social partners they see infrequently. As mentioned at the start of this chapter, theorists have emphasized frequent and repeated interactions as an element of intimate relationships, but such repetition is not requisite for peripheral liaisons. For example, the pediatrician or family doctor, people who have season tickets in adjacent seats at the ballpark, a local bartender, and a sister's best friend may all be peripheral ties. Despite periodic contact, these peripheral ties can be important in individuals' lives. For example, community psychology documents that clients confide in bartenders, haircutters, and divorce lawyers and thus derive mental health benefits from these ties (Cowen, 1982; Cowen, Gesten, Boike, Norton, Wilson, & DeStefano, 1979; Cowen, McKim, & Weissberg, 1981). There is considerable individual variability in these periodic peripheral ties. Some individuals establish a relationship with a specific barber and have him cut their hair every few weeks; other individuals go to whichever haircutter is available at that time. Indeed, some people actively avoid making connections with partners encountered so infrequently and in such structured settings.

Finally, whether peripheral ties are connected to other social partners also varies. In the United States, a popular game demonstrates that every movie star appears in a film with at least one actor who performed in a film with Kevin Bacon: Every actor is but one actor removed from Kevin Bacon. The peripheral social network is filled with such Kevin Bacon liaisons. The friend of a friend, the parent of a child's classmate, and the business contact of a coworker, all constitute peripheral liaisons of this type. Indeed, initial investigations of peripheral ties focused primarily on these types of connections. Granovetter (1973) proposed that individuals gather information and bridge ties to other social enclaves through social partners who connect them to people they do not already know. Of note is that our close partners may also be interconnected – our friends may all be friends, our sisters feel close to one another, and so forth. The distinction in the peripheral network is that the *only* tie an individual maintains to a peripheral partner may be a link through another social partner.

In sum, members of the peripheral network include kin and non-kin, individuals seen on a daily basis and an infrequent basis, individuals with whom interactions are highly formal and individuals with whom individuals are less formal, and individuals who are connected to other people we know as well as individuals not so connected. The next section discusses further variability in the nature of the peripheral network as a function of position in the social structure.

Social Structures and the Peripheral Network

Throughout this volume, scholars describe important associations between culture, social structure, and personal relationships (for explicit discussions see Antonucci, Langfahl, & Akiyama, 2003; Takahashi, 2003). The nature and parameters of an individual's peripheral network largely reflects his or her position within the social structure and culture. Whereas individuals from a variety of social classes, ethnicities, and gender report five to seven close or intimate relationships (Antonucci, 2001; Antonucci & Akiyama, 1987; House, Kahn, McLeod, & Williams, 1985), the number and types of peripheral ties individuals encounter differs based on their social setting. Individuals who reside in urban settings may encounter a different suite of peripheral partners on a daily basis than individuals who reside in small towns. The network density or interconnectedness of a peripheral network may vary based on geographic location, in- and out-migration in the area, ethnicity, social class, and gender. People in small towns may have more peripheral partners who know one another. Furthermore, the emotional tenor of peripheral ties may vary by neighborhood, corporate organization, school district, or region of the country. For example, some management styles encourage teamwork and bonding among coworkers, other companies encourage at-home offices, telecommuting, and therefore little contact with coworkers. It would be inappropriate to consider peripheral ties without recognizing the variability in the nature of these liaisons.

The next section describes the functions the peripheral ties might serve in linking individuals to larger social structures such as social class and ethnicity.

FUNCTIONS OF THE PERIPHERAL NETWORK

Many chapters in this volume describe the functions of close relationships on individual development. In considering the functions of peripheral ties across the life span, we might consider these relationships in comparison to close relationships in three ways : 1) peripheral and close ties may influence one another in a reciprocal fashion, 2) peripheral ties may serve distinct functions not offered by close ties, or 3) peripheral ties may serve functions that close ties also serve for individual development. This section provides a brief overview of each of these types of functions.

Reciprocal Influences between Close and Peripheral Social Ties

It would be a gross oversimplification to presume that close and peripheral social ties function independently or even in parallel. Rather, these relationships influence one another and, in turn, the developing individual. At a certain level, peripheral ties serve as an interface between social structures, close relationships, and individuals. Further, the peripheral network and the close social network are intertwined ; an individual who is a peripheral social tie may later become a close friend and vice versa.

Peripheral Ties, Close Ties, and Social Structures. Elsewhere, scholars have argued that close relationships and peripheral ties serve as segues from larger social structures to individual development. For example, ecological theory (e.g., Bronfenbrenner, 1979 ; Bronfenbrenner & Morris, 1997) deals with the interplay between social structures and the developing child. This research literature provides indirect evidence that peripheral partners influence close ties. For example, studies suggest that individuals who encounter high levels of stress at work tend to be less warm with their children after work and to experience more family conflict ; these familial patterns, in turn, are associated with problematic adjustment for children and adolescents (see Crouter & Bumpus, 2001, for a review). A single mother who must commute an hour each way to a ten-hour factory shift cannot engage in lengthy discussion with her child's day care provider each morning. She gets up early, scrambles to prepare the children, and hurries to work, sleeping on the bus. She worries because she does not feel connected to the care provider ; her concern taints her encounters with her boss. At the end of the day, she returns tired from this fast-paced day, and initially withdraws from her children. Encounters in the peripheral network arise from social structures and color subsequent interactions with closer social partners.

In another example, early work on social class differences in autonomy suggested family patterns arise from, and are supported by, parents' encounters in the workplace. Kohn (1977) argued that social class differences in the value placed on autonomy and independence arise from social class differences in work contexts. Some work settings allow individuals greater independence than other work settings and these differences are translated into individual values for autonomy. Baumrind (1971) further indicated that social class differences are transmitted in the way parents raise their children. In other words, peripheral partners may develop shared ideas about treatment of various members, which in turn are transmitted to children through their families.

Other scholars have shown that peripheral ties may function differently depending on an individual's position within the social structure. In a large study of over six hundred German adults of differing socioeconomic background, Wegener (1991) found that individuals of higher social status successfully used their peripheral partners to find new jobs, whereas individuals of lower social status did not access peripheral partners in this manner. The role of peripheral partners in job seeking is equivocal and varies by nationality (as Wegener pointed out, German law precludes use of informal connections in hiring practice that are commonly used in the United States). Nonetheless, his study suggests peripheral ties are subject to variability across social strata.

Unfortunately, empirical studies examining social structures, peripheral partners, and close partners are indirect and largely limited to examination of work and family stress. Such stress may stem from encounters with coworkers and bosses (Birditt, 2002). Yet it is also plausible that specific demands of the job (rather than peripheral partners in the workplace) generate stress. For example, Repetti (1989) studied air traffic controllers who track airplanes in busy Los Angeles skies for a living ; stress in their work roles tended to reflect weather and flight patterns rather than coworkers per se. Likewise, Bolger and Eckenroade (1991) described marital stress when individuals study for an important medical examination. It is not that work stress, per se, stems from peripheral partners, but rather that research on family and work suggests there are reciprocal influences between peripheral and close relationships.

Peripheral Ties Preceding and Arising from Close Social Ties. In addition to mutual influences between peripheral and close social ties, peripheral ties and close ties are intertwined in a fluid state across the life span. Ties that are peripheral at one point in time may become close and intimate at another point in time. Elsewhere, we proposed that peripheral ties have three distinct associations with close social partners (Fingerman & Griffiths, 1999) : 1) peripheral partners may later become more intimate social contacts (e.g., a coworker who becomes a friend); 2) individuals on the periphery of a social network may remain there (e.g., a hairstylist or attorney, a longtime neighbor who has never become a more intimate social partner); 3) close partners may shift to the periphery for any number of reasons (e.g., geographic moves, changes in jobs, their children are grown).

In other words, the peripheral arena can serve as a staging ground or storage area for intimate ties. Indeed, scholarship examining social networks over time has used the term "peripheral" to refer to partners who are named in a social network at one point in time but not at a subsequent time. These ties are often latent or inactive, but available to become close again (Hammer, 1983; Lang, 2000; Morgan, Neal, & Carder, 1996). Likewise, relationships can end in good stead and become peripheral ties. Close ties take time and energy, but time constraints do not require individuals to sever relationships completely. Rather, a former roommate, a neighbor who lived next door to the first house you purchased, a coworker after retirement may all become peripheral ties.

In summary, peripheral ties may remain peripheral for long periods of time, can evolve into closer ties, or can arise from closer ties. The next section describes developmental functions of peripheral ties that may differ from or complement functions of closer relationships.

Discrete Functions of Peripheral Ties

Scholarly interest in peripheral ties in a developmental context involves debate over whether children and adolescents derive greater socialization experiences from larger peer groups than from familial experiences (Harris, 1995, 2000; Maccoby, 2002; Vandell, 2000). Yet discrete analysis of close and peripheral ties is impossible. Peripheral ties arise in schools and neighborhoods where families reside. Parents select day care settings and play activities for children in early life that reflect the child's temperament, the parents' personality, their reciprocal relationship, and available resources. The work world and the family world influence one another reciprocally in adulthood. Rather than consider whether peripheral ties or close ties are more important at any given stage of life, I attempt to delineate functions of peripheral ties less available in closer social ties.

Novelty and Information. As mentioned previously, descriptions of weak social ties initially emphasized the idea that such ties provide access to social resources not available from closer social ties (Granovetter, 1973). In this regard, peripheral ties may serve unique functions by providing models of cultural behaviors not readily available from a smaller network of close ties. Indeed, group socialization theories suggest that children and adolescents derive experiences from their peer groups not available with their parents or siblings (Harris, 1995, 2000; Maccoby, 2002). Harris specifically argues that intra- and intergroup processes, not dyadic relationships, are

responsible for the transmission of culture and for environmental modification of children's personality characteristics. This premise has been subject
to considerable debate and questioning in the field of child development
(see Vandell, 2000, for a critique). Yet of note is that scholarly discussion has
focused primarily on the larger aggregate groups of children rather than intimate dyads. Indeed, Maccoby (2002) explicitly points out that boys play
in larger groups than do girls, and group size itself may have differing
socialization experience. From a peripheral tie perspective, these theories
suggest that extra-familial social partners present children with socialization experiences not available in their families or close friends. It remains to
be seen, however, whether this novelty reflects a lack of intimacy between
partners and exposure to a variety of behaviors, group processes available in aggregates of familial or non-familial members, or a combination
of these factors.

Peripheral Ties and Regulation of Behavior. The opening vignette described a crowded parking lot filled with cooperative parents. This example suggests individuals may regulate their behaviors when in the presence of peripheral partners. Scholars have found that some people feel
free to act badly or with aggression when in a crowd of strangers. Likewise,
close social partners may accept poor behaviors on occasion. Peripheral
partners are not so forgiving. Indeed, social partners may view peripheral partners in a particularly negative light when they behave badly. In
a study of close, problematic, and ambivalent social ties, we found that
individuals aged 13 to 99 were most likely to name peripheral partners as
solely "problematic," but to view close social partners and family members
who cause aggravation as "ambivalent" (Hay, Birditt, Cichy, & Fingerman,
2001). Two theoretical explanations exist for these findings. Investment
theory suggests that when individuals value social partners highly, they
forgive annoying behaviors because they do not wish to risk severing their
ties (Rusbult, Johnson, & Morrow, 1986; Rusbult, Verette, Whitney, Slovik,
& Lipkus, 1991). By contrast, peripheral partners may view one another
as expendable at some level. Further, attribution theory explains differences in the way close and peripheral social partners may perceive one
another's behaviors. In a close relationship, a partner may assume bad
behavior stems from the situation. In peripheral relationships, partners
are more likely to make internal attributions and assume poor behavior
reflects something negative about the other party (Jones & Nisbett, 1972;
Ross & Nisbett, 1991). Of course, this does not mean that people feel free
to behave *badly* with close social partners. Rather, peripheral partners may
expect social partners to behave in more regulated ways.

Indeed, individuals recognize the need to regulate behaviors with peripheral partners from an early age. For example, in laboratory settings,
preschool children work hard to find equitable outcomes when they play in

"open field settings" with many other children. By contrast, when pairs of young friends play together in laboratory settings, they are more competitive and contentious (Berndt, Hawkins, & Hoyle, 1986; Hartup, French, Laursen, Johnston, & Ogawa, 1993; Laursen & Collins, 1994).

Developmental Functions. Finally, peripheral partners, such as distant kin or a client at work, may provide a form of "meta-development," or developmental awareness for individuals. When individuals have not seen a social partner in weeks or even months, the social partner may comment on differences or stability from the prior encounter. For children, the comment "My, how you've grown!" evokes feelings of pleasure. "You haven't changed a bit" can have a comparable effect at midlife. Such peripheral partners narrate the course of human development, particularly in adulthood, when changes may take place slowly and may be imperceptible to intimate partners with whom individuals interact on a frequent basis.

In other words, peripheral ties allow for relaxed behaviors in some contexts, and demand more regulated behaviors in other contexts. They may provide ties to new social partners at some stages of life and ties to the past at other stages of life. Development in a social arena comprised solely of close and intimate ties would look different, yet, as the next section describes, the peripheral network may also parallel functions served by closer social ties.

Similarities in Functions of Peripheral and Intimate Ties

Scholars have argued that close relationships support and even foster individual development across the life span (Erikson, 1950; Hartup, 1989; Hogan, 1985). Similarly, peripheral ties may serve to support or enhance developmental functions. Yet, as I described previously, the manner in which peripheral ties do so may vary from the way in which close ties do so.

As an example, peripheral ties may support individuals' sense of identity. Workers at a sawmill have a sense of themselves as "mill workers" derived in part from their encounters at that mill and the world around them. As will be discussed, peripheral partners may also allow individuals to try out aspects of their identity not as readily supported by close social partners who have established ideas about who they are. Adolescents may engage in experimentation with peers at school and older adults may relive a time when they were young and vital with an old friend passing through town – peripheral ties of different sorts allow individuals to enjoy different facets of their identities.

Finally, throughout life, peripheral partners may offer social support to individuals, just as close social partners do. Scholars have been interested in the role of mentorship and support provided by non-familial adults to children and adolescents (Werner 1989, 1995). Older adults also derive support from peripheral partners. Cantor (1979) interviewed over 1,500 older adults living in New York City and found that nearly two-thirds of the sample knew at least one of their neighbors well, and relied on these neighbors in emergencies for support. More recently, Barker (2002) reported findings from a study examining care to frail older adults provided by neighbors and other non-kin associates. As will be discussed, the types of support that individuals solicit from peripheral ties may vary across the life span.

   In sum, peripheral partners may enhance developmental functions just as close ties do. Although people may not connect to specific peripheral ties as a result of their own motivation for social contact, individuals' motivation for specific developmental goals may be manifest in peripheral relationships. The next section describes age differences in the types and functions of peripheral ties across the life span.

AGE DIFFERENCES IN PERIPHERAL TIES ACROSS THE LIFE SPAN

The prior sections dealt with parameters of peripheral ties and functions of peripheral ties in contrast to close social ties. This section highlights the ways in which peripheral ties might vary at different stages of life. Of course, tasks and goals carry over throughout life; it is merely the salience that varies. For example, although issues of independence may be particularly important in adolescence, individuals of all ages value aspects of autonomy. Further, it is not my intention to imply that peripheral and close ties are in competition with regard to developmental influences. Nonetheless, individuals appear to use peripheral partners in specific ways at specific stages of the life span, deriving benefits not clearly available in closer ties. This section briefly describes this progression of peripheral ties at different phases of life.

Infancy

Ties to caregivers dominate the infant's social world in the first months of life (Hartup, 1989). One of the most distinct social behaviors in the first year, however, involves infants' recognition of strangers beginning in the eighth or ninth month of life (Mangelsdorf, Shapiro, & Marzolf, 1995; Sroufe, 1977). Babies show individual differences in their reactions to these strangers (Kagan, 1984). Yet early cognitive and social abilities permit babies to make distinctions between intimate social contacts and other social contacts prior to the end of the first year, suggesting that this distinction is hard-wired and serves purposes for survival. Yet it is not clear whether infants conceptualize a fine-tuned hierarchy of social partners involving peripheral ties. As Spitze (1945) demonstrated decades ago, infants require warm contact with a consistent care provider. Repeated exposure to tangential social partners in the absence of such an attachment figure is deleterious. In certain respects, to infants, peripheral partners are strangers.

In the presence of a secure attachment figure, however, infants may benefit from exposure to less familiar partners. For example, many children spend their weekdays in care settings with non-familial adults and children. It is beyond the scope of this chapter to discuss variability in qualities of care settings, but in general, infants who have opportunities to develop early competence with peers demonstrate greater social skills in childhood (Howes, 1988, 1998). Furthermore, infants may benefit from exposure to peripheral contacts in their parents' presence, such as the parents' friends. Here, babies use social referencing to ascertain how to respond to peripheral partners. Cross-cultural studies show that babies who are frequently exposed to such ties show less distress than babies who are rarely exposed to extra-familial adults (Briggs, 1970 ; Chisholm, 1983). Such exposure may help suppress neophobic responses ; these babies learn to accept novelty and new people. They also acquire skills in transforming peripheral liaisons into intimate social ties.

In summary, during the first years of life, contact with consistent, warm care providers serves fundamental purposes for development. Yet for children who have such ties, exposure to peripheral ties may provide benefits with regard to the acceptance of novel social partners and the ability to form new relationships.

Childhood

Throughout childhood, children garner increasing exposure to peripheral social contacts, particularly in industrialized countries. By middle childhood, children spend six to eight hours a day surrounded by classmates, teachers, coaches, peers, and other peripheral partners, rather than with their families. At a general level, in childhood, the family serves as a forum for stability. (Of course, some families are more disorganized and chaotic than other families.) As mentioned with regard to infancy, the ability to understand and predict consistent social behavior in the family is undeniably important in the early years of life (and throughout life), but the peripheral arena allows development of other social skills, including the ability to master novel situations. Further, in societies that value independence and autonomy, the family cannot fully socialize children toward these goals. Rather, peripheral partners provide opportunities for the child to separate from close ties.

Children are clearly able to distinguish people who are close to them from people who are not. Over forty years ago, scholars demonstrated that children (like adults) can be induced to reject a group of peers whom they view as an "out-group" and to become belligerent and aggressive toward members of this group (Sherif, Harvey, White, Hood, & Sherif, 1961). News stories of shootings in American schools notwithstanding, however, most children do not spend their day in adversarial confrontations with peripheral partners. Rather, children's contact with schoolmates, teachers, neighbors, and other peripheral partners helps them acquire skills negotiating with people who are not intimate, skills that are essential in modern economies. Furthermore, even in small communities in nonindustrialized countries, children are often allowed into the huts or living quarters of nonfamily members to which adults are not privy (Briggs, 1970; Gardner, 1991) and develop similar skills.

Yet, distinctions between peripheral and close peers may be vague in childhood. Children's friendships are more fluid than adolescents' or adults' friendships, and are often based on proximity and availability rather than distinct characteristics of the other party (Hartup, 1989; Selman, 1981). Nonetheless, beginning in the preschool years, children show different behaviors when with friends and when with "other kids" (Hartup, 1989; Hartup et al., 1993), and by middle childhood, children can verbally identify who is a friend and who is on the periphery of their social network (Parker & Asher, 1993).

Children may expand their own repertoire of behaviors from observations of cultural models in the peripheral network. Family members could not possibly display the range of behaviors evident in a larger set of human beings. The oft-repeated refrain "But that's not how they do it at Susie's house..." reflects the child's increasing sense of how his or her family compares to other available models in the culture. In addition, children, like other young mammals, enjoy playing (Lorenz, 1952; Wallace, 1973). Of course, family members can provide fun times, but other children are more likely to have the energy to play. As Howes (1988) pointed out, a small child is unlikely to be willing to listen to his peer sing the alphabet out of tune but would be perfectly willing to join in and jump off a step twenty times in a row.

Peripheral ties also contribute to self-definition, even at this early stage of life. Children interact with other children based on ideas about status, and these interactions may accumulate into beliefs about the self over time; evidence suggests that children who achieve a status as particularly popular or rejected at one point in time will show effects of this status into puberty and even adulthood (Bagwell, Newcomb, & Bukowski, 1998; Dodge, 1983; Kuperschmidt & Coie, 1990; Parker & Asher, 1987). Of course, persistence in patterns of rejection or popularity could reflect stable traits within the child, such as a sour demeanor or an easygoing manner. Yet data suggest that continuity involves reciprocal influences of the individual's characteristics and transactions with social partners (e.g., Caspi, Elder, & Bem, 1987).

In sum, children gain increasing exposure to peripheral social partners as they enter cultural institutions and spend time away from their parents. Peripheral partners may include like-age peers, teachers, coaches, family friends, and neighbors. These partners provide exposure to the larger world at this stage of life and practice interacting with it.

Adolescence

Regardless of their beliefs about the influence of parents, scholars concur that the peer group in adolescence influences developmental outcomes (Harris, 1995, 2000; Vandell, 2000). Mentors, teachers, and other adults also serve peripheral roles in adolescents' daily lives. In essence, the peripheral network may serve several functions as adolescents prepare for adulthood, including: 1) processes in the formation of identity; 2) practice distinguishing behaviors between intimate and non-intimate social partners; 3) expanding models of cultural behaviors; 4) opportunities for definition of sexuality; and 5) provision of guidance, advice, or support. Given the plethora of writings on peers and identity formation, it would not be possible to do justice to that issue here. Instead, I focus on what peripheral ties add to adolescents' lives that intimate ties might not.

As mentioned previously, in many cultures children experience freedom from social barriers that exist for adults. Therefore, at some point adolescents must begin to distinguish between intimate and non-intimate social partners and to differentiate their behaviors accordingly. Although children *can* distinguish between friend and peer as early as preschool, in adolescence, these distinctions appear more explicitly in the social world. Adolescents have the cognitive capacities to form friendships based on psychological characteristics such as intimacy, loyalty, and disclosure (Selman, 1981; Sullivan, 1953). Several decades ago, Dunphy (1963) observed that adolescents belong to cliques of closer friends while also maintaining contact with peripheral partners in the larger crowd. In other words, hierarchies of intimacy are evident in adolescents' social worlds, with a larger group of peripheral ties, and a smaller group of intimate ties. This social organization provides adolescents a forum for learning appropriate behaviors with intimate partners (e.g., self-disclosure) and less intimate social partners (e.g., self-presentation) – an essential function in the adult social world.

Furthermore, adolescents spend increasing periods of time in extra-familial settings, at least in the United States (Larson & Richards, 1994). Adolescents' developmental needs may enhance the influence of these social partners. Conformity pressures intensify and the persuasiveness of peripheral ties as cultural models may become heightened. In establishing their identities, adolescents may take on attributes and behaviors from observations in this milieu.

Finally, teachers, coaches, supervisors at work (should the adolescent have a job), and adult neighbors are part of adolescents' lives. Many adolescents develop ties to such adults, who serve as "mentors." Research suggests adult mentors can help alleviate problems for adolescents who are at risk for poor outcomes due to poverty or disturbances in the family (Werner, 1989, 1995). For the adolescent, the tie may involve a subjective sense of intimacy and stability, rather than a sense that this tie is on the periphery. Yet scholarship tends to treat these ties as peripheral.

In sum, adolescence is a period of increasing interaction with the world outside the family. Adolescents engage in contact with a larger peer group and with adults who are not directly connected to their families. Peripheral ties at this stage of life facilitate entry into adulthood.

Young Adulthood

Young adulthood may include several transitions, such as completion of education, entry into the work world, finding a romantic partner, and having children. Peripheral partners in the young adult period vary as a function of these transitions. Individuals who are enrolled in college or postgraduate education spend much of their time surrounded by like-aged peers. By contrast, in the work world, individuals generally interact with a much wider age range of people. As individuals enter the adult world, peripheral ties serve several functions, such as 1) defining social status within the larger society, 2) supplying social connections and information, and 3) providing opportunities for fun, activities, and companionship.

The conceptualization of peripheral ties presented in this chapter portrays a set of social partners who exist regardless of individuals' desire to be involved with these partners. Yet, at certain phases of life, motivation to accrue a larger peripheral arena may also be heightened. In young adulthood, the peripheral arena is a form of social capital. Carstensen and her colleagues argue that individuals seek novel social partners in order to learn new information at this stage of life (Carstensen, Isaacowitz, & Charles, 1999). In addition to providing information, peripheral partners may introduce individuals to other social partners and potential mates. Indeed, as mentioned previously, scholars interested in "weak ties" report that some individuals use such ties to find jobs or social resources (Granovetter, 1973; Wegener, 1991).

Although class differences in the nature of peripheral ties are evident at all phases of life, completion of education and entrance into the work world make these issues particularly stark in young adulthood. The type of job or career that adults enter influences the types of peripheral ties to which they are exposed. In young adulthood, peripheral liaisons may be both an outcome and an underlying cause of socioeconomic disparities.

For example, young adults from higher socioeconomic backgrounds are more likely to know people who can provide information about a high-paying job (Wegener, 1991). Further, peripheral liaisons in work settings may have an impact on individuals' values, beliefs, and even their person-alities (Hughes & Perry-Jenkins, 1996; Kohn, 1977). Work is not simply a set of tasks individuals complete each day – the work world is comprised of other people. Individuals discuss their values and mimic behaviors of the people around them, including peripheral partners.

In sum, in young adulthood the peripheral network can provide op-portunities and resources that establish individuals in the larger society. Scholars have suggested that certain transitions, such as becoming a par-ent, induce individuals away from peers and activities (Noller, Feeney, & Peterson, 2001). As individuals accumulate increasing responsibilities through romantic partnership and children, the nature of their peripheral arena may shift toward that found in midlife.

Midlife

The period of midlife is broad, with few clear-cut developmental mark-ers. Middle age is often defined as beginning around age 40 and end-ing when adults retire around age 65, but extant definitions encompass adults as young as 25 and as old as 75 (Lachman, 2001). There is con-siderable diversity in the peripheral ties individuals in this age range en-counter. Middle-aged adults are exposed to different types of peripheral partners as a function of their work situation, marital status, familial con-texts (e.g., having children of their own, having living parents), and avail-able resources. Nonetheless, in comparisons to younger and older adults, middle-aged adults incur certain shared experiences in their peripheral ties.

In general, the network of intimate social ties expands at this stage of life (Antonucci & Akiyama, 1987). Life in the middle is rich with social contacts above, below, and in the same generation as oneself. In fact, in a recent study, we asked individuals of different ages about their living rel-atives (regardless of whether these relatives involved intimate social part-ners). Middle-aged and young-old adults had a considerably larger trove of relatives than did adolescents, young adults, or oldest old adults (e.g., siblings, parents, romantic partners/spouses, children, and even grandchil-dren) (Fingerman & Birditt, in press).

Given this array of close ties, two patterns are possible with regard to the peripheral network: 1) close social ties may use up available time and energy, leaving little time to interact with peripheral partners; or 2) the peripheral network may parallel the intimate network by expanding as well. Theoretically, we might expect to see the latter pattern. Middle-aged adults' lives may be saturated with liaisons to peripheral partners.

Individuals' investment in the larger family appears to increase at midlife, particularly for women; as a result, middle-aged adults may incur contact with distant kin such as grown siblings, in-laws, nieces, nephews, and so forth (Fingerman, 2001). Men and women in the work world may also find their positions have expanded to include increased contact with a wide array of daily contacts (clients, coworkers, or supervisees). Further, middle-aged adults may have more ties through their intimate partners; they may interact with their children's friends, husband's sister-in-law, and coworker's spouse.

Given the variety of social contacts individuals encounter at midlife it is difficult to speculate about the functions peripheral ties serve. By midlife, the network of close and peripheral ties may work in tandem to provide individuals with a sense of well-being. Young adults may be viewed as in-experienced, and older adults may suffer ageism, but middle-aged adults garner a degree of respect in society. The peripheral network may rein-force these perceptions. Further, in midlife individuals reap the benefits and harms of decisions and changes made in young adulthood. Periph-eral partners may reinforce middle-aged adults' sense of self-definition. Earlier in life, individuals may have relied on peripheral ties for exper-imentation with identity. In midlife, peripheral partners may provide a sense of stability.

Late Life

Theories of social development and empirical studies suggest that the over-all size of the social network decreases dramatically in late life, with much of that change occurring through selective exclusion of less rewarding so-cial partners (Carstensen, Isaacowitz, & Charles, 1999; Lang, 2001). This evidence applies primarily to the social support network, where it is clear that peripheral ties diminish with age. It is less clear how many peripheral ties remain or how peripheral ties function in daily life. Daily activities shift such that interactions with peripheral ties may diminish. For example, it is unlikely that individuals interact with as many peripheral partners after retirement as they did while in the workforce.

The specific types of partner in the peripheral network may also vary in late life. For example, as they incur health impairments, older adults have more frequent contact with health practitioners. These formal care providers – doctors, nurses, pharmacists – may serve as peripheral ties in the older adults' world. It is an empirical question whether such pe-ripheral partners have an impact on older adults' mood and psychological well-being, above and beyond the disease state and the network of close supportive ties.

Further, older adults' daily contacts may involve connections to the community rather than the work world. Older adults appear to have more frequent contact with neighbors and church members than do younger adults. Scarce empirical work on these ties suggests that older adults find such peripheral partners valuable with regard to functions of daily living (Cantor, 1979; Johnson & Barer, 1997).

As with close partners, peripheral partners may lend individuals a sense of cohesion at the end of life. Theorists have argued that a central task of old age is to reflect on, and to make sense of, one's life (Butler, 1963; Erikson, Erikson, & Kivnick, 1986) and social partners may assist in this process. For example, a study of holiday card networks revealed that older adults sometimes continued to exchange cards with people they had not seen in thirty or forty years (Fingerman & Griffiths, 1999). Such ties may allow "social reminiscence." Continuous relationships, such as those found between spouses or friends, evolve over time. Individuals can reminisce about the past, but the present relationship intervenes to remind them that they have grown older. Ties to past partners allow individuals to take a psychological leap into memories. A reunion with an old friend is like time travel back to college days or younger times.

In sum, although the least intimate partners may fall off in late life, older adults retain ties to some peripheral partners. The social arena of late life may not involve the diverse array of social contacts evident in young or middle adulthood, but older adults retain peripheral ties to the community through neighbors and church. Further, peripheral ties to past partners may provide individuals a sense of cohesion.

FUTURE RESEARCH AND CONCLUSION

The territory available for future research on peripheral ties is vast and open. Few researchers have examined these ties. Indeed, a graduate student and I recently conducted a content analysis of extant studies published in major journals focusing on personal and family relationships from 1994 to 1999. Fewer than 5% of studies in these journals examined peripheral relationships. Indeed, 70% of studies focused on spouses, romantic partners, and parents and children (Fingerman & Hay, 2002).

This chapter is largely theoretical and speculative. A first step in future research involves documenting the types of peripheral social ties individuals encounter and the functions they serve. Who is in the peripheral network and how do we classify these individuals? Researchers might utilize Q-sort methodologies and multidimensional scaling to determine whether a shared taxonomy of peripheral ties exists. For example, we might consider distant kin, daily contacts (e.g., coworkers, classmates), service providers, and connected liaisons (e.g., friends of friends) as distinct categories of peripheral ties. Alternately, researchers might consider whether a more hierarchical approach to classification of relationships (from most intimate to most distant) would be more useful.

Assessments of peripheral ties warrant a variety of approaches. Researchers might utilize diary methodology, where they survey participants on a daily basis and ask about the nature of their contacts with peripheral partners that day. Alternately, scholars might utilize event sampling where they page participants at random intervals and ask about social contacts during the prior half hour. These approaches circumvent a principal difficulty in assessing peripheral ties: people have trouble remembering relationships that are not salient.

There are several weaknesses in using diary or event sampling, however. First, these measures rely on self-report. Alternate methodologies, such as observation, are necessary to assess peripheral ties among small children. As mentioned in the opening chapter of this book, however, use of disparate methodologies to assess different parts of the life span introduces problems of noncomparability. Further, periodic measurements involved in diary and event sampling are unlikely to tap less frequent peripheral contacts such as a family doctor or a member of a club.

To capture less frequent peripheral social contacts, approaches that focus on specific contexts may fare better. Address books, Internet searches, alumni associations, long-distance phone bills, and reunions might provide fodder to study such ties. A disadvantage of these assessments lies in predefining the settings where such ties might be found, however.

Further, a key class of ties remains to be considered. This chapter described social ties that are not "close" or "intimate" but where there is *mutual* recognition by the partners that a tie exists. Social ties based on cognitive representations were not considered. At all stages of life, individuals may retain emotional bonds to individuals or objects who do not return their esteem. The toddler's tie to a teddy bear, the adolescent's sense of connection to a famous rock star, and the older adult's conversations with a deceased relative are examples. These ties warrant additional attention for functions they serve in individuals' sense of social embeddedness, definition of self, and connections to other social partners. Of course, these ties may not be "peripheral" from the individual's perspective.

Finally, to conclude this chapter on a provocative note, I posit that peripheral liaisons are central to human development at a larger species level. Current understanding of our history suggests that early Homo sapiens lived in small groups of intimate social partners who wandered the savanna. Close, rather than peripheral, ties were pervasive within the social structure. At times, other groups were encountered, particularly around large bodies of water during the dry season. These gatherings gave opportunities for mate selection, but did not involve daily interactions for the entire clan (Diamond, 1997; Shostak, 1981). With urbanization nearly one thousand years ago, and mobility during the past century, the nature of human contact shifted. We now find small geographic areas occupied by masses of people who must interact with each other, but who do not know one another well. We are still evolving as a species, and current evolutionary pressures may favor the ability to adjust to encounters with relative strangers. We shall have to leave it to our descendants to see how things turn out.

In sum, other chapters in this volume demonstrate that close social ties shape individuals' lives. At the same time, social contacts on the periphery have an impact on development. Intimate partners may influence the trajectories of our lives, but the people we encounter in the parking lot outside the Henderson building set a tempo for our daily mood and tie us to larger social structures. As this chapter suggests, not all strangers are truly "strangers." Some strangers are more familiar than others, and *these* strangers have consequences for human development at many levels.

References

Antonucci, T. C. (2001). Social relations: An examination of social networks, social support, and sense of control. In J. E. Birren & K. W. Schaie (Eds.), *Handbook of the psychology of aging*. Orlando, FL: Academic Press.

Antonucci, T. C., & Akiyama, H. (1987). Social networks in adult life and a preliminary examination of the convoy model. *Journal of Gerontology, 42*, 519–527.

Antonucci, T. C., Langfahl, E. S., & Akiyama, H. (2003). Relationships as outcomes and contexts. In F. R. Lang & K. L. Fingerman (Eds.), *Growing together: Personal relationships across the life span* (Chap. 2). New York: Cambridge University Press.

Bagwell, C. L., Newcomb, A. F., & Bukowksi, W. M. (1998). Preadolescent friendship and peer rejection as predictors of adult adjustment. *Child Development, 69*, 140–153.

Barker, J. C. (2002). Neighbors, friends, and other nonkin caregivers of community-living dependent elders. *Journals of Gerontology: Psychological Sciences and Social Sciences, 57*, S158–S167.

Baumrind, D. (1971). Current patterns of parental authority. *Developmental Psychology Monographs, 4*.

Berndt, T. J., Hawkins, J. A., & Hoyle, S. G. (1986). Changes in friendship during a school year: Effects on children's and adolescents' impressions of friendship and sharing with friends. *Child Development, 57*, 1284–1297.

Birditt, K. S. (2002). Age and gender differences in reactions to interpersonal tensions: The daily experience of arguments and the avoidance of arguments. Unpublished doctoral dissertation, Pennsylvania State University, Pennsylvania.

Blieszner, R., & Roberto, K. A. (2003). Friendship across the life span: Reciprocity in individual and relationship development. In F. R. Lang & K. L. Fingerman (Eds.), *Growing together: Personal relationships across the life span* (Chap. 7). New York: Cambridge University Press.

Bolger, N., & Eckenrode, J. (1991). Social relationships, personality, and anxiety during a major stressful event. *Journal of Personality and Social Psychology, 3*, 440–449.

Briggs, J. (1970). *Never in anger: Portrait of an Eskimo family* (pp. 109–146). Cambridge, MA: Harvard University Press.

Bronfenbrenner, U. (1979). *The ecology of human development*. Cambridge, MA: Harvard University Press.

Bronfenbrenner, U., & Morris, P. A. (1997). The ecology of developmental processes. In W. Damon (Ed.), *Handbook of child psychology* (5th ed.) (pp. 993–1028). New York: Wiley.

Burton, L. M. (1995). Intergenerational patterns of providing care in African-American families with teenage childbearers: Emergent patterns in an ethnographic study. In V. L. Bengtson & K. W. Schaie (Eds.), *Adult intergenerational relations: Effects of societal change*. New York: Springer Publishers.

Butler, R. N. (1963). The life review: An interpretation of reminiscence in the aged. *Psychiatry, 256,* 65–76.

Cantor, M. H. (1979). Neighbors and friends: An overlooked resource in the informal support system. *Research on Aging, 1,* 434–463.

Carstensen, L. L., Isaacowitz, D. M., & Charles, S. T. (1999). Taking time seriously: A theory of socioemotional selectivity. *American Psychologist, 54,* 165–181.

Caspi, A., Elder, G. H., & Bem, D. J. (1987). Moving against the world: Life-course patterns of explosive children. *Developmental Psychology, 23,* 308–313.

Chisholm, J. S. (1983). *Navajo infancy: An ethological study in child development*. New York: Aldine.

Cowen, E. L. (1982). Help is where you find it: Four informal helping groups. *American Psychologist, 37,* 385–395.

Cowen, E. L., Gesten, E. L., Boike, M., Norton, P., Wilson, A. B., & DeStefano, M. A. (1979). Hairdressers as caregivers I: A descriptive profile of interpersonal help-giving involvement. *American Journal of Community Psychology, 7,* 633–648.

Cowen, E. L., McKim, B. J., & Weisberg, R. P. (1981). Bartenders as informal, interpersonal help-agents. *American Journal of Community Psychology, 9,* 715–729.

Crouter, A. C., & Bumpus, M. F. (2001). Linking parents' work stress to children's and adolescents' psychological adjustment. *Current Directions in Psychological Science, 10,* 156–159.

Diamond, J. (1997). *Guns, germs, and steel: The fates of human societies*. New York: W. W. Norton.

Dodge, K. A. (1983). Behavioral antecedents of peer social status. *Child Development, 54,* 1386–1399.

Dunphy, D. C. (1963). The social structure of urban adolescent peer groups. *Sociometry, 26,* 230–246.

Erikson, E. H. (1950). *Childhood and society* (pp. 247–273). New York: W. W. Norton.

Erikson, E. H., Erikson, J. M., & Kivnick, H. Q. (1986). *Vital involvement in old age: The experience of old age in our time*. New York: Norton & Company.

Fingerman, K. L. (2001). *Aging mothers and their adult daughters: A study in mixed emotions*. New York: Springer Publishers.

Fingerman, K. L., & Birditt, K. S. (in press). Do age differences in close and problematic family networks reflect the pool of available relatives? *Journals of Gerontology: Psychological Sciences*.

Fingerman, K. L., & Griffiths, P. C. (1999). Season's greetings: Adults' social contact at the holiday season. *Psychology and Aging, 14,* 192–205.

Fingerman, K. L., & Hay, E. L. (2002). Searching under the streetlight: Age biases in the personal and family relationships literature. *Personal Relationships, 9,* 415–433.

Fingerman, K. L., Hay, E. L., Porfeli, E., Mayger, H., & Birditt, K. S. (1999, November). Searching under the streetlight: Laypersons' and researchers' conceptions of important social ties. Symposium paper presented in K. L. Fingerman (chair), "Underresearched topics in social support," annual meeting of the Gerontological Society of America, San Francisco, CA.

Gardner, K. (1991). *Songs at the river's edge: Stories from a Bangladesh village*. Chicago, IL: Pluto Press.

Granovetter, M. S. (1973). The strength of weak ties. *American Journal of Sociology*, *78*, 1360–1380.

Hammer, M. (1983). 'Core' and 'extended' social networks in relation to health and illness. *Social Science and Medicine*, *17*, 405–411.

Hansson, R. O., Daleiden, E. L., & Hayslip, B., Jr. (2003). Relational competence across the life span. In F. R. Lang & K. L. Fingerman (Eds.), *Growing together: Personal relationships across the life span* (Chap. 13). New York: Cambridge University Press.

Harris, J. R. (1995). Where is the child's environment? A group socialization theory of development. *Psychological Review*, *102*, 458–489.

Harris, J. R. (2000). Socialization, personality development, and the child's environment: Comment on Vandell (2000). *Developmental Psychology*, *36*, 711–723.

Hartup, W. W. (1989). Social relationships and their developmental significance. *American Psychologist*, *44*, 120–126.

Hartup, W. W., French, D. C., Laursen, B., Johnston, M. K., & Ogawa, J. R. (1993). Conflict and friendship relations in middle childhood: Behavior in a closed-field situation. *Child Development*, *64*, 445–454.

Hay, E. L., Birditt, K. S., Cichy, K., & Fingerman, K. L. (2001). Age differences in close, problematic, and ambivalent social ties. In K. L. Fingerman (chair), "Complexities in socioemotional experiences," symposium presented at the Gerontological Society of America meeting, Chicago, IL, November 2001.

Heider, F. (1958). *The psychology of interpersonal relations*. New York: Wiley.

Hinde, R. A. (1979). *Towards understanding relationships*. New York: Academic Press.

Hinde, R. A. (1995). A suggested structure for a science of relationships. *Personal Relationships*, *2*, 1–15.

Hogan, D. (1985). Parental influences on the timing of early life transitions. In Z. Blau (Ed.), *Current perspectives on aging and the life cycle* (pp. 1–59). Greenwich, CT: JAI Press.

House, J. S., Kahn, R. L., McLeod, J. D., & Williams, D. (1985). Measures and concepts of social support. In S. Cohen & S. L. Syme (Eds.), *Social support and health* (pp. 83–108). Orlando, FL: Academic Press.

Howes, C. (1988). Peer interaction of young children. *Monograph of the Society for Research on Child Development*, *Volume 53* (Serial 217).

Howes, C. (1998). The earliest friendships. In W. M. Bukowski & A. F. Newcomb (Eds.), *The company they keep: Friendship in childhood and adolescence* (pp. 66–86). New York: Cambridge University Press.

Hughes, R., & Perry-Jenkins, M. (1996). Social class issues in family life education. *Family Relations*, *45*, 175–182.

Johnson, C. L. (1995). Determinants of adaptation of oldest old black Americans. *Journal of Aging Studies*, *9*, 231–244.

Johnson, C., & Barer, B. (1997). *Life beyond 85 years: The aura of survivorship.* New York: Springer Publishing.

Jones, E. E., & Nisbett, R. E. (1972). The actor and observer: Divergent perceptions of the causes of behaviors. In E. E. Jones, D. E. Kanouse, H. H. Kelley, R. E. Nisbett, S. Valins, & B. Weiner (Eds.), *Attribution: Perceiving the causes of behavior.* Morristown, NJ: General Learning Press.

Kagan, J. (1984). *The nature of the child.* New York: Basic Books.

Kahn, R. L., & Antonucci, T. C. (1980). Convoys over the life course: Attachment, roles, and social support. *Life-span Development, 3,* 253–286.

Kelley, H. H. (1983). Love and commitment. In H. H. Kelley et al. (Eds.), *Close relationships* (pp. 265–314). New York: W. H. Freeman.

Kohn, M. L. (1977). *Class and conformity: A study in values.* Homewood, IL: Dorsey Press.

Kuperschmidt, J. B., & Coie, J. D. (1990). Preadolescent peer status, aggression and school adjustment as predictors of externalizing behaviors in adolescence. *Child Development, 61,* 1350–1362.

Lachman, M. E. (Ed.) (2001). *Handbook of midlife development.* New York: Wiley.

Lang, F. R. (2000). Endings and continuity of social relationships: Maximizing intrinsic benefits within personal networks when feeling near to death. *Journal of Social and Personal Relationships, 17,* 157–184.

Lang, F. R. (2001). Regulation of social relationships in later adulthood. *Journals of Gerontology: Psychological Sciences, 56,* P321–P326.

Lang, F. R. (2003). Social motivation across the life span. In F. R. Lang & K. L. Fingerman (Eds.), *Growing together: Personal relationships across the life span* (Chap. 14). New York: Cambridge University Press.

Larson, R., & Richards, M. (1994). *Divergent realities: The emotional lives of mothers, fathers, and adolescents.* New York: Basic Books.

Laursen, B., & Collins, W. A. (1994). Interpersonal conflict during adolescence. *Psychological Bulletin, 115,* 197–209.

Lorenz, K. Z. (1952). *King Solomon's ring* (trans. M. K. Wilson). New York: Thomas Y. Crowell.

Maccoby, E. E. (2002). Gender and group process: A developmental perspective. *Current Directions in Psychological Science, 11,* 54–58.

Mangelsdorf, S. C., Shapiro, J. R., & Marzolf, D. (1995). Developmental and temperamental differences in emotion regulation in infancy. *Child Development, 66,* 1817–1828.

Marsden, P. V., & Campbell, K. E. (1984). Measuring tie strength. *Social Forces, 63,* 482–501.

Morgan, D. L., Neal, M. B., & Carder, P. (1996). The stability of core and peripheral networks over time. *Social Networks, 19,* 9–25.

Noller, P., Feeney, J. A., & Peterson, C. (2001). *Personal relationships across the lifespan.* Philadelphia, PA: Taylor and Francis.

Parker, J. G., & Asher, S. R. (1987). Peer relations and later personal adjustment: Are low-accepted children at risk? *Psychological Bulletin, 102,* 357–389.

Parker, J. G., & Asher, S. R. (1993). Friendship and friendship quality in middle childhood: Links with peer group acceptance and feelings of loneliness and social dissatisfaction. *Developmental Psychology, 29,* 611–621.

Repetti, R. (1989). Effects of daily workload on subsequent behavior during marital interactions: The roles of social withdrawal and spouse support. *Journal of Personality and Social Psychology, 57,* 651–659.

Ross, L., & Nisbett, R. E. (1991). *The person and the situation: Perspectives of social psychology.* Philadelphia: Temple University Press.

Rusbult, C. E., Johnson, D. J., & Morrow, G. D. (1986). Determinants and consequences of exit, voice, loyalty, and neglect: Responses to dissatisfaction in adult romantic involvements. *Human Relations, 39,* 45–63.

Rusbult, C. E., Verette, J., Whitney, G. A., Slovik, L. F., & Lipkus, I. (1991). Accommodation processes in close relationships: Theory and preliminary empirical evidence. *Journal of Personality and Social Psychology, 60,* 53–78.

Selman, R. (1981). The child as a friendship philosopher. In S. R. Asher & J. M. Gottman (Eds.), *The development of children's friendships.* Cambridge: Cambridge University Press.

Sherif, M., Harvey, O. J., White, B. J., Hood, W. R., & Sherif, C. W. (1961). *Intergroup cooperation and competition: The robbers cave experiment.* Norman, OK: University Book Exchange.

Shostak, M. (1981). *Nisa: The life and words of a !Kung woman.* New York: Random House.

Spitze, R. A. (1945). Hospitalism: An inquiry into the genesis of psychiatric conditioning in early childhood. *Psychoanalytic Studies of the Child, 1,* 53–74. New York: International Universities Press.

Sroufe, L. A. (1977). Wariness of strangers and the study of infant development. *Child Development, 48,* 731–746.

Sullivan, H. S. (1953). *The interpersonal theory of psychiatry.* New York: W. W. Norton.

Takahashi, K. (2003). Close relationships across the life span: Toward a theory of relationship types. In F. R. Lang & K. L. Fingerman (Eds.), *Growing together: Personal relationships across the life span* (Chap. 6). New York: Cambridge University Press.

Vandell, D. L. (2000). Parents, peer groups, and other socializing influences. *Developmental Psychology, 36,* 699–710.

Wallace, R. A. (1973). *The ecology and evolution of animal behavior.* Pacific Palisades, CA: Goodyear Publishing Company.

Wegener, B. (1991). Job mobility and social ties: Social resources, prior job, and status attainment. *American Sociological Review, 56,* 60–71.

Werner, E. E. (1989). Children of the garden island. *Scientific American, 260,* 107–111.

Werner, E. E. (1995). Resilience in development. *Current Directions in Psychological Science, 4,* 81–85.

9

Stress in Social Relationships: Coping and Adaptation across the Life Span

Karen Rook, Dara Sorkin, and Laura Zettel

Social relationships are an important source of support and companionship, but they can be a source of considerable frustration and disappointment as well. Stress in important social relationships has been found to detract from emotional and physical health, but coping responses may mitigate (or exacerbate) these adverse effects. We examine how people cope with two broad categories of interpersonal stress – conflict and loss – and discuss the implications of coping goals for understanding the nature and effectiveness of coping responses. We also consider some of the ways in which the process of adapting to relationship tensions and losses may vary across the life span and suggest directions for future research.

Social relationships are an important source of support and companionship throughout the life span, and empirical evidence amply demonstrates that involvement in satisfying social relationships is associated with enhanced emotional and physical health (House, Umberson, & Landis, 1988). Yet social relationships also can be a source of intense anxiety, anger, sorrow, and other negative emotions that detract from health and well-being (Rook, 1998). How people respond to the frustrations and disappointments they experience in their social relationships may affect the resulting toll on health and well-being. Relatively little work has investigated the nature or effectiveness of people's responses to stressors in their relationships with members of their social networks. In this chapter, we consider two broad categories of stress in social network relationships – conflict and loss – and examine how people might cope with each kind of interpersonal stress. We also discuss the effectiveness of such coping responses, as gauged in terms of their impact on personal well-being as well as their implications for relationship functioning.

We begin by considering the conflictual and disappointing interactions that sometimes occur between members of a social network. Both members of a relationship often recognize such interactions because a disagreement erupts between them or because one member of the relationship brings a perceived transgression to the attention of the partner. At other times, however, such shared recognition is absent because only one member of a relationship perceives a misdeed to have occurred and refrains from communicating this to the interaction partner. Resentments may remain dormant in such cases, with the potential to surface at a later point (Peterson, 1983). Such unilaterally experienced relationship disappointments are probably quite common, and they present additional challenges to the individual who seeks to cope with them. We accordingly discuss both unilaterally and mutually recognized relationship stressors. We then turn our attention to a second broad category of interpersonal stress – the loss of a close relationship or significant disruption of established patterns of interaction and exchange within a close relationship. Relationship losses arise from such events as the death or residential relocation of important members of one's social network. Relationship disruptions occur when access to a network member continues but when deteriorating health or other life circumstances sharply limit the network member's ability to participate in established patterns of interaction and exchange. Such losses or disruptions represent forms of interpersonal stress because, like relationship conflicts and disappointments, they tax the individual's coping resources and require adaptive responses.

We will provide examples of interpersonal stressors in each category and will discuss the relatively scant research that has investigated how people seek to respond to such stressors. We recognize that the motivation to respond to interpersonal stressors varies across people, and that their responses may not always be directed toward a resolution of the interpersonal problem. Sometimes their responses will be focused on managing their own emotional distress rather than remedying a disagreement or conflict. At other times, coping responses may directed primarily toward preserving goodwill in the relationship. Evaluating the effectiveness of responses to interpersonal stressors, therefore, may require attention to the coping objective(s) that motivate and direct coping responses (Coyne & Racioppo, 2000). We will discuss the implications of coping goals for understanding the nature and effectiveness of the coping responses that people draw upon in dealing with relationship disappointments or losses.

We also recognize that coping responses and outcomes may vary across different kinds of relationships and may change over time, as interpersonal stressors either dissipate or persist. The social environment is also likely to influence coping efforts and outcomes. For example, efforts to establish new friendships after a relationship major loss or disruption may be influenced by the pool of similar others in the social environment and by the response of individuals to whom overtures of friendship are made. We will consider how such contextual factors may influence the process of adapting to interpersonal stressors.

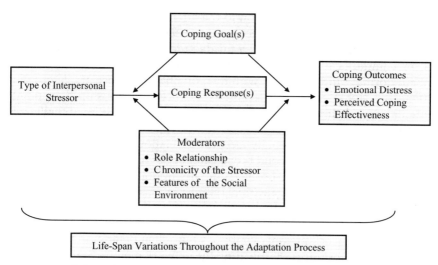

FIGURE 9.1. Adaptation to Interpersonal Stressors: Theoretical Model.

The framework that guides our discussion in the chapter, accordingly, includes attention to coping responses, coping goals, coping effectiveness, and several important contextual factors that influence the adaptation process. We apply this framework, shown in Figure 9.1, to each of the two categories of interpersonal stressors. We also consider some of the ways in which the adaptation process may vary across the life span, although the sparse empirical evidence on age differences in coping with interpersonal stressors makes our discussion of life-span variations necessarily speculative. Finally, the chapter concludes with suggestions for future research.

INTERPERSONAL CONFLICTS AND DISAPPOINTMENTS

Interpersonal conflicts and disappointments can take many forms, but they tend to have at their core the perception of a misdeed or transgression by a member of one's social network that causes one to experience distress and possible reservations about the interaction partner or the relationship itself. This can include acts of omission, such as excluding a friend from a social gathering, as well as acts of commission, such as criticizing a friend. Because our focus is on negative exchanges that occur between social network members, we do not examine exchanges that may be aversive but that occur between strangers (e.g., a shopkeeper and customer) (see Miller, 2001, for a treatment of such exchanges). We also focus on relatively commonplace, but nonetheless distressing, forms of negative social interactions, such as criticism, rejection, demands, and intrusions. Other authors have examined more extreme forms of negative social interactions, such as abusive or violent behavior (Emery & Laumann-Billings, 1998) as well as pathogenic interaction patterns that may play a role in the onset or maintenance of serious psychiatric disorders (Leff & Vaughn, 1981).

Kinds of Interpersonal Conflicts and Disappointments

The literature on negative exchanges in social network relationships evolved, in large part, to complement the very substantial literature on social support. As such, it reflects many of the substantive emphases and methodological approaches that have dominated the literature on social support. Just as social support researchers have been interested in social interactions that may enhance everyday functioning, foster adaptation to life stress, or facilitate the pursuit of personal goals, researchers who investigate negative social interactions have been interested in interactions that have the opposite effect – disrupting everyday functioning, interfering with adaptation to life stress, or undermining the pursuit of personal goals. This has led researchers to emphasize relatively delimited typologies of positive and negative social exchanges that are believed either to fulfill or thwart general needs for a sense of allegiance with others or situation-specific needs created by particular life challenges or goals (Lakey & Cohen, 2000; Wills & Shinar, 2000). In addition, much of this research emphasizes the positive and negative exchanges that people experience in a wide array of social network relationships, rather than within a specific dyadic relationship, such as the marital relationship or parent-child relationship. This is because the emphasis in such research tends to be on understanding, in an epidemiological sense, how the full range of support or conflict that people experience in their social network relationships influences their health and well-being. Other literatures provide more in-depth analyses of the conflictual and distressing interactions that occur in specific relationships, such as the marital relationship (Gottman & Notarius, 2000).

A review of the existing literature on negative exchanges in social networks provides a basis for distinguishing four common domains of negative social exchanges: intrusive or unsound advice provided by others, failure by others to provide tangible (instrumental) support in times of need, insensitive or critical behavior by others, and rejection or neglect by others (Newsom, Morgan, Nishishiba, & Rook, 2002). These correspond to four domains of positive social exchanges that have been emphasized in the literature: informational support, instrumental support, emotional support, and companionship. Differentiation of these four domains of negative social exchanges does not mean that they are mutually exclusive. To the contrary, the boundaries between domains can be fuzzy. For example, others' failure to provide help in times of need can be painful not only because it leaves a person without needed resources but also because it conveys disregard for the person, much like criticism or other insensitive behavior.

Adverse Effects of Interpersonal Conflicts and Disappointments. Negative social exchanges such as these detract significantly from psychological and physical health, despite the fact they tend to occur infrequently. In fact, studies that have compared the effects of positive and negative social exchanges have often found that negative exchanges are more strongly or reliably related to health outcomes (Rook, 1998). Not all research yields evidence of a disproportionate effect of negative social exchanges (Finch, Okun, Pool, & Ruehlman, 1999), but ample evidence documents that negative exchanges detract considerably from health and well-being.

Evidence of the damaging effects of negative social interactions has emerged in longitudinal as well as cross-sectional studies, including carefully controlled prospective studies. These effects persist when researchers include controls for potentially confounded factors, such as socioeconomic status, personality characteristics, and initial health status (Rook, 1998). In addition, in the few studies that have obtained reports of negative social exchanges from both members of a relationship, such as husbands and wives, significant correlations have emerged (Vinokur & Vinokur-Kaplan, 1990), suggesting that the findings reported in this literature do not solely reflect biased perceptions of relationships.

Coping Responses

Despite evidence documenting the harmful effects of negative social exchanges, relatively little research has examined how people cope with such exchanges. Much of the coping literature has examined how people cope with stressors that are not interpersonal in nature, such as life-threatening illness or financial stress. The theoretical perspectives that have guided investigations of coping with such non-interpersonal stressors may be useful, nonetheless, in examining how people cope with interpersonal stressors.

Problem-Focused and Emotion-Focused Interpersonal Coping Responses. Coping researchers have distinguished between two basic kinds of coping: problem-focused coping (externally directed responses aimed at changing the stressful situation itself) and emotion-focused coping (internally directed responses aimed at managing the negative emotions generated by the stressful event) (Lazarus & Folkman, 1984). This distinction between problem-focused and emotion-focused coping has been incorporated in the small body of research that has begun to examine how people cope with interpersonal stressors (e.g., Bolger & Zuckerman, 1995; O'Brien & DeLongis, 1996; Rahim, 1986; Suls, David, & Harvey, 1996). Varying labels have been used to describe specific kinds of interpersonal coping, but researchers have converged in identifying several common forms of problem-focused and emotion-focused coping responses. Problem-focused forms of interpersonal coping emphasized in this literature include compromise (efforts to achieve with the interaction partner a mutually satisfactory resolution of the problem), assertion or confrontation (efforts to change the interaction partner's behavior), and support seeking (solicitation of advice or support from others about the problem). Some researchers include interpersonal distancing (avoiding or distancing oneself from the interaction partner) as a form of problem-focused coping because it may prevent a recurrence of the interpersonal problem even though it is unlikely to resolve the problem. Emotion-focused forms of interpersonal coping emphasized in this research include cognitive distancing (efforts to keep from thinking about the interpersonal problem or to minimize its significance), emotional restraint or self-control (efforts to keep one's feelings about the problem to oneself), and self-blame (efforts to accept responsibility for the problem).

An additional interpersonal coping strategy that has received attention in the literature recently is forgiveness. In a study of married couples, greater forgiveness was associated with less retaliatory behavior and more conciliatory behavior toward the spouse, after controlling for marital quality (Fincham, 2000). Jones and his colleagues (Jones, Moore, Schratter, & Negel, 2000) have cautioned, however, that "forgiving is not the same as forgetting" (p. 249). In their research, nearly one-third of participants who had experienced a betrayal reported that they had forgiven the betrayer, but further examination revealed that their forgiveness was often qualified and that resentments persisted.

These coping responses do not exhaust the possible ways that people might respond to a perceived infraction in one of their relationships. Other strategies, such as revenge, have been mentioned in the literature. Jones et al. (2000) argue that retaliation is a relatively rare response to interpersonal conflicts among adults, although it may be more common among children and adolescents (Jensen-Campbell, Graziano, & Hair, 1996). Similarly, we have not emphasized relationship dissolution as a possible coping response to a relationship conflict, but it could be considered to represent an extension or final expression of interpersonal distancing. Relationship dissolution (whether active or passive) may be perceived to be the only viable option for dealing with serious breaches of trust and loyalty (Jones et al., 2000), and may occur most often when the relationship is no longer judged to have redeeming value.

Research is just beginning to investigate the factors that lead people to engage in particular kinds of interpersonal coping responses. This work generally has not differentiated among particular kinds of stressors, but it is plausible that the type of conflict or disappointment experienced would influence the nature of one's coping responses. For example, an experience such as being excluded by others from social activities can be quite debilitating because the harm goes beyond the denial of opportunities to enjoy companionship. The damage extends, as well, to feelings of self-worth (Nezlek, Kowalski, Leary, Blevins, & Holgate, 1997) inasmuch as exclusion by others conveys the message that one's company is not desired – a fundamental rejection of the self. The options for addressing rejection, without risking further rejection, are probably rather limited. It is difficult to imagine that confronting or seeking to reach a compromise with the "rejecter" would prove to be comfortable or effective since people cannot compel others to like them or want to spend time with them. A negative exchange like receiving unwanted advice, in contrast, presents more coping options because it is culturally appropriate to request others to refrain from intrusive behavior.

In addition, whether the interpersonal stressor is unilaterally or mutually recognized is likely to influence the nature of individuals' coping responses. Overt conflicts make broaching the possibility of problem discussion and resolution a relatively straightforward (if not necessarily easy) task. When only one individual, however, perceives an interpersonal problem to have occurred, he or she is necessarily forced to bring this to the attention of the interaction partner, before joint efforts directed toward problem resolution can even be considered. This process of bringing the problem to the attention of the other individual may involve additional risks, such as creating conflict or subjecting oneself to criticism or rejection. Contemplation of these risks may lead people to refrain from discussing them (Fingerman, 1998), causing relationship problems to remain submerged.

Coping Goals

How people respond to interpersonal stressors also may be influenced by implicit or explicit goals that are paramount at the time. This is not to imply that either coping goals or responses to interpersonal stressors are always, or even often, conscious. Some coping responses may occur with little conscious deliberation, prompted by largely unconscious needs or desires rather than explicit goals. Different coping responses, nonetheless, may be directed toward different objectives, and people appear to be able to identify their interpersonal coping goals if prompted to reflect on them (Rook, Sorkin, David, Newsom, & Morgan, 2001). For these reasons, we think it is useful to explore how coping goals may influence coping responses to interpersonal stressors.

Coping theorists generally have assumed that coping efforts are directed either toward resolution of the problem or the reduction of emotional distress (Lazarus & Folkman, 1984; Pearlin & Schooler, 1978). Yet other goals may be served by coping responses as well (Coyne & Racioppo, 2000). In the interpersonal domain, these goals could include not only reducing one's own emotional distress or inducing the interaction partner to change his or her behavior but also preserving goodwill in the social relationship (O'Brien & DeLongis, 1996; Rook et al., 2001). These goals, in turn, are likely to influence coping responses. For example, if an individual's goal is to prevent a recurrence of the problem, he or she may be motivated to discuss the issue with the interaction partner in an effort to bring about a change in the partner's behavior. If the individual's goal, however, is to maintain harmony in the relationship, he or she may forgo discussing the problem with the other person as a means of avoiding tensions.

Responses to interpersonal stressors also may be driven by multiple goals or motivations, rather than one goal alone. The vast majority (95%) of college students in one study identified more than one goal as important to them in responding to an interpersonal conflict (Ohbuchi & Tedeschi, 1997). Similarly, over 80% of older adults in another study reported having had more than one goal in mind when they responded to a recent interpersonal stressor (Rook et al., 2001). Such multiple goals are sometimes compatible, at least in the short run, as when a person tries to forget about the problem or to construe it in more benign terms in order to reduce his or her own emotional distress and to avoid tensions that might arise from discussing the problem with the interaction partner. At other times, multiple coping goals may be incompatible, as when a person wants an interaction partner to change an offensive behavior but also wishes to preserve harmony in the relationship. Confronting the interaction partner about the perceived relationship violation entails the risk of deterioration in relationship quality. When goals are fundamentally incompatible, an individual's coping responses are likely to be influenced by the most salient goal, but we also suspect that coping responses in such cases will often reflect a mix of different approaches aimed at reconciling seemingly incompatible coping goals.

Coping goals and, therefore, coping responses, may also change over time if an interpersonal stressor is chronic or reoccurring. For example, the first few times an interpersonal stressor occurs, a person may try to reach a compromise with the interaction partner. If these efforts prove unsuccessful, the person may forgo externally directed coping efforts, coming to rely, instead, on internally directed strategies to reduce emotional distress. Such a shift would be consistent with the work of control theorists, who suggest that it is functionally adaptive to begin by pursuing goals aimed at achieving desired outcomes in one's environment. If such attempts fail, however, and the goals prove to be unattainable, it becomes adaptive to disengage from the goals and to turn one's attentions toward the pursuit of more attainable goals (Heckhausen & Schulz, 1995; Rothbaum, Weisz, & Snyder, 1982). In the interpersonal domain, such disengagement might entail withdrawal or distancing from the interaction partner.

Coping Effectiveness

A central issue in seeking to understand how people deal with stressors in their social relationships concerns the effectiveness of their coping responses. Coping effectiveness has been investigated most often for stressors that are not interpersonal in nature. In the work, problem-focused coping responses have been found to be related more reliably to reduced emotional distress than have emotion-focused coping responses (e.g., Mitchell, Cronkite, & Moos, 1983). Moreover, some emotion-focused coping responses, such as self-blame or avoidant coping, have been linked to increased, rather than decreased, psychological distress (Smith, Patterson, & Grant, 1990).

Although emotion-focused strategies are generally regarded as less adaptive than problem-focused strategies (Smith et al., 1990), their effectiveness appears to be contingent on the perceived changeability of the stressor (Compas, Malcarne, & Fondacaro, 1988; Vitaliano, DeWolfe, Maiuro, Russo, & Katon, 1990). Lazarus and Folkman (1984) argued that coping strategies directed toward action and perseverance should be most frequent and adaptive when people believe they can do something about a stressor. Within the interpersonal domain, when stressors are regarded as controllable or changeable, problem-focused coping efforts have the potential to be effective. Recurring interpersonal stressors, in contrast, are likely to come to be regarded as unchangeable, and for such stressors, emotion-focused strategies may prove to be more effective than problem-focused strategies (Compas, Banez, Malcarne, & Worsham, 1991). Consistent with this, Compas et al. (1988) found that young adolescents' efforts to change a stressor were associated with fewer psychological symptoms when the stressor was perceived as controllable, whereas efforts to regulate emotional distress were associated with fewer symptoms when the stressor was perceived as uncontrollable.

Consideration of the role of goals in the coping process also has important implications for gauging the effectiveness of coping efforts. In the general literature on coping, a common barometer of effectiveness is the extent to which coping efforts reduce emotional distress caused by a stressor (Coyne & Racioppo, 2000). Yet some coping goals may be pursued at the expense of reducing emotional distress. In the interpersonal context, for example, if the individual's paramount goal is to maintain harmony in an important relationship, coping efforts may be directed toward this goal even if doing so contributes to a slower or less complete decay of emotional distress. The individual might engage in problem minimization or might refrain from expressing feelings of anger in the interest of avoiding tensions in the relationship.

In such scenarios, people may consider their coping efforts to be effective even if their emotional distress declines relatively little. Coping strategies that have been identified in the literature as ineffective, there-fore, might prove to be effective when evaluated with reference to spe-cific coping objectives. In a study of older adults' responses to interper-sonal stressors, some combinations of coping goals and responses that were associated with lengthier, rather than briefer, emotional distress were associated, nonetheless, with greater perceived coping success (Rook et al., 2001). Among elderly participants whose primary goal was to get a social network member to change an offensive behavior, assertive coping was related both to longer-lasting emotional distress and to greater perceived coping success. Such "mixed" coping outcomes underscore the usefulness of seeking both to assess people's coping goals and to evaluate coping effectiveness through multiple lenses.

The effectiveness of a given coping response depends not only on the kinds of actions taken by a focal person, but also on the responses of the other individual involved in the negative social exchange. For example, if the focal person cannot successfully engage the interaction partner in efforts to reach a compromise, a normally constructive strategy (compro-mise) could be associated with a poor outcome (continued emotional dis-tress). Such an association might seem paradoxical without taking into account the responses of the interaction partner. Taking a dyadic per-spective on the coping process also reminds us that the members of a dyad may differ in their perceptions of the severity or causes of a con-flict and in their analyses of optimal strategies for addressing the problem (Fingerman, 1995). These differences themselves can become grist for subsequent disagreements and misunderstandings (Kelley, 1987). Such a dyadic perspective also encourages attention to issues such as the impetus for, and sequence of, coping responses to interpersonal stressors. Efforts to resolve an interpersonal problem may be initiated by the interaction partner or a third party, rather than by the focal person. Other- versus self-initiated interpersonal coping responses may be differentially effective in reducing emotional distress or contributing to feelings of coping efficacy, but this issue has received little empirical attention.

LOSSES AND DISRUPTIONS OF SOCIAL RELATIONSHIPS

The second broad category of interpersonal stress that we wish to explore involves the loss or disruption of an important relationship with a social network member. This section defines and categorizes various types of re-lationship loss and disruption and describes research on the consequences of such losses for emotional and physical health. We then discuss coping responses, goals, and effectiveness, emphasizing the phase of the adapta-tion process that follows the resolution of acute sadness and grief, when people begin to make efforts to reorganize their social lives. We focus on this latter phase of the adaptation process because an extensive literature has examined how people resolve the acute grief associated with the loss or disruption of an important relationship (Stroebe, Hansson, Stroebe, & Schut, 2001).

Kinds of Relationship Losses and Disruptions

Relationship losses refer to relationships that have ended or effectively ended, such as those terminated by death or divorce. Relationship disruptions, in contrast, refer to relationships in which the potential for contact still exists, but in which existing patterns of interaction and exchange have been restricted or suspended on an indefinite basis. For instance, residential relocation may create obstacles to maintaining a relationship by diminishing opportunities for contact and complicating the performance of relationship functions. Relationships can be disrupted, as well, by serious illness or disability that limits a role partner's ability to perform important relationship functions that he or she previously performed (Williamson & Schulz, 1990), such as providing emotional or instrumental support. Significant life stress, or other competing claims on a role partner's time or emotional resources, also may interfere with his or her ability to continue providing support and companionship at previously established levels.

Some relationship losses that originate with members of a specific dyad can disrupt relationships beyond the dyad. Parental divorce, for example, not only severs a relationship between spouses but also alters the relationships between children and their parents (Stewart, Copeland, Chester, Malley, & Barenbaum, 1997). Similarly, widowed individuals often experience a dwindling of contacts with in-laws and couples with whom they once socialized (Lamme, Dykstra, & Broese van Groenou, 1996).

Adverse Effects of Interpersonal Losses and Disruptions. Relationship losses and disruptions, such as divorce or the death of a spouse or close family member, are among the most stressful of life experiences (Holmes & Rahe, 1967). Declines in both psychological and physical health often follow such a loss, with the greatest declines generally occurring when the lost relationship was especially close or important to the individual (Murphy, 1988). Divorced individuals have been found to be at risk for physical and mental health problems (Jones, 1992), and widowed individuals exhibit a marked increase in depression immediately following the death of the spouse (Morgan, Neal, & Carder, 1997). Adults who experience the death of an adult child tend to suffer from increased depression and decreased physical health (De Vries, Davis, Wortman, & Lehman, 1997).

Relationship losses in childhood can also be distressing. Children who lose a best friend to a geographical move, for example, experience increased loneliness and sadness (Park, 1992). The loss of a parent in childhood appears to have adverse effects that persist into adulthood. Middle-aged men and women who experienced parental divorce in childhood report more physical health problems than do middle-aged adults who did not experience parental divorce, and women who experienced parental death in childhood exhibit elevated rates of depression (Maier & Lachman, 2000).

Thus, the loss or disruption of an important social relationship can undermine emotional and physical health. Yet is it also possible for substantial recovery of mental and physical health to occur. In a study of older widows, for example, Morgan et al. (1997) found that although depression rates increased immediately following the spouse's death, they declined to normal levels after about two years. Coping responses may play a role in explaining such long-term recovery, but few empirical studies have looked systematically at how people cope and what works and what does not work (Folkman, 2001).

Coping Responses

As noted earlier, our analysis of coping responses focuses not on the resolution of acute grief following a significant relationship loss or disruption but, rather, on the long-term task of reconstituting one's social ties as a means of deriving some of the support and companionship that has been lost. We accordingly emphasize coping responses that address the specific social needs or yearnings that may emerge in the wake of the relationship loss, after acute feelings of sadness and grief have subsided. These needs – such as the need for day-to-day companionship or emotional intimacy – may motivate people to reorganize their social lives in some way, turning to other social network members to meet these needs or, when this is not possible, seeking to expand their social networks by establishing new social ties. In this sense, people who have sustained a relationship loss may be seeking to "replace" some of the relationship functions formerly performed by a role partner, such as a spouse, adult child, or close friend.

In suggesting this, we do not mean to imply that important social relationships can be reduced to a set of functions they perform or that long-term relationships can readily be replaced, or perhaps ever truly replaced, by other social ties (Kahn & Antonucci, 1980; Lofland, 1982). Shared memories, intimacies, worldviews, and finely tuned patterns of interaction that have evolved over many years cannot be replicated. Nonetheless, people typically do seek to fill the gaps created in their lives by a relationship loss or disruption (Ferraro, Mutran, & Barresi, 1984; Morgan et al., 1997), and this process can be conceptualized in terms of their efforts to derive needed forms of support and companionship from others.

Construing people's responses to a relationship loss in terms of the core forms of support and companionship they might seek to derive from alternate relationships has value if one accepts the notion that many relationships become specialized in the functions they perform (Weiss, 1974).

Friends, for example, often provide emotional support and companionship, but they less often function as a source of instrumental support. Family members, in contrast, regularly provide instrumental support and often provide emotional support as well, but they less often serve as a source of companionship (Rook & Schuster, 1996). Relationships with a primary partner, such as a spouse, represent an exception to this general pattern of relationship specialization in that intimate partners often perform many of the essential functions of close relationships (Weiss, 1974). A person who loses a primary partner, therefore, may be forced to turn to multiple others to derive the various kinds of support and companionship once provided by the partner.

Problem-Focused and Emotion-Focused Interpersonal Coping Responses.
The long-term process of seeking to reorganize one's social ties after experiencing a major relationship loss or disruption may involve both problem-focused and emotion-focused coping. Our primary emphasis, however, will be on a problem-focused strategy that may be unique to this particular kind of interpersonal stressor: substitution. Substitution refers to the process by which people seek to derive lost relationship functions from other sources.

Substitution can take several different forms. First, substitution can involve the formation of a new social relationship. For example, widows may try to establish new ties, such as befriending other widows to whom they can turn for some of the support and companionship previously provided by their spouses (Morgan et al., 1997). Lamme et al. (1996) asked elderly widowed individuals whether they had undertaken "many efforts to obtain, maintain, or intensify contact with [their] friends and acquaintances" after the death of the spouse. Of the participants who reported having made a deliberate effort to establish new social ties or intensify existing ties after becoming widowed, 44% reported new relationships in enumerating the current membership of their social networks.

Another form of substitution involves turning to existing social network members to derive support and companionship. This would occur, for example, when widowed individuals turn to their adult children to assume some of the support roles once performed by the spouse (Connidis & Davies, 1992). The children may already have been considered to be important support providers within the bereaved person's social network, yet they may be expected to assume additional support roles, taking over those previously performed by the deceased parent. Similarly, children who are rejected by peers at school may turn to their siblings for emotional support and companionship (East & Rook, 1992).

A third form of substitution involves attempting to rekindle social ties that have been dormant or relatively inactive. Dormant ties refer to friendships and family relationships in which contact dwindled because of such factors as time conflicts or competing role demands. Because the largely dormant status of the relationship does not reflect tensions or estrangement, the possibility exists for the relationship to be "rekindled" or "rejuvenated." For example, a divorced man might reinitiate contact with a neighbor who was seen intermittently preceding his divorce but with whom he now has more frequent or more intimate contact. Thus, he has deepened an existing relationship as a means (whether conscious or unconscious) of replacing some of the support and companionship functions once performed by his spouse.

Some forms of substitution may be perceived to be unattainable by a person who has sustained a relationship loss, either at the outset or after initial substitution attempts prove unsuccessful. In such cases, people may rely on emotion-focused coping responses to deal with the absence of desired support and companionship. Especially relevant in this context are internally directed coping responses that involve efforts to minimize the need for the missing relationship functions and to protect feelings of self-worth through self-protective attributions and social comparisons (cf. Brandtstadter & Renner, 1990; Heckhausen & Schulz, 1995). People may resign themselves to the idea that they no longer need the kind of relationship they have lost or the various forms of support and companionship they once derived from it. Consistent with this, Dykstra (1995) found in a study of widows that the perceived desirability of being married declined as the duration of widowhood increased, suggesting a shift over time in relationship aspirations. People also may seek to convince themselves that others have worse life circumstances, as a means of dealing with the disappointment of the loss and the perceived difficulty of establishing substitute ties.

Alternatively, some people may turn to nonsocial activities, such as solitary hobbies, to obtain emotional gratification and a sense of engagement that does not require the participation of an interaction partner (Rook & Schuster, 1996). Whether nonsocial activities such as reading, gardening, or working on crafts by oneself can compensate for social activities has been debated in the literature on loneliness (Young, 1982), with little consensus. Solitary hobbies and interests can serve to elevate mood, however, and they have been incorporated in some behaviorally oriented treatments for depression and loneliness (e.g., Lewinsohn & Amenson, 1978; Young, 1982).

Coping Goals

Coping goals in response to the loss or disruption of a major social relationship may vary across phases of the adaptation process. As noted earlier, immediately following the loss, the primary goal may be to come to terms with the loss, and coping responses may be dedicated to resolving feelings of sadness or grief. Over time, the coping goal, and consequently the coping responses, may shift to replacing the lost relationship (e.g., Walker, MacBride, & Vachon, 1997). For example, immediately following the death of the spouse, widows are striving to maintain a sense of identity and stability, and they rely heavily on their closest ties, especially family members, for assistance in accomplishing these goals. As time passes, however, widows often become interested in branching out and may turn to friends and new social ties in an attempt to reconstruct a satisfying social life, even if it differs in major respects from the one led previously.

Different types of relationship loss or disruption, and the accompanying needs they create, may also influence coping goals during the process of efforts to reconstruct one's social life. The loss of a primary partner who provided key forms of emotional support, advice, instrumental support, and companionship may prompt the search for a new primary relationship. Loss of a relationship with someone who performed a more delimited set of functions (a more specialized relationship in Weiss's (1974) terms), such as the provision of emotional or instrumental support but not companionship, may prompt efforts to derive this support from existing social ties, rather than efforts to establish new ties altogether. Thus, some circumstances may make the formation of a new relationship the paramount coping goal, whereas other circumstances may make the modification of existing relationships the paramount coping goal.

Goals are also shaped by perceived constraints and opportunities in the social environment, such as the extent to which similar others (e.g., age peers) are available with whom one might be able to establish a relationship and the availability of contexts for meeting others that are conducive to relationship formation (Rook, 1984). A classic study by Blau (1961) of adjustment to widowhood in different geographic regions revealed that the social lives of widowed individuals were influenced by the prevalence of widowhood in the local social structure. Widowed individuals, particularly widowed men, tended to have fewer social ties in areas where widowhood was uncommon, and the constraints imposed by the social environment may have had an impact on their coping goals.

Coping goals also may be influenced by people's perceptions of their resources (e.g., social skills) for initiating and maintaining new social ties or for seeking needed forms of support and companionship from existing social ties. For example, people who might wish to establish a new relationship, following a major relationship loss, may be thwarted in their efforts to do so by a perceived or real shortage of opportunities in the social environment or by doubts about their own ability to take advantage of existing opportunities. This may lead to the abandonment of the preferred goal of establishing a new relationship in favor of goals that might be regarded as more attainable, such as increasing one's contact with family members or friends.

Coping goals may change over time as well, as people experience success or failure in their initial coping efforts. The effectiveness of interpersonal coping responses depends not only on the actions taken by a focal person but also on the responses of others. Substitution will only take place, for example, if the potential social partner is willing to establish a new or deeper tie with the focal person. If the focal person tries unsuccessfully to initiate a relationship with someone who appears to share similar interests, emotional distress may result and may prompt both a coping response in its own right (cf. Dixon & Backman, 1995) and a reevaluation of coping goals. Repeated experiences of rejection may lead to a shift in coping goals, including possible disengagement altogether from the goal of replacing the missing forms of support and companionship.

This discussion is not meant to imply that we regard coping goals in response to a significant relationship loss or disruption as necessarily falling within the realm of awareness and subject to conscious deliberation. Coping goals may vary on these dimensions. Many individuals who experience a divorce in early or middle adulthood, for example, may endorse remarriage as an explicit goal and may be quite aware of the strategies they pursue with the hope of establishing a new relationship with a partner. Other people may engage in coping responses without actually being aware of these responses or their underlying motivations (Cramer, 2000; Dixon & Backman, 1995). A widower, for example, might linger in his interactions with his existing acquaintances to fulfill needs for companionship, even though he is unaware of doing this or even of his own needs for increased social contact. Thus, people may engage in unconscious efforts to increase their contact with others (Peplau, 1955), although it is unclear how often such unconscious efforts foster effective coping (Cramer, 2000).

Coping Effectiveness

Substitution involves efforts to find one or more people to assume the functions previously performed by a missing social tie. There is no guarantee, however, that the substitute social tie(s) will yield psychological benefits comparable to those derived from the lost tie. That is, there is no guarantee that a substitute relationship will actually compensate for the lost relationship (Rook & Schuster, 1996). A child who has lost his friends as a result of a residential move may turn to his siblings or parents for companionship, at least until new friendships can be forged. This companionship may differ qualitatively from that provided by his former friends, however, thereby limiting its potential to boost the child's spirits and reduce feelings of loneliness. Thus, while substitution occurs when a new or existing network member assumes functions previously performed by a lost social tie, actual compensation can be considered to occur only if the focal person derives benefits from the substitute tie that resemble those derived from the former tie. From this perspective, coping effectiveness can be evaluated in terms of complementary, but distinct, outcomes – the extent to which efforts to derive missing support and companionship from alternate sources (new or existing social ties) succeed and the extent to which these new sources of support and companionship yield discernible psychological benefits.

Mixed evidence currently exists regarding social network substitution and compensation. Johnson and Troll (1992) found little evidence that un-married and childless older adults were able to draw upon extended family members to assume the support functions ordinarily performed by adult children. Simons (1984), in contrast, found that childless older widows fulfilled their needs for intimacy through contacts with a confidant or sib-ling and fulfilled their needs for a sense of belonging through interaction with friends or organizational participation. His study yielded evidence of relationship specialization, consistent with the theoretical perspective of Weiss (1974), in that needs for intimacy could not be met through involve-ment with friends or organizations and, conversely, needs for a sense of belonging could not be met through contacts with a confidant or sibling. Such results suggest that substitution is possible, but that social needs fol-lowing a major relationship loss may be difficult to meet through just one substitute tie.

It may be possible to establish substitute relationships following a ma-jor relationship loss, but it may be more difficult to derive psychological benefits from these alternative relationships that approximate those de-rived from the lost relationship. Because prospective studies of relation-ship loss are quite scarce (see Carr, House, Wortman, Neese, & Kessler, 2001, for an exception), tests of compensation are usually conducted by comparing the post-loss emotional health of two or more of the follow-ing groups: individuals who have not sustained a loss, individuals who have sustained a relationship loss and who have established substitute social tie(s), and individuals who have sustained a relationship loss and who have not established substitute social tie(s). Rice (1989), for example, contrasted the latter two groups in a study of adaptation to widowhood and found that among older childless, widowed women, those who had established a confidant relationship reported greater life satisfaction than did those who lacked a confidant. In our own research on compensation among older widowed women, we have not found evidence of the psycho-logical benefits of substitute ties. Widows who had established substitute relationships to assume some of the roles and functions once performed by their husbands did not exhibit gains in emotional health, relative to the widows who had not established substitute relationships (Zettel, Rook, & Morgan, 2001). Similarly, only limited evidence of the compensatory ben-efits of substitute social ties emerged in a study of children who had been rejected by peers at school. Lacking friends at school, the rejected children turned to their siblings for social support, but this sibling support was not associated with substantially better psychological health and functioning (East & Rook, 1992).

Limits may exist on the degree of compensation that is possible following the loss or disruption of an important relationship, particularly a long-term relationship. This may account for the mixed evidence that has emerged in studies conducted thus far. Partial compensation (some rebound in well-being) following a major relationship loss may be possible, but complete compensation (complete rebound in well-being) may prove to be difficult. Normative patterns of relationship specialization, for example, may require a match between the kind of support that is needed and the kind of relationship (e.g., role relationship) in which it can be derived optimally, and such matches may be difficult to achieve. Empirical work is needed to investigate variations in the effectiveness of substitution and compensation processes for different kinds of relationship loses.

Relatively little is known about the effectiveness of internally directed coping responses, such as a redefinition of one's social needs, when efforts to establish substitute relationships prove unsuccessful. Some theorists argue that psychological well-being is maintained when personal goals and aspirations are brought into line with objective circumstances that make their attainment unlikely (Brandstadter & Renner, 1990; Wrosch & Heckhausen, 1999). Other theorists believe that the need for close, stable social bonds is universal and essential to human health and well-being, with negative consequences stemming from the deprivation of this need (Baumeister & Leary, 1995). Denial of this need, accordingly, is unlikely to protect well-being. Weiss (1974) observed in this regard that lonely individuals rarely succeed in alleviating their loneliness by attempting to deny their needs for social contact.

Whether solitary activities serve to preserve well-being in the face of a significant relationship loss or disruption also requires further empirical investigation. Greater involvement in leisure activities was associated with lower anxiety in a study of recently bereaved older adults, but solitary versus social activities were not distinguished, making the results inconclusive with respect to the benefits of solitary leisure (Patterson, 1996).

In concluding this discussion of coping responses and outcomes following a major relationship loss, we wish to acknowledge that the long-term adaptation process may involve fundamental changes in the worldviews and self-concepts of people who have sustained such losses (Harvey & Miller, 1998). The processes we have termed substitution and compensation, therefore, are not necessarily directed toward the preservation of a static self or way of life; rather, they may occur in concert with other processes that involve the forging of new identities and new aspirations and assumptions about the future. Understanding how psychological well-being is maintained through a mix of these different processes is a challenge for future research.

LIFE-SPAN VARIATIONS

We have explored some of the ways in which people might seek to cope with conflicts and disappointments, as well as losses or disruptions of established patterns of exchange and interaction, in their social relationships. We have also considered how coping goals and responses may change over time, as a function of prior coping success or failure. In this section, we suggest some of the ways these processes may vary across the life span.

Kinds of Interpersonal Stressors across the Life Span

Life-span variations in responses to interpersonal stressors may arise, in part, from differences in the kinds of interpersonal stressors that are experienced over the life span. Developmental tasks and challenges that vary across the life span may predispose people to experiencing particular kinds of conflicts or disappointments in their interactions with others, as well as particular kinds of losses. For example, conflicts related to issues of autonomy and control are common between children and parents (Noller, Feeney, & Peterson, 2001). Children and adolescents, accordingly, may be particularly likely to feel that others make unreasonable demands on them or give unwanted advice. Issues of peer acceptance and the desire to form romantic relationships in late adolescence and young adulthood may make people particularly vulnerable to real or perceived experiences of rejection. In middle adulthood, the challenges of child rearing, coupled with work obligations, may leave adults feeling unsupported by their spouses. In later life, declining health and other major stressful events can create long-term needs for support that strain the caregiving resources of a social network. Older people whose social network members cannot provide sustained support over time may be particularly likely to experience feeling let down by others in terms of needed help and assistance (Johnson & Catalano, 1983). Similarly, many older people experience the loss of a spouse or other close relationships through death or residential relocation, and such losses may prompt them to turn to existing friendships and family relationships for some of the companionship and emotional support formerly provided by others. If these efforts meet with only limited success, they may become vulnerable to feelings of rejection or neglect.

Coping Responses, Goals, and Effectiveness across the Life Span

Life-span variations may exist not only in the kind of interpersonal stressors that people experience but also in the nature, goals, and effectiveness of their coping responses (Lang, 2001). Responses to interpersonal stressors are likely to be influenced by self-regulatory capacities, which may be integrally linked to psychosocial maturation and to the specific objectives that motivate and direct coping responses. Studies of coping suggest that the skills necessary for problem-focused versus emotion-focused coping emerge at different points in childhood and adolescence. Problem-focused coping skills appear to develop as early as the preschool years, with further development continuing through early adolescence. In contrast, emotion-focused coping skills do not appear to develop until late childhood or early adolescence (e.g., Altshuler & Ruble, 1989). This delay in the development of emotion-focused strategies may be a function of younger children's inability to recognize their own internal emotional states, coupled with limited ability to observe and model the emotion-focused coping efforts of adults (Compas et al., 1991).

These changes in the capacity for emotion-focused coping in childhood and adolescence have implications for managing interpersonal stressors. Young children have difficulty containing strong emotions aroused by interpersonal stressors (Compas et al., 1991) and tend to make greater use of problem-focused than emotion-focused coping strategies (Compas et al., 1991). As the capacity to regulate emotions develops, it allows individuals to consider a broader range of responses and to forecast the effects of emotional expression (Altshuler & Ruble, 1989; Compas et al., 1988). Lawton (2001, p. 122) observed in this regard, "Emotion may act an intrusive element in social decisions among developmentally immature people but as a source of differentiation among social situations for mature people." Growth in the capacity for empathy and perspective taking allows the individual to consider the implications of potential responses not only for oneself but also for the interaction partner and the relationship itself.

Throughout adulthood, people generally exhibit a preference for problem-focused coping over emotion-focused coping as a means of dealing with many kinds of stressors (Blanchard-Fields & Chen, 1996). This preference extends into later life, but evidence also points to an increased reliance on emotion-focused coping strategies in later life. Older adults make greater use than younger and middle-aged adults of such emotion-focused coping strategies as cognitive distancing (Blanchard-Fields & Chen, 1996; Brandstadter & Renner, 1990). This shift does not appear to reflect a decline with age in the capacity to engage in active, problem-oriented coping (though see Folkman, Lazarus, Pimley, & Novacek, 1987, for an exception); rather, coping repertoires appear to expand with age to include emotion-focused as well as problem-focused coping. Some researchers have argued that this shift reflects an integration of cognitive and affective processes that comes to fruition in late middle age and beyond (Labouvie-Vief, Hakim-Larson, DeVoe, & Schoeberlein, 1989). This shift allows older adults to regulate their emotions more effectively, to have greater tolerance of uncertainty and complexity in their social relationships, and to discriminate more effectively among alternative options for coping with interpersonal stressors (Blanchard-Fields, 1998; Lawton, 2001). Over the course of a lifetime, people also experience a wide variety of stressors, and through the process of managing these stressors they develop coping skills and acquire insights about the types of coping strategies that can help them achieve their goals and the types of strategies that are generally less effective (Aldwin, 1994).

Life-span variations in coping responses, goals, and effectiveness may be shaped not only by internal processes but also by the social environment. Opportunities and constraints encountered in the social environment may influence the perceived and actual viability of possible coping options. The range of viable coping responses to conflicts in one's relationships may be restricted, for example, by differences in status or power that exist in some relationships, with individuals who have less status or power tending to exhibit more constrained and deferential responses to higher-status interaction partners (Noller et al., 2001). Such power differentials in relationships may be more common at certain stages of the life course. For example, dependence on parents early in life creates a clear difference in power between parents and children, limiting the range of coping options available to children. Similarly, ill or disabled older adults who depend on family members for day-to-day care may feel constrained in how they can respond to interpersonal difficulties with these caregivers.

The social environment may influence the viability of responses to relationship losses as well. Individuals who occupy few social roles may discover that they have limited opportunities to establish new social relationships. Thus, when an important relationship is lost or disrupted, it may be harder for those with fewer connections to others to replace the lost relationship. Similarly, one's place in the life course may limit the opportunities that exist to establish new social relationships. For example, the statistical probabilities of establishing a partner relationship (such as a marital relationship) diminish considerably after middle age, particularly for women (Guttentag & Secord, 1983). Efforts to establish a new relationship after the loss or termination of a partner relationship may be thwarted if scarce opportunities exist in the social environment, prompting the individual to relinquish this goal and to shift to internal coping responses (such as minimizing the importance of establishing a new relationship or engaging in self-protective social comparisons). Wrosch and Heckhausen (1999) have found that such a shift is adaptive and functions to preserve psychological well-being when efforts to establish a desired partner relationship prove futile.

In a related vein, prior coping successes and failures may influence the perceived viability of particular coping goals and strategies. A history of unsuccessful coping with a recurring interpersonal stressor is likely to prompt a shift to alternative coping responses that are perceived to be more viable. For example, people who feel repeatedly rebuffed in their efforts to establish greater intimacy with a family member may be forced to seek intimacy from an alternative – and possibly less preferred – relationship. This lack of success, moreover, may be sufficiently distressing as to require a coping response in its own right (cf. Dixon & Backman, 1992; Heckhausen & Schulz, 1995). Developmental differences may exist in the ability to recognize that a particular coping strategy has been unsuccessful and to protect one's motivational resources for a redirection of coping efforts toward more attainable goals (cf. Heckhausen & Schulz, 1995).

FUTURE DIRECTIONS

In this chapter we have suggested a framework for thinking about the nature and effectiveness of people's responses to interpersonal stressors, taking into account the specific kind of stressor experienced, the individual's coping repertoire, and the specific goals that motivate and direct coping responses. We regard this framework, shown in Figure 9.1, as preliminary because little empirical work has examined how people adapt to stressors in their important social relationships, making inferences about the strength or direction of the hypothesized associations premature. We also regard this framework as skeletal, because it could be elaborated substantially with the addition of antecedents, mediators, and moderators of the adaptation process that go beyond the scope of this chapter. In this section, we highlight some of the substantive and methodological issues that could be pursued in future research and that would provide a basis for evaluating and elaborating the framework we presented in this chapter.

Substantive Issues

A great deal remains to be learned about how the characteristics and perceptions of interpersonal stressors influence the adaptational process. Interpersonal conflicts, for example, may vary not only in their content but also in their specificity, ranging from disagreements about specific behaviors to resentments about violations of relationship rules to disputes about the core traits and motives of interaction partners (Kelley, 1987). The level of specificity, in turn, may influence the nature and effectiveness of problem resolution efforts, with more global conflicts tending to be more difficult to resolve (Kelley, 1987). Interpersonal stressors also vary in their severity. Those that fall below a subjective threshold for action may go unaddressed, whereas those that surpass this threshold may be sufficiently dislocating as to interfere with coping efforts. Thus, the relationship between severity and coping efforts may be curvilinear, although relatively little research has examined this possibility. Perceptions of the causes of an interpersonal stressor or its "changeability" may influence the coping goals that are perceived to be viable and, in turn, the coping responses that are undertaken (Bradbury, Beach, Fincham, & Nelson, 1996). A conflict that is perceived to stem from an intractable personality trait in an interaction partner, for example, may lead to relationship disengagement or to internally directed coping responses. Examination of such perceptions of interpersonal stressors will help to advance our understanding of the adaptation process.

Aspects of the social and temporal contexts in which an interpersonal stressor occurs may also influence the adaptation process and warrant greater attention in future research. The role relationship in which the stressor occurs is an important defining feature of the social context. A given interpersonal stressor, such as receiving unwanted advice, may elicit different affective reactions and coping responses when it occurs in a friendship versus a family relationship. Norms that vary across role relationships may influence what is perceived to constitute a relationship violation and what are regarded as appropriate ways of responding. Consideration of the role relationship is important in analyzing responses to a relationship loss or disruption as well, because normative patterns of relationship specialization may require a match between the kind of support that is needed and the kind of relationship (e.g., role relationship) in which it can be derived optimally. The broader social environment also has a bearing on the coping process, and more research needs to examine how the opportunities and constraints associated with different environmental contexts influence coping goals, responses, and outcomes for different kinds of interpersonal stressors. Interpersonal stressors also vary in the extent to which they recur or persist, thus defining an important aspect of their temporal context. The chronicity of an interpersonal stressor and the prior history of success or failure with specific coping responses are likely to play an important role in shaping coping goals and responses at a given point in time. Little is known, however, about the key transitions that occur in the course of coping with a chronic interpersonal stressor and, particularly, about the transition from externally directed to internally directed coping that may occur when prior coping efforts have proven unsuccessful. Understanding how the adaptation process is influenced by these and other features of the context in which interpersonal stressors occur points to many specific issues that can be investigated in further research.

With respect to the effectiveness of coping responses, we have suggested that coping effectiveness can be gauged with reference to distinct, and sometimes divergent, outcomes, including the reduction of emotional distress, the preservation of relationship harmony, and the degree of perceived success in meeting a personal coping objective. Expanding the criteria by which coping effectiveness is evaluated raises interesting questions that could be pursued in future studies. For example, do coping outcomes that diverge in the short run tend to converge in the long run, or do they remain divergent over time? Preserving goodwill in a relationship by refraining from venting one's feelings of resentment following a relationship disagreement could lead, over time, to reduced emotional distress. Alternatively, relationship resentments could remain dormant in such cases, allowing emotional distress to accumulate, rather than dissipate, over time. These kinds of questions need to be grappled with conceptually and methodologically, as we note below, in future studies that evaluate coping effectiveness through multiple lenses.

Methodological Issues

A number of methodological issues also warrant attention in future research directed toward increasing our understanding of how people adapt to interpersonal stressors. Methodologies that do not rely exclusively on self-reports would help to address concerns about the validity of such data and also would provide a means of identifying coping responses or other aspects of the adaptation process that fall outside the realm of individual awareness (and, therefore, beyond self-reports). Behavioral observations or reports of significant others may help to shed light on coping responses that occur with little conscious processing and that cannot readily be recalled. Study designs that examine the adaptation process from the perspective of both members of a relationship, when this is feasible and appropriate to the kind of interpersonal stressor experienced, would help to document the sequential and contingent nature of many responses to interpersonal problems. For example, gaining information from both members of a relationship could help illuminate how contingent relationships that exist between a focal person's coping responses and those of his or her partner serve to escalate conflicts and disagreements or, alternatively, serve to contain anger and curb destructive communications (Gottman & Notarius, 2000).

Longitudinal research designs are needed to capture the transitions or shifts in coping goals and strategies that may occur over time in the course of experiencing and responding to a recurring interpersonal stressor. Such longitudinal studies will help to fill in gaps in knowledge regarding the natural history of coping attempts and the role of coping successes or failures in prompting the modification of coping goals. Longitudinal research designs also make it possible to investigate the reciprocal associations that may exist between some elements of the adaptation process. For example, the link between coping outcomes and goals may be bidirectional, rather than unidirectional, as implied in Figure 9.1, but this possibility requires longitudinal studies to be explored successfully.

Life-span variations in the coping responses, goals, and outcomes associated with particular kinds of interpersonal stressors can be examined most effectively in longitudinal studies that span two or more developmental periods. Cross-sectional studies that examine age differences in aspects of the coping and adaptation process often will be more feasible, of course, and they can offer insights about life-span variations if care is given to disentangling the effects of age per se from the effects of the particular type of interpersonal stressor experienced. This potential confounding of age and the type of stressor experienced can be avoided in experimental studies that make use of vignette methodologies, for example, thereby holding the type of stressor constant across age groups (e.g., Blanchard-Fields & Chen, 1996).

Finally, the outcome measures chosen to evaluate the effectiveness of efforts to cope with an interpersonal stressor need to be considered carefully in future research. For example, the effectiveness of coping responses to an interpersonal conflict could be evaluated in terms of the extent to which they reduce emotional distress, preserve or undermine goodwill in the relationship, or achieve a personal coping goal. These coping outcomes sometimes may diverge for reasons that reflect the implicit or explicit assignment of a higher priority to one coping over other goals, and detecting systematic patterns of divergence among coping outcomes will require researchers to assess personal coping goals in some fashion. In the context of adaptation to a relationship loss, we have argued that substitute social ties cannot be assumed to have compensatory effects on emotional health. Research designs are needed that evaluate substitution and compensation as conceptually distinct aspects of the adaptation process.

CONCLUSION

Evidence from several different literatures has demonstrated convincingly that satisfying social relationships are an important source of meaning in most people's lives and a significant determinant of their emotional and physical health. Threats to close relationships, in the form of corrosive interactions or significant losses, often prompt "corrective action" to limit the resulting toll on health and well-being. Given this, more needs to be learned about how people respond to tensions and disappointments in their social relationships and to the loss or disruption of important relationships. Embedding the investigation of these coping processes in a developmental framework that examines the interplay of internal and external conditions and processes across the life span is likely to yield the richest insights about the process of adaptation in this important life domain.

References

Aldwin, C. M. (1994). *Stress, coping, and development: An integrative perspective.* New York: Guilford.

Altshuler, J. L., & Ruble, D. N. (1989). Developmental changes in children's awareness of strategies for coping with uncontrollable stress. *Child Development, 60,* 1337–1349.

Baumeister, R. F., & Leary, M. R. (1995). The need to belong: Desire for interpersonal attachments as a fundamental human motivation. *Psychological Bulletin, 117,* 497–529.

Blanchard-Fields, F. (1998). The role of emotion in social cognition across the life-span. In K. W. Schaie & M. P. Lawton (Eds.), *Annual review of gerontology and geriatrics Vol. 17* (pp. 238–265). New York: Springer.

Blanchard-Fields, F., & Chen, Y. (1996). Adaptive cognition and aging. *American Behavioral Scientist, 39,* 231–248.

Blau, Z. (1961). Structural constraints on friendship in old age. *American Sociological Review,* 1961, 26, 429–439.

Bolger, N., & Zuckerman, A. (1995). A framework for studying personality in the stress process. *Journal of Personality and Social Psychology, 69,* 890–902.

Bradbury, T. N., Beach, S. R. H., Fincham, F. D., & Nelson, G. M. (1996). Attributions and behavior in functional and dysfunctional marriages. *Journal of Consulting amd Clinical Psychology, 64,* 569–576.

Brandstadter, J., & Renner, G. (1990). Tenacious goal pursuit and flexible goal adjustment: Explication and age-related analysis of assimilative and accommodative strategies of coping. *Psychology and Aging, 5,* 58–67.

Carr, D., House, J. S., Wortman, C., Neese, R., & Kessler, R. C. (2001). Psychological adjustment to sudden and anticipated spousal loss among older widowed persons. *Journal of Gerontology: Social Sciences, 56,* S237–S248.

Compas, B. E., Banez, G. A., Malcarne, V., & Worsham, N. (1991). Perceived control and coping with stress: A developmental perspective. *Journal of Social Issues, 47,* 23–34.

Compas, B. E., Malcarne, V. L., & Fondacaro, K. M. (1988). Coping with stressful events in older children and young adolescents. *Journal of Consulting and Clinical Psychology, 56,* 405–411.

Connidis, I. A., & Davies, L. (1992). Confidants and companions: Choices in later life. *Journal of Gerontology: Social Sciences, 47,* S115–S122.

Cramer, P. (2000). Defense mechanisms in psychology today. *American Psychologist, 55,* 637–646.

Coyne, J. C., & Racioppo, M. W. (2000). Never the twain shall meet? Closing the gap between coping research and clinical intervention research. *American Psychologist, 55,* 655–664.

De Vries, B., Davis, C. G., Wortman, C. B., & Lehman, D. R. (1997). Long-term psychological and somatic consequences of later life parental bereavement. *Omega: Journal of Death and Dying, 35,* 97–117.

Dixon, R. A., & Backman, L. (1995). Concepts of compensation: Integrated, differentiated, and Janus-faced. In R. A. Dixon & L. Backman (Eds.), *Compensating for psychological deficits and declines: Managing losses and promoting gains* (pp. 3–19). Mahwah, NJ: Lawrence Erlbaum.

Dykstra, P. A. (1995). Loneliness among the never married and the formerly married: The importance of supportive friendships and a desire for independence. *Journal of Gerontology: Social Sciences, 50,* S321–S329.

East, P. L., & Rook, K. S. (1992). Compensatory patterns of support among children's peer relationships: A test using school friends, nonschool friends, and siblings. *Developmental Psychology, 28,* 163–172.

Emery, R. E., & Laumann-Billings, L. (1998). An overview of the nature, causes, and consequences of abusive family relationships: Toward differentiating maltreatment and violence. *American Psychologist, 53*, 121–135.

Ferraro, K. F., Mutran, E., & Barresi, C. M. (1984). Widowhood, health, and friendship support in later life. *Journal of Health and Social Behavior, 25*, 245–259.

Finch, J. F., Okun, M. A., Pool, G. J., & Ruehlman, L. S. (1999). A comparison of the influence of conflictual and supportive interactions on psychological distress. *Journal of Personality, 67*, 581–621.

Fincham, F. D. (2000). The kiss of the porcupines: From attributing responsibility to forgiving. *Personal Relationships, 7*, 1–24.

Fingerman, K. L. (1995). Aging mothers' and their adult daughters' perceptions of conflict behaviors. *Psychology and Aging, 10*, 639–649.

Fingerman, K. L. (1998). Tight lips?: Aging mothers' and adult daughters' responses to interpersonal tensions in their relationships. *Personal Relationships, 5*, 121–138.

Folkman, S. (2001). Revised coping theory and the process of bereavement. In M. S. Stroebe, R. O. Hansson, R. O. W. Stroebe, & H. Schut (Eds.), *Handbook of bereavement research: Consequences, coping, and care* (pp. 563–584). Washington, DC: American Psychological Association.

Folkman, S., Lazarus, R. S., Pimley, S., & Novacek, J. (1987). Age differences in stress and coping processes. *Psychology and Aging, 2*, 171–184.

Gottman, J. M., & Notarius, C. I. (2000). Decade review: Observing marital interaction. *Journal of Marriage and the Family, 62*, 927–947.

Guttentag, M., & Secord, P. F. (1983). *Too many women: The sex ratio question.* Beverly Hills, CA: Sage.

Harvey, J. H., & Miller, E. D. (1998). Toward a psychology of loss. *Psychological Science, 9*, 429–434.

Heckhausen, J., & Schulz, R. (1995). A life-span theory of control. *Psychological Review, 102*, 284–304.

Holmes, T. H., & Rahe, R. H. (1967). The social readjustment rating scale. *Journal of Psychosomatic Research, 11*, 213–218.

House, J. S., Umberson, D., & Landis, K. (1988). Structures and processes of social support. *Annual Review of Sociology, 14*, 293–318.

Jensen-Campbell, L. A., Graziano, W. G., & Hair, E. C. (1996). Personality and relationships as moderators of interpersonal conflict in adolescence. *Merrill-Palmer Quarterly, 42*, 148–164.

Johnson, C. L., & Catalano, D. J. (1983). A longitudinal study of family supports to impaired elderly. *The Gerontologist, 23*, 612–625.

Johnson, C. L., & Troll, L. (1992). Family functioning in late late life. *Journal of Gerontology: Social Sciences, 47*, S66–S72.

Jones, S. L. (1992). Physical and psychological illness as correlates of marital disruption. In T. J. Akamatsu & M. A. Parris Stephens (Eds.), *Family health psychology* (pp. 151–168). Washington, DC: Hemisphere.

Jones, W. H., Moore, D. S., Schratter, A., & Negel, L. A. (2000). Interpersonal transgressions and betrayals. In R. M. Kowalski (Ed.), *Behaving badly* (pp. 233–256). Washington, DC: American Psychological Association.

Kahn, R. L., & Antonucci, A. (1980). Convoys over the life course: Attachment, roles, and social support. In P. B. Baltes & O. G. Brim (Eds.), *Life-span development and behavior* (Vol. 3, pp. 253–286). New York: Academic Press.

Kelley, H. H. (1987). Toward a taxonomy of interpersonal conflict processes. In S. Oskamp & S. Spacapan (Eds.), *Interpersonal processes* (pp. 127–147). Newbury Park, CA: Sage.

Labouvie-Vief, G., Hakim-Larson, J., DeVoe, M., & Schoeberlein, S. (1989). Emotions and self-regulation: A lifespan view. *Human Development, 32,* 279–299.

Lakey, B., & Cohen, S. (2000). Social support theory and measurement. In S. Cohen, B. H. Gottlieb, & L. G. Underwood (Eds.), *Social support measurement and interventions: A guide for health and social scientists* (pp. 29–52). New York: Oxford University Press.

Lamme, S., Dykstra, P. A., & Broese van Groenou, M. I. (1996). Rebuilding the network: New relationships in widowhood. *Personal Relationships, 3,* 337–349.

Lang, F. R. (2001). Regulation of social relationships in later adulthood. *Journal of Gerontology: Psychological Sciences, 56,* P321–P326.

Lawton, M. P. (2001). Emotion in later life. *Current Directions in Psychological Science, 10,* 120–123.

Lazarus, R. S., & Folkman, S. (1984). *Stress, appraisal, and coping.* New York: Springer.

Leff, J. P., & Vaughn, C. E. (1981). The role of maintenance therapy and relatives' expressed emotion in relapse of schizophrenia: A two-year follow-up. *British Journal of Psychiatry, 139,* 102–104.

Lewinsohn, P. M., & Amenson, C. S. (1978). Some relations between pleasant and unpleasant mood-related events and depression. *Journal of Abnormal Psychology, 87,* 644–654.

Lofland, L. H. (1982). Loss and human connection: An exploration into the nature of the social bond. In W. Ickes & E. S. Knowles (Eds.), *Personality, roles, and social behavior* (pp. 219–233). New York: Springer-Verlag.

Maier, E. H., & Lachman, M. E. (2000). Consequences of early parental loss and separation for health and well-being in midlife. *International Journal of Behavioral Development, 24,* 183–189.

Miller, R. S. (2001). Breaches of propriety. In R. M. Kowalski (Ed.), *Behaving badly: Aversive behaviors in interpersonal relationships* (pp. 29–58). Washington, DC: American Psychological Association.

Mitchell, R. E., Cronkite, R. C., & Moos, R. H. (1983). Stress, coping, and depression among married couples. *Journal of Abnormal Psychology, 92,* 433–448.

Morgan, D. L., Carder, P. C., & Neal, M. B. (1997). Are some relationships more useful than others? The value of peers in the support networks of recent widows. *Journal of Social and Personal Relationships, 6,* 745–759.

Morgan, D. L., Neal, M. B., & Carder, P. C. (1997). Both what and when: The effects of positive and negative aspects of relationships on depression during the first three years of widowhood. *Journal of Clinical Geropsychology, 1,* 73–91.

Murphy, S. (1988). Mental distress and recovery in a high-risk bereavement sample three years after untimely death. *Nursing Research, 37,* 30–35.

Newsom, J. T., Morgan, D. L., Nishishiba, M., & Rook, K. S. (2002). Development of new comparable measures of negative and positive social exchanges. Manuscript under review.

Nezlek, J. B., Kowalski, R. M., Leary, M. R., Blevins, T., & Holgate, S. (1997). Personality moderators of reactions to interpersonal rejection: Depression and trait self-esteem. *Personality and Social Psychology Bulletin, 23,* 1235–1244.

Noller, P., Feeney, J. A., & Peterson, C. (2001). *Personal relationships across the life span*. East Sussex, UK: Psychology Press.

O'Brien, T. B., & DeLongis, A. (1996). The interactional context of problem-, emotion- and relationship-focused coping: The role of the big five personality factors. *Journal of Personality, 64*, 775–813.

Ohbuchi, K., & Tedeschi, J. T. (1997). Multiple goals and tactical behaviors in social conflicts. *Journal of Applied Social Psychology, 27*, 2177–2199.

Park, K. A. (1992). Preschoolers' reactions to loss of a best friend: Developmental trends and individual differences. *Child Study Journal, 22*, 233–252.

Patterson, I. (1996). Participation in leisure activities by older adults after a stressful life event: The loss of a spouse. *International Journal of Aging and Human Development, 42*, 123–142.

Pearlin, L. I., & Schooler, C. (1978). The structure of coping. *Journal of Health and Social Behavior, 19*, 2–21.

Peplau, H. E. (1955). Loneliness. *American Journal of Nursing, 55*, 1476–1481.

Petersen, D. R. (1983). Conflict. In H. H. Kelley, E. Berscheid, A. Christensen, J. H. Harvey, T. L. Huston, G. Levinger, E. McClintock, L. A. Peplau, & D. R. Peterson (Eds.), *Close relationships* (pp. 360–396). New York: W. H. Freeman.

Rahim, M. A. (1986). Referent role and styles of handling interpersonal conflict. *Journal of Social Psychology, 126*, 79–86.

Rice, S. (1989). Single, older childless women: Differences between never-married and widowed women in life satisfaction and social support. *Journal of Gerontological Social Work, 13*(3/4), 35–47.

Rook, K. S. (1984). Promoting social bonding: Strategies for helping the lonely and socially isolated. *American Psychologist, 39*, 1389–1407.

Rook, K. S. (1998). Investigating the positive and negative sides of personal relationships: Through a lens darkly? In B. H. Spitzberg & W. R. Cupach (Eds.), *The dark side of close relationships* (pp. 369–393). Mahwah, NJ: Lawrence Erlbaum.

Rook, K. S., & Schuster, T. L. (1996). Compensatory processes in the social networks of older adults. In G. R. Pierce, B. R. Sarason, & I. G. Sarason (Eds.), *Handbook of social support and the family* (pp. 219–248). New York: Plenum.

Rook, K. S., Sorkin, D. H., David, J., Newsom, J., & Morgan, D. (2001, November). Adaptation to interpersonal stressors: The role of control strivings, coping responses, and coping goals. Paper presented at the annual meeting of the Gerontological Society of America, Chicago, IL.

Rothbaum, F., Weisz, J. R., & Snyder, S. S. (1982). Changing the world and changing the self: A two-process model of perceived control. *Journal of Personality and Social Psychology, 42*, 5–37.

Simons, R. L. (1984). Specificity and substitution in the social networks of the elderly. *International Journal of Aging and Human Development, 18*, 121–139.

Smith, L. W., Patterson, T. L., & Grant, I. (1990). Avoidant coping predicts psychological disturbance in the elderly. *Journal of Nervous and Mental Disease, 178*, 525–530.

Stewart, A. J., Copeland, A. P., Chester, N. L., Malley, J. E., & Barenbaum, N. B. (1997). *Separating together: How divorce transforms families*. New York: Guilford Press.

Stroebe, M. S., Hansson, R. O., Stroebe, W., & Schut, H. (Eds.) (2001). *Handbook of bereavement research: Consequences, coping, and care.* Washington, DC: American Psychological Association.

Suls, J., David, J. P., & Harvey, J. H. (1996). Personality and coping: Three generations of research. *Journal of Personality, 64,* 711–735.

Vinokur, A. D., & Vinokur-Kaplan, D. (1990). "In sickness and in health": Patterns of social support and undermining in older married couples. *Journal of Aging and Health, 2,* 215–241.

Vitaliano, P. P., DeWolfe, D. J., Maiuro, R. D., Russo, J., & Katon, W. (1990). Appraised changeability of a stressor as a modifier of the relationship between coping and depression: A test of the hypothesis of fit. *Journal of Personality and Social Psychology, 59,* 582–592.

Walker, K. N., McBride, A., & Vachon, M. L. S. (1997). Social support networks and the crisis of bereavement. *Social Science and Medicine, 2,* 35–41.

Weiss, R. S. (1974). The provisions of social relationships. In Z. Rubin (Ed.), *Doing unto others* (pp. 17–26).

Williamson, G. M., & Schulz, R. (1990). Relationship orientation, quality of prior relationship, and distress among caregivers of Alzheimer's patients. *Psychology and Aging, 5,* 502–509.

Wills, T. A., & Shinar, O. (2000). Measuring perceived and received social support. In S. Cohen, B. H. Gottlieb, & L. G. Underwood (Eds.), *Social support measurement and interventions: A guide for health and social scientists* (pp. 86–135). New York: Oxford University Press.

Wrosch, C., & Heckhausen, J. (1999). Control processes before and after passing a developmental deadline: Activation and deactivation of intimate relationship goals. *Journal of Personality and Social Psychology, 77,* 415–427.

Young, J. E. (1982). Loneliness, depression and cognitive therapy. In L. A. Peplau & D. Perlman (Eds.), *Loneliness: A sourcebook of current theory, research and therapy* (pp. 379–405). New York: Wiley.

Zettel, L. A., Rook, K. S., & Morgan, D. (2001, November). Substitution and compensation in the social networks of older widowed women. Poster presented at the annual meeting of the Gerontological Society of America, Chicago, IL.

10

Social Support and Physical Health across the Life Span: Socioemotional Influences

Susan Turk Charles and Shahrzad Mavandadi

The socioemotional health model posits that emotion regulation is the central mechanism mediating the link between social relationships and physical health. The four tenets of the model maintain that: (1) emotions and social relationships share a complex interplay developed over the millennia; (2) emotion regulation is the central mechanism linking social relationships with health; (3) emotion regulation includes physiological, cognitive, and behavioral processes, all three of which influence health, and (4) socioemotional processes affect health throughout the life span, but will be most evident at the very beginning and end of the life cycle when people are most physically vulnerable. We present the model and provide an overview of how socioemotional processes influence health throughout the life span via physiological, cognitive, and behavioral pathways.

Magazines and newspaper columns often highlight stories of people surviving seemingly insurmountable physical hardships: people who live with a terminal illness longer than any physician had anticipated, or someone lost for weeks in the wilderness with little to eat or drink who, miraculously, is found alive. When queried about their success, many of these people mention the presence or thoughts of a loved one as a critical factor in their survival. Viktor Frankl wrote poignantly about this subject, describing how thoughts of his wife sustained him during his internment at a Nazi concentration camp: "In a last violent protest against the hopelessness of imminent death, I sensed my spirit piercing through the enveloping gloom. . . . The guard passed by, insulting me, and once again I communed with my beloved. More and more I felt that she was present, that she was with me" (1959, pp. 51–52). These accounts seem extraordinary, but empirical studies have confirmed the link between social relationships and many physical health outcomes.

Social support predicts mortality, a finding documented in multiple longitudinal studies (see reviews by Cassel, 1976; Cobb, 1977; House,

Landis, & Umberson, 1988). After controlling for physical activity, blood pressure, smoking, obesity, cholesterol, respiratory functioning and other known medical indicators, men and women low in social support are two to three times more likely to die than those high in support (Berkman & Syme, 1979; House, Robbins, & Metzner, 1982). Moreover, the effects of social support on mortality are as strong as other risk factors, such as smoking and cholesterol levels (see review by House et al., 1988). Social support is also linked to overall health status (e.g., see reviews by Ryff & Singer, 2001; Seeman, 1996; Uchino, Cacioppo, & Kiecolt-Glaser, 1996), exerting both direct effects on the trajectory of physical disease and illness (House et al., 1988), as well as buffering effects when people are faced with stressful situations (cf. Cohen & Wills, 1985). This phenomenon is present across many disease processes and occurs throughout the life span, but no specific physiological process linking health to social support has been determined (see reviews by Seeman, 1996; Uchino et al., 1996).

The current chapter discusses the link between physical health and social relationships throughout the life span. In the first section, we present the socioemotional health model and describe its four tenets explaining how emotion regulation mediates the association between social support and physical health. The second and third sections review studies supporting each of these tenets. In the second section, we briefly mention psychoevolutionary underpinnings for the interplay between social relationships and emotion. In the third and main section, we review findings documenting the influence of socioemotional processes on health outcomes from the prenatal period to the end of the life span. For each life stage, we describe how socioemotional processes influence current and future health status through physiological, cognitive, and behavioral pathways. The final section includes future directions in the study of socioemotional processes affecting physical health.

SOCIOEMOTIONAL HEALTH MODEL

We propose that emotion regulation is the central mechanism mediating the association between social relationships and physical health. The first tenet of the socioemotional health model maintains that relationships are integral to health because they are inherently tied to emotion regulation, an association interwoven across the millennia and present throughout an individual's life course. For this reason, social processes *by definition* entail emotional outcomes. Second, the model posits that the most important element of social relationships is the emotional regulatory benefits derived from them. Emotion regulation in this chapter is conceptualized as the ability to regulate one's emotional state to promote higher levels of affective well-being and lower emotional reactivity throughout daily life.

Humans are inherently emotional creatures, and successful social relationships include those where relational needs and high levels of intimacy are met (Reis, 2001). In this chapter, we will focus predominantly on the importance of positive emotional experiences, although we do recognize that negative emotions in the context of a supportive relationship can also be valuable for emotion regulation and consequent positive mental and physical health. For example, disciplining a child can be a negative experience for all involved, but this experience also teaches the child to manage his or her emotions and to navigate social environments (e.g., Gottman, 2001). Also, we understand that not all social relationships are defined by high levels of intimacy. Researchers have studied a variety of functional and structural qualities of the social system, including network size, social control, companionship, and reciprocity (see review by Rook, 1994), and many of these measures correlate with well-being outcomes (see review by Cohen & Wills, 1985). Perceived support, however, is a more robust predictor of well-being (Cohen & Wills, 1985) and captures the perceived fulfillment of relational needs central to this model. Moreover, meaningful social relationships offer the emotion regulatory benefits that we describe in this model.

The third tenet posits that because emotions are comprised of physiological, cognitive, and behavioral processes, socioemotional influences on health will be exerted directly via physiological processes (e.g., Seeman, 1996), and indirectly via cognitions (e.g., will to live) and behaviors (e.g., proper nutrition and health care visits). We recognize that positive emotions, and positive socioemotional experiences, are related to better health (see review by Salovey, Rothman, Detweiler, & Steward, 2000), even though we focus primarily on studies showing the negative effects of poor socioemotional experiences when we explain these processes in the following sections of this chapter.

The fourth and last tenet of the socioemotional health model is that although socioemotional processes influence health throughout the life span, the effects are most evident when people are most physically vulnerable, which normatively occurs at the very beginning and end of the life cycle. The most critical time is arguably at the beginning of life, when socioemotional experiences have long-term consequences in addition to immediate effects (Coe & Lubach, 2001). Researchers posit that many diseases occurring in later life including hypertension, hyperlipidaemia, non-insulin-dependent diabetes mellitus, stroke, breast and testicular cancer, and coronary heart disease and allergies have "fetal origins" influenced by both intrauterine environment and birth outcomes (Barker, 1997; Phillips et al., 1998; Swerdlow, De Stavola, Swanwick, & Maconochie, 1997; Warner, Jones, Jones, & Warner, 2000). On the other extreme, the end of life is generally in very old age, but also includes terminally ill younger adults – all people who are nearing the end of their life and who are therefore physically most vulnerable.

No Man Is an Island – Evolutionary Models of Social Relationships and Emotion

The socioemotional health model holds that emotions and social relationships have evolved together to create an interdependent association. Researchers have compared humans to other animal species, examined universal principles invariant across cultures, and documented innate mechanisms exhibited at birth to find patterns suggestive of psychoevolutionary influence. Through these investigations, scientists have determined that evolutionary processes have shaped humans into socioemotional creatures.

Emotions are present at birth, universal, and similar to those of more primitive species. Emotions serve to motivate the self and others and, in so doing, promote survival. Because emotions are located in the primitive limbic lobe (LeDoux, 1996), they are believed to have influenced the evolution of more recent brain structures, including those responsible for cognitions and social behavior (Zajonc, 1998). In addition, emotions are innate and unfold in distinct patterns throughout the first few years of life (Izard, 1978); even blind children smile. Emotions are defined as action tendencies developed over the millennia and are social in nature, such as fear promoting the flight response, anger promoting aggression, or happiness promoting reproduction and bonding (Ekman & Davidson, 1994; Fredrickson, 2000).

Social behavior is also innate in humans as well as in a variety of different species (see discussion by Ryan, 1993). Many researchers believe that the ability to perceive faces is innate (e.g., Bowlby, 1969), an argument bolstered by studies finding that infants recognize faces uniquely from other types of stimuli (cf. Morton & Johnson, 1991; Slater & Quinn, 2001; but see Nelson, 2001). In fact, human and monkey brain regions contain neurons that respond selectively to faces, bodies, and eye gaze (Emery, 2000). In addition, humans and other primate species have elaborate muscle systems around their eyes, and scientists posit that these muscles evolved specifically to enable social gaze to communicate to others not only focused attention, but also emotional information (Emery, 2000).

Further physiological evidence points to the interdependence of social and emotional experiences. The primary physiological mechanisms responsible for feelings of social attachment and emotional feelings of love are hypothesized to be located in the neuropeptides oxytocin and vasopressin, based in the hypothalamic-pituitary-adrenal (HPA) axis (see review by Carter, 1998). Oxytocin is a hormone implicated in animals' ability to bond with potential mates as well as to nurture their offspring (Liu, Curtis, & Wang, 2001). Carter (1998) maintains that these processes are evident in humans as well. Perhaps not surprising, researchers are hypothesizing a link between oxytocin and autism, a developmental disorder whose symptoms include poor emotional attachment with others (Insel, O'Brien, & Leckman, 1999).

Many emotional and social processes appear to be innate, universal among humans, and dependent on similar physiological processes. As brain size increases in mammals, so do the number and complexity of social relationships (see discussion by Harcourt, 1992) as well as, arguably, the complexity of emotional feelings. In general, the most intense emotional experiences are social experiences. The most basic social stimulus – the human face – is thought to have evolved for the functional purpose of communicating emotions (Ekman, 1973; Izard, 1978). The primary functions of emotions, to motivate and communicate, are embedded in social processes and serve social goals. For these reasons, social and emotional processes are intertwined. For humans, social relatedness – the desire to feel connected to others, to feel loved, and to care for others – is an innate motivational drive (see reviews by Baumeister & Leary, 1995; Deci & Ryan, 1991; Ryan & Deci, 2000), and a socioemotional construct.

EMOTION, SOCIAL SUPPORT, AND HEALTH ACROSS THE LIFE SPAN

For each phase of the life cycle, we first outline findings relating physical health status to social support and then discuss the emotional processes – physiological, cognitive, and behavioral – accounting for this association. We maintain that these three processes influence health outcomes for each age group. Our review is not parallel across age groups; studies vary in the types of health outcomes and types of social support measured, methodological variations most likely stemming from differences in health problems commonly experienced at different points in the life cycle. Examining patterns of morbidity and mortality across the life span helps to clarify these differences. For example, the vast majority of children in the United States (over 98%) are born healthy and only a small percentage of children under eighteen years old, 6.5%, have a functional limitation (National Center for Health Statistics, 2001). When children die, the most common reasons are SIDS, for which we have little information regarding its etiology, and accidents and homicides, factors unrelated to physical health (National Center for Health Statistics, 2001). The effects of variations in normative social behavior among this relatively healthy population may be hard to detect, and for this reason our review focuses on the effects of gross social neglect on health outcomes.

Young adulthood, between the ages of eighteen and thirty-five, is considered the apex for reproductive, cognitive, and overall physical functioning.

Most young adults have no major chronic illnesses or functional limitations; the most common reasons for death in this age group (i.e., accidents and homicide) are not related to disease processes, and thus socioemotional influences are more often measured by physiological reactivity than by morbidity or mortality. In contrast, among older adults, physical resilience and physical reserve capacity decreases, chronic illness is the norm rather than the exception, and the prevalence rates of chronic illnesses increase with each older age group (Ory, Abeles, & Lipman, 1992). These chronic diseases include cancer and diseases of the heart, which together are responsible for over half of the deaths in the United States (U.S. Department of Health and Human Services, 2000). Physiological, cognitive, and behavior mechanisms have been studied among adults who have these, as well as other, chronic illnesses.

The Prenatal Period

Social Support and Health Outcomes in Pregnancy. Anne Boleyn's pregnancy was one of joyous anticipation, but when she gave birth to a healthy girl instead of the promised son, the king's disappointment grew into contempt and anger toward his wife. Her next two pregnancies ended in miscarriage (Weir, 2001). Historians have pondered whether Anne Boleyn's miscarriages were partly related to her stressful relationship with her husband during her pregnancies. Most likely we will never know the exact reason, but recent findings suggest that stress during pregnancy influences pregnancy outcomes.

This chapter emphasizes the socioemotional health model, which focuses on the individual's socioemotional system and how it influences his or her health. This agentic view, however, ignores social influences over which an individual has no control but which may affect health from birth to death: the socioemotional experience of his or her mother. The quality of social relationships throughout the course of pregnancy is related to an array of health indices affecting the future child, including fetal growth, the likelihood of preterm labor, birth weight, and labor complications.

Maternal perception of emotional support exerts unique influences on birth outcomes. The importance of emotional support is posited to increase throughout pregnancy, exerting its greatest influence the three months before and after delivery; during these months, emotional support is believed to outweigh other functional aspects of social support, such as the fulfillment of informational or instrumental needs (Jacobsen, 1986; Power & Parke, 1984). Perceived support from one's family and partner is related to preterm birth (Collins, Dunkel-Schetter, Lobel, & Scrimshaw, 1993; Lidderdale & Walsh, 1998) and low birth weight among both African- and European-American women (Abell, Baker, Clover, & Ramsey, 1991). Moreover, perceived meaningful social support predicts fetal growth (birth weight adjusted for length of gestation) after controlling for infant sex, ethnicity, and obstetric risk (Feldman, Dunkel-Schetter, Sandman, & Wadhwa, 2000). Emotional support accounts for 31% of the variance in fetal growth, which is comparable to the effects of well-accepted biomedical determinants of birth weight (Feldman et al., 2000).

Labor complications are also related to lower levels of emotional support during pregnancy. In a study of African American and Caucasian women, low social support from one's mother during pregnancy was associated with a higher likelihood of all gestational and labor complications, including a long labor and the need for a cesarean section (Norbeck & Anderson, 1989). Further, among African Americans, greater partner support was related to fewer pregnancy complications (Norbeck & Anderson, 1989). Higher levels of social support during pregnancy is related to fewer labor difficulties, an increased likelihood of a normal delivery, higher birth weight babies, a greater likelihood of delivering a baby with a normal fetal heart rate, and higher Apgar scores for the newborn (Collins et al., 1993; Lidderdale & Walsh, 1998). Higher levels of emotional support at the time of labor and delivery (e.g., verbal encouragement, touch, and mere physical presence of a loved one or birth companion) are also associated with fewer delivery complications, a factor related to newborn health status (Gjerdingen, Froberg, & Fontaine, 1991; Lidderdale & Walsh, 1998).

Using non-human subjects, researchers can experimentally control levels of maternal social support and examine its effects on the health of the offspring. In a study by Schneider and Coe (1993), chronic disruption of female primates' social relationships during the course of pregnancy was significantly associated with declines in subsequent neonatal/infant performance on numerous neuromotor tasks (e.g., poor motor abilities and balance reactions and inability to cope in the face of stressors). These infant primates also had shorter attention spans and impaired orientation abilities, suggesting that the development of vestibular proprioceptive functions was altered due to the chronic stress experienced by the mother.

Possible Physiological Pathways. The emotion regulatory functions of meaningful social support are believed to exert their influence on maternal-fetal health along two physiological axes, the hypothalamic-pituitary-adrenal (HPA) axis and the sympathetic-adrenal-medullary (SAM) axis. Both axes are involved in emotional reactivity and maternal and fetal health outcomes. The hypothalamic, pituitary, adrenal and placental stress hormones (e.g., corticotropin releasing hormone) are involved in reproduction, growth, and immunity, and their elevation is related to intrauterine growth retardation (IUGR), a precursor to low birth weight (Feldman et al., 2000). The activation and release of hormones associated with the SAM axis, which may occur as a result of experienced stressors, may result in vasoconstriction and hypoxia, two factors associated with fetal growth restriction and low birth weight.

Social support helps to decrease maternal depression, anxiety, and overall reports of feelings of stress, which in turn acts to dampen activation of the SAM and HPA axes. Greater levels of emotional support from close friends and spouse are related to lower maternal depression and better mental health both during and after pregnancy (O'Hara, 1986; Power & Parke, 1984). Lack of emotional support from others, in contrast, may lead to increased maternal anxiety, resulting in both elevated levels of these circulating catecholamines and decreased uterine contractility (Kennell, Klaus, McGrath, Robertson, & Hinkley, 1991). In addition, greater social support is related to decreased anxiety, which is associated with lower plasma levels of ACTH and cortisol (hormones in the HPA and SAM axes) and a reduced likelihood of preterm labor onset (Feldman et al., 2000; Lederman, 1995), two factors associated with preterm birth (Lederman, 1995).

Behaviors and Cognitions. Enhanced emotion regulation motivates maternal behaviors and cognitions that affect the health outcomes of the child, such as IUGR and low birth weight. For example, pregnant women reporting high levels of perceived support, as compared to those with low levels of social support, are more likely to seek health-related information, receive prenatal care earlier in their pregnancy, attend prenatal classes, and receive treatment for diseases such as hypertension, all factors related to IUGR (Feldman et al., 2000; Gjerdingen et al., 1991). In addition, women who report greater satisfaction with their social ties are less likely to report prenatal substance use (Collins et al., 1993) and more likely to engage in behaviors that promote infant health, such as breast-feeding (Oakley, 1988), compared to their less satisfied counterparts. Greater emotional support is related to cognitions as well, such as greater perceived parenting competence, which in turn protects against the occurrence of postpartum depression among new mothers (Gjerdingen et al., 1991), a factor important in caring for the new infant.

Infancy and Early Childhood

Social Support and Health in Infancy and Early Childhood. In Harlow's classic studies, he documented that young monkeys prefer a non-living mother substitute who fulfilled needs of warmth and comfort over one that offered sustenance (Harlow & Zimmerman, 1959). Relational needs are essential in the earliest days and months of life, a time during which critical developmental periods for the immune system and other physiological systems take place; for this reason, insufficient relational needs have long-lasting consequences for health outcomes (see review by Coe & Lubach, 2001).

Parents' and caregivers' anticipation of and sensitivity to an infant's needs are essential to the baby's well-being and subsequent physical and psychosocial development (Maudner & Hunter, 2001), and gross neglect and deprivation can have extreme physical consequences. One negative outcome is termed "psychosocial dwarfism," a condition defined by insufficient levels of growth hormone and growth retardation (Hofer, 1994). In addition, poor attachment has been related to failure to thrive (FTT), a condition affecting approximately 5–10% of children observed in outpatient clinics and defined as weight-for-age at or below the 5th percentile, weight-to-height ratio less than the 25th percentile, and a deceleration in the rate of weight gain from birth to the time of evaluation based on standardized growth charts (Coolbear & Benoit, 1999; Dykman, Ackerman, Loizou, & Casey, 2000). FTT is also related to problems with later physical development (Coolbear & Benoit, 1999; Skuse, Wolke, & Reilly, 1992), cognitive deficits, behavioral problems (Dykman et al., 2000), and deficits in neurological development (Boddy, Skuse, & Andrews, 2000).

FTT was originally considered a disorder stemming from purely biological causes because almost all children with this disease have a serious medical or organic problem, such as undernutrition. Now, however, researchers consider multiple features of the parent, child, and the environment in the pathogenesis (Casey, 1987), and distinguish the type of FTT as either *organic* (i.e., when there is an underlying medical problem that is causally linked to undernutrition) or *nonorganic* (i.e., when no underlying medical problem except for undernutrition is present). Interestingly, the most common nonorganic factors associated with the development of FTT are largely relationship factors, including deficient parental care, disturbed relationship between the infant and caregiver, insecure attachment to the caregiver, and family dysfunction and poverty (Iwaniec & Sneddon, 2001).

Possible Physiological Pathways. Mothers and other caregivers serve as external regulators for an infant's emotional reactivity (Liu et al., 1997; see discussion by Coe & Lubach, 2001). Children often exhibit increased cortisol responses after the departure of their mother, but these responses are attenuated if the child has access to a "warm, responsive, and interactive" caregiver (Gunnar et al., 1992). In addition, studies using animal samples provide controlled examinations of these processes over a longer period of time, and researchers argue that the findings can be generalized to humans (Maudner & Hunter, 2001).

Emotional attachment and maternal-infant bonding in early life are hypothesized to influence the development of both viscera and neuroanatomy (Gorski, 2001). Affective experience is one of the primary forms of stimulus for early brain growth, and chronic deprivation of an emotional attachment has been suggested to result in inadequate development of the right hemisphere of the brain. During the first two years of life, the majority of the organization of the brain's right hemisphere dominant cortico-limbic system occurs. This system is critical for the development of sensorimotor pathways, processes of brain bioamine metabolism, emotion regulation, cardiovascular stress reactivity, immune system function, and conceptual learning styles throughout the course of life (Gorski, 2001). When early relationships and patterns of attachment and bonding are threatened or damaged, a wide array of short- and long-term alterations in endocrine, immune, and autonomic system functioning can result.

In primates, for example, short-term maternal deprivation and inadequate levels of handling lead to suppressed levels of growth hormone, prolactin, and insulin, reductions in DNA synthesis in most organ tissues, a slowing of insulin catabolism, and increases in the secretion of corticosterone (see review by Schanberg, 1995). In addition, brief disruptions in the maternal-infant bond affect the integrity of the indigenous, intestinal microflora (responsible for warding off infection and reducing pathogen colonization and growth) for several days, leaving the immune system weakened and the infant susceptible to disease (Bailey & Coe, 1999).

Primate infants experiencing prolonged separation from their mothers evidence decreased heart rate and lowered body temperature (Hofer, 1994), and monkeys remaining in isolation during critical periods of infant development exhibit reduced cerebellar and motor cortical dendritic branching and altered hormonal functioning (Maudner & Hunter, 2001; Lewis, Gluck, Petitto, Hensley, & Ozer, 2000). These negative effects remain in adulthood; for example, non-mother-reared monkeys demonstrate abnormally high levels of lymphocyte proliferation in response to mitogen exposure even at 1.5 years of age (Coe, Lubach, Ershler, & Klopp, 1989; Lewis et al., 2000). This reduced efficiency in cell-mediated immune functioning may be one reason monkeys deprived of maternal nurturing have shorter life spans compared to non-deprived monkeys (Coe et al., 1989; Lewis et al., 2000).

Similarly, rats who received brief periods of maternal licking and grooming during the first ten days of life had lower levels of plasma adrenocorticotropin hormone (ACTH), lower adrenal corticosterone (i.e., the main stress hormone in rats), lower hypothalamic corticotropin-releasing hormone messenger RNA, increased hippocampal glucocorticoid receptor messenger RNA expression, and greater glucocorticoid feedback sensitivity in response to acute stressors than rats without maternal care. Importantly, these physiological differences persist in adulthood (Liu et al., 1997).

Cognitions and Behavior. Without the mother's ability to provide external emotion regulation, the child's resultant poor emotion regulation, and the behaviors that ensue, are linked to later health problems. Deprivation of an attachment figure exerts long and short-term effects on psychosocial processes in domains such as affiliation, communication, social responsiveness, learning, and exploratory, consumption behaviors, sexual and maternal behavior in nonhuman and human species (Lewis et al., 2000). During World War II, for example, infants who were orphaned, hospitalized, or placed in residential nurseries often displayed a predictable sequence of behavioral responses following separation – protest, despair, and detachment (Field, 1990). Babies who experience separations and other object losses exhibit affective behavior suggestive of depression, helplessness and hopelessness, and attitudes of "having given up" (Taylor, Bagby, & Parker, 1997). Paralleling these findings, primate infants separated from their mothers for a prolonged period first exhibit protest behavior (e.g., high intensity vocalizations) and then reduced responsiveness and behavior indicative of affective shifts from anxiety and anger to sadness and despair (Hofer, 1994). Among humans, maternal separation and poor caregiver-infant attachment may have detrimental effects upon social outcomes regarding peer relationships and later romantic attachments (Ainsworth, 1989), and as we describe in the following sections, engaging in emotionally meaningful relationships in adulthood is strongly related to physical health status.

Later Childhood and Adolescence

In childhood, social relationships broaden to include siblings, peers, teachers, and other extra-family sources of support. In adolescence, social companionship with peers (i.e., belongingness) is especially important in that it decreases stress by allowing the adolescent to affiliate with others, distracts them from worries, aids in coping with problems, and facilitates positive mood states (see review by Seiffge-Krenke, 1998). The importance of the relationship with one's parents, however, is arguably the most important social tie. Negative correlations between adolescent depression and family cohesion are stronger than those between depression and peer companionship (Seiffge-Krenke, 1998).

Possible Physiological Pathways. Childhood has been identified as the most important period in the development of emotional control and regulatory processes, and families provide the basis for shaping these processes (Gottman & Katz, 1989). For example, four-to-five-year-olds who have parents who model poor emotion regulation skills exhibit more emotional and physiological distress than children whose parents model emotion regulation effectively (Gottman & Katz, 1989). In addition, distressed couples are more likely to have children who are under a high level of chronic stress than non-distressed children (Gottman & Katz, 1989). Furthermore, couples who are unhappy and physiologically underaroused tend to have parenting styles that are cold, detached, and angry, which subsequently results in increased levels of anger and noncompliance, high vagal tone, and high levels of urinary catecholamines in their children (Gottman & Katz, 1989). Chronically high levels of catecholamines and feelings of anger and disgust create a cascade of events ending in poor emotion regulation styles. As a result, these children may be more reactive and therefore more susceptible to feelings of negative affect, leading to lower levels of peer play and, as a consequence, greater impairment of his or her ability to regulate negative emotions once they are elicited. Poorly regulated emotions may subsequently lead to greater SAM/HPA activation, which suppresses the immune system and leaves the individual more susceptible to disease. In contrast, supportive and cohesive family relationships serve a protective function in adolescence; parental support has both a main effect on physical and psychological symptoms and a stress buffering effect under conditions of high stress (Seiffge-Krenke, 1998). The few studies analyzing the protective function of peers and friends, on the other hand, yield inconsistent evidence (Seiffge-Krenke, 1998).

Cognitions and Behaviors. Negative emotions, particularly depression, are also related to unhealthy cognitions and poor health behavior, which in turn influence health (Salovey et al., 2000). When preadolescent children report that their social relationships lack emotional closeness, they also report more infrequent exercise, poor self-reported health, and more smoking and alcohol use compared to children reporting emotional satisfaction in their relationships (McLellan, Rissel, Donnelly, & Bauman, 1999). Social interactions with peers can also be influenced by negative affect; children whose parents are in distressed marriages tend to participate in low, conflict-free types of play with peers (Gottman & Katz, 1989). The importance of emotional connection on health behavior remains in adolescence. Both family and peer relationship quality are related to health behaviors, including dieting and exercise (Byely, Archibald, Graber, & Brooks-Gunn, 2000; Field, Diego, & Sanders, 2001), cigarette, drug, and alcohol use (Beal, Ausiello, & Perrin, 2001; Conrad, Flay, & Hill, 1992; Friedman, Lichtenstein, & Biglan, 1985), and contraception use (Nathanson & Becker, 1986). For most of these behaviors, lifetime patterns are set in late childhood (Conrad et al., 1992).

Participation in high-risk behaviors, such as smoking and substance use, is closely linked to the experience of negative emotions such as depression, hostility, and anxiety and the cognitions related to these negative emotions. These cognitive factors, including decision making, self-efficacy, and self-esteem, not only have a role in the initiation of problem behaviors, but they may also play an important role in maintaining the behavior over time (Botvin et al., 1993). Greater perceived emotional support has been linked to reduced negative affect and reduced likelihood of one's participation in high-risk behaviors as a means of coping; in contrast, poor social relationships are linked to more negative emotions and more high-risk behaviors as a means of coping, such as smoking to reduce anxiety and to "fit in" (Ewart & Kolodner, 1994; Mueller, Grunbaum, & Labarthe, 2001; Patton et al., 1998; Smith & Furlong, 1994). Middle and junior high school students with deficiencies in personal competence (e.g., poor decision-making skills and low personal efficacy) are more likely to perceive social benefits from smoking and to initiate smoking behavior (Epstein, Griffin, & Botvin, 2000). Among high school students, other types of problem behaviors, such as alcohol or drug use, are also associated with problem behavior patterns and lower levels of self-efficacy (Chung & Elias, 1996).

Adulthood

Methodological Considerations. Adulthood spans many decades. Although older adults are actuarially more physically vulnerable than younger adults, the great variation in physical functioning throughout the adult age range makes distinctions by chronological age difficult. Many studies determine populations by health symptom or diagnosis, not age. As a result, the wide age range, and the limited number of people representing each of these decades, makes examining age differences difficult. With few exceptions, studies often do not report any interaction with age, and when age is mentioned, similarities between the influences of socioemotional processes on health are generally emphasized over differences.

Socioemotional Processes and Health in Adulthood. One of the most powerful kings of Scotland, Malcolm III, died in battle in 1098. According to historians, Queen Margaret heard of her husband's death and died three days later from grief. She was forty-eight years old. Declines in health after the death of a spouse, both during the acute grieving period and in the years following, are well documented, and the life span of widows and widowers is significantly shorter compared to their married counterparts (see review by Stroebe & Stroebe, 1987). Effects are even stronger for men than women, and socioemotional processes such as emotional expression and the amount of relational closeness to other members of the social network have been hypothesized to play a role in this gender difference (Stroebe, 2001). For all adults, however, deprivation of emotionally meaningful relationships through bereavement, divorce, or geographical relocation has profound influences on morbidity and mortality.

As stated in the introduction and noted above, social relationships strongly predict mortality, a topic comprehensively reviewed elsewhere both in articles (e.g., House et al., 1982) and edited volumes (e.g., Ryff & Singer, 2001). People throughout the entire adult life span, from those in their twenties to people in their eighties, are more likely to die from all causes if they report low social support (House et al., 1988). The sheer volume of findings is too great to review adequately here, and thus we provide a limited overview (please refer to Ryff & Singer (2001) for a comprehensive review).

Presumably, low social support is not a sufficient requisite for death. Returning to the story of Queen Margaret, she was already ill when she heard the news of her husband's demise, and her emotional distress presumably exacerbated her already weakened physical state. This does not suggest, however, that seemingly physically robust people are impervious to the effects of social relationships.[1] Among healthy adults, greater socioemotional support is related to fewer physical symptoms for men and women (Krantz & Oestergren, 2000) and lower levels of prostate-specific antigens (PSA) among men (Stone, Mezzacappa, Donatone, & Gonder, 1999). Greater numbers of physical health symptoms are associated with lower perceived social support at work and home (Holahan & Moos, 1982), and self-rated health is lower among people getting a divorce who report low levels of social support compared to those with high perceived social support (Richmond, Steenbergen, & Hendrickson, 2000). In addition, socioemotional stressors leave relatively healthy people more susceptible to viruses. Cohen and his colleagues have found that stressors, as measured by recent life events, are related to a greater susceptibility to the flu virus, and people with interpersonal life stressors are at greatest risk for infection (see review by Cohen, 2001). Psychosocial factors also play a role in the etiology of peptic ulcers, a condition caused by Helicobacter pylori bacteria (Levenstein, 2000); specifically, marital distress and problems experienced by one's children are related to greater likelihood of developing a peptic ulcer among adult women (Levenstein, Kaplan, & Smith, 1995).

For people who are vulnerable to assaults on their health, socioemotional stressors may result in more observable negative health outcomes, with mortality being the most extreme health outcome measured. Using social support as a strategy to cope with stressors is related to better functioning among people with rheumatoid arthritis, chronic obstructive lung disease, and psoriasis (e.g., Scharloo et al., 1998). For people with rheumatoid arthritis, higher marital quality buffered the effects of stressful weeks, such that those with greater spousal support did not show the increase in disease activity exhibited by those reporting lower levels of spousal support (Zautra et al., 1998).

Cancer is also subject to the influence of socioemotional factors (e.g., Tominaga, Andow, Koyama, Numao, Kurokawa, Ojima, & Nagai, 1998; but see Cassileth, Lusk, Miller, Brown, & Miller, 1985; Cassileth, Walsh, & Lusk, 1988). Social support is consistently linked to survival from cancer among European- and African-Americans (Creagan, 1997; Reynolds et al., 1994). Among women with breast cancer, socioemotional support predicts

---

[1] Although insidious processes leading to later disease are posited to be present since birth (Lucas, Fewtrell, & Cole, 1999), problems are often undetected at this time.

survival for people representing three age groups: 15–45, 46–60, and 61 and older (Funch & Marshall, 1983). For the younger and older members, social support is an even stronger predictor of survival than stage of the cancer at time of diagnosis (Funch & Marshall, 1983). In another study examining emotional expressiveness at home, low anger and greater extroversion predicted survival four years later after controlling for objective health measures, and researchers suggest that these findings attest to the importance of social emotional networks (Hislop, Waxler, Coldman, Elwood, & Kan, 1987).

The effects of meaningful social relationships are prevalent across many chronic illnesses, but they arguably have the strongest effects for those with cardiovascular disease (i.e., heart attacks and strokes), the number one cause of mortality for adults in the United States. For older adults with heart disease or a history of heart attacks, greater emotional support is associated with decreased mortality (Berkman, Leo-Summers, & Horowitz, 1992); among women aged fifty-five and older, those who are socially isolated, are three times more likely to die compared to those highly integrated in a social network (LaVeist, Sellers, Brown, & Nickerson, 1997). Among middle-aged and older men, reports of social isolation and high levels of distress were related to a four-fold increased risk of death compared to those with lower levels of both factors (Ruberman, Weinblatt, Goldberg, & Chaudhary, 1984).

Social support predicts survival after a myocardial infarction for both European- and Hispanic-American men and women after controlling for objective health indicators including hypertension, diabetes, and hypercholesterolemia (Farmer, Meyer, Ramsey, Goff, & Wear, 1996), but these effects may be even stronger among the Hispanic Americans (Farmer et al., 1996). Compared to European Americans, Mexican Americans are more likely to have comorbid diabetes and lower socioeconomic status, two risk factors associated with mortality from cardiovascular diseases, strokes and heart attacks, yet their mortality rates from cardiovascular disease are lower than non-Hispanic Americans (Howard, Anderson, Sorlie, Andrews, Backlund, & Burke, 1994; Sorlie, Backlund, Johnson, & Rogot, 1993). These researchers interpret this ethnicity disparity as a result of better social connectedness among the Hispanic Americans relative to European Americans.

Possible Physiological Pathways. Researchers have examined the effects of social relationships on physiological processes directly and speculate that chronic physiological reactivity – from poor emotion regulation – will lead to impaired immune system functioning and other physiological dysregulation, leaving people more susceptible to disease (Seeman, 1996). Cacioppo and his colleagues compared college students who self-reported experiencing high levels of loneliness to those reporting close social ties

(Cacioppo et al., 2000). Loneliness is the epitome of lack of social support, defined as the reaction to unfulfilled intimate and social needs (Cacioppo et al., 2000). They found that people who were chronically lonely had less heart rate reactivity than either their normally socially embedded or highly connected counterparts. In addition, they found that although diurnal patterns of salivary cortisol levels were comparable in the morning for both groups, lonely students had higher cortisol levels in the evenings. The researchers conjecture that the evening is the usual time of social activity, and a time when the emotional reaction to one's lonely state may be experienced to a greater degree.

The effects of socioemotional processes may moderate reactions to other physical or psychological stressors, either buffering or exacerbating physiological response. In studies of young adults, medical students faced with the stress of exams who were lonely had a greater number of Epstein-Barr virus (EBV) titers compared to medical students who reported low levels of loneliness (Glaser, Kiecolt-Glaser, Speicher, & Holliday, 1985). In another study, greater social support among young male firefighters was associated with greater cardiovascular reactivity and faster recovery, particularly when they had experienced many life events (Roy, Steptoe, & Kirschbaum, 1998). Among a more physically vulnerable sample – middle-aged women with breast cancer – low perceived social support was related to impaired natural killer cell activity (Levy, Herberman, Lippman, & D'Angelo, 1991).

Emotions and Cognitive Pathways to Health. Findings suggest that the link between socioemotional processes and health cannot be explained by the overlap in somatic symptoms used to define both constructs; expressive cognitions predict mortality independent of the somatic indicators of depression (Blazer, Hybels, & Pieper, 2001), and researchers suggest that the cognitions comprising depression directly influence health processes. Cognitions alter neurochemical activity (e.g., Sarter, Bruno, & Berntson, 2001); particularly for physically vulnerable adults, cognitions engendered through socioemotional processes may have significant health consequences.

Close social relationships often create emotionally meaningful interactions in a person's life, motivating their thoughts and actions (Carstensen, Isaacowitz, & Charles, 1999). Having meaningful social ties is related to less depression (Gotlib & Hammen, 1992) and greater positive well-being and life satisfaction. This overall more positive outlook is related to multiple health outcomes. Taylor and her colleagues have found that a fighting spirit is associated with greater longevity in cancer patients, and that finding meaning in one's life is associated with greater longevity for both terminally ill cancer patients and people with AIDS (see review by Taylor, Kemeny, Reed, Bower, & Gruenwald, 2000). Another study found that a pessimistic outlook on life is related to mortality from cancer after controlling for cancer site and symptomatology, but only among younger patients (Schulz, Bookwala, Knapp, Scheier, & Williamson, 1996).

Other studies provide direct tests for the mediation of emotional processes in the association between meaningful social relationships and health. For example, the will to live is associated with social support for both men and women, but this relationship is no longer significant when emotion variables such as life satisfaction are included in analyses (Carmel, 2001). In addition, although social support has been strongly associated with mortality in multiple studies (e.g., House et al., 1988), social support is not associated with mortality in studies that have controlled for depressive symptoms (Ahern et al., 1990), anxiety (Thomas, Friedmann, Wimbush, & Schron, 1997), or emotional functioning (Gorkin, Follick, Wilkin, & Niaura, 1994). In another study, social support was not related to mortality after controlling for quality of life and coping styles (Butow, Coates, & Dunn, 1999). Social support engenders the fighting spirit and promotes psychological well-being, providing people with reasons to live and maintaining or enhancing their physical health (e.g., Spiegel & Kimerling, 2001).

Emotions and Behavioral Pathways to Health. Research examining socioemotional processes and health behavior among adults has yielded inconsistent findings. Cacioppo and colleagues (2000) found that people who reported being lonely reported poorer sleep quality, longer sleep latency, longer perceived sleep duration, and greater daytime dysfunction due to sleepiness than their more emotionally embedded counterparts. They also took longer to fall asleep, evidenced longer REM latency, and awoke more frequently during the night; even though hours of sleep were equal, their sleep was less efficient. The health benefits of reporting less loneliness were tempered, however, by findings that less loneliness was related to other behaviors not beneficial to health, such as greater alcohol consumption, more smoking, and a lower likelihood of restorative behaviors such as meditation, exercise, and relaxing (Cacioppo et al., 2000). Similarly, another study found mixed support for health behaviors and social support when studying patterns of alcohol use and exercise (Alan, Markovitz, Jacobs, & Knox, 2001).

Less ambiguous are findings indicating that social support may act as its own health behavior by providing an emotional outlet through confiding with friends. Among spouses who lost their partners through sudden death, those who reported the greatest amount of confiding in friends were least likely to report increases in physical symptoms in the ensuing year (Pennebaker & O'Heeron, 1984). In a community sample of men and women, constructively discussing angry feelings correlated with lower resting blood pressure (Davidson, MacGregor, Stuhr, Dixon, & MacLean, 2000). Suppression of the behavioral expression of emotion, in contrast, was related to greater sympathetic activation of the cardiovascular system (Gross & Levenson, 1997) and to disease processes (see review by Pennebaker & Traue, 1993).

Examining more physically vulnerable populations, research by Spiegel and his colleagues suggests that social support is related to longevity among people with metastatic breast cancer (Spiegel, Bloom, Kraemer, & Gottheil, 1994). He and his colleagues propose that the ability to express emotions, as opposed to inhibiting emotional experiences, may play a role in increased survival (see review by Spiegel & Kimerling, 2001), which cannot be explained by differences in medical treatment or other health behaviors (Kogon, Biswas, Pearl, Carlson, & Spiegel, 1997). Cancer patients who are emotionally expressive also report better health, and being emotionally expressive is related to having a receptive social network (Stanton et al., 2000).

FUTURE DIRECTIONS

A growing volume of studies attests to the robust association between social support and health. In an early review, House and his colleagues (1988) mentioned the challenges of interpreting this literature from the many measures of social support and the myriad of social, psychological, and biological processes involved, and how little the scientific community knew of interconnecting pathways between these processes (House et al., 1988). In the nearly fifteen years since this critique, the social, psychological, and biological processes mentioned by House and his colleagues (1988) are still pertinent to the study of social support and its association with health, and the physiological links are ever elusive (Seeman, 1996). In this section, we focus on three specific areas in which this research can expand to fulfill many of the remaining gaps in the literature. These three areas are driven by our life-span model that holds that emotion regulation plays a pivotal role in this association.

Measurement

Both structural and functional aspects of social support are related to indices of physical health (e.g., see review by Cohen & Wills, 1985), but the mechanisms accounting for these associations remain, for the most part, unknown. In this chapter, we proposed that emotions mediate the association between social support and health. For this reason, we believe that emotion regulation needs to be assessed when examining the physical health/social support relationship. For example, when examining the association between network size and health status using a socioemotional view, network size may be indicative of greater extraversion, which is related to greater positive affect (Charles, Reynolds, & Gatz, 2001) and consequent improved health status (Salovey et al., 2000). Although we propose that having emotionally meaningful relationships where relational needs are met is fundamental in the association between social support and health, multiple aspects of the emotional experience may be involved. Including questions of emotion regulation when investigating the effects of social support – both structural and functional – on physical well-being could greatly advance our understanding of this complex association.

Life-Span Perspective

Biologists have long documented age-related physiological and biological declines, and the age-associated increases in the prevalence rates of chronic illnesses. In addition, researchers have also documented the age-related changes in emotional experience and the functional and structural qualities of social networks (Carstensen, Isaacowitz, & Charles, 1999). Given the age-related changes within social, emotional, and physical domains, as well as their complex interplay, researchers need to address these associations from a developmental perspective. Future examinations of these processes would enhance knowledge regarding both life-span development and health psychology.

Physiological, Behavioral, and Cognitive Pathways

Emotions are often defined as consisting of physiological, behavioral, and cognitive components (see Ekman & Davidson, 1994). In addition, many research findings, some of which are reviewed above, suggest that physical health is influenced directly through physiological mechanisms, and indirectly via cognitions and behaviors. In studies examining the nature of socioemotional processes on health, including all three components would provide a comprehensive view into the direct and indirect effects of social support on physical health outcomes.

CONCLUSION

Social support is related to physical health, an association highlighted in lay articles and studied extensively by researchers. In this chapter, we proposed the socioemotional health model, which posits that social support is associated with physical health to the extent that social support provides the context and experience of emotion regulation throughout daily life. Social processes are intertwined with emotional processes, an association that has evolved over the millennia. Meaningful, fulfilling social connections infuse life with meaning, allow self-expression, and provide emotional outlets. Nearly half a century ago, Victor Frankl (1959) wrote about the thoughts that sustained him when he was a prisoner in a concentration camp, stating that "I understood how a man who has nothing left in this world still may know bliss, be it only for a brief moment, in the contemplation of his beloved" (p. 49). Emotions are engendered, nurtured, and sustained in relationships, and this socioemotional process is intrinsically related to our physical well-being.

Acknowledgments

Work by the first author was supported by grant R03-AG19387 from the National Institute of Aging. We thank Melanie Horn for her comments on this chapter.

References

Abell, T. D., Baker, L. C., Clover, R. D., & Ramsey, C. N. (1991). The effects of family functioning on infant birthweight. *Journal of Family Practice, 32,* 37–44.

Ahern, D. K., Gorkin, L., Anderson, J. L., Tierney, C., Hallstrom, A., Ewart, C., Capone, R. J., Schron, E., Kornfeld, D., & Herd, J. A. (1990). Biobehavioral variables and mortality or cardiac arrest in the Cardiac Arrhythmia Pilot Study (CAPS). *American Journal of Cardiology, 66,* 59–62.

Ainsworth, M. S. (1989). Attachments beyond infancy. *American Psychologist, 44,* 709–716.

Alan, J., Markovitz, J., Jacobs, D. R., & Knox, S. S. (2001). Social support and health behavior in hostile Black and White men and women in CARDIA. *Psychosomatic Medicine, 63,* 609–618.

Bailey, M. T., & Coe, C. L. (1999). Maternal separation disrupts the integrity of the intestinal microflora in infant rhesus monkeys. *Developmental Psychobiology, 35,* 146–155.

Barker, D. J. P. (1997). Intrauterine programming of coronary heart disease and developmental psychobiology, *Acta Paediatrica Supplement, 423,* 178–182.

Baumeister, R. F., & Leary, M. R. (1995). The need to belong: Desire for interpersonal attachments as a fundamental human motivation. *Psychological Bulletin, 117,* 497–529.

Beal, A. C., Ausiello, J., & Perrin, J. M. (2001). Social influences on health-risk behaviors among minority middle school students. *Journal of Adolescent Health, 28,* 474–480.

Berkman, L. F., Leo-Summers, L., & Horowitz, R. I. (1992). Emotional support and survival after myocardial infarction. A prospective, population-based study of the elderly. *Annals of Internal Medicine, 117,* 1003–1009.

Berkman, L. F., & Syme, S. (1979). Social networks, host resistance, and mortality: A nine-year follow-up study of Alameda County residents. *American Journal of Epidemiology, 109,* 186–204.

Blazer, D. G., Hybels, C. F., & Pieper, C. F. (2001). The association of depression and mortality in elderly persons: A case for multiple, independent pathways. *Journal of Gerontology: Medical Sciences, 56,* M505–M509.

Boddy, J., Skuse, D., & Andrews, B. (2000). The developmental sequelae of nonorganic failure to thrive. *Journal of Child Psychology and Psychiatry and Allied Disciplines, 41,* 1003–1014.

Botvin, G. J., Baker, E., Botvin, E. M., Dusenbury, L., et al. (1993). Factors promoting cigarette smoking among Black youth: A causal modeling approach. *Addictive Behaviors, 18*, 397–405.

Bowlby, J. (1969). Disruption of affectional bonds and its effects on behavior. *Canada's Mental Health Supplement, 59*, 12.

Butow, P. N., Coates, A. S., & Dunn, S. M. (1999). Psychosocial predictors of survival in metastatic melanoma. *Journal of Clinical Oncology, 17*, 2256–2263.

Byely, L., Archibald, A. B., Graber, J., & Brooks-Gunn, J. (2000). A prospective study of familial and social influences on girls' body image and dieting. *International Journal of Eating Disorders, 28*, 155–164.

Cacioppo, J. T., Ernst, J. M., Burleson, M. H., McClintock, M. K., Malarkey, W. B., Hawkley, L. C., Kowalewski, R. B., Paulsen, A., Hobson, J. A., Hugdahl, K., Spiegel, D., & Bernston, G. G. (2000). Lonely traits and concomitant physiological processes: The MacArthur social neuroscience studies. *International Journal of Psychophysiology, 35*, 143–154.

Carmel, S. (2001). The will to live: Gender differences among elderly persons. *Social Science and Medicine, 52*, 949–958.

Carstensen, L. L., Isaacowitz, D. M., & Charles, S. T. (1999). Taking time seriously: A theory of socioemotional selectivity. *American Psychologist, 54*, 165–181.

Carter, C. S. (1998). Neuroendocrine perspectives on social attachment and love. *Psychoneuroendocrinology, 23*, 779–818.

Casey, P. H. (1987). Failure to thrive: Transitional perspective. *Developmental and Behavioral Pediatrics, 8*, 37–38.

Cassel, J. (1976). The contribution of the social environment to host resistance: The fourth Wade Hampton Frost lecture. *American Journal of Epidemiology, 104*, 107–23.

Cassileth, B. R., Lusk, E. J., Miller, D. S., Brown, L. L., & Miller, C. (1985). Psychosocial correlates of survival in advanced malignant disease? *New England Journal of Medicine, 312*, 1551–1555.

Cassileth, B. R., Walsh, W. P., & Lusk, E. J. (1988). Psychosocial correlates of cancer survival: A subsequent report 3 to 8 years after cancer diagnosis. *Journal of Clinical Oncology, 6*, 1753–1759.

Charles, S. T., Reynolds, C. A., & Gatz, M. A. (2001). Age related differences and change in positive and negative affect over 23 years. *Journal of Personality and Social Psychology, 80*, 136–151.

Chung, H., & Elias, M. (1996). Patterns of adolescent involvement in problem behaviors: Relationship to self-efficacy, social competence, and life events. *American Journal of Community Psychology, 24*, 771–784.

Cobb, S. (1977). Presidential address-1976. Social support as a moderator of life stress. *Psychosomatic Medicine, 38*, 300–314.

Coe, C. L., Lubach, G. R., Ershler, W. B., & Klopp, R. G. (1989). Influence of early rearing on lymphocyte proliferation responses in juvenile rhesus monkeys. *Brain, Behavior and Immunity, 3*, 47–60.

Coe, C. L., & Lubach, G. R. (2001). Social context and other psychological influences on the development of immunity. In C. D. Ryff & B. H. Singer (Eds.), *Emotion, social relationships, and health* (pp. 243–261). New York: Oxford University Press.

Cohen, S. (2001). Social relationships and susceptibility to the common cold. In C. D. Ryff & B. H. Singer (Eds.), *Emotion, social relationships, and health* (pp. 221–232). New York: Oxford University Press.

Cohen, S., & Wills, T. A. (1985). Stress, social support and the buffering hypothesis. *Psychological Bulletin, 98*, 310–357.

Collins, N. L., Dunkel-Schetter, C., Lobel, M., & Scrimshaw, C. M. (1993). Social support in pregnancy: Psychosocial correlates of birth outcomes and postpartum depression. *Journal of Personality and Social Psychology, 65*, 1243–1258.

Conrad, K. M., Flay, B. R., & Hill, D. (1992). Why children start smoking cigarettes: Predictors of onset. *British Journal of Addiction, 87*, 1711–1724.

Coolbear, J., & Benoit, D. (1999). Failure to thrive: Risk for clinical disturbance of attachment? *Infant Mental Health Journal, 20*, 87–104.

Creagan, E. T. (1997). Attitude and disposition: Do they make a difference in cancer survival? *Mayo Clinic Proceedings, 72*, 160–164.

Davidson, K., MacGregor, M. W., Stuhr, J., Dixon, K., & MacLean, D. (2000). Constructive anger verbal behavior predicts blood pressure in a population-based sample. *Health Psychology, 19*, 55–64.

Deci, E. L., & Ryan, R. M. (1991). A motivational approach to self: Integration in personality. In Richard A. Dienstbier (Ed.), *Nebraska symposium on motivation, 1990: Perspectives on motivation* (pp. 237–288). Lincoln, NE: University of Nebraska Press.

Dykman, R. A., Ackerman, P. T., Loizou, P. C., & Casey, P. H. (2000). An event-related potential study of older children with an early history of failure to thrive. *Developmental Neuropsychology, 18*, 187–212.

Ekman, P. (Ed.). (1973). *Darwin and facial expression: A century of research in review.* New York: Academic Press.

Ekman, P., & Davidson, R. J. (1994). *The nature of emotion: Fundamental questions.* New York: Oxford University Press.

Emery, N. J. (2000). The eyes have it: The neuroethology, function and evolution of social gaze. *Neuroscience and Biobehavioral Reviews, 24*, 581–604.

Epstein, J. A., Griffin, K. W., & Botvin, G. A. (2000). A model of smoking among inner-city adolescents: The role of personal competence and perceived social benefits of smoking. *Preventive Medicine: An International Journal Devoted to Practice and Theory, 31*, 107–114.

Ewart, C. K., & Kolodner, K. B. (1994). Negative affect, gender, and expressive style predict elevated ambulatory blood pressure in adolescents. *Journal of Personality and Social Psychology, 66*, 596–605.

Farmer, I. P., Meyer, P. S., Ramsey, D. J., Goff, D. C., & Wear, M. L. (1996). Higher levels of social support predict greater survival following acute myocardial infarction: The Corpus Christi heart project. *Behavioral Medicine, 22*, 59–65.

Feldman, P. J., Dunkel-Schetter, C., Sandman, C. A., & Wadhwa, P. (2000). Maternal social support predicts birth weight and fetal growth in human pregnancy. *Psychosomatic Medicine, 62*, 715–725.

Field, T. (1990). *Infancy.* London, UK: Harvard University Press.

Field, T., Diego, M., & Sanders, C. E. (2001). Exercise is positively related to adolescents' relationships and academics. *Adolescence, 36*, 105–110.

Frankl, V. E. (1959). *Man's search for meaning: An introduction to logotherapy.* New York: Simon & Schuster.

Fredrickson, B. L. (2000). The role of positive emotions in positive psychology. The broaden-and-build theory of positive emotions. *American Psychologist, 56*, 218–226.

Friedman, L. S., Lichtenstein, E., & Biglan, A. (1985). Smoking onset among teens: An empirical analysis of initial situations. *Addictive Behaviors, 10,* 1–13.

Funch, D. P., & Marshall, J. (1983). The role of stress, social support and age in survival from breast cancer. *Journal of Psychosomatic Research, 27,* 77–83.

Gjerdingen, D. K., Froberg, D. G., & Fontaine, P. (1991). The effects of social support on women's health during pregnancy, labor and delivery, and the postpartum period. *Family Medicine Special Articles, 23,* 370–375.

Glaser, R., Kiecolt-Glaser, J. K., Speicher, C. E., & Holliday, J. E. (1985). Stress, loneliness, and changes in herpesvirus latency. *Journal of Behavioral Medicine, 8,* 249–260.

Gorkin, L., Follick, M. J., Wilkin, D. L., & Niaura, R. (1994). Social support and the progression and treatment of cardiovascular disease. In S. A. Shumaker & S. M. Czajkowski (Eds.), *Social support and cardiovascular disease.* New York: Plenum Press.

Gorski, P. A. (2001). Contemporary pediatric practice: In support of infant mental health (imaging and imagining). *Infant Mental Health Journal, 22,* 188–200.

Gotlib, I. H., & Hammen, C. L. (1992). *Psychological aspects of depression: Toward a cognitive-interpersonal integration.* New York: John Wiley & Sons.

Gottman. J. M. (2001). Meta-emotion, children's emotional intelligence, and buffering children from marital conflict. In C. D. Ryff & B. H. Singer (Eds.), *Emotion, social relationships, and health* (pp. 23–40). New York: Oxford University Press.

Gottman, J. M., & Katz, L. F. (1989). Effects of marital discord on young children's peer interaction and health. *Developmental Psychology, 25,* 373–381.

Gross, J. J., & Levenson, R. W. (1997). Hiding feelings: The acute effects of inhibiting negative and positive emotion. *Journal of Abnormal Psychology, 106,* 95–103.

Gunnar, M. R., Larson, M. C., Hertsgaard, L., Harris, M. L., et al. (1992). The stressfulness of separation among nine-month-old infants: Effects of social context variables and infant temperament. *Child Development, 63,* 290–303.

Harcourt, A. H. (1992). Coalitions and alliances: Are primates more complex than non-primates? In A. H. Harcourt & F. B. M. De Waal (Eds.), *Coalitions and alliances in humans and other animals* (pp. 445–471). New York: Oxford University Press.

Harlow, H. F., & Zimmerman, R. R. (1959). Affectional responses in the infant monkey. *Science, 130,* 421–432.

Hislop, T. G., Waxler, N. E., Coldman, A. J., Elwood, J. M., & Kan, L. (1987). The prognostic significance of psychosocial factors in women with breast cancer. *Journal of Chronic Diseases, 40,* 729–35.

Hofer, M. A. (1994). Early relationships as regulators of infant physiology and behavior. *Acta Paediatrica Supplement, 397,* 9–18.

Holahan, C. J., & Moos, R. H. (1982). Social support and adjustment: Predictive benefits of social climate indices. *American Journal of Community Psychology, 10,* 403–415.

House, J. S., Landis, K. R., & Umberson, D. (1988). Social relationships and health. *Science, 241,* 540–544.

House, J. S., Robbins, C., & Metzner, H. L. (1982). The association of social relationships and activities with mortality: Prospective evidence from the Tecumseh community health study. *American Journal of Epidemiology, 116,* 123–140.

Howard, G., Anderson, R., Sorlie, P., Andrews, V., Backlund, E., & Burke, G. L. (1994). Ethnic differences in stroke mortality between non-Hispanic whites,

Hispanic whites, and blacks. The national longitudinal mortality study. *Stroke*, 25, 2120–2125.

Insel, T. R., O'Brien, D. J., & Leckman, J. F. (1999). Oxytocin, vasopressin, and autism: Is there a connection? *Biological Psychiatry, 45*, 145–57.

Iwaniec, D., & Sneddon, H. (2001). Attachment style in adults who failed to thrive as children: Outcomes of a 20 year follow-up study of factors influencing maintenance or change in attachment style. *British Journal of Social Work, 31*, 179–195.

Izard, C. E. (1978). Emotions as motivations: An evolutionary-developmental perspective. In *Nebraska symposium on motivation* (pp. 163–200). Lincoln, NE: University of Nebraska Press.

Jacobsen, D. E. (1986). Types and timing of social support. *Journal of Health and Social Behavior, 27*, 250–264.

Kennell, J., Klaus, M., McGrath, S., Roberston, S., & Hinkley, C. (1991). Continuous emotional support during labour in a U.S. hospital: A randomized control trial. *Journal of the American Medical Association, 265*, 2197–2201.

Kogon, M. M., Biswas, A., Pearl, D., Carlson, R. W., & Spiegel, D. (1997). Effects of medical and psychotherapeutic treatment on the survival of women with metastatic breast carcinoma. *Cancer, 80*, 225–230.

Krantz, G., & Oestergren, P. (2000). Common symptoms in middle aged women: Their relation to employment status, psychosocial work conditions and social support in a Swedish setting. *Journal of Epidemiology and Community Health, 54*, 192–199.

LaVeist, T. A., Sellers, R. M., Brown, K. A. E., & Nickerson, K. J. (1997). Extreme social isolation, use of community-based senior support services, and mortality among African American elderly women. *American Journal of Community Psychology, 25*, 721–732.

Lederman, R. P. (1995). Relationship of anxiety, stress, and psychosocial development to reproductive health. *Behavioral Medicine, 21*, 101–109.

LeDoux, J. E. (1996). *The emotional brain: The mysterious underpinnings of emotional life*. New York: Simon & Schuster.

Levenstein, S. (2000). The very model of modern etiology: A biopsychosocial view of peptic ulcer. *Psychosomatic Medicine, 62*, 176–185.

Levenstein, S., Kaplan, G. A., & Smith, M. W. (1995). Psychological predictors of peptic ulcer incidence in the Alameda County study. *Journal of Clinical Gastroenterology, 24*, 140–146.

Levy, S. M., Herberman, R. B., Lippman, M., & D'Angelo, T. (1991). Immunological and psychosocial predictors of disease recurrence in patients with early-stage breast cancer. *Behavioral Medicine, 17*, 67–75.

Lewis, M. H., Gluck, J. P., Petitto, J. M., Hensley, L. L., & Ozer, H. (2000). Early social deprivation in nonhuman primates: Long-term effects on survival and cell-mediated immunity. *Biological Psychiatry, 47*, 119–126.

Lidderdale, J. M., & Walsh, J. J. (1998). The effects of social support on cardiovascular reactivity and perinatal outcome. *Psychology and Health, 13*, 1061–1070.

Liu, Y., Curtis, J. T., & Wang, Z. (2001). Vasopressin in the lateral septum regulates pair bond formation in male prairie voles (Microtus ochrogaster). *Behavioral Neuroscience, 115*, 910–919.

Liu, D., Diorio, J., Tannenbaum, B., Caldji, C., et al. (1997). Maternal care, hippocampal glucocorticoid receptors, and hypothalamic-pituitary-adrenal responses to stress. *Science, 277*, 1659–1162.

Lucas, A., Fewtrell, M. S., & Cole, T. J. (1999). Fetal origins of adult disease – the hypothesis revisited. *British Medical Journal, 319*, 245–250.

Maudner, R. G., & Hunter, J. J. (2001). Attachment and psychosomatic medicine: Developmental contributions to stress and disease. *Psychosomatic Medicine, 63*, 556–567.

McLellan, L., Rissel, C., Donnelly, N., & Bauman, N. (1999). Health behaviour and the school environment in New South Wales, Australia. *Social Science and Medicine, 49*, 611–619.

Morton, J., & Johnson, M. H. (1991). CONSPEC and CONLERN: A two-process theory of infant face recognition. *Psychological Review, 98*, 164–181.

Mueller, W. H., Grunbaum, J. A., & Labarthe, D. R. (2001). Anger expression, body fat, and blood pressure in adolescents: Project HeartBeat! *American Journal of Human Biology, 13*, 531–538.

Nathanson, C. A., & Becker, M. H. (1986). Family and peer influence on obtaining a method of contraception. *Journal of Marriage and the Family, 48*, 513–525.

National Center for Health Statistics (2001). *Healthy people 2000 final review.* Library of Congress catalog card number 76–641496. Hyattsville, MD: Public Health Service.

Nelson, C. A. (2001). The development and neural basis for facial recognition. *Infant and Child Development, 10*, 3–18.

Norbeck, J. S., & Anderson, N. (1989). Life stress, social support, and anxiety in mid- and late-pregnancy among low income women. *Research in Nursing and Health, 12*, 281–287.

Oakley, A. (1988). Is social support good for the health of mothers and babies? *Journal of Reproductive and Infant Psychology, 6*, 3–21.

O'Hara, M. W. (1986). Social support, life events, and depression during pregnancy and the puerperium. *Archives of General Psychiatry, 43*, 569–573.

Ory, M. G., Abeles, R. P., & Lipman, P. D. (1992). Introduction: An overview of research on aging, health and behavior. In M. G. Ory, R. P. Abeles, & P. D. Lipman (Eds.), *Aging, health, and behavior* (pp. 1–23). Newbury Park, CA: Sage.

Patton, G. C., Carlin, J. B., Coffey, C., Wolfe, R., Hibbert, M., & Bowes, G. (1998). Depression, anxiety, and smoking initiation: A prospective study over 3 years. *American Journal of Public Health, 88*, 1518–1523.

Pennebaker, J. W., & O'Heeron, R. C. (1984). Confiding in others and illness rate among spouses of suicide and accidental-death victims. *Journal of Abnormal Psychology, 93*, 473–476.

Pennebaker, J. W., & Traue, H. C. (1993). Inhibition and psychosomatic processes. In H. C. Traue & J. W. Pennebaker (Eds.), *Emotion inhibition and health* (pp. 146–163). Kirkland, WA: Hogrefe & Huber Publishers.

Phillips, D. I. W., Barker, D. J. P., Fall, C. H. D., Seckl, J. R., Whorwood, C. B., Wood, P. J., & Walker, B. R. (1998). Elevated plasma cortisol concentrations: A link between low birth weight and the insulin resistance syndromes? *Journal of Clinical Endocrinology and Metabolism, 83*, 757–760.

Power, T. G., & Parke, R. D. (1984). Social network factors and the transition to parenthood. *Sex Roles, 1984*, 949–972.

Reis, H. T. (2001). Relationship experiences and emotional well-being. In C. D. Ryff & B. H. Singer (Eds.), *Emotion, social relationships, and health* (pp. 57–86). New York: Oxford University Press.

Reynolds, P., Boyd, P. T., Blacklow, R. S., Jackson, J. S., Greenberg, R. S., Austin, D. F., Chen, V. W., & Edwards, B. K. (1994). The relationship between social ties and survival among black and white breast cancer patients. National Cancer Institute black/white cancer survival study group. *Cancer Epidemiology, Biomarkers and Prevention, 3,* 253–259.

Richmond, L., Steenbergen, C., & Hendrickson, D. (2000). Coping strategies and postdivorce health outcomes. *Journal of Divorce and Remarriage, 34,* 41–59.

Rook, K. S. (1994). Assessing the health-related dimensions of older adults' social relationships. In M. P. Lawton & J. A. Teresi (Eds.), *Annual review of gerontology and geriatrics* (Vol. 14, pp. 142–181). New York: Springer Publishing Company.

Roy, M. P., Steptoe, A., & Kirschbaum, C. (1998). Life events and social support as moderators of individual differences in cardiovascular and cortisol reactivity. *Journal of Personality and Social Psychology, 75,* 1273–1281.

Ruberman, W., Weinblatt, E., Goldberg, J. D., Chaudhary, B. S. (1984). Psychosocial influences on mortality after myocardial infarction. *New England Journal of Medicine, 311,* 552–559.

Ryan, R. M. (1993). Agency and organization: Intrinsic motivation, autonomy and the self in psychological development. In J. Jacobs (Ed.), *Nebraska symposium on motivation: Developmental perspectives on motivation* (Vol. 40, pp. 1–56). Lincoln, NE: University of Nebraska Press.

Ryan, R. M., & Deci, E. L. (2000). Self-determination theory and the facilitation of intrinsic motivation, social development, and well-being. *American Psychologist, 55,* 68–78.

Ryff, C. D., & Singer, B. H. (2001). Introduction: Integrating emotion into the study of social relationships and health. In C. D. Ryff & B. H. Singer (Eds.), *Emotion, social relationships, and health* (pp. 3–22). New York: Oxford University Press.

Salovey, P., Rothman, A. J., Detweiler, J. B., & Steward, W. T. (2000). Emotional states and physical health. *American Psychologist, 55,* 110–121.

Sarter, M., Bruno, J. P., & Berntson, G. G. (2001). Psychotogenic properties of benzodiazepine receptor inverse agonists. *Psychopharmacology, 156,* 1–13.

Schanberg, S. (1995). The genetic basis for touch effects. In T. M. Field (Ed.), *Touch in early development* (pp. 67–79). Mahwah, NJ: Lawrence Erlbaum Associates, Inc., Publishers.

Scharloo, M., Kaptein, A. A., Weinman, J., Hazes, J. M., Willems, L. N. A., Bergman, W., & Rooijmans, H. G. M. (1998). Illness perceptions, coping and functioning in patients with rheumatoid arthritis, chronic obstructive pulmonary disease and psoriasis. *Journal of Psychosomatic Research, 44,* 573–585.

Schneider, M. L., & Coe, C. L. (1993). Repeated social stress during pregnancy impairs neuromotor development of the primate infant. *Journal of Developmental and Behavioral Pediatrics, 14,* 81–87.

Schulz, R., Bookwala, J., Knapp, J. E., Scheier, M., & Williamson, G. M. (1996). Pessimism, age, and cancer mortality. *Psychology and Aging, 11,* 304–309.

Seeman, T. E. (1996). Social ties and health: The benefits of social integration. *Annals of Epidemiology, 6,* 442–451.

Seiffge-Krenke, I. (1998). *Adolescents' health: A developmental perspective*. Mahwah, NJ: Lawrence Erlbaum Associates, Inc., Publishers.

Skuse, D., Wolke, D., & Reilly, S. (1992). Failure to thrive: Clinical and developmental aspects. In H. Remschmidt & M. H. Schmidt (Eds.), *Developmental psychopathology* (pp. 46–71). Kirkland, WA: Hogrefe & Huber Publishers.

Slater, A., & Quinn, P. C. (2001). Face recognition in the newborn infant. *Infant and Child Development, 10*, 21–24.

Smith, D., & Furlong, M. J. (1994). Correlates of anger, hostility, and aggression in children and adolescents. In M. J. Furlong and D. C. Smith (Eds.), *Anger, hostility, and aggression: Assessment, prevention, and intervention strategies for youth* (pp. 15–38). Brandon, VT: Clinical Psychology Publishing Co.

Sorlie, P. D., Backlund, E., Johnson, N. J., & Rogot, E. (1993). Mortality by Hispanic status in the United States. *JAMA, 270*, 2464–2468.

Spiegel, D., Bloom, J. R., Kraemer, H. C., & Gottheil, E. (1994). Effect of psychosocial treatment on survival of patients with metastatic breast cancer. In A. Steptoe & J. Wardle (Eds.), *Psychosocial processes and health: A reader* (pp. 468–477). New York: Cambridge University Press.

Spiegel, D., & Kimerling, R. (2001). Group psychotherapy for women with breast cancer: Relationships among social support, emotional expression, and survival. In C. D. Ryff & B. H. Singer (Eds.), *Emotion, social relationships, and health* (pp. 97–123). New York: Oxford University Press.

Stanton, A. L., Danoff-Burg, S., Cameron, C. L., Bishop, M., Collins, C. A., Kirk, S. B., Sworowski, L. A., & Twillman, R. (2000). Emotionally expressive coping predicts psychological and physical adjustment to breast cancer. *Journal of Consulting and Clinical Psychology, 68*, 875–882.

Stone, A. A., Mezzacappa, E. S., Donatone, B. A., & Gonder, M. (1999). Psychosocial stress and social support are associated with prostate-specific antigen levels in men: Results from a community screening program. *Health Psychology, 18*, 482–486.

Stroebe, M. (2001). Gender differences in adjustment to bereavement: An empirical and theoretical review. *Review of General Psychology, 5*, 62–83.

Stroebe, W., & Stroebe, M. S. (1987). *Bereavement and health: The psychological and physical consequences of partner loss*. Cambridge: Cambridge University Press.

Swerdlow, A. J., De Stavola, B. L., Swanwick, M. A., & Maconochie, N. E. S. (1997). Risks of breast and testicular cancers in young adult twins in England and Wales: Evidence on prenatal and genetic aetiology. *The Lancet, 350*, 1723–1728.

Taylor, G. J., Bagby, R. M., & Parker, J. D. A. (1997). *Disorders of affect regulation: Alexithymia in medical and psychiatric illness*. New York: Cambridge University Press.

Taylor, S. E., Kemeny, M. E., Reed, G. M., Bower, J. E., & Gruenwald, T. L. (2000). Psychological resources, positive illusions, and health. *American Psychologist, 55*, 99–109.

Thomas, S. A., Friedmann, E., Wimbush, F., & Schron, E. (1997). Psychological factors and survival in the cardiac arrhythmia suppression trial (CAST): A reexamination. *American Journal of Critical Care, 6*, 116–26.

Tominaga, K., Andow, J., Koyama, Y., Numao, S., Kurokawa, E., Ojima, M., & Nagai, M. (1998). Family environment, hobbies and habits as psychosocial predictors of survival for surgically treated patients with breast cancer. *Japanese Journal of Clinical Oncology, 28,* 36–41.

Uchino, B. N., Cacioppo, J. T., & Kiecolt-Glaser, J. K. (1996). The relationship between social support and physiological processes: A review with emphasis on underlying mechanisms and implications for health. *Psychological Bulletin, 119,* 488–531.

U.S. Department of Health and Human Services (2000). *Healthy People 2010: Tracking healthy people 2010.* Washington, DC: Department of Health and Human Services.

Warner, J. A., Jones, C. A., Jones, A. C., & Warner, J. O. (2000). Environmental and inflammatory mechanisms: Prenatal origins of allergic disease. *Journal of Allergy and Clinical Immunology, 105,* S493–S496.

Weir, A. (2001). *Henry VIII: The king and his court.* New York: The Ballantine Publishing Group.

Zajonc, R. (1998). Emotions. In D. T. Gilbert, S. T. Fiske, & G. Lindzey (Eds.), *The handbook of social psychology,* Vol. 1 (4th ed.) (pp. 591–632). Boston: McGraw-Hill.

Zautra, A. J., Hoffman, J. M., Matt, K. S., Yocum, D., Potter, P. T., Castro, W. L., & Roth, S. (1998). An examination of individual differences in the relationship between interpersonal stress and disease activity among women with rheumatoid arthritis. *Arthritis Care and Research, 11,* 271–279.

11

Social Cognition and Social Relationships

Fredda Blanchard-Fields and Carolyn Cooper

From a social cognitive and developmental perspective, we offer a content-based explanation for age differences in social judgment biases when individuals are presented with relationship dilemmas. Older adults' tendency to blame individuals for negative outcomes in relationship situations may reflect age-related differences in the nature and content of information stored in long-term memory (knowledge, beliefs, and values) that are relevant to the particular social judgment. Older adults may have highly schematized social rules for appropriate behavior that are chronically accessible and drive social judgments in particular situations, especially in the domain of marital relationships. In addition, we suggest that changes in emotional functioning as we grow older also impact the attributional processes in the context of marital relationships.

There is a substantive body of research examining the importance of social cognitive mechanisms in understanding adaptive social relationships. These include how relationship enhancing attributions relate to marital satisfaction (Bradbury & Fincham, 1990; Lopez, 1993), how selectively attending to negative aspects of a relationship creates relationship distress (Baucom, Epstein, Sayers, & Sher, 1989; Sillars, Roberts, Leonard, & Dun, 2000), how individuals preserve positive self-views in the context of a relationship (Fincham & Beach, 1999), and the accessibility of attitudes, values, and beliefs when engaging in interpersonal interactions (Baldwin, 1992; Fincham & Beach, 1999). Individual differences in the influence of such cognitive representations and processes may help us to differentiate adaptive from dysfunctional cognitions in dealing with relationship situations across the life span.

This chapter will focus on adult developmental differences in social cognitive processing as it relates to personal relationships. Such mechanisms impact the nature of functional and dysfunctional interpersonal judgments among partners in personal relationships across the adult life span. Personal relationships encompass a wide arena of partners, from friendships to families to romantic partners. We will focus primarily on the research related to romantic partners in general, and marital relationships in particular, for two reasons. First, the focus of this chapter is on social cognitive processes and relationships. The lion's share of research examining social cognition and personal relationships focuses on marital relationships. Research on friendship and family typically takes a broader social psychological perspective. Second, there is a growing literature on marital partners in an aging context, on the one hand, and interpersonal social cognition and aging, on the other hand, that lends itself to an integrative social cognitive analysis. Finally, it should be noted that we focus on intimate relationships in general, and marital relationships more specifically, primarily for illustrative purposes. It is in this context that the interface between cognition and emotion is most clearly demonstrated.

We will begin with a brief review of social cognitive mechanisms typically examined in the context of personal relationships, primarily focusing on attributional processes. Information processes will be reviewed in the context of attribution theory with particular emphases on social knowledge structures, cognitive representations, and social judgment biases. We will then explore the question, "What does aging tell us about social cognitive processes in personal relationships?" In this case, we will explore social cognitive mechanisms as they interface with emotional processes within an adult developmental framework. In particular, the role of emotion in social cognitive processes will be explored as it applies to judgments about relationship dilemmas. We will end the chapter with future directions for understanding how the nature of personal relationships changes as we grow older.

THE NATURE OF ATTRIBUTIONS IN PERSONAL RELATIONSHIPS

When an interpersonal exchange occurs, individuals make attributions to explain why another person behaved or communicated information in a certain manner or why a negative outcome occurred (Manusov & Koeing, 2001). Individuals can attribute behaviors and outcomes to something about the situation (situational attributions), to internal characteristics of the person involved (dispositional attributions), or to a combination of factors (interactive attributions; Heider, 1958). Although such attributions allow individuals to interpret situations, they often lead to biased and erroneous explanations of behavior.

In fact, research in social psychology has persuasively shown that college-aged youth make biased attributions about the degree to which a person's attitude, for example, is strongly in favor of a particular topic despite the fact that the person was coerced into conveying a favorable attitude. In this case, the young adult does not take into consideration the situational constraints, that is, the coercive factors. This bias is typically labeled the "correspondence bias." Another form of the correspondence bias is a dispositional bias. Dispositional biases reflect blame or responsibility placed on an individual for causing a negative outcome, again ignoring the causal implications of other powerful situational constraints operating.

Research suggests that cognitive effort plays an important role when making bias-free causal attributions (Gilbert & Malone, 1995; Gilbert & Osborne, 1989; Gilbert, Pelham, & Krull, 1988). Gilbert and colleagues posit three attributional processing stages. The first stage involves categorization of the behavior, that is, labeling the behavior performed. Second, characterization of the action occurs that typically takes the form of a dispositional attribution. Finally, a correction or adjustment process is performed at the third stage of processing. This involves an adjustment of the original dispositional attribution by taking into consideration situational information (thus theoretically eliminating the correspondence bias). This final stage is deliberate and effortful and requires considerable cognitive effort, whereas both categorization and characterization require little cognitive effort. Let us now consider the following vignette to illustrate how dispositional biases arise.

Alan had been dating Barbara for over a year. At Barbara's suggestion, they moved in together. Everyone kept asking when they were getting married. Alan found it extremely uncomfortable to live with Barbara and not be married to her. Even though Barbara disagreed, Alan kept bringing up the issue of marriage. Eventually, they broke up.

In this case the negative outcome is the breakup of the relationship. Social psychologists are typically interested in the factors an individual takes into consideration in determining whether the cause of the breakup was due to something about Alan (dispositional attribution) or situational factors such as peer pressure, Barbara's concerns, etc. For example, Alan could possibly have foreseen the outcome, yet he most likely did not intend the outcome. Thus, factors that impel individuals to be dispositionally biased (e.g., blaming or holding Alan responsible) toward Alan and to ignore external factors when making causal attributions include ambiguity as to Alan or Barbara's intentions to produce the negative outcome, the fact that the situation involved a hypothetical other as opposed to the self, and the fact that the outcome was negative.

However, from an individual difference perspective, individuals with varying backgrounds and different belief systems could also differ in their causal attributions. For example, the degree to which an individual identifies with a character influences the use of dispositional attributions toward that character (Cooper & Blanchard-Fields, 2001). If individuals identify with a character it is because they see that character as similar to themselves. Subsequently, they tend to absolve the "similar" character and blame the one seen as dissimilar to them. If individuals identified with Alan they would absolve him of culpability whereas they would tend to blame Barbara (with whom they did not identify) for the breakup of the relationship. We will return to such factors that influence dispositional biases again when we address social cognitive processes and aging. For now it is important simply to note that this exemplifies the typical type of paradigm employed in social psychology research in this domain.

Attributions and Personal Relationships

In the context of personal relationships, attribution theorists examine types of causal attributional biases that occur as a result of negative behavior performed by a spouse or partner. For non-distressed couples, causal attributions about the negative behavior of a partner tend to minimize the negativity, intentionality, and globality of the event (Baucom, Epstein, Daiuto, Carels, Rankin, & Burnett, 1996; Bradbury & Fincham, 1990; Fincham & Beach, 1999; Lopez, 1993). In other words, these couples engage in relationship enhancing attributions that are transient and interpersonal in nature. For example, if Michelle forgets an important date with Andy, Michelle may attribute the cause to the fact that this is a busy time of the year at work for Andy and she may also consider that both partners may have had differing expectations for this event. These explanations emphasize how situational factors influence explanations for why the date was forgotten and they entertain the notion that the expectations of both partners are taken into consideration when attempting to understand the event. The focus is on explanations of behavior that deal with perceptions of self in regard to other and other in regard to self (Newman, 1981).

On the other hand, a heavy reliance on negatively valenced dispositional attributions is more typical of distressed couples, that is, attributing the cause to Andy's insensitivity while ignoring situation-based information such as the busy time of year. These explanations represent more distress-maintaining attributions designed to heighten negative affect and produce blaming and provocative behavior directed at the partner (Lopez, 1993). In both cases, the nature of the attributions tends to snowball and shape the ongoing relationship process. In fact, one of the more consistent findings in the literature indicates a strong relationship between marital satisfaction and types of attributions made by the respective spouses (Baucom et al., 1996; Bradbury & Fincham, 1990; Lopez, 1993).

The literature also highlights the finding that this type of attributional activity is more frequent at early stages of dating, when attributions are needed to assist in establishing relationship stability. It is also more frequent at later points in the relationship when important choices are typically made or when the relationship is perceived as unstable. At this point attributions are employed to reestablish relationship equilibrium (Holtzworth-Munroe & Jacobson, 1985; Lopez, 1993). Interestingly, as in most of the social cognition literature no mention is made of the possibility that attributional processes may differ for older versus middle-aged versus younger couples. For example, recent research suggests that older adults weigh negative information more heavily when processing social information (Hess & Pullen, 1994). However, this was not examined in the context of personal relationships.

Given that non-distressed and distressed couples make functional and dysfunctional attributions respectively, what are the mechanisms governing their differential attributional processing? It appears that the two different types of couples selectively attend to positive or negative information respectively. For example, because of prior negative expectations and relationship history distressed couples may selectively attend to negative relationship events, bad feelings, and undesirable partner acts resulting in negative dispositional attributions of intentionality on the part of the partner's behavior (Baldwin, 1992; Lopez, 1993). Thus it is important that we next focus on the content of such knowledge structures and memory representations and how they influence attributional processing.

The Social Content of Memory Representations and Attributional Processing

The content of socially relevant information (e.g., relationship expectations and social beliefs about how individuals should behave in order to have a successful intimate relationship) in memory plays an important role in attributional processing (e.g., Fincham & Beach, 1999; Fiske, 1993; Wyer & Srull, 1989). Social context and social knowledge (e.g., the social content of information in semantic memory) guide cognitive processing by determining what types of information are attended to, how that information is interpreted, and how it is applied to the particular social situation in question. In this section, we consider the specific ways in which memory content influences attributional processing.

First, we must consider the stored representations of relationship scripts, interpretive rules based on the nature of these representations, and episodic memory of past relationship events that are available to the individual. For example, when knowledge consisting of traits, behaviors, and memories of past experiences involving interactions with particular persons are assessed they are shown to influence when positive and negative communication processes occur in personal relationships (Scott, Fuhrman, & Wyer, 1991; Sillars, Roberts, Leonard, & Dun, 2000).

However, determining the availability of information in memory does not necessarily imply that this relationship information can be easily accessed. Thus, a second way in which memory content influences attributions is the degree to which the available information in memory is easily accessible. Accessibility of information determines the extent to which the available information will guide social judgments and/or behavior.

Accessibility depends on the strength or schematicity of the information stored in memory. In this case the strength of beliefs about personal relationships is related to belief-related behaviors (Baldwin, 1992; Fletcher, Rosanowski, & Fitness, 1994). For example, a strong belief that partners in a relationship should engage in activities together is related to the degree of sharing behavior experienced in the context of the respective partners' interests and hobbies. In addition, in comparison to individuals with weak beliefs in the importance of intimacy, those with strong beliefs have strong links between levels of reported relationship quality and self-reported levels of intimate behavior (Fletcher et al., 1994).

Accessibility also depends upon the particular history of prior processing of relevant relationship representations. This is exemplified best in research that experimentally manipulates relationship representations through priming techniques. Relationship constructs are presented unobtrusively in order to influence the subsequent social judgment or behavior (Baldwin, 1992; Holmes, 2000). The heightened accessibility of the construct results in a perceptual readiness to respond in accordance with the particular relationship construct. For example, priming hostility changes responses to particular partner behaviors, for example, ratings of the partner's hostility (Fincham & Beach, 1999). Activating attachment representations increases one's attraction to a potential date (Baldwin, Keelan, Fehr, Enns, & Koh-Rangarajoo, 1996). Priming positive interpersonal expectations increases support seeking and the use of positive coping strategies (Pierce & Lydon, 1998).

Finally, accessibility involves the extent to which processing requires automatic or controlled activation of relationship information. Concurrent demands on cognitive resources may cause an individual to rely more heavily on easily accessible social representations such as schemas and not engage in an effortful, deliberate analysis of the situation (Gilbert, Taforodi, & Malone, 1993). To test if social-relational knowledge structures can automatically drive processing in personal relationships, Fletcher et al. (1994) used a reaction paradigm to examine the importance of passion and intimacy beliefs on the formation of successful romantic relationships. Findings revealed that in comparison to individuals with strong beliefs concerning the importance of passion and intimacy in relationships those with weak beliefs were slower to decide whether adjectives accurately described their own relationships, especially in a memory-load condition. Participants with strong beliefs made faster decisions under both memory load and no memory load conditions. Those with strong beliefs may have developed chronically accessible judgments concerning aspects characteristic of specific intimate relationships that are automatically processed, whereas those individuals with weak beliefs engaged in a more effortful, controlled processing when making judgments in a relationship context (Fletcher et al., 1994).

A third type of content-processing influence on attributions highlights the role that well-learned processing rules stored in memory play in influencing the accuracy of social judgments. This may determine what information is attended to and how extensively resources are allocated to processing the information. In this case, naturally occurring individual differences in the elicitation of aspects of one's marriage are important for understanding the correlates of the nature of marital interaction. For example, spouses whose marital quality is spontaneously elicited in conflict situations behave toward their partner in a more consistent manner than spouses whose marital quality is not spontaneously elicited (Fincham, Garnier, Gano-Phillips, & Osborne, 1995).

Elicitation of well-learned processing rules can explain differential attributions of non-distressed and distressed couple attributions discussed earlier. Remember that happier couples' attributions for marital events serve to enhance their relationship happiness, whereas distressed couples focus on attributions that emphasize negative aspects of the relationship. Thus, a well-learned general set of feelings toward their partner may influence the way individuals perceive and interpret various marital events. This is referred to as sentiment override (Baucom, Sayers, & Duhe, 1989; Fincham & Beach, 1999). Sentiment override stipulates that spouses respond to their partners according to a dominant sentiment about their marriage rather than on the basis of the specific behavior the partner has emitted (Weiss, 1980).

A fourth way in which processing-content interaction impacts attributions involves the automatic activation of goals that guide social judgments and interpersonal behavior. There is a substantial body of research suggesting that preconscious goals influence behavior (Bargh, 1997). In the relationship domain, researchers find that pro-relationship intentions prior to an interpersonal interaction with a partner can be transformed into defensive patterns and conflict. The good intentions may represent salient goals at first, but if defensive-avoidant goals are activated simultaneously, they may replace the good intentions because the emergent goal of self-protection comes into play (Fincham & Beach, 1999).

A final type of processing-content interaction includes how prior processing context influences social judgments, more formally labeled as a framing effect (Schwarz, Strack, & Mai, 1991). Contextual information that may or may not have been previously stored in long-term memory may have an effect when it precedes a social judgment. When individuals were asked about their life satisfaction before their marital satisfaction the correlation between the two constructs was low (Schwarz et al., 1991). However, if they were asked about their marital satisfaction first, the correlation was high. Accessing the quality of one's marriage subsequently influences or "frames" one's overall life satisfaction.

Conclusion

At this point, we find that social content and/or the social context of memory increases our understanding of how social knowledge influences the way individuals in relationship contexts process information about each other and their relationship. We would now like to explore the extent to which age-related considerations factor into how the accessibility of social memory content influences social judgments, in general and then more specifically in personal relationships.

AGING AND ATTRIBUTIONAL JUDGMENT BIASES

Recall that research on attributional processing suggests that individuals rely too heavily on dispositional information in making causal attributions while ignoring situational information. In the social cognition literature, this bias has been primarily documented on college-aged youth. In our research, we have examined the extent to which this general dispositional bias persists beyond young adulthood (Blanchard-Fields, 1994, 1996, 1999). Consider the previously presented vignette involving Alan and Barbara's romantic dilemma. We presented adults with this vignette situation among many others all of which resulted in a negative outcome. Situations were ambiguous as to the degree that each character was involved in producing the negative outcome. Participants rated the extent to which something about the main character (in this case Alan) was the cause of the outcome (i.e., the breakup of the relationship with Barbara). We have found that older adults (i.e., 65 to 80 years) are more likely than younger adults to attribute the cause of negative outcomes, such as the breakup of the relationship, to personal characteristics of the main character (e.g., Alan). This has been a consistent finding over a number of studies (Blanchard-Fields, 1994; Blanchard-Fields & Norris, 1994; Blanchard-Fields, Chen, Schocke, & Hertzog, 1998).

One possible explanation for this well-replicated finding are age-related limitations on processing resources and the processing consequences of cognitive load. Recall that making accurate causal attributions requires integrating both dispositional and situational information into one's evaluation of the situation (Gilbert et al., 1988; Gilbert & Osborne, 1989; Gilbert & Malone, 1995). Again, this requires elaborative processing that is deliberate and effortful. Accordingly, older adults should rely on highly accessible initial judgments, such as dispositional causes inherent in the character, like Alan, given resource limitations related to age. Processing would typically stop short of considering situational information such as peer pressure felt by Alan. In a study conducted by Chen and Blanchard-Fields (1997), older adults' dispositional biases were reduced when they were given more time to contemplate their ratings than when they were forced to make an immediate judgment. It may be the case that age-related reduction in processing capacity (Salthouse, 1991) would result in higher dispositional ratings due to the cognitive demands necessary to integrate situational information.

However, age-related differences in resource capacity represent an insufficient explanation of age differences in dispositional attributions. Studies in our lab have not necessarily supported a general, content-free dispositional bias by older adults. Older adults have demonstrated a dispositional bias only for negative outcomes in interpersonal relationship situations. The bias has not been evident for positive relationship outcomes or for either positive or negative outcomes in achievement vignettes (i.e., vignettes where the main character strives to accomplish a self-defined goal). Thus, the bias appears to be specific to the domain of interpersonal relationships. In fact, a recent study shows that when vignettes are rated as high versus low in interpersonal involvement, age differences in dispositional biases only occur in the highly interpersonal situations (Cooper & Blanchard-Fields, 2001). Apparently, the dispositional bias effect we have observed is subtle and does not represent a predominant and consistent effect of age on dispositional attributions. Instead, such age effects are elicited only under certain conditions.

The domain specificity of the age differences in dispositional attributions suggests that the heightened dispositional bias is not necessarily a function of a generalized resource deficit that prevents older adults from engaging in elaborative social inferencing. However, resource limitations operating in conjunction with other eliciting conditions could account for the phenomenon. Such conditions may include age-relevant interpersonal schemas, beliefs, and values that are activated when making attributions about interpersonal dilemmas (Baldwin, 1992; Bargh, 1989; Gilbert & Malone, 1995; Fazio, Sanbonmatsu, Powell, & Kardes, 1986). Adults of all ages may rely more on beliefs and values if they are elicited by a particular situation to guide their causal attributions rather than engage in elaborative processing.

As indicated earlier, a first step to understanding attributional processing is to assess the availability and accessibility of social cognitive representations such as beliefs and values. From an adult developmental perspective, the availability of stored representations varies as a function of age/cohort/life stage differences in social schemas and beliefs about how partners in a relationship should behave. Second, in line with the importance of the accessibility of social schemas and beliefs, it is necessary to ascertain the degree to which activation of these schemas and beliefs mediate age differences in the types of causal attributions made about relationship dilemmas. Activated schemas regarding appropriate relationship behaviors can promote a dispositional bias in causal explanations by suppressing an elaborated search for other possible explanations of the behavior beyond those dispositional characteristics associated with the activated schema (Blanchard-Fields, 1999).

Let us return to the situation described above regarding the dissolved romantic relationship between Alan and Barbara. Assume that Alan is the target character for a dispositional attribution. Given the negative outcome (the breakup of the relationship) and the ambiguity of causal factors leading to the negative outcome, initial dispositional information is automatically evoked suggesting that Alan is responsible for the breakup. Under the limited resources hypothesis, older adults would be less likely to adjust this initial dispositional judgment by considering other extenuating circumstances leading up to the breakup. Instead, they would engage in more schema-driven processing, leading to a greater dispositional bias.

However, older adults may make more attributional processes because they do rely more on effortless schema-driven processing, but not because of cognitive limitations. First, older adults may exhibit a cognitive processing style that forecloses any further consideration of other explanations for the behavior of Alan. Such styles include a need for structure or intolerance for ambiguity in situations. The literature suggests that such age-related decreases in attitudinal flexibility may lead to biases in social judgment (Blanchard-Fields & Norris, 1994; Schaie, 1996). Second, strong social beliefs and values may be evoked by the presented situation when the main character (e.g., Alan) violates such strongly held beliefs. This encourages a blame-oriented bias toward the violator of the beliefs, in this case Alan (Blanchard-Fields, 1996; Blanchard-Fields et al., 1998). Negative relationship situations may trigger relatively automatic trait- and rule-based schemas relevant to the actor in the problem situation (Blanchard-Fields & Norris, 1994). For example, an individual can strongly believe that "You don't need to be married to be happy in a relationship." In the Alan and Barbara vignette, Alan violated this schema. Thus, the individual would blame Alan for the breakup of the relationship. Because of the relatively automatic activation of well-instantiated schemas, the individual may not have engaged in intentional and effortful processing of individuated, detailed information regarding the entire scope of the problem situation (e.g., other factors besides the characteristics of the actor). Instead, they may have relied more on activated schemas, resulting in dispositional attributional inferences. Under the latter two hypotheses, older adults have sufficient processing capacity to engage in elaborative social inference, but do not do so in certain contexts due to overriding considerations (e.g., the naturally occurring accessibility and irrepressibility of beliefs, values, and attitudes).

Age Differences in Social Schemas

Again, a first step is to examine the differential availability of stored representations of social schemas in different age groups. The assumption is that relationship vignettes evoke schemas containing societally prescribed

rules and values regarding relationships and appropriate behavior in relationship situations. Written justifications of attribution ratings from the attributional studies conducted in our lab (Blanchard-Fields & Norris, 1994)
were examined, post hoc, for social schema content for a selected sample of
relationship vignettes that were particularly high in emotional and value-
laden content. From the written justifications we were able to extract social
schemas, which appeared to be evoked as a function of the value-laden
content of several of the negative relationship vignettes (Blanchard-Fields,
1996). We found age differences in various types of social schemas evoked.
An illustrative social schema from this study is "Marriage comes before
one's career." Older adults and adolescents produced this social rule more
than young and middle-aged adults did (Blanchard-Fields, 1996). This and
other social schemas may have been particularly salient for older cohorts,
given their years of accumulated experience, stage in life, and the particular
cohort in which they were socialized. Compared to younger adults, such
schemas may have triggered a different orientation and approach to the
task for older adults. The question remains as to the degree to which these
social schemas are accessible in the context of making social judgments
and how they influence those judgments.

Social Schemas and Attributional Processing

We conducted a study to assess age-related differences in schematic beliefs
and rules and their impact on social judgments (Chen & Blanchard-Fields,
1997). We proposed a belief content hypothesis to explain the dispositional
bias found in older adults. In this case, the violation of social schemas
or beliefs about a certain type of person or event may inhibit adjustment
of one's initial attributions, resulting in a higher degree of dispositional
attributions.

We presented twelve relationship vignettes to participants similar to the
one described earlier about Alan and Barbara. Embedded within each vignette was a representative social schema or rule about what is appropriate
relationship behavior in the specific type of situation. Within each vignette,
the main character and/or other characters violated the relationship rule
or schema. For example, in the vignette about Alan and Barbara, the rule
"You should never cohabitate before marriage" is violated.

We hypothesized that strong negative reactions about a violated relationship belief or schema may be activated for older adults (and possibly
for young adults). The question was, could older adults adjust their initial tendency to blame the violator of the rule, given other extenuating
information in the vignette?

As typical of our previous work, older adults made higher dispositional
ratings than young adults did. We also asked individuals to complete brief
written essays as to what were the important themes and issues related to

each vignette. The content of their statements was used to identify each individual's schematic beliefs regarding appropriate behaviors in the social situations portrayed in the vignettes. These variables produced outcomes that support the belief-based view of age differences in the initial causal attributions. Chen and Blanchard-Fields (1997) coded the themes and issues in terms of schematic social beliefs and rules (evaluative statements) from participants for each vignette. We found that older adults made more evaluative rule statements about the main character (e.g., similar to the rule "you shouldn't cohabitate before marriage"). In addition, high dispositional attributional ratings were positively correlated with such evaluative schema statements about the main character. Finally, the ratio of content-evoked evaluative schema statements about the main character statistically mediated the relationship between age and dispositional ratings about the main character in the immediate rating condition.

The findings of this study can be taken as evidence consistent with a schema-content-based explanation of dispositional biases. However, it should be noted that the evidence for the schema-content view is somewhat weak and indirect. It is limited by the fact that social schemas and beliefs were extracted from post-attribution essays explaining the attribution ratings. In more recent work, we assessed social schemas a priori to performing the causal attribution task and found that, again, schematic beliefs mediated age differences in dispositional biases (Blanchard-Fields & Hertzog, 2000).

IMPLICATIONS FOR PERSONAL RELATIONSHIPS IN OLDER ADULTHOOD

The majority of research on attributional processing and beliefs and aging has focused primarily on social judgments of events and people outside of the self, that is, focusing on hypothetical situations. Again, evidence suggests that at least in hypothetical relationship situations that are highly interpersonal and emotionally salient older adults rely on dispositional explanations of causes to negative outcomes. Is this the case in the context of older adults' own relationship situations? For young adults, the marital literature suggests that when partners in conflict attribute the source of conflict to stable and pervasive personality traits (as in the case of dispositional attributions), it influences the overall view of their respective partner in the context of the entire relationship (Solomon, 2001). In turn, this may serve to promote persistent conflict across a multitude of personal relationship situations. Attributional systems such as this serve to unify the various interpersonal episodes and ultimately support negative global evaluations of relationship quality (Solomon, 2001). Again, to what extent does this apply to the context of older adults' marital relationships?

Contrary to the implications of the above research, a consistent find-ing in the adulthood and aging literature on marital relationships is that older adults tend to deal with conflict quite well, better than middle-aged and younger adults do. For older adults there is a greater focus on the positive and less focus on the negative in conflict situations (Levenson, Carstensen, & Gottman, 1993; Carstensen, Graff, Levenson, & Gottman, 1996). In order to help explain this finding, Levenson argues that older adults are skilled at creating a "comfort zone," which is a constructed space where partners in a marriage can work through emotion-laden conflicts at a level of emotional intensity that is both comfortable and productive (Levenson, 1997). Affective relationships in the space of the comfort zone encourage a different and more positive pattern of communication after a negative emotion, such as anger, is displayed in the context of a conflict situation (i.e., how expressions of anger are dealt with or resolved). These developmental findings inform, as well as confirm, the mainstream litera-ture on marital and relationship satisfaction, which asserts that the degree to which one's current affective relationship in a marriage is related to mar-ital satisfaction is highly influenced by patterns of interaction (Forgas, 2001; Solomon, 2001). What they do not take into consideration is the dynamic changes that take place when considering the developmental trajectory of affect and cognition. It may be the case that patterns of interaction change with increasing longevity in marriage and age-related changes in emotion regulation.

There are other aspects of the mainstream literature on marital satisfac-tion that also inform the aging literature and suggest potential explanations for understanding the quality of older adults' marital relationships. Neff and colleagues (Neff & Karney, 2002) demonstrate how the differential im-portance of positive and negative perceptions in the context of a relation-ship influences marital quality. Positive perceptions contribute to marital satisfaction more than negative ones. In addition, the ability to alter beliefs as they change over time results in increased marital satisfaction. In other words, if positive perceptions in a marriage are seen as more important than negative perceptions, the higher is the level of one's marital satisfac-tion. Highlighted in this profile of marital quality is that greater flexibility of an intimate partner's importance ratings results in positive changes in marital satisfaction. Thus, lower marital satisfaction is related to greater negative perceptions and the inability to engage in the reorganization of one's positive and negative beliefs within the context of the relationship.

This is an interesting form of flexibility. As we indicated earlier, there is evidence of foreclosed flexibility in the thinking of older adults (e.g., Schaie, 1996). However, flexibility in changing the relative importance of positive and negative perceptions accompanying relationship situations for older adults is a relatively new context to examine flexibility. It may be the case that older adults display greater flexibility given their propensity to positively resolve interpersonal conflicts in a marriage. Future research is warranted to examine flexibility in social cognitive thinking in personal relationships across the latter half of the life span.

As the above research suggests, adaptive functioning in marital relationships is highly dependent upon positive and accurate perceptions and interpretations of the actions of one's partner. Another important implication of the above research is that cognitive structures play a crucial role in mediating emotional reactions to relationship events. In fact, cognition appears to play a role in eliciting emotion only when the evoked cognitive representation relates to an event of significance to the individual (Campos, Campos, & Barrett, 1991). The complex interactions between emotional functioning and interactions play an important role in maintaining the integrity of a marital relationship. The literature maintains that it is important to consider the reciprocal relationship between cognition and emotion in explaining individual differences in marital satisfaction. At the same time, the developmental literature suggests that older adults are more competent in or at least more aware of regulating their emotions in the context of a relationship (see Schaie & Lawton, 1997). We now explore the interface between these two literatures.

THE ROLE OF EMOTION IN SOCIAL JUDGMENTS ABOUT PERSONAL RELATIONSHIPS

In general, there is a growing emphasis in the literature on exploring the relationship between emotion and cognition in order to understand human functioning in general and personal relationships more specifically (Damasio, 1994; Forgas, 2001). In addition, research suggests that cognition only plays a role in affective responses when values and significance are placed on the cognitive interpretation of the event (Campos et al., 1991). In the social cognitive literature, research on motivated processing suggests that goals such as mood repair and maintenance, ego enhancement, among others, guide information search as well as social judgments (e.g., Erber & Erber, 1994). Forgas (1991, 2001) demonstrates strong evidence for a mood-related bias in social judgments in a relationship context. For example, mood can influence the likelihood that an individual will commit an attributional error in that happy people are more likely to commit the correspondence bias, whereas sad people pay more attention to situational constraints on behavior (Forgas, 1998). When in a negative mood, individuals process information more deeply, whereas a happy mood results in shallower processing.

Interestingly, mood has a greater influence on attributions about complex and serious aspects of relationship conflicts than on those about simple ones. Again, this is because more complex events require a greater degree of elaborate and constructive processing, thus rendering judgments susceptible to affective priming effects (Forgas, 1995). Furthermore, evidence converges on the finding that partners in a relationship primed to be happy are more likely to focus on external, unstable, and specific explanations of their partner's role in real-life relationship conflict. By contrast, partners primed to be sad attribute the cause of conflict to internal, stable, and global causes (Forgas, 2001). Implications of these findings suggest that sad partners could feel guilty and blame themselves more for negative outcomes in relationship conflict (Forgas, 2001). This fits well with Damasio's claim that emotional functioning has a critical influence on adaptive thinking and decision making. In this case, attribution judgments play a critical role in maintaining the integrity of relationships. Furthermore, these lines of theorizing lend themselves to recent theorizing and findings on the importance of affect regulation goals in older adulthood and age-related differences in affect intensity, quality, and frequency.

From an adult developmental perspective, changing social roles, life goals, and life contexts influence emotions and subsequently adaptive thinking and decision making across the latter half of the life span. Studies demonstrate that as adults grow older and change life contexts, their goals become more concerned with other people, intimacy, and generativity as well as reflect cohort-related socioemotional rule systems that influence reasoning and behavior (Blanchard-Fields, 1999; Sansone & Berg, 1993). Along the same lines, Carstensen's (1992) theory of socioemotional selectivity suggests that older adults place a greater value on quality of relationships than younger adults do. Similarly, evidence suggests that older adults have a greater diversity of goals with a heavy emphasis on interpersonal goals and affective regulation than do younger adults (Lawton, Kleban, Rajagopal, & Dean, 1992; Sansone & Berg, 1993; Strough, Berg, & Sansone, 1996). Finally, the literature on age differences in various dimensions of emotion demonstrates the importance of emotion as a motivating force in triggering social judgments and cognitive strategies (Blanchard-Fields, 1997). For example, in highly emotional situations older adults use both emotion regulation and direct problem solving strategies, whereas younger adults adopt a more exclusive direct problem solving approach.

It is also important to take into consideration the physiological experience of affect. Both physiological and self-report data suggest that affect intensity decreases with age as a function of inevitable biological aging (Diener, Sandvik, & Larsen, 1985; Levenson, Carstensen, Friesen, & Ekman, 1991), although this may be tempered by individual variability (Filipp, 1996). Research on frequency of positive and negative affect suggests that older adults do not experience more negative affect than younger adults (Ferring & Filipp, 1995; Levenson, Carstensen, & Gottman, 1994; Smith & Baltes, 1993). It appears that the basic emotional system remains stable throughout adulthood. Lower emotional intensity in older adults may, therefore, be due to preferred affect regulation strategies used to avoid potentially negative emotionally arousing situations (Levenson et al., 1991). Finally, the quality of affective valence has been shown to change with age. For example, younger adults define positive affect more in terms of psychophysiological arousal and excitement (Lawton et al., 1992). Such age-related differences in the experience of emotion correspond well with the notion that older and younger adults may have differential motivational goals that influence social judgments, the selection of problem solving strategies, and decision making in social contexts, discussed above.

How do these developmental differences in affective functioning interface with attributional processing in the context of a marital relationship? It may be the case that the ability on the part of older adults to maintain positivity and attenuate negativity when experiencing relationship conflicts may allow for more adaptive attributional explanations of the conflict situation. For example, they may attribute the cause of conflict to external, relatively impermanent factors as opposed to stable, internal, and pervasive factors. This ability could serve to facilitate emotion regulation in older couples as evidenced in the literature and mediate the relationship between experienced emotion in a relationship and relationship satisfaction. These hypotheses are speculative and deserve more empirical attention.

An alternative hypothesis suggests that, in the context of working through marital conflicts and creating the comfort zone, older adults may actually strive to maintain civility in dealing with emotions without resolving the emotional conflict in order to establish a new and desired level of symbiosis or synergy between the two partners. In other words, it appears from Levenson and colleagues' work that older couples do engage in emotional strategies and cognitive appraisals or attributions to limit the experience of negative affect. Is this the case no matter how intense the situation? And what implications does this have on one's emotional well-being? Here, reduced conflict may reflect the successful downplaying of nagging issues rather than effective emotional regulation. Consonant with the beliefs and values of the older generation, it may be that the goal of this cohort is to keep a marriage intact irrespective of these issues. Let us consider a real world example.

An older man and woman, from all appearances, seem to have maintained a high quality marital relationship. However, the older man had been keeping love letters of another woman outside of his marriage. Despite the fact that the wife was aware of this, their relationship, again, remained intact. However, when the man died, his wife vigorously burned the letters. In this case, the exhibited positive affect and reduced negative affect in the context of the "living" relationship could result from the active suppression of the desire to achieve a different emotional goal (to confront the husband with the affair). This goal is very different from that of maintaining the integrity of the marriage (resolving the conflict about this other woman) and could only be released outside the context of the marriage (i.e., when the husband died). Again, goals and attributional processes need to be carefully examined for underlying cause and explanation.

Another issue to consider is the negative emotions themselves. Levenson and colleagues (Levenson et al., 1991, 1993, 1994) do argue that it is not necessarily the quelling of negative emotions that operationalize the comfort zone (i.e., the safe space to work out conflicts). However, negative disruption can be facilitative toward growth – a form of level building, a positive disintegration in order to move toward another level of functioning. Given cohort differences between middle-aged and older adult couples, is this a part of older couples' functioning or a part of middle-aged couples' functioning? Are there positive components of the greater negative affect perceived in middle-aged couples? These issues need to be clarified in the context of the gains in emotional regulation and emotional appraisals demonstrated in older couples. Along these lines, we need to specify emotional elicitors, their cognitive appraisal (i.e., attributions), and strategies used to deal with them. In what contexts do emotions as regulators of behavior serve an adaptive role, a minimal role, or a disruptive role?

CONCLUSIONS AND FUTURE DIRECTIONS

There is a growing literature that continues to provide evidence for adulthood changes in attributional processes in relationship situations, as well as the influence of one's social knowledge base and emotional regulation of these attributions. Thus, it is important for future research to examine social cognitive functioning within the context not only of marital relationships but also personal relationships in general. There are a number of areas that need further elaboration and examination. First, there is an accumulation of evidence suggesting changes in motivation and goals as we grow older. In concert, there is much theoretical speculation suggesting that these changes should influence social judgments. However, there is a need for more empirical work to substantiate such a relationship. For example, if, indeed, older adults are motivated to reduce negative affect, studies need to assess this motivational structure (e.g., the goal to increase or decrease emotional stimulation) and relate it to attributions explaining marital conflict, selection of problem solving strategies, interpretation of problems, or the selection of intimate contacts.

Second, there is a proliferation of research in mainstream social cognition suggesting that one's current mood or emotional state influences relationship judgments. Such on-line assessment of current emotional states in older adults as compared to other age groups would help determine whether changes in emotional experience (e.g., affect intensity) modifies this relationship (e.g., between mood and memory, affect and causal attributions) as a function of age. In this way, important factors (such as changes in processing capacity) can be identified that may not have been considered because of the limited age range typically used in social cognition research. In other words, developmental changes in knowledge systems and processing operations may impact how social-cognitive functioning proceeds. It may be the case that the models developed in mainstream social cognition are too static and therefore unable to incorporate such developmental phenomena.

Third, changes in affective functioning in older adulthood may serve an important adaptive role in social cognitive functioning. For example, a general reduction in affect intensity may represent effective self-regulation, without eliminating the possibility of intense emotional responses under other specific eliciting conditions. The search for aspects of the aging process that have adaptive value for developing adults may be advanced by more studies that examine the interface between cognition appraisal, affect, and the quality of personal relationships.

Finally, there are a number of developmental dimensions that need to be considered when examining social cognition in personal relationship situations. To what degree is attributional processing and its influence on marital satisfaction an age-related dimension such as the accumulation of experience? Or is it a life stage effect, where retirement years or a career stage do not carry as much pressure to prove oneself (in contrast to the importance of career in middle age)? Finally, do older adults today represent a cohort that values the need to reduce negative affect because negative feelings are considered inappropriate? Overall, the area of adult development and aging has witnessed a recent proliferation of studies in emotion and strategy selection. However, these questions suggest that more research is needed.

In conclusion, age/cohort differences in social attitudes, beliefs, values, and expectations and their relationship to interpersonal reasoning have implications for understanding the nature of functional and dysfunctional attributions in the context of personal relationships and their relation to marital satisfaction. From a more applied perspective, they are suggestive for counseling couples of different age/cohort groups. Thus, an important long-term goal in the literature may be to develop a more systematic assessment of functional and dysfunctional attributions as they relate to instantiated social schemas. This should have predictive utility for other variables of adaptive significance as well as providing diagnostic tools for healthy functioning in adulthood and aging (i.e., maintenance of mental and physical health).

References

Baldwin, M. W. (1992). Relational schemas and the processing of social information. *Psychological Bulletin, 112,* 461–484.

Baldwin, M. W., Keelan, J. P. R., Fehr, B., Enns, V., & Koh-Rangarajoo, E. (1996). Social-cognitive conceptualization of attachment working models: Availability and accessibility effects. *Journal of Personality and Social Psychology, 71,* 94–109.

Bargh, J. A. (1989). Conditional automaticity: Varieties of automatic influence in social perception and cognition. In J. S. Uleman and J. A. Bargh (Eds.), *Unintended thought* (pp. 3–51). New York: The Guilford Press.

Bargh, J. A. (1997). The automaticity of everyday life. In R. S. Wyer, Jr. (Ed.), *The automaticity of everyday life: Advances in social cognition* (Vol. 10, pp. 1–61). Mahwah, NJ: Lawrence Erlbaum Associates.

Baucom, D. H., Epstein, N., Daiuto, A. D., Carels, R. A., Rankin, L. A., & Burnett, C. K. (1996). Cognitions in marriage: The relationship between standards and attributions. *Journal of Family Psychology, 10,* 209–222.

Baucom, D. H., Epstein, N., Sayers, S., & Sher, T. G. (1989). The role of cognitions in marital relationships: Definitional, methodological, and conceptual issues. *Journal of Consulting and Clinical Psychology, 57,* 31–38.

Baucom, D. H., Sayers, S. L., & Duhe, A. (1989). Attributional style and attributional patterns among married couples. *Journal of Personality and Social Psychology, 54,* 596–607.

Blanchard-Fields, F. (1994). Age differences in causal attributions from an adult development perspective. *Journal of Gerontology, 49,* P43–P51.

Blanchard-Fields, F. (1996). Causal attributions across the adult life span: The influence of social schemas, life context, and domain specificity. *Applied Cognitive Psychology, 10,* 137–146.

Blanchard-Fields, F. (1997). The role of emotion in social cognition across the adult life span. In K. W. Schaie & M. P. Lawton (Eds.), *Annual review of gerontology and geriatrics* (Vol. 17, pp. 238–265). New York: Springer Publishing Company, Inc.

Blanchard-Fields, F. (1999). Social schematicity and causal attributions. In T. M. Hess & F. Blanchard-Fields (Eds.), *Social cognition and aging.* San Diego, CA: Academic Press, Inc.

Blanchard-Fields, F., Chen, Y., Schocke, M., & Hertzog, C. (1998). Evidence for content-specificity of causal attributions across the adult life span. *Aging, Neuropsychology, and Cognition, 5,* 241–263.

Blanchard-Fields, F., & Hertzog, C. (2000). Age differences in schematicity. In U. von Hecker, S. Dutke, & G. Sedek (Eds.), *Processes of generative mental representation and psychological adaptation.* Dordrecht, The Netherlands: Kluwer.

Blanchard-Fields, F., & Norris, L. (1994). Causal attributions from adolescence through adulthood: Age differences, ego level, and generalized response style. *Aging and Cognition, 1,* 67–86.

Bradbury, T. N., & Fincham, F. D. (1990). Attributions in marriage: Review and critique. *Psychological Bulletin, 107,* 3–33.

Campos, J. J., Campos, R. G., & Barrett, K. C. (1991). Emergent themes in the study of emotional development and emotion regulation. *Developmental Psychology, 24,* 394–402.

Carstensen, L. L. (1992). Selectivity theory: Social activity in life-span context. *Annual Review of Gerontology and Geriatrics, 11,* 195–217.

Carstensen, L. L., Graff, J., Levenson, R. W., & Gottman, J. M. (1996). Affect in intimate relationships: The developmental course of marriage. In C. Magai & S. H. McFadden (Eds.), *Handbook of emotion, adult development, and aging* (pp. 227–247). San Diego, CA: Academic Press.

Chen, Y., & Blanchard-Fields, F. (1997). Age differences in stages of causal attributional processing. *Psychology and Aging, 12,* 694–703.

Cooper, C., & Blanchard-Fields, F. (2001, November). Do personal identification and interpersonal involvement explain age differences in attributional biases? Poster session presented at the annual meeting of the Gerontological Society of America, Chicago, IL.

Damasio, A. R. (1994). *Descartes' error*. New York: Grosset Putnam.

Diener, E., Sandvik, E., & Larsen, R. J. (1985). Age and sex differences for emotional intensity. *Developmental Psychology, 21*, 542–546.

Erber, R., & Erber, M. W. (1994). Beyond mood and social judgment: Mood incongruent recall and mood recognition. *European Journal of Social Psychology, 24*, 79–88.

Fazio, R. H., Sanbonmatsu, D. M., Powell, M. C., & Kardes, F. R. (1986). On the automatic activation of attitudes. *Journal of Personality and Social Psychology, 50*, 229–238.

Ferring, D., & Filipp, S. H. (1995). The structure of subjective well-being in the elderly: A test of different models by structural equation modeling. *European Journal of Psychological Assessment, 11*, 32.

Filipp, S. H. (1996). Motivation and emotion. In J. E. Birren & K. W. Schaie (Eds.), *Handbook of psychology and aging* (4th ed., pp. 218–235). San Diego, CA: Academic Press.

Fincham, F. D., & Beach, S. R. H. (1999). Marriage in the new millennium: Is there a place for social cognition in marital research? *Journal of Social and Personal Relationships, 16*, 685–704.

Fincham, F. D., Garnier, P. C., Gano-Phillips, S., & Osborne, L. N. (1995). Preinteraction expectations, marital satisfaction, and accessibility: A new look at sentiment override. *Journal of Family Psychology, 9*, 3–14.

Fiske, S. (1993). Social cognition and social perception. *Annual Review of Psychology, 44*, 155–194.

Fletcher, G. J. O., Rosanowski, J., & Fitness J. (1994). Automatic processing in intimate contexts: The role of close-relationship beliefs. *Journal of Personality and Social Psychology, 67*, 888–897.

Forgas, J. P. (1991). Affect and cognition in close relationships. In G. Fletcher & F. D. Fincham (Eds.), *Cognition in close relationships* (pp. 151–174). Hillsdale, NJ: Lawrence Erlbaum Associates.

Forgas, J. P. (1995). Mood and judgment: The affect infusion model (AIM). *Psychological Bulletin, 117*, 39–66.

Forgas, J. P. (1998). Happy and mistaken? Mood effects on the fundamental attribution error. *Journal of Personality and Social Psychology, 75*, 318–331.

Forgas, J. P. (2001). Affective influences on communication and attribution in relationships. In V. Manusov & J. H. Harvey (Eds.), *Attribution, communication behavior, and close relationships* (pp. 3–20). Cambridge: Cambridge University Press.

Gilbert, D. T., & Malone, P. S. (1995). The correspondence bias. *Psychological Bulletin, 117*, 21–38.

Gilbert, D. T., & Osborne, R. E. (1989). Thinking backward: Some curable and incurable consequences of cognitive busyness. *Journal of Personality and Social Psychology, 57*, 940–949.

Gilbert, D. T., Pelham, B. W., & Krull, D. S. (1988). On cognitive busyness: When person perceivers meet persons perceived. *Journal of Personality and Social Psychology, 54*, 733–740.

Gilbert, D. T., Tafarodi, R. W., & Malone, P. S. (1993). You can't not believe everything you read. *Journal of Personality and Social Psychology, 65*, 221–233.

Heider, F. (1958). *The psychology of interpersonal relations.* New York: Wiley.

Hess, T. M., & Pullen, S. M. (1994). Adult age differences in impression change processes. *Psychology and Aging, 9*, 237–250.

Holmes, J. G. (2000). Social relationships: The nature and function of relational schemas. *European Journal of Social Psychology, 30*, 447–495.

Holtzworth-Munroe, A., & Jacobson, N. S. (1985). Causal attributions of married couples: When do they search for causes? What do they conclude when they do? *Journal of Personality and Social Psychology, 48*, 1398–1412.

Lawton, M. P., Kleban, M. H., & Rajagopal, D., & Dean, J. (1992). Dimensions of affective experience in three age groups. *Psychology and Aging, 7*, 171–184.

Levenson, R. (1997, August). "The social context of emotion throughout the life span," symposium for the APA Presidential Mini-convention on Psychology and the Aging Revolution, annual American Psychological Association Conference, Chicago, IL.

Levenson, R. W., Carstensen, L. L., Friesen, W. V., & Ekman, P. (1991). Emotion, physiology, and expression in old age. *Psychology and Aging, 6*, 28–35.

Levenson, R. W., Carstensen, L. L., & Gottman, J. M. (1993). Long-term marriage: Age, gender, and satisfaction. *Psychology and Aging, 82*, 301–313.

Levenson, R. W., Carstensen, L. L., & Gottman, J. M. (1994). The influence of age and gender on affect, physiology, and their interrelations: A study of long-term marriages. *Journal of Personality and Social Psychology, 67*, 56–68.

Lopez. F. G. (1993). Cognitive processes in close relationships: Recent findings and implications for counseling. *Journal of Counseling and Development, 71*, 310–315.

Manusov, V., & Koenig, J. (2001). The content of attributions in couples' communication. In V. Manusov & J. H. Harvey (Eds.), *Attribution, communication behavior, and close relationships. Advances in personal relations.* New York: Cambridge University Press.

Neff, L. A., & Karney, B. R. (2002, February). Differential importance and relationship maintenance: The dynamic structure of relationship beliefs. Paper presented at the meeting of the Society for Personality and Social Psychology, Savannah, GA.

Newman, H. (1981). Communication within ongoing intimate relationships: An attributional perspective. *Personality and Social Psychology Bulletin, 7*, 59–70.

Pierce, T., & Lydon, J. (1998). Priming relational schemas: Effects of contextually activated and chronically accessible interpersonal expectations on responses to a stressful event. *Journal of Personality and Social Psychology, 75*, 1441–1448.

Salthouse, T. A. (1991). *Theoretical perspectives on cognitive aging.* Hillsdale, NJ: Lawrence Erlbaum Associates.

Sansone, C., & Berg, C. A. (1993). Adapting to the environment across the life span: Different process or different inputs? *International Journal of Behavioral Development, 16*, 215–241.

Schaie, K. W. (1996). *Intellectual development in adulthood.* Cambridge: Cambridge University Press.

Schaie, K. W., & Lawton, M. P. (Eds.) (1997). *Annual review of gerontology and geriatrics* (Vol. 17). New York: Springer.

Schwarz, N., Strack, F., & Mai, H. P. (1991). Assimilation and contrast effects in part-whole question sequences: A conversation logic analysis. *Public Opinion Quarterly*, 55, 3–23.

Scott, C. K., Fuhrman, R. W., & Wyer, R. S. (1991). Information processing in close relationships. In G. J. O. Fletcher & F. D. Fincham (Eds.), *Cognition in close relationships* (pp. 37–67). Hillsdale, NJ: Lawrence Erlbaum Associates.

Sillars, A., Roberts, L. J., Leonard, K. E., & Dun, T. (2000). Cognition during marital conflict: The relationship of thought and talk. *Journal of Social and Personal Relationships*, 17, 479–502.

Smith, J., & Baltes, P. B. (1993). Differential psychological ageing: Profiles of the old and very old. *Ageing and Society*, 13, 551–587.

Solomon, D. H. (2001). Affect, attribution, and communication: Uniting interaction episodes and global relationship judgments. In V. Manusov & J. H. Harvey (Eds.), *Attribution, communication behavior, and close relationships* (pp. 79–90). Cambridge: Cambridge University Press.

Strough, J., Berg, C. A., & Sansone, C. (1996). Goals for solving everyday problems across the life span: Age and gender differences in the salience of interpersonal concerns. *Developmental Psychology*, 32, 1106–1115.

Weiss, R. L. (1980). Strategic behavioral marital therapy: Toward a model for assessment and intervention. In J. P. Vincent (Ed.), *Advances in family intervention, assessment, and theory* (Vol. 1, pp. 229–271). Greenwich, CT: JAI Press.

Wyer, R. S., Jr., & Srull, T. K. (1989). *Memory and cognition in its social context.* Hillsdale, NJ: Lawrence Erlbaum Associates.

12

Dyadic Fits and Transactions in Personality and Relationships

Franz J. Neyer

Starting out with the premises of the dynamic interactionistic paradigm, the chapter discusses how personality and relationships develop and influence each other over the life course. Two basic rules of personality-relationship transaction are proposed: First, individual differences in personality become increasingly stable and exert long-term and accumulative effects on relationships, whereas relationship experiences have only short-term effects that do not accumulate because they are interpreted in a way that suits the individual personality. Second, new relationships may offer a turning point for personality change, especially when accompanying age-related and socially scripted life transitions. The chapter is organized around these basic tenets and describes the mechanisms that promote personality-relationship transaction beyond initial assortment, and summarizes the empirical findings relevant to these assumptions.

At the time when two people, let's say two students at college, become committed to their relationship, they not only bring life experiences and histories but also enduring personality characteristics to their relationship. Whether they get on well with each other or whether their relationship breaks up following repeated quarrels is related not only to how they deal with each other in everyday or critical situations, but also depends on their personalities. Whereas one student may appear confident and agreeable, another one may appear wary, reserved, and fearful. These and other personality characteristics are relatively stable, albeit not unchangeable over the life course, and not only affect one as an individual, but also, and even more importantly, influence one's personal relationships and the related outcomes. Although such interaction between personality and relationships is obvious, personality psychology has unaccountably ignored social relationships for a long time. It is only recently that personality researchers have discovered social relationships as one of the main places where dynamic interactions between the individual and his or her environment occur.

This chapter is guided by the dynamic-interactionistic paradigm of individual development over the life span (Caspi, 1998; Caspi & Roberts, 1999; Magnusson, 1990; Sameroff, 1983). The paradigm assumes that individuals generally develop over time through a dynamic, continuous, and reciprocal *transaction* with their environment, and there is good reason to believe that the environment is above all else social. People may become influenced or even socialized by relationship partners such as parents, siblings, children, friends, colleagues and others, but at the same time they may actively search, create, and change relationships in a way that suits them, which in turn gives feedback to their further development. Thus, *personality-relationship transaction* is not just a special kind of transaction between the individual and his or her environment; it is the most central one. In order to understand how these transactions unfold, the chapter is organized as follows: First, stability and change of personality and relationships are considered from a life-span perspective. Second, two basic rules of personality-relationship transaction are proposed, one claiming that in general relationships are the outcome of personality differences, whereas the other states that in times of developmental transition emerging new relationships may have the potential to bring about personality change. Third, how the personality-relationship transaction can be studied from an individual and a dyadic perspective is discussed. Fourth, the question of who suits whom will be addressed. Finally, the empirical evidence will be considered regarding how personality and relationship influence each other over time.

PERSONALITY AND RELATIONSHIPS ACROSS THE LIFE SPAN

Personality is the characteristic way in which one thinks, feels, behaves, and relates to others. The personality makeup therefore comprises a set of characteristics that differs between individuals, such as temperament, attitudes, goals, and intellectual and social abilities. This set is also assumed to be relatively stable over time and marks individual behavior across different situations and, analogously, across different kinds of relationships. The contemporary version of a general trait theory is represented by the Five Factor Theory (FFT) that describes in depth a range of broad traits used by most people around the world to evaluate each other (i.e., extraversion, neuroticism, conscientiousness, agreeableness, and openness) (McCrae & Costa, 1999). Since personality psychology has been long dominated by a plethora of more or less interrelated personality constructs, the consensual use of five basic traits unifies the field of trait psychology, and many studies on relationship outcomes of personality, either study directly the Big Five or use concepts that can be related to FFT. More recently, McCrae and Costa (1996) suggested two classes of traits to be distinguished, *basic tendencies* and *characteristic adaptations*. Whereas basic tendencies such as the Big Five are viewed as cross-culturally invariant and genetically based temperament-like dispositions, which are not at all influenced by the environment, the other more malleable parts of personality, such as attitudes, goals, and the self-concept, are viewed as characteristic adaptations assisting the individual to fit into the demands of the external world. Therefore, characteristic adaptations are more prone to environmental influences. The position is provocative and controversial, although empirical evidence from longitudinal, behavior genetics, and cross-cultural research gives some support (see McCrae, Costa, Lima et al., 1999; McCrae, Costa, Ostendorf et al., 2000).

Personal relationships, in contrast, are characterized by patterns of repeated interaction of at least two independent persons. For example, the relationship between the two students mentioned above may be considered as "personal" if it appears unique, in being, for example, harmonious and collaborative, or conflictual and antagonistic. These unique characteristics have emerged from their relationship history and have also been affected by other experiences outside of the college context. But in addition, both partners' individual personalities uniquely contribute to the specific characteristics of the relationship (Asendorpf, 2002). Whether these constituents of personal relationships interplay additively or synergistically in such a way that this relationship is more than the sum of its parts is a question that can be studied only empirically. Both personality and personal relationships develop over time and increasingly stabilize when people grow older. However, stability and change of personality and relationships can be both studied from (at least) two broad perspectives, mean-level and rank-order stability, and it is important to be explicit about these perspectives because each has different implications for personality-relationship transaction.

Stability and Change of Personality

The perspective of *mean-level stability and change* addresses the general or normative age-related trajectory of personality development. Basic personality traits emerge from childhood temperament, and crystallize in adolescence and early adulthood (Caspi, 1998, 2000; Shiner, 1998). As various longitudinal studies have shown, personality in young adults generally changes toward maturity (e.g., Haan, Millsap, & Hartka, 1986; Helson & Moane, 1987; Roberts, Caspi, & Moffitt, 2001), a stage that may be ideally characterized by being happy, lacking neurotic and abnormal tendencies, and being able to maintain warm and compassionate relationships, especially with a romantic partner (Allport, 1961).

From adolescence to middle adulthood basic personality traits related to extraversion, neuroticism, and openness decrease, whereas traits like conscientiousness and agreeableness increase. This was the first general conclusion from two cross-cultural studies by McCrae and collaborators (McCrae, Costa, Lima et al., 1999; McCrae, Costa, Ostendorf et al., 2000), who observed that cross-sectional age differences in the mean levels of the Big Five personality traits appeared cross-culturally consistent. Because these age-related trends emerged in different cultures that surely represent extremely diverse environments, the second major and somewhat provocative conclusion by McCrae et al. was that this kind of personality change is due to intrinsic maturation and not at all contingent on environmental influences. The conclusions by McCrae et al. certainly seem plausible from an evolutionary perspective: Neuroticism, extraversion, and openness decrease when people settle down after having engaged in mating and reproduction (i.e., beginning a partnership, giving birth to children, starting a career), whereas agreeableness and conscientiousness increase with generativity (i.e., raising offspring, mentoring the young). It is nevertheless important to realize that the evolutionary explanation is not in conflict with a contextual view of personality change, one that views maturation as contingent on new relationship experiences.

The perspective of *rank-order stability and change*, in contrast, taps the relative standing of individuals on specific personality traits and relationship characteristics. Thus, a high rank-order stability does not necessarily imply high mean-level stability. For example, although mean-level neuroticism may decline in early adulthood, individual differences may remain quite stable over four years, as was observed by Neyer and Asendorpf (2001) in young adults. Over the life span, the rank-order stability of personality is expected to increase, implying that personality traits become more crystallized when people grow older. Recent longitudinal studies suggest substantial stability from childhood temperament to the personality of adolescents or young adults (e.g., Caspi, 2000; Caspi & Silva, 1995), but inconsistent findings on stability in adulthood led to contradictory conclusions. For example, Costa and McCrae (1994) expected almost perfect stability beyond age thirty, while Aldwin and Levenson (1994) expected personality change even in old age. More recently, the question was settled by Roberts and DelVecchio (2000), who concluded from an extensive meta-analysis that the rank-order stability of the Big Five personality traits, when controlled for retest intervals of about 6.7 years, increases in a step-like function from childhood ($r = .31$), adolescence (.54), to young and middle adulthood (.64), but reaches its plateau not before the sixth decade of life (.71). The less than perfect stability beyond age fifty, however, also suggests that personality may still change in old age. Although increases in personality stability are mostly associated with life phases that typically involve developmental transitions such as beginning a career, empty nest, etc., it is not clear whether such transitions set in motion personality stabilization or vice versa. Nevertheless, these findings show that personality development is not completed by age thirty and suggest substantial plasticity of personality across the adult life span.

The growing stability of personality differences depends on the following mechanisms (Caspi & Roberts, 1999; Conley, 1984; Roberts & DelVecchio, 2000): First, the stability increases because the reliability of personality assessment rises when people grow older. Second, the stability of personality increases with the growing stability of the environment. That is, with increasing age people have fewer new and unfamiliar experiences. For example, the frequency of changing romantic partners or close friends is likely to decrease over the life span. Third, genetic factors not only substantially influence the variability of personality traits, but also contribute to the long-term stability of individual differences, as was shown by McGue, Bacon, and Lykken (1993), who observed from a ten-year longitudinal twin study that 80% of the stability of personality traits could be explained by genetic differences. Fourth, the ability to control one's emotions and impulses, a general trait called *resiliency*, has been shown to support the stability of personality characteristics. Asendorpf and van Aken (1991), for example, observed that resiliency predicted the stability of children's personality from preschool to school age, and that resilient children were more stable in their personality profiles. Fifth, the stability of personality increases with the growing stability of the self-concept and a firm identity: People with a coherent schema of themselves will not fall down easily when slipping into crises and other calamities. Finally, the goodness of fit between personality and the environment enhances the stability of both sides. For example, the personalities of two friends, each representing a part of the other's environment, may show a fit with respect to their basic traits and views on their relationship, although this fit may not necessarily be a happy one.

Stability and Change of Relationships

Mean-level stability and change of personal relationships primarily pertain to age-related changes in size of personal networks. It is well backed up empirically that personal networks decrease in size when people reach old age (Lang, 2000; Lang & Carstensen, 1998). There is also evidence that specific types of relationships undergo normative changes across the life span. For example, the relationships between siblings develop in a U-shaped fashion from adolescence to old age (Cicirelli, 1995): After leaving family of origin, emotional closeness usually decreases until siblings reach their thirties and forties and are involved in raising children or in their careers. After reproductive and generative ages, however, closeness increases again, and siblings may rediscover each other as close companions when passing the empty-nest and retirement transitions.

The perspective of *rank-order stability and change* takes a different look at relationships by focusing on the relative standing of dyadic differences in relationship characteristics. For example, although the general developmental course of sibling relationships across adulthood takes on the gestalt of a U-shaped curve, it is likely that those sibling dyads feeling closer and contacting each other more frequently than others continue to do so over time. Exactly this pattern was observed by the retrospective evaluations of twin relationships, revealing that despite age-related relationship change the dyadic differences between relationship qualities remained highly stable across adulthood (Neyer, 2002a). Similarly, Lang (2000) observed substantial decreases in average network size in old age, whereas individual differences remained highly stable.

Whereas the stabilization of personality starts with the conception of the individual person, the rank-order stability of relationships begins to increase when relationship partners meet for the first time. In principle, it may be expected that the stability of relationship characteristics increases with the age of both relationship partners and the relationship duration. The mechanisms responsible for increasing relationship stability are presumably comparable with those supporting the stability of personality. That is, first, the stability of relationships increases with reliability of measurement. Second, relationship stability increases with growing environmental stability. For example, stable working conditions will support the stability of a colleagueship irrespective of whether the relationship is experienced as positive or negative. Third, to the extent to which heritable personality traits are involved in relationships, the increasing relationship stability should also be due to genetic influences. Fourth, the stability of relationship characteristics should also depend on the resiliency of the relationship itself, which may be conceived as the ability of relationship partners to flexibly and adequately deal with stress and conflict, for example, at the workplace or in the family. Fifth, the relationship stability should increase with the self-concepts and identities of dyad members. That is, the more consistent partners are in the views of themselves, the more consistently will they experience their dyadic relationship. Finally, the goodness of fit between the personalities of both relationship partners is likely to enhance relationship stability, that is, stability increases the more personality traits of relationship partners match with each other.

Because a relationship quality such as frequency of contact, conflict, or satisfaction basically is the outcome of two interacting persons, it is likely that these relationship characteristics are typically less stable than individual personality traits. Unfortunately, there are to the best of my knowledge no meta-analytic studies or comparative reviews of the rank-order stability of relationship characteristics across a broad range of different types of relationships. Two longitudinal studies on personality-relationship transaction in young adults, however, make it possible to contrast the rank-order stability of personality and self-reported qualities of various relationship types, such as with partners, parents, other family members, and peers. In a study of younger students, the mean 18-month stability was .76 for personality and .30 for relationship quality (Asendorpf & Wilpers, 1998). In a more representative study on young adults, the four-year stability was .64 for personality and .39 for relationship qualities (Neyer & Asendorpf, 2001). This unbalance of personality stability versus relationship stability has clear implications for the nature of personality-relationship transaction.

PERSONALITY-RELATIONSHIP TRANSACTION

It is argued here that, in principle, personality effects dominate over relationship effects. This prediction is based on the assumption that individual personality traits are more stable than relationship characteristics, which is because relationships are inherently dyadic and include two separate personalities plus the relationship history, and the relationship outcome should therefore be less stable than its underlying factors. This fundamental difference affects the relative strengths of personality and relationship effects in that the more stable parts exert more powerful effects on the less stable parts. People bring individual characteristics and histories to their relationships that shape the way that social experiences become integrated instead of the other way around. To bring about far-reaching personality change, in contrast, relationship experiences must be novel and profound, and, at least in part, not due to preexisting individual differences.

Two Basic Rules of Personality-Relationship Transaction

Caspi and Moffitt (1993) have called attention to an apparent paradox of personality coherence and argued that most external and atypical discontinuities in life tend to accentuate rather than change individual differences, because these differences may have led, at least partly, to these discontinuities. In contrast, other expectable and age-graded life transitions, especially when highly scripted, may have the potential to "catalyze" change in personality. Based on these assumptions, two basic rules of personality-relationship transaction are proposed here: Whereas the first pertains to the general dominance of personality effects over relationship effects, the second rule outlines a condition under which relationships may have strong effects on personality.

First, at least since childhood, individual differences in personality become more stable, thereby exerting long-term and accumulative effects on relationships, which reveal that people react to social experiences due to their individual dispositions; relationship experiences, in contrast, have only short-term effects that do not accumulate because they are interpreted in a way that suits the individual personality. Discontinuities in relationship experiences, therefore, may be conceived of as the outcome of individual differences in personality, which in turn may become accentuated instead of being changed.

Second, it can nevertheless be expected that new relationships may have the potential of bringing about personality change, especially when they accompany age-related and socially scripted life transitions. New relationships may offer turning points for personality change, leading the individual person to accomplish new social tasks and obligations. More generally speaking, normative life transitions as experienced by most people in Western cultures are typically accompanied by relationship change such as the establishment of new ones or the dissolution of others. For example, the transition to kindergarten or school usually involves new relationships with peers, whereas the transition to professional training contexts or the occupational world offers new social opportunities. Also, other transitions that are more related to one's private life, like falling in love and engaging in a serious partnership for the first time, or becoming a responsible and dutiful parent, involve the establishment of new significant relationships that change one's life dramatically and, perhaps, induce personality change. The empirical evidence supporting these two basic rules is presented in the last section of this chapter (e.g., Asendorpf & Wilpers, 1998; Neyer & Asendorpf, 2001).

Mechanisms of Personality-Relationship Transaction

Viewed from a dynamic transactional perspective, personality and relationships continuously influence each other such that individuals begin and maintain relationships in a manner that suits them. Once established, the congruence of personality and relationships can be considered in terms of a *goodness of fit* (Wachs, 1994), a concept to which personality and developmental psychologists refer differently: Whereas from a developmental perspective the goodness of fit stands for the optimal outcome of the codevelopment of personality and relationships, the personality perspective views the goodness of fit as the result of a mutual increase in stability of both personality and relationships regardless of whether this fit is healthy or not. That is, a personality profile that matches one's relationships may engender stabilizing reactions from relationship partners, which in turn may foster the stabilization of one's personality. It is in this sense that the goodness of fit strengthens the stability of both personality and relationships. But how does this goodness of fit come about?

The goodness of fit results from continuous transactions between personality and relationships, which may be conceptualized by borrowing the idea of *genotype→environment correlation* from behavior genetic theory. According to this idea, genotypes stay in specific environments, because they look for, create, and simply find themselves in environments that suit them and which may, in turn, influence their further development. Such genotype→environment effects are genetic mechanisms designed to control the extent to which genotypes are exposed to specific environments, thereby increasing phenotypic variability (Plomin, DeFries, & Loehlin, 1977; Scarr & McCartney, 1983). When transferring the idea of genotype→environment effects to transactions between personality and the environment it is important to bear in mind that the origin of personality is of course due to both genetic and environmental influences, which is why several authors have suggested considering *personality→environment transaction* in a broader sense (e.g., Buss, 1987; Caspi 1998, 2000; Caspi & Roberts 1999; Roberts & DelVecchio, 2000). From this perspective, four basic kinds of personality-environment transactions can be distinguished, labeled as *reactive, evocative, proactive,* and *manipulative.*

These mechanisms also apply to transactions between personality and relationships: *Reactive* transactions emerge when an individual person perceives and interprets relationship experiences in keeping with his or her personality and self-concept. For example, one student may interpret the constructive comments by a teacher regarding his or her seminal paper as destructive and severe criticism because this perception corresponds with his or her self-concept as depressed and devalued. *Evocative* transactions occur if an individual causes or provokes reactions from relationship partners consistent with his or her personality. Thus, the student just mentioned may also induce derogative reactions by teachers and other students because his or her behavior conveys the impression of somebody who is insecure and incompetent. *Proactive* transactions result from one's tendency to search for relationship partners who are compatible with one's personality. Therefore, our student may make extremely high self-demands that he or she can never meet. The student may be then inclined to look for especially rigid teachers who suit these high standards, and who in turn react according to his or her self-devaluation. Finally, *manipulative* transactions are due to one's tendency to actively change or manipulate the behavior of his or her relationship partners. The student may then become increasingly enmeshed in a vicious circle of self-devaluation and negative responses by teachers and fellow students that additionally may be driven by the active attempts to bias the others' attitudes toward him or her, regardless of whether these manipulative attempts are pursued consciously or not.

Of course, such transactions may also produce positive outcomes, for example, regarding personality growth and happy relationships, though it is important to keep in mind that these transactions emerge over longer time periods through the continuous interplay of stable personality traits with repeated relationship experiences. Moreover, it might be expected that these transactions become more powerful across the life span. Because the stability of personality steadily increases from childhood to adulthood, it is highly probable that the effects of personality accumulate over time, whereas the short-term effects of relationships are likely to fluctuate and may even cancel each other out. Therefore it is basically assumed that the individual personality is the active creator of his or her social relationships, although this does not exclude the possibility that new relationships offer a turning point for personality change. In the end, however, the strength of personality and relationship effects is a research question only to be answered by empirical studies, whose methodological standards are considered in the next section.

INDIVIDUAL AND DYADIC PERSPECTIVES

Transactions between personality and relationships can be viewed from two perspectives, an individual and a dyadic one. Each perspective will be discussed separately, since each has different implications for the theory and research of personality-relationship transaction across the life span. The ideal study of personality-relationship transaction should be dyadic, but research has only recently begun to design studies that meet these standards (e.g., Caughlin, Huston, & Houts, 2000; Karney & Bradbury, 1997; Robins, Caspi, & Moffitt, 2000).

Individual Perspective

How personality traits in general influence change in social relationships, and the reverse, can be considered at the level of the individual. To perform strict tests on personality versus relationship effects, it is necessary that both be measured on at least two occasions (Figure 12.1). The concurrent correlation *a* between a personality trait and a relationship measure is not informative about personality-relationship transaction because it may be

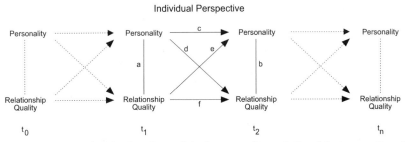

FIGURE 12.1. Individual path model of personality-relationship transaction: Personality effects on relationship quality (d) are controlled for the synchronic correlation (a) and relationship stability (f). Analogously, relationship effects (e) are controlled for the synchronic correlation (a) and personality stability (c). Personality and relationship effects can be studied over more than two subsequent occasions (t_0, t_n).

due to both personality and relationship effects as well as to other unknown factors. But also a cross-lagged correlation between personality measured at Time 1 and relationship measured at Time 2 does not allow for the prediction of relationship change, unless indirect effects are controlled for (Asendorpf, 2002; Campbell & Kenny, 1999; Rogosa, 1980, 1988).

Path analysis is an appropriate tool to disentangle the effects of antecedent personality on relationship qualities and vice versa. Consider a personality trait at Time 1 (e.g., neuroticism) showing a cross-lagged correlation with a relationship quality at Time 2 (e.g., conflict). When the whole correlational pattern is examined, the predictive correlation between both measures may even turn out to be spurious because neuroticism and conflict were already positively correlated at Time 1 (correlation a), and conflict proved to be a stable relationship quality across time (path f). Now, path analysis separates the *direct effect* (e.g., path d) from the *indirect effects* $(a \rightarrow f)$. In other words, the path d indicates the prediction of change in conflict by initial neuroticism, controlling not only for the concurrent correlation at Time 1 (a) but also for the stability of conflict (f). The individual perspective is restricted to general patterns of personality-relationship transaction rather than addressing the transaction between two personalities and their relationship over time. Thus, this perspective is essentially not more than a suboptimal solution in cases where dyadic information on relationship quality and the personality of relationship partners is not available. Because relationships consist of two persons, however, it is generally preferable to take a dyadic perspective.

Dyadic Perspective

The dyadic perspective considers the compatibility of both partners' personalities and their relationship experiences, and how this changes over time. The dyadic perspective can be illustrated with a path model that is alike the individual perspective (Figure 12.2). It applies to each type of dyadic relationship regardless of whether dyad members are exchangeable (e.g., same-sex siblings, friends, colleagues, or gay and lesbian couples), or whether dyad members are distinguishable (e.g., heterosexual couples, opposite-sex siblings or friends, hierarchical relationships), although this distinction has methodological implications (see Griffin & Gonzalez, 1995; Gonzalez & Griffin, 1997).

Dyadic compatibility can take the form of either correspondence or complementarity, and is expressed by how similar or dissimilar relationship partners are with regard to their personality, and how this similarity or dissimilarity changes over time (correlation a). Accordingly, the dyadic compatibility of relationship experiences is expressed by how similar or dissimilar both dyad members perceive the quality of their relationship (correlation b), and how this correlation changes over time. In general, the

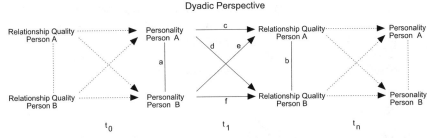

FIGURE 12.2. Dyadic path model of personality-relationship transaction: Actor effects from personality on relationships (c, f) are controlled for similarity (a) and partner effects (d, e). Analogously, partner effects (d, e) are controlled for similarity (a) and actor effects (c, f). Actor and partner effects unfold over time and can also run from relationship to personality (t_0, t_n).

dyadic similarity in perceived relationship quality is much higher than the actual similarity in personality traits. This is not surprising, because relationship qualities are inherently dyadic, and therefore interdependent between relationship partners, whereas personality traits are characteristics of the individual person. For example, the similarity in perceived relationship quality usually ranges between .40 and .80 in marital partners (e.g., Karney, Bradbury, Fincham, & Sullivan, 1994), while the personalities of marital partners are usually not very similar (mean $r = .15$, as reviewed by Lykken & Tellegen, 1993). The same applies to genetically related partners whose personalities resemble each other for genetic and shared environmental reasons, as is the case in parent-child or sibling relationships. The only case where both personality similarity and similarity in relationship experiences may approach comparable levels is in that of monozygotic twins who are genetically identical (Neyer, 2002a, 2002b).

Reciprocal transactions between personality and relationship quality can be also studied from a dyadic perspective. The dyadic perspective not only reflects that both partners are independent personalities but also accounts for the fact that most features of the relationship are non-independent or, in other words, systematically correlated between relationship partners. For example, although relationship dissatisfaction is likely to be correlated between both members of a dyad, the unique dissatisfaction felt by a dyad member can partly result from his or her own neuroticism as well as from the partner's neuroticism. The effect of one's own neuroticism is called *actor effect* (paths c and f), whereas the effect of one's partner's personality trait is called *partner effect* (paths d and e). As in the individual path model, the paths in the dyadic design control for indirect effects, that is, the actor effects (c, f) control for partner effects (d, e) and similarity (a), and the reverse (Gonzalez & Griffin, 1997; Kenny, 1996). It should be noted that dyadic transactions emerge and unfold over time.

Thus, in principle a longitudinal dyadic research strategy would be highly desirable in order to separate out actor and partner effects beyond initial assortment. But up to now, such extremely costly research projects have been rare, although in the future they will probably become the ideal way to research the personality-relationship transaction.

WHO SUITS WHOM?

Lay psychology knows two rules about why people become committed in relationships, one claiming that birds of a feather flock together, and one that opposites attract. Regarding personality traits, interests, attitudes and other enduring characteristics, the empirical evidence is quite clear that similarity effects are stronger than dissimilarity effects (Berscheid & Reis, 1998). However, this rule applies differently for different kinds of relationships depending on whether attraction is based on similarity in non-kin relationships, or genetic relatedness in kin relationships. Assortative mating effects occur in romantic or marital relationships, but assortment effects also occur in other relationships where partners are non-kin, such as friends, acquaintances, or colleagues. In contrast, kin relationships are given and favored over non-kin relationships because kin are genetically related by descent (Daly, Salmon, & Wilson, 1997; Neyer & Lang, 2003).

Birds of a Feather Flock Together

Assortative mating is the tendency to select a mating partner not by chance but instead due to similarity in genetically influenced traits. Assortative mating is not very strong but substantial. As was reviewed by Lykken and Tellegen (1993), heterosexual partners usually resemble each other strongly in ethical orientations and attitudes (correlations ranging from .20 and .70), followed by intellectual abilities (.37), physical attractiveness (.38 to .53), and physical characteristics such as weight and height (.10 to .30), but not very much in personality traits (−.23 to .45). Particularly low correlations of partners' self-ratings were found in neuroticism and extraversion; one exception is openness to experience with a moderate correlation (McCrae, 1996; Watson, Hubbard, & Wiese, 2000). Marital partners usually do not become more similar in basic personality traits (Buss, 1984; Caspi, Herbener, & Ozer, 1992). However, the similarity in intellectual abilities seems to increase over time, because marital partners share specific environmental influences such as socioeconomic status and academic achievement (Gruber-Baldini, Schaie, & Willis, 1995).

From an evolutionary perspective, assortative mating is a powerful tool to maintain and increase the genetic variability in a population. For example, body height is a highly heritable trait, which is modestly correlated between partners (.25) (Plomin, DeFries, McClearn, & Rutter, 1997).

Although on average husbands tend to be taller than their wives, relatively tall men tend to mate women who are taller than other females, and the reverse is also true. Therefore, marriages of relatively tall men and relatively small women are quite uncommon. If partners do not select each other for body height and produce offspring regardless of this criterion, this would in the long run lead to a restricted genetic variability. The example of body height nicely illustrates why assortative mating is such an important mechanism: Even if assortment effects are small, as it is true for most traits, the effects accumulate over generations and thus maintain and even increase genetic and phenotypic variability. Also, assortative mating with regard to personality traits seems not useless from an evolutionary point of view, because many traits, such as the Big Five and characteristic adaptations, show substantial heritability (.40 on average, as summarized by Plomin et al., 1997). Small assortment effects are sufficient, since the effect of increasing variability unfolds across many generations.

Assortment effects also apply for other non-kin relationships, such as with friends or acquaintances. It is empirically well backed up that similarity plays an important role in friendship formation. The similarity of friends in personality traits is smaller even than in dating and married couples, but stronger regarding attitudes, leisure interests, and other social attributes, especially academic achievement (e.g., Berscheid & Reis, 1998; Blieszner & Adams, 1992; Funder, Kolar, & Blackman, 1995; Watson et al., 2000). Friends' similarity reflects the structure of their shared social environment. That is, people become friends because they have the opportunity to interact, for example, in educational contexts or neighborhoods. But more than that, friends may actively attract each other because they share specific interests. Over the life span, the active choice of friends seems to increase, as was observed by Duck (1975) in adolescents: Friends in early adolescence are usually more similar in objective characteristics such as school grade, while in middle and late adolescence friends tend to resemble each other more in psychological characteristics.

Finally, similarity effects apply to kin relationships that are given, although their maintenance may be a case of deliberate choice: Kin are favored over non-kin because kin carry copies of one's genes, and this indirect investment serves the inclusive fitness just as direct investment in sexual reproduction and raising offspring (Hamilton, 1964). Moreover, within the kinship system, more closely genetically related persons are preferred over less closely related kin. For example, it is likely that full siblings are emotionally closer than half-siblings, who are in turn closer than step siblings. One reason for this is that the degree of genetic relatedness is .50 in full siblings, .25 in half-siblings, and 0 in step siblings (Daly et al. 1997; Jankowiak & Diderich, 2000; Neyer & Lang, 2003; White & Riedmann, 1992). For the same reasons, genetic relatives resemble each other in personality traits, as various twin, family, and adoption studies have shown.

Higher correlations in the Big Five traits are usually observed in MZ twins (ranging between .42 and .54), and lower correlations in DZ twins or full siblings (ranging between .14 and .24). Correlations with adoptive siblings and adoptive parents, in contrast, are usually not substantive, and have shown that, in general, shared environmental influences of the family of origin do not contribute to personality similarity (see Loehlin, 1992; Plomin et al., 1997).

Proactive and Evocative Transactions in Interpersonal Attraction

Assortment effects are prototypes of proactive personality→relationship effects. People actively seek relationship partners who suit their interests and preferences, and perhaps also their basic personality traits. At the same time, assortment effects may be evocative, because people stay in environments where they have a higher chance to meet others who feel attracted toward them. In all these cases, people become attracted by phenotypic characteristics including personality traits, influenced by genetic as well as environmental factors. Thus, the extent to which assortment effects are driven by genetic and environmental influences cannot ultimately be disentangled.

A strict test for genotype→environment effects, however, offers a comparison of twin relationships. MZ and DZ twins are an experiment of nature, because they differ in the degree of genetic relatedness (i.e., 1 vs. .50), but not in how much they share environmental influences. Therefore, differences in their relationship qualities can be primarily attributed to gene→environment effects: In fact, in a recent study of twins over the adult life course MZ twins contacted each other more frequently, felt closer, and gave more support to each other as compared with DZ twins. Moreover, MZ twins reported that they lived at a closer distance to one another than DZ twins (Neyer, 2002a). Although twin relationships are unique and unrepresentative of the variety of relationships in general, these results highlight that gene→environment effects substantially contribute to interpersonal attraction.

Assumed Similarity

Although genetically unrelated relationship partners do not, in general, resemble each other very much with regard to personality traits, they usually believe themselves to be similar. The effect of assumed similarity, or projection, has been consistently shown in many studies on interpersonal perception, and is especially strong with regard to affective states, but also to enduring personality traits (e.g., Cronbach, 1955; Kenny, 1994; Kenny & Acitelli, 2001; Watson et al., 2000). In relationships with close relatives, whose personalities are similar for genetic reasons, perhaps with a degree of relatedness of 50% and more, the tendency to assume the other's personality as similar to oneself may provide a valid and useful heuristic strategy. This was shown in a study of dyadic perception between older twins (Neyer, Banse, & Asendorpf, 1999): In each domain of dyadic perception (i.e., the perception of the co-twin's emotional state, preference for emotional situations, and personality) the projection of the twins reached the level of the reliability of measures. Moreover, measures of projection and empathic accuracy were highly correlated, indicating that the accurate perception of the co-twin was in part achieved through projection. Further mediation analyses revealed that once the similarity of the twins in self-perception was controlled for, the levels of empathic accuracy substantially decreased. Therefore, the conclusion of this study was that in cases where dyad members resemble each other very much, as with genetically related twins, assuming similarity and projecting one's self-concept onto the partner serve as a valid heuristic that helps to improve the understanding of the other.

However, assumed similarity is invalid in dyadic perception between relationship partners whose personalities are not very similar, such as marital or romantic partners, or in friendship dyads. In these cases, the projection of one's self-concept onto the relationship partner will not improve accurate perception and the understanding of the other. Nevertheless, it seems unfair to ignore assumed similarity as a defective by-product of dyadic perception, because it is so common. For example, Watson et al. (2000) studied dyadic perception of personality traits in couples and friendship dyads, and found evidence of a high cross-situational consistency of assumed similarity, with especially high levels when self-other agreement was low. It is therefore useless to ask whether assumed similarity improves accuracy or leads to inaccuracy. Rather it seems reasonable to ask for the interpersonal function of assumed similarity in everyday life. For example, Thomas, Fletcher, and Lange (1997) showed in laboratory experiments on on-line empathic accuracy in romantic couples that the tendency to assume similarity was positively correlated with relationship satisfaction. This result was consistent with other findings on the benefits of assumed similarity, showing that, when in doubt, it may be adaptive to assume that the partner is experiencing thoughts and feelings similar to one's own (e.g., Acitelli, Douvan, & Veroff, 1993; Sillars, Pike, Jones, & Murphy, 1984).

PERSONALITY-RELATIONSHIP TRANSACTION OVER TIME

How do personality and relationships influence each other beyond initial assortment? Although from a naïve transactional perspective it would be reasonable to expect reciprocal influences in both directions, it was argued above that personality effects dominate over relationship effects, although new relationships potentially may induce personality change. These basic tenets refer to "normal" variation in personality and relationships, but not to clinical instances, and are now illustrated by empirical studies from the literature.

Personality Effects on Relationships

A plethora of studies has addressed personality effects on relationships, although rigorous cross-lagged panel designs were rarely realized. Asendorpf (2002) reviewed four areas of research that have provided evidence of personality effects. First, children's temperament and parents' personality influence the quality of infant-caregiver attachment (e.g., van Ijzendoorn, 1995). Second, childhood aggressiveness influences the quality of different relationships in childhood, adolescence, and adulthood (e.g., Coie, Dodge, & Kupersmidt, 1990; Hartup, 1996). Third, shyness has long-lasting effects on the quality and the number of relationships (e.g., Asendorpf & Wilpers, 1998). Finally, emotional instability has detrimental effects on both the stability and satisfaction of marital relationships (e.g., Kelly & Conley, 1987; Kurdek, 1993). The overwhelming evidence from these research lines is quite clear and supports the first rule of personality-relationship transaction outlined above. But until now only two studies have used the rigorous power of a cross-lagged panel design as depicted in Figure 12.1 to the full.

Asendorpf and Wilpers (1998) studied personality and relationship development of 132 young Berlin students aged 20 after entering university. Personality (Big Five traits including extraversion's sub-factors, shyness and sociability) and relationships were assessed up to 7 times over a period of 18 months. Social relationships were assessed using a personal network questionnaire covering a broad range of types of relationship (e.g., parents, siblings, friends, peers, etc.), and relationship qualities (e.g., support, conflict, contact, etc.). A clear pattern of personality relationship-transaction emerged: Once initial correlations between personality and relationships were controlled for, the personality traits influenced change in social relationships, but virtually no relationship effect on personality emerged. Specifically, extraversion, agreeableness, and conscientiousness predicted change in relationship characteristics, such as the number of peers, peer conflict, falling in love, and the development of relationships with the family of origin. Thus, despite the tremendous environmental changes during the transition to college (e.g., moving to a new city, new contacts, peers, and academic challenges), the personality of students was already so crystallized that it was insensitive to relationship influences.

Neyer and Asendorpf (2001) used the same methodology as Asendorpf and Wilpers and observed similar results with a general population sample of 489 young German adults who were assessed at ages 18–30 and

4 years later. Path analyses revealed again a clear dominance of personality effects over relationship effects. Specifically, extraversion, shyness, neuroticism, self-esteem, and agreeableness predicted change in various qualities of relationships. Interestingly, at the level of specific kinds of relationships, personality effects were exclusively limited to peer relationships (i.e., with friends and colleagues), while other relationships (e.g., with family members) were completely unaffected by personality effects. Whereas the general fit between personality and other relationships (e.g., with parents) might have been achieved earlier, peer relationships, especially work relationships, are newly, albeit not always deliberately, established when young adults enter the occupational world. It is often ignored that people spend more time with colleagues in professional contexts than with the family of origin, and perhaps even more than with romantic partners. This relatively new social context gave rise to personality effects shaping relationships usually located at the periphery of one's personal network.

Until now personality-relationship transactions have been rarely studied from the dyadic perspective outlined in Figure 12.2, and the few existing studies have been primarily concerned with romantic or marital relationships. Cross-sectional studies on these relationships have shown that neuroticism and negative emotionality not only predict one's own marital dissatisfaction (actor effect) but also dissatisfaction of partner (partner effect) (e.g., Eysenck & Wakefield, 1981; Karney et al., 1994; Robins et al., 2000). One recent study has followed the course of 168 newlywed marital couples over a period of 13 years (Caughlin et al., 2000): Initial trait anxiety was related to relationship satisfaction and interpersonal negativity assessed at the same time and three subsequent occasions using a telephone diary procedure. Trait anxiety of wives especially had enduring effects not only on their own negativity (actor effect) but also on husbands' negativity (partner effect). In turn, interpersonal negativity predicted later relationship dissatisfaction of the partner, showing that the link between trait anxiety and relationship dissatisfaction was in part mediated by interpersonal negativity. The study also gave some support to the idea that trait anxiety yielded direct actor and partner effects on marital dissatisfaction, independent of marital negativity. The authors concluded from this dyadic study that the disagreeable impact of trait anxiety was already evident at the outset of marriage, and stable over time. This conclusion was consistent with findings by Karney and Bradbury (1997), who followed 60 newlywed couples over a period of 4 years, and studied both intrapersonal processes and marital interactions as explanations of the link between neuroticism and marital dissatisfaction. Although a negative correlation was observed between neuroticism and dissatisfaction at the start of marriage, neuroticism did not predict longitudinal change in dissatisfaction. Instead, the initial marital interaction quality predicted change in marital dissatisfaction. Karney and Bradbury suggested from this that neuroticism influences dissatisfaction through intrapersonal processes that are not at all mediated by interpersonal behavior, although the latter uniquely predicted change in dissatisfaction.

Unfortunately, Caughlin et al. (2000) and Karney and Bradbury (1997), as well as other longitudinal studies on personality effects on marital stability and satisfaction (e.g., Kelly & Conley, 1987; Kurdek, 1993), measured personality only once at the beginning of marriage, because it was implicitly assumed that personality remained unchanged over time. Personality development, though, is not completed by age 30, and individual differences are still malleable until the sixth decade of life (Roberts & DelVecchio, 2000). Thus, it cannot be ruled out that interpersonal negativity or marital dissatisfaction might produce retroactive effects on trait anxiety or neuroticism of both partners. A final conclusion on the issue of personality versus relationship effects in marital relationships as well as in other types of relationships in adulthood is premature and awaits future studies that rigorously use cross-lagged panel designs following dyads from the very beginning of their relationship formation.

Relationship Effects on Personality

Social relationships influence personality in childhood and adolescence, although the traditional view of unidirectional effects from parent-child or peer relationships to children's personality is antiquated (e.g., Bell, 1968). Such naïve environmentalism has been overcome by behavior genetic research (among other research lines), which ironically has provided the most convincing evidence that environmental influences on personality are powerful: Nearly half of the variance in basic personality traits and characteristic adaptations is, of course, due to genetic variation, whereas the remaining variance is nearly completely due to unshared environmental variance (e.g., Loehlin, 1992; Plomin et al., 1997). Unshared environmental variance originates from unique experiences that are not shared by children within a family, making siblings within the same family dissimilar from one another. It is very likely that these unique experiences mostly take place in the context of personal relationships, such as unique social experiences with parents, siblings, and outside of the family context, especially with peers. It should be acknowledged, though, that these unique experiences may partly be driven by genetically influenced personality traits (i.e., genotype→environment effects), making it even more difficult to disentangle the causes of relationship and personality effects (Rowe, 1997).

A large body of research has addressed how relationship experiences affect personality development in childhood and adolescence. Important relationship effects include: parent-infant attachment and parental insensitivity in early childhood; escalating coercive parent-child interactions in childhood; peer rejection, peer acceptance, and number of peers in child-hood and adolescence. These and other relationship domains were shown to have substantive influences on children's and adolescents' personality and further development (see Hartup & Laursen, 1999; von Salisch, 2000, for a review). However, cause and effect are not always clearly distinguishable, because relationship experiences may in fact be due to preexisting differences in personality or temperament dispositions, as would be expected from the first rule of personality-relationship transaction.

Can social relationships change personality in adulthood where individual differences are already crystallized but still malleable? According to the second rule of personality-relationship transaction it is expected that new relationships may have the potential to induce personality change. Neyer and Asendorpf (2001) observed effects of two new relationships in young adulthood, one being with one's preschool-aged children, and the other pertaining to the developmental transition from being single to having a romantic partner for the first time. Whereas effects of children were related to the prediction of change in the rank order of personality traits, the effects of partners were related to the prediction of mean-level changes toward personality maturation.

Although personality effects clearly dominated over relationship effects in the Neyer and Asendorpf study, relationship experiences with one's preschool children predicted differential personality change. Specifically, conflict with children predicted later increases in extraversion, and perceived insecurity with children predicted later increases in neuroticism. Whereas the effect on neuroticism appears reasonable in light of the demanding challenges of having children who are experienced as difficult, the effect on extraversion was surprising. However, repeated constructive confrontations with children, as is normal in numerous parent-child relationships, could lead a parent to come out of his or her shell repeatedly, and thereby to become more extraverted. The child effects support again the long-standing observation that "socializing" effects in parent-child relationships are not necessarily unidirectional from parents to children (Bell, 1968).

The effects of partnership transition were also studied because it appeared in the first assessment of the Neyer and Asendorpf study that personality profiles differed strongly due to whether participants were in a partnership (Neyer, 1999): Singles reported lower levels of extraversion, conscientiousness, and self-esteem, and were higher in neuroticism and shyness as compared with participants in a partnership. Because this finding left open whether single status leads to this socially undesirable personality profile, or vice versa, personality development was compared longitudinally between "single continuers" (i.e., stable singles) and "relationship beginners" (i.e., former singles who had entered into a partnership in between). In addition to this test for the effect of the transition from being single to being in a partnership, a second comparison between "committed continuers" (i.e., participants in stable relationships with the same or other partner) and "discontinuers" (i.e., participants who returned to single status) enabled the effect of partnership dissolution to be tested. In fact, once initial individual differences in personality were controlled for, it appeared that relationship beginners had changed their personality, and reported increases in extraversion, self-esteem, and conscientiousness, and decreases in neuroticism and shyness, while single continuers, committed continuers, and discontinuers remained stable. In other words, the maturation of personality (i.e., decreases in neuroticism and increases in conscientiousness) was moderated by the transition to partnership, whereas partnership dissolution had no effect on personality change. This finding reveals an important environmental effect on personality change in adulthood, and argues against the purist view of intrinsic personality maturation suggested by McCrae et al. (1999, 2000). If both transitions are considered in terms of successive developmental stages, starting with being single, then initiating and maintaining a close relationship, and perhaps dissolving the relationship later on, these findings suggest that the developmental benefits one is gaining from a close relationship seem to be irreversible. However, this finding does not exclude the possibility that partnership dissolutions have short-term effects on personality traits, or long-term effects that will not be evident until later in life.

Costa, Herbst, McCrae, and Siegler (2000) studied personality and reactions to life events over a 7-year and 9-year period in a sample of 2,274 middle-aged adults (between 39 and 45 years at first assessment). Stability of the Big Five was higher than 60. Explorative data analyses revealed that divorce and (re-)marriage had different effects on personality change in men and women: Extraversion and openness increased in women after divorce relative to married women, whereas men showed increases in a facet of neuroticism, depression, and decreases in facets of conscientiousness (e.g., competence, self-discipline). In contrast, men who had married decreased in neuroticism. Thus, in contrast with men, women even seemed to benefit from divorce, at least regarding their personality. These findings of Costa et al. (2000) are explorative because they did not control for pre-selection effects (e.g., for initial differences between comparison groups).

Taken together, the results of Neyer and Asendorpf (2001) and Costa et al. (2000) indicate that even basic tendencies are not immune against environmental influences such as important relationship transitions, and generally speak for a contextual rather than an essentialist model of personality development. Partnership transitions such as constitution and dissolution may have different meanings and consequences at different stages of the adult life course, depending on future perspectives and other pursued life goals.

CONCLUSIONS AND FUTURE DIRECTIONS

The consideration of dyadic fits and long-term transactions between personality and relationships leads to four major conclusions with strong implications for future research. Although it is fashionable to assume balanced reciprocal transactions between personality and relationships in each direction, empirical evidence and theoretical assumptions lead to the conclusion of two basic rules of personality-relationship transaction: First, at least since childhood, personality effects are more powerful than relationship effects. Second, only new significant relationships that are involved in major developmental transitions have the potential to bring about personality change. Because these major conclusions were drawn from studies in young adulthood (e.g., Asendorpf & Wilpers, 1998; Neyer & Asendorpf, 2001), the first requirement for future research is the study of personality-relationship transaction at other stages of the adult life course involving transitions like the loss of parents, the empty nest, retirement, and others.

Second, the interplay between personality and relationships has to be viewed from a dynamic transactional perspective that moves beyond unidirectional and individualistic views on personality and relationships by assuming that dyadic relationships are among the most central settings where interactions between the individual and the environment occur. The empirical study of personality-relationship transaction is costly in terms of time and methodology. The second requirement for future research is to include both longitudinal cross-lagged panel and dyadic designs, thus doing justice to both individual traits and dyadic relationships.

Whereas during the last two decades personality psychology has successfully proceeded in gaining knowledge about the origins of individual differences and the development of personality over the life course, it is my impression that the field of personal relationships is more diverse but lacks sufficient knowledge on the emergence, stability, and change of various relationships and their qualities. For example, to date no meta-analytic study or comparative review has addressed stability and change of different relationship qualities across various kinds of relationships. The third requirement therefore pertains to the comparative study of relationship stability and change.

Comparative knowledge on relationship stability and change could complement the growing knowledge on personality development, and help further the understanding of the domain specificity, relationship specificity, and age specificity of personality-relationship transactions. Because it seems reasonable to expect that certain domains of personality interact with specific types of relationships differently at various ages, the fourth requirement is to systematically address the specificities of transaction. If future research meets at least a few of these requirements, the study of personality-relationship transaction will become an exciting adventure, perhaps even with surprising and unexpected findings.

References

Acitelli, L. A., Douvan, E., & Veroff, J. (1993). Perceptions on conflict in the first year of marriage: How important are similarity and understanding? *Journal of Social and Personal Relationships, 10,* 5–19.

Aldwin, C. M., & Levenson, M. R. (1994). Aging and personality assessment. In M. P. Lawton & J. A. Teresi (Eds.), *Annual review of gerontology and geriatrics: Focus on assessment* (pp. 182–209). New York: Springer.

Allport, G. W. (1961). *Pattern and growth in personality.* New York Holt, Rinehart, & Winston.

Asendorpf, J. B. (2002). Personality effects on personal relationships over the life span. In A. L. Vangelisti, H. T. Reis, & M. A. Fitzpatrick (Eds.), *Stability and change in relationships* (pp. 35–56). Cambridge, UK: Cambridge University Press.

Asendorpf, J. B., & van Aken, M. A. G. (1991). Correlates of temporal consistency of personality patterns in childhood. *Journal of Personality, 59,* 689–703.

Asendorpf, J. B., & Wilpers, S. (1998). Personality effects on social relationships. *Journal of Personality and Social Psychology, 74,* 1531–1544.

Bell, R. Q. (1968). A reinterpretation of the direction of effects in studies of socialization. *Psychological Review, 22,* 595–603.

Berscheid, E., & Reis, H. T. (1998). Attraction in close relationships. In D. T. Gilbert, S. T. Fiske, & G. Lindzey (Eds.), *The handbook of social psychology* (4th ed., Vol. 2, pp. 193–281). New York: McGraw-Hill.

Blieszner, R., & Adams, R. G. (1992). *Adult friendships.* Newbury Park: Sage Publications.

Buss, D. M. (1984). Marital assortment for personality dispositions: Assessment with three different data systems. *Behavior Genetics, 14,* 111–123.

Buss, D. M. (1987). Selection, evocation, and manipulation. *Journal of Personality and Social Psychology, 53,* 1214–1221.

Campbell, D. T., & Kenny, D. A. (1999). *A primer on regression artifacts.* New York, London: The Guilford Press.

Caspi, A. (1998). Personality development across the life course. In W. Damon & N. Eisenberg (Eds.), *Handbook of child psychology: Vol. 3. Social, emotional, and personality development* (pp. 311–388). New York: Wiley.

Caspi, A. (2000). The child is the father of the man. Personality continuities from childhood to adulthood. *Journal of Personality and Social Psychology, 78,* 158–172.

Caspi, A., Herbener, E. S., & Ozer, D. J. (1992). Shared experiences and the similarity of personality. *Journal of Personality and Social Psychology, 62,* 281–291.

Caspi, A., & Moffitt, T. E. (1993). When do individual differences matter? A paradoxical theory of personality coherence. *Psychological Inquiry, 4,* 247–271.

Caspi, A., & Roberts, B. W. (1999). Personality continuity and change across the life course. In L. Pervin & O. P. John (Eds.), *Handbook of personality* (2nd ed., pp. 300–326). New York: Guilford Press.

Caspi, A., & Silva, P. A. (1995). Temperament qualities at age 3 predict personality traits in young adults: Longitudinal evidence from a birth cohort. *Child Development, 66,* 486–498.

Caughlin, J. P., Huston, T. L., & Houts, R. M. (2000). How does personality matter in marriage? An examination of trait anxiety, interpersonal negativity, and marital satisfaction. *Journal of Personality and Social Psychology, 78,* 326–336.

Cicirelli, V. G. (1995). *Sibling relationships across the life-span.* New York: Plenum Publishing.

Coie, J. D., Dodge, K. H., & Kupersmidt, J. B. (1990). Peer group behavior and social status. In S. R. Asher & J. D. Coie (Eds.), *Peer rejection in childhood* (pp. 17–59). Cambridge, UK: Cambridge University Press.

Conley, J. J. (1984). The hierarchy of consistency: A review and model of longitudinal findings on adult individual differences in intelligence, personality, and self-opinion. *Personality and Individual Differences, 5,* 11–26.

Costa, P. T., Herbst, J. H., McCrae, R. R., & Siegler, I. C. (2000). Personality at midlife: Stability, intrinsic maturation, and response to life events. *Assessment, 7,* 365–378.

Costa, P. T. Jr., & McCrae, R. R. (1994). Set like plaster? Evidence for the stability of adult personality. In T. F. Heatherton & J. L. Weinberger (Eds.), *Can personality change?* (pp. 21–40). Washington, D.C.: American Psychological Association.

Cronbach, L. J. (1955). Processes affecting scores on "understanding of others" and "assumed similarity." *Psychological Bulletin, 52,* 177–193.

Daly, M., Salmon, C., & Wilson, M. (1997). Kinship: The conceptual hole in psychological studies of social cognition and close relationships. In J. Simpson & P. T. Kenrick (Eds.), Evolutionary psychology (pp. 265–296). Mahwah, NJ: Erlbaum.

Duck, S. (1975). Personality similarity and friendship choices by adolescents. *European Journal of Social Psychology, 5,* 351–365.

Eysenck, H. J., & Wakefield, J. A., Jr. (1981). Psychological factors as predictors of marital satisfaction. *Advances in Behavior Research and Therapy, 3,* 151–191.

Funder, D. C., Kolar, D. C., & Blackman, M. C. (1995). Agreement among judges of personality. Interpersonal relations, similarity, and acquaintanceship. *Journal of Personality and Social Psychology, 69,* 656–672.

Gonzalez, R., & Griffin, D. (1997). On the statistics of interdependence: Treating dyadic data with respect. In S. Duck (Ed.), *Handbook of personal relationships.* (2nd ed.) (pp. 271–302). Chichester, UK: Wiley.

Griffin, D., & Gonzalez, R. (1995). The correlational analysis of dyad-level data: Models for the exchangeable case. *Psychological Bulletin, 118,* 430–439.

Gruber-Baldini, A. L., Schaie, K. W., & Willis, S. L. (1995). Similarity in married couples: A longitudinal study of mental abilities and rigidity-flexibility. *Journal of Personality and Social Psychology, 69,* 191–203.

Haan, N., Millsap, R., & Hartka, E. (1986). As time goes by: Change and stability in personality over fifty years. *Psychology and Aging, 1,* 220–232.

Hamilton, W. D. (1964). The genetic evolution of social behavior. *Journal of Theoretical Biology, 7,* 1–52.

Hartup, W. W. (1996). The company they keep: Friendships and their developmental significance. *Child Development, 67,* 1–13.

Hartup, W. W., & Laursen, B. (1999). Relationships as developmental contexts. *Minnesota Symposia on Child Psychology, 30,* 13–35.

Helson, R., & Moane, G. (1987). Personality change in women from college to midlife. *Journal of Personality and Social Psychology, 53*, 176–186.

Jankowiak, W., & Diderich, M. (2000). Sibling solidarity in a polygamous community in the USA: Unpacking inclusive fitness. *Evolution and Human Behavior, 21*, 125–139.

Karney, B. R., & Bradbury, T. N. (1997). Neuroticism, marital interaction, and the trajectory of marital satisfaction. *Journal of Personality and Social Psychology, 72*, 1075–1092.

Karney, B. R., Bradbury, T. N., Fincham, F. D., & Sullivan, K. T. (1994). The role of negative affectivity in the association between attributions and marital satisfaction. *Journal of Personality and Social Psychology, 66*, 413–424.

Kelly, E. L., & Conley, J. J. (1987). Personality and compatibility: A prospective analysis of marital stability and marital satisfaction. *Journal of Personality and Social Psychology, 52*, 27–40.

Kenny, D. A. (1994). *Interpersonal perception: A social relations analysis.* New York, London: The Guilford Press.

Kenny, D. A. (1996). Models of non-independence in dyadic research. *Journal of Social and Personal Relationships, 13*, 279–294.

Kenny, D. A., & Acitelli, L. (2001). Accuracy and bias in the perception of the partner in a close relationship. *Journal of Personality and Social Psychology, 80*, 439–448.

Kurdek, L. A. (1993). Predicting marital dissolution: A 5-year prospective longitudinal study on newlywed couples. *Journal of Personality and Social Psychology, 64*, 221–242.

Lang, F. R. (2000). Endings and continuity of social relationships: Maximizing intrinsic benefits within personal networks when feeling near to death. *Journal of Social and Personal Relationships, 17*, 155–182.

Lang, F. R., & Carstensen, L. L. (1998). Social relationships and adaptation in late life. In A. S. Bellak & M. Hersen (Eds.), *Comprehensive clinical psychology* (Vol. 7, pp. 55–72). Oxford, UK: Pergamon Press.

Loehlin, J. C. (1992). *Genes and environment in personality development.* Newbury Park, CA: Sage.

Lykken, D. T., & Tellegen, A. (1993). Is human mating adventitious or the result of lawful choice? A twin study of mate selection. *Journal of Personality and Social Psychology, 65*, 56–68.

Magnusson, D. (1990). Personality development from an interactional perspective. In L. Pervin (Ed.), *Handbook of personality: Theory and measurement* (pp. 193–22). New York: Guilford Press.

McCrae, R. (1996). Social consequences of experiential openness. *Psychological Bulletin, 120*, 323–337.

McCrae, R. R., & Costa, P. T. Jr. (1996). Toward a new generation of personality theories: Theoretical contexts of the five-factor model. In J. S. Wiggins (Ed.), *The five-factor model of personality: Theoretical perspectives* (pp. 51–87). New York: Guilford Press.

McCrae, R. R., & Costa, P. T. Jr. (1999). A five-factor theory of personality. In L. Pervin & O. P. John (Eds.), *Handbook of personality* (2nd ed., pp. 139–153). New York: Guilford Press.

McCrae, R. R., Costa, P. T. Jr., Lima, M. P., Simoes, A., Ostendorf, F., Angleitner, A., Marusic, I., Bratko, D., Caprara, G. V., Barbaranelli, C., Chae, J. H., & Piedmont, R. L. (1999). Age differences in personality across the adult life span: Parallels in five cultures. *Developmental Psychology, 35,* 466–477.

McCrae, R. R., Costa, P. T. Jr., Ostendorf, F., Angleitner, A., Hrebickova, M., Avia, M. D., Sanz, J., Sanchez-Bernardoz, M. L., Kusdul, M. E., Woodfield, R., Saunders, P. R., & Smith, P. B. (2000). Nature over nurture: Temperament, personality, and life span development. *Journal of Personality and Social Psychology, 78,* 173–186.

McGue, M., Bacon, S., & Lykken, D. T. (1993). Personality stability and change in early adulthood: A behavioral genetic analysis. *Developmental Psychology, 29,* 96–109.

Neyer, F. J. (1999). Die Persönlichkeit junger Erwachsener in unterschiedlichen Lebensformen [The personality of young adults with different life patterns]. *Kölner Zeitschrift für Soziologie und Sozialpsychologie, 51,* 491–508.

Neyer, F. J. (2002a). Twin relationships in old age: A developmental perspective. *Journal of Social and Personal Relationships, 19,* 155–177.

Neyer, F. J. (2002b). The dyadic interdependence of attachment security and dependency: A conceptual replication across older twins and younger couples. *Journal of Social and Personal Relationships, 19,* 483–504.

Neyer, F. J., & Asendorpf, J. B. (2001). Personality-relationship transaction in young adulthood. *Journal of Personality and Social Psychology, 81,* 1190–1204.

Neyer, F. J., Banse, R., & Asendorpf, J. B. (1999). The role of projection and empathic accuracy in dyadic perception between older twins. *Journal of Social and Personal Relationships, 16,* 419–422.

Neyer, F. J., & Lang, F. R. (2003). Blood is thicker than water: Kinship orientation across adulthood. *Journal of Personality and Social Psychology, 84,* 310–321.

Plomin, R., DeFries, J., & Loehlin, J. C. (1977). Genotype-environment interaction and correlation in the analysis of human behavior. *Psychological Bulletin, 84,* 309–322.

Plomin, R., DeFries, J. C., McClearn, G. E., & Rutter, M. (1997).*Behavioral genetics* (3rd ed.). New York: W. H. Freeman.

Roberts, B. T., Caspi, A., & Moffitt, T. E. (2001). The kids are alright: Growth and stability in personality development from adolescence to adulthood. *Journal of Personality and Social Psychology, 81,* 670–683.

Roberts, B. T., & DelVecchio, W. F. (2000). The rank-order consistency of personality traits from childhood to old age: A quantitative review of longitudinal studies. *Psychological Bulletin, 126,* 3–25.

Robins, R. W., Caspi, A., & Moffitt, T. E. (2000). Two personalities, one relationship: Both partners' personality traits shape the quality of their relationship. *Journal of Personality and Social Psychology, 79,* 251–259.

Rogosa, D. (1980). A critique of cross-lagged correlation. *Psychological Bulletin, 88,* 245–258.

Rogosa, D. (1988). Myths about longitudinal research. In K. W. Schaie, R. T. Campbell, & W. Meredith (Eds.), *Methodological issues in aging research* (pp. 171–209). New York: Springer.

Rowe, D. (1997). *The limits of family influences: Genes, experiences, and behavior.* New York: The Guilford Press.

316   F. J. Neyer

Salisch, M. von (2000). The emotional side of sharing, social support, and conflict negotiation between siblings and between friends. In R. Mills & S. Duck (Eds.), *Developmental psychology of personal relationships* (pp 49–69). Chichester, UK: Wiley.

Sameroff, A. J. (1983). Developmental systems: Contexts and evolution. In W. Kessen (Ed.), Handbook of child psychology. Vol.1, History, theory, and methods (4th ed.) (pp. 237–294). New York: Wiley.

Scarr, S., & McCartney, K. (1983). How people make their own environment: A theory of genotype-environment effects. *Child Development, 54,* 424–435.

Shiner, R. L. (1998). How shall we speak of children's personalities in middle childhood? A preliminary taxonomy. *Psychological Bulletin, 124,* 308–332.

Sillars, A. L., Pike, G. R., Jones, T. J., & Murphy, M. A. (1984). Communication and understanding in marriage. *Human Communication Research, 10,* 317–350.

Thomas, G., Fletcher, G. O., & Lange, C. (1997). On-line empathic accuracy in marital interaction. *Journal of Personality and Social Psychology, 72,* 839–850.

van Ijzendoorn, M. H. (1995). Adult attachment representations, parental responsiveness, and infant attachment: A meta-analysis on the predictive validity of the adult attachment interview. *Psychological Bulletin, 117,* 387–403.

Wachs, T. D. (1994). Fit, context, and the transition between temperament and personality. In C. F. Halverson, Jr., G. A. Kohnstamm, & R. P. Martin (Eds.), *The developing structure of temperament and personality from infancy to adulthood* (pp. 209–220). Hillsdale, NJ: Erlbaum.

Watson, D., Hubbard, B., & Wiese, D. (2000). Self-other agreement in personality and affectivity: The role of acquaintanceship, trait visibility, and assumed similarity. *Journal of Personality and Social Psychology, 78,* 546–558.

White, L. K., & Riedmann, A. (1992). When the Brady Bunch grows up: Step/half and full sibling relationships in adulthood. *Journal of Marriage and the Family, 54,* 197–208.

13

Relational Competence across the Life Span

Robert O. Hansson, Eric L. Daleiden,
and Bert Hayslip, Jr.

Important personal relationships can at times become stressed, conflicted, unpredictable, and a poor fit to our needs. At such times, adaptation depends largely on one's ability to successfully access, initiate, develop, and maintain support relationships. The chapter describes the theoretical and empirical efforts that led to the formulation of a two-component model of "relational competence," emphasizing competencies and perspectives relevant to the initiation and enhancement of relationships. We examine developmental processes characteristic of populations ranging in age from infancy to late life, with an eye to (a) the nature and development of relational competence, (b) links to early developmental phenomena such as temperament, attachment, and self-concept, and to (c) psychological processes in adulthood such as hardiness, resilience, and adaptation to dependency.

From the beginning, relationships shape and influence our lives. They provide nurturance, security, support, and companionship. They are our inspiration, our links to the broader social world, and the contexts for our emotional and cognitive development.

Yet the nature and composition of our relationships and the functions they serve tend to change across the life span. Unfortunately, personal relationships can also become problematic. At each phase of development, important peer, friendship, and support relationships can become stressed, conflicted, overwhelmed, unpredictable, and a "poor fit" to one's needs. Our personal and support relationships cannot, therefore, always be taken for granted. Such events present complex adaptive challenges for those in need of a support network, and the ability to successfully cope with these "relational challenges" varies considerably across individuals.

In this context, the concept of relational competence was proposed to encompass those characteristics and social competencies that enable a person to successfully access, initiate, develop, and maintain relationships important to support and well-being (Hansson & Carpenter, 1994; Hansson,

Jones, & Carpenter, 1984). In the first section of this chapter, we will briefly introduce the construct of relational competence and the kinds of research it has generated. In keeping with the intent of the present volume, however, the main thrust of the rest of the chapter will be to explore the functions and processes of relational competence more broadly, within a life-span framework.

A person's relational competencies are thought to reflect continuity of disposition, skills and perspectives acquired in early life, and developmental adaptations to normative and nonnormative life events. By old age, they should also reflect a lifetime of experience, and (for better or for worse) the emergence of fairly well established patterns of cognitive style, motivation, and emotion regulation. Diversity of experience, learning, personality, and maturation will have exerted considerable influence. Stable individual differences in relational competence would be expected, with some older adults quite successfully managing the social transitions of their lives and some not. Among younger persons, however, the influence of experience, learning, and maturation should be less developed. In nonsupportive or discordant social environments, some children would therefore be expected to be at risk for poor outcome. In this context, developing relational skills and emotional competencies could make a difference in a child's ability to adapt.

The construct of relational competence involves a number of assumptions: (a) successful adaptation to changing or stressful life circumstances can be greatly enhanced by the support of others; (b) our natural family, friendship, and community support networks are usually a reliable resource in this connection; (c) such relationships, however, can often become complex, problematic, overburdened, and an ineffective match to the individual's needs; (d) among certain groups of persons (e.g., children, ill or disabled persons, or the elderly) who may experience more complex, progressive, and long-term needs for assistance and security, relational networks are more likely to become overwhelmed, problematic, and ineffective; (e) some potential care recipients may therefore find it difficult to access or benefit from effective support relationships; and (f) a recurring interpersonal issue throughout the life span will involve one's ability to manage such social transition, an ability that will reflect individual differences.

It is useful at the outset to identify some core tasks of relating in such interpersonal contexts. These can be construed as the need to access, initiate, develop, and maintain supportive relationships under changing and difficult conditions. Such tasks are particularly important among the elderly (Hansson & Carpenter, 1994), who typically experience a growing dependency on support relationships, which can become more burdened, unpredictable, and formal over time. A broader view, however, suggests similar possibilities at critical points throughout the life span.

That individual differences would play a role in this process is consistent with Lawton and Simon's (1968) widely supported "environmental docility" theorem, which holds that persons of diminished competence (in terms of age, health, psychological or social competence) should have a narrower range of adaptability to decreasingly supportive environments, including one's interpersonal environment. Persons of diminished competence, thus construed, have consistently been found to be less able to accommodate to an environment (in the present instance, one's social or caregiving relationships) that has become a "poor fit" to current needs. The consequences of such a situation would likely include the potential for breakdown of informal caregiving and an increasing need for institutionalization. Some persons, however, would be expected to be more successful than others in managing these difficult social transitions. It is therefore important to focus on individual differences in social skills, cognitive and affective dispositions, or characteristics that might make a difference. In the sections that follow, we describe a two-component model of relational competence, and consider how these components might influence social process from early to later life.

THE TWO-COMPONENT MODEL OF RELATIONAL COMPETENCE

Research on a variety of subject populations (ranging in age from college students to older adults) led Carpenter (1987) to propose a two-component model of relational competence that broadly sampled the important competency domains. The first component of this model is termed *initiation*. This component includes characteristics and skills that should make it easier for an individual to make necessary demands on existing support networks, initiate new personal relationships as a basis of support, and assert a degree of control over the direction a relationship takes. Characteristics in this component of the model, then, might include assertiveness, self-confidence, extraversion, and well-developed communication skills. These kinds of skills should be especially useful when a person's natural family or friendship support networks have become overwhelmed, lost important members, or suffered other disruptions.

The second component of the model is termed *enhancement*. The skills and attributes included in this component are those that should be useful in maintaining, nurturing, and enhancing the personal relationships on which social or caregiver support may depend. Such skills might include flexibility, empathy, friendliness, likability, and the ability to find ways to make the relationship rewarding for the caregiver or members of one's support network. To the extent that many dependency situations are intense and long-term (e.g., childhood, illness, disability, or age-related decline), these skills should serve an important function.

Our understanding of relational competence was advanced considerably by early psychometric research on the construct. Carpenter (1987,
1993) developed the Relational Competence Scale (RCS) to assess individuals on the characteristics proposed to fall into the two domains of relational competence. In the RCS, five personal attributes are assessed which
broadly sample relational competencies within the *initiation* domain. These
include (lack of) shyness, (lack of) social anxiety, dominance, assertiveness,
and instrumental competence. Five personal attributes are also assessed
which broadly sample relational competencies within the *enhancement* domain. These include *interpersonal sensitivity, intimacy, trust, altruism, and
perspective taking*.

The two-component model, then, provided an organizing structure for
thinking about the diverse relational competencies that might (a) contribute either to the initiation or development of personal/support relationships, and those that (b) maintain and nurture them. Psychometric work with the RCS demonstrated that scores on the subscales within
each of the components are substantially intercorrelated. However, overall scores on the initiation and enhancement domains are only slightly
related.

In the last two decades, considerable research has focused on many of
the attributes associated with relational competence (see Adkins, Martin,
& Poon, 1996 ; Carpenter, 1993 ; & Hansson & Carpenter, 1994, for reviews
of this research). In most instances, these attributes tend to be associated
with more competent and more satisfying relational functioning. For example, lower scores on the attributes associated with the initiation component are related to less frequent social participation, less active, assertive,
and effective communication styles, increased loneliness, reports of fewer
friends, and unduly negative and suspicious attributions to other persons
who might have been cultivated as friends or supporters. Among elderly
persons, they have been associated with fear of crime and perceptions that
help from others in the community will be unavailable if needed. Similarly,
among older people, initiation characteristics predict level of anxiety over
approaching retirement, and level of comfort with community support
services.

Studies also suggest support for the relevance of enhancement-related
attributes to successful relationships (see reviews in Carpenter, 1993 ;
Hansson & Carpenter, 1994). Enhancement attributes are, for example, related to satisfaction with friends, marital satisfaction, and to increased trust
in forming workplace relationships.

Persons scoring higher on both the initiation and enhancement domains
of the RCS have been found to have greater confidence in the coping resources they have available for dealing with a stressful situation. RCS scores
are also related positively to self-esteem in a wide range of populations,
and negatively to neuroticism. Alcoholics and psychiatric patients tend to

score lower on relational competence (especially on the initiation-related attributes) than do individuals in the general population (Carpenter, 1993).

DEVELOPMENTAL ISSUES IN RELATIONAL COMPETENCE

Early research on relational competence focused on adults. However, related issues have long been of interest to developmental psychologists studying the life span (from infancy to old age). Given the goals of the present volume, we will broaden the focus of our discussion of relational competence and the two-component model to consider its application to the entire life span, from infancy to old age. As a general framework, we will adopt a theoretically based, organizational approach to development.

Theoretically based approaches to developmental adjustment (e.g., Cicchetti & Cohen, 1995) often describe development as oriented toward age- or stage-specific developmental tasks. Humans are thought to be active agents in their development and to construct an increasingly differentiated but hierarchically integrated and organized set of capacities for adjusting to the world. Adaptive behaviors are those that focus on achieving relevant developmental tasks. Maladaptive behaviors, in contrast, interfere with developmental task completion. Within this perspective, competence is defined as the successful negotiation of developmental tasks. At any given point, growth is constrained by previous development. Thus, competence tends to beget competence and the failure to develop competence places an individual at increased risk for difficult adjustment to subsequent developmental adaptational challenges.

Adopting a life-span perspective on relational competence requires an assumption that there is sufficient continuity to discuss the relevant skills as a coherent construct. Adequate theory must specify whether developmental continuity is expected at the level of specific behaviors or broader patterns of adaptation to age- or stage-specific developmental tasks (Garber & Strassberg, 1991). The organizational perspective on development expects that continuity at the level of molecular behaviors is unlikely (e.g., Cicchetti & Schneider-Rosen, 1986). Accordingly, we expect that the specific behaviors emitted by a relationally competent four-year-old to initiate social interchange with peers in a playroom are not likely to be the same as an adult in that playroom. For example, the child might hold a colorful toy in the visual field of a peer to initiate associative play, whereas the adult may listen to an ongoing conversation and then gradually interject relevant verbal comments. Despite differences in molecular behavior, both the child and adult are demonstrating competent relational initiation. This example illustrates how the construct of relational competence may show sufficient continuity across the life span to be a useful developmental notion.

Given the assumption of meaningful continuity for the relational competence construct, the burden of elaborating an organizational developmental theory falls on specifying characteristic points of reorganization, factors influencing such reorganization, and an account of the role of relational competence in predicting adjustment at each step in the process of reorganization. We will discuss two primary periods of reorganization in the development of relational competence in childhood (i.e., the interaction of temperament and parenting in the development of attachment style, and the interaction of attachment style with broader social influences in the child's formation of a more stable skill set and self-concept regarding relational competence). We also discuss our expectation that the role of relational competence in adjustment will change from one of mediation to one of moderation (see Fig. 13.1 for an overview).

Reorganizations in the Development of Relational Competence

Relational competence in adulthood is viewed to reflect an interaction of personality and social experience. A variety of theoretical perspectives have highlighted stabilities in child temperament as the root of adult personality (cf. Roberts & DelVecchio, 2000), and thus nominate temperament as a starting point for a developmental theory of relational competence. Temperament identifies a set of individual differences variables

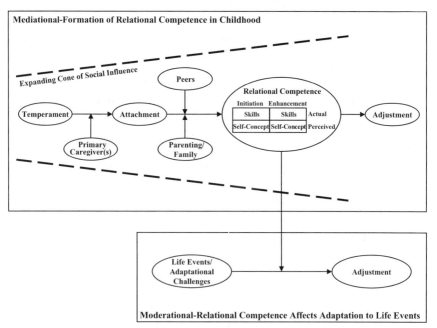

FIGURE 13.1. Mediational – Formation of Relational Competence in Childhood.

(e.g., distress proneness, behavioral inhibition, approach, activity, and persistence; cf. Rothbart & Mauro, 1990) that are thought to be present at or near birth. Among the most salient aspects of the child's social experience during the first year of life are exchanges with a primary caregiver. As a result of such interaction, the first major organization to the child's relational world occurs in the form of an attachment style. As part of the attachment process, children are thought to form "internal working models" of the social world, which are sets of expectancies that guide their subsequent relational behavior (Bowlby, 1973).

Increasing evidence has been emerging that individual differences in temperament interact with the caregiving relationship in the development of children's attachment. For example, Van den Boom (1989) found that the temperamental dimension of distress proneness at age 15 days was related to an increased likelihood of the child receiving an avoidant attachment classification at age 12 months. Analysis of parent-child observations revealed that the mothers of distress-prone infants tended to increasingly ignore and engage in less positive play with their infants over time. Therefore, Van den Boom (1989) investigated the effects of a maternal training program that taught mothers to persist in soothing and playing with their distress-prone six-month-old infants. Relative to control participants, the experimental group demonstrated more positive and less negative parent-child interactions. Children in the experimental group engaged in more exploratory play and were less likely to be classified in the avoidant attachment group at age 12 months.

In a related vein, Kagan (1994) reviewed evidence that some infants inherit a high level of biological reactivity and commonly respond to unfamiliar events with excessive motor activity and crying. Kagan suggested that as this predisposition interacts with social experience the majority of such children will respond to novelty by freezing, fretting, and withdrawing and thus may be classified as behaviorally inhibited. As these children mature, their social environment assumes increasing importance, such that environmental factors (e.g., parent behaviors that encourage children's behavioral approach to novelty) may moderate the ongoing expression of this inhibited behavioral style. In addition to such environmental factors, Kagan argues that once inhibited children become self-aware, some deliberately try not to be afraid and some are successful in changing their behavioral style. This latter example highlights the possibility of a second reorganization to the child's relational competence that coincides with elaboration of self-awareness and self-concept through childhood to seven-eight years of age.

As children age, their social world commonly expands to include more exchanges with other family members, peers, and the broader community. These social experiences involve increasing demands for relating in both individual and social group situations. Equipped with their temperamental tendencies and their attachment style, children interact with the social world to develop more stable and generalized self-concepts (cf. Harter, 1986). The elaboration of self-concept and self-awareness supports the possibility of a discrepancy between a child's perceived and actual competence. Perceived relational competence involves children's expectancies and judgments about their capacity to initiate and maintain relationships. Actual relational competence refers to the child's skills and abilities to successfully initiate and maintain relationships.

Discrepancies between perceived and actual competence have been found to be important predictors of adjustment in other contexts. For example, Weisz, Rudolph, Granger, and Sweeney (1992) noted that there are developmental differences in the association between perceived and actual competence such that the correlation between perceived and actual academic competence in children increases from first or second grade to sixth grade, but that for those children who change schools around seventh grade this correlation drops again. Moreover, Cole (1990) found that not only did depressed children underestimate their academic competence compared to their peers and teachers, but also that the tendency to do so significantly predicted depression.

With respect to relational competence, the two factors of initiation and enhancement may interact with perceived and actual competence. Due to its anticipatory nature, perceived competence may be a better predictor of whether individuals engage in initiation-related behaviors. Anxious apprehension and low self-efficacy regarding successful relational initiation may prevent individuals from even attempting to initiate relational behaviors despite the fact that if relational initiation were attempted, the individual might successfully achieve relational goals due to sufficient skills. Alternatively, once relationships are initiated, perceived enhancement skills may be less influential than actual competence at relational enhancement. In other words, the social world may respond more to competent performance of relational behaviors than to self-perceptions of relational competence.

Through adolescence and young adulthood, the social world and friendships of youth develop along a variety of avenues. For example, friendships become increasingly centered on intimacy, loyalty, and exclusivity (cf. Damon, 1977). The type of relationship with the strongest influence on behavior evolves from the family of origin to peers to romantic relationships. Relationships tend to be more enduring and individuals tend to increasingly differentiate their view of social relationships into more precise categories, such as best friend, close friends, coworkers, neighbors, acquaintances, strangers, etc. (Berndt, 1996). These years are also characterized by a host of intraindividual changes such as increasing emotional competence, the development of formal cognitive operations, the crystallization of an identity, and further stabilization of personality traits. These changes present youth with a variety of adaptational challenges, and we expect continued evolution in one's relational behaviors, but not fundamental reorganization in their relational competence. We expect that the basic components of relational competence should be established by middle childhood and that its role in adaptation may change from a mediator to a moderator of life events.

Given their early history, youth enter adolescence with an established pattern and self-concept of their relational competence. As they face their rapidly expanding social world and confront the diversity of new relationship structures, they do so with an organized pattern of relational responding. This organization of relational competence provides the youth with a "default" response style when faced with adaptational challenges. As Neyer (chap.12, this volume) notes, over time, the effect of preestablished individual differences on relationships tends to be more powerful than the effect of relationships on such individual differences. Accordingly, adolescents are expected to select and shape their relationships to provide a "goodness of fit" to their established relational style. Nevertheless, an individual's specific social behaviors are also continually shaped through interactions within any given relationship. Therefore, an individual's behaviors within a particular relationship are expected to have relationship-specific characteristics in addition to reflecting general relational competence. Again, variability in molecular behavior is expected but molar reorganization is not.

Through adolescence and young adulthood, individuals will continue to develop more sophisticated relational skills, social-cognitive information-processing systems, and emotional competence. Relationally competent individuals should be more adept at adapting to changing social circumstances by readily acquiring these skills. Relationally competent individuals are also expected to successfully modulate their relational behaviors to achieve relevant developmental tasks, such as distancing from their family of origin and increasing their interactions with peers and coworkers during adolescence and forming romantic relationship(s) in late adolescence and young adulthood.

During adolescence and young adulthood, individuals may actively apply their relational skills to assemble "convoys of support" (Kahn & Antonucci, 1980) that follow them through separation from home and establishment of adult lives. Formation of these convoys places a premium on relational initiation skills to expand their size. However, enhancement skills are likely tantamount to maintaining these convoys through major life transitions such as changing schools, leaving home, entering a career, and marrying. Indeed, it appears that a friendship may only attenuate the effect of a negative life event on youth if that friendship survives the stressor (Parker et al., 1995).

Developmental Challenges to Relational Competence

The general pattern of competence begetting competence may be disrupted in childhood. Shapiro (1995) has argued that there is an "increasing cone" of social influence moving from the primary caretaker to the parenting dyad, to family, friends, school, teachers, employers, etc., as children get older. Thus, for younger children, parenting may be a more powerful influence on relational competence because of the relative centrality of parents in children's social environment and because parents may play a larger role as "gatekeepers" in children's exposure to other social influences. For older children and adolescents, parenting behaviors may have relatively less impact on children due to increased diffusion of social influence and increased child autonomy from the family environment.

Also, Patterson, Reid, and Dishion (1992) have discussed the concept of "limited shopping" to describe the increasing deviancy of antisocial boys' social environments. The limited shopping notion suggests that abrasive interactions between a child and the social environment lead to dyadic avoidance that becomes more pronounced over the years. This relational avoidance results in an accumulation of missed opportunities for corrective experiences. Meanwhile, the expanding cone of social influence is presenting peers with a variety of new social contexts for skill development and practice. Although Patterson et al. (1992) discuss limited shopping in the context of antisocial youth, this notion has also been applied to the characteristic avoidance of anxious youth (Daleiden, Vasey, & Brown, 1999) and to the failure to develop cognitive skills due to limited engagement in epistemic activities (Case et al., 1988). Limited shopping, then, offers a mechanism by which early relational incompetence could be propagated across the life span and result in increasingly stable individual differences on this dimension.

Relational Competence and Adjustment

So far, our discussion has emphasized developmental pathways in the formation of relational competence, but has not addressed the links between relational competence and adjustment. One approach to understanding the potentially changing role of relational competence across the life span is to distinguish between mediational and moderational models. In a mediational model, the child is thought to develop relational competence as a result of the mechanisms described above. In turn, relational competence would be expected to directly contribute to the child's adjustment and adaptation. A moderational model would suggest that the causal relationship between life experiences and adjustment depends on a child's level of relational competence.

To illustrate, Cole and Turner (1993) provided an excellent discussion of the mediational and moderational roles of attributional style in influencing the relation between negative life events and depression. The mediational model suggests that the experience of negative life events contributes to the development of a negative attributional style, which in turn causes depression. However, attributional style may moderate the relationship between negative life events and depression such that the experience of negative life events causes depression in those children with negative attributional styles, but may be unrelated to depression in children without negative attributional styles. Studies suggest that during the early school years children's cognitive style is still under development and does not predict depression (e.g., Nolen-Hoeksema, Girgus, & Seligman, 1992). Negative life events may predispose young children to depression or precipitate a depression episode, whereas negative life events only precipitate depressive episodes in those late middle school children and adolescents predisposed to depression by a negative cognitive style.

The adult literature has emphasized the moderational role that relational competence may play in adaptation to life events. We hypothesize that relational competence will evolve into the role of a moderating variable as it becomes integrated into a more stable organization of self-concept and relational skills. Once an individual's relational competence is organized in this fashion, it is expected that high competence will be protective in the face of adverse events and that low competence will be a risk factor throughout normative developmental transitions (see Fig. 13.2). Evidence

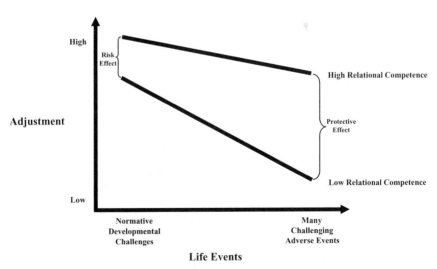

FIGURE 13.2. Conceptual Illustration of Moderational Role of Relational Competence.

from childhood and adolescence suggests that friendships buffer children from the negative effects of life stressors if (a) the friendship survives the stressor, (b) the friendship provides the specific type of support needed to cope with the specific stressor, and (c) children seek out and take advantage of the support (see Parker et al., 1995, for a review). The role of relational competence as a moderator of adjustment in adulthood will be further illustrated in the specific contexts of productivity in later life, and the increasing dependency in later life.

RELATIONAL COMPETENCE IN LATER LIFE

The preceding section dealt with the nature and likely functions of relational competence, with an emphasis on early development. In the following sections, we turn to implications and issues emerging in later life. Specifically, this section will explore the implications of relational competence for psychological hardiness and resilience, successful and productive aging, and adaptation to increasing dependency. In addition, we outline potential implications of relational competence for two social processes of current interest in the gerontological literature (socioemotional selectivity and the management of social involvements with one's convoy of support). Finally, we examine the question of expanding the two-component model of relational competence to incorporate the potential for age-related changes in expertise and in emotion regulation, and the influence on relational competence (well into later life) of continuing social-cognitive processes and internal representations of self-other relationships.

Hardiness/Resiliency

Relational competence may contribute to psychological hardiness in older adults and in turn influence their responses to stressful life events. Hardy individuals, by disposition, tend to view stressors with a greater sense of commitment, control, and challenge (Kobasa, Maddi, & Kahn, 1982). Hardiness appears to contribute to psychological resiliency in later life as it relates to physical health and psychological well-being (Bergeman & Wallace, 1999). For example, hardy persons appear to be in better health (Huang, 1995). Also, among family caregivers hardiness is related to lower levels of experienced stress associated with the demands of caring for an elderly family member (Clark & Hartman, 1996). Brandtstadter (1999) argues that resilience in later life reflects assimilative, accommodative, and immunizing processes that permit one to tenaciously pursue a priori defined goals, to redefine goals in light of changes in one's skills or life situation, or to protect oneself from self-discrepancies.

Interpersonally speaking, resilience in later life might be expressed via 1) the maintenance and/or redefinition of friendship networks, or 2) reliance on a confidant as an interpersonal buffer from isolation or depression associated with disruptions in one's network of support. Thus, hardiness emerges as both a determinant and a consequence of positive efforts at coping with negative life events in adulthood, and may help to codefine the role of relational competence in coping with such changes. In this connection, Ryff, Kwan, and Singer (2001) proposed the concept of "relational flourishing," referring to evidence that those who are more socially integrated demonstrate less morbidity and delayed mortality. A focus on relational competence may help us to understand such linkages, and suggests that older persons who are relationally skilled may evidence both health-related and interpersonal benefits. Such adaptability presumes a certain degree of "selectivity" (Filipp, 1996) regarding who one can count on and whether requests for support are likely to be honored or not.

Relational Competence and Productive, Successful Aging

In later life, relational competence can be understood as either an antecedent or a consequence of positive adaptive functioning. In this context, relational competence might be viewed as a heretofore unrecognized core characteristic of "successful aging" (Friedrich, 2001 ; Rowe & Kahn, 1998), as it is central to being able to continually "engaged with life" (Rowe & Kahn, 1998) via the maintenance of relationships with others and being able to perform productive activities (see also Baltes & Baltes, 1990). Similarly, relational competence should be associated with "productive aging" (Bass & Caro, 2001), defined in terms of one's ability to engage in activities that have either social or economic value, maximizing reliance on one's life experience, skills, and accumulated expertise.

The development of cognitive expertise in later life has been widely studied (see Park & Gutchess, 2000). Such expertise is acquired by selecting specific, valued skills to maintain, and by optimizing such skills via practice or training. Such expertise can help to maximize important areas of performance, enhance quality of life, and compensate for age-related declines in other life domains (Baltes, 1997). We propose, then, that relational competence could be viewed as a form of expertise (in life), experiential in nature, and subject to a process of selective optimization and compensation. As such, it should differentiate persons who are or are not aging successfully. In this respect, gerontological treatments of personality styles (e.g., Neugarten, 1977) have long acknowledged that some individuals are more adept at either maintaining friendships or family support networks or eliciting support from others, enabling them to maintain a consistent interpersonal framework within which they age. Consistent with the reasoning in the earlier section on childhood, successes (interpersonally speaking) breed successes, and failures in eliciting support from others predict future such failures, thus contributing to individual differences in consistency of personality styles over time. Relational competence might then be viewed as one of many internal resources older persons draw upon in coping with later life events (Ruth & Coleman, 1996). As the accurate cognitive appraisal of one's resources in light of the demands of negative life events is key to successful coping efforts (see Ryff et al., 2001, for a discussion), individual differences in life histories should parallel variations across persons in the ability to initiate and maintain relationships over time.

Key to a definition of either productive or successful aging is the fact that the activities in which one is involved must be both voluntary and personally meaningful. These parameters may help us identify those contexts in which relational competence is critical to adaptive coping. For example, it is not uncommon to find older persons in diverse caregiving roles, which by virtue of their economic, emotional, physical, or interpersonal demands isolate them from others, underscoring the need for meaningful contact and relationships with others. An emerging concern in this regard is the role of custodial grandparent (Hayslip et al., 1998 ; Shore & Hayslip, 1994), which can involve isolation, loneliness, a lack of social support, and depression. Even among traditional grandparents, there is evidence that persons are anticipatorily socialized into the grandparent role prior to the birth of their grandchild (Somary & Stricker, 1998). Thus, such persons may feel the need to anticipate their interpersonal requirements for support and to evaluate changes in their relationships with others. It is also relevant that the roles of both traditional and custodial grandparent result from the actions of others. Relational competence should then be construed as having both reactive and proactive aspects, as when one establishes a network of age peers to help one cope with unanticipated role demands, as is clearly the case among custodial grandparents, who often assume care of their grandchildren during a family crisis (Hayslip et al., 1998). In the broader context of productive aging, having loving grandparents may be a key element in producing future generations of older persons who are themselves productive (Birren, 2001). Thus, being able to model appropriate role-specific behavior or pass along family traditions to one's grandchildren or maintain the family in the face of stressful events involves considerable interpersonal skill (Hayslip & Goldberg-Glen, 2000).

Relational competence could also shape our anticipatory assessments of future needs for meaningful relationships, for example, to help in the occurrence of unforeseen life events. In this context, relational competence may reflect the integrity of one's executive functions (see Waldstein, 2000), allowing planful (re)organizations of one's interpersonal life when necessary. Relational competence would be expected to be pertinent to the process of building a support network of age peers who are faced with similar caregiving or other role demands. Older persons who possess such skills would therefore be expected to adapt more easily to nonnormative life events, such as being asked to care for a grandchild (Hayslip & Goldberg-Glen, 2000), as well as to a variety of normative life events such as illness or death of a spouse. Moreover, accurately anticipating one's interpersonal needs when facing a normative life event (e.g., becoming a grandparent), dependency or institutionalization (due to an inability to care for oneself, poor health, or the death of a spouse) may reflect accumulated relational competence. (N.B. Although older adults are the focus of this discussion, we believe that these principles apply to persons at most stages of development.)

Enhanced interpersonal skills may also facilitate the ability to successfully access social services, especially mental health services. Many older persons are not comfortable in approaching mental health services (Currin et al., 1998), resulting in the underutilization of such services. However, this might be minimized among older persons who are interpersonally skilled enough to identify others as sources of support in the face of a crisis. This might be especially important for older minorities (African Americans, Hispanics) who may be more reluctant to rely on formal service providers, in contrast to seeking support from age peers or extended family networks (Williams & Wilson, 2001). The degree to which one is interpersonally skilled may enable some minority aged to reach out more effectively to others in times of need. On the other hand, the embeddedness of many older minority persons in their respective extended family networks, and the resulting exchange of help (Mutran, 1985), could reduce the necessity for the development of initiation skills but place a premium on enhancement skills.

Convoys of Support

In later life, social support is critical to mental health, well-being, physical health, and even mortality (see Antonucci, 2001). However, support networks change and evolve throughout one's later years, and relational competence may play an important role in how changes in the social convoy of support (Kahn & Antonucci, 1980) come about. For example, relational competence may moderate the extent to which social support is beneficial (see our earlier discussion, and Filipp, 1996), or the extent to which some older persons are better able to provide support to others, due to their ability to anticipate others' needs or requests for help. These observations about the role of relational competence in both accessing and providing support to others are especially noteworthy given that for many persons, the social convoy of support becomes less dense with age, and relationships that are intimate in nature tend to replace those that are instrumental (role-specific) (see Antonucci, 2001 ; Kahn & Antonucci, 1980).

Individual differences in relational competence should then influence one's ability to maintain one's convoy of support over time, in the face of relocation, illness, or the loss of significant others through death. Indeed, changes in one's convoy of support do not happen by chance ; they must

be actively and successfully (re)negotiated for the convoy to fulfill its protective function. This may co-occur with the process of socioemotional
selectivity (Charles & Carstensen, 1999), wherein, given an awareness of
the finiteness of time, older persons selectively disengage from relationships that are no longer critical to the development of self-knowledge or
are no longer emotionally salient.

Thus, it is at the interface between developmental change and relational
competence that social convoys of support are key to understanding the
importance of relational competence in maintaining one's independence
and quality of life in later adulthood. Convoys that are functional may provide physical safety, enhance well-being, provide resources, and generally
speaking, serve as a buffer in times of crisis or distress. Older persons, however, must actively construct such convoys, so that support is given freely
when requested and offered in a timely manner. Smith and Goodnow (1999)
underscored the importance of the voluntary, purposeful nature of such
requests. These authors found that persons of all ages disliked unsolicited
support from others, with offers of such support implying incompetence.
Alternatively, being able to ask for and receive support from others is also
likely to enhance one's own sense of relational competence. Persons who
lack relational competence may be unable to negotiate relationships that
provide such support, and not receive positive feedback regarding the
success of their efforts to evoke financial, spiritual, or emotional aid and
comfort from formal support agencies, family, friends, or coworkers.

Similarly, people who lack relational competence may be forced into a
disengaged lifestyle, born of negative feedback from others regarding the
quality of their interpersonal, communicative, or listening skills. This could
lead to missed opportunities to perform personally and societally valued
roles, causing them to occupy a "tenuous" or a "roleless" role later in life
(Rosow, 1985). Such persons may feel isolated, marginalized, or discrimi-
nated against. They may cease to be viewed by others as productive and
important, and come to define themselves as having little to offer (Rosow,
1985). Consequently, persons who would otherwise be available to help
the individual cope with both normative and nonnormative changes may
not be willing to help, and become inaccessible. This process of actively
forming and redefining one's convoy of support and exercising decisions
to reorder relationships with others is the essence of socioemotional selectivity (Carstensen, Isaacowitz, & Charles, 1999).

Over and above the importance assigned to planful and accurate appraisal of one's interpersonal needs, relational competence may have a
distinctly cognitive quality to it. Age-related changes in social competence
are an important avenue by which persons adapt to life contexts and are influenced by changes in such contexts (Blanchard-Fields & Hess, 1999). For
example, adaptation could involve changes in representations of the self
with respect to others via the construct of possible selves (Cross & Markus,

1991 ; Hooker, 1999), which might vary along a solitary-other oriented continuum. Thus, the social-cognitive processes by which older persons internally represent information regarding self-other relationships, the accuracy of such representations, and their health-related, emotional, vocational, or cognitive consequences may codefine relational competence in later life. Older adults who are more interpersonally skilled may be better able to anticipate future needs for support from others. They may also be more accurate in defining such estimates due to the nature of the information that is internally represented regarding others and one's relationships to them.

Increasing Dependency (and Loss) in Later Life

It is a matter of concern that as older adults begin to experience significant age-related declines and dependency, their families are also aging and becoming more frail. It can thus be a difficult time to begin to deal with increased dependency of an older person, and concerns are likely to arise regarding the family's ability to handle successive levels of case management or caregiving (Moss, Moss, & Hansson, 2001). Families may lack information and understanding regarding aging and the changing needs of an elderly parent. They may lack the motivation or resources to effectively engage this role. In many families, also, a problematic history of family relationships can undermine efforts to cooperate to support an elderly family member. Such circumstances, then, suggest a need for the older adult (and potential support recipient) to exhibit relational competencies appropriate to the demands of the interpersonal context (Hansson & Carpenter, 1994). Older persons who are more sensitive to the status and maintenance needs of their family network, and who have the skills and dispositions to more effectively contribute to the functioning and stability of the family, should then be more adaptable. In this connection, the quality of the personal relationship between a family caregiver and elderly care recipient has been found to mediate the impact of caregiver stressors on feelings of being overwhelmed as well as on depressive symptoms (Townsend & Franks, 1995 ; Williamson et al., 2001 ; Yates, Tennstedt, & Chang, 1999). In contrast, the quality and emotional tone of elderly parents' communication and interaction style is one of the most frequently reported themes in their children's descriptions of intergenerational conflict and tension (Clarke, Preston, Raskin, & Bengtson, 1999).

In addition, those older individuals who have the skills and emotional competence that allow them to assert their needs, preferences, and rights, negotiate ground rules for caregiving efforts, monitor the dynamics of their care relationships and make necessary adjustments, minimize conflict, and so on, should experience more effective support relationships. For example, older persons who are high on social self-efficacy are more likely to perceive greater availability of personal relationships (Lang, Featherman, & Nesselroade, 1997). In later life, however, several factors emerge that could alter the nature of relational demands in one's environment.

For example, a lifetime of managing difficult transitions can provide considerable *expertise* in the pragmatics of life (Ericsson & Charness, 1994; Staudinger, Smith, & Baltes, 1992). Older persons who have tried to learn the lessons of life should therefore have achieved a more realistic future view of their later years, better understand how they may have to respond to the adaptive challenges (including interpersonal challenges) of later life, and be better prepared. Similarly, a lifetime of coping with stressful life (and interpersonal) events can produce coping skills that can have a preventive, protective, or mediating influence on the experience of stress in old age (Lazarus, 1996). We might expect, then, a diminishing demand for relational competencies focused on initiation or accessing support networks.

Moreover, the processes of emotion regulation may shift in emphasis in late life. Old age brings greater risks of disability, decline, and loss. Yet reports of emotional well-being actually tend to increase. A number of explanations seem possible for such counterintuitive phenomena (Magai & McFadden, 1996). For example, older persons may appraise life stressors differently; they may report fewer life problems in comparison to middle-aged counterparts, and be less upset or challenged when problems are encountered. Although they more frequently experience loss and decline, they may feel relatively confident that they will be able to deal with such emotionally demanding events. Some evidence now also suggests that older adults experience a dampening of emotions, both positive and negative. Physiological assessments of emotional responsiveness support this hypothesis (Lawton, Kleban, Rajagopal, & Dean, 1992; Tsai, Levenson, & Carstensen, 2000). This may be a reflection of age-related changes in the brain's emotion systems. Alternatively, it may be that older persons are more likely to have come to terms with age-related problems, and that experience has taught them how they might manage or prevent the consequences of life stress associated with old age, minimizing demands to cope with a crisis. Finally, coping styles may change somewhat in later life, from problem-focused to emotion-focused forms of coping. For example, older persons may realistically lower their standards for coping, reappraise their circumstances to acknowledge a balance of positive and negative consequences, and so on. Lazarus (1996) has argued that this may not so much reflect a developmental change in coping style but be a logical adaptation to the changing kinds of stress and irrevocable loss experienced in old age (dependency becoming increasingly medical, partner loss, etc.). We speculate that these changes in emotion regulation, then, may reduce experience with stress quite generally, and thus allow a reduction of demands for support by members of one's support networks.

In addition, research guided by socioemotional selectivity theory (Carstensen et al.,1999) suggests that changing sensitivities among older persons to time left to live may result in a reprioritization of social goals, with an increasing emphasis on existing relationships that are emotionally fulfilling. This is viewed to result in a conscious narrowing of social networks to emotionally close members of one's network, and a reduction in attention to or involvement with relationships that might serve some other, more peripheral or instrumental purpose. Such a shift might be expected to alter the relative importance of the two components of relational competence, reducing especially demands for those abilities and attributes associated with the initiation component.

CONCLUSIONS AND DIRECTIONS FOR FUTURE RESEARCH

The construct of relational competence appears meaningful within the framework of the full life span. Its nature and development can be delineated within the context of related early developmental processes such as temperament, attachment, and developing self-concept. Connections can also be drawn between the construct and important psychological and social processes in later life (e.g., hardiness and resilience, successful and productive aging, adaptation to dependency, socioemotional selectivity, and so on). The functions of relational competence across the life span are amenable to specification and confirmation.

The two-component model for construing and measuring relational competence (Carpenter, 1987) seems relevant across a wide age range, and provides a useful vehicle for integrating research on related, but more narrowly focused, social competence variables. As we have discussed above, the model also quite effectively guides the formulation of predictions regarding the implications of initiation and enhancement competencies for important social and developmental processes. It may also prove helpful in the continuing and broadening exploration of mediating and moderating influences in development.

Examining relational competence in the context of the life span, however, has generated a number of intriguing questions for future research. For example, it would be interesting to explore the issue of which types of relational competence skills or attributes might appear or develop earlier (and why). Some of these would likely require more learning, experience, or maturation within the cognitive and emotional systems more broadly. We note that no longitudinal studies of relational competence (as construed here) have been conducted to date.

It would be interesting, too, to systematically explore the implications of developing relational competence in early life for important social processes such as socialization, moral development, and development of self-concept. Each of these processes depends in great part on effective interactions with others.

Broadening our perspective on relational competence to reflect the life span has also suggested to us the potential value of revisiting and refining the construct itself. For example, the cognitive and affective components of relational competence would be expected to continue to evolve and differentiate across the life span, in response to changes in the individual and the nature of demands for adaptation faced by the individual. For example, it may therefore be worth proposing the addition of a third component (expertise in life pragmatics) to Carpenter's (1987) relational competence model.

Finally, there is clearly much to do before a general life span view of the construct of relational competence can be proposed. Two issues seem especially relevant in this connection. First, it is a concern that we have had little to say in this chapter regarding midlife issues. Research focusing on a number of topics could aid in filling that gap. For example, it would be interesting to explore contextual and age variations in relational competence as they (a) moderate response to such events as divorce, child abuse, retirement, empty nesting, custodial grandparenting, caregiving, hospice care, or widowhood, or (b) influence health and risk-taking behavior. Second, we have described a variety of developmental insights drawn from either the early developmental years or from later life, but an examination of the generalizability of such insights to each stage of social development is beyond the scope of this chapter. For example, it would be useful in future investigations to ask whether hardiness and resiliency (discussed in the context of old age) might emerge from relational competence at any age. Also, we discussed the notion of mediational and moderational models that become dominant at different points in early development. From a broader life span viewpoint, however, it may be the selective, reactive, and adaptive qualities of relational competence that become more interesting. For example, rather than cast the construct in purely age-specific, developmental terms, it may be more fruitful to see individuals regardless of age as being ordered along a proactive to reactive continuum. Depending on life experience and on one's particular contextual demands and resources, either a proactive relational style or a reactive interpersonal style could be more adaptive.

References

Adkins, G., Martin, P., & Poon, L. W. (1996). Personality traits and states as predictors of subjective well-being in centenarians, octogenarians, and sexagenarians. *Psychology and Aging, 11,* 408–416.

Antonucci, T. C. (2001). Social relations: An examination of social networks, social support, and sense of control. In J. E. Birren & K. W. Schaie (Eds.), *Handbook of the psychology of aging* (pp. 427–453). San Diego: Academic Press.

Baltes, P. B. (1997). On the incomplete architecture of human ontogeny: Selection, optimization, and compensation as foundation of developmental theory. *American Psychologist, 52*, 366–380.

Baltes, P. B., & Baltes, M. M. (1990). *Successful aging: Perspectives from the behavioral sciences.* New York: Cambridge University Press.

Bass, S. A., & Caro, F. G. (2001). Productive aging: A conceptual framework. In N. Morrow-Howell, J. Hinterlong, & M. Sherraden (Eds.), *Productive aging: Concepts and challenges* (pp. 37–80). Baltimore, MD: Johns Hopkins University Press.

Bergeman, C., & Wallace, K. (1999). Resiliency in later life. In T. L. Whitman & T. Merluzzi (Eds.), *Life span perspectives on health and illness* (pp. 207–225). Mahwah, NJ: Erlbaum.

Berndt, T. J. (1996). Friendships in adolescence. In N. Vanzetti & S. Duck (Eds.), *A lifetime of relationships* (pp. 181–212). New York: Brooks/Cole.

Birren, J. E. (2001). Psychological implications of productive aging. In H. Morrow-Howell, J. Hinterlong, & M. Sherraden (Eds.), *Productive aging: Concepts and challenges* (pp. 102–119). Baltimore, MD: Johns Hopkins University Press.

Blanchard-Fields, F., & Hess, T. M. (1999). The social cognitive perspective and the study of aging. In T. M. Hess & F. Blanchard-Fields (Eds.), *Social cognition and aging* (pp. 2–16). San Diego: Academic Press.

Bowlby, J. (1973). *Attachment and loss. Vol. 2, Separation.* New York: Basic Books.

Brandtstadter, J. (1999). Studies of resilience in the aging self: Toward integrating perspectives. In T. M. Hess & F. Blanchard-Fields (Eds.), *Social cognition and aging* (pp. 125–144). San Diego: Academic Press.

Carpenter, B. N. (1987, August). Development, structure, and concurrent validity of the relational competence scale. Paper presented at the annual convention of the American Psychological Association, New York, NY.

Carpenter, B. N. (1993). Relational competence. In D. Perlman & W. H. Jones (Eds.), *Advances in personal relationships* (Vol. 4, pp. 1–28). New York: Jessica Kingsley.

Carstensen, L. L., Isaacowitz, D. M., & Charles, S. T. (1999). Taking time seriously: A theory of socioemotional selectivity. *American Psychologist, 54*, 165–181.

Case, R., Hayward, S., Lewis, M., & Hurst, P. (1988). Toward a neo-Piagetian theory of cognitive and emotional development. *Developmental Review, 8*, 1–51.

Charles, S. T., & Carstensen, L. L. (1999). The role of time in the setting of social goals across the life span. In T. M. Hess & F. Blanchard-Fields (Eds.), *Social cognition and aging* (pp. 319–345). San Diego: Academic Press.

Cicchetti, D., & Cohen, D. J. (1995). Perspectives on developmental psychopathology. In D. Cicchetti & D. J. Cohen (Eds.), *Developmental psychopathology (Vol. 1): Theory and methods* (pp. 3–20). New York: John Wiley.

Cicchetti, D., & Schneider-Rosen, K. (1986). An organizational approach to childhood depression. In M. Rutter, C. Izard, & P. Read (Eds.), *Depression in young people: Developmental and clinical perspectives* (pp. 71–134). New York: Guilford.

Clark, L., & Hartman, M. (1996). Effects of hardiness and appraisal on the psychological distress and physical health of caregivers to elderly relatives. *Research on Aging, 18*, 379–401.

Clarke, E. J., Preston, M., Raskin, J., & Bengtson, V. L. (1999). Types of conflicts and tensions between older parents and adult children. *The Gerontologist, 39*, 261–270.

Cole, D. A. (1990). The relation of social and academic competence to depressive symptoms in childhood. *Journal of Abnormal Psychology, 99*, 422–429.

Cole, D. A., & Turner, J. E. (1993). Models of cognitive mediation and moderation in childhood depression. *Journal of Abnormal Psychology, 102*, 271–281.

Cross, S., & Markus, H. (1991). Possible selves across the life course. *Human Development, 34*, 230–255.

Currin, J., Hayslip, B., Schneider, L., & Kooken, R. (1998). Cohort differences in attitudes toward mental health services among older persons. *Psychotherapy: Theory, Research, Practice and Training, 35*, 506–518.

Daleiden, E., Vasey, M. W., & Brown, L. M. (1999). Internalizing disorders. In W. K. Silverman & T. H. Ollendick (Eds.), *Developmental issues in the clinical treatment of children and adolescents* (pp. 259–278). Boston: Allyn and Bacon.

Damon, W. (1977). *The social world of the child*. San Francisco: Jossey-Bass.

Ericsson, K. A., & Charness, N. (1994). Expert performance: Its structure and acquisition. *American Psychologist, 49*, 725–747.

Filipp, S. H. (1996). Motivation and emotion. In J. E. Birren & K. W. Schaie (Eds.), *Handbook of the psychology of aging* (pp. 218–235). San Diego: Academic Press.

Friedrich, D. D. (2001). *Successful aging: Integrating contemporary ideas, research findings, and intervention strategies*. Springfield, IL: C. C. Thomas.

Garber, J., & Strassberg, Z. (1991). Construct validity: History and application to developmental psychopathology. In W. M. Grove & D. Cicchetti (Eds.), *Thinking clearly about psychology. Vol. 2, Personality and psychopathology* (pp. 219–258). Minneapolis, MN: University of Minnesota Press.

Hansson, R. O., & Carpenter, B. N. (1994). *Relationships in old age: Coping with the challenge of transition*. New York: Guilford.

Hansson, R. O., Jones, W. H., & Carpenter, B. N. (1984). Relational competence and social support. In P. Shaver (Ed.), *Review of personality and social psychology. Vol. 5, Emotions, relationships, and health* (pp. 265–284). Beverly Hills: Sage.

Harter, S. (1986). Cognitive-developmental processes in the integration of concepts about emotions and the self. *Social Cognition*, 119–151.

Hayslip, B., & Goldberg-Glen, R. (2000). *Grandparents raising grandchildren: Theoretical, empirical, and clinical perspectives*. New York: Springer.

Hayslip, B., Shore, J., Lambert, P., & Henderson, C. (1998). Custodial grandparenting and the impact of grandchildren with problems on role satisfaction and role meaning. *Journal of Gerontology: Social Sciences, 53B*, S164–S174.

Hooker, K. (1999). Possible selves in adulthood: Incorporating telenomic relevance into studies of the self. In T. M. Hess & F. Blanchard-Fields (Eds.), *Social cognition and aging* (pp. 99–124). San Diego: Academic Press.

Huang, C. (1995). Hardiness and stress: A critical review. *Maternal-Child Nursing Journal, 23*, 82–89.

Kagan, J. (1994). On the nature of emotion. *Monographs of the Society for Research in Child Development, 59* (2–3, Serial No. 240).

Kahn, R. L., & Antonucci, T. C. (1980). Convoys over the life course: Attachments, roles, and social support. In P. B. Baltes (Ed.), *Life span development* (pp. 253–286). New York: Academic Press.

Kobasa, S. C., Maddi, S. R., & Kahn, S. (1982). Hardiness and health: A prospective study. *Journal of Personality and Social Psychology, 42*, 168–172.

Lang, F. R., Featherman, D. L., & Nesselroade, J. R. (1997). Social self-efficacy and short-term variability in social relationships: The MacArthur successful aging studies. *Psychology and Aging, 12,* 657–666.

Lawton, M. P., Kleban, M. H., Rajagopal, D., & Dean, J. (1992). Dimensions of affective experience in three age groups. *Psychology and Aging, 7,* 1171–184.

Lawton, M. P., & Simon, B. B. (1968). The ecology of social relationships in housing for the elderly. *Gerontologist, 8,* 110–115.

Lazarus, R. S. (1996). The role of coping in the emotions and how coping changes over the life course. In C. Magai & S. H. McFadden (Eds.), *Handbook of emotion, adult development, and aging* (pp. 289–306). San Diego: Academic Press.

Magai, C., & McFadden, S. H. (Eds.) (1996). *Handbook of emotion, adult development, and aging.* San Diego: Academic Press.

Moss, M. S., Moss, S. Z., & Hansson, R. O. (2001). Bereavement and old age. In M. S. Stroebe, R. O. Hansson, W. Stroebe, & H. Schut (Eds.), *Handbook of bereavement research* (pp. 241–260). Washington, DC: American Psychological Association.

Mutran, E. (1985). Intergenerational family support among blacks and whites: Response to culture or to socioeconomic differences? *Journal of Gerontology, 40,* 382–389.

Neugarten, B. L. (1977). Personality and aging. In J. E. Birren & K. W. Schaie (Eds.), *Handbook of the psychology of aging* (pp. 626–649). New York: Van Nostrand Reinhold.

Neyer, F.-J. (2003). Dyadic fits and transactions in personality and relationships. In F. R. Lang & K. L. Fingerman (Eds.), *Growing together: Personal relationships across the life span* (chap.12). New York: Cambridge University Press.

Nolen-Hoeksema, S., Girgus, J. S., & Seligman, M. E. P. (1992). Predictors and consequences of childhood depressive symptoms: A 5-year longitudinal study. *Journal of Abnormal Psychology, 101,* 405–422.

Park, D. C., & Gutchess, A. H. (2000). Cognitive aging and everyday life. In D. C. Park & N. Schwarz (Eds.), *Cognitive aging: A primer* (pp. 217–232). Philadelphia, PA: Taylor & Francis.

Parker, J. G., Rubin, K. H., Price, J. M., & DeRosier, M. E. (1995). Peer relationships, child development, and adjustment. In D. Cicchetti & D. J. Cohen (Eds.), *Developmental psychopathology (Vol. 2): Risk, disorder, and adaptation* (pp. 96–161). New York: Wiley.

Patterson, G. R., Reid, J. B., & Dishion, T. J. (1992). *Antisocial boys.* Eugene, OR: Castalia Publishing.

Roberts, B. W., & DelVecchio, W. F. (2000). The rank-order consistency of personality traits from childhood to old age: A quantitative review of longitudinal studies. *Psychological Bulletin, 126,* 3–25.

Rosow, I. (1985). Status and role change through the life cycle. In R. H. Binstock & E. Shanas (Eds.), *Handbook of aging and the social sciences* (pp. 693–701). New York: Academic Press.

Rothbart, M. K., & Mauro, J. A. (1990). Questionnaire measures of infant temperament. In J. W. Fagen & J. Colombo (Eds.), *Individual differences in infancy: Reliability, stability, and prediction* (pp. 411–429). Hillsdale, NJ: Erlbaum.

Rowe, J. W., & Kahn, R. L. (1998). *Successful aging.* New York: Pantheon.

Ruth, J., & Coleman, P. (1996). Personality and aging: Coping and management of the self in later life. In J. E. Birren & K. W. Schaie (Eds.), *Handbook of the psychology of aging* (pp. 308–322). San Diego: Academic Press.

Ryff, C. D., Kwan, C. M., & Singer, B. H. (2001). Personality and aging: Flourishing agendas and future challenges. In J. E. Birren & K. W. Schaie (Eds.), *Handbook of the psychology of aging* (pp. 477–499). San Diego: Academic Press.

Shapiro, T. (1995). Developmental issues in psychotherapy research. *Journal of Abnormal Child Psychology, 23,* 31–44.

Shore, R. J., & Hayslip, B. (1994). Custodial grandparenting: Implications for children's development. In A. S. Gottfried & A. W. Gottfried (Eds.), *Redefining families: Implications for children's development* (pp. 172–220). New York: John Wiley.

Smith, J., & Goodnow, J. (1999). Unasked-for support and unsolicited advice: Age and the quality of social experience. *Psychology and Aging, 14,* 108–121.

Somary, K., & Stricker, G. (1998). Becoming a grandparent: A longitudinal study of expectations and experiences as a function of sex and lineage. *The Gerontologist, 38,* 53–61.

Staudinger, U. M., Smith, J., & Baltes, P. B. (1992). Wisdom related knowledge in a life review task: Age differences and the role of professional specialization. *Psychology and Aging, 7,* 271–281.

Townsend, A. L., & Franks, M. M. (1995). Closeness and conflict in adult children's caregiving relationships. *Psychology and Aging, 10,* 343–351.

Tsai, J. L., Levenson, R. W., & Carstensen, L. L. (2000). Autonomic, subjective, and expressive responses to emotional films in older and younger Chinese Americans and European Americans. *Psychology and Aging, 15,* 684–693.

Van den Boom, D. (1989). Neonatal irritability and the development of attachment. In G. Kohnstamm, J. Bates, & M. K. Rothbart (Eds.), *Temperament in childhood.* Chichester, UK: Wiley.

Waldstein, S. R. (2000). Health effects on cognitive aging. In P. C. Stern & L. L. Carstensen (Eds.), *The aging mind: Opportunities in cognitive research* (pp. 189–217). Washington, DC: National Research Council.

Weisz, J. R., Rudolph, K. D., Granger, D. A., & Sweeney, L. (1992). Cognition, competence, and coping in child and adolescent depression: Research findings, developmental concerns, therapeutic implications. *Development and Psychopathology, 4,* 627–653.

Williams, D. R., & Wilson, C. M. (2001). Race, ethnicity, and aging. In R. H. Binstock & L. K. George (Eds.), *Handbook of aging and the social sciences* (pp. 160–178). San Diego: Academic Press.

Williamson, G. M., Shaffer, D. R., & The Family Relationships in Late Life Project (2001). Relationship quality and potentially harmful behaviors by spousal caregivers: How we were then, how we are now. *Psychology and Aging, 16,* 217–226.

Yates, M. E., Tennstedt, S., & Chang, B. H. (1999). Contributors to and mediators of psychological well-being for informal caregivers. *Journal of Gerontology: Psychological Sciences, 54B,* P12–P22.

14

Social Motivation across the Life Span

Frieder R. Lang

The chapter addresses mechanisms and processes underlying the life span ontogeny of social motivation. Six propositions on the life span development of personal relationships are presented. From birth to death individuals are active agents, who coregulate the structure, function, and quality of their social worlds in accordance with their age-specific needs and resources. An individual's developmental resources determine the lifelong salience and outcomes of two kinds of basic goal commitments, a striving for social agency and a striving for belongingness in one's social world. The interplay and dynamic between these two sets of goals determines an individual's interpersonal functioning and competence. A *goal-resource-congruence* model of social self-regulation suggests that individuals may benefit from matching their social strivings to their resources and potentials.

Why do individuals seek to maintain personal relationships over time? Few issues appear as self-evident and yet at the same time inexplicable. At birth everyone has a mother and a father. Most people have siblings, uncles and aunts, cousins, nephews and nieces. Very rarely do people grow up without an intimate partner, a close friend, or acquaintances. It seems impossible to imagine a well-functioning society without the networks of strong and weak ties that transmit social information, sanction desirable or undesirable behaviors, and provide a social backup in times of misery (Fiske, 1992; Granovetter, 1973; Parsons, 1961; Wiese, 1955). An individual's personal network of relationships constitutes a complex structure and is as much an outcome as it is a determinant of behavioral development. People's lives are social, and their everyday living is imbued with personal relationships. Individuals feel strongly about the social ties they maintain and strictly differentiate the specific roles and functions of their relationship partners. For example, people typically know who they can turn to with their problems, who they enjoy having a fancy dinner with, who they can trust, who will help if asked, and who will be a good companion for a two-week journey overseas. People of all ages are regularly confronted with such everyday decisions about social partners in kindergarten, in school, at work, and at home. What are the developmental mechanisms underlying these choices over the life course?

This chapter advances and extends the proposition that individuals actively influence the course and outcomes of their personal relationships from childhood to later adulthood (e.g., Hinde, 1997; Lang, 2001; Lewis & Rosenblum, 1975; Youniss, 1980). The individual's regulation of personal relationships is described in the following pages as a motivational process that reflects a dynamic interplay between one's developmental resources and one's aspirations. While the human need to belong is known to exist at all phases of the human life course, from neonates to centenarians (Baumeister & Leary, 1996), it is still not well understood in what ways individuals are active in molding their social environments at various phases of the life span. For example, only after children have developed a capacity to theorize about the reasoning that goes on in other people's minds (Watson, Nixon, Wilson, & Capage, 1999) will they also be able to consider long-term consequences of beginning or ending a personal relationship. This chapter focuses on how individuals regulate their individual development via the influence they exert on their personal relationships. Of course, such processes and outcomes involve at least two partners who are interdependent. In personal relationships, having influence inevitably and necessarily implies that one is influenced back. For example, wanting to help another person depends on the other person's willingness or resistance to being helped. The quality of a personal relationship depends on the expectations, intentions, and behaviors of two partners. When one is satisfied but the other is not, it won't work for long. For reasons of clarity and space, however, I focus exclusively on an individual-centered perspective on one's personal relationships. This means that the developmental processes that are involved in dealing with others are discussed here with respect to the behavioral development of only one individual in a dyad.

The first section of this chapter discusses in what ways the understanding of motivational processes in personal relationships contributes to an understanding of human ontogeny across the life span. Empirical findings on this issue are summarized in six propositions on the life span development of personal relationships. In the second section I address the specific mechanisms and processes that regulate an individual's personal relationships and personal networks over the life course. A resource-goal-congruence model of social motivation is presented suggesting that when matching one's goals to one's developmental and psychosocial resources, individuals will experience enhanced social functioning. A final section of this chapter ends with an outlook on future research on this issue. It is suggested that a focus on dyadic perspectives promises to shed further light on the specific regulatory processes that lead to enhanced social adaptation.

Personal relationships are defined as a relatively stable pattern of behavior and cognition between at least two individuals who are socially interacting in at least one recurrent situation. This implies that a personal relationship refers to a series of social interactions between individuals that occur in clearly defined and relatively stable contexts (e.g., during the daily subway ride to work, at school, at an annual conference). In addition, a personal relationship pertains to both partners' social behaviors as well as to their mutual feelings and cognitive representations of each other (e.g., Hinde, 1997). The regulation of personal relationships entails an individual's behaviors and cognitions that are related to the choice, activation, continuation, change, or discontinuation of social ties. This implies that the individual regulates both the self and the world that the individual inhabits. However, in accordance with Heckhausen and Schulz (1995) it is argued that seeking to influence the social world has a functional primacy over seeking to influence oneself. Individuals seek to regulate the social world so that it fits with their resources and needs. If that is not possible, internal standards are adapted.

One premise is that individuals seek to achieve goals that represent age-specific needs and tasks. However, an individual's commitment to a specific goal may not be functional at every stage of the life course, because there are different costs and benefits associated with pursuing a specific goal at different points in the life course (e.g., J. Heckhausen & Schulz, 1995; Lang & J. Heckhausen, 2001). For example, seeking a new job or profession may involve more effort and greater risks in middle adulthood than a job change involves in adolescence or early adulthood. As already stated above, the costs and benefits of personal relationships depend on at least two interdependent partners (Kelley, 1997). Consequently, individuals may not always be able to successfully attain what they want from others. There are basically three possible alternatives when a goal is not attained: give up on the goal, look for another partner, or try again. In the following it is suggested that the content and adaptive outcomes of such decisions depend on the extent to which one's goals are in accordance with one's developmental resources.

A LIFE SPAN PERSPECTIVE ON THE REGULATION
OF PERSONAL RELATIONSHIPS

Why should one consider changes in social motivation and personal relationships from a life span perspective? In what ways do motivational and developmental processes contribute to an improved understanding of personal relationships? There is a considerable amount of empirical findings that speak for a proactive role of individuals in the construction

TABLE 14.1. *Six Propositions on the Life-Span Development of Personal Relationships*

Perspective	Proposition	Implications for Individual
1. Evolved nature	Seeking personal relationships is a ubiquitous motif of individual action at all phases of the human life span.	• Individuals do not develop to become socially motivated; rather, social motivation changes across the life span.
2. Contextual influence	Contextual influences determine the course and outcome of personal relationships.	• Individuals' personal relationships reflect contextual opportunities. • Interweaving of personal relationships networks, and society.
3. Multidirectionality and multidimensionality	The structures and functions of personal relationships show different age-associated trajectories across the life span.	• Individuals' experience decline but also growth with respect to differing aspects of personal relationships over time.
4. Resource adequacy	Personal relationships may contribute to adaptation and mastery at all stages of life when age adequate.	• Individuals use personal relationships as a resource for improved mastery at a risk of experiencing distress.
5. Vulnerability and resilience	When experiencing aversive events, each and every personal relationship can be ended. Some are not ended even in the most extreme adversity.	• Individuals deliberately decide how long and in what ways they maintain contact with relationship partners.
6. Diversity and variability	There is much diversity and variability between and among the relationships that individuals maintain over the life course.	• Individuals maintain a basic inventory of different types of personal relationships. • Functions of relationships may change or fluctuate over time.

of age-specific and age-adequate social environments. I will discuss six propositions that highlight some of the most pertinent insights on the development of personal relationships across the life span. Table 14.1 summarizes the theoretical perspective, contents, and implications of each of the six propositions. Each of these six propositions is discussed in detail in the following.

(1) Seeking Personal Relationships Is a Ubiquitous Motive of Individual Action throughout the Life Course

Humans have evolved as social creatures and social life has become the core of human existence (e.g., Gaulin & McBurney, 2001). From the moment of birth, individuals approach others in their social environment and develop intentions and plans of social behavior. Newborns quickly learn how to smile. Newborns also learn to smile even with those persons in their environment who do not feed them. Most seven-to-nine-month-old toddlers express joy when seeing someone they already know, and toddlers express fear when a stranger appears. Children seek contact with their peers and thus acquire new social or cognitive skills (Harris, 1995; Hartup, 1989). Improved social and prosocial behavior is associated with enhanced popularity among peers as well as enhanced academic achievement (e.g., Wentzel, 1998, 2000). Adolescents seek to establish a sense of autonomy from their parents while continuing to rely on them as an emotional resource (Larson & Richards, 1994). Young adults seek to establish their independent lives in society and seek to find a reliable and stable partnership (e.g., Bierhoff & Schmohr, Chap. 5, this volume). Middle-aged adults experience their children growing up while their own parents grow old (e.g., Fingerman, 1996; Lang, in press; Rosenthal, Martin, & Matthews, 1996). Older adults are confronted with personal and social losses and limitations of life, which may render meaningful social contact more precious than ever.

(2) Contextual Influences Determine the Course and Outcome of Personal Relationships

The contextual perspective builds on the central premises that individuals develop in transaction with their respective context, and that this transaction or "dynamic interaction" between the person and the context changes over time (Lerner & Kauffman, 1985). There are three basic sources of change and stability of personal relationships across the life span: A first influence relates to biological and physical influences that shape and structure the individual's life course. For example, individuals may suffer from physical handicaps for a longer or for a shorter period of their lives, which may affect their relationships with others when they develop a need for help. A second influence relates to the age-graded opportunity structures of the human life course that are related to age-specific norms and social timetables, for example, about when to move out from one's parents' home, when to become a parent, or when to have grandchildren (J. Heckhausen, 1999). A third influence relates to an individual's own active efforts to master his or her own life. Individuals may either seek to change their social world in accordance with their goals or they may adapt their goals in response to the social opportunities of their environment. Both strategies imply that the individual remains an active agent who seeks to remain in control over his or her life (J. Heckhausen & Schulz, 1995; Lang, 2001).

Another issue of a contextual perspective on social development pertains to the interweaving of social structures and personal networks of relationships. Personal networks mediate between the individual and the society, for example, by transmitting and controlling social norms (e.g., Parsons, 1961). It is only in the course of continuous personal relationships that individuals learn what is socially desirable and what is undesirable. Personal relationships constitute a frame of reference for comparing and evaluating one's goals and behaviors. In many ways, the personal networks of an individual serve as a proxy of the larger society and the social opportunity structures. We learn about the world through those people we know. The interweaving of personal relationships and the larger society is also illustrated in the "small world problem" first introduced by Stanley Milgram in 1967 (see also Travers & Milgram, 1969). The small world problem is better known under the popular but equivocal and misleading title of a play and movie, "six degrees of separation." According to the "small world" concept, any two citizens in the United States of America (or of the entire world) are likely to be linked through an average number of four to six intermediary acquaintances (see Fingerman, Chap. 8, this volume). However, there is not much empirical evidence for the theory, mostly because of the difficulties in operationally defining what is an "acquaintance" (e.g., two people who know each other by name versus two people who meet each other regularly). More importantly, the small world problem illustrates that the social connections between individuals constitute large communicative mega-networks in which the information about social events and norms flows to and from each single person through their personal relationships. This implies that the relationship behaviors of each individual contribute in some way to the quality and functions of the larger societal structure.

(3) The Structure and Function of Personal Relationships Are Differently Associated with Age

The social worlds of children, adolescents, and adults are characterized by substantive structural and functional differences. From birth until early adulthood, individuals continually increase the number of their personal relationships. In a longitudinal study, Feiring and Lewis (1991a) interviewed mothers when their children were three, six, and nine years old. According to their mothers' reports, three-year-old children, on average, had weekly social contacts with about five or six persons, who were either kin ($M = 2.6$), non-kin adults ($M = 1.5$), or peer friends ($M = 1.5$). The number of persons contacted at a weekly rate increased to an average of seven persons at the time when the children were nine years old. More importantly, there was much change with respect to the type of children's personal relationships: While the number of peer friends doubled between age three and age nine ($M = 3.2$), the number of relatives decreased at age nine ($M = 1.5$). In a second longitudinal study, Feiring and Lewis (1991b) used the same procedure to investigate changes in children's social contacts between ages nine and thirteen. The total number of weekly social contact partners increased from an average 7.5 at age nine to about 10 persons at age thirteen. Again, the contacts with kin and non-kin adults showed a considerable decrease, while the number of peer friends nearly doubled (from an average of 3.5 to 6.6 personal relationships). The findings serve to illustrate the relative importance of relationships with friends or peers in childhood and early adolescence as they contribute to the child's social development (Hartup, 1989; Harris, 1995; Youniss, 1980). One difficulty is that empirical findings on personal relationships in childhood or adolescence have rarely been compared with findings on personal relationships of adults. For example, there is robust evidence that the number of personal relationships markedly decreases when individuals approach the end of their lives (e.g., Lang, 2000). Is it possible that the same underlying motivations that lead to an enlargement of personal networks in early and middle childhood are also responsible for the reduction of the social worlds in late adulthood? What do we know about early and middle adulthood? First of all, one difficulty of comparing findings across life phases lies in the multitude of different existing methods to assess the availability and quality of personal relationships (e.g., Neyer, 1997). One exemplar illustration of the lifelong pattern of age differences in personal relationships can be gained when comparing findings of studies that have relied on similar methods to assess personal relationships at different life phases.

Figure 14.1 shows a hypothetical trajectory of the number of very close and less close personal relationships from infancy until late life based on findings from several cross-sectional empirical studies that have used the Antonucci (1976) circle diagram method to assess personal networks (Fung, Carstensen, & Lang, 2001; Levitt, Guacci-Franco, & Levitt, 1993; Lang, 2000; Lang & Carstensen, 2002; Lang, Staudinger, & Carstensen, 1998). As Figure 14.1 illustrates, the total number of close personal relationships follows an inverted U-shape pattern across the life span with a broad peak in midlife. While this pattern holds for less close relationships, there is much

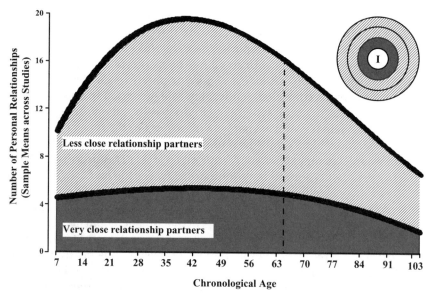

FIGURE 14.1. Hypothetical Trajectory of Personal Network Size across the Life Span Based on Findings of Four Empirical Studies Using the Circle-Diagram Method.

stability with respect to the number of very close social partners. The pattern displayed in this illustration is based on one instrument that has been used in different cultures and with people of all ages between 7 and 103 (Antonucci et al., 2001). In developmental psychology it is a rare case that the same method yields comparable, reliable, and adequate findings across a broad age range.

(4) Personal Relationships May Contribute to Mastery at All Stages of Life When Age Adequate

Other people give support in a myriad of different ways such as encouraging, mentoring, cheering up, intimate confiding, helping with practical problems, teaching, giving positive feedback, or just tenderly touching. Personal relationships are often known to be helpful in overcoming the hardships and setbacks of one's life. At all phases of life there are other people who encourage and assist the individual. And even if others are not physically present, individuals represent them cognitively (e.g., Baldwin, 1992). When the system of social resources breaks down, individuals may easily drop out of their social roles and vice versa. When developmental tasks are not mastered successfully, social resources diminish or become unavailable. However, this view of personal relationships as an individual resource is also problematic if one ignores that not all features of personal relationships are equally resourceful at all phases of the life span. Many personal relationships entail risks and negative experiences as well. For example, three-year-old children often express their wish to do a task all by themselves and reject any offer for help. This phenomenon has been proposed as being a central mechanism in the development of achievement motivation (Geppert & Kuester, 1983). This early striving for autonomy then fully disappears within subsequent years, showing up again in different forms at later stages. One implication is that there are no benefits without costs in social interactions. Most people appear to learn over the life course how to disentangle and how to balance the resourceful and the stressful sides of their personal relationships. However, the underlying processes of such regulations are still not well understood.

The age-associated trajectories of structural and functional aspects of personal relationships (Propositions 4 and 5) may serve to underscore the notion that individuals are active in choosing, maintaining, or discontinuing their personal relationships depending on the challenges and constraints of a specific life phase. This points to another relatively neglected issue in research and theory on social motivation, the risk of a personal relationship ending.

(5) Each and Every Personal Relationship Is Vulnerable and at Risk of Being Ended

In the literature, it is often stated that friendship relationships differ from family relationships with respect to their voluntary nature (e.g., Hinde, 1997). One argument is that because friendships and romantic ties are deliberately chosen they are more likely to be dissolved. There is much empirical and theoretical work on the processes and determinants that lead to dissolution of romantic partners (e.g., Battaglia, Richard, Datteri, & Lord, 1998) or of friendships (e.g., Roberto, 1989; Wiseman, 1986). It cannot be doubted that a friendship is based on the voluntary and mutual agreement of two interaction partners. This, however, applies to other role relationships as well. It is often ignored that all other types of relationships, even those in the nuclear family, can in principle be dissolved. In fact, the use of the term *voluntary* is quite equivocal and might even be misleading.

In Western societies involuntary or forced personal relationships do not in principle legally exist. Friends can decide to end their friendship. Similarly most other personal relationships can, at least in theory, be deliberately dissolved by one of the partners. Many other personal relationships may be temporarily discontinued in the course of life. However, many social contexts such as school settings, hospitals, nursing homes, prisons, one's neighborhood, or one's workplace involve personal relationships that are not fully self-selected and that typically cannot be ended without enormous costs (e.g., moving, job change). In some cultures there still exists a tradition of parentally arranged marriages (Mullatti, 1995) that involves negative sanctions when adolescents decide against the parents' wishes. Ending a relationship always incurs costs. In severe cases, family members can decide to break off a relationship with a relative who has betrayed, abused, or severely neglected them. Relatives may lose contact with each other for some period of time. Personal relationships may thus be described along a continuum of negative consequences that result when one or both of the individuals decides to end the relationship.

Even the strongest bond between a father or mother and his or her child does not persist against all odds, as illustrated in those extreme cases in which biological parents are willing to abandon their newborn baby who is physically deformed or impaired (e.g., Weiss, 1998). Furthermore, even parents and their adult child may break off their contacts, for instance after one has abused the other (see Luescher & Pillemer, 1998). When parents separate, noncustodial fathers are at risk of losing contact with their children (e.g., Kruk, 1991; Lewis, Maka, & Papacosta, 1997). It can be argued that certain types of relationships continue to exist even if there is no contact and no desire to have contact among the partners. Some personal relationships are merely cognitively represented without any occurrence of real social contact (e.g., Gleason, Sebanc, & Hartup, 2000; Seiffge-Krenke, 1997). Moreover, some personal relationships that have ended continue to exist as a biological or legal association (e.g., father, siblings). In each of these cases, there exist underlying motivations that guide the individual's relationship behavior and thus influence his or her relationships. Finally, one may also want to ask why people maintain personal relationships that are perceived as unsatisfying or strained (e.g., Drigotas & Rusbult, 1992). Sometimes, individuals show a remarkable resilience in terms of keeping up a social tie with another person even in the face of the most aversive experiences.

(6) There Is Much Diversity and Variability between and among the Personal Relationships that Individuals Maintain over the Life Course

Personal relationships may be characterized and classified with respect to specific social roles (e.g., parent, sibling, colleague, classmate), specific functions they fulfill (e.g., companion, confidant, mentor, collaborator), or specific characteristics of interaction styles (e.g., peripheral, exchange, communal, intimate). Each personal relationship can be characterized in different ways on each of these dimensions. Some personal relationships even serve in a multiplicity of diverse functions and situations. Moreover, in our everyday experience no two personal relationships are the same.

And even at the empirical level, if one assumes that all relationship behavior is determined by the stable personality characteristics of the partners, there may remain some variation that can be attributed to the unique effects of a specific relationship (cf. Kenny & LaVoie, 1984).

In this context, it is necessary to make a distinction between the diversity of the personal relationship of one individual and the individual differences of the characteristics of personal relationships. The former emphasizes that there is much interindividual difference with respect to the kinds of personal relationship that people maintain, whereas the latter pertains to the issue that personal networks are typically composed of a diversity of relationships that differ with respect to social roles, functions, and types. One explanation for this diversity is that personal networks serve to meet and fulfill a variety of needs of one individual; friends, for instance, serve different functions than family members. Also, if an individual already has many friendships, the likelihood of gaining an additional new friend may be smaller than if the same person has only a few friends. In modern societies, most married people have just one spouse and this means that a married individual is less likely to engage in a new romantic relationship than the same individual would be if unmarried. However, not much is known about how the availability of a certain relationship quality (e.g., companionship, intimacy) affects the quality of other personal relationships of the same individual. One common influence that affects all personal relationships in equal ways pertains to individual differences in personality (e.g., Asendorpf & Wilpers, 1998; Neyer & Asendorpf, 2001). However, other aspects of the individual personal relationships may be less stable and instead be strongly associated with the individual's current life situation and goals (e.g., Wrosch & J. Heckhausen, 1999). Thus, interindividual differences in personal relationships may also reflect the individual's strategies of adapting to the constraints and tasks of specific life phases.

To sum up, the quality of one's personal relationships are not just due to fate, to which one has to adhere under all and even the most aversive conditions. Rather, personal relationships occur as the result of enduring but generally reversible decisions that reflect the individual's needs and goals at various points of time in one's life. This implies that change and stability of personal relationships over the life course follow predictable patterns of individual preferences and behaviors. What factors determine these patterns of change?

In the following, I address in which ways personal relationships and the regulation of personal relationships change over the life course. In which ways do individuals change their social motivation in response to the availability of individual resources such as health or remaining life expectancy? An integrative goal-resource-congruence model of the

regulation of personal relationships is suggested and illustrated with selected empirical findings in childhood, adolescence, and adulthood. A final
section discusses future directions of this research and gives an outlook on
some of the most pertinent issues in this field.

MOTIVATION OF PERSONAL RELATIONSHIPS ACROSS
THE LIFE SPAN: GOALS AND RESOURCES

Modern theories of human development emphasize the active role
of individuals in regulating their development over the life course
(Brandtstaedter, 1989; J. Heckhausen, 1999; Lerner & Walls, 1999). A central proposition of this perspective is that all human behavior is directed at producing contingencies in one's environment (DeCharms, 1968;
J. Heckhausen & Schulz, 1995; Schulz & J. Heckhausen, 1996; White, 1959).
At all phases of the life course, individuals are motivated to maximize
their abilities to influence the world they inhabit. The life span theory of
control developed by Heckhausen and Schulz (1995) contends that individuals seek to enhance their action potentials through the use of two
general control strategies, primary control and secondary control. Primary control involves the shaping of one's environment in accordance
with one's goals, while secondary control means the shaping of one's
goals and internal states in accordance with environmental constraints.
A basic tenet of the theory is the primacy of primary control (Schulz &
J. Heckhausen, 1996). This implies that whenever it is possible people
seek to make use of primary control strategies, and that secondary control strategies are in the service of the individual's striving for primary
control (i.e., action potential). Personal relationships represent the most
central components of the individual's environment. Consequently, most
control strategies of individuals are implicitly or explicitly directed at one's
social world or personal relationships. Individuals actively influence their
relationship partners in order to produce a goal-congruent social environment, which, in turn, influences the course and direction of their own
development.

     As suggested above (see Proposition 5), in some social contexts personal
relationships are not self-controlled (i.e., workplace, school, prison). Thus,
individuals are also confronted with unexpected and undesirable social
experiences. Moreover, individuals have only limited possibility to control
the behavior of their relationship partners. One consequence is that when a
personal relationship does not match with one's goals or plans and one sees
no way to influence it, one may have to decide whether to adapt one's internal standards and goals to the new situation or to end the relationship for
some time or forever. This underscores that relationship behaviors depend
on the contents of one's goals and on one's capacities to pursue these goals.
This has two implications, which I will discuss in the following: (a) The

structure and functions of personal relationships are associated with specific contents of goals; and (b) goal contents are associated with individual resources. Depending on resource availability, pursuing a specific goal may lead to more positive outcomes in one's social environment than pursuing some other goal.

SOCIAL MOTIVATION AND THE MAINTENANCE OF PERSONAL RELATIONSHIPS: TYPES OF GOALS

Goal commitment is known to be a central feature of adaptive social functioning (e.g., Emmons, 1986; J. Heckhausen, 1997; Little, 1989; Omodei & Wearing, 1990). A critical question is to what extent the contents of one's goals are relevant to social functioning. Do people behave differently in a personal relationship depending on which goal they are currently pursuing? For example, do people who wish to obtain social recognition and popularity for their deeds prefer other contents in social interactions than people who seek a romantic and intimate experience? Obviously they do. Goals determine what one expects from others and how one responds to expectations of others. People often seek comfort from social interactions with their colleagues but also seek help in accomplishing career goals. Children seek to obtain rewards and recognition for their accomplishments from their parents but also wish to share their most intimate feelings and sorrows with them. However, the provisions that can be obtained from different relationships differ, and thus people are more likely to attain certain goals (e.g., social recognition) in some relationship types (e.g., workplace relationships) than in other types of relationships (e.g., intimate relationships). The priority of specific goals will thus influence the kinds of personal relationships that one maintains. A central proposition of this chapter lies in the contention that personal networks and social relationships are regulated in congruence with one's most salient goals. The pursuit of specific goal contents is known to play an important role in the maintenance of personal relationships and social functioning in childhood (Wentzel, 1994, 1998), adolescence (e.g., Jarvinen & Nicholls, 1996), and adulthood (Lang & Carstensen, 2002).

How can the content of goals be classified? In psychology, there is a long tradition of taxonomies of goal contents (for an overview, see Austin & Vancouver, 1996). One challenge of such attempts lies in the obstacle of classifying the content of an individual's goal independent of the specific developmental context in which the goal arises. The specific content of a goal is the result of the interaction between an individual's personality and the individual's environment (cf. H. Heckhausen, 1991). This implies that any taxonomy of goals is incomplete as long as it does not reflect all the possible transactions (and combinations) of stable personality with environmental characteristics, in which a goal commitment is situated. Obviously this can never be fully achieved, and may not even appear desirable. For this reason, I focus on those contents of goals that are most relevant in the domain of interpersonal functioning and personal relationships. There are two general classes of goals that are typically associated with personal relationships: (1) belonging goals, which are directed at social integration and attachment (e.g., Baumeister & Leary, 1996; Bowlby, 1969); and (2) social agency goals, which aim at self-determination, individuality, and control over social events (e.g., Hansson & Carpenter, 1994; Lang, Featherman, & Nesselroade, 1997; Rook, 1995).

Goals of belongingness pertain to the quality of one's relationships (e.g., seeking the companionship of a friend, avoiding states of anger) or to the well-being of a relationship partner (e.g., caring for a close partner, avoiding unpleasant behaviors). A central feature of belonging goals is that they are directed at establishing a mutually satisfactory state for both partners in a relationship. The desired end state lies in a specific quality of that relationship. In most cases this means that one uses strategies that serve both partners equally well while excluding competitive or instrumental strategies in a relationship. For example, one implication is that when a relationship partner behaves in unexpected or undesirable ways, one may seek to reestablish a state in which one feels comfortable with one's partner rather than breaking the tie.

Goals of social agency aim at seeking personal relationships as a means to an end (e.g., to enhance social recognition). The desired end state of agency goals lies in the relative status of the self as compared to others. For example, an individual may seek to convince others of their capabilities in certain areas of expertise in order to achieve a higher social status. Individuals may seek social contact in order to gain information, because this can enhance one's competence and self-determination. Competition is another example of social agency. People often measure their own abilities and performance by comparing themselves with similar others (Festinger, 1954). Thus, relating with others constitutes a frame of reference for social comparisons, which contributes to personal growth and to the development of the self (e.g., J. Heckhausen & Krüger, 1993; J. Heckhausen & Lang, 1996). In more general terms, social agency goals are directed at getting others to behave, act, or think in specific ways that are not relationship specific.

The difference between belonging goals and social agency goals may not always be obvious and clear-cut, because goals are hierarchically structured at different levels. For example, a child may seek the social recognition of his or her peers because this enhances one's popularity in the classroom. In contrast, the child may also seek the social recognition of a father because he or she feels close to him. While the latter implies a belonging goal, the former implies an agency goal. In addition, goals of belonging and social agency are not mutually exclusive. Although the distinction is of theoretical importance, agency and belonging goals are often mixed with

TABLE 14.2. *Theoretical Concepts Related to Goals of Belonging and to Goals of Social Agency*

Sources	Goals of Belonging	Goals of Social Agency
Murray (1938); McClelland (1951)	Need of affiliation, need of intimacy	Need of dominance, need of achievement
Maslow (1954)	Needs of safety, dependency, belongingness, and love	Needs of esteem and self-actualization
Bakan (1966); McAdams (1980)	Communion	Agency
Clark (1983); Clark & Mills (1979)	Communal orientation	Exchange orientation
Markus & Kitayama (1991); Raeff (1997)	Interdependent self	Independent self
Triandis (1995)	Allocentric orientation (collectivism)	Idiocentric orientation (Individualism)
Austing &Vancouver (1996)	Self-assertive social relationship goal	Integrative social relationship goal
Carstensen, Isaacowitz, & Charles (1999)	Emotion regulation	Information seeking

respect to the maintenance of a specific personal relationship. For example, a graduate student may seek contact with an academic advisor because this may further future career options, while at the same time the student may experience a strong sympathy and admiration for the mentor and may want to gain his or her friendship. The central proposition here is that there is continuous change in the priority of the two motives.

The proposition that there is a dynamic interplay between both motives has a long tradition in the literature on social motivation. Table 14.2 shows an overview of selected theories that rely on related concepts. For example, scholars in motivational psychology have long emphasized the "big four" of motivation, that is, the needs of affiliation and of intimacy on one hand, and the needs of achievement and of dominance or power on the other hand (H. Heckhausen, 1991; McClelland, 1951; Murray, 1938). Each of these four basic motive dispositions has been investigated in a large number of theoretical and empirical studies over the past decades. The findings have shed much light on the determinants, functions, and processes underlying these motives. However, the interplay and dynamic between the different motivation systems is still not well understood. Few textbooks of human motivation provide an introduction to all four motive systems (e.g., H. Heckhausen, 1991). Maslow (1954) suggested a hierarchy of human needs in which goals related to esteem and self-actualization are viewed as hierarchically superior to social needs (e.g., belongingness, love, protection, dependency) and to safety needs.

In his classic monograph, Bakan (1966) distinguished between "communion" and "agency" as a basic "duality of human existence" in which agency stands "for the existence of an organism as an individual…" (p. 15) and communion pertains to "the participation of the individual in some larger organism of which the individual is a part" (p. 15). The thread of this distinction was picked up again in the work of McAdams (e.g., 1985), who applied the concepts of communion and agency to issues of social motivation and generativity (e.g., McAdams, Hart, & Maruna, 1996). In another line of reasoning, Margret Clark (1984; Clark & Mills, 1979) differentiated two dimensions of orientations toward potential new social partners, an exchange orientation geared toward short-term exchanges with others and a communal orientation geared toward a long-term commitment with another person. Differentiation of motives of belongingness and of social agency also pertains to the distinction between an idiocentric versus an allocentric social orientation that appears to prevail in different cultures (i.e., individualistic vs. collectivistic; Triandis, 1995) as well as to the distinction between independence and interdependence as opposing dimensions of self-development (Markus & Kitayama, 1991; Raeff, 1997). In a similar vein, Austin and Vancouver (1996) distinguished between goals of self-assertive social relationships and goals of integrative social relationships. In her theory of socioemotional selectivity, Laura Carstensen and her colleagues (e.g., Carstensen, Isaacowitz, & Charles, 1999) suggested that there are two fundamental social motivations relevant to age-associated adaptation across the life span, emotion regulation and seeking information.

SOCIAL GOALS AND PERSONAL RELATIONSHIPS OVER THE LIFE COURSE: MODERATING INFLUENCES OF RESOURCES

Individual development is associated with changes of one's psychological, physical, social, and sociocultural resources. For example, when individuals are healthy, physically and cognitively well-functioning, well educated and equipped with a positive personality they make better use of adaptive strategies in response to experiences of loss or aging (M. Baltes & Lang, 1997; Lang, Rieckmann, & M. Baltes, 2002). Individual resources thus determine the individual's goals. For example, there are stable and consistent individual differences with respect to an individual's needs. When people have a strong desire for control, they may be generally more likely to seek relationships with people who enhance their sense of agency (e.g., Burger, 1992). In contrast, introverted and emotionally unstable people may generally prefer contacts with partners, who are reassuring, warm, and comforting (Lang et al., 1998). One explanation is that individuals select those goals that best match with their individual resource status.

The availability of individual resources may moderate the relation between goals and the actual quality of one's personal relationships. In a study with young adults, Brunstein and his colleagues (Brunstein, Schultheiss, & Grassman, 1998) found that the pursuit of goals that are congruent with one's motive disposition (e.g., intimacy motive) contributes to enhanced subjective well-being. For example, when an individual is committed to intimacy-related goals while having a strong power or achievement motive disposition, progress toward the intimacy goals (e.g., finding a romantic partner) may not lead to increased well-being.

Individuals shift their priorities between goals across the life course in response to and in accordance with developmental resources and opportunity structures (Carstensen et al., 1999; J. Heckhausen, 1999; Lang, 2001; Lang & Carstensen, 2002). When individuals have many resources available, they seek to enhance their agentic control over social events, for example, by seeking social recognition or power. When individuals have few resources, belonging goals are prioritized, for example, seeking to find a satisfying and meaningful experience in one's personal relationships. In response to resource loss, individuals may shift their goal priorities to find comfort, a sense of belonging, familiarity, and security in their social ties. Such a shift of goal priorities in response to resource loss reflects a secondary control strategy, which secures the individual's capability of soliciting or evoking contingent experience from the social environment (e.g., care or attentiveness of partners). Figure 14.2 illustrates the hypothesized relation between developmental resources and the salience (and adaptiveness) of the two goal domains.

According to this goal-resource-congruence model, both sets of goals are differently associated with the developmental resources. There is a

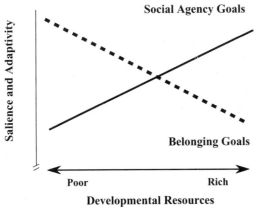

FIGURE 14.2. A Theoretical Model of the Dynamic Interplay between Resources and Goals on Social Functioning.

linear and positive association between the availability of developmental resources and the salience of social agency goals as well as the adaptive outcomes of pursuing social agency goals: Resource-rich individuals are more likely to pursue and benefit from pursuing social agency goals. In addition a linear negative relationship is assumed between developmental resources and the salience as well as the pursuit of belonging goals: The fewer the available resources, the more likely and the more beneficial is the pursuit of belonging goals. The basic tenet of this model of relationship regulation is that there are continuous and situational shifts in the priority between both goal sets. In a given situation, individuals prioritize either seeking emotional comfort with their partner or enhancing their competence. When individuals are in a resource-poor state, they prefer to seek a sense of belongingness in their personal relationships, rather than social agency. And vice versa, when individuals are in resource-rich states they seek to maximize their efficacy in the social world. Neither belonging nor agency goals are ever fully abandoned. Both sets of goals are expected to remain active in the regulation of personal relationships throughout all phases of the life span.

How are developmental resources defined? The use of the term *resources* has a long tradition in theorizing about life span developmental processes (e.g., M. Baltes & Lang, 1997; Lawton, 1989; Steverink, Lindenberg, & Ormel, 1998). In general, resources refer to an individual's capacities and assets. This involves objective and subjective as well as internal and external resources such as a positive agreeable and outgoing personality, interpersonal skills, high education, economic wealth, or strong cognitive capabilities. For example, perceiving one's future time as being relatively open-ended constitutes an important individual resource even if objectively there is only a limited number of remaining years in one's life. All resources of the individual, taken together, represent the constraints and opportunities of specific life phases. In the following, the term *developmental resource* is preferred here to characterize those resources that are relevant for the mastery of developmental challenges and tasks over the life course. Changes in such resources follow age-graded patterns that serve as a scaffold of lifelong development (Brandtstaedter, 1989; J. Heckhausen, 1999).

Developmental resources are defined as resources that are developmentally salient at specific phases of the life span. This implies that only age-related resources affect the life course trajectories of goal priority. Developmental resources influence how individuals respond to the constraints and challenges of each life phase and to transitions such as entering elementary school in childhood, the turmoil of puberty in early adolescence, leaving one's parents' home, finding a romantic partner, and having children who grow up and leave home to eventually have their own children. One prominent developmental resource concerns the ways in which individuals construe their future time over the life course. The next section illustrates selected findings on the influences of future time perspectives as a developmental resource on the regulation of personal relationships across the life span.

PERCEPTIONS OF THE FUTURE AS A DEVELOPMENTAL RESOURCE: EMPIRICAL ILLUSTRATIONS ACROSS THE LIFE SPAN

The ways in which individuals construe their future time determines their commitment to goals (e.g., Nuttin, 1985). What one expects in the future influences one's beliefs about one's present action potentials, and vice versa. Future time perspectives relate to beliefs about what one thinks one is able to achieve in the future (Bandura, 1997; Lang & J. Heckhausen, 2001) and what one thinks the future will be like (e.g., Zimbardo & Boyd, 1999). The latter aspect also implies beliefs about the relationship between means and ends (Skinner, 1996). For example, an individual may expect that under certain conditions (e.g., "when remaining healthy"), he or she will have many chances to make new plans in the future. From this perspective, individuals generally consider what they expect in the future before they commit to a specific goal. What one expects in the future thus constitutes a powerful resource of human development across the life span (Carstensen et al., 1999; Kastenbaum, 1982; Lewin, 1948; Mischel, Shoda, & Peake, 1988; Trommsdorff, 1983). In what ways do future time perspectives moderate the associations between goals and interpersonal functioning across the life span?

At preschool age, children develop the capacity of delaying expected rewards, which may be seen as an important precursor of the development of future time perspectives (e.g., Klineberg, 1967). Delay of gratification at preschool age has been shown to be a valid precursor of competence in late adolescence and early adulthood (Mischel et al., 1988). In a longitudinal study with 156 children aged 11, Ayduk, Mendoza-Denton, Mischel, Downey, Peake, and Rodriguez (2000; Study 2) investigated children's delay of gratification in relation to the fear of social rejection and interpersonal functioning as rated by the child's teacher. Expressing great fear of being rejected by peers indicates a strong social motivation to be socially accepted, which is a social agency goal. Fear of social rejection was assessed with children's ratings of vignettes of ambiguous social situations. Children who expressed a great fear of rejection and displayed high delay of gratification were rated as maintaining the most positive personal relationships. In contrast, those children who expressed great fear of rejection but displayed low delay of gratification were rated by teachers as having the least positive personal relationships. This finding serves to underscore that delay of gratification is an important resource that moderates the association between striving for social agency (fear of rejection) and social functioning. Notably though, no belonging goal was assessed in this study.

For example, children who are low in delayed gratification may have benefited when pursuing a belonging goal (e.g., seeking close friendship, fear of losing an intimate friend).

In another series of studies with adults, Lang (2000, 2001) investigated the moderating role of future time perspectives on associations between goals and social embeddedness. For example, Lang and Carstensen (2002) used a card-sort technique to assess goal priorities and partner preferences in a cross-sectional study with 480 young, middle-aged, and old adults. The card sort was used to assess four different goal types, that is, goals of social agency such as autonomy and social acceptance, and goals of belongingness such as generativity and emotion regulation. A first question pertained to the association between future time perspective and the priority of belonging versus social agency goals. Time perspective was assessed with a 10-item questionnaire assessing the perceived extension of one's future time. Results showed that when participants perceived their future time as limited, they prioritized belonging goals such as generativity goals (e.g., "leave my mark on this world") and goals of emotion regulation (e.g., "know my feelings very well"). In contrast, when participants perceived the future time as open-ended, they prioritized social agency goals related to autonomy (e.g., "be financially independent") and those related to social acceptance (e.g., "have good friends who accept me the way I am").

A second question concerns the associations between goal priorities and the structure of personal relationships. Findings suggest that social environments are reflective of the individual's social goals and future time perspective. For example, prioritizing emotion regulation goals was associated with smaller personal networks, whereas importance of social acceptance was associated with larger personal networks. Theoretically more important was the finding that future time perspective also moderated the associations between goals and characteristics of social relationships. For example, the association between priority of emotion regulation goals and smaller personal networks was strongest among participants who perceived their future time as limited. In addition, among individuals who perceived their future as limited, prioritizing emotionally meaningful goals was associated with improved perceived quality of social relationships.

To sum up, future time perspectives related to delay of gratification and to perceived extension of future time are shown to moderate the associations between an individual's social motivation and social functioning. Age differences in personal relationships across the life span are shown to be associated with individual differences in future time perspectives and contents of goals. The pursuit of belonging goals appears to be an adaptive strategy for dealing with low-resource situations for two reasons. First, when individuals have few resources to engage in agency goals, pursuing belonging goals evokes contingent responses from one's social world and thus maximizes one's action potentials. Second, when individuals engage in belonging goals this implies an enhanced quality of their personal relationships over time that compensate for resource losses.

FUTURE DIRECTIONS AND OUTLOOK

Motivational processes contribute to the development of personal relationships across the life span. Individuals actively produce their own social worlds, and they construct their social worlds in order to match with their capabilities, plans, and tasks in life. The goal-resource-congruent model of regulation of personal relationships emphasizes mechanisms of social adaptation over the life course. Individuals are motivated to seek personal relationships that provide them with a sense of personal causation (DeCharms, 1968) and social rewards. Two broad types of social rewards motivating an individual's relationship behaviors are distinguished: belongingness and social agency.

It is argued that in the absence of developmental resources individuals focus on goals that serve to enhance their social integration and maximize their sense of safety. This enhances their social resources in the long run. However, there is one caveat that should be considered with respect to the status of social resources. In the empirical literature, structural or functional aspects of personal relationships such as the size of personal networks or the availability of social support are often treated as coping resources. However, this perspective falls short. Personal relationships are not just a passive resource of the individual (e.g., Hansson & Carpenter, 1994; Hansson, Daleiden, & Hayslip, Chap. 13, this volume). Rather, personal relationships are both a determinant and an outcome of motivational processes through which individuals regulate their lifelong development. This implies a theoretical distinction between the resourceful characteristics of personal relationships and those qualities of relationships that result from goal-regulatory processes. For example, when individuals experience a lack of social resources (e.g., when feeling lonely or needing emotional support), they may invest more time and energy in achieving belonging goals, which in turn may increase the availability of social support resources.

Dyadic perspectives are needed. How do the goals of one partner affect the goals of the other? How do individuals in social relationships acknowledge and respond to each other's goals and resources? Dyadic perspectives are needed that focus on the transactions of motivational and regulatory processes within a system of personal relationships. For example, the goals of intimate partners are typically studied in married couples without considering that the same partners also maintain close relationships with other people as well (e.g., relatives, colleagues, friends). It is common sense that what happens in one relationship may affect all other personal relationships. However, I am not aware of any empirical study that has investigated such a network process. For example, when do conflicts of one individual in one relationship carry over to his or her other relationships and when not? How do relationships with others contribute to the maintenance and continuation of other relationships?

There are also clinical implications. When individuals experience a change in the availability of developmental resources, their goals and plans may have changed automatically as they engage in social contact. This may increase the risk of experiencing dissatisfying social interactions. Moreover, while spending time with others people may not be aware that their feelings of dissatisfaction may be related to an incongruence of their goals with their current situation and capacities. At times, individuals may feel overwhelmed by the demands of others whereas at other times they are happy to take over these responsibilities. Perceiving personal relationships as a developmental product rather than as a resource may help to underscore the individual's self-regulatory influence on the course and quality of personal relationships.

References

Antonucci, T. C. (1976). Hierarchical mapping technique. *Generations, 10*, 10–12.

Antonucci, T. C., Lansford, J. E., Schaberg, L., Smith, J., Baltes, M., Akiyama, H., Takahashi, K., Fuhrer, R., & Dartigues, J.-F. (2001). Widowhood and illness: A comparison of social network characteristics in France, Germany, Japan, and the United States. *Psychology and Aging, 16*, 655–665.

Asendorpf, J. B., & Wilpers, S. (1998). Personality effects on social relationships. *Journal of Personality and Social Psychology, 74*, 1531–1544.

Austin, J. T., & Vancouver, J. B. (1996). Goal constructs in psychology: Structure, process, and content. *Psychological Bulletin, 120*, 338–375.

Ayduk, O., Mendoza-Denton, R., Mischel, W., Downey, G., Peake, P. K., & Rodriguez, M. (2000). Regulating the interpersonal self: Strategic self-regulation for coping with rejection sensitivity. *Journal of Personality and Social Psychology, 79*, 776–792.

Bakan, D. (1966). *The duality of human existence*. Boston: Beacon Press.

Baldwin, M. W. (1992). Relational schemas and the processing of social information. *Psychological Bulletin, 112*, 461–484.

Baltes, M. M., & Lang, F. R. (1997). Everyday functioning and successful aging: The impact of resources. *Psychology and Aging, 12*, 433–443.

Bandura, A. (1997). *Self-efficacy. The exercise of control*. New York: Freeman & Company.

Battaglia, D. M., Richard, F. D., Datteri, D. L., & Lord, C. G. (1998). Breaking up is (relatively) easy to do: A script for the dissolution of close relationships. *Journal of Social and Personal Relationships, 15*, 829–845.

Baumeister, R. F., & Leary, M. R. (1996). The need to belong: Desire for interpersonal attachments as a fundamental human motivation. *Psychological Bulletin, 117*, 497–529.

Bierhoff, H.-W., & Schmohr, M. (2003). Romantic and marital relationships. In F. R. Lang & K. L. Fingerman (Eds.), *Growing together: Personal relationships across the life span* (Chap. 5). New York: Cambridge University Press.

Bowlby, J. (1969). *Attachment and loss. Vol. 1, Attachment.* New York: Basic Books.

Brandtstaedter, J. (1989). Personal self-regulation of development: Cross-sequential analyses of development-related control beliefs and emotions. *Developmental Psychology, 25*, 96–108

Brunstein, J. C., Schultheiss, O. C., & Grassman, R. (1998). Personal goals and emotional well-being: The moderating role of motive dispositions. *Journal of Personality and Social Psychology, 75*, 494–508.

Burger, J. M. (1992). *Desire for control: Personality, social, and clinical perspectives.* New York: Plenum Press.

Carstensen, L. L., Isaacowitz, D. M., & Charles, S. T. (1999). Taking time seriously: A theory of socioemotional selectivity. *American Psychologist, 54*, 165–181.

Clark, M. S. (1984). A distinction between two types of relationships and its implications for development. In J. C. Masters & K. Yarkin-Levin (Eds.), *Boundary areas in social and developmental psychology* (pp. 241–270). New York: Academic Press.

Clark, M. S., & Mills, J. (1979). Interpersonal attraction in exchange and communal relationships. *Journal of Personality and Social Psychology, 37*, 12–24.

DeCharms, R. (1968). *Personal causation.* New York: Academic Press.

Drigotas, S. M., & Rusbult, C. E. (1992). Should I stay or should I go? A dependence model of breakups. *Journal of Personality and Social Psychology, 62*, 62–87.

Emmons, R. A. (1986). Personal strivings: An approach to personality and subjective well-being. *Journal of Personality and Social Psychology, 51*, 1058–1068.

Feiring, C., & Lewis, M. (1991a). The development of social networks from early to middle childhood: Gender differences and the relation to school competence. *Sex Roles, 25*, 237–253.

Feiring, C., & Lewis, M. (1991b). The transition from middle childhood to early adolescence: Sex differences in the social network and perceived self-competence. *Sex Roles, 24*, 489–509.

Festinger, L. (1954). A theory of social comparison processes. *Human Relations, 7*, 117–140.

Fingerman, K. (1996). Sources of tension in the aging mother and adult daughter relationship. *Psychology and Aging, 11*, 591–606.

Fingerman, K. L. (2003). The consequential stranger: Peripheral relationships across the life span. In F. R. Lang & K. L. Fingerman (Eds.), *Growing together: Personal relationships across the life span* (Chap. 8). New York: Cambridge University Press.

Fiske, A. P. (1992). The four elementary forms of sociality: Framework for a unified theory of social relations. *Psychological Review, 99*, 689–723.

Fung, H., Carstensen, L. L., & Lang, F. R. (2001). Age-related patterns of social relationships among African-Americans and Caucasian-Americans: Implications for socioemotional selectivity across the life span. *International Journal of Aging and Human Development, 52*, 185–206.

Gaulin, S. J. C., & McBurney, D. H. (2001). *Psychology. An evolutionary approach.* Upper Saddle River, NJ: Prentice-Hall.

Geppert, U., & Kuester, U. (1983). The emergence of "wanting to do it oneself": A precursor of achievement motivation. *International Journal of Behavioral Development, 6*, 355–369.

Gleason, T. R., Sebanc, A. M., & Hartup, W. W. (2000). Imaginary companions of preschool children. *Developmental Psychology, 36*, 419–428.

Granovetter, M. (1973). The strength of weak ties. *American Journal of Sociology, 78*, 1360–1380.

Hansson, R. O., & Carpenter, B. N. (1994). *Relationships in old age.* New York: Guilford.

Hansson, R. O., Daleiden, E., & Hayslip, B. Jr. (2003). Relational competence across the life span. In F. R. Lang & K. L. Fingerman (Eds.), *Growing together: Personal relationships across the life span* (Chap. 13). New York: Cambridge University Press.

Harris, J. R. (1995). Where is the child's environment? A group socialization theory of development. *Psychological Review, 102*, 458–489.

Hartup, W. W. (1989). Social relationships and their developmental significance. *American Psychologist, 44*, 120–126.

Heckhausen, H. (1991). *Motivation and action.* New York: Springer.

Heckhausen, J. (1997). Developmental regulation across adulthood: Primary and secondary control of age-related challenges. *Developmental Psychology, 33*, 176–187.

Heckhausen, J. (1999). *Developmental regulation in adulthood.* New York: Cambridge University Press.

Heckhausen, J., & Krüger, J. (1993). Developmental expectations for the self and most other people: Age grading in three functions of social comparison. *Developmental Psychology, 29*, 539–548.

Heckhausen, J., & Lang, F. R. (1996). Social construction in old age: Normative conceptions and interpersonal processes. In G. Semin & K. Fiedler (Eds.), *Applied social psychology* (pp. 374–398). London: Sage.

Heckhausen, J., & Schulz, R. (1995). A life-span theory of control. *Psychological Review, 102*, 284–304.

Hinde, R. A. (1997). *Relationships. A dialectical perspective.* Hove, East Sussex, UK: Taylor & Francis.

Jarvinen, D. W., & Nicholls, J. G. (1996). Adolescents' social goals, beliefs about the causes of social success, and satisfaction in peer relations. *Developmental Psychology, 32*, 435–441.

Kastenbaum, R. (1982). Time course and time perspective in later life. In C. Eisdorfer (Ed.), *Annual review of gerontology and geriatrics* (pp. 80–101). New York: Springer.

Kelley, H. H. (1997). Expanding the analysis of social orientations by reference to the sequential-temporal structure of situations. *European Journal of Social Psychology, 27*, 373–404.

Kenny, D. A., & LaVoie, L. (1984). The social relations model. In L. Berkowitz (Ed.), *Advances in experimental social psychology* (Vol. 18, pp. 141–182). Orlando: Academic Press.

Klineberg, S. L. (1967). Changes in outlook on the future between childhood and adolescence. *Journal of Personality and Social Psychology, 7*, 185–193.

Kruk, E. (1991). Discontinuity between pre- and post-divorce father-child relationships: New evidence regarding paternal disengagement. *Journal of Divorce and Remarriage, 16,* 195–227.

Lang, F. R. (2000). Endings and continuity of social relationships: Maximizing intrinsic benefits within personal networks when feeling near to death. *Journal of Social and Personal Relationships, 17,* 157–184.

Lang, F. R. (2001). Regulation of social relationships in later adulthood. *Journal of Gerontology: Psychological Sciences, 56B,* P321–326.

Lang, F. R. (in press). The filial task in midlife: Ambivalence and the quality of adult children's relationships with their old-aged parents. In K. Luescher & K. Pillemer (Eds.), *Intergenerational ambivalence.* Belgium: Elsevier/JAI Press.

Lang, F. R., & Carstensen, L. L. (2002). Time counts: Future time perspective, goals, and social relationships. *Psychology and Aging, 17,* 125–139.

Lang, F. R., Featherman, D. L., & Nesselroade, J. R. (1997). Social self-efficacy and short-term variability in social relationships: The MacArthur successful aging studies. *Psychology and Aging, 12,* 657–666.

Lang, F. R., & Heckhausen, J. (2001). Perceived control over development and subjective well-being: Differential benefits across adulthood. *Journal of Personality and Social Psychology, 81,* 509–523.

Lang, F. R., Rieckmann, N., & Baltes, M. M. (2002). Adapting to aging losses: Do resources facilitate strategies of selection, compensation, and optimization in everyday functioning? *Journal of Gerontology: Psychological Sciences, 57B,* P501–P509.

Lang, F. R., Staudinger, U. M., & Carstensen, L. L. (1998). Socioemotional selectivity in late life: How personality and social context do (and do not) make a difference. *Journals of Gerontology: Psychological Sciences, 53B,* P21–P30.

Larson, R., & Richards, M. (1994). *Divergent realities: The emotional lives of mothers, fathers, and adolescents.* New York: Basic Books.

Lawton, M. P. (1989). Behavior-relevant ecological factors. In K. W. Schaie & C. Schooler (Eds.), *Social structure and aging: Psychological processes* (pp. 57–78). Hillsdale, NJ: Erlbaum.

Lerner, R. M., & Kauffman, M. B. (1985). The concept of development in contextualism. *Developmental Review, 5,* 309–333.

Lerner, R. M., & Walls, T. (1999). Revisiting individuals as producers of their development: From dynamic interactionism to developmental systems. In J. Brandtstädter & R. M. Lerner (Eds.), *Action and self-development: Theory and research through the life span* (pp. 3–36). Thousand Oaks, CA: Sage Publications.

Levitt, M. J., Guacci-Franco, N., & Levitt, J. L. (1993). Convoys of social support in childhood and early adolescence: Structure and function. *Developmental Psychology, 29,* 811–818.

Lewin, K. (1948). Time perspective and morale. In K. Lewin (Ed.), *Resolving social conflicts* (pp. 103–124). New York: Harper.

Lewis, C., Maka, Z., & Papacosta, A. (1997). Why do fathers become disengaged from their children's lives? Maternal and paternal accounts of divorce in Greece. *Journal of Divorce and Remarriage, 28,* 89–117.

Lewis, M., & Rosenblum, L. A. (Eds.) (1975). *Friendship and peer relations.* New York: Wiley.

Little, B. R. (1989). Personal projects analysis: Trivial pursuits, magnificent obses-
sions, and the search for coherence. In D. M. Buss & N. Cantor (Eds.), *Personality
psychology: Recent trends and emerging directions* (pp. 15–31). New York: Springer.
Luescher, K., & Pillemer, K. (1998). Intergenerational ambivalence: A new approach
to the study of parent-child relations in later life. *Journal of Marriage and the Family,
60*, 413–425.
Markus, H. R., & Kitayama, S. (1991). Culture and the self: Implications for cognition, emotion, and motivation. *Psychological Review, 98*, 224–253.
Maslow, A. H. (1954). *Motivation and personality*. New York: Harper & Row.
McAdams, D. P. (1985). *Power, intimacy, and the life story: Personological inquiries into
identity*. New York: Guilford press.
McAdams, D. P., Hart, H. M., & Maruna, S. (1996). The anatomy of generativity.
In D. P. McAdams & E. de St. Aubin (Eds.), *Generativity and adult development*
(pp. 7–43). Washington, DC: APA.
McClelland, D. C. (1951). *Personality*. New York: Holt, Rinehart &Winston.
Milgram, S. (1967). The small-world problem. *Psychology Today, 1* (1), 60–67.
Mischel, W., Shoda, Y., & Peake, P. K. (1988). The nature of adolescent competen-
cies predicted by preschool delay of gratification. *Journal of Personality and Social
Psychology, 54*, 687–696.
Mullatti, L. (1995). Families in India: Beliefs and realities. *Journal of Comparative
Family Studies, 26*, 11–25.
Murray, H. A. (1938). *Explorations in personality*. New York: Oxford University Press.
Neyer, F. (1997). Free recall or recognition in collecting egocentered networks: The
role of survey techniques. *Journal of Social and Personal Relationships, 14*, 305–316.
Neyer, F. J., & Asendorpf, J. B. (2001). Personality-relationship transaction in young
adulthood. *Journal of Personality and Social Psychology, 81*, 1190–1204.
Nuttin, J. (1985). *Future time perspective and motivation*. Hillsdale, NJ: Lawrence
Erlbaum.
Omodei, M. M., & Wearing, A. J. (1990). Need satisfaction and involvement in
personal projects: Toward an integrative model of subjective well-being. *Journal
of Personality and Social Psychology, 59*, 762–769.
Parsons, T. (1961). An outline of the social system. In T. Parsons, E. A. Shils, K. D.
Naegele, & J. R. Pitts (Eds.), *Theories of society. Foundations of modern sociological
theory* (pp. 30–79). New York: Free Press.
Raeff, C. (1997). Individuals in relationships: Cultural values, children's social interactions, and the development of an American individualistic self. *Developmental
Review, 17*, 205–238.
Roberto, K. A. (1989). Exchange and equity in friendships. In R. G. Adams &
R. Blieszner (Eds.), *Older adult friendship: Structure and process* (pp. 147–165). Thou-
sand Oaks, CA: Sage Publications.
Rook, K. S. (1995). Support, companionship, and control in older adults' social net-
works: Implications for well-being. In J. F. Nussbaum & J. Coupland (Eds.), *Hand-
book of communication and aging research* (pp. 437–463). Hillsdale, NJ: Lawrence
Erlbaum Associates.
Rosenthal, C. J., Martin, M. A., & Matthews, S. H. (1996). Caught in the middle?
Occupancy in multiple roles and help to parents in a national probability sample
of Canadian adults. *Journal of Gerontology: Social Sciences, 51B*, S274–S283.

Schulz, R., & Heckhausen, J. (1996). A life span model of successful aging. *American Psychologist, 51,* 702–714.

Seiffge-Krenke, I. (1997). Imaginary companions in adolescence: Sign of a deficient or positive development? *Journal of Adolescence, 20,* 137–154.

Skinner, E. A. (1996). A guide to constructs of control. *Journal of Personality and Social Psychology, 71,* 549–570.

Steverink, N., Lindenberg, S., & Ormel, J. (1998). Towards understanding successful ageing: Patterned change in resources and goals. *Ageing and Society, 18,* 441–467.

Travers, J., & Milgram, S. (1969). An experimental study of the small world problem. *Sociometry, 32,* 425–443.

Triandis, H. C. (1995). *Individualism and collectivism.* Boulder, CO: Westview Press.

Trommsdorff, G. (1983). Future orientation and socialization. *International Journal of Psychology, 18,* 381–406.

Watson, A. C., Nixon, C. L., Wilson, A., & Capage, L. (1999). Social interaction skills and theory of mind in young children. *Developmental Psychology, 35,* 386–391.

Weiss, M. (1998). Parents' rejection of their appearance-impaired newborns: Some critical observations regarding the social myth of bonding. *Marriage and Family Review, 27,* 191–209.

Wentzel, K. R. (1994). Relations of social goal pursuit to social acceptance, classroom behavior, and perceived social support. *Journal of Educational Psychology, 86,* 173–182.

Wentzel, K. R. (1998). Social relationships and motivation in middle school: The role of parents, teachers, and peers. *Journal of Educational Psychology, 90,* 202–209.

Wentzel, K. R. (2000). What is it that I'm trying to achieve? Classroom goals from a content perspective. *Contemporary Educational Psychology, 25,* 105–115.

White, R. W. (1959). Motivation reconsidered: The concept of competence. *Psychological Review, 66,* 297–333.

Wiese, L. v. (1955). *System der allgemeinen Soziologie als Lehre von den sozialen Prozessen und den sozialen Gebilden der Menschen* [A system of general sociology as a theory of social processes and social relations of humans]. Berlin: Duncker & Humblot.

Wiseman, J. P. (1986). Friendship, bonds and binds in a voluntary relationship. *Journal of Personal and Social Relationships, 3,* 191–212.

Wrosch, C., & Heckhausen, J. (1999). Control processes before and after passing a developmental deadline: Activation and deactivation of intimate relationship goals. *Journal of Personality and Social Psychology, 77,* 415–427.

Youniss, J. (1980). *Parents and peers in social development.* Chicago: University of Chicago Press.

Zimbardo, P. G., & Boyd, J. N. (1999). Putting time in perspective: A valid, reliable individual-differences metric. *Journal of Personality and Social Psychology, 77,* 1271–1288.

15

A Lifetime of Relationships Mediated by Technology

Rebecca G. Adams and Michelle L. Stevenson

Although recent technological developments have made transportation and communication faster, more efficient, and more accessible, relationship theorists and researchers have been slow to adapt. This chapter outlines a *synthetic dynamic framework for the study of a lifetime of relationships mediated by technology*, which integrates theories of individual development, life course, family development, and network change. Although this framework could be used to generate questions about the effects of any type of technology on social relationships, because communication via the Internet has become common and has already contributed dramatically to the reduction of geographic constraints on relationships, we illustrate the use of this framework by generating questions about its effects.[1]

Research has repeatedly verified Homans's (1950) proposition that increased interaction leads to increased liking (e.g., Hays, 1984, 1985). This suggests that any change in technology that facilitates increased contact among family and friends would contribute to the solidarity of relationships. It is common knowledge that changes in communications and transportation technologies during the last 150 years have made contact among kin and friends, whether separated by small or great distances, less expensive, faster, and easier. Although numerous studies have been conducted on the social impact of previous technological developments, such as the telephone and automobile (e.g., Fischer & Carroll, 1988; Martin, 1991; Pool, 1983), the effects of the most recent developments in electronic communications on social relationships have not been studied extensively (see Parks & Floyd, 1996, and Watt & White, 1999, for exceptions). Furthermore, researchers who have studied the effects of technology on social relationships have not examined how these effects might vary by stage of individual or life course development. As a first step toward addressing these deficits

[1] The authors would like to thank Matthew Hembree and George Sanders for assistance in developing the bibliography for this chapter and Jenny Berggren for editorial comments.

in the relationship literature, we provide a theoretical framework to guide future research on how communications and transportation technology might facilitate or inhibit the evolution of family and friend relationships at various stages of individual or life course development. Although this framework could be used to generate questions about the effects of any type of communications or transportation technology on relationships, because communication via the Internet is "becoming normalized as it is incorporated into the routine practices of everyday life" (Wellman, Haase, Witte, & Hampton, 2001), has already contributed dramatically to the reduction of geographic constraints on social relationships, and will continue to have a tremendous impact on social relationships in the future, we focus here on the generation of questions regarding its effects.

Although the main purpose of this chapter is to suggest directions for future research, it is useful first to examine the extent and variety of changes in transportation and communications technology and the state of the literature on Internet technology as a mediator in social relationships. Examining the changes in technology serves as a reminder of how dramatically the context for social relationships has changed as geographic constraints on social interaction have been reduced. Surveying the literature on technology as a relationship mediator serves to demonstrate how slowly researchers have changed their perspectives to adapt to recent changes and how little attention they have given to the potential interaction effect among age of relationship participants, use of technology to communicate, and the character of social relationships.

After summarizing recent changes in communications and transportation technology and reviewing the literature on Internet communications as a social relationship mediator, we present our framework, which integrates four dynamic social theories, and discuss the implications of each of the four theories for understanding the impact of Internet technology on relationships. The dynamic perspectives we examine include structural theories of the life course and network change and process theories of individual and family development. In conclusion, we suggest directions for future research on a lifetime of relationships mediated by technology.

CHANGES IN THE TECHNOLOGICAL CONTEXT[2]

In this chapter, we focus on one type of communications technology, namely the Internet, as a mediator of social relationships. In order to understand the changing context of social relationships, however, it is important to examine the history of transportation technology in addition to the history of communications technology, because a mere two hundred years ago, communication across distances was dependent on transportation.

---

[2] The information in this section was previously reported in Adams (1998).

Messages could only be sent via animals or people who were traveling. Letters were sent when someone happened to be going in a certain direction or, later, by the Pony Express ("Pony Express," Encyclopedia Britannica, 1997; "Postal System," Encyclopedia Britannica, 1997).

When the telegraph was developed in 1844, communication was no longer dependent on transportation. For the first time, messages could be sent without someone traveling, and they could be sent faster than someone could carry them (Carey, 1983). By 1861, the Pony Express had ceased operation and the transcontinental telegraph system had been fully established (Klein, 1993; "Pony Express," 1997). On December 12, 1901, forty years after the first transatlantic telegraph cable had been laid, Marconi sent a message by wireless telegraph across the Atlantic. Although the wireless was used mainly to send commercial messages, amateur enthusiasts, forebears of the current Internet junkies, began communicating socially with one another (Warthman, 1974; Reynolds, 1977–79).

During the twentieth century, both communications and transportation have become faster, more efficient, and more accessible. Although Bell invented the first telephone transmitter in 1876, the diffusion of the telephone started out slowly (Warthman, 1974). By 1900, only two out of every one hundred Americans had telephones, and even most of these were instruments of convenience and commerce rather than tools for friends to use in keeping in touch (Fischer & Carroll, 1988). By 1915, transcontinental telephone service was possible (Warthman, 1974). According to Fischer and Carroll (1988), on the eve of the Great Depression, 41% of all homes in the United States were equipped with a telephone, and it had become firmly established as a social instrument, at least among the middle class. Full saturation did not occur until the 1960s.

Transportation technology developed rapidly over this same period. In the early nineteenth century, commercial steamships began operation in the United States and Great Britain and shortly thereafter steam locomotives were available as transportation ("History of Technology," Encyclopedia Britannica, 1997). Then came automobiles and airplanes. In 1895, there were 3,700 car owners in the United States; by 1900, there were 8,000. In 1903, both the first flight by the Wright brothers and the first continental crossing by automobile occurred (Hokanson, 1988). The Lincoln Highway opened in 1915, making it possible for people to cross the United States by car relatively easily (Hokanson, 1988). In 1918, the first airline was formed in Germany. By the 1930s, three airlines were developing worldwide fight patterns, and one-fifth of all Americans owned automobiles ("Formation of airlines," Encyclopedia Britannica, 1997; Fischer & Carroll, 1988). By the 1960s, most people owned cars and air transportation was easily available to passengers who could afford it.

By the 1970s, it was relatively easy for people with adequate financial resources to talk and visit with people who lived all over the globe. The development of the Internet facilitated almost instant and easier communication with large numbers of people worldwide. According to Castells (1996), there were only twenty-five computers on the Internet in 1973. As late as the 1980s, there were only a few thousand Internet users. By 1997, 37.4 million American households had computers, and 56.7 million Americans aged three years and above used the Internet (U.S. Census Bureau, 1997). Experts predict that one day the Internet could connect 600 million computer networks (Castells, 1996). Although most electronic communication is currently mainly text-based, multimedia applications for on-line communication are being developed (Paccagnella, 1997). We are now hearing about the possibilities of virtually projecting people to another location, once again blurring the distinction between transportation and communications (Rheingold, 1991). This time, however, rather than communication being dependent on transportation, transportation-like experiences will be dependent on communications technology.

TECHNOLOGY AS A MEDIATOR OF SOCIAL RELATIONSHIPS

Despite the constant changes in the technological context of social relationships, most of the theory that researchers use to guide their endeavors is based on the assumption that kin and friend relationships are formed and maintained primarily, if not exclusively, through face-to-face interaction (Adams, 1998). For example, psychologists who study interpersonal attraction have focused on the importance of visual cues, including how physical appearance plays a role in attraction, what gestures, facial expressions, and tie-signs people use to indicate involvement, and how spatial placement varies by closeness of relationships (see Short, Williams, & Christie, 1976). Similarly, sociologists are still influenced by classic conceptions of the groups (or "primary groups") through which the individual becomes integrated into society as involving repeated, intimate, face-to-face contact (Cooley, 1983 [1909]). In the context of these intellectual traditions, scholars focus their research on understanding face-to-face relationships to the exclusion of relationships that exist across distances.

As Adams (1998) has argued elsewhere, the focus on physically copresent relationships made some sense in the technological context in which these territorially bound theories developed. After all, it was not possible until recently to travel or communicate with people who lived at a distance with enough frequency to form a relationship with them. Even maintaining already established relationships across distances was problematic until recently, due to the expense and amount of time required to travel or communicate. On the other hand, at least since industrialization and urbanization took root at the turn of the nineteenth and twentieth centuries, some people have maintained relationships with friends they had previously met in face-to-face encounters, and it has been fairly common for families to be dispersed around the globe.

Nonetheless, even as recently as the fifties and sixties, both quantitative and qualitative researchers focused their attention almost exclusively on local relationships. Survey researchers demonstrated their blindness to the importance of long-distance relationships by relying mainly on global questions regarding the frequency of face-to-face interaction with friends and family members to measure social integration (e.g., Blau, 1961; Pihlblad & McNamara, 1965; Rose, 1965). Most of the questions they posed about relationships were designed to measure face-to-face contact specifically and thus asked about how frequently the respondents "saw " or "visited" their family and friends (see Adams, 1989, for a discussion of measurement issues in relationship research). Even when they did not use wording that assumed face-to-face contact, the issue remained "frequency of contact," not "quality of interactions," and they made no attempt to study long-distance and face-to-face relationships separately.

Perhaps more understandable given their focus on studies of various "settings," during this same period of intellectual history, ethnographers also focused on physically proximate relationships to the exclusion of long-distance ones. It is probable that the relatively poor inhabitants of *Tally's Corner* (Liebow, 1967) did not have any ties outside of their neighborhood, but it is more difficult to believe that the *Organization Man* (Whyte, 1956) and his family and the *Levittowners* (Gans, 1967), all now famous middle-class transients, did not. Even the working-class inhabitants of *Street Corner Society* (Whyte, 1943) and the *Urban Villagers* (Gans, 1962) probably maintained ties with their relatives who still lived in Italy, but these relationships are not discussed in these volumes. Although these ethnographers did not chronicle everyday life in these mid-century communities in the idealistic way it is now often depicted in the media, their descriptions do remind us of the fictitious community portrayed in the film *Pleasantville* (Soderbergh & Ross, 1998). Pleasantville was an island of civilization with nothing beyond its borders. In these ethnographies, the term "the outside world" was used to mean the worlds of work, education, and health care. Participation in these worlds did not necessarily take the inhabitants outside of the geographic boundaries of the neighborhood (Gans, 1962). The implications of close connections with significant others beyond these neighborhood boundaries were not considered. It was as if the outside world, and the friends and relatives who inhabited it, did not exist.

In the late 1960s, however, researchers began to question the territorially bound assumptions that formed the foundation for earlier research. For example, Litwak and Szelenyi (1969) challenged Parsons's (1949) argument that the nuclear family is the most adaptive form in contemporary society because geographic mobility was common and long-distance connections were difficult to maintain. They posited that changes in technology had led to new forms of primary groups and that "contacts among extended kin can be maintained despite breaks in face-to-face contact; neighborhoods can exist despite rapid membership turnover; and friendships can continue despite both of these problems" (Litwak & Szelenyi, 1969, p. 465). At the same time, survey researchers began to ask questions about letter writing and telephone calls or at least eliminated the wording from their questions that implied that they were only interested in face-to-face contact. A decade later, including such questions on survey instruments was common, and theorists began arguing that "intimacy at a distance" was the type of relationship people preferred with their family members (Rosenmayr, 1977).

Similarly, as communications and transportation technology developed, theorists began addressing the topic of communities based on beliefs and interests rather than on shared territory (Webber, 1973; Effrat, 1974). Once these scholars recognized that "despatialized communities can cross city – and national – boundaries" (Craven & Wellman, 1974, p. 78), the theoretical climate made it sensible for researchers to focus on long-distance relationships in addition to the physically proximate ones that had always demanded their attention. Survey researchers began asking "how far away" friends and family members lived, recognized the existence of commuter marriages and long-distance romantic relationships, stopped eliminating nonlocal friends and family from consideration, and started conducting separate analyses on information about local and nonlocal relationships.

It has been over two decades since theorists gave researchers permission to study long-distance relationships, but very little work in this area has been published. Exceptions include Rohlfing's (1995) study of long-distance friendships and Cuba's (1991, 1992; Cuba & Hummon, 1993) research program on the effect of geographic location on older families. This relative lack of studies on long-distance relationships is unfortunate, because now that the Internet and other forms of electronic communication are common and begging to be studied, relationship researchers are left only with the territorially bound theories of a much earlier intellectual age to guide them.

Although researchers have now been studying on-line interactions for some time (e.g., Smith & Kolluck, 1999), they have not paid much attention to the effect of technology on personal relationships. Perhaps this is because the theoretical perspectives that inspired the early research on this topic suggested that relationships would be unlikely to develop in an electronic context. For example, in an early publication on this topic, social presence theorists argued that on-line communications are not perceived to be as intimate as face-to-face exchanges because they are asynchronous and text-based (Short et al., 1976). Similarly, others argued that due to the reduced number of social cues available for participants to use and interpret, electronic communication is seen as less personal and more negative (Siegal,

Dubrovsky, Kiesler, &McGuire, 1986). The on-line context is evolving, however, and now not all communication is asynchronous or text-based and
an increasing number of social cues are available. Furthermore, although
not many researchers have studied on-line relationships, enough of them
have for it to be clear that relationships do develop on-line (e.g., Parks &
Floyd, 1996).

Few scholars have studied relationships that develop on-line. Of these
scholars an even smaller number have paid attention to the effect that
the use of electronic means of communication has on relationships that
originally develop in face-to-face contexts and morph into long-distance
relationships, or to the effect it has on relationships between people who
still live near each other (see Wellman, Haase, Witte, &Hampton, 2001,
for an exception). E-mail, instant messaging, and chat rooms all provide
people with opportunities to keep in touch with their family and friends between face-to-face encounters, no matter how frequently those face-to-face
encounters take place or how little distance people have to travel to have
them. Electronic communication can mediate all types of relationships.

RESEARCH FINDINGS ON THE EFFECTS OF INTERNET
TECHNOLOGY ON SOCIAL RELATIONSHIPS

While the focus of this chapter is on Internet technology and relationships
over the life span, current studies do not extend to all stages of development. Most studies focus on adults, although a small amount of work has
been done involving children. The group almost entirely absent from this
literature is that of old age.

Although researchers primarily have focused on relationships involving adult Internet users, a University of California–Los Angeles research
study (2001) shows that all ages report using this form of communication
technology. Of the sample of 2,002 participants, 72% reported Internet use
in 2001, an increase from 67% in the year 2000. Fifteen percent of Internet users were children ages 18 years and younger, 69% were ages 19 to
55 years, while only 16% were older adults ages 56 years and older. Perhaps
the research focus on adults merely results because they are a more viable
pool of participants.

The following review of the literature is organized by stage of the life
course – childhood, adulthood, and old age – and within adulthood into
the major topics found in both academic journals and the popular press, including the major foci of activities (education, work, and leisure activities)
and types of relationships and processes (mate selection, dating, friendship, and social isolation). Although the popular press, such as newspapers
and magazines, would typically not be included in an academic literature
review, our search for information on this topic had to be expanded beyond peer-reviewed journals because little research exists in this area. As

a result, few of the articles that are reviewed here are theoretically driven or methodologically sound. We can say, with confidence, that there is considerable room for future research on the mediating effect of technology on relationships.

Childhood

Most children are familiar with computers. In 1997, about three out of four children had access to computers (U.S. Census Bureau, 1997). The most abundant information regarding children concerns parental fears about the on-line experiences their children might have and the resulting need to monitor their computer use. For example, journalists suggest the importance of regulating children's access to information and of monitoring the information to which they are exposed (Carlin & Surk, 2000; Gibson, 2001). One author (Gibson, 2001) discussed the privacy policies of children-targeted sites. While parents might assume that historically child-friendly agencies and companies will remain so in virtual space, Gibson shows that this is not always the case. Many sites require children to log in in order to gain access to their sites. How safe is it for children to provide personal information in order to play a game or gain information about a treasured character? On the other hand, to what kinds of information do these sites expose children? The point made here is that children's behavior on the Internet should be monitored in order to preserve their safety and age-appropriate education.

Iliff (2002), a high school student herself, designed a study of middle school students to challenge these conclusions. In her study of all students who had Internet access who attend one middle school in a southeastern city, she found that students were exposed to some of the dangers that concern parents and the media – personal questions posed by strangers, pornography, cons, and foul language, but that most of the students handled these problems effectively, eliminating any threat to their safety or well-being. She argues that many of the restrictions parents impose on their children's on-line activity are unnecessary for this reason and, furthermore, that these restrictions undermine the parent-child relationship. The atmosphere of distrust thus created can interfere with the children's social life, which is increasingly supplemented by on-line interactions with school friends.

Adulthood: Foci of Activities

The Internet is not only used for social activities, it is also used to acquire an education, accomplish work-related activities, and pursue leisure interests. In this section, we summarize some of the research on on-line activities in these areas and discuss its implications for social relationships.

Education. Examinations of technological influences on education suggest that faculty contact with students is enhanced. For example, in their focus-group study of active on-line teachers, web enhancers, and faculty interested in teaching on-line, Adams and Ammons (2000) found that faculty who taught on-line felt that they interacted more with students than they did when they were teaching traditional face-to-face classes. They warned faculty who were thinking about teaching on-line that "you really have to enjoy interacting with students" to be a successful on-line instructor. Tiene (2000) investigated the advantages and disadvantages of on-line discussion groups, or class listservs, in graduate courses, and found that students enjoyed the asynchronous aspect of the written form of discussion. Mild frustrations arose, however, with technical barriers (limited access when network was down, losing a post) and the lack of visual cues (possible misinterpretation of statements). The authors concluded that the on-line discussion forums were a good supplement to, but should not replace, in-class discussions. An article published in the Chronicle of Higher Education (O'Donnell, 1998) described a college professor's positive experience with e-mail communication with students. He suggests that contact may overcome difficulties posed by illness, studies or visits abroad, social apprehensions, and time.

Work and Work Environments. Research on the interplay between work and the Internet primarily focuses on physically absent employees and outcomes such as feelings of social isolation. The creation of "virtual offices" portrays an image of an employee, primarily female, working from her home office and enjoying the advantages created by being physically absent from the workplace (Duxbury, Higgins, & Thomas, 1996). Some of these advantages include flexibility in time (i.e., setting one's own hours, breaking up the workday into several segments) and physical location (i.e., working from a remote setting, geographic mobility, ability to work from vacation locale) (Duxbury et al., 1996). The primary disadvantage that employees of virtual work environments report is social isolation (Duxbury et al., 1996; Tolson, 2000). However, it is unclear whether social isolation is actually an outcome of a virtual work environment. For example, are people who prefer little social interaction simply drawn to jobs that enable remote communication? Also, how different are the growing number of cubicle-style offices from virtual work environments? Researchers need to be sensitive to these questions while developing research methods to investigate this area.

Leisure. While many people suggest that technology is a form of leisure, few social scientists or media journalists have discussed the outcomes of technology on leisure behavior. In fact, our review found only one article with this specific focus and it was written as an investigation of possible outcomes with hopes of providing the catalyst for more research in this area (Bryce, 2001). Bryce points out that the Internet blurs domestic, virtual, and commercial leisure by redefining our concept of space. We use the Internet for a variety of tasks, such as communicating, disseminating and gathering information, socializing, shopping, and entertaining (games). Instead of the traditional means of completing these leisure tasks that require one to be in a specific physical space, the Internet has provided the opportunity for virtual spaces. The Internet, one type of virtual space, allows individuals to partake in various types of leisure activities without changing physical space.

It is important to note that cyberspace enables deviant leisure activities as well as nondeviant ones (Bryce, 2001). That is, the possible anonymity and solitary nature of Internet use provides a safer environment than non-Internet leisure for activities such as pornographic viewing, criminal activity (e.g., pedophilia, obtaining information illegally, on-line stalking), and sexual experimentation. The ability to act freely on deviant desires (e.g., to access pornography) may influence social and intimate relationships by decreasing satisfaction with intimate partners (Zillmann & Jennings, 1988). Further information is not known about the effect of open access to deviant leisure activities on relationships.

Adulthood: Types of Relationships and Processes

Theoretically, any type of relationship can develop or be maintained through on-line interaction. The popular media has focused most of its attention on mate selection and dating and on sexual relationships, but the limited research by scholars examines on-line friendships and the potential of the Internet to provide computer users an excuse to avoid face-to-face interaction and therefore isolate them from others.

Mate Selection and Dating. The literature regarding mate selection and dating (i.e., beginning relationships) via computer technologies is sparse when articles on sexual relationships are excluded. A content analysis of one hundred personal ads on the Internet placed by college students suggests that security is an important issue to these young adults (Milewski, Hatala, & Baack, 1999). That is, on-line personal ads contained little personal information when compared to newspaper ads. However, some of the advantages of on-line personals over newspaper ads include: 1) ease of locating people with similar interests; 2) use of search engines to create selective search criteria for possible dates; 3) fast and low-cost nature of the Internet; 4) possible anonymity; and 5) portrayal of one's own or socially expected ideal.

Some people may benefit more than others by using the Internet to locate a possible date. For example, people with relationship inhibitions, such as shyness or low self-esteem associated with appearance, use the Internet to find an appropriate match more often than those who are less shy or have higher self-esteem (Scharlott & Christ, 1995). In addition, those persons interested in locating a dating partner, particularly women, may feel more secure by the anonymity the on-line search offers. Additional research must be conducted, however, to confirm and expand these findings. Scharlott and Christ (1995) used a convenience sample with a problematic method-ology, thereby restricting the type of conclusions that may be drawn from their efforts.

A popular press article may assist these women by providing advice for moving the on-line relationship to one that is off-line (Goldsborough, 1998). In general, Goldsborough suggests that women use common sense, understand the risks, and recognize that negative experiences, however rare, may occur. This advice is likely to enable women to feel more confident and comfortable in their on-line search for partners.

Sexual Relationships. A high proportion of the traffic on the Internet is sexual in nature (Mills, 1998; Waskul et al., 2000). Waskul and colleagues (2000) used participant observation and qualitative interviews through sex-ually oriented on-line chat rooms and discussion forums to investigate the use of the Internet in sexual relationships. Specifically, these authors were interested in the "disembodiment of self," or the virtual portrayal of the human body and human interactions. The Internet was found to provide a mechanism for the "experience of multiplicity" (p. 394), or the ability to portray numerous selves that are situationally defined. Waskul and col-leagues (2000) suggest that these on-line portrayals of selves are unique because of the disembodiment of self, or the absence of a physical body that usually restricts the fluidity between the self and portrayals of the self to others. As such, participants have the ability to become their ideal self, which may or may not be consistent with their physical characteristics. In addition, these multiple selves facilitate involvement in situations not otherwise experienced, such as various experimental sexual relationships. Waskul and colleagues (2000) suggest that newer communication technolo-gies, such as Internet chat rooms, challenge traditional assumptions about the interplay between body, self, and the social environment. The body can no longer be thought of as a starting point or anchor for our self, but is open to redefinition. Once defined as the most stable characteristic, our sense of who we are and where we are in physical space is now malleable due to virtual space. These unreliable characteristics of our selves invari-ably influence interactions with others and subsequent reactions to these relationships.

Rather than merely limiting his study to sexual encounters on-line, Mills (1998) provided support for the suggestion that Internet sexual relation-ships influence relationships off-line through his research using participant observation and ten on-line interviews of "randomly chosen people in a number of different chat rooms" (p. 43). Instead of focusing on the self, however, Mills approached the use of sexually oriented Internet conversation as a threat to off-line intimate relationships. While the absence of physical contact may suggest that the cyber encounters are innocent, infidelity has occurred in the mind of the participant. Mills (1998) argues that more traditional types of threats to intimate relationships have had time for responses to develop to prevent encounters from expanding into an affair. Internet-based communication, however, is a novel temptation that may pique curiosity and progress into intimate exchanges before a conscious decision is made. This process may evolve from the lack of identified cues and previous experience with "virtual" relationships. Research may assist in this area by identifying and describing the early stages of interactions between people in virtual communication settings and distinguish between relationships that progress into intimate exchanges from those that do not.

Friendships. Although very few researchers are focusing attention on on-line friendships, the research in this area tends to be of higher quality than the research in some of the other areas we have discussed. On-line friendships are found to be common among Internet users belonging to a variety of Internet newsgroups (Parks & Floyd, 1996). The progression of these friendships has been found to follow similar paths of development as off-line relationships (Parks & Floyd, 1996). The relationships that form are typically transformed into off-line relationships, indicating that Internet newsgroups serve as another context for personal relationship formation.

On-line friendships are not a substitute for off-line relationships, but may precede them in some instances. In fact, the Internet may facilitate the identification of appropriate friends for individuals who want to meet someone with specific characteristics, qualities, or interests. For example, someone may join a newsgroup related to a specific hobby or political concern to meet people who share this concern or knowledge (Parks & Roberts, 1998). In their study of visitors to the National Geographic Society web site, however, Wellman, Haase, Witte, and Hampton (2001) found that people's on-line interaction supplements their face-to-face and telephone interaction without increasing or decreasing it.

Social Isolation. Next to sexual relationships, the literature on social isolation and current technologies contains the largest number of articles. Overall, there is a debate over whether or not computers, especially the Internet, lead to socially isolated individuals or provide a vehicle for interaction. A lack of consistency in findings likely stems from an absence of appropriate research methods. Using convenience samples, disregarding

important mediating factors, and using poor measurements result in findings that should be considered as the basis for future research rather than
as a basis for practice or policy. Unfortunately, the popular media pub-
lishes research findings without weighing the potential importance of these
methodological deficiencies.

A controversial longitudinal study published in *American Psychologist*
(Kraut, Patterson, Lundmark, Kiesler, Mukopadhyay, & Scherlis, 1998) followed new Internet users and their household companions over a one to
two year time period. They found that frequent Internet use was associated with less communication with household members, declines in the
size of social networks, and increased depression and loneliness. Several
responses challenged the findings of Kraut and his colleagues. First, it was
noted that these researchers did not take into account the expected increase or decrease of social network size given one's position in the life
course (Shapiro, 1999). Second, Kraut et al. (1998) selected their sample
from citizens who were highly involved in their community. Shapiro (1999)
explained "whenever a sample is selected on the basis of high values of
some variable, there is a tendency for that variable to decline (regress) toward more average values (the mean) over time." Third, the effect sizes
Kraut and colleagues (1998) found for outcomes of distress were minimal
(Rierdan, 1999). In addition, the infrequent use of the Internet (average
of less than three hours per week) led Rierdan (1999) to discount Kraut
and associates' suggestions for political and personal implications. The
fact that the article received front-page attention from the New York
Times (Harmon, 1998) suggests the importance of carefully conducted
research.

In the investigation of the relationship between computer-mediated
communication and social isolation, it may be important to ask whether the
Internet will replace face-to-face communication. Research conducted by
Flaherty and colleagues (1998) suggests that on-line communication is not
a functional alternative to face-to-face communication. Likewise, a review
by Galston (2000) suggests that on-line groups fulfill certain emotional and
psychological needs, but do not meet all needs of individuals or society.
For example, several articles suggest that information technology such as
the Internet influences lifestyles by making it possible to shop from home,
to cut back hours at the office to work from home (O'Toole, 2000), and
to spend less time in recreation, social interaction, and social gatherings
(Perry, 2000). Nonetheless, the Internet allows communication between
family members who are geographically distant and searching capabilities
for friends and family whose contact information has been lost. Galston
(2000) points out that while computers facilitate contact over distances, one
cannot share a cup of coffee, give a hug, or offer touches of understanding. Such restrictions may, depending on the conceptual definition used,
be classified as social isolation.

OLD AGE

Census data shows that 21% of adults aged 55 and older have a computer in their household, yet little is known about their use of computers and how it affects their relationships and daily lives (U.S. Census, 1997). Although we found no published studies of the use of the Internet by older adults, Jennings's (2001) observations, written as part of the requirements for a graduate student internship, are thought-provoking. Her internship involved helping older adults who lived in a multilevel care residential community use their computers. She found that the majority of the residents did not own computers but those who did showed a great deal of interest. Interest and use was not correlated with age, suggesting that previous exposure to computers did not affect their attitudes. On the other hand, their physical and mental health did affect residents' use of computers. Residents who were physically healthier were more interested in using a computer and had better control of the devices needed to access information, such as a keyboard and a mouse. Residents who were mentally healthier and had no memory problems were more interested in using the computer because they had an easier time understanding and remembering instructions. These findings suggest that without the development of more age-appropriate equipment, the frail elderly will be unlikely to use the computer to maintain relationships.

Conclusions

Research on relationships and Internet technology is in its infancy. Consequently, current information is generally not theoretically grounded nor has it been rigorously tested. Computer use is on the rise in the United States and is expected to continue to increase (U.S. Census Bureau, 1997). What we know thus far suggests that computer technology may affect various aspects of relationships, increasing interactions in some cases while decreasing them in other contexts. Some relationships may be nurtured using information technology, while others may suffer neglect. Furthermore, computers have an age-related yet complex impact on the formation, process, and structure of relationships.

SYNTHETIC DYNAMIC FRAMEWORK FOR THE STUDY OF A
LIFETIME OF RELATIONSHIPS MEDIATED BY TECHNOLOGY

Although we have organized the review of the literature on on-line relationships roughly by stage of the life course, the literature in each category is too sparse and the topics vary too much across age categories to enable us to make generalizations about how the use of the Internet to establish and maintain relationships varies by age. Furthermore, none of these studies,

whether they were scholarly or popular, specifically examined the effects
of age on any computer use or relationship outcome variables. Perhaps
the neglect of this topic by researchers can be explained by the lack of a
theoretical framework to guide their endeavors. In the face of the absence
of empirical data from which to derive grounded theory, in order to develop a *synthetic dynamic framework for the study of a lifetime of relationships
mediated by technology,* we rely on four existing dynamic social theories for
guidance about what elements to include in the model and what issues
scholars might want to address.

Two of these dynamic theories address aging, and two of them address
group development and change. These four theories share a focus on systematic and patterned changes over time. They vary on two dimensions:
whether they examine these changes from a structural perspective or a
developmental one and whether they focus on changes in the individual
or changes in the family or friendship group.

Individual development theory, as we will call the first type, focuses
on systematic and patterned *developmental* changes in *individuals.* Here we
draw on the work of Erikson (1959; Erikson, Erikson, & Kivnick, 1989).

The second type of theory, which we call life course theory, examines
systematic and patterned *structural* changes in the life course of *individuals.*
Informed by sociological stratification scholarship, this approach was developed by Cain (1964), Clausen (1972), Ryder (1965), Riley, Johnson, and
Foner (1972), and was more recently summarized by Bengtson and Allen
(1993).

Family development theory is the third type. This approach features an
interdisciplinary progression that integrates concepts and ideas from sociologists, demographers, economists, life course and human developmental
theorists, and, more recently, family theorists. Scholars whose work is most
prominent in the current application of family development theory include
Glick (1947), Duvall (1957), Hill (1971), Rodgers (1977), Aldous (1978),
Hill and Mattessich (1979), and, most recently, White (1991). Researchers
who use this approach focus on the systematic and ordered sequence of
developmental changes in *families* through attention to relationships within
the group and on the construction of internal norms and roles (Aldous,
1978).

Network change theory, the fourth and final type, focuses on systematic and patterned *structural* changes in *social networks* (Suitor, Wellman, &
Morgan 1997). Although some network analysts study the interconnections
among all of the individuals in a bounded population (e.g., an apartment
building or a company), here we are interested in the literature examining
"personal networks," or sets of ties developed and maintained by individuals that may extend beyond any identifiable boundaries.

See Figure 15.1 for the synthetic dynamic framework for the study of
a lifetime of relationships mediated by technology integrating all four of

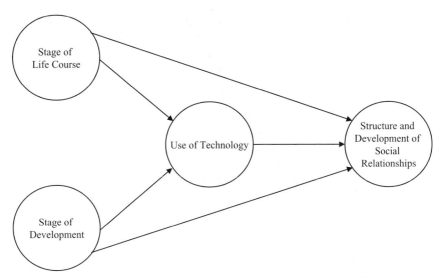

FIGURE 15.1. Synthetic Dynamic Model for the Study of a Lifetime of Relationships Mediated by Technology.

these perspectives. This model can be used to guide studies designed to answer the questions: "How do changes in the life course and developmental stages of individuals affect their use of the technology?" and "How, in turn, does the use of this technology change the structure and development of social relationships?" Note that this framework also recognizes that stage of life course and stage of development have direct effects on the structure and development of social relationships, which researchers have studied extensively (see Blieszner & Adams, 1992, for a review of relevant literature). Here we are more interested in the indirect effects than the direct ones. In this section, we therefore use individual development theory and life course theory to derive research questions regarding the effects of age on use of technology. Similarly, we use family development theory and network change theory to derive questions regarding the effects of the use of technology on the structure and development of social relationships. In each of the four following subsections, we elaborate on one of these theoretical approaches and discuss the research questions regarding the technological mediation of relationships that each of them raises.

Individual Development Theory

The basic premise of Erik Erikson's theory (1959) of individual psychosocial development is that increased social demands and responsibilities occur with physical maturation. As an individual acquires skills and abilities through physical development, she or he experiences growing pressure to change the way they interact with their environment. For example, as a child acquires language skills, she is expected to talk instead of cry for something she wants. These new social demands evoke a *crisis* the individual must overcome in order to advance toward healthy development.

Erikson (1959) proposed eight such crises during loosely defined ages and a psychosocial strength that is associated with the resolution of each crisis. The first crisis, *trust versus mistrust*, is experienced during infancy, and its resolution results in feelings of hope. Second, *autonomy versus shame and doubt*, is the stage associated with early childhood, leading to the development of will power. Third, *initiative versus guilt* occurs during what Erikson calls "play age" (i.e., around ages three or four years), leaving the child with a sense of purpose. Fourth, *industry versus inferiority* is the crisis school-age children face and is associated with the development of competence. Fifth, adolescents experience *identity versus identity confusion*, leading to fidelity in social relationships. Sixth, *intimacy versus isolation* occurs during young adulthood and is associated with the strength of love. Seventh, adults who successfully negotiate *generativity versus stagnation* develop their ability to care. Lastly, adults in old age face *integrity versus despair* and have the potential to find wisdom. Note that Erikson's later work (Erikson et al., 1989) described wisdom as the ability to maintain and learn to convey the integrity of experience, despite mental and physical decline. Each of these eight stages is influenced by and based on specific experiences at earlier ages. As a result, individuals continue to cope with an unresolved crisis throughout life while adding new issues with each stage.

Research Questions. How does this individually focused, developmental theory inform research on technology and relationships? Erikson's stages lend information about what issues are most important to individuals at a given stage of development. One example of a research question from this frame of reference is, "How does the stage of early childhood influence one's use of technology to interact in a social environment?" Issues surrounding this question might include: 1) how the degree of autonomy the child has developed facilitates or inhibits on-line communication and information exploration; 2) how the degree of shame and doubt a child feels has an impact on the use of technology to interact with and maintain the interest of adults; and 3) the degree to which the use of communication technology facilitates or inhibits the development of will power acted out in relationships.

A second example of a research question that follows from Erikson's stage theory is, "How does the emphasis on intimacy and isolation during early adulthood influence the use of technology as a social vehicle?" This line of research is currently most popular among researchers interested in the interplay between technology and relationships, as shown in the literature previously reviewed. Other issues that might be important here are: 1) types of communication technologies used by young adults who have successfully achieved intimacy (e.g., chat rooms, individual e-mail contact, sex-based communication, technology as a supplement to face-to-face interaction, or technology as a way to initiate a relationship); 2) types of communication technologies used by young adults who have yet to resolve the intimacy-isolation crisis (e.g., on-line-only communication, chat rooms, sex-based communication); and 3) the circumstances under which young adults in intimate relationships use technology to maintain or further develop love.

Life Course Theory

Sociologists of age stratification developed life course theory, which focuses on the role of age in the social structure, and how, in turn, age affects the opportunities and constraints imposed on individuals. Building on the work of Cain (1964), Ryder (1965), and Clausen (1972), life course theorists view society as a succession of age cohorts of individuals who, as they age, are allocated to fill roles open to individuals of specific ages and are socialized regarding age-related expectations and sanctions (Riley et al., 1972). Successive cohorts are socialized differently and have different opportunities available to them because the characteristics of social contexts, including the age composition of society, change over time (Ryder, 1965). For this reason, behaviors, norms, and values are affected by the age of the individual, by the current period, and by the cohort of which the individual is a member.

Some life course researchers have focused their efforts on developing methods to specify the effects of age, period, and cohort and have developed cross-sequential longitudinal study designs for this purpose. Finding funding for such ambitious projects has proven difficult, so other life course researchers have developed less comprehensive study designs, focusing on how transitions from one stage of the life course to another affect the lives of individuals and the development of their friendship networks and families (e.g., Feld & Carter, 1998; Lamme, Dykstra, & Broese van Groenou, 1996; Leik & Chalkley, 1997; Wellman, Wong, Tindall, & Nazer, 1997).

Research Questions. The life course framework is useful for addressing questions related to understanding how technology mediates social relationships at different stages of the life course. The main question on this topic that can be derived from this theory is: How does the social context during which people are socialized, their biological age (i.e., physical and mental abilities), and their current social context affect their attitudes toward the use of technology and their use of technology to develop and maintain relationships? More specifically, what opportunities are offered for people at various stages of life to access technology and to use it to develop and maintain relationships? What relevant constraints are imposed on them? Do certain social roles provide occupants with more access to technology or more opportunities to learn how to use it to maintain and develop relationships than others? Are these social roles allocated based on age? Are people at some stages of life expected to use technology or to use it to maintain social relationships more than those at other stages of life? What are these expectations, what positive sanctions are given to those who meet them, and what negative sanctions are applied to those who fail to do so?

Family Development Theory

The basic premise of family development theory is that families continuously change and develop as prompted by the demands of family members (e.g., biological, psychological, and social needs), social expectations, and ecological constraints (Mattessich & Hill, 1987). Each family member performs roles within the family over time, although the norms and specific behaviors in those roles are likely to be modified as family members mature and family interaction patterns evolve (Aldous, 1978). During this restructuring, families engage in *developmental tasks*, or activities that prepare them for the upcoming stage. The process of moving from one stage to another is dependent upon prior experiences (i.e., previous stages) and the length of time within the previous stage. Traditional stages include marriage without children, marriage with various aged children (e.g., infant, preschool, school age, adolescent, young adult), marriage with children who live outside the household, grandparenting, and marriage in late life. White (1991) has expanded these traditional stages to include divorce and remarriage, stages that were previously classified as *nonnormative*, or not widely accepted, but are now considered *normative*, or less deviant, family configurations. The classification of normative or nonnormative also refers to the *timing* of a particular stage. For example, the birth of the first child is expected to occur (normative) before the parents reach age forty and children are expected to leave (normative) their parents' home in their early to mid-twenties.

Family development theory allows scholars to organize family experiences into specific categories while recognizing the dynamic nature of stage progression. This classification identifies different issues and opportunities likely to face families at distinct points of development. White (1991) suggests that it is possible to investigate macro-level influences on the group level (i.e., family development), which provides a solid foundation for understanding the influence of technology on family relationships.

Research Questions. The primary research question offered by family development theory is, "How does technology influence family change over time?" More specifically, how does the use of on-line communication influence the norms and roles of family members? How is technology used in the developmental tasks that contribute to stage transitions? In what ways is the use of technology different across various stages of development and where is technology more influential? Does technology affect or contribute to the experience of off-time, or nonnormative stage transitions? How is the use of technology in early development qualitatively different from its use in later stages? A final question may be more relevant before communication technology further infiltrates families but may be impossible in the near future: How does family development occur in families equipped with technology allowing continuous availability and how does this process compare to families without access to these tools? Note that parallel questions could be posed about the development of friendship groups or networks.

Social Network Change Theory

The goal of social network analysis is the formal representation of the structure of personal relationships beyond the dyad (Feger, 1981). Over the past twenty-five years, social network researchers have focused their efforts on measuring and describing various characteristics of social networks (e.g., size, density, hierarchy, homogeneity, and solidarity, Adams & Blieszner, 1994). Only recently have they begun to study changes in social networks over time and the processes underlying such changes (Suitor et al., 1997). It is thus a bit premature to use the phrase "social network change" as an adjective phrase modifying "theory." Nonetheless, we do so here because network researchers study changes in friendship networks as well as changes in social networks in general, including families. Furthermore, family developmental theorists emphasize internal process issues more than internal structural issues, and social network change theorists do the opposite (Blieszner & Adams, 1992). Deriving research questions from both of these theories thus leads to a more comprehensive coverage of possible topics.

Research Questions. The main relevant question derived from the network change literature is: How does the use of technology change the structure of social networks (see Adams, 1998, for an earlier discussion of this topic)? Does on-line interaction affect the structure of face-to-face networks as well as the structure of virtual networks? More specifically, do people who spend time on-line have larger networks because more people with whom they share interests are easily available for interaction? Does time on-line detract from the time spent in face-to-face interaction and therefore lead to a deterioration in traditional relationships? Are on-line networks less dense because the people in them are less likely to know each other? Does on-line interaction increase the overall density of social networks because it is possible for people who would normally not cross paths do so easily and inexpensively in chat rooms and other virtual spaces? Are on-line networks less homogeneous than face-to-face networks because, in on-line contexts, structural barriers do not inhibit people occupying different social statuses from interacting with each other? If so, how does this affect the homogeneity of face-to-face networks? How are social hierarchies developed on-line? Is the process similar to the way that hierarchies develop in face-to-face groups? Are on-line networks lower in solidarity than face-to-face networks? Finally, and of great demonstrated interest to journalists, does on-line interaction strengthen or weaken face-to-face relationships?

CONCLUSIONS

Since the development of the telegraph, communications technology has not been dependent on transportation technology. This means that communication is faster, more efficient, and more accessible than it was two hundred years ago. Although it is clear that these contextual changes have affected the way in which people develop and maintain relationships, theorists and researchers have been slow to adapt. With the "normalization" of Internet communication as part of everyday life (Wellman, Haase, Witte, & Hampton, 2001), the need to study its effects has increased. Journalists have written a great deal about on-line relationships, but carefully designed, theoretically based research on the topic is rare. Furthermore, the sparse research literature does not address the effects of age on the use of technology or the potential interaction effect between age of participant, use of technology, and the development, structure, and process of family relationships and friendships. Most of the relevant research narrowly focuses on the use of on-line technology by one age group, particularly adults. The literature is thus not developed enough to inform policy or to suggest applications, but this has not stopped journalists from publishing articles including practical recommendations. These developments make it very important that scholars begin considering the implications of technological change for theory, conduct carefully conceived research on the mediating effect of technology on relationships of people of different ages, and disseminate confirmed results to the media and to appropriate agencies.

In this chapter, we have outlined a *synthetic dynamic framework for the study of a lifetime of relationships mediated by technology*. This framework integrates four dynamic social theories, individual development theory, life course theory, family development theory, and network change theory. We used individual development theory and life course theory to generate research questions regarding the effects of age on the use of technology. Similarly, we used family development theory and network change theory to derive questions regarding the impact of technology on the structure, process, and development of social relationships. Although we hope that this framework will inspire some well-designed research on the mediating effect of technology on relationships across the life span, even more do we hope that this chapter will inspire social relationship theorists from a variety of traditions to consider how current perspectives must be modified or expanded to adapt to recent changes in technology.

References

Adams, R. G. (1989). Conceptual and methodological issues in studying friendships of older adults. In R. G. Adams & R. Blieszner (Eds.), *Older adult friendship: Structure and process* (pp. 17–41). Newbury Park, CA: Sage.

Adams, R. G. (1998). The demise of territorial determinism: Online friendships. In *Placing friendship in context* (pp. 153–182). Cambridge: Cambridge University Press.

Adams, R. G., & Ammons, S. K. (2000, August). Face-to-face faculty discussions about teaching online. Paper presented at the annual meetings of the American Sociological Association, Washington, DC.

Adams, R. G., & Blieszner, R. (1994). An integrative conceptual framework for friendship research. *Journal of Social and Personal Relationships, 11*, 163–184.

Aldous, J. (1978). *Family careers: Developmental change in families*. New York: Wiley.

Bengtson, V. L., & Allen, K. R. (1993). The life course perspective applied to families over time. In P. G. Boss et al. (Eds.), *Source book of family theories and methods* (pp. 469–499). New York: Plenum.

Blau, Z. S. (1961). Structural constraints on friendship in old age. *American Sociological Review, 26*, 429–439.

Blieszner, R., & Adams, R. G. (1992). *Adult friendship*. Newbury Park: Sage.

Bryce, J. (2001). The technological transformation of leisure. *Social Science Computer Review, 19*(1), 7–16.

Cain, L. D., Jr. (1964). Life course and social structure. In R. E. L. Faris (Ed.), *Handbook of modern sociology* (pp. 272–309). Chicago: Rand McNally.

Carey, J. W. (1983). Technology and ideology: The case of the telegraph. *Prospects, 8*, 302–325.

Carlin, P. A., & Surk, B. (2000). Cyber survivor. *People Weekly, 53* (21), 95–96.

Castells, M. (1996). *The rise of the network society*. Cambridge, UK: Blackwell.

Clausen, J. A. (1972). The life course of individuals. In M. W. Riley, M. E. Johnson, & A. Foner (Eds.), *Aging and society: A sociology of age stratification* (Vol. 3, pp. 457–514). New York: Russell Sage.

Cooley, C. H. (1983 [1909]). *Social organization: A study of the larger mind*. New York: Charles Scribner's Sons.

Craven, P., & Wellman, B. (1974). The network city. In M. P. Effrat (Ed.), *The community: Approaches and applications*. Glencoe, IL: The Free Press.

Cuba, L. (1991). Models of migration decision making reexamined: The destination search of older migrants to Cape Cod. *The Gerontologist, 31*, 204–209.

Cuba, L. (1992). Families and retirement in the context of elderly migration. In M. Szinovacz, D. J. Ekerdt, & B. H. Vinick (Eds.), *Families and retirement* (pp. 205–211). Newbury Park, CA: Sage.

Cuba, L., & Hummon, D. M. (1993). Constructing a sense of home: Place affiliation and migration across the life cycle. *Sociological Forum, 8,* 547–572.

Duvall, E. M. (1957). *Family development* (1st ed.). Philadelphia: Lippincott.

Duxbury, L. E., Higgins, C. A., & Thomas, D. R. (1996). Work and family environments and the adoption of computer-supported supplemental work-at-home. *Journal of Vocational Behavior, 49*(1), 1–23.

Effrat, M. P. (1974). Approaches to community: Conflicts and complementarities. In M. P. Effrat (Ed.), *The community: Approaches and applications.* Glencoe, IL: The Free Press.

Encyclopedia Britannica, Inc. (1997). Formation of airlines. [Computer software].

Encyclopedia Britannica, Inc. (1997). History of technology. [Computer software].

Encyclopedia Britannica, Inc. (1997). Pony Express. [Computer software].

Encyclopedia Britannica, Inc. (1997). Postal system. [Computer software].

Erikson, E. H. (1959). *Identity and the life cycle.* New York: Norton.

Erikson, E. H., Erikson, J. M., & Kivnick, H. Q. (1989). *Vital involvement in old age.* New York: Norton.

Feger, H. (1981). Analysis of social networks. In S. Duck & R. Gilmour (Eds.), *Personal relationships* (Vol. 1, pp. 91–108). London: Academic Press.

Feld, S., & Carter, W. C. (1998). Foci of activity as changing contexts for friendship. In *Placing friendship in context* (pp. 136–152). Cambridge: Cambridge University Press.

Fischer, C. S., & Carroll, G. R. (1988). Telephone and automobile diffusion in the United States, 1902–1937. *American Journal of Sociology, 93*(5), 1153–1178.

Flaherty, L. M., Pearce, K. J., & Rubin, R. B. (1998). Internet and face-to-face communication: Not functional alternatives. *Communication Quarterly, 46,* 250–269.

Galston, W. A. (2000). Does the Internet strengthen community? *National Civic Review, 89*(3), 193.

Gans, H. (1962). *The urban villagers.* Glencoe, IL: The Free Press.

Gans, H. (1967). *The Levittowners.* New York: Pantheon.

Gibson, J. (2001). Don't forget kids' privacy. *Library Journal, 126* (1), 7.

Glick, P. C. (1947). The family cycle. *American Sociological Review, 12,* 164–174.

Goldsborough, R. (1998, Jan.-Feb.). The curious phenomenon of online romance. *Link-Up, 15*(1), 15.

Harmon, A. (1998, August 30). Sad, lonely world discovered in cyberspace. *The New York Times,* p. 1.

Hays, R. B. (1984). The development and maintenance of friendship. *Journal of Social and Personal Relationships, 1,* 75–98.

Hays, R. B. (1985). A longitudinal study of friendship development. *Journal of Personality and Social Psychology, 48,* 909–24.

Hill, R. (1971). Modern systems theory and the family: A confrontation. *Social Science Information, 10,* 7–26.

Hill, R., & Mattessich, P. (1979). Family development theory and life span development. In P. Baltes & O. Brim (Eds.), *Life span development and behavior* (Vol. 3). New York: Academic Press.

Hokanson, D. (1988). *The Lincoln Highway: Main Street across America.* Iowa City, IA: University of Iowa Press.

Homans, G. C. (1950). *Social behavior: Its elementary forms.* New York: Harcourt, Brace, and Jovanovich, Inc.

Iliff, H. A. (2002). Middle school Internet usage: Is there a gender difference? Paper presented at the annual meetings of the Southern Sociological Society, Baltimore, MD, April.

Jennings, S. R. (2001). Older adults and computers: A study of Wellspring Retirement Community residents. Report on internship submitted as partial fulfillment of requirements for the Master's of Arts degree in Sociology, Department of Sociology, University of North Carolina at Greensboro, Greensboro, NC, December 4.

Klein, M. (1993). What hath God wrought? *American Heritage of Invention and Technology, 8*(4), 34–43.

Kraut, R., Patterson, M., Lundmark, V., Kiesler, S., Mukopadhyay, T., & Scherlis, W. (1998). Internet paradox: A social technology that reduces social involvement and psychological well-being? *American Psychologist, 53*, 1017–1031.

Lamme, S., Dykstra, P. A., Broese van Groenou, M. I. (1996). Rebuilding the network: New relationships in widowhood. *Personal Relationships, 3*(4), 337–349.

Leik, R. K., & Chalkley, M. A. (1997). On the stability of network relations under stress. *Social Networks, 19*, 63–74.

Liebow, E. (1967). *Tally's corner.* Boston: Little, Brown.

Litwak, E., & Szelenyi, I. (1969). Primary group structure and their functions: Kin, neighbors, and friends. *American Sociological Review, 34*(4), 465–481.

Martin, M. (1991). Communication and social forms: The development of the telephone, 1876–1920. *Anitpode, 23*(3), 307–333.

Mattessich, P., & Hill, R. (1987). Life cycle and family development. In M. B. Sussman & S. K. Steinmetz (Eds.), *Handbook of marriage and the family* (pp. 437–469). New York: Plenum.

Milewski, K., Hatala, M. N., & Baack, D. W. (1999). Downloading love: A content analysis of Internet personal advertisements placed by college students. *College Student Journal, 33*(1), 124.

Mills, R. (1998). Cyber: Sexual chat on the Internet. *Journal of Popular Culture, 32*(3), 31–46.

O'Donnell, J. J. (1998, February 13). Tools for teaching: Personal encounters in cyberspace. *The Chronicle of Higher Education.*

O'Toole, K. (2000, May). How the Internet is changing daily life. *Direct Marketing, 63*(1), 50.

Paccagnella, L. (1997). Getting the seats of your pants dirty: Strategies for ethnographic research on virtual communities. *Journal of Computer Mediated Communication, 3*(1), http://jcmc.huji.ac.il/vol3/issue1/.

Parks, M. R., & Floyd, K. (1996). Making friends in cyberspace. *Journal of Communication, 46*, 80–97.

Parks, M. R., & Roberts, L. D. (1998). "Making MOOsic": The development of personal relationships on-line and a comparison to their off-line counterparts. *Journal of Social and Personal Relationships, 15*, 517–537.

Parsons, T. (1949). The social structure of the family. In R. N. Anshen (Ed.), *The family: Its function and destiny.* New York: Harper and Row.

Perry, J. (2000, February 28). Only the cyberlonely. *U. S. News & World Report, 128*(8), 62.

Pihlblad, C. T., & McNamara, R. L. (1965). Social adjustment of elderly people in three small towns. In A. Rose & W. A. Peterson (Eds.), *Older people and their social world.* Philadelphia: F. A. Davis.

Pool, I. de S. (1983). *Forecasting the telephone: A retrospective technology assessment.* Norwood, NJ: Ablex.

Reynolds, G. F. (1977–79). Early wireless and radio in Manitoba, 1909–1924. *Transactions of the Historical and Scientific Society of Manitoba, 34–35,* 89–113.

Rheingold, H. (1991). *Virtual reality.* New York: Summit Books.

Rierdan, J. (1999). Internet-depression link? *American Psychologist, 54,* 781–782.

Riley, M. W., Johnson, M., & Foner, A. (1972). *Aging and society: A sociology of age stratification* (Vol. 3). New York: Russell Sage.

Rodgers, R. H. (1977). The family life cycle concept: Past, present, and future. In J. Cuisenier (Ed.), *The family life cycle in European societies.* Berlin: Mouton de Gruyter.

Rohlfing, M. E. (1995). "Doesn't anybody stay in one place anymore?" An exploration of an understudied phenomenon of long-distance relationships. In J. T. Wood & S. Duck (Eds.), *Understudied relationships: Off the beaten track.* Newbury Park, CA: Sage.

Rose, A. M. (1965). Aging and social interaction among the lower classes of Rome. *Journal of Gerontology, 20,* 250–253.

Rosenmayr, L. (1977). The family: A source of hope for the elderly? In E. Shanas & M. B. Sussman (Eds.), *Family, bureaucracy, and the elderly* (pp. 132–157). Durham, NC: Duke University Press.

Ryder, N. B. (1965). The cohort as a concept in the study of social change. *American Sociological Review, 30,* 843–861.

Scharlott, B. W., & Christ, W. G. (1995). Overcoming relationship-initiation barriers: The impact of a computer-dating system on sex role, shyness, and appearance inhibitions. *Computers in Human Behavior, 11,* 191–204.

Shapiro, J. S. (1999). Loneliness: Paradox or artifact? Response to Kraut et al., 1998. *American Psychologist, 53,*1017.

Short, J., Williams, E., and Christie, B. (1976). *The social psychology of telecommunications.* New York: John Wiley and Sons.

Siegal, J., Dubrovsky, V., Kiesler, S., & McGuire, T. (1986). Group processes in computer-mediated communication. *Organizational Behavior and Human Decision Processes, 37,* 157–87.

Smith, M. A., & Kolluck, P. (1999). *Communities in cyberspace.* London, Boston: Routledge.

Soderbergh, S. (Producer), & Ross, G. (Director). (1998). *Pleasantville.* Film. (available from Warner Home Video). Theatrical release: October 23.

Suitor, J. J., Wellman, B., & Morgan, D. L. (1997). It's about time: How, why and when networks change. *Social Networks, 19,* 1–7.

Tiene, D. (2000). Online discussions: A survey of advantages and disadvantages compared to face-to-face discussions. *Journal of Educational Multimedia and Hypermedia, 9,* 371.

Tolson, J. (2000, May 15). A not-so-lonely crowd: Wired loners business-personality. *U.S. News & World Report, 128*(19), 46.

UCLA Center for Communication Policy (2001). *Surveying the digital future. The UCLA Internet Report 2001.* Los Angeles: UCLA Center for Communication Policy.

U.S. Census Bureau (1997). *Computer use in the United States.* Current Population Reports P20–522.

Warthman, F. (1974). Telecommunication and the city. *Annals of the American Academy of Political and Social Sciences, 412*, 127–137.

Waskul, D., Douglass, M., & Edgley, C. (2000). Cybersex: Outercourse and the enselfment of the body. *Symbolic Interaction, 23*(4), 375–397.

Watt, D., & White, J. M. (1999). Computers and the family life: A family development perspective. *Journal of Comparative Family Studies, 30*, 1–15.

Webber, M. M. (1973). Urbanization and communications. In G. Gerbner, L. P. Gross, & W. H. Melody (Eds.), *Communications, technology, and social policy*. New York: John Wiley & Sons.

Wellman, B., Haase, A. Q., Witte, J., & Hampton, K. (2001). Does the Internet increase, decrease, or supplement social capital? *American Behavioral Scientist, 45*(3), 436–455.

Wellman, B., Wong, R. Y., Tindall, D., & Nazer, N. (1997). A decade of network change: Turnover, persistence and stability in personal communities. *Social Networks, 19*, 27–50.

White, J. M. (1991). *Dynamics of family development: The theory of family development*. New York: Guilford.

Whyte, W. F. (1943). *Street corner society*. Chicago: University of Chicago Press.

Whyte, W. H. (1956). *The organization man*. New York: Doubleday.

Zillmann, D., & Jennings, B. (1988). Effects of prolonged consumption of pornography on family values. *Journal of Family Issues, 9*, 518–544.

Subject Index

Author Index